seventh edition

The Whole Child

Developmental Education for the Early Years

JOANNE HENDRICK

UNIVERSITY OF OKLAHOMA, EMERITA

Merrill
Prentice Hall

Upper Saddle River, New Jersey
Columbus, Ohio

Library of Congress Cataloging in Publication Data

Hendrick, Joanne

 The whole child : developmental education for the early years / Joane Hendrick.—7th ed.
  p. cm.
 Includes bibliographical references (p.) and index.
 ISBN 0-13-022606-8
 1. Education, Preschool—United States. 2. Early childhood education—United
States. 3. Preschool teachers—Training of—United States. I. Title.
 LB1140.23.H46 2001
 372.21'0973—dc21

                     99-058488

Vice President and Publisher: Jeffery W. Johnston
Executive Editor: Ann Castel Davis
Editorial Assistant: Pat Grogg
Production Editor: Sheryl Glicker Langner
Design and Cover Coordinator: Diane C. Lorenzo
Cover Designer: Ceri Fitzgerald
Cover photo: Joanne Hendrick
Production Manager: Laura Messerly
Electronic Text Management: Marilyn Wilson Phelps, Karen L. Bretz, Melanie N. Ortega
Photo Coordinator: Sherry Mitchell
Director of Marketing: Kevin Flanagan
Marketing Manager: Amy June
Marketing Services Manager: Krista Groshong

This book was set by in Goudy Old Style and Humanist by Prentice Hall. It was printed and
bound by R. R. Donnelley & Sons Company. The cover was printed by Phoenix Color Corp.

Photo Credits: Children's Place, Integris Baptist Medical Center, Oklahoma City,
Oklahoma; Institute of Child Development, University of Oklahoma, Norman, Oklahoma;
Oaks Parent-Child Workshop, Starr King Parent-Child Workshop, and San Marcos Parent-
Child Workshop, Santa Barbara, California; Discoveries, Santa Barbara, California; East
and West Tinker Air Force Base Child Development Centers, Midwest City, Oklahoma; p.
210 by Barbara Schwartz, Merrill/Prentice Hall.

10 9 8 7 6 5 4
ISBN 0-13-022606-8

Revising this book about
early childhood education is
always stimulating. It has been
an interesting task for me to
set down what I know about
this area and then to witness
the changing needs the past
few years have brought to the
fore. If it is also helpful to
beginning teachers and to the
children they serve, I will be
pleased indeed.

Joanne Hendrick

Overview

The Whole Child is a practical methods book that explains how to teach young children in ways that foster healthy development. It shifts the attention of the teacher away from "art" or "science" to what the child *is* and what he needs from the learning environment in order to thrive. For that reason, it focuses on the child and pictures him as composed of a number of selves: the physical self, the emotional self, the social self, the creative self, and the cognitive self.

The physical self includes not only large and fine muscle development but also the handling of routines because such things as eating, resting, and toileting contribute much to physical comfort and well-being. For the emotional self, the book considers ways to increase and sustain mental health, to cope with crises, to use discipline to foster self-control, to cope with aggression, and to foster self-esteem. Included for the social self are ways to build social concern and kindliness and learning to value the cultures of other people. The creative self covers the areas of self-expression through the use of art materials and creativity as expressed in play and applied in thought. Finally, the cognitive, or intellectual, self is considered in terms of language and literacy development, the development of reasoning and thinking skills via the emergent approach, and the development of specific reasoning abilities.

The Whole Child is based on the premises that physical and emotional health are fundamental to the well-being of children, that education must be developmentally appropriate if that well-being is to prosper, and that children need time to be children—time to be themselves, to do nothing, to stand and watch, to repeat again what they did before—in short, they need time to live in their childhood rather than through it. If we offer the young children we teach rich and appropriate learning opportunities combined with enough time for them to enjoy and experience those opportunities to the fullest, we will enhance childhood, not violate it.

Inviting Features of This Textbook

New to This Edition

- New information on the development of the brain and the implications of those findings for early childhood education is included in relevant chapters.

- Additional new material is as diverse as discussions of asthma, obesity, and universal precautions and revised charts on the development of block play and Reggio-inspired examples of emergent curriculum.

- The basic tenets of Vygotsky's and Piaget's theories are explained, as well as their implications for early childhood education.

- The chapters on cognition have been reformulated to provide an even greater emphasis on the development of reasoning and thinking skills via the emergent approach.

- Annotated references have been completely revised and updated, including a new feature, "Pick of the Litter," that identifies especially interesting and perhaps offbeat references.

- *The Whole Child* is coordinated with the popular television series based on *The Whole Child*, funded by the Annenberg CPB Project. This series, available in Spanish and English, was produced under the guidance of an Advisory Committee that included Lilian Katz, Joan Costley, Irving Siegel, Carol Phillips, Ruby Burgess, Eli and Rosaline Saltz, Barbara Ferguson-Kamara, Frederich Goodman, and Jane Squires.

Continuing Features

- Material is presented in a warm, practical approach based on more than 30 years of experience teaching adult students and young children.

- Emphasis is on teaching methods that focus on children and their developmental needs rather than on science or art per se.

- The author, who recently edited *First Steps Toward Teaching the Reggio Way*, includes explanations of the Reggio Emilia approach and suggestions for integrating aspects of that philosophy.

- Entire chapters are included on multicultural, nonsexist education (Chapter 13) and welcoming children who may have special educational requirements into the life of the school (Chapter 9).

- An expanded Instructor's Manual is available at no charge to instructors which includes transparency masters describing "predicaments" for class discussion, suggested assignments, and a variety of test questions.

Acknowledgments

I owe so much to so many people that it is a well-nigh impossible task to mention them all. The contributions of students and parents to my knowledge and point of view have been considerable, as have the contributions of the members of my staff. In addition, I am forever in the debt of my mother, Alma Berg Green, who not only began some of the first parent education classes in Los Angeles but also taught me a great deal about young children and their families.

I am also indebted to Sarah Foot and her wonderful Starr King Parent/Child Workshop, which convinced me that my future lay in early childhood education, and to my own children, who bore with me with such goodwill while I was learning the real truth about bringing up young people.

The seventh edition has moved with the times and includes much new material. For their many suggestions in this regard, I would like to thank Susan Gomez, California State University at Sacramento; Peggy O. Jessee, University of Alabama; Janie H. Humphries, Louisiana Tech University; Mary Virginia Peaslee, Florida Southern College; Pauline Davey Zeece, University of Nebraska-Lincoln.

As far as the book itself is concerned, I would like to thank Murray Thomas for teaching me, among other things, how to write and John Wilson for convincing me that some things remained to be said and changed in early education. To Chester and Peggy Harris, I am forever indebted for a certain realistic attitude toward research, particularly in the area of cognitive development.

The people at Merrill/Prentice Hall have, as always, been of great assistance. In particular I want to thank Ann Davis and Pat Grogg for their encouragement. The contributions of Linda Poderski, freelance copy editor; and Sheryl Langner, production editor, also deserve grateful notice. Without their careful help, the book would not exist.

Nor would my photographs be nearly as attractive without the advice and services provided by Color Chrome Photographic Laboratories. Along this same line I am indebted to the staff and children from several centers for making their schools and lives available for me to portray. These schools are The Children's Place at Integris Baptist Medical Center, Oklahoma City; The Institute of Child Development, University of Oklahoma; The Oaks Parent/Child Workshop, San Marcos Parent/Child Workshop, Starr/King Parent/Child Workshop and Discoveries (all of Santa Barbara, California); and East Tinker Air Force Base Child Development Center, Midwest City, Oklahoma.

Discover the Companion Website Accompanying This Book

The Prentice Hall Companion Website: A Virtual Learning Environment

Technology is a constantly growing and changing aspect of our field that is creating a need for content and resources. To address this emerging need, Prentice Hall has developed an online learning environment for students and professors alike—Companion Websites—to support our textbooks.

In creating a Companion Website, our goal is to build on and enhance what the textbook already offers. For this reason, the content for each user-friendly website is organized by chapter and provides the professor and student with a variety of meaningful resources. Common features of a Companion Website include:

For the Professor—

Every Companion Website integrates **Syllabus Manager**™, an online syllabus creation and management utility.

- **Syllabus Manager**™ provides you, the instructor, with an easy, step-by-step process to create and revise syllabi, with direct links into Companion Website and other online content without having to learn HTML.

- Students may logon to your syllabus during any study session. All they need to know is the web address for the Companion Website and the password you've assigned to your syllabus.

- After you have created a syllabus using **Syllabus Manager**™, students may enter the syllabus for their course section from any point in the Companion Website.

- Class dates are highlighted in white and assignment due dates appear in blue. Clicking on a date, the student is shown the list of activities for the assignment. The activities for each assignment are linked directly to actual content, saving time for students.

- Adding assignments consists of clicking on the desired due date, then filling in the details of the assignment—name of the assignment, instructions, and whether or not it is a one-time or repeating assignment.

- In addition, links to other activities can be created easily. If the activity is online, a URL can be entered in the space provided, and it will be linked automatically in the final syllabus.
- Your completed syllabus is hosted on our servers, allowing convenient updates from any computer on the Internet. Changes you make to your syllabus are immediately available to your students at their next logon.

For the Student—

- **Chapter Objectives** — outline key concepts from the text
- **Interactive Self-quizzes** — complete with hints and automatic grading that provide immediate feedback for students

After students submit their answers for the interactive self-quizzes, the Companion Website **Results Reporter** computes a percentage grade, provides a graphic representation of how many questions were answered correctly and incorrectly, and gives a question by question analysis of the quiz. Students are given the option to send their quiz to up to four email addresses (professor, teaching assistant, study partner, etc.).

- **Message Board** — serves as a virtual bulletin board to post-or respond to-questions or comments to/from a national audience
- **Net Searches** — offer links by key terms from each chapter to related Internet content
- **Web Destinations** — links to www sites that relate to chapter content

To take advantage of these and other resources, please visit *The Whole Child: Developmental Education for the Early Years* Companion Website at

www.prenhall.com/hendrick

Part II   Fostering Physical Well-Being   77

chapter 4
Handling Daily Routines   78

chapter 5
Development of the Physical Self   106

Part III   Nourishing and Maintaining Emotional Health   133

chapter 6
Fostering Mental Health in Young Children   134

There was a child went forth every day,
And the first object he look'd upon, that object
he became,
And that object became part of him for the day or
a certain part of the day,
Or for many years or stretching cycles of years.

The early lilacs became part of this child,
And grass and white and red morning-glories, and
white and red clover, and the song of the
phoebe-bird,
And the Third-month lambs and the sow's pink-
faint litter, and the mare's foal and the
cow's calf,
And the noisy brood of the barnyard or by the
mire of the pond-side,
And the fish suspending themselves so curiously
below there, and the beautiful curious liquid,
And the water-plants with their graceful flat
heads, all became part of him.

The field-sprouts of Fourth-month and Fifth-
month became part of him,
Water-grain sprouts and those of the light-yellow
corn, and the esculent roots of the garden,
And the apple-trees cover'd with blossoms and the
fruit afterward, and wood-berries, and the
commonest weeds by the road,
And the old drunkard staggering home from the
outhouse of the tavern whence he had
lately risen,
And the schoolmistress that pass'd on her way to
the school,
And the friendly boys that pass'd, and the
quarrelsome boys,
And the tidy and fresh-cheek'd girls, and the
barefoot negro boy and girl,
And all the changes of city and country wherever
he went.

His own parents, he that had father'd him and she
that had conceiv'd him in her womb and
birth'd him,
They gave this child more of themselves than that,
They gave him afterward every day, they became
part of him.

The mother at home quietly placing the dishes on
the supper-table,
The mother with mild words, clean her cap and
gown, a wholesome odor falling off her person
and clothes as she walks by,
The father, strong, self-sufficient, manly, mean,
anger'd, unjust,
The blow, the quick loud word, the tight bargain,
the crafty lure,
The family usages, the language, the company, the
furniture, the yearning and swelling heart,
Affection that will not be gainsay'd, the sense of
what is real, the thought if after all it should
prove unreal,
The doubts of day-time and the doubts of night-
time, the curious whether and how,
Whether that which appears so is so, or is all
flashes and specks?
Men and women crowding fast in the streets, if
they are not flashes and specks what are they?
The streets themselves and the facades of houses,
and goods in the windows,
Vehicles, teams, the heavy-plank'd wharves, the
huge crossing at the ferries,
The village on the highland seen from afar at
sunset, the river between,
Shadows, aureola and mist, the light falling on
roofs and gables of white or brown two miles off,
The schooner near by sleepily dropping down the
tide, the little boat slack-tow'd astern,
The hurrying tumbling waves, quick-broken crests,
slapping,
The strata of color'd clouds, the long bar of
maroon-tint away solitary by itself, the spread of
purity it lies motionless in,
The horizon's edge, the flying sea-crow, the
fragrance of salt marsh and shore mud,
These became part of that child who went forth
every day, and who now goes, and will always go
forth every day.

Walt Whitman
There Was a Child Went Forth (1871)

part I

Beginning to Teach

chapter one

How to Survive While Teaching: Suggestions and Guidelines for the First Few Weeks

chapter two

What Makes a Good Day for Children?

chapter three

What Parents Need

How to Survive While Teaching

Suggestions and Guidelines for the First Few Weeks

Whether you'll ever get used to teaching?

What to do about feeling helpless and incompetent?

Whether anyone else ever hated a child in her class?

Why you feel terribly tired?

. . . IF YOU HAVE, THE MATERIAL IN THE FOLLOWING PAGES WILL HELP YOU.

Wanting to teach is like wanting to have children or to write or paint or dance or invent or think through a mathematical problem that only a few have been able to solve. It has an element of mystery, involving as it does the yearly encounter with new people, the fear that you will be inadequate to meet their needs, as well as the rewards of seeing them become stronger because of your work. And as is true of the other creative challenges, the desire to teach and the ability to teach well are not the same thing. With the rarest of exceptions, one has to learn how to become a good teacher just as one has to learn how to become a scientist or an artist.

Herbert Kohl (1984, p. 16)

At the core of all education that makes a difference in children's lives—beneath all the methods, materials, and curricula—is a teacher who cares about each child, who teaches from the heart.

Mimi Brodsky Chenfield (1993, p. 56)

3

Teaching preschool children can be one of the best, most deeply satisfying experiences in the world. Children ages 2 to 5 go through fascinating, swiftly accomplished stages of development. They are possessed of vigorous personalities, rich enthusiasms, an astonishing amount of physical energy, and strong wills. With the exception of infancy there is no other time in human life when so much is learned in so brief a period (Bloom, 1964).

This phenomenal vigor and burgeoning growth present a challenge to the beginning teacher that is at once exhilarating and frightening. The task is a large one: The teacher must attempt to build an educational climate that enhances the children's development and whets their appetites for further learning. The milieu must also nourish and sustain emotional health, encourage physical growth and muscular prowess, foster satisfying social interactions, enhance creativity, develop language skills, and promote the development of mental ability. Moreover this must all be garbed in an aura of happiness and affection to establish that basic feeling of well-being that is essential to successful learning.

With such a large task at hand it is not surprising that the beginning teacher may wonder somewhat desperately where to begin and what to do—and that is what this chapter is all about. It is intended to start you on the right track and help you survive those first perilous but exciting days of student teaching.

Granted, the first weeks of teaching are not easy, but they need not be impossible either. However, it is wise for you to make allowances for possible stress and not to be disappointed if you feel more tired than usual, or occasionally disheartened, or bewildered. These feelings will become less frequent as time passes and the children, staff, and routine become more familiar. They will also diminish as you gain more skill and confidence.

SOME THOUGHTS ABOUT GETTING STARTED

Think of Yourself As Providing a Life-Affirming Environment and Use That As a Yardstick When Working With Children

Life-affirming teachers see children and themselves as being involved in a positive series of encounters intended to facilitate growth and happiness. They have faith that children want to do the right thing—that they can grow and change for the better—and they have confidence that teachers and parents can assist them in that task.

Such teachers accept their own humanness and that of other people. They know it takes strength, determination, and knowledge to sustain these life-affirming policies in situations in which children are just learning the rudiments of socially acceptable behavior in a time when many families are disorganized and unhappy.

They realize that sometimes a child can seem lost in a morass of angry feelings and strike out at others, but they also have confidence that she knows deep inside that this behavior is not working well. They know it is possible for a life-affirming teacher to lead that child onto the firmer ground of being socially acceptable if she is patient, positive, and consistent.

Enjoying animals together is part of providing a life-affirming environment.

Increase Your Self-Esteem by Realizing You Are Part of a Noble, Though Young, Tradition

Interest in the study of children and awareness of the value of educating their parents in wholesome child-rearing practices began to grow around the turn of the 20th century. My own mother was one of the first parent education leaders in Los Angeles, and I well remember her going off to speak to other earnest mothers at various school-sponsored gatherings more than 65 years ago. That this interest continues today is shown by the continued popularity of child-rearing books and the growing awareness that what parents and teachers do during the early years of childhood can make a significant contribution to the future well-being of the child. The newest indication of such concern is the addition of parenting classes by many high schools throughout the United States.

Along with the burgeoning interest in child development came a companion interest in preschool education and child care. This began abroad, where such leaders as Maria Montessori and the McMillan sisters pioneered child care as a means of improving the well-being of children of the poor.

In 1907 Maria Montessori, an ardent young reformer-physician, began her *Casa dei Bambini* (Children's House). That child care center was originally founded as part of an experiment in refurbishing slum housing in an economically distressed quarter of Rome (Loeffler, 1992). Supporters of that cooperative housing venture found that young children left unattended during the day while their parents were away at work were getting into trouble and destroying the property that people had worked so hard to restore. They therefore wanted to work out some way for the children to be cared for. Under Montessori's guidance, Children's House emphasized health, cleanliness, sensory training, individual learning, and the actual manipulation of materials (Hainstock, 1997; Montessori, 1912). Since Montessori believed that individual experience with self-correcting materials must come before other learning could take place, language experience, the use of imagination, and dramatic play were not recognized as being of much importance (Beatty, 1995). Montessori stressed that the teacher should be a cultivated woman and live in the community wherein she taught.

In England, too, the pathetic condition of young slum children was being recognized. In 1911 two English sisters, Margaret and Rachel McMillan, founded their open-air nursery school. The McMillans had been interested in socialism and the women's movement and through these concerns came to know the condition of the London poor. They were horrified to discover that many children were running around shoeless in the London slums, suffering from lice, malnutrition, and scabies. Like Children's House, their school stressed good health, nourishing food, and adequate medical care. Unlike Children's House, it emphasized the value of outdoor play, sunshine, sandboxes, and regular baths. (The school featured deep tubs wherein the children were regularly bathed.) The McMillans advocated teaching children together in small groups. They stressed building independence and self-esteem. They also believed that young girls had natural gifts for working with children, so they gave them paid, on-the-job training as they worked with the children (Bradburn, 1989; McMillan, 1929).

Nursery education in the United States witnessed a flowering of interest in the early 1920s. In 1915 a short-lived Montessori school was founded in New York by Eva McLin. The Montessori philosophy was severely criticized on a variety of grounds, however, including that children had no opportunity for self-expression, that children were not encouraged to play together, and that the conception of freedom was inadequate (Beatty, 1995). Therefore, that school of thought failed to take strong root in the United States until the 1950s, when increasing concern about cognitive learning sparked by *Sputnik*, combined with the war on poverty, produced renewed interest in the Montessori program.

At about the same time the McLin school was established, a group of women at the University of Chicago began the first parent cooperative nursery school in 1916 (Osborn, 1991). In 1919 Harriet Johnson opened the City and County School, which later metamorphosed into Bank Street. Abigail Eliot began the Ruggles Street Nursery School in Boston in 1921—the same year that Patty Smith Hill founded a laboratory nursery school at Columbia Teachers College.

As interest in nursery-level education grew, the academic community began to offer training in the field and professional associations were formed. For example, at the Merrill Palmer School of Motherhood and Home Training (which later became the prestigious Merrill Palmer Institute), a nursery school was provided where students participated in an 8-hour laboratory experience each week. They studied child care management, health, nutrition, and social problems—not very different from what students do, at least in part, today! Other academically based centers included those at Iowa State, Ohio State, Cornell, Georgia, Purdue, Kansas, Nebraska, Oklahoma A&M, Cincinnati, and Oregon State (Osborn, 1991).

Shortly afterward, in 1925, Patty Smith Hill (1942/1992) called a meeting of early leaders in the field to discuss issues of concern in the care of young children. In 1929 the National Association of Nursery Education was founded. That association has continued and is now known as the National Association for the Education of Young Children (NAEYC). At last report that association has grown to more than 106,000 members and provides an annual conference attended by 24,000 people (NAEYC, 1998c).

Despite Some Government Support, Providing Adequate Funding for Child Care Remains a Problem

Various government agencies in the United States have participated in the field of child care and education from time to time, but until the current era of Head Start, they were never a consistent source of support (Cahan, 1989). During the Great Depression of the 1930s, the government did add impetus to the growth of child care by sponsoring nearly 3,000 such programs in 31 states. These were intended to provide work for unemployed women, as well as to care for children of the poor. This federal support continued during World War II so that women who worked in war-related industries could have their children cared for (Hurwitz, 1998). (I recall Edith Dowley, a longtime professor of early childhood education, telling me what it had been like to work in one of those 24-hour-a-day centers during the war. At one point she suddenly realized she was tripping over her feet because her shoes were so loose. When she weighed herself, she found she had lost 40 pounds in 3 months while struggling to get one of the wartime centers started.) Although these federally supported programs are now largely defunct (one or two states, such as California, have continued to operate them), they may have helped pave the way for the most widely known government-supported program currently in place: Head Start.

Since Head Start's inception in 1965, when 561,000 4-year-olds were enrolled for only a summer program, the ranks have swelled so that by 1997 more than 16 million youngsters have participated. Although the primary focus of the program continues to be on providing low-income children and their families with health, nutritional, and social services, as well as with educational skills, Head Start has moved with the times and now includes more 3-year-olds and children with disabilities. Some Early Head Start programs are specifically for families with infants and toddlers. About half of the programs also provide some full-day services to families who need child care services (Head Start Bureau, 1998).

In addition to Head Start the federal government has also increased child care support during the past decade by funding the Child Care and Development Block Grant, the Child and Adult Food Program, the Child and Dependent Care Tax Credit, and the Individuals with Disabilities Education Act. Although many would argue that an even more extensive system of subsidies is required to ensure reasonable quality in the majority of child care centers, this increase in funding is at least a heartening step in the right direction. (Child Care Information Exchange 1998b; Neubert, 1997).

Support at the state level varies widely; some monies are required to "match" federal funding. Other support differs as much as do the states themselves, ranging from prekindergarten programs for 4-year-olds to full-day child care situations beginning in infancy (Clifford, 1998).

The recent successful settlements between the tobacco industry and various states ("Tobacco Settlement," 1999) and the possible reopening of charges against those companies at the federal level may produce an additional source of revenue for child care and education. Despite this government support, though, *the fact remains that the majority of half- and full-day early education programs receive no subsidies.* Their growth has been gradual and marked by inspired teachers, hard work, and somewhat precarious financing.

Meanwhile the Demand for Child Care Continues to Increase

As the Research Study in this chapter reveals, the demand for child care and early education continues to rise. Census Bureau predictions anticipate that the number of children under age 5 will increase from 18,900,000 in 1990 to 20,000,000 by 2005 and that a "slow, steady growth rate of about .75% a year for the next 25 years" will continue after that (D. Allen, 1998, p. 8). Coupled with this population trend is the increase in the number of mothers of young children working outside the home. That number has grown from 54% in 1986 to 59% in 1990 to 62% in 1997 (Children's Defense Fund, 1998). The recent federal welfare-to-work legislation has also increased the need for child care as more young mothers are required to enter the labor force. Clearly this trend toward women working outside the home implies an increasing need for additional child care and education for their children (Zaslow, Oldham, Moore, & Magenheim, 1998).

IMPLICATIONS FOR THE PROFESSION: WHAT DO THESE FACTS HAVE TO DO WITH ME?

Basically what the foregoing data predicts is that early childhood people are never going to run out of work and that some of that work is likely to provide adequate pay and benefits because of various government subsidies. What may not be so evident to the beginner is the increasing variety of work and student teaching situations available to choose from.

Kinds of Child Care

To begin, the part of the profession that cares for children from infancy to age 5 in centers offers possibilities to suit almost every philosophical taste and interest. Teaching situations range from half to full day care of infants up through prekindergarten children. The center could be funded by parents, the state, a parent employer, a church, a private charity, and/or the federal government. It could be part of a chain or operate as an independent center. It might be located in a new facility or in make-do circumstances, or on a college campus or in a church, a public school, or its own building. It could be a public preschool program for 4-year-olds or a Head Start Center, part of the military child care system

Research Study

Who Is Caring for America's Young Children

Results of the 1995 National Household Education Survey

Research Question: The investigators who conducted the National Household Education Survey wanted to obtain current information about how many and what kinds of children were participating in child care and early education programs in the United States. To obtain that information they repeated and extended a study originally conducted in 1991 (National Center for Education Statistics [NCES], 1993).

Research Method: The information was gathered by means of a telephone survey using randomly selected numbers. The survey used a sample drawn from "the civilian noninstitutionalized population in households with telephones in the 50 states and the District of Columbia" (NCES, 1995, p. 7). For the first time it included infants and toddlers in the under-6 portion of the inquiry, and 7,557 interviews were completed. Respondents were asked who provided nonparental care for their young children, care that was either center or family-home-based care.

Research Results: The study found that in the spring of 1995 about 6 out of every 10 children under age 6 and not yet in kindergarten received some type of care and education on a regular basis from persons other than their parents. In terms of actual numbers this translated "to more than 12.9 million infants, toddlers, and preschool children receiving nonparental care" (p. 2).

Additional interesting information included the facts that, as children grow older, the percentage of children in care rises from 45% of children under 1 year of age to 84% of 5-year-olds, that Black children participate at a slightly higher rate (66%) than do White children (62%), and that the current rate of participation for both groups is higher than the rate for Hispanic children (45%). As one might expect, children whose mothers are employed participate at a higher rate than do other children. About 88% of children whose mothers work full-time and 75% of children whose mothers work part-time were in some type of care, as contrasted with 32% of children whose mothers were not in the workforce.

Implications for Teaching: The fact that more than 12,000,000 preschool-age children are in nonparental care on a regular basis makes it plain that the debate about child care can no longer be *whether* such care should be provided, but rather *how* such care should be provided. It reminds us ever more forcefully of how seriously we caregivers must take our role. On the personal, one-to-one level, we must do everything possible to be the best we can be when so many parents entrust such an important portion of their children's lives to our care. On a broader level, we must continually monitor state and federal decisions to make certain that all proposed regulations truly enhance the quality of care and education we provide the children.

Source: Child Care and Early Education Program Participation of Infants, Toddlers, and Preschoolers: National Household Education Survey (NCES-95–213), by National Center for Education Statistics (NCES), 1995, Washington, DC: Author.

The ability to enjoy children is one of the basic elements of good teaching.

operated by the U.S. Department of Defense, or restricted to serving families of low income. It may be staffed by teachers with a Child Development Associate or college degree in early childhood, by people working on those degrees, by staff who depend on occasional conferences for education, by parents participating in a cooperative, or by people who meet only the criteria of being 16 years old and having a high school degree and no criminal record. The choices are truly bewildering. Salary, job satisfaction, and other employment benefits vary as much as job possibilities do, with pay ranging from minimum wage to the equivalent of a primary school teacher's salary. In general, child care situations that are subsidized in some way in addition to or instead of parent fees provide the better salaries.

Day Care Centers

Full-day centers usually serve the children of working parents, some of whom are fairly well-to-do and some not. Funds for such care may be provided by parents or, less frequently, by public agencies of various kinds. Although the growth rate has declined during the past decade, private for-profit child care chains continue to make a significant contribution in this area (Neugebauer, 1999). For example, in 1998 the 20 largest chains reported they had a total capacity of more than 500,000 child care slots (Child Care Information Exchange, 1998c). These enterprises may offer teachers such possibilities as packaged curriculum written by professionals, centralized methods of accounting, and clearly prescribed policies based on keeping costs down while, in many cases, maintaining a reasonable level of care for children.

Good day care programs are delightful and valuable because of the potential for the leisurely pace and extended learning experiences they can provide. Mediocre custodial day care services are still a stain on the conscience of some communities and need to be remedied and modified for the welfare of the children (Helburn, 1995).

Independent Schools

Independent (or "private") schools are so named since they do not depend on public funding for support. They may be half- or full-day programs and tend to offer a traditional curriculum based on the individual needs of the children. The programs are likely to stress creativity and social and emotional adjustment. Such schools usually serve middle-class families, and they meet a real need for early childhood education in this portion of the community. They are often located in church buildings because many churches offer these facilities at nominal or no cost. Neugebauer (1998) reports that 1.5 million children attended weekday programs in church facilities in 1997.

Cooperatives

As previously noted cooperative nursery schools have been a tradition in the United States since 1916 (Hewes, 1998). They usually have fewer professional teachers and more mothers and fathers participating than independent schools do, although they, too, are independent in the sense that they are not usually supported by public funds. They offer the special enrichment provided by a high adult-child ratio, and the children who attend them also profit from the abundance of ideas furnished by such a wide variety of adults. It is still the case that many teachers enter the profession by participating in a well-run co-op when their children are young, finding that they love to teach, and going on to further training in early childhood education.

Compensatory Programs

Head Start is the best known of the compensatory programs since it exists on a nationwide basis. Some states also fund additional preschool programs designed to educate children from low-income families. Although termed *compensatory* because they were originally intended to compensate for deficiencies in the child's home environment, current investigations have found greater strengths in the homes than had previously been noted. Now the programs seek to honor these strengths, as well as to compensate for lags in verbal and mental development.

Kindergarten Programs and Public School Programs for 4-Year-Olds

During teacher training, some students have the opportunity to split their teaching experience between the kindergarten, first, or second grade, and the preprimary level in a public school setting. Such assignments, which are more typically the case for university rather than community college students, are almost always arranged between the college of education and the public school in question. Even in that circumstance it may be possible for students to express interest in working with a particular teacher if they are willing to be tactfully assertive. A good way to identify a congenial teacher is to keep your eyes open during visitations or during early aiding experiences and to ask other students for their opinions. Just bear in mind that different students can have radically different feelings about the same teacher, so reserve the right to make the final decision for yourself.

Montessori Schools

Placement of student teachers in schools that base their curriculum on the teachings of Maria Montessori is usually quite difficult to arrange unless the students are participating in an academic program philosophically based in the same tradition. This is because Montessori schools require their teachers to undergo training specifically related to Montessori's precepts. Occasionally students who do not meet this criterion can find employment as an aide or during the summer in such schools, thereby gaining at least some exposure to the methods and philosophy of that distinguished educator (Hainstock, 1997).

Demonstration or Laboratory Schools

Demonstration or laboratory schools are typically connected with teacher-training institutions or with research programs. They can be wonderful places for young students to begin their teaching since they are the most likely of all the kinds of schools to be child and *student* centered. Ideally students should have teaching opportunities in both laboratory and real-life schools so that they receive a balance of ideal and realistic teaching experiences.

Family Child Care

Family child care for the youngest children is another facet of the profession. Family child care has the virtues of providing children with a smaller, more intimate environment, more flexible hours, and a more homelike atmosphere. Many families prefer this kind of care particularly for infants and toddlers. Providers often prefer this setting because it offers opportunities for increased income while keeping their own youngsters as part of the group, and it offers personal independence in curriculum planning and scheduling. As is true for center-based care, fees, and hence a provider's income, vary widely, depending on quality of service and what the traffic will bear.

One alternative to using the caregiver's home as a base is having caregivers reside in the children's homes. Although nannies do not constitute a very large segment of the early childhood care population, they are popular with more affluent families who can provide both the living space and the money that makes such care feasible.

Related Opportunities for People with Additional Experience

One thing that makes early childhood education such an interesting field is the increasing variety of related positions available. Although these generally require applicants to have had a combination of education, perhaps even advanced degrees, and practical early childhood experience, it is well for the beginning teacher to be aware of future possibilities.

For example, as experience and skills are developed, many teachers find they are challenged to assume more and more responsibility. Perhaps they wish to move from being an aide to becoming a teacher in the Head Start program and so begin work on becoming a Child Development Associate (Council for Early Childhood Professional Recognition, 1997). Perhaps they become directors of centers, curriculum specialists and advisers, or officers of early childhood organizations. Sometimes they even become college professors! Other teachers decide they want to apply concepts of early childhood education to the primary school and either continue or return to college to qualify for an early childhood credential entitling them to teach in elementary school.

An early childhood background also provides an excellent foundation for teachers who find that, because of the emphasis in our field on developmental appropriateness and attention to the emotional, physical, and social well-being of children, they are drawn to working with children who have disabilities. Likewise, Child Life Specialists (Kingston et al., 1996) who work with children in hospitals, providing activities and emotional support, find an early childhood background to be invaluable.

Many programs, such as *Parents and Teachers* and *Hippy* (Behrman, 1999), include a home visiting component. These positions often require the visitors to have social and cultural ties to the community they will serve and sometimes bilingual expertise. Home visitors usually work with the children and other family members, too. The continuing warm, personal contact thus provided often enriches the parents' repertoire of educational activities to do with their youngsters (Baker, Piotrkowski, & Brooks-Gunn, 1998; Dunst, 1995).

Resource/referral centers are now present in every state and provide information for parents and employers seeking licensed child care. However, that aspect of service is just the tip of the iceberg; such centers may also provide training opportunities for child care staff, toy- and book-lending services, and on-site advice to the centers. They serve as advocates for better quality child care and also compile, analyze, and share information about child care (National Association of Child Care Resource and Referral Agencies, 1998).

Working for the state agency that inspects and licenses center-based and (sometimes) home-based care is yet another important early childhood-related job. It is mainly through licensing and follow-up inspections that children and families can be assured that at least minimum standards of health and safety are enforced.

Preparation for the Most Valuable Occupation of All

The most valuable occupation is, of course, *parenthood*. I can think of no other educational training that has such a direct benefit to family life than studying and learning about young children and how to help them develop into balanced, secure, loving adults. No matter how much we already know and how much our parents taught us, there is always more to learn about ways of caring for young children so that they flourish. Early childhood education provides an unequaled opportunity for doing this.

SOME COMFORTING THOUGHTS

The Mentor Teacher Is Probably Ill at Ease, Too

During the early days of student teaching students can be so wrapped up in their own shyness that they fail to realize that the teachers they are working with are shy of them as well. They attribute all the awkwardness of the first days on the job to their own insecurities and inexperience. Actually a mentor, while wanting to be helpful, may be somewhat uncomfortable, too, particularly if she has not had many student teachers before. It will help her help the student if she knows the student likes her.

One Poor Experience with a Student Will Not Ruin a Child's Life

Some conscientious new teachers are almost too sensitive to the effect their actions will have on the children. It is true that young children are more vulnerable to influences than older children are, and for this reason everyone attempts to do his or her best. But the significance of the single traumatic experience has been overrated. Usually it is the continuing approach or climate that molds the child (Rouse, 1998; Werner & Smith, 1992). Therefore, the student need not agonize over one mishandled situation on the grounds that it may have scarred the child for life; this is a most unlikely result.

Reflecting on Past Activities Can Turn a Student Into a Better Teacher

Analyzing an activity after presenting it by noting its strengths, as well as its weaknesses, is one of the quickest ways to improve one's teaching. When things have not gone exactly right, it's easy to dwell on the negative aspects and forget the positive ones. Even when the experience could have gone better, rather than investing a lot of energy in regretting the errors, it is more healthy and productive to figure out what went wrong and decide how to be more effective next time. It is also helpful to repeat the experience as soon as possible (rather like getting back on a horse and riding again right after you've fallen off) so that bad memories are supplanted by better ones.

Remember That There Is a Wide Variety of Places to Use Your Training in Addition to Conventional School Situations

Sometimes students become baffled and discouraged when after giving it a fair chance they just do not like teaching a group of children in a half- or full-day setting of any kind, yet they know in their hearts they wish to continue working with young children. This is the time to remember the numerous related possibilities discussed on page 13. In recent years students from my program, in addition to teaching in conventional school situations, have pursued the following careers: Child Life Specialist in a children's hospital, resource referral adviser about children's services, motherhood, home visitor, teacher of children with disabilities, nanny, child care licensing agent, child abuse counselor, family services provider in Head Start, college professor, toy store owner, director of a children's center, and family child care provider. The possibilities are growing all the time.

Remember That Age Can Be a Positive Factor When Learning to Teach Young Children

One of the most interesting trends in recent years has been the return to school by women who for one reason or another have decided to reenter the working world outside the home. Sometimes it can be a bit daunting to women in their middle years to take classes surrounded by people newly graduated from high school. A number of such women have confided to me that it is frightening to return and have to compete with those they perceive as brighter or at least younger than they are.

The truth is that every age brings with it some special assets. It may well be the case that younger students are more accustomed to managing the routines of studying and campus life. It can be a comforting thought to more mature learners, however, to realize that they, in turn, bring special skills and benefits to the college experience. These usually include more experience with children (there's nothing like having children of your own to breed humility and compassion for other parents) and a wider perspective on life that can serve reentry students well as they work to increase their teaching skills.

BASIC PROFESSIONAL ETHICS

Now that the student is becoming a member of a profession, it will be helpful to know from the beginning some ethical guidelines that are followed by most preschool teachers. The National Association for the Education of Young Children (NAEYC) provides a complete summary of those guidelines, which are included in Appendix A (Feeney & Freeman, 1999; NAEYC, 1998b).

Some of the most fundamental ethical principles teachers should observe include the following items.

When in Doubt About the Value of a Decision, Put the Child's Welfare First

Granted, what is "best" may not always be easy to determine. Special circumstances in which we cannot be certain what is best for the child's welfare will always remain. For example, is it better for a 3-year-old to stay with a loving but emotionally disturbed and disoriented single parent or to place her with a less disturbed but apparently cold and emotionally remote grandmother? But it is also true that much of the time, if teachers honestly try to do what is best for the child rather than what is merely convenient or "the rule," they will be on the right ethical track.

Strive to Be Fair to All Children

Another important guideline to observe is that all children deserve a fair chance and a reasonable amount of concern from each teacher. Perhaps the student will recall situations in his or her own school life in which a teacher made a scapegoat of some child and picked on her continually, or another teacher never seemed to notice some of the youngsters. Although nobody intends to have this kind of circumstance happen, sometimes it does, and teachers should be warned against behaving in this way. Every child is important and is entitled to be valued by the teacher.

Keep Personal Problems Private During the Day

Teachers should not discuss their personal problems or emotional difficulties with parents, nor should they discuss them with other teachers while school is in session. Teachers need to leave personal problems at the door as they begin the day, since the time at school rightfully belongs to the children. Discussion of personal matters should take place after the children have gone home. Many a teacher has discovered that shutting out such troubles during the teaching day can provide interludes of relief and happiness that can make otherwise intolerable situations bearable.

Show Respect for the Child

One important way teachers of young children demonstrate basic respect for others is by refraining from discussing a child in her presence unless she is included directly in the conversation. Sometimes teachers thoughtlessly talk over the children's heads, assuming the youngsters are unaware of what is being said. But students who have had the experience of eavesdropping while people were discussing them will no doubt remember the special potency of that overheard comment. Anything said about a child in her presence needs to be said with her included. Thus it is more desirable to say, "Peg, I can see you're feeling pretty tired and hungry," than to cock an eyebrow in her direction and remark to another teacher, "Oh, brother! Are we ever in a nasty temper today!"

An even more fundamental aspect of respect between teacher and child can best be described as a valuing of the person: The teacher who truly respects and values the child pauses to listen to her with full attention whenever this is possible, remembering that each child is a unique person, relishing her for her differences from her companions and allowing her to generate ideas of her own, rather than subtly teaching her that it is better to accept unquestioningly the teacher's ideas as being best.

This kind of respect is, of course, a two-way street. Teachers who hold a child in such respectful regard set a model for the youngster, who will in time reflect this same fundamental consideration back to them. This process can be accelerated and strengthened if the teacher quietly makes a point of protecting her own rights, as well as the children's. She may say something as simple as, "Now, Ashley, I've listened to you; take just a minute and hear what I want to say," or she may make this same point with another child by saying, "You know, my desk is just like your cubby. I don't take your things out of that, and you must never take anything from my desk, either."

Observe Professional Discretion

Still another aspect of respect for people is respect for the family's privacy. Family affairs and children's behavior should not be discussed with people outside the school who have no need to know about them. Even amusing events should never be told unless the names of the children either are not mentioned or are changed. Most communities are smaller worlds than a beginning teacher may realize, and news can travel with astonishing rapidity.

In general, student teachers should be wary of being drawn into discussions with parents about their own or other families' children. This kind of discussion is the teacher's prerogative, and it is a wise student who passes off questions about youngsters by making some pleasant remark and referring the parent to the teacher. Nobody is ever antagonized by a student who does this in a tactful way, but disasters can result from well-meant comments by ill-informed or tactless beginners.

In addition, students should not discuss situations they disapprove of at the school where they work or say anything critical about another teacher to outsiders. These remarks have an unpleasant way of returning to the source, and the results can be awkward, to say the least. The principle "If you don't say it, they can't repeat it" is a sound one here. It is better instead to talk the problem over in confidence with the college supervisor.

Observe the Chain of Command

Just about every organization has a chain of command. It is always wise to avoid going over anyone else's head when making a comment or request. Understandably, teachers hate being put in a bad light by a student's talking a problem over with the school director or principal before talking it over with the teacher first.

A related aspect of this authority structure is being sure to get permission *before* planning a special event such as a field trip or getting out the hoses after a videotape on water play. Answers to such requests are generally yes, but it is always best to check before embarking on a major venture.

SOME RECOMMENDATIONS FOR STARTING OUT

Although not always possible, it helps to find out some things before beginning the first student-teaching day. For example, it is helpful to talk with the teacher and determine the expected arrival time and recommended style of clothing. Most school guidelines are reasonable and will recommend sensible but professional-looking clothes.

Some schools have written guidelines they can give the student to read. Time schedules and lists of rules are also very helpful to review. (For a typical schedule, see chapter 4.) If the school does not have these items written down, ask the teacher how basic routines such as eating and taking children to the toilet are handled, and ask about crucial safety rules and for a brief review of the schedule. If the student can come for a visit when the children are not there, the teacher will have a better opportunity to chat. During this visit make a special point of finding out where the children's cubbies are, where sponges and cleanup materials are kept, and where various supplies are stored. Don't hesitate to ask questions; just do your best to remember the answers!

PRACTICAL THINGS TO DO TO INCREASE COMPETENCE

Gain Confidence in Your Ability to Control the Group

Almost invariably the first thing students want to discuss is discipline. Because this is the point everyone seems most concerned about, it is recommended that the reader begin preparation for work by reading the chapters on discipline and aggression in order to build skills in this area. Even though those reviews will help, observation, practice, and seeing situations all the way through are the best ways to gain competence in controlling children.

Get to Know the Children as Soon as Possible

One way to become familiar with each of the children is to make a list of their names from the sign-in sheet and then jot down a few adjectives or facts to remember about each one. Calling the children by name at every opportunity will help, too. It will not take more than a day or two to become well acquainted, and it will help you belong to the group more quickly.

Develop the Proverbial "Eyes in the Back of the Head"

One of the most common failings of inexperienced teachers is their tendency to focus on only one child at a time. It is pleasant and much "safer" to sit down and read a favorite book with one or two lovable children and ignore the chaos going on in the block corner, but good teachers form the habit of total awareness. They develop a sense of what is happening in the entire area. This is true outdoors as well as indoors. But to say that the teacher should never plan to settle down with any group would be an exaggeration. Of course, teachers have to center their attention on specific children from time to time or else there is little satisfaction in the experience for teacher or child, but teachers must keep tuned in to the whole room as well. Sometimes such a simple technique as learning to look up frequently will help build skills in this area. Another technique is sitting so that the whole room or whole playground can be seen. Many beginning students sit with their backs to half the room; this is simply courting trouble.

Take Action in Unsafe Situations Immediately

Since students are sometimes afraid of appearing too restrictive in a liberal atmosphere, they may allow dangerous incidents to happen because they do not know the rule or school policy about it. The general rule of thumb is that when one is unsure whether an activity is dangerous, it is better to stop it and then check to see what the teacher thinks. Stopping a few activities that are safe is better than letting two children wrestle each other off the top of the slide while the student debates indecisively below. Children's behaviors generally look less dangerous to students as they gain experience and feel less anxious, *but it is always better to be safe than sorry.*

Encourage the Growth of Independence and Competence; Avoid Overteaching, Overhelping, and Overtalking

As a general principle, we encourage children at the preprimary level to do everything they can for themselves and for other children, too. This is different from the behavior of the teacher who sees the role of the teacher as doing *to* and doing *for* children. It takes self-control to wait while Katy fumbles for the zipper, insight to see how to assist her without taking over, and self-discipline not to talk too much while she is learning. But building competencies in the children by encouraging them to do things for themselves and for others increases their self-esteem so much that practicing restraint is worth the effort.

Encourage Originality of Self-Expression

One of the most frowned-on things students can do is to make models of something for the children to copy when they are working with creative materials. It is easy to be trapped into making one child a clay snake or drawing a man for another youngster, but early childhood teachers dislike providing such models since they limit children's expression of their own feelings and ideas. It is better to relish the materials with the children and help them use the materials for their own purposes.

Keep Contacts with the Children as Quiet and Meaningful as Possible

Except in a real emergency, walk over to the child to talk with her, rather than call across the room. Use a low voice and bend down so that she can see your face and be less overwhelmed by your size. (An excellent way to find out how big an adult is from a child's point of view is to ask a friend to stand up and teach you something while you remain seated on the floor. It's enlightening.)

Expect to Do Menial Tasks

No other profession requires the full range of abilities and effort that preschool teaching does. These extend from inspiring children and counseling parents to doing the most menial types of cleanup. Sometimes students do not realize this, so they feel imposed upon when they are asked to change a child's pair of pants or to mop the floor or clean the guinea pig cage. This kind of work is expected of almost all early childhood teachers as just being part of school life. Not only is cleaning up to be expected, but continual straightening up is also necessary as the day progresses. Blocks should be arranged on shelves and dress-up clothes rehung several times to keep the room looking attractive. (Unfortunately there is no good fairy who will come along and do this.)

Learn From the Start to Be Ingenious About Creating Equipment and Scrounging Materials

Early childhood programs almost always operate on lean budgets, and every school develops some ingenious ways to stretch money and invent equipment. Students can learn from each place they work by picking up these economical ideas from the staff, and they can contribute much by sharing their own ideas about the creative use of materials and new sources of free supplies. Be on the lookout for so-called waste materials that other businesses throw away. The carpet company's colorful scraps can make handsome additions to the collage box, for example, and rubber tires can be used in fascinating ways to make sturdy play equipment.

Organize Yourself Before Beginning to Teach

It is very helpful to arrive early on each teaching day so that there is time to get everything together in advance for the morning or afternoon. Nothing beats the feeling of security this preparation breeds. Life is also easier if before going home the student asks what will be happening during the next teaching session. Asking in advance makes reading up on activities ahead of time possible—a real security enhancer!

It increases confidence when you know the schedule well enough to tell what is going to happen next, as well as what time it is likely to happen. This allows time for cleanup and helps avoid the disappointment of moving into a new activity just as the group is expected to wash up for lunch. For these reasons, it is advisable always to wear a watch.

When You Need Help, Ask for It

Mentors usually are not critical when beginners admit they do not know something and have the courage to ask, but they are inclined to resent students who protect themselves by appearing to know everything already or who defend themselves by making constant excuses. When one is unsure of a policy at the school, it never does any harm to say to the child, "I don't know if it's all right to climb on the fence. Let's ask Mrs. Green, and then we'll both know."

The chance to chat with your mentor while cleaning up at the end of the morning or at some other convenient time of day is an invaluable time to raise problems and ask questions. During the day itself students often have to muddle through—learning by observation and using their own common sense. Nothing disastrous is likely to take place, and teachers are usually too busy to be corralled for more than a sentence or two of explanation while school is in progress.

RECOGNIZE STRESS AND DEAL WITH IT AS EFFECTIVELY AS POSSIBLE

It is inevitable to feel stress when dealing with a new situation such as beginning to teach, and it is valuable to recognize this fact so that you can deal with it effectively, rather than

Allowing children to do things "on their own" helps them build sound feelings of self-esteem.

just feel anxious, overwhelmed, or disappointed because sometimes you are exhausted at the end of the day. So much about the experience is new. There are so many personalities to deal with and so much to learn, so much uncertainty and excitement, and such a great desire to please without knowing exactly what is expected. This situation is clearly a lot to handle. These stresses do not mean that teaching is bad or unpleasant. Many novel situations such as getting married or receiving a promotion are delightful; but nonetheless they are stressful since they represent change, and change requires learning and adaptation.

Symptoms of stress vary with the individual. Some people lose their appetites; others try to comfort themselves by eating too much. Still others suffer from loss of sleep or find that they get angry at the slightest provocation.

Wise teachers acknowledge the possibility of stress and make practical plans for coping so that they can avoid coming down with various ailments or experiencing the excessive fatigue that prevents them from functioning effectively. Unfortunately such plans require a certain amount of self-discipline. Deciding to get plenty of rest, for example, is rarely a favorite prescription for the young, and yet it really does reduce stress, as do adequate nutrition and provision for having fun off the job (Gruenberg, 1998).

Truthful analysis of what is causing the most intense stress also helps. It might be apprehension about a child's threat to bite you, or it might be worry over how to keep the group attentive during story time, or it might be concern about whether other teachers or parents like you. Whatever it is, identifying the source is the first step toward reducing worry and strain. Solutions beyond that point vary according to case, but after identification, successful reduction of stress depends on making some kind of plan for coping with it and then having the fortitude to carry through with the plan. Selye (1981) was certainly correct when he commented that "action absorbs anxiety." For example, rather than just worrying over the coming group time, it is better to take action by acquainting yourself with the materials in advance, planning for variety, choosing activities that interest the children, and having the children actively participate.

Making realistic estimates about how long it will take you to accomplish something takes the strain and worry out of trying to get it done at the last minute. It is better to allow yourself too much time for planning than to come up short. Prioritizing helps, too. Choosing things that must be done and doing those first is a great stress-reducer. Concentrating on just one thing at a time also blocks out worry and helps you appreciate the current experience to its fullest. After all, all anyone really has is the current moment of existence. Why not seek to be aware of it fully while it is here?

Deliberately creating opportunities for relaxation is still another effective way of handling stress (McKay & Fanning, 1996). Finding a quiet place and letting go from the toes all the way to the forehead and ears can be quieting and refreshing. Such strategies need not take long, but it is necessary to make a point of remembering to use them from time to time.

The final suggestion that can help reduce stress is having a safety valve available. All of us should be aware of things we can do for ourselves that take the pressure off for a while when life is too demanding. These solutions vary a lot. I have had people tell me they do activities as diverse as going shopping, taking a swim, reading a detective story, and telling another person how they feel. The important thing about such strategies is that they should not be used as ways of permanently avoiding the stressful situation, because ultimately they can increase anxiety. At best they are stopgap measures that provide temporary relief and refreshment so that the person can pick up and go on in a reasonable period of time. When they are used, I believe they should be done deliberately, purposefully, and without guilt. When used in that manner, such indulgence provides maximum refreshment and benefit.

SOME SPECIAL PROBLEMS

The following problems have come up often enough with students that they deserve discussion. Of course, since each situation is different, recommendations are risky. Nevertheless the following suggestions may provide solutions that may not have occurred to the student.

What to Do If You Hate the School to Which You Are Assigned

I have already mentioned the several types of preschool, child care, and kindergarten situations, and even the same type varies a good deal from school to school and teacher to teacher. Some schools seem to suit some students, and others fit other students better. Therefore, do not conclude that teaching is not for you just because one placement is less than satisfactory. Maybe a change to another school is the answer to the problem; maybe it is not. At any rate the way to begin solving the difficulty is by talking over the reason for the unhappiness with the supervising teacher from the college. This is a more productive, as well as a more ethical, solution than complaining to a friend.

It is also wise to refrain from making snap judgments about a teacher or placement. The first 2 or 3 weeks in any school will be some of the most stressful weeks of the student's career, and it is essential to realize that some people react to stress by attacking what is frightening them and by criticizing it and that others shrink up and feel paralyzed or disillusioned. As time passes, the strain will probably lessen, and the school may seem more attractive, somewhat in the way hospital food mysteriously improves as the patient recovers.

What to Do If You Don't Like a Child

It is no sin to dislike a child, but it *is* a sin not to admit your dislike, come to terms with it, and try to do something about it. Sometimes what will help most is getting to know him or her better since insight often breeds compassion. Sometimes making progress of some sort with the child helps. Sometimes figuring out why you dislike the youngster will ease the feeling. With beginning students this can often be traced to the fact that some children challenge adults or put them on the spot. Students who already feel insecure find this behavior particularly trying. Whatever the reason it is healthier to risk admitting your dislike to yourself and perhaps to your mentor teacher, if you feel safe with that person, and then to work toward resolving the problem. Although the suggested remedies may not overcome the dislike completely, they should help. At the very least it is always possible to be fair and decent to all the children. The liking will probably come in time.

THE WAY TO YOUR MENTOR'S HEART

I have already talked about the fact that it takes time to feel at home and to build a friendship with a mentor. Six more specific practices the student can follow will help generate friendliness. The first thing is to remember that the teacher is *not* your mother! Perhaps this sounds like silly advice, but experience has taught me how easy it is to drag along the excess baggage of a former relationship when starting to work with an unfamiliar older person—often a woman—who is in a position of power. Far better to dump that burden and start a fresh relationship as two adults together.

The second thing to remember is to be prepared to make the small, extra contribution of time and energy *beyond* what is expected. The student who stays the extra 10 minutes on potluck night to dry the coffee pot is well on the way to becoming a popular member of the staff.

The third thing sounds simple but is often overlooked because new teachers tend to be nervous. It is to *listen* to what the teacher tells you, and do your best to remember it!

The fourth thing is to offer help *before* being asked to lend a hand. Some students are so afraid of being pushy or of making mistakes that they never volunteer. But always having to request help gets tiresome for the mentor teacher, even if the student is willing when asked. It is better to develop an eye for all the little things that must be done and then to do them quietly. Such students are treasured by their mentor teachers.

Fifth, besides volunteering to help, teachers also appreciate the student who contributes ideas for projects and activities. After all, it is not the mentor teacher's responsibility to provide all the ideas for your teaching days. Come prepared with a variety of suggestions so that if one or two turn out to be impractical, you can be flexible and propose alternative possibilities.

The sixth and final thing is for the student to let enthusiasm show through. The vast majority of teachers follow their profession since they love it; the rigors of the job and the relatively low pay weed the others out very quickly. The teachers are therefore enthusiastic themselves. They are often "born" teachers, and they love teaching students as well as young children. Expressing thanks by being enthusiastic yourself will encourage them to keep on making the extra effort entailed in guiding student teachers.

SUMMARY

The student should grasp three basic principles before beginning to teach: (a) Mentors are human, too; (b) one poor experience won't ruin a child's life; and (c) mistakes can be turned into valuable learning opportunities.

Even beginning students need to observe professional ethics when they are teaching. It is particularly important to respect each child and to preserve the privacy of the families whose children attend the school.

Gaining knowledge of the school's basic routines, schedules, and policies will make the early days of teaching a more comfortable experience for the young teacher. Some practical pieces of advice that will increase the student's competence include gaining confidence in handling discipline situations, getting to know the children, being alert to the whole environment, taking swift action in situations that are dangerous, encouraging the growth of independence and originality of self-expression, making contact with the children as quietly and meaningfully as possible, being organized, realizing that age need not be a negative factor when learning to teach, and asking for help when it is needed.

Probably no other time in the life of the teacher is so exciting, unsettling, and challenging as the first days of student teaching. Teachers are fortunate who manage to retain at least some of this flutter of anticipation throughout their teaching lives.

Questions and Activities

1. Getting started in the first days of student teaching can be a special challenge, and it is helpful to know yourself and your own reactions well enough to be able to control them. How do you anticipate you will cope with the strangeness and unfamiliarity of the student-teaching experience when you are just beginning? Close your eyes and think back to the last two or three occasions when you entered a new group and got acquainted. What was your personal mode of adapting? Did you talk a lot? Clam up? Act extremely helpful?

2. If you were guiding a young, new teacher, what advice would you give him or her that might help that person through the first days of teaching?

3. Do you believe that mentor teachers and professors are ever nervous or frightened when dealing with students, or do they seem invulnerable to such difficulties?

4. If you have ever had the good fortune to exist in a "life-affirming environment," identify the qualities you believe helped create that kind of emotional climate.

5. List some effective *do's* and *don'ts* for getting acquainted with young children. What are some effective ways of establishing friendly yet respectful relationships with them?

6. Do you know of some remedies that seem to help other people deal effectively with stress but that do not seem to help you? What are they, and why do you think they work for some people and not for others?

Self-Check Questions for Review

Content-Related Questions

1. Briefly outline the general history of the child care movement in the United States.

2. The text discusses the educational philosophies of two English women and an Italian woman who helped begin the child care movement in their countries. What are their names, and what are some facts about the schools they founded?

3. Name several kinds of child care situations and describe each of them in a general way.

4. Give some examples of ethical principles that teachers of young children should follow.

5. Name some practical things beginning teachers can do that will help them become competent as quickly as possible.

Integrative Questions

1. This book begins with a poem by Walt Whitman. What does the poem really mean, and how is it related to teaching young children?

2. The text lists some basic tenets of the Montessori and McMillan nursery schools. Compare the two schools. What do they have in common, and how do they differ?

3. At this point in your experience which kind of school (e.g., independent, Head Start, cooperative) do you think would best meet your needs as a student teacher? Discuss what might be the strong points and drawbacks of making that particular choice.

4. This chapter offers suggestions for coping successfully with stress. Which of these suggestions do you feel would be the most helpful ones for you to use?

5. Compare the advantages and disadvantages of being an independent child care provider paid by parents with the advantages and disadvantages of receiving financial support from a nonparental source such as the federal government or a church congregation.

References for Further Reading

Pick of the Litter

Note: The "Pick of the Litter" selection that begins each reference list in this book is a special, often offbeat book the reader might not otherwise encounter. I hope you will enjoy them!

Brosterman, N. (1997). *Inventing kindergarten.* New York: Abrams. I happened on this extraordinary book, anticipating "another" routine discussion. Instead it turned out to be an excellent description of primarily Froebel's theory, complete with beautiful illustrations and discussions of each of his "gifts."

This was followed by a discussion of Froebelian philosophy in relation to its influence on such modern artists as Klee, Mondrian, Wright, and LeCorbusier.

Overview

Morrison, G. (1998). *Early childhood education today* (7th ed.). Upper Saddle River, NJ: Merrill/Prentice Hall. This helpful book offers a current overview of some kinds of early childhood settings and philosophies that exist in the United States.

Maintaining Good Relationships with Children

Ayers, W. (1989). *The good preschool teacher: Six teachers reflect on their lives.* New York: Teachers College Press. This book is a collection of interviews given by six very different teachers of preschool children, combined with descriptions of events in their child care situations. It provides a variety of viewpoints and how teachers put their philosophies into action.

Maintaining Good Relationships with Other Adults

Blanchard, K. (1992). *The one minute manager.* New York: Berkley. What this book has to say about communicating with people is valuable for all of us, not just managers!

Learning About Our Roots: Historical Approaches to Teaching Young Children

Beatty, B. (1995). *Preschool education in America: The culture of young children from the colonial era to the present.* New Haven, CT: Yale University Press. Beginning with a thorough survey of European antecedents, the author traces the development of child care and particularly kindergarten programs throughout their development in the United States.

Bradburn, E. (1989). *Margaret McMillan: Portrait of a pioneer.* London: Routledge. This is an inspiring book about an early advocate of nursery education. *Highly recommended.*

Greenberg, P. (1992). *The devil has slippery shoes: A biased biography of the Child Development Group of Mississippi.* Washington, DC: Youth Policy Institute.

(Original work published 1970) The trials and tribulations of the Child Development Group in the early days of Head Start are described. Wonderful reading.

Hainstock, E. G. (1997). *The essential Montessori: An introduction to the woman, the writings, the method, and the movement.* New York: Plume. Many direct quotations by Dr. Montessori convey the true flavor of this innovative early childhood pioneer.

Mills, K. (1998). *Something better for my children.* New York: Dutton. Replete with anecdotes about what Head Start is really like, this book also discusses some current difficulties and what may lie ahead.

Osborn, D. K. (1991). *Early childhood education in historical perspective.* Athens, GA: Education Associates. This is a chronology of significant events in early childhood education, with brief synopses of their significance. A one-of-a-kind book.

Pratt, C. (1990). *I learn from children.* New York: Harper & Row. (Original work published 1948) It is wonderful having this classic of early childhood literature available once again. *Highly recommended.*

Dealing Effectively with Stress

Gruenberg, A. (1998). Creative stress management: "Put your own oxygen mask on first." *Young Children,* 53(1), 38–42. This article is filled with practical advice about handling stress. *Highly recommended.*

Jorde, P. (1982). *Avoiding burnout: Strategies for managing time, space, and people in early childhood education.* Washington, DC: Acropolis Books. This is a wonderful, relevant book stuffed with ideas for managing one's life as a teacher and as a human being. *Highly recommended.*

Miller, L. H., Smith, A. D. & Rothstein, L. (1993). *The stress solution: An action plan to manage the stress in your life.* New York: Pocket Books. This easy-to-read book provides a comprehensive, practical discussion of sources of stress and suggests a great variety of ways to relieve it. *Highly recommended.*

For the Advanced Student

Ellsworth, J., & Ames, L. J. (1998). *Critical perspectives on Head Start.* Albany: State University of New York. Of course, no program is perfect, and Head Start is no exception. A series of chapters, many research based, detail aspects of that program that merit changing.

Feeney, S., & Freeman, N. K. (1999). *Ethics and the early childhood educator: Using the NAEYC code.* Washington, DC: National Association for the Education of Young Children. The authors present the National Association for the Education of Young Children standards for ethical behavior and follow that with common place situations where reference to the code might resolve a variety of frequently experienced dilemmas—a good starting place for more in-depth discussion than *The Whole Child* has space to provide.

Humphryes, J. (1998). The developmental appropriateness of high-quality Montessori programs. *Young Children, 53*(4), 4–24. This article is an interesting attempt to explain some principles of the Montessori Method and to reveal what they have in common with other contemporary early childhood approaches.

Kagan, S. L., & Bowman, B. T. (Eds.). (1997). *Leadership in early care and education.* Washington, DC: National Association for the Education of Young Children. Of particular interest to someone entering the early childhood field might be the discussion of new directions in which a variety of related careers may be heading in future years.

Lehrer, P. M., & Woolfolk, R. L. (Eds.). (1993). *Principles and practice of stress management* (2nd ed.). New York: Guilford Press. This book presents numerous effective methods for alleviating stress that are described by authorities in their fields. *Highly recommended.*

Mitchell, A., Stoney, L., & Dichter, H. (1997). *Financing child care in the United States: An illustrative catalog of current strategies.* Ewing Marion Kaufmann Foundation and the Pew Charitable Trusts. This one-of-a-kind catalog is an invaluable compilation of sources and strategies for financing child care at the present time.

The future of child care: Financing child care. (1966). *Future of Children, 6*(2). For a complete survey of the current confusing situation, this free publication is hard to beat. Available from the David and Lucille Packard Foundation, 300 2nd St., Suite 102, Los Altos, CA 94022.

What Makes a Good Day for Children?

In the evaluation of the dominant moods of any historical period it is important to hold fast to the fact that there are always islands of self-sufficient order—on farms and in castles, in homes, studies, and cloisters—where sensible people manage to live relatively lusty and decent lives: as moral as they must be, as free as they may be, and as masterful as they can be. If we but knew it, this elusive arrangement is happiness.

Erik Erikson (1958)

Child care is only easy when you don't know what you're doing.

Jim Greenman (1998d, p. 6)

What to reply when a friend says your job is really just baby-sitting?

Whether early education really makes any difference?

What a good program should include?

Why people are so excited about something called *Reggio Emilia*?

. . . IF YOU HAVE, THE MATERIAL IN THE FOLLOWING PAGES WILL HELP YOU.

No doubt the reader is anxious to press on to discussions of discipline or eating problems or teaching children to share; these are valid concerns of all teachers of young children. However, it seems wise to take time first for an overview of whether early education is effective and what should go into a good day for young children. What elements should be included when planning the overall curriculum? Once these elements are clearly in mind, we can consider more specific problems and recommendations.

CAN EARLY EDUCATION MAKE A DIFFERENCE?

For more than two decades, research on approaches to early childhood education has sought to investigate the effectiveness of various kinds of programs in changing the behavior and enhancing the development of young children. The results of these investigations have been at times discouraging and at times heartening. On the one hand the Westinghouse Report (Cicerelli, Evans, & Schiller, 1969), the Hawkridge study (Hawkridge, Chalupsky, & Roberts, 1968), and a report by Abt Associates (Stebbins, Pierre, Proper, Anderson, & Cerva, 1977) found little evidence of persistence across program change on measures of intellectual ability.

If IQ tests are to be accepted as the sole indicator of valuable changes that can result from early education, then these investigators are quite correct. Preschool programs have not been shown to produce measurable, long-term (continuing beyond the fourth grade) changes in the intelligence quotients of children attending such programs (Barnett, 1995). When additional measures of ability are included, however, hundreds of studies now confirm the value of early educational intervention. Many of these are reviewed by Barnett and Boocock (1998) in their landmark book *Early Care and Education for Children in Poverty*. Moreover, additional recent investigations measuring the development of the brain reveal that early prevention and intervention activities can have a significant positive effect on the overall development of the brain itself (Lally, 1998; R. Shore, 1997). It is crucial that such support be provided during the early years of childhood because waiting until later sharply reduces the chances of permanent improvement.

It is important to know about the results of such studies since most members of the general public, including parents and legislators, are still uninformed about the potential value of early education and persist in seeing it as "just baby-sitting." If we are tired of this misguided point of view, we need to have the results of these studies on the tips of our tongues so that we can explain the value of our work with young children to those who need to be better informed about it.

The first and therefore particularly important retrospective study was published by Irving Lazar (Lazar & Darlington, 1978, 1982; Lazar, Hubbell, Murray, Rosche, & Royce, 1977). Additional studies of the Perry Preschool Project detailed by Schweinhart, Barnes, and Weikart in *Significant Benefits: The High/Scope Perry Preschool Study Through Age 27* (1993), by Schweinhart and Weikart in *Lasting Differences: The High/Scope Preschool Curriculum Comparison Study Through Age 23* (1997), by Gray, Ramsey, and Klaus in *From 3 to*

20 (1982), and by McKay and colleagues (1985), who reviewed 210 Head Start studies, have supported and enriched these findings.

Lazar's consortium study (Lazar, Darlington, Murray, Royce, & Snipper, 1982) followed up on some infant and preschool programs (including the work by Gray [Gray et al., 1982] and Weikart [Schweinhart et al., 1993; Schweinhart & Weikart, 1997]) that took place in the 1960s. These were special, high-quality programs that used both experimental and control groups and drew their subjects from families of the poor. Members of each experimental group participated in a preschool program, whereas their similar control companions did not have that advantage.

At the time of the follow-up, the questions Lazar and his coworkers (Lazar & Darlington, 1978, 1982; Lazar et al., 1982; Lazar et al., 1977) wanted to answer about both groups were "Now that these children are either in their teens or early twenties, what has become of them?" "How have they turned out?" and "Did early intervention make a difference in their lives?" To answer these questions, each project traced as many of the experimental and control children as possible, retested them on the Wechsler Intelligence Test, and among many other questions asked whether they had ever repeated a grade in school or had been placed in a class for educable mentally retarded children (an EMR classroom).[1]

An analysis of the intelligence test material (both current and prior tests) led the investigators to conclude that "although evidence showed that early education can produce significant increases in IQ (compared to a control group) which last for up to three years after the child leaves the program . . . it appears that the effect . . . is probably not permanent" (Lazar et al., 1977, pp. 19, 20).

The information related to grade retention and placement in EMR classrooms was much more encouraging in part because of its implications for saving public monies (Barnett & Escobar, 1990; Schweinhart et al., 1993) but also because of what the findings mean in terms of human happiness.

Even though these data vary considerably between programs (probably since different school districts have different policies on having children repeat grades), they clearly indicate that early education can reduce the rate of repeating grades for low-income children, thereby preventing much humiliation and loss of self-esteem. And if repetition of a grade is humiliating to a youngster, one can only surmise how bad it feels to be placed in a classroom for cognitively delayed children. Here, once again, the Lazar data provide convincing evidence that early education is worthwhile because substantially fewer project children were found to have been placed in such classes.

The research on children in the Perry Preschool Project carried these studies even further. Begun in 1962, that research is still continuing, and the data have been consistent over more than three decades of investigation. Table 2.1 illustrates the substantial differences between the experimental group of children who had experienced the benefits of a good preschool program combined with home visiting and a similar group of children who had not had those experiences (Weikart, 1990). Note that fewer of the Perry Preschool children had been in trouble with the law, more of them had graduated from high school, and more of them had jobs after graduation. The most recent data, published in 1993 by

---

[1] *For a more complete interpretation and explanation of this study, the reader should refer to the original reports, which are well worth reading.*

Table 2.1
Summary of the results of the Perry Preschool Project*

	Experimental Group (%)	Control Group (%)
In Education		
Classified as mentally retarded	15	35
Completed high school	67	49
Attended college or job-training programs	38	21
In Employment		
Hold jobs	50	32
Support themselves or are supported by spouse	45	25
Satisfied with work	42	26
In the Community		
Arrested for criminal acts	31	51
Birth rate†	64*	117*
Public assistance	18	32

*Age of subjects was 19 years.
†Birth rates are per 100 women.

Source: From Quality Preschool Programs: A Long-Term Social Investment *(p. 7), by D. Weikart, 1990, New York: Ford Foundation. Reprinted with permission.*

Schweinhart and Weikart, indicate that this trend toward self-sufficiency was continuing as the group neared age 27. They continued to have fewer arrests and significantly higher incomes, and many more of them owned homes than did those in the control group. When these results are translated into taxpayer dollars saved, the money amounts to about $76,077 (1992 dollars) per participant—a return of $7.16 for every dollar originally invested in the preschool program.

The Lazar and Perry Preschool studies are selected since they are the most widely publicized pieces of research on this subject, but the reader should realize that they are but two of many studies that now support the value of well-planned early education for children who come from families of low income.[2]

DO DIFFERENT EDUCATIONAL APPROACHES PRODUCE DIFFERENT RESULTS?

The Perry Preschool study has also been used for another interesting research project: *Lasting Differences: The High/Scope Preschool Curriculum Comparison Study Through Age 23* (Schweinhart & Weikart, 1997). This project compared three models of early childhood

[2] *For additional information, the reader should refer to Barnett & Boocock (1998) or to the entire issue of* The Future of Children *(1995, vol. 5, no. 3).*

instruction: (a) The High/Scope model, which engaged children as active learners, emphasized "key experiences" focusing learning in intellectual, social, and physical domains, and encouraged children to plan, do, and review what they had done; (b) the traditional nursery school model, which focused on a child-centered approach with unit- or theme-based curriculum emphasizing social skills; and (c) the direct instruction model, which emphasized teacher-directed academic instruction using workbooks and rigorously planned question-and-answer lessons.

In the early years of the follow-up study results from all three models were about the same. Or, as the investigators phrased it, it appeared that "well-implemented preschool curriculum models have similar [desirable] effects on children's intellectual and academic performance" (Schweinhart & Weikart, 1997, p. xi).

However, as time went on, the effect of using the different instructional models became more and more apparent. At age 23, when children from the High/Scope curriculum and/or the nursery school curriculum were compared with children from the direct instruction program, many differences became evident. Among the most important were that children who had participated in "the High/Scope and Nursery School groups . . . had significantly fewer felony arrests, fewer years of special education for emotional impairment, and more members doing volunteer work" than did the direct instruction children (Schweinhart & Weikart, 1997, p. xii).

The authors concluded, "This study supports the idea that early childhood programs in which children initiate their own learning activities are superior to programs based on teacher-directed instruction." Further, it identifies "the High/Scope Curriculum and a traditional Nursery School curriculum as particular methods that are effective in helping children to make decisions, solve problems, and get along with others—and in the long run, to avoid crime" (Schweinhart & Weikart, 1997, p. xii).

UNDERLYING PHILOSOPHY OF THIS BOOK

The Whole Child is based on the traditional nursery school model and uses an eclectic approach that draws from several theoretical bases: (a) the application of behavior modification strategies when appropriate; (b) the application of Piagetian and Vygotskian principles as expressed in the *constructivist, developmental, interactionist approach;* and (c) the application of the philosophical principles exemplified by the schools of Reggio Emilia whenever possible. All these approaches offer material of great value in relation to understanding and teaching young children.

Uses and Values of Behavior Modification

The term *behavior modification* tends to bring scowls to the faces of many teachers who object to the potential for manipulation inherent in that approach. However, it is important to understand its positive value as well. Learning theorists who practice behavior modification have accumulated a great deal of carefully documented research that substantiates their claims that this approach, which rewards desirable behavior and discourages undesirable actions, can be a powerful avenue for teaching (Thomas, 1999; Witt, Elliott, & Gresham, 1988). It has proved its usefulness particularly in work with children with a variety of disabilities (Bailey & Wolery, 1992; Berkson, 1993).

Behavior modification theorists stress the importance of the influence of environment on behavior. They maintain that children learn various behaviors as a result of experiencing pleasant or unpleasant outcomes or reinforcements. Pleasant outcomes or rewards such as teacher attention, praise, or candy tend to cause the behavior to persist, whereas unpleasant negative consequences such as scolding or writing the child's name on the chalkboard discourage it. If the child receives neither positive nor negative reinforcement,

No matter what philosophy is involved, warm, caring relationships are the cornerstones of all good early childhood programs.

then he will gradually abandon the behavior. Critics complain that this approach to human development emphasizes the role of external rewards and sees the child as a passive recipient of stimuli that regulate behavior, rather than as a human being capable of initiating novel ideas and behavior.

It is true that the cut-and-dried, deliberately orchestrated manipulation of behavior that might be possible if such a program were carried out in its purest form is repugnant, but it is also true that *all teachers use this technique constantly and extensively whether they realize it or not.* Every smile, every frown, every positive or negative bit of attention a child receives either encourages or discourages future behavior. Therefore, rather than blindly condemning such theory, why not become aware of how often we employ such strategies on an informal basis and acknowledge their power? To use behavior modification effectively it is not necessary to agree with Skinner (1974) and Goodwin (1999) that positive or negative reinforcement is the only activator of behavior. Indeed it seems impossible to use learning theory satisfactorily to explain how people generate original ideas or how they formulate language patterns they have not heard before. In my opinion, learning theory is simply a useful tool that explains a great deal, but not all, of why human beings behave as they do. As such it cannot be ignored.

Uses and Values of Piagetian, Constructivist Theory

The reader will find that the work of the great theorist and investigator Jean Piaget is referred to again and again throughout this volume. His more than half-century of research into the developmental stages and characteristics of children's cognitive processes is invaluable, as are both his emphasis on the importance of dynamic interaction between the child and the environment as the child *constructs* what he knows for himself, and his emphasis on the significance of play as a medium for learning (DeVries & Kohlberg, 1990).

However, many scholars and teachers, including myself, are not satisfied with restricting themselves solely to Piagetian constructivist theory because we believe that Piaget did not say enough about social relationships, creativity, or emotional health. This is because Piaget's primary interest was the investigation of children's thought processes. Although we must incorporate his work, we cannot limit ourselves only to his theory in a textbook of this scope.

A point of view closely related to Piagetian constructivism but more comprehensive is the developmental-interactionist approach of the Bank Street program described by Biber (1981, 1984). It sees children as developing human beings in whom knowing about things (the intellectual self) combines with feeling about them (the emotional self). In this point of view the impetus for growth lies in part within the maturing individual but also occurs in part as a result of the interaction between the child and the environment and people to whom the child relates.

This interaction is important since the child is regarded as being an active participant in his own growth. He learns by constructing and reconstructing what he knows as he encounters a variety of experiences and people that widen and enrich his knowledge. The teacher's role is one of guiding, questioning, and enabling—not just stuffing the child with an assortment of facts and rewards for good behavior.

Because the child is a complex, interacting being composed of many attributes and aspects both social and intellectual, we must see teaching as stimulating and enhancing the development of all these aspects, not just the cognitive one. That is why this book concentrates on the five selves of the child, rather than on specific topics such as art or science. It is an attempt to shift the attention of the teacher to what the child *is* and what he needs from the learning environment to realize his tremendous potential. Only when this is done can it be truly said that we are educating the whole child.

Contributions of Vygotsky

In recent years the Russian Lev Vygotsky (1978) has become known as yet another educational theorist who has contributed helpful insights about the way young children learn and develop. Vygotsky reminds us how important the influence of culture and social interchange is to mental growth. Adults and more knowledgeable peers who transmit these social values and information assist the child's growth. They do this by interacting and encouraging him to operate at the growing edge of his mental abilities—the area of "assisted performance" termed by Vygotsky *the zone of proximal development* (often abbreviated as the *ZPD*).

Vygotsky identified social play as the premier or "leading" activity that enables young children to operate in that zone since play requires the use of imagination, symbolic language, and observation of social "rules" requiring self regulation. In addition to play Vygotsky devoted considerable time to defining the role of the teacher. He advocated that teachers should sense which skills are about to emerge in each child and seek to develop them. Development should be accomplished by delicately assisting the child—first by finding out what he already knows and then by using dialogue and various experiences to assist him to advance to a further point in his growth.

Contributions from Reggio Emilia

In addition to drawing on the behavior modification and constructivist points of view advocated by Piaget and Vygotsky the current edition of this book recognizes that a newer approach to early childhood education is gaining prominence. Ever since 1987, when the 100 Languages of Children exhibit began its still-continuing tour of the United States, interest in some remarkable Italian schools situated in the city of Reggio Emilia has been growing. These schools enable very young children to explore and express their ideas through an astonishing array of media. Their productions, though lovely, are not only aesthetically pleasing but also represent a level of creative thought and problem-solving ability that goes far beyond American expectations of what young children can do. These results are causing many American teachers to reassess their current approaches to early education.[3]

The teachers at Reggio Emilia are confident about the preschool child's abilities (Malaguzzi, 1998; Rinaldi, 1993). They see him as strong, competent, capable of con-

---

[3] *Space permits only a brief overview of the Reggio approach in this chapter. Additional information is provided at appropriate points throughout the book.*

structing his own thoughts, and having great potential to offer to the world. In this approach the teacher becomes a compass that may point the child in a particular direction, and education is seen as an ever-developing process that cannot be predetermined because it emerges bit by bit.

The children's centers at Reggio Emilia are places where children and teachers interact—listening and talking with each other—to explore subjects in depth by exchanging ideas and trying out those ideas. Teachers select an aspect of the children's interests to develop further—an aspect that presents problems for them to consider and solve (or, as Reggian teachers put it, "provokes" the children into thought). A particular interest may be pursued in depth over several months, depending on how intrigued the children become with the topic.

The results of these joint investigations are then transformed by the children into visible products that communicate what they have found out to other people. As the staff members often say, "You don't know it until you can express it." Since the children are too young to write, the staff encourages them to express what they know by using all sorts of other languages. It might be the language of paint, or clay, or cardboard structures, or concoctions of bent wire bedecked with tissue paper, or shadow plays.

American preschools already espouse many ideas basic to the Reggian philosophy: parent involvement; fostering creativity; learning by doing; inquiry-based, child-centered, hands-on, cooperative learning. But we are also tantalized by evidence of the exceptional abilities demonstrated by these young Italian children, particularly because observers report that it is really the children themselves who are doing the work and accomplishing it without strain. It is my hope that inclusion of information about the Reggio approach in *The Whole Child* will encourage the application of many of its principles in our own work with children in this country.

BASIC PREMISES OF THIS BOOK

Besides advocating that a curriculum be provided for every self, this book is based on additional basic premises. The first premise is that the purpose of education is to increase competence and mastery in all aspects of the developing self. It is much more important to teach children to cope by equipping them with skills than to stuff them full of facts. This is so because confidence in their coping ability is what underlies children's sense of self-worth. Skills empower children.

The second premise is that physical and emotional health are absolutely fundamental to the well-being of children. Any program that ignores that fact is building its curriculum on a foundation of sand.

The third premise is that children learn most easily by means of actual, involving experiences with people and activities. This is best accomplished in an open, carefully planned yet flexible environment where children must take responsibility and make decisions for themselves and where they have ample opportunity to learn through play.

The fourth premise is that children pass through various stages as they develop. Piaget has, of course, thoroughly demonstrated this in regard to intellectual development, but it has been heavily documented for the other selves as well (K. E. Allen & Marotz, 1990; Brittain, 1979; Gesell, Halverson, Thompson, & Ilg, 1940; R. Shore, 1997; Shotwell, Wolf, & Gardner, 1979; Wickstrom, 1983).

It is important to realize that having a general sense of these landmark stages in mind can be both an asset and a liability for the teacher. Such knowledge is an asset if it fosters the development of activities and expectations that are known to be generally appropriate for a particular age. On the other hand, knowledge of developmental stages can be a liability if that information is used to blindly restrict what is offered to the children to encourage their development. The most sensible approach is to remain aware of the developmental level of the children we teach and then to provide education that fits that level while encouraging children to reach a little beyond it (Vygotsky, 1978).

The fifth premise is that children do not exist in isolation as they develop. As Bronfenbrenner (1979) and Vygotsky (1978) remind us, we are all surrounded by ever-widening worlds of family, community, and the wider world beyond all of which influence the direction and degree of our growth.

The final premise is that children need time to be children. The purpose of preprimary education and child care should not be to pressure and urge youngsters on to the next step in a hurried way. The current term *hothousing* well describes the effect of such forced learning on the unfortunate children who experience it. Recent research provides evidence that placing academic pressure on preschool children is a precursor to negative attitudes toward school and decreased creativity in kindergarten and academic accomplishments in later grades (Hyson & Hirsh-Pasek, 1990; Marcon, 1992, 1994a, 1994b; Schweinhart & Weikart, 1997).

Children need time and personal space in which to grow. They need time to be themselves—to do nothing, to stand and watch, to repeat again what they did before; in short, they need time to live *in* their childhood, rather than *through* it. If we are sensitive to their concerns and offer the young children we teach rich and appropriate learning opportunities combined with enough time for them to enjoy and experience those opportunities to the fullest, we will be enhancing that era of childhood, not violating it.

PUTTING PREMISES INTO PRACTICE: PLANNING A GOOD DAY FOR CHILDREN

A Good Day Is a High-Quality Day

At a time when research reveals that only one in seven child care centers could be rated as excellent it is clear that careful attention must be paid to changing some prevailing conditions (Helburn, 1995).[4] During the past few years research has begun to identify the

---

[4] Excellent quality *was defined as health and safety needs are met, warmth and support are provided for all children, many ways of learning through interesting and pleasureful activities are provided, encouragement toward independence is evident, individual learning needs are planned for, and close personal relationships are maintained with each child (Helburn, 1995).*

various components that contribute to producing high-quality care. Some of these, such as stronger, firmly enforced licensing standards, national accreditation, higher ratios of teachers to children, well-trained staff, and adequate salaries, require concerted group action to bring into being (Helburn, 1995; S. L. Kagan & Cohen, 1996; Kinch & Schweinhart, 1999). However, others are within the reach of everyone working at the preschool level, so these are discussed in the following paragraphs. Better to light a candle than to curse the darkness!

Good Human Relationships Are a Fundamental Ingredient of a Good Day

All good programs are built on the foundation of sound human relationships. Warmth and empathic understanding have been shown to be effective means of influencing young children's positive adjustment to school (Zanolli, Saudargas, & Twardosz, 1997). It is apparent that genuine caring about the children and about other adults in the program is fundamental to success.

For warmth and personal contact to flourish, the day must be planned and paced so that opportunities for person-to-person, one-to-one encounters are numerous. In practical terms this means groups must be kept small and the ratio of adults to children must be as high as possible. Many occasions must also be provided for the children to move freely about, making personal choices and generating individual contacts. Such arrangements permit numerous interludes in which informal learning experiences can be enjoyed and human caring can be expressed. The moments may be as fleeting as a quick hug when the teacher ties a pair of trailing shoelaces or as extended as a serious discussion of where babies come from. It is the *quality* of individualized, personal caring and the chance to talk together that are significant.

Parents Must Be Included as Part of the Life of the School

The day is past when parents were expected to pay their bill but leave their children at the preschool or center's door. Of course, cooperative schools have long demonstrated the feasibility of including the family in the school experience, but today we can also point to mounting research confirming that inclusion of the parent in the educational process, whether in home tutoring programs or the school itself, results in longer lasting educational gains for the child (Olds & Kitzman, 1993). Parent inclusion is also a fundamental cornerstone of the Reggio approach, in which parents participate in day-to-day interactions, discussions of relevant issues, excursions, and celebrations (Spaggiari, 1998).

Now parent involvement goes far beyond attending parent education meetings and open houses. Parents serve as indispensable volunteers in the classroom, where their duties are as diverse as tutoring and sharing their cultural backgrounds with the youngsters. They serve on powerful advisory boards, raise money, and provide ideas and criticism about the curriculum.

Rather than feeling threatened by this vigorous interest, wise teachers do all they can to get to know the children's parents well in order to use their talents most effectively. There is no more valuable way to widen everyone's horizons than by strengthening the link between home and school. Chapters 3, 8, and 13 provide more detailed suggestions of practical ways to welcome parents into the life of the school.

A Good Program Must Be Developmentally Appropriate

Developmentally appropriate means the learning activities planned for the children are placed at the correct level for their age and are suited to individual children's tastes, abilities, and cultures. This definition is important because if the material is at the right developmental level, the children will be drawn to it and want to learn about it (Bredekamp & Copple, 1997).

In contrast, when children are pushed too far ahead of their current levels and the curriculum is unsuited to their abilities, it's like pushing them into deep water before they can swim: They're likely to dread the water and avoid it when they can. Herein lies one peril of misinterpreting Vygotsky's recommendation that the teacher lead the child to reach beyond his current ability to the edge of his zone of proximal development. In the hands

A good program needs to be developmentally appropriate. This is just about challenging enough to intrigue but not discourage these young threes.

of an insensitive and overzealous teacher this recommendation could be wrongly interpreted and translated into too high expectations and overbearing pressure.

At this early stage of schooling it is crucial for children to decide that learning is something to be pursued with verve, not that it is difficult and anxiety-provoking. For this reason it is vital that teachers have a good grasp of the developmental characteristics of children at various ages, understand how they are likely to progress as they grow, and plan the curriculum to stimulate that growth without making it so difficult that children give up in despair.

A Good Program Is Individualized

The teacher must see every youngster not only in terms of what he knows in general about child development but also in terms of what that particular child is like developmentally and culturally. This is the real art of teaching—being able to clothe overall bare-bones educational goals in the raiment of individual children's abilities, needs, interests, and pleasures. Fortunately the small size and intimacy of preschool groups make it possible for teachers to know each youngster well and to plan with particular individuals in mind.

A Simple Test to Determine Whether the Curriculum Is Individualized

The teacher can use four questions to determine whether the curriculum is individualized:

1. Are there numerous recent instances in which the curriculum was based on a child's specific interests?
2. Can examples be cited in which curriculum plans were changed since a child revealed an unanticipated interest or enthusiasm during the day?
3. Can examples be identified in which a child was deliberately provided opportunities to learn what observation and evaluations had indicated that he especially needed to know?
4. Can recent examples be cited in which the children had opportunities to perceive and *value* the cultural and physical diversity of other youngsters in the group?

A Good Program Honors Diversity in Its Many Forms

Ever since its original publication in 1973, *The Whole Child* has included an entire chapter advocating cross-cultural education and another on inclusion of children who have special needs into the preschool group. Since this is the case, I will content myself here with reminding the reader that everyone's experience is enriched when children from a variety of backgrounds are included in the school.

A Good Program Uses Reasonable and Authentic Methods of Assessment to Find Out More About the Children

Although space does not permit an extensive discussion of assessment methods in a beginning text, even teachers who are just starting out need to know that assessing children of preschool age is a risky and problematic business (Meisels & Atkins-Burnett, 1994). At best assessments can identify skills, needs, and promising potentials of such young children; at worst they can use totally inappropriate methods of evaluation (McAfee & Leong, 1994).

Perhaps the most desirable way to think of assessment for the majority of preschool children is as an opportunity to record growth and deepen teachers' and parents' insights about particular children. There are a variety of ways that teachers can generate such records. These include information contributed by families, simple checklists based on developmental charts, snapshots or even videotapes of children's special accomplishments such as block structures or other creations, an occasional painting, and weekly anecdotal records citing events or interactions related to the child that the teacher thinks are significant (Hendrick, 1998; McAfee & Leong, 1994). Remember that records are most helpful when they are begun early in the year so that progress can be noted as it occurs.

When more comprehensive assessments are needed, it is best to refer the family to someone who specializes in that area. See chapter 9 for a discussion about how to make effective referrals.

A Good Program Has a Balance Between Self-Selection and Teacher Direction; Both Approaches Are Valuable

Value of Self-Selection

The idea that young children can be trusted to choose educational experiences for themselves that will benefit them goes all the way back in educational theory to Jean Jacques Rousseau and John Dewey. Currently this concept is being used at Reggio Emilia, as well as continuing its tenure in the majority of American child care centers.

It is important to understand that those daily activities should be thought through and planned intentionally to provide a comprehensive array of educational benefits even though these benefits may not be readily perceived by visitors who are most aware of the children circulating freely from one activity to another as their interests dictate. The other aspect of the program that may not be apparent to the casual visitor is the planned though flexible purpose and overall direction to the entire program—a continuing vision of "becoming." The daily curriculum is developing with a long-term goal in view as the teacher and children move along a pathway of interests and problem solving together.

Of course, no plan should be interpreted so rigorously that it leaves no room for momentary spontaneity. At times the marvelous welling up of an idea or activity suddenly occurs, and these teachable moments are to be sought after and treasured—but this does not happen all the time. Nor does reliance on such events ensure that every important area of the self will be educated, that necessary goals will be achieved, or that the needs of individual children will be considered. *Only planning coupled with consistent evaluation can ensure that these objectives are accomplished.*

Self-selection needs to be balanced with opportunities for group experiences, too. Some of those experiences are small, casual, and informal, as when a group of interested children gathers around the teacher to discuss where the snow went and how to make it return. Some, such as large-group times (chapter 16) and mealtimes (chapter 4), require more management by the teacher. These more formal situations are essential ingredients

Summertime provides special opportunities to experience the delights of water play.

in the early childhood program because they provide opportunities to make certain that all the children are included in thinking and reasoning activities every day. Without these planned participation times, occasional children might graduate from preschool with a degree in trike riding coupled with a deadly inability to put five words together into a coherent sentence.

A Good Program Should Be Comprehensive

One aspect of planning that deserves special consideration is that the curriculum should be comprehensive in coverage. As mentioned earlier, a valuable way to think about this is to picture the child as being composed of a number of selves: the physical self, the emotional self, the social self, the creative self, and the cognitive self. This book is based on this division of the child into selves, since experience has shown that various aspects of the curriculum fall rather neatly under these headings and that the five selves succeed in covering the personality of the child.

The *physical self* includes not only large and fine muscle development but also the handling of routines because such things as eating, resting, and toileting contribute much to physical comfort and well-being. For the *emotional self* we consider ways to increase and sustain mental health, to use discipline to foster self-control, to cope with aggression, and to foster self-esteem. Included for the *social self* are ways to build social concern and kindliness, learning to enjoy work, and learning to value the cultures and abilities of other people. The *creative self* covers the areas of self-expression through the use of art materials and creativity as expressed in play and applied in thought. Finally, the *cognitive*, or *intellectual*, *self* is considered in terms of the development of language and generalized and specific reasoning abilities. This last self is the newest one to receive intensive consideration and analysis in early childhood education, and much remains to be learned in this area.

Formulating an Effective Daily Plan

One way of ensuring that the curriculum is both comprehensive and purposeful is to discipline oneself by filling out the Curriculum Analysis and Planning Chart each week (shown in Figure 2.1) to make certain something is deliberately planned for each self of the child every day to enhance his growth.

In the space where Activity is specified, the name of the activity—for example, "clay"—should be written in. The specific purpose that day for offering clay might be "to relieve aggressive feelings." If so, clay would best fit the Emotional category. Or if the primary purpose is to provide the materials as an opportunity for creative self-expression, then the clay activity would be listed in the Creative space. Or if the intention is make a model using clay to show how pipes would be arranged to carry water to the duck pond it would go in the Cognitive category.

Although I would not advocate such detailed planning as a usual occurrence, the staff at the Institute of Child Development at the University of Oklahoma has found it helpful for beginning teachers to use since it requires them to think through the purposes or reasons for selecting activities for their curriculum. The bonus is that once teachers learn to think this clearly, they not only stop offering educational trash and time fillers to children but also have no difficulty justifying the educational purposes of the activities to inquiring parents.

An example of a daily plan is included in Figure 2.1. The children's interests were focused on letting a friend know they cared about him.

Formulating a Longer Term Plan

Of course, planning needs to extend beyond the day and even the week. There is, however, a difficulty associated with a longer term plan: Formulating a detailed plan far in advance (or worse yet, repeating the same plan year after year!) is likely to push teacher and children into a lockstep of unchangeable direction and activity. That is why it is most helpful to think of long-term planning as "a vision of becoming." Doing this encourages the planner to stay open to several directions the children's interests might take—pathways down which teacher and children might venture together in their quest for knowledge.

For example, a longer term plan continuing the children's interest in fish might pursue trying out ways to keep the aquarium from getting mossy and then investigating ways to

Long-Term Interest: How Animals Live

Date: 5/11/99

Age of Children: 4½–5

Self	Physical: Large muscle	Physical: Fine muscle	Emotional: Understanding feelings	Social	Multicultural	Nonsexist	Creative	Cognitive: Mental ability	Cognitive: Language
Activity	Trike ride to family's pond	Catching fish; Setting up aquarium	Hospital play; Discussions of hospital during group time	Make aquarium and get-well notes; Visit child's family	Lunch	Discuss who cares for fish pond	Collaged get-well soon cards; Arrange aquarium	Finding out about goldfish and aquarium	Dictate get-well messages; Listen to books about fish or giving presents
Educational purpose	Bilateral coordination of legs and arms. Increase fitness and endurance.	Use nets to catch elusive baby goldfish—eye/hand coordination. Embed plants in rocks—dig, hold, press plants down under water.	Play out feelings about hospitals. Cope with worries about friend. Think about how to comfort someone else.	Do something kind for someone else. Do meaningful work. Consider what someone, *not yourself,* would really like for a present. Negotiate who will go to hospital to deliver aquarium. Help bond shy child and her family closer to school.	Food from another culture tastes good (tacos, fruit salad, milk).	Everyone in family takes turns maintaining pond, feeding and caring for fish and plants.	Fosters sense of balance, color, and design. Use of own ideas and inspirations.	Opportunities for problem solving: What kind of present is practical in a hospital? How can we catch the fish? What can we use to transport them? How can we keep the plants from floating up in the aquarium? Specific Mental Abilities: *Cause/Effect:* What happens to fish out of water? *Common Relations:* Pair real fish and water plants to pictures in fish book. *Facts about goldfish:* They require cool, non-salty water. They can live a long time. There are many kinds: fantails, pop-eyes, etc.	Writing is a useful way to send a message. Reading helps us find out things we want to know. New vocabulary—such as "fins," "scales," "aquarium," etc. Group discussions of putting ideas and plans into words. *Fish stories* *Swimmy* (Lionni, 1987). *Stories about presents* Ask *Mr. Bear* (Flack, 1932) *No Roses for Harry* (Zion, 1958)

WEDNESDAY

Note: On this particular day the teacher had several primary educational purposes in mind: She wanted the children to deal with their feelings about hospitals and about their friend's injury; the previous day the children had proposed sending a little fish to keep him company and a child volunteered fish from her family's pond—hence the trike ride. The teacher hoped that visiting that particular family would also strengthen home/school bonds for one of the shyer children. She was pleased, also, with the possibilities the children's idea about giving the aquarium presented for being kind to someone else and for figuring out how to solve some interesting problems as well.

Figure 2.1

Daily analysis and planning chart

keep water fresh in general so animals and people want to drink it. Or another pathway might lead to investigating fish tails and other ways to make things move through water, and then trying some of those ideas out to see if they work. The choice of subject depends on two things—the direction the children's interests take combined with the potential for learning the subject presents that is perceived by the teacher.

There are some alternative terms for this linked kind of topic development, such as *chaining, webbing,* and *project work.* I prefer *pathways* because a pathway has direction to it, but at the same time a pathway can lead to adventure—walkers don't always know at the beginning of the path exactly where they will end up. The teacher who is truly sensitive to helping children advance down pathways of their true interests cannot predict at the beginning of an investigation where they will end up, either. However, he *can* make certain that along the way the children have direction and focus and that they are provided opportunities to practice some basic mental ability skills, solve problems, and use a variety of graphic materials to express what they have learned. (For a more in-depth discussion of how to develop inquiry pathways, refer to chapter 18.)

A Good Program Has Stability and Regularity Combined with Flexibility

Young children need to know what is likely to happen next during the day. This means that the order of events should be generally predictable. Predictability enables children to prepare mentally for the next event; it makes compliance with routines more likely and helps them feel secure.

At the same time, time schedules and routines should not be allowed to dominate the school.[5] Sometimes this happens because of a strong-minded custodian or cook. I know of a school where it was necessary for the children to use only half their room from 10:30 until nap time because of the custodian's routine. Sometimes overconformance to time schedules happens because teachers are creatures of habit and simply do not realize that juice and raisins do not have to be served at exactly 9:15. Rather than sticking right to clock time, it is better to maintain an orderly but elastic schedule wherein play periods and investigative activities can be extended at those times when the majority of the children are involved in activities that interest them intensely.

A Good Program Has Variety

Children Need Many Different Kinds of Experiences, as Well as Changes in Basic Experiences

Research on the effects of stimulus deprivation (W. Dennis, 1960; Walk, 1981) and early stimulation (B. L. White, 1979) has highlighted the value of supplying a variety of experi-

---

5   *Schedules are discussed in more detail in chapter 3.*

Here are some examples of ways caregivers have been inspired to produce creative and inexpensive solutions that make their lives easier. It is my dearest wish that the following pictures will inspire readers to pursue the possibilities and satisfactions of creativity in their own settings.

Creativity can be as spontaneous as answering the phone à la banana wire!

asoning = physical self = emotional heal
mpetence = creativity = language = literac
physical self = emotional health = self-est

Here, everything needed for the story is available for the teacher to use without fumbling and without distracting the children's attention from what is being said.

Is your housekeeping corner tucked away in a windowless corner— how about turning it into a room with a view, as this teacher did?

A brush in time saves lots of sandy, slippery floors later on.

Storage, always at a premium in child care centers, can save space and add an attractive note as well.

Colorful ribbons are lovely to use for dancing and to look at, too.

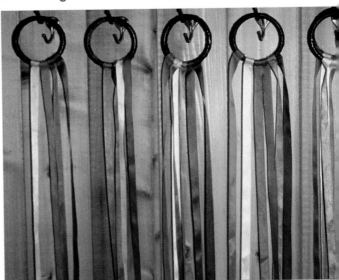

What could be more attractive than these colorful hand puppets?

Here the instruments contribute beauty to the room while, at the same time, are being protected from unsupervised little hands.

When there's no closet space left—and we've all been there—how about storing bulky items up here?

Children are such voracious consumers of materials it's always interesting to see some economical possibilities for activities.

A dash of food coloring was all it took to spark investigation of ice and its properties.

Jared was captivated by counting up how many days there were until his birthday— a **LONG** time!

Heaven bless Mother Nature for the lovely bounty of free collage materials.

Here's an excellent, inexpensive safety measure to protect children from running into the path of the swings.

Although this happens to be a commercial example, the same equipment could easily be made using a piece of chain covered with an old hose.

In Oklahoma I've actually seen children kept indoors because it was too hot outside to play. How much better it was to invest in a couple of umbrellas and set up shady areas for their enjoyment and the teacher's relief.

I couldn't conclude this series without including an example of water play. All it took was an old gutter, a bucket, a hose, and, of course, a boy!

ences even for babies, and variety should certainly be incorporated into a program for preschool children. Many teachers think of variety of experience in terms of field trips or covering different topics such as families or baby animals. But another kind of variety that should also be considered is variety in everyday basic learning experiences. What a difference there is between the school that has the same pet rat and bowl of goldfish all year and the school that first raises a rabbit, then borrows a brood hen, and next has two snakes as visitors. Lack of variety is also apparent in schools that offer the omnipresent easel as their major "art" experience or others that set out all the blocks at the beginning of the year and leave it at that.

Children Should Be Offered Various Levels of Difficulty in Activity Materials

If the children's center combines age levels during the day so that 3-, 4-, and 5-year-olds play together, it is important to provide materials that are challenging for all the ages within the group. Teachers need to be especially careful to offer materials that are genuinely interesting to the older 4-year-olds and young 5-year-olds. A dearth of stimulating, fresh curricular activities is the most common cause of a posse of children galloping through block areas and housekeeping corners, spreading destruction as they go.

Even when the group is composed predominantly of children of one age, the teacher will still need to provide a variety of activities for different developmental levels because of the great difference, for example, between what younger and older 4-year-olds can achieve.

The curriculum not only should offer a variety of levels of difficulty every day but also *should become more challenging and move from simple to more complex activities as the year progresses* and as the children mature and gain competence. The curriculum should not look the same in May as it did in September.

Children Need Changes of Pace During the Day to Avoid Monotony and Fatigue and to Maintain a Balance of Kinds of Experiences

The most obvious way to incorporate variation of pace is to plan for it in the overall schedule. For example, a quiet snack can be followed by a dance period.

Additional opportunities to meet individual temperamental requirements of children must be allowed for. The quieter, less gregarious child needs to have places available where he can retreat from the herd, and the more active youngster needs the escape hatch of moving about when the group has sat beyond his limit of endurance.

Some kinds of programs appear to have special problems associated with pacing. For example, some compensatory programs attempt to cram so much into such a short time (playtime, story time, snack, lunch, special activity time, not to mention visits from the psychologist, field trips, and special visitors) that the day goes by in a headlong rush of children being hurried from one thing to the next without the opportunity to savor any experience richly and fully. At the other extreme some day care programs offer a variety of activities and changes of pace during the morning but turn the children loose in the play yard for 3 interminable hours in the afternoon. Such consistent conditions of hurried stress or unalleviated boredom, unless analyzed thoughtfully and modified, can ultimately have only a deleterious effect on children (Hosfield, 1998).

Learning Must Be Based on Actual Experience and Participation

Anyone who has ever taken a young child to the market knows how strong his impulse is to touch and smell and taste everything he encounters. Although occasionally inconvenient, the child's behavior illustrates a fundamental fact of early childhood learning: Children learn best when they are allowed to use all their senses as avenues of learning. Participatory experience is an essential ingredient in preschool education. This means the curriculum of the preschool must be based on real experiences with real things, rather than limited to the verbal discussions and pictures commonly (though not necessarily ideally) used when teaching older children.

Because educators ranging from Piaget to Vygotsky to Reggio Emilia have emphasized the value of real experience as being fundamental to successful education since the turn of the century, one might think this principle need not be reiterated. The persistent influx of word-oriented rather than action-oriented teaching materials on display in the commercial exhibits of most conferences on early childhood, however, and the fact that these materials continue to sell make it evident that this point must be stated very clearly: Young children learn best when they can manipulate material, experiment, try things out, and talk about what is happening as it takes place. Talking without doing is largely meaningless for a child of tender years.

Play Is an Indispensable Avenue for Learning

Another long-held value in early childhood education is an appreciation of play as a facilitator of learning. Although research is still lacking in this area, evidence is beginning to accumulate (Fromberg & Bergen, 1998) that lends support to something generations of teachers of young children have learned through experience. Teachers who have watched young children at play know the intense, purposeful seriousness they bring to this activity. Play is the medium used by children to translate experience into something internally meaningful to them. Piaget (1962) and Vygotsky (1978) agree with teachers and maintain that children use play as an important symbolic activity, but it serves many purposes beyond this function. Play clarifies concepts, provides emotional relief, facilitates social development, and creates periods of clearly satisfying delight. Sometimes teachers see its value only as a teacher-controlled, structured experience used to achieve a specific educational end (e.g., role playing after visiting the fire station), but it is crucial that there be ample time in the curriculum for self-initiated play. There is no surer way to tap into the children's real concerns and interests.

The Program Should Be Reflected on Daily

Once a curriculum is planned and put into action, it is also necessary to evaluate the results, and these reflections need to go beyond such statements as "My gosh! What a terrible day!" or "Things went well!"

Instead teachers should ask themselves the following questions:

What special interests emerged that I can respond to when planning curriculum pathways?

How did the day go? Did any hitches and glitches occur?

If so, how can I rearrange plans and activities so that they move more smoothly for the children next time?

What did the children learn today?

How are the children with special problems getting along?

And finally the most valuable question of all:

How can I help each child experience success tomorrow?

Thoughtful answers to questions like these will go a long way toward helping build a more effective curriculum for the children as the year moves on.

The Day Should Be Pleasurable

Probably the most significant value a teacher can convey to children is the conviction that school is satisfying and that they want to return the next day. This point has been deliberately left until last to give it special emphasis in case the reader, having waded through the other elements of a good program, has begun to feel bogged down with the sober-sided responsibilities of running a good program for young children.

The experience not only should be pleasurable for the children but also should be a joy for the adults. Young children have their trying moments, but they are also delightful. They see the world in a clear-sighted way that can lend fresh perspective to the eyes of their teacher, and their tendency to live for the present moment is a lesson to us all. Pleasure, enjoyment, humor, and laughter should be very much a part of each preschool day.

PUTTING THE ELEMENTS TOGETHER

What Does a Day Look Like That Combines These Basic Elements Into a Coherent Whole?

The setting is established with children in mind: Furniture is scaled to the right size, the building has easy access to the yard, and the general air of orderly yet easygoing comfort and beauty does not put people off because of its newness or perfection. This kind of atmosphere goes a long way toward making parents feel at home and part of the school family.

When it is necessary to form groups, the children are formed into small gatherings. Story hours, investigations, and snack tables of four or five children and a grown-up, for example, should be the rule to facilitate conversation and participation. (My staff refers to this as Hendrick's law: "The larger the group, the smaller the learning.") The daily pace is easy enough and the staff unharrassed enough that there are many intimate little opportunities for teachers to talk with the children individually.

There is a reasonably repetitious scheduling of basic experiences planned to provide alternate periods of quiet and active experience. These periods include a morning welcome for each child as he arrives, a snack in the morning and the afternoon, and lunch and rest in the middle of the day.

Between these landmark times many interesting events take place. These are developed with individual and group goals in mind, and they should include every day some activity that is creative, another that is messy, something that is new, something that requires the children to think and generate ideas, some carefully varied activities that foster motor development, some opportunity for the children to engage in meaningful work, and many chances to use books, pictures, poetry, and to listen and be listened to. Intertwined among these activities lie all the situations the teacher must seize and use as they arise to develop social learning and emotional strength in the children.

For at least one generous block of time during the morning and afternoon, materials and possibilities are set out and the child is expected to take the responsibility of selecting for himself what he wants to pursue. During this time the teacher moves from one place to another as the occasion demands, talking first with one child, helping another group settle a fight, and getting out a piece of equipment for a third. Another part of the day involves more focused participation but should not be cast in the mold of 15 children doing the same thing in one large group at the same time.

If staffing and weather permit, children have access to indoors and outdoors as they prefer. Failing this, large muscle activities are available indoors, and small muscle and more cognitive and creative materials are available outdoors to avoid the "recess" concept so common in elementary school.

This then is the overall framework of a sound preschool day. It provides opportunities for children to learn all kinds of things and to enjoy both the process and satisfaction of the results. It includes many diverse experiences and many diverse people. The miracle of a good school is that somehow these all go together to produce a good day for both children and staff.

SUMMARY

After more than three decades of research, the accumulation of evidence indicates that early intervention in the form of quality education for young children and their families can make a difference.

The Whole Child advocates the use of four theoretical bases as the philosophical foundation for teaching young children: (a) behavior modification, (b) Piagetian constructivism, (c) the sociocultural theory of Vygotsky, and (d) the pedagogical theory exemplified by the schools of Reggio Emilia.

Certain elements are emerging that appear to be common to the majority of effective early childhood programs. These include good human relationships, parent inclusion, and a curriculum that is developmentally, individually, and culturally appropriate. A good program uses reasonable and authentic methods of assessment, incorporates a balance of self-selection and teacher direction, educates all the child's five selves, and is based on both daily and longer term planning.

A good program for young children is basically orderly but also flexible; it provides for variety in experience, levels of difficulty, and pacing; and it is based on the principles that learning should be the result of actual experience, that play is a significant mode of learning, and above all that the center should be a place of joy for both children and staff.

Questions and Activities

1. *Predicament*: Suppose a parent said to you after touring the school, "My heavens, your fees are high. Why, my baby-sitter charges less than you do, and she comes to the house and does the ironing while she takes care of little Jennifer. I don't see what costs so much about just taking care of little children!" What should you reply?

2. Describe some situations in your own educational background in which the learning was primarily accomplished by means of language and other situations in which the emphasis was on learning by means of experience and participation. Which method did you prefer? What were the advantages and disadvantages of each of these approaches?

3. What guidelines would you suggest to help a teacher determine whether the children's day includes enough free choices or too much structure?

4. As a beginning teacher, how do you feel about the prospect of having parents at school? If a mother is helping at school on the day her youngster has a temper tantrum and refuses to come in to lunch, would it be easier to handle this situation if the mother were not there? Do you agree completely that parents should be welcomed at school? Why or why not?

5. Select a basic activity, such as using tricycles or easel painting, that tends to stay the same throughout the year in many schools and suggest some variations that would add interest and learning to the activity.

Self-Check Questions for Review

Content-Related Questions

1. Name two important research studies having to do with the effectiveness of preschool education. List three or four important findings from these studies.

2. *The Whole Child* uses both behavior modification and Piagetian and Vygotskian theory as partial theoretical bases. According to the author, what are the strengths and weaknesses of these three theories?

3. Describe several ways in which the preschools of Reggio Emilia appear to differ from those of the United States.

4. List several ways in which teachers might generate records that will help them and the parents assess how much a child has learned and what he is like.

5. What is the chief difficulty or problem associated with planning a curriculum far in advance of what the children are currently doing? Does this mean that long-term planning should be completely avoided?

6. Name the five selves discussed in this chapter and tell what aspects of the child each self includes.

7. List and discuss the ingredients that should go into a good day for young children.

Integrative Questions

1. Suppose a friend says to you, "What I don't understand is why you have to go to school so long to learn to take care of little kids; after all, it's just glorified baby-sitting." Explain what you might produce in the way of evidence to educate this person.

2. Compare the findings for the experimental and control groups from the Perry Preschool Project (Table 2.1). In which categories did the greatest differences between the groups show up? Imagine you are explaining these differences to a state legislator. What basic points would you stress from the results as being most likely to influence her or him to vote for more money to finance preschool programs?

3. Give an example of a situation with a 3-year-old in which it would be appropriate to use a behavior modification technique.

4. Compare the developmental-interactionist philosophy of teaching to a behavior modification approach. What do they have in common, and in what ways do they differ?

5. Describe some benefits children receive from the self-select parts of an early childhood program, and contrast these with the benefits they gain from activities they participate in together as a group. Be sure to include consideration of social and emotional benefits, as well as cognitive ones.

6. During the past year the following topics were proposed as possible educational interests to be used with 3-year-olds: kittens, shapes, space travel, Hawaii, air, and snow. Which of these would you select as being most appropriate, and which as being least appropriate? Explain the reasoning behind your answer.

7. This chapter describes several concepts common to both American and Reggian teaching philosophies. These include learning by doing, inquiry-based learning, and child-centered learning. Explain what you think each of these terms means, and provide a specific example that illustrates how you might implement each of these practices in your classroom of 4-year-olds.

References for Further Reading

Pick of the Litter

Greenman, J. (1998d). *Places for childhoods: Making quality happen in the real world.* Redmond, WA: Child Care Information Exchange. At last! Greenman's columns are gathered in one place for reference. The mixture of practicality, good sense, and inspiration illustrates the way child care ought to be and how to make it that way.

Overviews

Beardsley, L. (1990). *Good day, bad day: The child's experience of child care.* New York: Teachers College Press. This book contrasts fictitious good and mediocre schools by describing imaginary situations and how the schools handle them. These are followed by knowledge-based comments. *Highly recommended.*

Bredekamp, S., & Copple, C. (Eds.). (1997). *Developmentally appropriate practice in early childhood programs* (Rev. ed.). Washington, DC: National Association for the Education of Young Children. This indispensable resource spells out good teaching practices that are appropriate at the preschool level. It remains the most influential publication on this subject in the field.

Koralek, D. G., Colker, L. J., & Dodge, D. T. (1993). *The what, why, and how of high-quality early childhood education: A guide for on-site supervision.* Washington, DC: National Association for the Education of Young Children. This wonderful book discusses programs divided according to age and includes a helpful chapter on family child care. It approaches the curriculum by describing what one should see and why and identifies warning signs, suggests the cause of the trouble, and recommends what might be done to correct the difficulty. *Exceptionally helpful.*

National Association for the Education of Young Children (NAEYC). (1998a). *Accreditation criteria & procedures of the National Association for the Education of Young Children.* Washington, DC: Author. Accreditation by the association means the individual center or preschool has met very good standards for caring for young children that almost always exceed those required by state licensing. This book describes the process involved in qualifying for accreditation and includes clear descriptions of each standard and explanations of why each one is important. *An indispensable reference.*

Specific Curricula

Curtis, D., & Carter, M. (1996). *Reflecting children's lives: A handbook for planning child-centered curriculum.* St. Paul, MN: Redleaf. The authors provide many examples that contrast a traditional, overly planned approach with curriculum having a more child-centered approach.

Hendrick, J. (Ed.). (1997). *First steps toward teaching the Reggio way.* Upper Saddle River, NJ:Merrill/Prentice Hall. *First Steps* includes clear descriptions of the Reggio approach, followed by many chapters depicting steps taken by American teachers to implement aspects of that philosophy in their classrooms.

Hohmann, M., & Weikart, D. (1995). *Educating young children: Active learning practices for preschool and child care.* Ypsilanti, MI: High/Scope. *Educating Young Children* is the comprehensive teachers' manual that explains the philosophy and implementation of the High/Scope (Perry Preschool) model.

Planning the Environment

Note: Remember to peruse the Greenman book listed as Pick of the Litter!

Carter, M., & Curtis, D. (1996). *Spreading the news: Sharing the stories of early childhood education.* Beltsville, MD: Gryphon House. This delightful, brief book is crammed with discussions and examples of how to use bulletin boards for many purposes; emphasis is on communicating while also using good design. *Highly recommended.*

Greenman, J. (Ed.). (1998c). A guide to equipping the developmentally appropriate center. In *Places for childhoods: Making quality happen in the real world.* Redmond, WA: Child Care Information Exchange. Here, on 3 pages, is a basic, suitable list of equipment grouped according to activity area and children's age. *Highly recommended.*

Vogel, N. (1997). *Getting started: Materials and equipment for active learning preschools.* Ypsilanti, MI: High/Scope. A concise explanation of practical room arrangements is provided here complete with careful lists of equipment needed for each learning area.

Conducting Authentic Assessments

Hendrick, J. (1998). *Total learning: Developmental curriculum for the young child* (5th ed.). Upper Saddle River, NJ: Merrill/Prentice Hall. Chapter 7, "Practical Methods of Recording and Evaluating

Behavior," suggests many ways to generate effective assessments.

McAfee, O., & Leong, D. (1994). *Assessing and guiding young children's development and learning.* Boston: Allyn & Bacon. A very thorough treatment of this subject is provided by two authors who know their children *and* the subject, too. *Highly recommended.*

For the Advanced Student

Barnett, W. S., & Boocock, S. S. (1998). *Early care and education for children in poverty: Promises, programs, and long-term results.* Albany: State University of New York. This invaluable reference provides an extensive summary of long-term effects of early education programs on children of the poor. *Highly recommended.*

Edwards, C., Gandini, L., & Forman, G. (1998). *The hundred languages of children: The Reggio Emilia approach—advanced reflections.* Greenwich, CT: Ablex. This revised and expanded edition is the comprehensive resource in the English language that explains the philosophy and implementation of the Reggio approach in its homeland of Italy and in the United States. *Highly recommended.*

Goffin, S. G. (1994). *Curriculum models and early childhood education: Appraising the relationship.* Upper Saddle River, NJ: Merrill/Prentice Hall. Goffin provides in-depth appraisals of several early childhood education models: Montessori, developmental-interaction, direct instruction, High/Scope, and Kamii/DeVries constructivist. She includes excellent appraisals, as well as a thoughtful discussion of implications for future investigations. *Highly recommended.*

Kagan, S. L., & Cohen, N. E. (1996). *Reinventing early care and education: A vision for a quality system.* San Francisco: Jossey-Bass. A readable, comprehensive description of the present state of child care and its condition is followed by discussions of ways to bring about necessary changes. *Highly recommended.*

Malaguzzi, L. (1998). History, ideas, and basic philosophy: An interview with Lella Gandini. In C. Edwards, L. Gandini, & G. Forman (Eds.). *The hundred languages of children: The Reggio Emilia approach—advanced reflections*. Greenwich, CT: Ablex. If this revised edition of *The Hundred Languages* is the American "bible" of the Reggio movement, then Malaguzzi is its prophet.

Shore, R. (1997). *Rethinking the brain: New insights into early development*. New York: Families and Work Institute. This book provides badly needed documentation of up-to-date evidence demonstrating how important early stimulation and education are to fostering the positive development of the brain. *Highly recommended*.

Singer, D. G., & Revenson, T. A. (1997). *A Piaget primer: How a child thinks* (Rev. ed.). Madison, CT: International Universities Press. The authors clarify explanations of the essential elements of Piaget's theory by tying them to examples of behavior from familiar literature. *Highly recommended*.

Thomas, R. M. (1999). *Comparing theories of child development* (5th ed.). Monterey, CA: Brooks/Cole. Thomas presents a readable overview of Piagetian theory, complete with discussion of implications for teachers.

Vygotsky, L. (1978). *Mind in society: The development of higher psychological processes* (M. Cole, V. John-Steiner, S. Scribner, & E. Souberman, Eds.). Cambridge, MA: Harvard University Press. Vygotsky sets forth his basic theories in this very readable book.

chapter three

What Parents Need

Why a mother seems to avoid talking with you?

How to open a discussion with parents about a problem their child is having?

How to deal with your disappointment when parents refuse your advice?

. . . IF YOU HAVE, THE MATERIAL IN THE FOLLOWING PAGES WILL HELP YOU.

Who takes the child by the hand, takes the mother by the heart.

Danish proverb

No matter how dedicated and meticulous we are about establishing a good life for the child at school, teachers must never forget that the most significant part of the young child's environment lies outside the school. Quite wholesomely and rightly, there is a much more profound influence in the child's life: her home and the members of her family. Thus it makes good sense, if we hope to establish the best total environment for the child, to include her family as an important part of the preprimary experience (D. R. Powell, 1998; Workman & Gage, 1997).[1]

There are a number of formal and informal ways to build these links between home and school. The current interest at the elementary and secondary levels in developing parent advisory boards and in encouraging parent participation in the classroom offers interesting confirmation of principles that early childhood teachers have championed for many years (Taylor, 1981). Such involvement can be as varied as making home visits, inviting parents to volunteer in the classroom, or asking them to serve on the parent board. All these avenues encourage interchange and communication between families and teachers if they are well done. One teacher-parent skill lies at the heart of them all: the ability to talk together in a sincere, nonthreatening way.

PROBLEMS THAT INTERFERE WITH GOOD COMMUNICATION

Despite the important advantages of keeping communication open, many parents and teachers do not get along comfortably together. The teacher may dread the parents' criticisms ("Oh, no! Not paint on his shirt again?") or feel financially at their mercy because displeased parents may take their child out of the center. Or the teacher may blame the parents for the child's shortcomings; this is bound to interfere with a good relationship between them.

In these times when more than 62% of all mothers with preschool-age children work outside the home (Children's Defense Fund, 1998), the additional burdens of fatigue and guilt that such added responsibilities may entail take an additional toll on parent energies. The results can be that although the parents remain as loving and concerned as ever, the time for contact between school and home is diminished.

When parents *do* have contact, they, like the teacher, feel vulnerable to criticism. After all, their child, who is an extension of themselves, is on view. First-time parents particularly can be quite frightened of the teacher's opinion, and all parents yearn to know that the teacher likes their child and that she is doing well. The relationship is doubly touchy since a parent, particularly the mother, may be seeking validation of her own worth as a person by ascertaining that the teacher approves of her offspring. She is all too ready to believe the teacher (and also to feel threatened and angry) if blame is implied (Daniel, 1998; Maccoby, 1999).

---

[1] *For additional material on parents' participation in the school, refer to chapter 13, "Providing Cross-Cultural, Nonsexist Education."*

Parents may also fear that if they speak frankly and mention something they do not like about the school or about what their child is doing there, they will antagonize the teacher. They may worry about the possibility of reprisals against the child when they are not there. This is comparable to the parent who fears complaining to hospital personnel lest they discriminate against the child. The fact that most professional people are more mature than this may not affect the parent's innate caution in this matter.

Besides being vulnerable to criticism and wishing to protect her child, the mother may dread being displaced by the teacher in the child's affections. Separation involves mixed feelings for her. On the one hand, she deeply wants to wean her child: She is tired of changing his pants and tying his shoes and never going anywhere alone. On the other hand, something inside her resents having the teacher take over. To add to her confusion, the mother may also be struggling with guilty feelings over the relief she feels at being able to parcel her child out for a few days a week. Surely, if she were a "good mother," she wouldn't feel so elated at the thought of going shopping by herself! So she worries about what the teacher would think of her if the teacher only knew.

For both parents and teacher there is also the residue of all the past experiences and previous relationships with other teachers and parents that color what each anticipates of the other. In addition to pleasant memories may be the emotionally powerful ones of the principal's office, of having to stay after school, of authoritarian teachers, and of militant, unreasonable parents that lie at the back of consciousness and plague parents and teacher during their initial contacts. It is no wonder then, with all these things conspiring to build walls between families and teachers, that we must invest some effort and understanding if we wish to establish a more rewarding relationship between the adults who are so important in the life of the young child.

SUGGESTIONS FOR ESTABLISHING A GOOD RELATIONSHIP BETWEEN PARENT AND TEACHER

Surely there must be some way to establish a bond that leads to problem solving, rather than to defense building. The question is, How can the teacher go about doing this?

Probably the most essential ingredient in a more satisfactory relationship between teacher and parent is that the teacher have the child's welfare truly at heart and that she be genuinely concerned about her. My experience has been that when parents believe this to be true—which means, of course, that it has to *be* true and not just something the teacher *wishes* were true—when parents really sense the teacher's goodwill, they will forgive the teacher her inadvertent transgressions, and the relationship will warm up as trust develops.

Genuine concern and caring can be expressed in a variety of ways. Faithful caretaking is one way. The teacher takes pains to see that everything the child has made is valued by being put in her cubby for her to take home, her belongings are kept track of, her nose is wiped when it needs to be, and although she may not be the pristinely clean youngster at the end of the day that she was upon arrival, she is tidied up and has had her face washed before her parent picks her up. The teacher also shows she cares by carefully enforcing the health and safety regulations and by planning a curriculum that is interesting, varied, and suited to the needs of individual children.

Another way for the teacher to show concern is by expressing genuine interest in each child to her parent. For example, it is always sound practice to comment on something the youngster has enjoyed that day. It may be the friendly statement, "Jessie really loves our new bunny; she fed him and watched him half the morning," or it might be, "I think Jerry is making friends with our new boy, Manuel; they spent a lot of time with the trains in the block corner today." These comments assure the parent that the child has had attention from the teacher and that she is aware of her as an individual, rather than as just one of the troop.

Teachers can also demonstrate they truly care about the children and their families by taking special care to learn about differing points of view concerning child rearing that families from cultures other than the teacher's own may have (Sturm, 1997). As Tutwiler (1998) points out, not only may points of view differ in a general way from group to group, but also attitudes toward the value of their own backgrounds vary within members of that group. These attitudes range from the desire of the parents to have their children blend completely with the dominant culture to an equally strong desire to have their youngsters respect and retain the parents' personal values related to their own culture.

This contrast in value systems can be complex and bewildering at times but is not impossible to resolve. For example, Tutwiler (1998) identifies some broad characteristics of "typical" American families as encouraging individualism and making decisions for themselves, valuing punctuality, emphasizing personal accomplishment and the competitive spirit, and valuing athletic achievement, just to name a few. When this description is contrasted with Japanese ideals of the importance of maintaining harmonious relationships, of not "letting their heads show above the crowd," and of never bringing shame on the family, the possibility for potential cultural conflicts becomes apparent. Perhaps once these cultural mores are recognized, when conferencing with Japanese parents the teacher might evaluate the child in terms of parental values and so place more emphasis on how smoothly their child gets along with her peers, rather than worrying over her lack of assertiveness. Several resources on recognizing the cultural strengths and values of various groups are included at the end of this chapter, as well as in chapter 13, "Providing Cross-Cultural, Non-Sexist Education."

Still another kind of caring can be indicated on a subtler level by letting the parent know that the teacher is on the child's side *but not on the child's side as opposed to the family's*. Occasionally teachers fall into the fantasy of thinking, "If only I could take that child home with me for a week and give her a steady, loving environment." Or sometimes a child will say in a rush of affection, "Oh, I wish *you* were my mother!" To avoid an emotionally confusing and difficult situation for the child, it is important that the teacher clarify her role. She can handle this by gently replying, "We *are* having fun, and I like you, too; but, of course, you already have a mother—I'm not your mother, I'm your *teacher*. I take care of you at school, and your mother takes care of you at home." This avoids rivalry and makes a friendly alliance between mother and teacher more likely.

It is difficult to be on the family's side if the teacher blames the parent for all the child's problems. Such disapproval, even if unspoken, cannot help being sensed by parents (Murphy, 1997). In any situation in which I feel critical of a parent, I have found it helpful to remember what Beth Leonhard (1963) recommends: "Ask yourself, if *I* were that mother, with that set of problems and that background, could I do any better with that child?"

Another thing to remember, as any parent of more than one child knows, is that children are born with different temperaments. No matter what fathers and mothers do, children are different to start with and remain so, no matter what their environment. It is therefore ridiculous to hold the parent accountable for all the child's shortcomings.

Thus we see that the teacher can put parents at ease by letting them know that she is concerned about the child, that she is on both the child's and the parents' sides, and that she does not think everything the child does is the family's fault. After all, parents, like teachers, also want what is best for their children. A sense of common, shared concern is worth working for because once parents feel its existence, they are freer to work with the teacher on the child's behalf.

Of course, sometimes, despite our best intentions, a relationship with a parent may not be so harmonious. When this is the case, it can be helpful to know how to handle such encounters.

WHAT IF THE RELATIONSHIP IS NOT GOOD?

It is inevitable that, from time to time, parents will make teachers so angry it is almost impossible to resist the temptation to lose one's temper in return—a response that usually just makes things worse. Fortunately there are alternative ways of coping with angry feelings that can help teachers (and other people) retain control of themselves and the situation—an important skill for a person to acquire (Samalin, 1991).

The Preamble: What to Do Before the Situation Arises

A good way to begin is to know one's own points of vulnerability. I picture these points as being a series of red buttons people can push—red buttons that, when pushed, make me see red, too! Different things make different people angry. For some teachers it's the parent who is bossy and domineering, whereas for others it's the parent who is always late or who sends her child to school with a deep cough and runny nose. Whatever the buttons are, it is helpful to identify them in advance since once they are identified it is possible to summon up the extra reserves of self-control that are needed when someone begins to push one.

Coping with the Initial Encounter: What to Do When That Button Is Pushed

Surviving an encounter with an angry parent is really a three-part process. It includes the immediate first encounter, what happens afterward, and the final resolution of the situation.

For the sake of example, let's take an angry complainer, because teachers do have to deal with such people from time to time. The usual response to complaints is to give in to the impulse to defend and explain. However, this is not what complainers want. They want to complain and have the teacher apologize and do what they wish. Now sometimes an apology is justified, but sometimes it is not! Either way, the teacher is likely to feel angry in return.

Rather than jumping right in with a defensive reply, the more effective approach is to wait a minute before responding and actually *listen* to what the parent is saying (Phipps, 1998). These precious seconds provide valuable lead time that allows an opportunity to recognize the anger inside oneself and to consider the reply before saying something you'll regret later.

Next, instead of defending or explaining, take time to rephrase what the complainer is saying, adding a description of her feelings. This is exactly the same strategy advocated in chapter 6 on emotional health and emphasized again in chapter 11 on self-discipline. *There is no more effective way of dealing with strong feelings than using this response.* Admittedly it can be even harder to remember to do this with a grown-up than with a child since grown-ups are so much more threatening than children, but it does work like magic. For example, you might say, "You don't want me to . . . ," or, "You're upset because I . . . "

After the person has calmed down, it may be appropriate to explain your side of the situation, or it may not. Many times, when a matter of policy is in question ("You mean you lost his mittens again?" or, "If you let that kid bite Ann once more, I'm calling licensing"), the wisest thing to do is refer it to the director or at least say you'll need to discuss it with the person in charge.[2] This tactic is called "referring it to a committee," and it serves the invaluable purposes of spreading around the responsibility for the decision, as well as providing a cooling-off period.

For the bravest and securest teachers there is another way to cope with the initial encounter. After listening and rephrasing an attack, some people are comfortable enough to put their own honest feelings into words. "I'm feeling pretty upset (angry, frightened, worried) right now about what you've said. I don't know what to say. Let me think it over, and I'll get back to you." This kind of self-disclosure is too risky for some people to attempt, but it is an effective way of dealing with feelings for those who feel able to try it.

In the following anecdote, Docia Zavitkovsky (1990) provides us with an example of how such self-disclosure can be effective.

> There is always the element of the unpredictable at first. My first presentation to the Santa Monica Board of Education is a good example. I remember it as though it happened yesterday.
>
> It was budget time and I was asked to come and explain to the Board why more money was needed to operate the Children's Centers. The staff and I had worked long and hard compiling the necessary material, so I felt relaxed and confident that all would go well.
>
> When I arrived at the Board Room, every seat was occupied . . . and when my name was called, I walked to the front of the room and instantly became aware that seven pairs of eyes were looking at me intently and expectantly. I suddenly had butterflies in my middle, a quiver in my voice, and a slight trembling of the legs. I took a deep breath and said the first thing that came to mind: "I like and respect each of you as individuals, but collectively you scare me to pieces." There were smiles and chuckles from Board members and then each one went out of his/her way to put me at ease. They nodded with approval, asked good questions, and, after some discussion, said they couldn't see why additional funds could not be made available.

---

[2] *Student teachers should* always *follow this procedure.*

Somehow these seven people no longer seemed formidable. Though in the future they might not agree with me on some issue or vote favorably for a request, they were human beings and they were interested, concerned, and friendly. It is amazing how one's perception changes when fear and anxiety are acknowledged and eliminated, and a situation takes on realistic proportions. (p. 62)[3]

What to Do After the Complainer Departs

The problem with controlling anger as I have suggested is that it does not always melt away after the attacker has left. A common but undesirable way teachers and other people deal with this residue is to justify themselves to other people, describe the situation (perhaps slanted a trifle in their favor!), and explain why they were right, thereby getting other people to take their side of the argument. Or they take revenge by undercutting the attacker, saying bad things about her so that the staff or director is turned against the parent.

A third, equally undesirable way of unloading anger is to pick on some hapless victim who cannot defend herself. This is called *displacement*. For example, parents may yell at a child when they fear confronting a spouse, or teachers may pick on a child when they are afraid of antagonizing another adult.

But is there a better way—one that doesn't require us to swallow our anger and that does no harm to other people? There is. And it is simple and available to everyone. All it requires is a good friend with a listening, uncritical ear.

Everyone needs someone to talk with—someone who has confidence enough in us that she or he can listen while we express our feelings without arguing with us or telling us we shouldn't feel that way, someone who knows we can draw the line between talking about what we would like to do for revenge and actually doing it. This opportunity to ventilate feelings in a safe place is a wonderful luxury that eventually can lead to forming constructive solutions to whatever problem exists.

It is also helpful to think through the best- and worst-case scenarios during that discussion. Facing up to the worst that could happen when you speak with the parent again and the best that might happen will reduce anxiety a great deal and increase confidence when the meeting actually takes place.

The Return Engagement

One benefit of waiting and then returning to discuss an emotion-laden problem is that the other person has had time to calm down, too. She may even be a little ashamed about how she behaved, so it may be necessary to help her save face.

It can also be helpful to include a third person in the discussion, particularly if the problem has been "referred to a committee." Many times this person is the director or someone else who can support both teacher and parent.

This is the point at which various alternatives for solving the problem can be proposed, so it is a good idea to have several such possibilities in mind that are acceptable to the school and that allow the parent the opportunity to participate in the final solution, too.

---

[3] *Reprinted with permission of Exchange Press, Inc., publisher of* Child Care Information Exchange *(a bimonthly management magazine for owners and directors), P.O. Box 2890, Redmond, WA 98073–9977.*

Whatever that solution turns out to be, if the teacher has listened, rephrased, dealt with her own anger in safe surroundings, and offered explanations or solutions, it is probable that the parent will see the teacher as a reasonable person. The teacher will have the comfort of knowing she has done nothing that she need be ashamed of at a later date.

MAINTAINING GOOD RELATIONSHIPS: KEEPING THE LINES OF COMMUNICATION OPEN

Fortunately most relationships with parents do not involve such difficult encounters. For these parents, too, it is important to keep communication lines open. Thus it is necessary for the teacher to be accessible in two senses of the word. First, she must be approachable because she cares about the child; second, she must be physically available when the parent is around the school. In some schools availability can be hard to come by. The teacher

Informal contacts as families come and go build comfortable relations between teachers and parents.

may be occupied with setting up as the children arrive and able to give the parent only a passing word, or at the end of the day she may be so harassed that she has no time or energy to talk.

It is possible and even desirable to arrange the schedule so that one teacher is free to greet parents during the first and last 15 minutes of the day or during peak arrival and departure times. If she is free from other responsibilities at that time, she can see each parent for countless casual meetings and can build relationships of friendliness and trust more easily. The sheer informality of this encounter robs it of a good deal of threat. Chatting right by the gate, the parents know they can hasten away if the conversation takes too threatening a turn. In addition they are likely to see the teacher in a variety of moods and predicaments, which increases the teacher's humanity.

This repeated, consistent contact is far superior to relying solely on the more formal and frightening "conference" that may occur once or twice a semester. After a comfortable, everyday relationship is well established, an occasional conference with a longer uninterrupted opportunity to talk can be used to better advantage.

A helpful way to broaden teacher-parent communication skills is to think over past encounters with a parent to determine who is doing most of the talking. If this analysis reveals that the teacher is talking most of the time, then it probably means that either the chats are too hurried or the teacher needs to monitor herself to make certain she is truly listening to what the parent has to say. The Research Study in this chapter, which is about the quality and frequency of teacher-parent communication in child care situations, can help teachers become more aware of another potential problem.

COUNSELING WITH PARENTS

Once lines of communication are open, the question remains, "What do we do then?"

When people talk together, many levels of relating can exist between them. During the year all these levels can be used by the teacher, depending on the situation.

The simplest level is a verbal or written message in which the teacher may say to the parent, "This is what we did in school today," or, "Samantha learned to ride the scooter today." On this level at least the parents know that the teacher wants them to know what is happening at school. Most new relationships have to start about here.

On another level the teacher acts as the supportive information provider and general comforter. In this guise she interprets the child's behavior to the parents on the basis of her extensive experience with other children. For example, the simple information that many 4-year-olds relish "disgraceful" language can be a great relief to a family secretly tormented by the worry that they suddenly have a pervert on their hands.

At yet another level the parent-teacher relationship has more of a counseling flavor to it. This is guidance, but not guidance in the sense that the teacher tells the parents what to do. Guidance means the teacher works with the parents in terms of conscious motivation and behavior to help them discover what may be causing various behavior problems in the child and to help them figure out how to cope with them.

Research Study

Which Kinds of Children's Centers Are Likely to Do the Best Job Communicating with Parents?

Research Question: Ghazvini and Readdick wanted to find out whether the frequency of various kinds of communication between parents and children's center teachers was related to the overall quality of the child care center.

Research Method: The investigators surveyed the parents, teachers, and directors of 12 centers. Four centers were completely government subsidized, four were a combination of profit and nonprofit settings providing a mix of private pay and subsidized child care, and four were completely nonsubsidized, private, for-profit programs. The investigators studied three kinds of communication: one-way (teacher to parent), two-way (teacher to parent and parent to teacher), and three-way (parent to teacher to community resource). (For the purposes of simplicity only one- and two-way exchanges are considered in this review.)

Ghazvini and Readdick had the parents and teachers complete questionnaires about parental perceptions of communication and caregiver perceptions of communication. The questionnaires asked about the frequency and kind of communication that took place. Examples of what the researchers considered to be one-way communication are parents reading items on the bulletin board, getting a newsletter, and seeing a calendar of daily activities planned for the children. Examples of two-way communication are teachers talking with parents during arrival or departure times, parent-teacher conferences, and parents attending field trips or special events. In all, 201 parents and 49 caregivers returned the questionnaires.

My impression is that teachers who have had special training are more likely to have the aplomb to attempt this third level. However, all teachers could increase their skills and do no harm and probably considerable good by offering themselves in a guidance role to parents in need of help, especially if they concentrate on listening rather than prescribing. The truth is that even when parents ask for help, they usually know the answer already. They are simply having difficulty applying it.

Excluding the occasional special situation in which more professional help is required, what parents need in order to work out a difficulty is the chance to talk out how they feel and evaluate whether a tentative solution is right for them and their unique child. Tremendous comfort comes to a distressed family when they are given the opportunity to air a problem with someone who can listen attentively and who is not too shaken by the confession that Jennifer and Mary have been sitting behind the back fence doing you know what! Allowing them to express their feelings of shame, or occasionally even anguish, over their child's behavior is a positive benefit to offer parents in a counseling situation.

It is also true that teachers who have known literally hundreds of youngsters do have a broader background of experience than most parents. It seems only right to pool this

= physical self = emotional health = self-esteem = social competence =

The investigators also rated the quality of the 12 center environments by using The Early Childhood Environment Rating Scale (Harms & Clifford, 1980).

Research Results: The subsidized or partially subsidized centers were judged to be of higher quality than the nonsubsidized, private, for-profit centers. In those higher quality centers both parents and caregivers reported greater frequency of both one- and two-way communication than did parents and caregivers in private settings. In those same higher quality centers, however, the teachers rated all forms of parent communication as occurring more often and being more important than did the parents.

Implications for Teaching: For one thing, teachers and directors should note that private, for-profit centers evidently tend to be weak in the area of talking with parents. Thus everyone who works in those settings should make more of an effort to communicate with parents.

Why teachers in the higher quality centers thought that they did more communicating with parents than the parents thought they did is an interesting question. The researchers suggest it may *seem* to the teacher that more communication is taking place since she is talking to 15 or 20 parents each day, whereas individual parents do not have that experience. The result is that these teachers may think they are doing a better job of talking with parents than they really are. Whatever the reason for insufficient contact, it seems reasonable to conclude that *all* teachers in *all* settings should make more of an effort to talk with every parent as often as possible. Doing so is absolutely the most effective way to build wholesome bonds between home and school.

Source: "Parent-Caregiver Communication and Quality of Care in Diverse Child Care Settings," by A. S. Ghazvini & C. A. Readdick, 1994, Early Childhood Research Quarterly, 9(2), pp. 207–222.

knowledge with the family's as long as the teacher's alternatives are offered in such a way that parents feel free to accept or reject them. Parents will be able to use the teacher's range of knowledge most easily if the teacher points out to them that no matter how much she knows in general about children, she will *never* know as much about the individual child as the parent does.

Instead of providing instant answers to all problems posed by parents, the teacher will find it more useful to ask such questions as "Why don't you tell me what you've tried already?" or "What are your thoughts about what to do next?" When a mother comes to say that her child has begun "misbehaving" in some new way (perhaps she is fighting a great deal with her sister or has begun having nightmares), the best question to ask is "I wonder if you could tell me what else happened at about the same time?" The typical response is "Well, nothing much. Let me see, now, I guess that was about the time my in-laws came to visit, and, oh yes, her little dog was run over, and . . . " By this means the mother gains useful insight into what has upset her child and usually can formulate a plan about what she might do to help the youngster get on an even keel again (Koulouras, Porter, & Senter, 1986).

Another cornerstone of good counseling is patience. It seems to be human nature that we want instant results, but change often takes a long time. I used to despair when I made a suggestion that a parent ignored. I was most concerned on the occasions when I referred a family to a specialist and the parent declined to act on the referral. My implicit assumption was that if the family did not do it then, they never would. Happily I have found this to be a false assumption. To be sure, parents may not be ready this year to face the problem of Brody's temper tantrums and hyperactivity, but they have at least heard that the possibility of a problem exists, and the next professional person who approaches them may have greater success because the ground has been prepared.

Nowadays I am more wary of the person who agrees completely and instantly with my suggestions. Usually there is not very much movement in these cases. The chance to think out, backtrack, consider various solutions, and take time to get used to an idea is indispensable in a guidance situation.

PRACTICAL POINTERS ABOUT CONDUCTING A PARENT CONFERENCE

Getting ready for the conference is as important as the conference itself since neither teachers nor parents want to waste time just chatting. Preparation may involve accumulating a series of quick observations or developmental checklists if these are used by the school. Some teachers also take photographs of significant events or activities the youngster has participated in and find that sharing these at the beginning of the conference starts conversation off on a friendly note. When these as well as other materials are assembled in a portfolio, it provides a useful, consistent record of how and what the child is doing during her time at the center.

In addition to these tangible documents, it helps focus the conference to think through the points to be covered before beginning, but at the same time it is important to remember that a conference is just that: It is an opportunity to *confer and collaborate*. So, while making plans on what to cover, it is also essential to allow plenty of time and opportunity for parents to talk and to raise concerns of their own. Always bear in mind that even more important than exchanging information is building and maintaining the bond of warmth and trust between teacher and family (Koch & McDonough, 1999).

As obvious as it may sound, a conference consists of three parts: a beginning, a middle, and an end. It is a good idea during the conference to convey a sense of this structure as things move along.

In particular it is helpful to *set a clear time limit at the beginning* so that you and the parent can pace yourselves. This avoids a sense of rejection when the teacher suddenly jumps up like the white rabbit in *Alice in Wonderland* and says she must hurry away! Perhaps you might say, "I'm so glad we have this half hour to talk together; I've been looking forward to it," or, "It's wonderful you're so prompt; that gives us our whole 45 minutes for discussion," or (over the telephone) "That'll be fine if you come at 2:00; that should allow us to finish by the time the children are due to go home."

Avoid Interruptions

Of course, avoiding interruptions is easier said than done sometimes, but most parents resent the teacher's or director's taking a telephone call during a conference. Doing so not only interrupts the flow of talk but also infringes on the parents' rightful time, and parents of young children are often paying a baby-sitter for the privilege of attending. So it is best to find a place to talk that cuts intrusions to the minimum. It might be outside in an undisturbed corner of the play yard during nap, or it might be in the teacher's office, or even the parent's car will do in a pinch. The essentials are privacy and quiet. The child, of course, should not be present.

Some Ways to Begin

In addition to the common pleasantries about weather and being busy, other ways of opening a conference can get things off to a businesslike and not too threatening start. For example, one of the best therapists I ever knew often began conferences with the friendly question, "Well, what's new?" Some additional nonthreatening ways to get the ball rolling suggested by Rue Watkins (1993) include asking parents what they are most

When talking with parents, always remember that old adage, "Who takes the child by the hand takes the mother by the heart."

proud of about their child, where her favorite place to play is, what the child has recently learned to do, or what the family enjoys doing together. Watkins suggests the teacher might make a point of sharing with the parents what the teacher likes about the child, whom their child plays with and what they enjoy doing together at school, and new things their youngster is interested in or learning.

Sometimes it works well to begin with a quick explanation of what you want to talk about. "Shawntell tells me you're moving soon, and I thought, if you like, we might do a little talking about how to help her adjust to the change." Or you might mention a concern expressed by the parent at a previous meeting: "I remember last time we were talking about Janie's stuttering. How's that coming along now at home?"

An even *better* way to begin is to encourage parents to express their concerns first. "Have you special things in mind you want to talk over about Brian?" Even though their initial response may be, "Well, no, not really," this kind of early opening question often enables parents to bring something up later in the conference they were too shy to mention at first. More frequently, however, the parent will leap at this chance and start right in with a genuine concern, often phrased as a return question: "Well, I was wondering, how is he . . . ?" It is gratifying how often this concern is related to that of the teacher.

During the Conference, Stay as Relaxed as Possible

Take time to really listen to what the parent says. (A good way to monitor yourself is to check whether during conversations you are usually busy formulating a reply in your own mind. If you find yourself doing this habitually, then it is probably an indication that you should focus your attention more completely on the speaker and be less concerned about your response.) If you think of the conference as being a time for the parent to do most of the talking, it will help you at least share the time more equally.

It is all right to admit to a parent that you are unsure about something. A parent asked me last week whether her youngster was acting "mopey" at snack time. I had no idea because I am never with that child at that time, but it was easy to promise to find out and get back to her, and then to ask, "Are you wondering about that for some special reason?" This led to a helpful talk about this 4-year-old's sulkiness and belligerence at home since her grandfather, who had recently moved in with the family, was insisting she eat everything on her plate. (Ultimately I anticipate offering some appropriate referrals or activities that will facilitate the grandfather's making friends in his new community and perhaps recommending family therapy to help them get their shifting roles straight under these new circumstances.)

Avoid Sharing Your Personal Experiences

It is commonplace to respond to another's concern or tale of misfortune by saying, "I know just what you mean. When my mother died. . . . " or, "I had a neighbor child like that and I . . . " Apparently people do this to express sympathy and show they understand because of a similar experience. However, for several reasons it is better to avoid this kind of response. First, it uses up precious conference time. Second, other people really are not interested; they are there to discuss *their* child, not your experiences. Third and finally, doing this may shift the focus of discussion to an entirely different topic. A better response is to rephrase what they have just said—"You mean you feel like there's no one left to talk to now that your mother has died?" or, "Are you feeling that the neighbor boy gets Alec into trouble and you don't know what to do about it?"

Drawing the Conference to a Close

As the time to close draws near, you can signal this in several ways. (Remember that the wise teacher has mentioned the potential limit in the beginning in some tactful fashion.) These ending signals are as varied as shifting a little in your chair and (in desperate circumstances in which past experience has indicated that a parent is insensitive to time limits) having someone primed to interrupt in a casual way.

It is always worthwhile to sum up what has been said as part of the closing process: "I am really glad we had a chance to talk. Even though Mike is getting along so well, it never hurts to touch base, does it? I'll remember what you said about the allergy tests. We'll make sure he gets water instead of milk and that the other children understand and don't tease him about it," or, "I'm sure sorry to hear your family's going through that. We're here if there's something we can do to help. Give me a ring any time, and meanwhile we'll do those special things with Jennifer we worked out today and let you know how they turn out."

What to Do After the Conference

It is vital to follow up on any promises or plans you and the parents have made together. For the teacher who has spoken with 15 families, it can be all too easy to forget something or to defer doing it since she is so busy. But for the parents who have only that one particular conference to recall, it is much easier to remember! If you wish to maintain a condition of trust between you and the families you serve, it is necessary that *you* remember, too. This is one reason why it is valuable to make notes immediately following the conference. They can serve as a reminder of promises and plans that should be carried out.

Notes also provide useful take-off points for the next conference. I have even known them to be valuable in court, when the teacher was asked to document that a parent had demonstrated a faithful interest in the well-being of her child by attending a series of conferences during the year.

Finally, Remember That Information Shared by Parents During a Conference Is Confidential

It is unethical, as well as unwise, to repeat what was said in private to anyone else unless that person (the director perhaps or another teacher who works with the child) has a genuine need to know that information. Indeed, if you foresee the need to share such material with another person, it is a good idea to ask the parents first. That way you do not risk violating their trust.

LIMITS TO GUIDANCE WORK

When planning and carrying out conferences, we must also recognize that some behavior and development problems are beyond the teacher's ability, training, and time to handle. It is vital to be clear about where to draw the line and how far to go in guidance work. My rule of thumb is "When in doubt, refer." If the situation looks serious or does not respond to matter-of-fact remedies, it is time to suggest a specialist. In general it is too risky and takes more advanced training than a typical preschool teacher possesses to draw implications and offer interpretations to parents about deep, complex reasons for behavior. Fortunately we can rely on highly trained, skilled specialists to solve serious problems, so let's leave Oedipus and his troublesome kin to our psychiatric cohorts.

SUMMARY

Sensible caution and referral to an expert are advisable under some circumstances, but teachers can offer a lot of help and work with parents in many ways to bring about a happier life for their children. To do this, it is first necessary to overcome various problems that make communication between parents and teachers difficult. One of the most effective things teachers can do is make it plain to the parent that they have the welfare of the child at heart and that they want to join with the family to help the child. Teachers can also take care to be available when the parent wants to talk, and they can provide the opportunity for many easygoing, casual contacts.

Once the lines of communication are open, teachers can offer help by serving as friendly listeners who assist the parent in assessing the nature of the difficulty and in proposing alternatives until they find the one best suited for parent and child. Teachers who assume this guidance function offer parents what they need the most: an accepting attitude, an open ear, and a warm heart.

Question and Activities

1. Have the class divide into pairs. One person in each pair should select a problem or difficulty to discuss while the other person listens. The only restriction on the listener is that, before making any other reply, she must first restate in her own words what she hears the speaker saying; that is, her primary task is to be open to the feelings and import of the communication. Then shift roles and have the speaker practice this sort of listening and responding.

2. Select children in your group who appear to require special diagnostic help of some kind. List the reasons for your conclusion that they need help. With another student, practice how you might broach the subject of referral with the family. It is helpful to practice this with a "parent" who is resistant, one who is overly agreeable, and one who is obviously upset about your suggestion.

3. If you have children of your own, have you ever been summoned to school to discuss a problem? Share with the class how you felt about being asked to come in and do this.

4. *Predicament:* You are now head teacher in a class of 3-year-olds. One afternoon a father is half an hour late picking up his child. When you ask why he is late, he snarls, "None of your damn business," and yanks his child out the door. How would you handle this situation?

5. *Predicament:* You are caring for a 4-year-old girl who is really acting like a bully. She shoves children out of the way to get the first cracker, she makes everyone move so that she can get the best view of the book, and when thwarted, she gets her own way by pinching whoever gets in front of her. When you raise this problem behavior with the parents, they say, "That's terrible! She shouldn't act that way. Don't let her do it. Just give her a good, hard smack—that's what we do!"

   The question for you to answer is *not* what to do about the child's behavior. The question to answer is this: "What should you do when you absolutely disagree with what parents tells you to do to manage their child?"

Self-Check Questions for Review

Content-Related Questions

1. What are some reasons that parents and teachers sometimes feel ill at ease with one other?
2. Give some practical examples of ways a teacher can show parents that she really cares about their child.
3. List and describe the three-part process involved in dealing with an angry parent.
4. What do parents really need in a parent conference?
5. List some practical pointers for conducting a successful conference.
6. Give two examples of one-way communication between teachers and parents. Then give two examples of two-way communication between teachers and parents.

Integrative Questions

1. How might the feelings of mothers who work outside the home and mothers who do not be similar when placing their 3-year-olds in child care?
2. Teddy, a 4-year-old boy in your group, has taken to pinching children when they sit next to him, tearing pages out of books when you aren't looking, and displaying other destructive behaviors. You are quite concerned and ask his mother whether she could come to a conference with you. Give three examples of what you would say to this parent during the conference that would blame her for her son's behavior. Be sure to use actual quotations.

3. Now that she's really mad at you, suggest an angry sentence or two she would say in reply. Then, for each of her sentences, phrase a response that would describe her feelings to her.

4. Now suggest some approaches you could use instead that would *not* blame Teddy's mother for his behavior.

5. Is it accurate to say that the research by Ghazvini and Readdick (1994) revealed that parents thought teachers in higher quality children's centers talked as much with them as the teachers themselves thought they did?

References for Further Reading

Coordinating Videotape

Listening to families. Tape #6. The whole child: A caregivers guide to the first five years. The Annenberg/CPB Collection, P.O. Box 2345, South Burlington, VT 05407-2345. *Listening to Families* prepares caregivers to welcome families into the life of the children's center. It demonstrates ineffective and more desirable ways to conduct parent interviews and suggests ways to help families and children deal with everyday problems and life crises.

Pick of the Litter

David L., & Keyser, J. (1997). *Becoming the parent you want to be: A sourcebook of strategies for the first five years.* New York: Broadway Books. This is an excellent resource for teachers seeking information to share with parents or to place on the parent bookshelf because it is filled with easy-to-read, sensible advice. *Highly recommended.*

Overviews

Berger, E. H. (2000). *Parents as partners in education: Families and schools working together* (5th ed.). Upper Saddle River, NJ: Merrill/Prentice Hall. This comprehensive textbook provides in-depth discussions of ways to foster the teacher-parent partnership. *Highly recommended.*

Daniels, J. (1998). A modern mother's place is wherever her children are: Facilitating infants' and toddlers' mothers' transitions in child care. *Young Children, 53*(6), 4–12. In these few pages Daniels identifies the key ingredients needed to establish trustful, sound relationships between the family and the child care situation—very practical. *Highly recommended.*

Hildebrand, V., Phenice, L. A., Gray, M. M., & Hines, R. P. (2000). *Knowing and serving diverse families.* Upper Saddle River, NJ: Merrill/Prentice Hall. *Knowing and Serving Diverse Families* should be in every teacher's library since it offers hard-to-find information on a wide range of families from various ethnic backgrounds and family structures. *Highly recommended.*

Aspects of Family Life

Coll, C. G., Surrey, J. L., & Weinharten, K. (1998). *Mothering against the odds: Diverse voices of contemporary mothers.* New York: Guilford Press. Anticipating just another book about mothers working in and out of the home? If so, you'll need to look elsewhere; instead, this book is a treasure trove of information about incarcerated, divorced, homeless, HIV-positive, and immigrant mothers, just to name a few of the special aspects of motherhood discussed here. *Highly recommended.*

Fenichel, E. (Ed.). (1997). Some kids have dads and some don't, right? Wrong. *Zero to Three, 18*(1).

Parke, R. D. (1996). *Fatherhood.* Cambridge, MA: Harvard University Press. It's just plain true that fathers fill a different role with children than mothers do, and the *Zero to Three* issue and Parke's book discuss many aspects of that relationship.

Szinovacz, M. E. (Ed.). (1998). *Handbook on grandparenthood.* Westport, CT: Greenwood Press. A comprehensive book on a seldom-addressed subject, the authors explore grandparents' diverse roles in our society.

Creating Family-Friendly Environments

Diffily, D., & Morrison, K. (Eds.). (1996). *Family friendly communication for early childhood programs.* Washington, DC: National Association for the Education of Young Children. This book presents reproducible, brief articles for potential inclusion in newsletters explaining the "why" of early education coupled with suggestions of appropriate activities for the children for staff and/or parents to use.

Schweikert, G. (1996). I confess, I've changed. *Child Care Information Exchange, #111,* 90–92. This article includes a practical list of ways to create family-friendly environments.

Workman, S. N., & Gage, J. A. (1997). Family-school partnerships: A family strengths approach. *Young Children, 52*(4), 10–19. Practical suggestions for increasing family participation at school are discussed here.

Talking Things Over with Parents

Dennis, R. E., & Giangreco, M. F. (1996). Creating conversation: Reflections on cultural sensitivity in family interviewing. *Exceptional Children, 63*(1), 103–116. These suggestions for conducting parent interviews with families from differing cultures are based on a research study that resulted in concrete, sensitive recommendations. *Highly recommended.*

Koch, P. K., & McDonough, M. (1999). Improving parent-teacher conferences through collaborative conversations. *Young Children, 54*(2), 11–15. The authors encourage using a third person to serve as facilitator during conversations when a child is having difficulty. Lots of practical examples are included.

Murphy, D. M. (1997). Parent and teacher plan for the child. *Young Children, 52*(4), 32–36. A "nice" example of a conference "gone wrong" with suggestions of what to do before and afterward to prevent that from happening.

Samalin, N. (1991). *Love and anger: The parental dilemma.* New York: Viking. Samalin provides sound advice for parents *and for teachers* for coping successfully with anger.

Making Friends with Parents from Other Cultures

Note also the Hildebrand et al. (2000) and the Dennis and Giangreco (1996) references listed above, the Mallory and New (1993) reference listed below, and also refer to chapter 13 for more information on this subject.

Lee, F. Y. (1995). Asian parents as partners. *Young Children, 50*(3), 4–9. Lee suggests many practical ways to reach out effectively to parents who may otherwise feel reticent about approaching their children's teachers. *Highly recommended.*

Lopez, A. (1996). Creation is ongoing: Developing a relationship with non-English-speaking parents. *Child Care Information Exchange, #107,* 56–62. This sensitive article focuses on the Latino point of view. Very helpful.

Sturm, C. (1997). Creating parent-teacher dialogues: Intercultural communication in child care. *Young Children, 52*(5), 34–38. Several actual examples combined with practical suggestions are included in this discussion.

Tutwiler, S. W. (1998). Diversity among families. In M. L. Fuller & G. Olsen (Eds.), *Home-school relations: Working successfully with parents and families.* Boston: Allyn & Bacon. Tutwiler's chapter identifies some possible cultural characteristics of major ethnic groups.

Wilson, M. N. (Ed.). (1995). African American family life: Its structural and ecological aspects. *New Directions for Child Development,* 68. A good range of information on African American family life from a variety of perspectives is included in this issue. Useful reading.

For the Advanced Student

Carter, B. C., & McGoldrick, M. M. (Eds.). (1999). *The expanded family life cycle: Individual, family, and social perspectives* (3rd ed.). Boston: Allyn & Bacon. For a comprehensive, scholarly treatment of just about every aspect of family life, this is a good source to turn to. *Highly recommended.*

Fuller, M. L., & Olsen, G. (Eds.). (1998). *Home-school relations: Working successfully with parents and families.* Boston: Allyn & Bacon. The editors provide a rich source of information as diverse as parent conferencing and parent involvement and home tutoring.

Mallory, B. L., & New, R. S. (Eds.). (1993). *Diversity & developmentally appropriate practices: Challenges for early childhood education.* New York: Teachers College Press. This book points out the differing values about education that parents from a variety of cultures may hold. Thought-provoking reading.

Powell, D. R. (1998). Research in review: Reweaving parents into the fabric of early childhood programs. *Young Children, 53*(5), 60–67. Powell reviews essential ingredients of a sound relationship between parents and teachers and offers information on concrete ways to involve parents.

Additional Resources

Zero to Three: Bulletin: National Center for Infants, Toddlers, and Families, 734 15th Street, NW, Suite 1000, Washington, DC 20005–1013. Issues generally focus on a single subject each time and include book and videotape reviews. *Highly recommended.*

part II

Fostering Physical Well-Being

chapter four
Handling Daily Routines

chapter five
Development of the Physical Self

Handling Daily Routines

How to stop nagging the children through transition times?

Why Miguel won't eat his lunch?

How to get Maggie off the climbing gym when it's time to go indoors?

. . . IF YOU HAVE, THE MATERIAL IN THE FOLLOWING PAGES WILL HELP YOU.

The lunch period should be an occasion for the enjoyment of good food in a social situation. I can remember my first experience as an assistant teacher in an all-day program. Lunch was rolled into the classroom on a wagon. Children (already bibbed) were lying on cots for a pre-lunch rest. Teachers served the plates and summoned the children to the tables. Everything on the plate had to be eaten before melba toast chunks were distributed (these were great favorites!) and finally dessert and milk. There was one particularly dismal meal which appeared weekly: a barely poached egg (the white still transparent) sitting on top of some dreary spinach. No one liked it, and one little girl finally refused to eat it. She sat stolidly before the offensive plate, quietly but firmly asserting, "I won't eat it. I hate it. It's not even cooked." The teacher finally removed the plate to the kitchen with the comment that it would be waiting for her after her nap.

After nap, Jill was escorted to the kitchen to be confronted with the cool mess of uncooked egg and spinach. She was told that she could return to the playroom after she had eaten it.

When she returned to the playroom, the teacher asked her if she had eaten her lunch. Jill answered, "Yes, and then I threw it up." And she had!

Evelyn Beyer (1968, p. 124)[1]

You can't hide a piece of broccoli in a glass of milk!

Anonymous

[1] From TEACHING YOUNG CHILDREN, by Evelyn Beyer, copyright © 1968, by Western Publishing Company, Inc., reprinted by permission of The Bobbs-Merrill Company, Inc.

Routines, those omnipresent recurring sequences of behavior, constitute the backbone of full- and half-day programs and serve as landmarks that divide the day into different sections. They typically include the activities of arriving, departing, eating, toileting, resting, and the transitions between them and the other daily activities of preschool life.

Adequate handling of routines can foster both emotional and physical health, but in recent years teachers have tended to be more aware of the significance of routines in relation to emotional health than of the physical significance of good nutrition and adequate rest. The pasty faces, vulnerability to illness, and low energy levels of many children in compensatory programs now serve to remind us, however, that physical health is vital to well-being and that our young children need these routines to help them build strong bodies as well as stable personalities.

It is surprising to discover that although routines involve a good portion of the day and although strong feelings and convictions of what is "right" abound, scant research has been carried out in these areas. What research there is deals with nutrition and the emotional process of attachment and separation, rather than with the investigation of alternative ways to handle routines in school. Therefore readers should understand that the following discussion is based on a consensus of generally followed practice and that the recommendations mainly rest on experience and opinion and are not validated by research.

One other note of caution about routines: If the teacher is unwise enough to go to war with a child on the subject of routines, the child, if he is so inclined, can always win. Thus a child who absolutely will not eat, will not use the toilet, or refuses to go to sleep can win any time he wants to; there is little the teacher can do about it. Fortunately teachers and children rarely reach this kind of impasse, but it is important to understand that such power struggles *can* happen and *have* happened and that the most common way to bring about such a disaster is to reduce oneself to attempting to force a child to comply with any routine absolutely against his will. It just does not work.

The best way to prevent conflicts from developing is to realize that children usually find comfort in reasonable routines that contribute to their physical well-being. It also helps if the teacher determines the most important learnings to be derived from each routine and then works toward achieving those goals, rather than becoming caught up in "winning for its own sake." For example, it is more important that a child enjoy food and take pleasure in mealtimes than it is that he clear his plate, wait until everyone is served, or not rap his glass on the table. Bearing this primary goal in mind will reduce the amount of criticism and control that may otherwise mar snack and lunch times.

SCHEDULES AND TRANSITIONS INTO ROUTINES

Schedules

Routines and transitions are best understood when seen in the perspective of the overall schedule, so a sample full-day schedule is provided (Figure 4.1).

7:00–7:30	Some teachers arrive, set out materials, and ready the environment for children.
7:30	Children begin to arrive. One teacher or the director is specially assigned to greet children and parents, chat, and carry out the health check. If possible, another staff member provides a cozy time reading books with those who desire it. Self-select materials are also available.
8:30–9:15	Breakfast available for children who want it. Breakfast area set up near school-room sink to facilitate hand washing before and after eating. Self-selected activity continues until 9:15 for those who are not hungry.
9:15–9:45	Small- or large-group time: this often continues quite a while for 4-year-olds, less time for younger children. Its length should vary each day in order to adapt to the changing needs of the group.
9:45–10:00	Transition to activities.
10:00–11:40/11:45	Mingled indoor-outdoor experience or outdoor followed by indoor activity, depending on staffing and weather. Small-group experiences and field trips occur during this time. Self-selected activities, changed from the ones available in the early arrival period, are also provided.
11:40–11:45/12:00	Children help put things away, prepare gradually for lunch. Children go to toilet; children *and teachers* wash hands.
12:00–12:35/12:45	Family-style lunchtime; children are seated with adults in groups as small as possible.
12:35–12:45/1:00	Children prepare for nap: toilet, wash hands, brush teeth, disrobe, snuggle down.
1:00–2:30/3:00	Nap time; children get up as they wake up, toilet, dress, and move out of nap area. Snack ready as they arrive and desire it.
By 3:30	All snacks completed. Indoor-outdoor self-select continues, again with special activities planned and provided for.
4:40	Children begin to put things away, freshen up (wash hands and faces, etc.), and have quiet opportunities to use manipulatives or sit with teacher for songs, stories, and general quiet, relaxing time as parents call for them.
5:30	Children picked up (except for the inevitable emergencies of course!)

Note: For a sample curriculum plan, see Chapter 18, Developing Thinking and Reasoning Skills: Using the Emergent Approach to Foster Creativity in Thought, and Chapter 19, Developing Thinking and Reasoning Skills: Using the Conventional Approach to Build Midlevel Mental Abilities.

Figure 4.1
Daily schedule for a full-day program for 3- and 4-year-olds

Remember that a schedule should be regarded as a guide, not as dogma. Allowance should always be made for deviations when these are desirable. Perhaps it took longer than anticipated for the bread to rise, or perhaps dramatic play is involving most of the group in an intensely satisfying way. Schedules need give and stretch to accommodate these kinds of possibilities. This is why overlap times and approximate times are listed in the schedule. Even a modest amount of latitude allows children to proceed gradually from one activity to the next without being hassled by the teachers (K. Miller, 1996).

physical self ~ emotional health ~ self-esteem ~ social competence

| Research Study |

Intentions Versus Reality

Research Question: Ostrosky and her associates asked how good the match was between the activities scheduled by teachers in preschool special education classes and the activities in which the children were actually involved.

Research Method: The researchers observed children in 24 preschool classrooms for children with disabilities during the morning periods. Three to five children were randomly selected in each class, with the total sample of 94 children ranging in chronological age from 38 to 89 months.

Time samples were taken of the children's behavior by using the Ecobehavioral System for the Complex Assessment of Preschool Environments (Carta, Greenwood, & Atwater, 1986). This system uses 12 activity categories such as stories, fine motor activities, music, language programming, play, and self-care. The children's behavior was classified according to these categories.

Detailed schedules of their class day were provided by the teachers, and the planned activities were classified according to the same system used to classify the children's bheavior.

Results: When the intended activities were compared with how the children actually spent their time, the researchers found a close match between the amount of time planned for some activities—namely, pre-academics and gross and fine motor activiites—and the amount of time the children actually spent doing them. However, significant discrepancies were found in other areas. In common with teachers in many preschool classrooms serving typical children, the teachers underestimated or did not even include the time required for transitions. They also underscheduled the amount of time children spent in independent storybook perusal. From an early childhood point of view, the most serious discrepancy was the difference

---

It can also happen that some schedules do not match what actually takes place in the classroom. The Research Study in this chapter, which describes the work done by Ostrosky, Skellenger, Odom, McConnell, and Peterson (1994) that observed children's participation in classrooms for preschool-age children with disabilities, reveals how in those classrooms some scheduled times were consistently short-changed.

Note that the schedule in Figure 4.1 allows for breakfast to be served only to those children who desire it. For years our center was plagued with the problem of having some children arrive at 8:30 or 9:00 stuffed to the gills, whereas others were clearly famished. If we waited for snack until 10:00, when everyone had at least a little appetite, then they were not hungry for lunch! We finally decided to solve this problem by offering breakfast on a self-select basis, with food kept appetizing on warming trays and with a friendly staff member sitting in the breakfast corner at all times to assist the children and welcome them for a quiet personal chat as they ate. This solution, though unconventional, has done a much better job of meeting all the children's needs by freeing more of the staff to work with the youngsters who are not hungry and by providing a homey, comfortable, slow-paced beginning of the day for children who are just waking up and do want break-

physical self = emotional health = self-esteem = social competence

between the amount of time the teachers planned for free play compared with the amount of time the children were actually involved in that activity. The researchers comment that "play may be perceived by early childhood special educators as the activity most easily given up by teachers" (p. 31).

Implications: This study illustrates a condition common to many teachers—a condition especially challenging for preschool teachers who work with children with disabilities: Teachers are experiencing tension between doing what they *have* to do versus doing what they *want* to do. Many teachers recognize the contribution play can make to children's development, and yet when push comes to shove, it is the first thing jettisoned from the schedule.

The value of this research to such teachers is that it may make them aware the play period is suffering most consistently from attrition. Once they realize that this is the case, it will be up to them to decide whether to reschedule the day to make

certain the children are no longer denied this important avenue of growth.

The basic implication to be drawn by teachers in more typical preschool classrooms is that they, too, should take a careful look at how realistic their schedules actually are. Is enough time being allotted for transitons or are the children constantly pushed to get ready for the next activity? Is sufficient time truly included for the children to become deeply involved in their play, or do they just get started and then have to put everything away? Might it be more satisfactory to rearrange the schedule into fewer, longer time blocks so that the number of transitions is reduced? These and other problems related to scheduling deserve consideration and reconsideration as the year progresses.

Source: From "Teachers' Schedules and Actual Time Spent in Activities in Preschool Special Education Classes," by M. M. Ostrosky, A. C. Skellenger, S. L. Odom, S. R. McConnell, and C. Peterson, 1994, Journal of Early Intervention, 18(1), 25-33.

fast. It also helps settle down children who may have been rushed off to school in too much of a hurry to have had more than a bite to eat before departure.

The same policy of eating by choice is followed after nap since children drift out of the nap area a few at a time. Almost all of them at that point, of course, are ready for something good to eat, but it is still a matter of self-decision for them. This not only prevents wasted food but also is part of our effort to encourage children to be aware of what their bodies are saying to them. Are they eating just because it is the thing to do, or are their bodies telling them they are really hungry?

The primary rule that applies to both breakfast and snack time is that, once seated, the child stays until he is finished eating. No one walks around with food in his hands, and a staff member is always seated at the table to keep the children company.

Transition Times

A study of several kinds of nursery schools (Berk, 1976) makes the point that *transitions* (the time spent in moving from one activity to the next) occupy from 20% to 35% of activity time in nursery school, depending on the school, the particular day, and the skill and planning contributed by the teacher. This surprising statistic certainly emphasizes that transitions are worth thinking about and managing well so that children can move as smoothly as possible from one activity to the next. It also reminds us how necessary it is to plan for enough time when shifting, for instance, from music to lunch or from lunch to nap so that children are not unnecessarily harried in the process.

If you find yourself continually nagging and urging the children to hurry through their paces, you may want to try the following suggestions to make transitions easier for you and them. In addition to allowing a realistic amount of time for transitions to take place, it always helps to warn *once* in advance when a change is in the offing, saying, "It's almost story time," or, "You can have a little more time with the beads, but then we'll have to put them away." This gives the children a chance to finish what they are doing and makes their compliance more likely. It also helps to remember that transitions do not usually present an opportunity for a real choice (the child is supposed to come, not linger in the yard), so it is best not to ask, "Would you like to come?" or, "It's time to come in, OK?" but to say more definitely, "In just a minute it's going to be time for lunch, and we will go indoors. What do you suppose we're having to eat today?" Occasionally singing a simple song such as "Here We Go A' Marching" will also help get children moving in the desired direction. Avoiding situations in which all the children have to do something at once is the best help of all since this avoids the noisy, crowded situations that seem to happen with particular frequency in the toilet room (Larson, Hawthorne, & Plum, 1994).

ROUTINES OF ARRIVAL AND DEPARTURE

It is natural for young children to feel anxious when their fathers or mothers leave them at school. This feeling, called *separation anxiety*, appears to be strongest in American children between the ages of 10 and 24 months (B. Z. Bailey, 1992). Even beyond this age, however, separation requires time and tactful handling by the staff so that the child and the parent come to feel comfortable about parting.

Introduce the Child to School Gradually

It is common practice and good sense to recommend a visit by parent and child for the first day, then another short stay while the parent leaves for a brief period, followed by a gradual extension of time as the child's ability to endure separation increases.

Another way of helping children become comfortable is by having an open house during which families can come and go at their convenience. Some schools begin the term with half the children coming on one day, and the other half coming on the next. At our center we send each child a personal letter with a name tag, an invitation to the open house, and a short description of what we will be doing at school. The children love these letters, and this preliminary contact does seem to overcome some of their initial apprehension.

These suggestions about gradual adaptation to the new environment are fine for many families whose schedules can be somewhat flexible, but they do not work for parents

Waiting can seem an eternity to a young child.

whose jobs demand that they appear promptly at 8:00 a.m. no matter what the teacher recommends or how hard the child is crying. If at all possible, special arrangements should be made for such families when their children begin attending. A grandfather or aunt might be pressed into service and stay while the child makes friends. Sometimes the parent can bring the child by for a visit around lunchtime, the teacher can make a Saturday visit to the home, or the child can come to school with a friend. Any of these arrangements, though not ideal, are preferable to allowing the child to walk in and simply be left in a strange place with strange people for 9 hours on his first day (Blecher-Sass, 1997).

Handle Outbursts of Emotion with Care

It helps to recognize that a child must often deal with three feelings when his mother leaves him: (a) grief (the emotion that seems most obvious and logical), (b) fear (also not very surprising), and (c) anger (the emotion the teacher is least likely to recognize in these circumstances) (Bowlby, 1973, 1980). It is often necessary not only to comfort and reassure the child but also to recognize with him that he feels angry with his mother because she left him at school. I recall one forthright 3-year-old who took real pleasure in biting the mama doll with our toothy rubber hippopotamus as soon as her mother departed. The teacher may also see this angry reaction at being left behind come out at the end of the day when the child insists (with just a touch of malice) that he wants to stay at school "for ever and ever" and does not want to go home. If the teacher interprets this reaction to his mother as being a way of relieving angry feelings, it will help maintain friendly relations all around.

Actually it is the children who make a forthright fuss as their mothers leave who seem to work through their feelings of loss with the greatest expedition, whereas the children who apparently make an easy adjustment by becoming instantly involved in activities often become downcast a few weeks later as they lower their defenses. If this happens 3 to 4 weeks after entry to school, the parent is likely to assume something has happened there that makes the child want to stay home. The best protection against this conclusion is to explain casually to the parent *before the child's facade crumbles* that he may show his grief at a later time and that most children feel some sadness and loneliness when left at school.

It is also wise to prepare parents for the fact that children may go through a milder attack of separation anxiety again when they return from vacation. Otherwise this repeated behavior can discourage parents who underwent a difficult separation experience at the beginning of school.

Other unexpected circumstances can also trigger anxiety. One spring the children in our center walked to the college cafeteria and met their parents there for lunch. All went well until it came time to part, and suddenly we had several very unhappy children on our hands. The unusual circumstances had made parting difficult once again for our small charges.

But learning to let go is part of becoming mature. A nice balance of comfort combined with a matter-of-fact expectation that he will feel better soon usually gets the child started on the day. Having something at hand that he especially enjoys will help, too. The teacher must take care to permit the child to form a relationship with him or her as a bridge to the other children yet at the same time not encourage this relationship so much that the youngster droops around longer than necessary or becomes a careerist hand-holder (Wilkerson, 1997).

ROUTINES THAT CENTER AROUND EATING

Adequate Nutrition Is Important

In these days of imitation foods and casual eating habits it is important to emphasize the value of good food for young children. Too many schools depend on artificial juices and a cracker for snack, supposedly on the grounds that the children are well fed at home. But the underlying reason for serving this kind of food is that it is convenient and cheap. Yet studies continue to accumulate that indicate good nutrition combined with other environmental factors is associated with the ability to pay attention and learn (Center on Hunger, Poverty, and Nutrition Policy, 1998).

Although nutritional problems are most severe among the poor, not only the children in compensatory programs are "orphans of wealth." An early 1990s study focusing on children ranging in age from 2 to 19 determined that only 1% of children actually ate the balanced diet recommended by the U.S. Department of Agriculture (USDA, 1985). Instead researchers found that 40% of children's diets came from fat and added sugars (Portner, 1997). With the increasing popularity of fast foods it is unlikely that children's diets have improved since then—and this is true for children of all economic classes. This is why, no matter the income level of the families of children served by the program, careful planning of nutritious meals is so important and why so much attention is devoted to it in the following pages.

Planning Appealing and Nutritious Meals

One fortunate fact about teaching at the preprimary level is that teachers and directors usually have opportunities to participate in planning what the children will eat. Even

When food is plain and tasty, children eat it with relish.

Table 4.1
U.S. Department of Agriculture Child Care Food Program required meal pattern

Foods	Ages 1 up to 3*	Ages 3 up to 6	Ages 6 up to 12
Breakfast			
Milk, fluid†	½ C	¾ C	1 C
Juice/vegetable(s) and/or fruits	¼ C	½ C	½ C
Bread/bread alternates‡			
Bread, cornbread, biscuits, rolls or	½ slice	½ slice	1 slice
Cereal:			
Cold, dry or	¼ C or ⅓ oz	⅓ C or ½ oz	¾ C or 1 oz
Hot, cooked, or	¼ C	¼ C	½ C
Cooked pasta, noodle products, or rice	¼ C	¼ C	½ C
Snack			
(Select 2 out of 4 components)			
Milk, fluid†	½ C	½ C	1 C
Meat/meat alternates§			
Lean meat, poultry, fish‖ or	½ oz	½ oz	1 oz
Cheese or	½ oz	½ oz	1 oz
Egg, large, or	½ egg	½ egg	1 egg
Cooked dried beans or peas or	⅛ C	⅛ C	¼ C
Peanut butter, soynut butter, other nut or seed butters	1 tbsp	1 tbsp	2 tbsp
or	½ oz	½ oz	1 oz
Peanuts, soynuts, tree nuts, or seeds	½ C	½ C	¾ C
Juice/vegetable(s) and/or fruit#			
Bread/bread alternates‡	½ slice	½ slice	1 slice
Bread, cornbread, biscuits, rolls or			
Cereal:	¼ C or ⅓ oz	⅓ C or ½ oz	¾ C or 1 oz
Cold, dry, or	¼ C	¼ C	½ C
Hot, cooked, or	¼ C	¼ C	½ C
Cooked pasta, noodle products, or rice			

when the menus are decided at a "higher" level, it can still be possible to influence the planning if this is attempted with tact and persistence!

A useful way to begin such planning is to become acquainted with the preschool lunch pattern required by the USDA (Table 4.1) since so many children's centers use funding from that agency to support their food services.[2] Or one can use the Food Guide Pyramid published by the USDA as an overall guide suitable for adults as well as children. Note the emphasis on complex carbohydrates, fruits, and vegetables (Figure 4.2).

These standards can serve as basic guidelines, but some additional points should be considered as well. Variety, particularly as the year progresses and the children feel at ease,

[2]   *For further information on obtaining funding from the Child and Adult Care Food Program, contact the U.S. Department of Agriculture office in your state capital. Many centers and day care homes that qualify for this assistance do not participate despite the fact that it can be a real budget saver.*

Foods	Ages 1 up to 3*	Ages 3 up to 6	Ages 6 up to 12
Lunch/Supper			
Milk, fluid, served as beverage	½ C	¾ C	1 C
Meat/meat alternates§			
Meat, poultry, fish‖ or	1 oz	1½ oz	2 oz
Cheese or	1 oz	1½ oz	2 oz
Egg, large, or	1	1	1
Cooked dry beans or peas or	¼ C	⅜ C	½ C
Peanut butter, soynut butter, other nut or seed butters or	2 tbsp	3 tbsp	4 tbsp
Peanuts, soynuts, tree nuts, or seeds**	½ oz = 50% ¼ C total	¾ oz = 50% ½ C total	1 oz = 50% ¾ C total
Juice/vegetable(s) and/or fruits‡‡			
Bread/bread alternates‡	½ slice	½ slice	1 slice
Bread, cornbread, biscuits, rolls or			
Cooked pasta, noodle products, or rice	¼ C	¼ C	½ C

*For required serving amounts for infants up to age 1 year, refer to program regulations.

†Fluid milk should be used as a beverage, on cereal, or in part for each purpose.

‡Or an equivalent serving of an acceptable bread, pasta, or noodle product. Cereals must be whole grain, enriched, or fortified.

§Or an equivalent quantity of any combination of foods listed under meat/meat alternates.

‖Cooked lean meat without bone, breading, or skin.

#Juice may not be served when milk is served as the only other component.

**Tree nuts and seeds, except acorns, chestnuts, and coconuts, may be used as meat alternates. Nuts and seeds may supply no more than half of the meat alternate requirement at lunch/supper. Nuts and seeds must be combined with another meat/meat alternate. For purposes of determining combinations, 1 ounce of nuts or seeds is equal to 1 ounce of cooked lean meat, poultry, or fish.

‡‡Serve two or more kinds of vegetable(s) and/or fruit(s) or a combination of both. Full-strength vegetable or fruit juice may be counted to meet not more than one-half of this requirement.

Source: From Food, Nutrition, and the Young Child (4th ed.), by J. B. Endres and R. E. Rockwell, 1993, Upper Saddle River, NJ: Merrill/Prentice Hall. Reprinted with permission.

should be a keynote of the food program. Snacks should be different every day and can be based on seasonal fruits and vegetables to help keep budgets within reason.

Dessert should be unsugared fruit and should be regarded as a nutritional component of the meal, not as a reward to be bargained for.

If the food is plain and familiar and a lot of it can be eaten with the fingers, children will eat more. As a general rule, young children are deeply suspicious of casseroles and food soaked in drab-looking sauces and gravies. They prefer things they can recognize, such as carrot sticks, hamburger, and plain fruit.

Table 4.2 provides some sample lunch menus that show how appealing plain, relatively inexpensive food can be. Even if all the children are from one particular ethnic group, it is desirable to vary the suggestions in Table 4.2 by incorporating food from many cultures bit by bit. For example, menus might include black-eyed peas with ham or pinto beans with

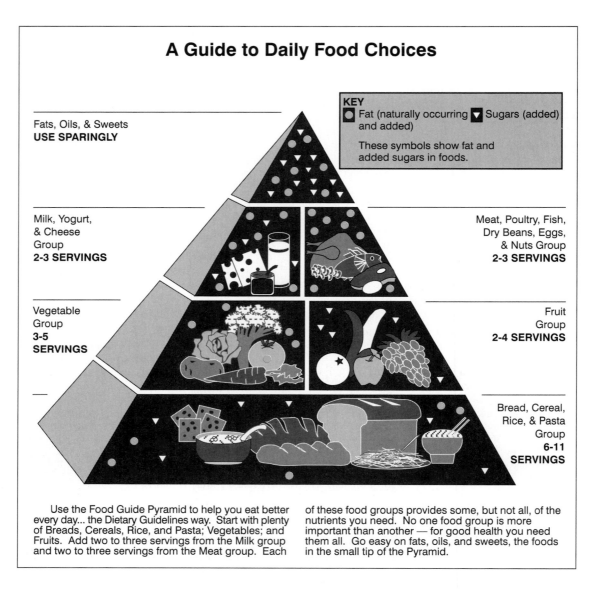

Figure 4.2
Food guide pyramid

Table 4.2

Sample lunch menus

Monday	Tuesday	Wednesday	Thursday	Friday
Week I				

Oven-baked fish
Green beans
Carrot sticks
Cheese biscuits
Milk
Fresh pear halves
	Beef balls
	Lima beans
	Tomato wedges
	Whole wheat
	  toast strips
	Milk
	Stewed prunes
		Stewed chicken
		Buttered noodles
		Grated carrot-
		  raisin salad
		Whole wheat
		  bread with
		  apricot spread
		Milk
		Orange slices
			Simmered steak
			Scalloped
			  potatoes
			English peas
			Whole wheat
			  muffins
			Milk
			Fresh fruit cup
				Chitterlings
				Stewed okra and
				  tomatoes
				Black-eyed peas
				Spoonbread
				  (corn type)
				Strawberries
				Milk

Week II				

Meat loaf
Buttered carrots
  and peas
Whole wheat
  bread and butter
Milk
Oatmeal muffins
	Creamed chicken
	Buttered rice
	French green
	  beans
	Cornbread sticks
	Milk
	Seedless grapes
		Oven-baked fish
		Buttered mixed
		  vegetables
		Whole wheat
		  toast strips
		Milk
		Apple wedges
			Toasted cheese
			  sandwich
			Tomato soup
			Chopped
			  broccoli
			Milk
			Cantaloupe slices
				Stir-fried beef
				  with assorted
				  leafy green
				  vegetables
				Rice
				Pineapple slices
				Lichees (seeded)
				  or raisins
				Milk

Week III				

Tostada with beef
  and cheese
Lettuce and
  tomato
Platano or
  spinach
Orange slices
Milk
	Meat balls with
	  tomato sauce
	Green beans
	Enriched bread
	  and butter
	Milk
	Banana bread
		Cheese cubes
		Twice-baked
		  potatoes
		Buttered beets
		Cooked spinach
		  with egg slices
		Milk
		Vanilla ice cream
			Beef stew with
			  peas, carrots,
			  and potatoes
			French bread
			  pieces
			Milk
			Cottage cheese
			  and peach slices
				Chicken
				  casserole
				Buttered broccoli
				Bran muffins
				Milk
				Fresh pineapple
				  and banana
				  slices

Week IV				

Hard-boiled eggs
Green beans with
  bacon
Drop biscuits
Milk
Orange slices in
  gelatin
	Braised calves
	  liver
	English peas
	Perfection salad
	Whole wheat
	  toast strips
	Milk
	Baked apple
		Tuna fish
		  sandwiches
		Lettuce pieces
		Buttered summer
		  squash
		Milk
		Fresh fruit cup
			Creamed chicken
			Buttered spinach
			Grated carrot-
			  raisin salad
			Whole wheat
			  bread
			Milk
			Applesauce
				Beef patty and
				  gravy
				Peas and
				  potatoes
				Tomato wedges
				Milk
				Sliced bananas in
				  orange juice

Source: Adapted from "Ideas for Administrators," The Idea Box, by the Austin Association for the Education of Young Children, © 1973, National Association for the Education of Young Children, 1834 Connecticut Ave., NW, Washington, DC 20009.

melted cheese. Introduction of such foods at this time of the child's life is particularly desirable for two reasons. First, good-tasting food that is identified as coming from a particular culture helps children feel friendly toward that culture. Second, research indicates that learning plays a big part in developing food preferences and that the preschool years may be a particularly sensitive period in the formation of such preferences (Birch, Johnson, & Fisher, 1995). If we wish to extend the range of children's food preferences, this is a good time to begin.

When there are children at the center of various ethnic and cultural backgrounds, it is even more crucial to include foods that they like and that are familiar. White, middle-class teachers need to remember that some foods they have eaten all their lives can be dishearteningly unfamiliar to the Navajo youngster who is accustomed to mutton and sheepherder's bread, or the Mexican American child whose diet staple is the tortilla. Table 4.3, A Sampling of Food Choices Often Preferred by Various Ethnic Groups, is included to remind readers of the wide variations in food preferences that may exist within the groups of children they teach. It is a plea for increased sensitivity to these variations so that menus might be revised to help some children feel more at home while widening the horizons of others beyond the scope of their ordinary diets. Of course, one should not assume that everyone from a particular cultural group necessarily likes all or any of the foods listed, but at least the table points the way to some enriched possibilities for menu planning. Additional resources for culturally familiar food are ethnic cookbooks and family recipes. A cook who comes from a background similar to that of the children can be a treasured asset. The references at the end of this chapter include readily available ethnic cookbooks.

Some Basic Principles Having to Do with Eating

Perhaps no area in our social life (except sex) has as many restrictions and regulations attached to it as eating does. A class of mine once counted up the rules enforced by their families about mealtimes. We thought of 43 rules within 10 minutes. They ranged from "no dessert until you clear your plate" to "wait until the men are fed before you sit down." We will content ourselves here with enumerating only the principles the majority of preprimary teachers have come to feel are important as they work with young children.

Some Children Eat More Than Others Do

The quantity of food a child consumes is related to his physiological makeup, as well as to his growth rate. Also, emotional states and needs can affect his appetite. All these factors must be considered when deciding whether a child's nutrition patterns are adequate. As long as the youngster remains healthy and his color is good, there is little need to worry about whether he is eating a lot or a little.

Eating Should Be a Pleasure, but Food Should Not Be Used as a Reward

Most of us are shocked when we hear of parents punishing their children by sending them to bed with no dinner, but how many of us would feel equally concerned about the adult who habitually rewards a child with a cookie or other desired food for being good? Yet this tying food together with behavior is one link in developing eating disorders in later years. Certainly eating should be (and is!) a satisfying pleasure, but that pleasure needs to be

Table 4.3

A sampling of foods often preferred by various ethnic groups

	Vegetables	Fruits	Meats and Alternatives	Grain Products	Others
Black	Broccoli, corn, greens (mustard, collard, kale, turnips, beets, etc.), lima beans, okra, peas, pumpkins	Grapefruit, grapes, nectarines, plums, watermelon	Sausage, pigs' feet, ears, etc., bacon, luncheon meat, organ meats, turkey, catfish, perch, red snapper, tuna, salmon, sardines, shrimp, kidney beans, red beans, black-eyed peas, peanuts, and peanut butter	Corn bread, hominy grits, biscuits, muffins, cooked cereal, crackers	Chitterlings, salt pork, gravies, buttermilk
Hispanic American	Avocados, chilies, corn, lettuce, onions, peas, potatoes, prickly pear (cactus leaf, called *nopales*), zucchini	Guava, lemons, mangoes, melons, prickly pear (cactus fruit called *tuna*), zapote (or sapote)	Lamb, tripe, sausage (*chorizo*), bologna, bacon, pinto beans, pink beans, garbanzo beans, lentils, peanuts, and peanut butter	Tortillas, corn flour, oatmeal, sweet bread (*pan dulce*)	Salsa (tomato, pepper, onion relish), chili sauce, guacamole, lard (*manteca*), pork cracklings
Japanese	Bamboo shoots, broccoli, burdock root, cauliflower, celery, cucumbers, eggplant, gourd (*kampyo*), mushrooms, napa cabbage, peas, peppers, radishes (daikon or pickles called *takuwan*), snow peas, squash, sweet potatoes, turnips, water chestnuts, yamaimo	Apricots, cherries, grapefruit, grapes, lemons, limes, melons, persimmons, pineapple, pomegranates, plums (dried pickled *umeboshi*), strawberries	Turkey, raw tuna or sea bass (*sashimi*), mackerel, sardines (*mezashi*), shrimp, abalone, squid, octopus, soybean curd (*tofu*), soybean paste (*miso*), soybeans, red beans (*azuki*), lima beans, peanuts, almonds, cashews	Rice crackers, noodles (whole-wheat noodle called *soba* or *udon*), oatmeal, rice	Soy sauce, Nori paste (used to season rice), bean thread (*komyaku*), ginger (*shoga*; dried form called *denishoga*)
Chinese	Bamboo shoots, bean sprouts, bok choy, broccoli, celery, Chinese cabbage, corn, cucumbers, eggplant, greens (collard, Chinese broccoli, mustard, kale), leeks, lettuce, mushrooms, peppers, scallions, snow peas, taro, water chestnuts, white turnips, white radishes, winter melon	Figs, grapes, kumquats, loquats, mangoes, melons, persimmons, pineapple, plums, pomegranates	Organ meats, duck, white fish, shrimp, lobster, oysters, sardines, soybeans, soybean curd (*tofu*), black beans, chestnuts (*kuri*)	Barley, millet, rice, wheat	Soy sauce, sweet and sour sauce, mustard sauce, ginger root, plum sauce, red bean paste

93

Table 4.3 *continued*

	Vegetables	Fruits	Meat and Alternatives	Grain Products	Others
Vietnamese*	Bamboo shoots, bean sprouts, cabbage, carrots, cucumbers, greens, lettuce, mushrooms, onions, peas, spinach, yams	Apples, bananas, eggfruit (*o-ma*), grapefruit, jackfruit, lychees, mandarins, mangoes, oranges, papaya, pineapple, tangerines, watermelon	Beef, blood, brains, chicken, duck, eggs, fish, goat, kidney, lamb, liver, pork, shellfish, soybeans	French bread, rice, rice noodles, wheat noodles	Fish sauce, fresh herbs, garlic, ginger, lard, MSG, peanut oil, sesame seeds, sesame seed oil, vegetable oil
Indian†	Cauliflower, carrots, cucumbers, corn-gourds, leeks, eggplant, beets, radishes, hot peppers, bell peppers, peas, French beans, okra, pumpkins, red and white cabbage, mung sprouts, bean sprouts, potatoes, tapioca root, sweet potatoes	Oranges, limes, grapes, watermelon, mangoes, guava, honeydew, chiku, cantaloupe, pineapple, green, yellow, and red bananas, berries, custard apples	Lamb, beef, duck, chicken, shrimp, catfish, buffalo, sunfish, sardines, fresh crab, lobster, peanuts, cashews, almonds, chickpeas, split peas, black-eyed peas, dry mung beans	Rice pancakes, wheat chapati, puri, mixed-grain flour bread	Fresh coconut juice, curries, tomato sauce, tamarind sauce, dried grain curries (*pulses*), yogurt-curry garnished with coriander (fresh leaves)
Navajo‡§	Home-grown corn, squash, melons, pumpkins, and some beans; some fresh vegetables available from trading posts; carrots, cabbage, lettuce, potatoes, and onions; also canned vegetables (these items take second priority to staples)	Canned or a little fresh fruit; fruit regarded as luxury	Mutton (name applies to both sheep and goat meat), horse, and beef; when meat is home slaughtered, almost all of animal is consumed; very little poultry	White flour has supplanted corn meal as most basic flour; blue corn flour regarded as specially nutritious	Canned, evaporated milk used almost exclusively; soft drinks in summer very popular

*Information supplied by Hanh-Trang Tran-Viet, Carbondale, IL.

†Refers to East Indian.

‡From "A Study of the Dietary Background and Nurtiture of the Navajo Indian" by W. J. Darby, C. M. Adams, M. Pollard, E. Dalton, and P. McKinley, 1956, *Journal of Nutrition, 60* (Supplement), pp. 3–83.

§There is little variation to daily food patterns. Bread and meat are the most crucial items. The chapter from which this material was taken also includes an interesting list of 20 native plants used as food by some Navajo families. Directions for preparing these plants are also included. Information on the Navajo Tribe was selected as an example for a specific group of American Indians and is not intended to be used as guidelines for menus for other American Indian groups.

Source: From *Food, Nutrition, and the Young Child (2nd ed., pp. 182–183)* by J. B. Endres and R. E. Rockwell, 1985, *Upper Saddle River, NJ: Merrill/Prentice Hall.* © 1985 by Prentice Hall. *Reprinted with permission.*

kept within bounds; it should not become the primary source of gratification in life. Food should not be used to punish or to bribe or to reward.

Eating Together Should Convey a Sense of Happy Family Life to the Children

There should be time both to eat and to chat. Discipline situations should be avoided whenever possible. Mealtime can also be a time to enjoy each other and to help the group by going for seconds, passing food to each other, and group cleanup.

Eating Should Help a Child Be Independent

When I think of the reason we encourage children to serve themselves, I remember the little girl who commented that when teachers are cold, they make the children put their sweaters on. The same thing is true of eating. When teachers are hungry, they serve the children too much; but if food is passed around the table, each child can take what he desires. It is up to him to choose. He knows how hungry he is, and he knows his preferences far better than his teacher does. Then, too, by serving himself he has the opportunity to learn to observe the social rule "Take some and leave some."

Having sponges close at hand also helps children become independent because they can mop up their own spills. Advertisements that stress the joys of carpeting to the contrary, it is much easier to clean up food from uncarpeted floors, so it is best to eat over a linoleum floor or even outdoors when possible.

Another way to help children retain independence is to make sure they do not have to wait to be fed. When children are hungry and their blood glucose level is low, they are in poor control of themselves, so food should be ready to be served as the children sit down. If it is placed on a low table or nearby shelf, the teacher can start passing around the serving bowls as soon as everyone has arrived.

Eating Should Be a Positive Experience

As the vignette in this chapter's opening quote so painfully reminds us, the quickest way to teach a child to hate a new food is to make him eat it all. It is desirable, though, to encourage (but not force) everyone to take a taste of everything served. Generally the teacher can count on the combination of good appetites and enthusiasm to foster venturesomeness, but sometimes a child will refuse to try something new. One teacher of my acquaintance handles these outright refusals by simply remarking, "Well, when you're older, I expect you'll want to try it," and then he changes the subject.

Some interesting and carefully controlled research by Birch (1980) indicates that children can also be influenced toward food in a positive way by the reactions of their peers. After determining who liked which vegetable, Birch studied groups of children who were seated so that a child who preferred one kind of vegetable was placed with a group who most preferred a second kind. After several days, during which the first child witnessed the others choosing her unpreferred vegetable as their first choice, Birch found that the child changed to selecting the second vegetable first, too. This change in preference remained constant over several weeks.

Unfortunately, negative comments can be just as influential as positive examples. Remarks such as, "It looks like dog poop!" should be discouraged. A wave of this kind of

talk can sweep through a group of 4-year-olds and actually spoil a meal if it is not controlled. The policy of "You don't have to eat it, but I won't let you spoil it for other people" is a sound one to enforce.

Perhaps one of the best ways to encourage children to try a new food is to allow them
to prepare it. Cooking is a fine learning experience, as well as a pleasure for preschoolers.
Making vegetable soup, deviling eggs, or baking whole wheat muffins can introduce them
to a whole range of taste experiences they might otherwise shun.

Eating Can Be a Learning Experience

Although the most important goal of the eating situation is to furnish nourishment and
pleasure, this experience can provide many opportunities for intellectual learning, too
(Dahl, 1998; Fuhr & Barclay, 1998). The lunch table is a fine place for conversation and
the development of verbal fluency. Children can be encouraged to talk about their pets,
what they did on the weekend, what they like best to eat, and what was fun at school during the morning. The opportunity can also be taken to talk about foods, textures, colors,
and more factual kinds of information, but some teachers seem to do this to excess and
forget to emphasize the more valuable goal of fluency. No matter what kinds of learning
experiences go along with the meal, the teacher should always remember that eating
should, first and foremost, be pleasurable and satisfying.

Children with Special Eating Problems

Allergies and Other Food Restrictions

Children who have allergies can have a difficult time at school, particularly at the lunch
table, and so deserve special mention. The allergies that occur most frequently are the
ones requiring a restriction on milk, milk products, eggs, soy, wheat, shellfish, and most
especially *peanuts*. According to Aronson (1997), peanuts are responsible for more allergic
reactions than any other food. Sometimes even being in the same room with a smidgen of
peanut butter can trigger a serious physiological crisis.

Allergic reactions can happen right away or take several hours to show up. Whichever
is the case, they must not be ignored since some of them are actually life threatening. It is
important to discuss the situation with parents and to develop a plan for dealing with a
possible reaction *before* it happens. This plan should include arrangements not only for
avoiding the food but also for storing medications or injections and for determining who
will administer them should the necessity arise.

At the same time it is necessary to consider the feelings of the youngster involved
because other children may be curious about why they cannot share a cookie with him or
why he isn't allowed to eat macaroni and cheese. It is wise to be as matter-of-fact as possible to avoid making the child feel regretful or persecuted about the restriction. Usually a
simple explanation that it is a physician's orders is sufficient.

The Child Who Won't Eat

Refusing to eat and obesity are luxuries that very few countries in the world can afford, so
I suppose we should count our blessings. For most children, taking the pressure off eating
at mealtimes and allowing a child to skip a meal if he so chooses will gradually solve the

problem of not eating. Although it may seem hard-hearted, I think it is a mistake to allow a recalcitrant child to repent suddenly when he realizes the food is going back to the kitchen. Good food should be set forth, a pleasant opportunity to eat should transpire, and when that time is past, it is past for everyone until it is time for snack. This policy should be carried out without vacillation or guilt on the teacher's part. It is up to the child to choose to eat or not eat; it is not the teacher's role to coax, bargain, or wheedle. No one ever starved to death because he missed his lunch.

On rare occasions the teacher will come across a youngster who either compulsively insists on eating only a narrowly circumscribed number of foods or refuses to eat altogether. This behavior is almost always duplicated at home as well. Taking the pressure off and handling mealtimes in a casual manner may not be enough in these special cases, and the condition can be difficult to ameliorate. Under these circumstances *it is important to suggest counseling promptly* for the family to relieve the situation.

The Child Who Grabs Everything

Whereas the noneater is likely to make teachers anxious, the grabber is likely to make them angry. Some grabbing is attributable to lack of social experience and consideration of others, some is attributable to enthusiasm or hunger, but some is attributable to feelings of emotional deprivation.

The teacher may need to remind the child many times to take some and leave some, as well as to recognize his feelings by commenting, "It looks so good to you that you just feel like taking it all, don't you?" It is also sound strategy to make sure that the hungry one gets a second helping and that he is delegated to go to the kitchen for refills. When he remembers to leave enough for the other children, his thoughtfulness should be commended.

When the grabbiness seems to be a symptom of emotional deprivation, particularly when children cram their mouths so full they cannot swallow, a more indirect approach is required that emphasizes meeting the youngster's emotional needs, rather than stressing consideration of others. Here again extreme cases may require psychological counseling.

THE PROCESS OF TOILETING

Taking Children to the Toilet

In general, preschools use the same toilet rooms for boys and girls. However, this rule always has exceptions such as some schools that serve mostly Mexican American youngsters, where families may feel strongly that open toileting violates the modesty of the little girls.

One benefit of toileting together is that children learn to treat sexual differences quite casually. They will ask or comment about differences from time to time, and this provides golden opportunities to give straightforward, simple explanations. (Refer to chapter 13 for a more detailed discussion about sex education.) Open toileting has the advantage of reducing the peeking and furtive inspections that may go on otherwise. It promotes a healthier attitude toward sexual differences and therefore should be encouraged.

The majority of children of preschool age can be expected to go to the toilet when they feel the need, but an occasional child will have to be reminded. Rather than lining up everyone at once and insisting they use the toilet, it is better to remind children while washing up for lunch or before nap that they will be more comfortable if they use the toilet first.

It will encourage children to take this responsibility for themselves if their parents dress them in pants with elastic tops or other easily managed clothing. It is also sound to remark to children that it certainly feels good to go to the toilet, a point of view with which most of them will concur.

Hand-washing should be a consistent part of the toilet routine, as well as of the food-handling routine. Children generally enjoy it and will gladly slick their hands with soap when they are reminded. *Teachers should always take time to wash their hands, too, and use soap as well.* Although this takes a little extra time, the reduction in colds and diarrhea that results for everyone is well worth the effort (Kendrick, Kauffman, & Messenger, 1995).

Thoughts About Flushing

Some children, most commonly between the ages of 2 and 3, are really afraid of sitting on a toilet while it is being flushed (perhaps they fear vanishing down the hole with their product). As a general practice, therefore, it is wise to wait until the child gets off before asking him to flush the toilet. We have achieved good cooperation at our center by suggesting to children that it is thoughtful to flush the toilet so that it is fresh for the next person, rather than constantly reminding, "Don't forget to flush it; go back and flush it."

Handling Mishaps

When children wet themselves or have a bowel movement in their pants, they should be changed without shaming or disgust, but without an air of cozy approval either. Such loss of control often happens when children are new to the school, are overly fatigued, or are coming down with an illness, as well as when they have not yet acquired the rudiments of control. Many children are humiliated by wet or soiled underwear, and the teacher should be sensitive to this and help them change in a quiet place. The inexperienced student may find it helpful to know it is easier to clean a child who has had a bowel movement if the child helps by bending over during the process.

Theoretically, the children should always have dry pairs of pants stowed in their cubbies, but actually these are often not there when needed; so it is necessary to have some extras on hand with the name of the school written prominently across the seat. It is helpful to have these changes of clothing available in a bureau in the toilet room itself.

Children with Special Problems

Once in a while a mother will worry aloud to the teacher that her child "never" has a bowel movement. By this she usually means the child does not have a bowel movement every day. This may be the child's natural pattern of defecation, or it may be true constipation. If the child is constipated, it is best to refer the mother to her pediatrician for help.

The same thing goes for a 3- or 4-year-old who leaks a little bowel movement in his pants from time to time and refuses to use the toilet. The child is often "clean" at school but messes his pants frequently at home. The name of this condition is *encopresis*, and it often becomes such a touchy issue between parent and child and can be so difficult to treat that it requires help from a pediatrician or, more likely, from a competent psychologist (Mash & Barkley, 1998).

HANDLING NAP TIMES

If eating in a strange place with unknown people is disturbing to young children, going to sleep under such circumstances can be even more so. Releasing oneself into sleep is, among other things, an act of trust, and it is not surprising that this can be difficult for a young child to allow during his first days at school. Fortunately there are some things the teacher can do to make this task easier for him.

Regularize the Routine

Keep daily expectations and the order of events the same when approaching the nap period. That is, try to do things the same quiet, steady way every day. One pattern that works well is to send the children one by one as they finish lunch to use the toilet, wash their hands, and brush their teeth. Remember that this is the only time some children ever brush their teeth. Then they are expected to settle down on their cots or mats with a book to look at quietly until all the children are ready to begin resting. Next the room is darkened, and the teacher moves quietly about, helping children take off their shoes, find their blankets, stuffed rabbits, and so forth, and set their books aside. This process should be accomplished with quiet affection combined with the clearly projected expectation that the youngster is going to settle down.

When the children are all snuggled in their blankets, some teachers prefer to read a story, whereas others sing softly or play a soothing recording. It helps to have the children spread out as far from each other as possible and to have them lie head to toe; this reduces stimulation and also keeps them from breathing in each other's faces. Restless children should be placed in out-of-the-way corners. Teachers need to be quiet and not talk among themselves, and other people must not be allowed to tiptoe in and out.

It takes at least two teachers to settle a roomful of children, and it may take as long as 30 to 45 minutes before all the children go to sleep. Some children will need their backs rubbed in a monotonous way to soothe them into slumber.

Allow the Children to Get Up as They Wake Up

Usually after about an hour some of the children will wake up by themselves and begin to stir about. This gradual awakening is convenient since it means that each child can be greeted and helped to dress one by one, and it presents a nice opportunity for friendly, quiet chats with the teacher. Children are more likely to wake up in a good mood if they are wakened gradually by the activity around them, rather than by having the teacher wake them up. They need time to collect themselves and to regain awareness before they begin their afternoon activities. It often works well to have a few staff members getting children up while the rest of the adults are in the play area, with snack being available as the children desire it and some quiet, attractive activity also available that the children may select when they feel ready for it.

How Long Should Children Sleep?

It is unfair to the parent to allow a child to sleep all afternoon—unless, of course, he does not feel well. A sleep of an hour or so is about right for most youngsters, but this does not include the time it takes for them to settle down (A. Griffin, 1998).

Should All Children Nap?

All children of preschool age should be expected to lie down and relax for a while in the middle of the day. The need for sleep itself varies considerably among different children,

Releasing oneself into sleep is an act of trust.

and this difference needs to be taken into consideration. Some youngsters, though, particularly older children who are approaching kindergarten age, never go to sleep during the daytime. They should not be expected to lie stiffly on their mats for 2 hours. Instead, after a reasonable rest period, they should be permitted to go outdoors or to another room and play under the supervision of a staff member. These more mature children often greatly enjoy helping prepare the afternoon snack; it makes them feel important and pays tribute to their own grown-up status.

Occasionally a child may need to rest but is so high strung and active that he disturbs everyone at nap time. Our staff has concluded that it is more satisfactory to take these youngsters out of the nap room and give them something quiet to do in the director's office than to become involved in angry, usually noisy confrontations, which upset all the children as well as frighten the restless one.

A Practical Note About Cots

Storage of cots can be a real problem in some schools. In some states licensing laws permit the use of folding mats instead of cots if the floor is not too drafty. These work well except for children who wet their beds at nap time. Saran-covered cots are better to use with these youngsters so that the urine drips through and does not collect in a puddle on the mat. Tiled floors are, of course, indispensable to use in areas where children wet their beds.

SUMMARY

Routines, which consist of arriving and departing, eating, toileting, and resting, are an important part of a child's day. If they are handled well, they can contribute to both the physical health and emotional well-being of young children.

Teachers will experience greatest success in handling routines if they avoid trying to win for the sake of winning, but work instead toward the more worthwhile goals of helping the children become competent, independent people who have healthy attitudes toward their bodily needs and who look forward to eating, toileting, and resting because of the comfort and pleasure associated with these activities.

Questions and Activities

1. What foods do you particularly dislike? Can you remember the reason for your original dislike? Do you feel you learned anything from the situation that could be transferred to the way you handle eating situations with young children?

2. List all the rules you can think of that applied to eating, sleeping, or toileting in your own family as you grew up. After recalling the stated rules, think of some of the deeper, unspoken ones that were also observed.

3. *Predicament:* You are the staff teacher delegated to greet children at the door every morning, and one little boy always begins to whimper as he arrives. At that point the father jollies him along and finally gives him a smack on the bottom, telling him firmly, "Little boys don't cry!" You have learned in your student teaching days that it is important for children to express their feelings. How would you handle this situation?

4. Try an experiment wherein you just tell the children for 3 or 4 days that it is time to come in for snack, and then for the next few days try warning them ahead of time that it will soon be time to come in. Is there any difference in the way they respond?

5. *Predicament:* Although you never meant to arrive at such an impasse, you have inadvertently made such an issue of a child's going to the toilet that he has become balky about it and will not use the toilet anymore, wetting his pants instead. At this point, what approach would you try next to solve this difficulty?

Self-Check Questions for Review

Content-Related Questions

1. Why is it wise to avoid "going to war" with a child about conforming to a particular routine?
2. Name two actions teachers can take to help children move easily through transitions.
3. Describe some sound procedures for helping children adjust to the new situation during their first days at a children's center.
4. What basic principles can you think of regarding the management of routines such as eating, naps, and toileting?

Integrative Questions

1. Identify two different transition times that take place at the school where you teach. Which one of the two goes more smoothly? Analyze why that is the case. Can procedures that are effective in managing that transition be applied to the less effective one?
2. Study Table 4.3, A Sampling of Foods Often Preferred by Various Ethnic Groups. Select one particular cultural group and plan a week's lunch menus using its preferred foods that also meet the

requirements of the USDA guidelines in Table 4.1, U.S. Department of Agriculture Child Care Food Program Required Meal Pattern.

Coordinating Videotape

It's the little things. Tape #1. The whole child: A caregiver's guide to the first five years. The Annenburg/CPB Collection, P.O. Box 2345, South Burlington, VT 05407–2345. *It's the Little Things* discusses the significance of plans and schedules and illustrates the importance of a well-ordered, predictable environment where arrivals, departures, toileting, meals, and naps are managed consistently and warmly by caregivers and parents.

References for Further Reading

Pick of the Litter

Katzen, M., & Henderson, A. (1994). *Pretend soup and other real recipes: A cookbook for preschoolers and up.* Berkeley, CA: Tricycle Press. Mollie Katzen, of *Moosewood Cookbook* fame, has produced a delightfully illustrated, child-tested cookbook. Each recipe is pictured so that very young cooks can "read" what to do. Sensible advice is also included.

Routines and Schedules

Berman, C., & Fromer, J. (1991a). *Meals without squeals.* Palo Alto, CA: Bull. A user-friendly book that should not be missed, it includes recipes, information on nutrition, cleanliness, recycling, feeding practices, and more! *Highly recommended.*

Gordon, S. A. M, Thomas, J. M., Pfeil, D. K., Guerra, F. A., Stephans, K., & Neugeberger, B. (1997, May/June). Beginnings workshop: "Mealtime." *Child Care Information Exchange,* #115, 39–58. Everything you might want to know about honoring the social aspects of mealtimes is presented here. *Highly recommended.*

Griffin, A. (1998). Infant/toddler sleep in the child care context: Patterns, problems, and relationships. *Zero to Three Bulletin: Babies, Parents and Sleep,* 19(2), 24–29. This article is noteworthy in particular because of the frank discussion of handling disagreements between parents and staff over sleep arrangements for their children—in this

case, babies, but comments apply to older youngsters as well.

Kinnell, G. (Ed.). (1995). Toilet learning in group care:
A resource for child care programs and parents.
Syracuse, NY: Child Care Council of Onondaga
County, Toilet Learning Task Force [3175 E.
Genesee Street, Suite 5, Syracuse, NY 13224].
This indispensable reference covers all aspects of
toilet training. *Highly recommended.*

Larson, N,. Henthorne, M., & Plum, B. (1994). *Transition magician: Strategies for guiding young children in
early childhood programs.* St. Paul, MN: Redleaf. A
myriad of transition tidbits are presented here
such as what to do while waiting for lunch or
moving from one activity to another. Lots of patterns are included in the back.

Poole, C., Miller, S. A., & Church, E. B. (1998). Reassuring routines & rituals. *Scholastic Early Childhood Today, 13*(1), 25–29. The authors explain
the value of schedules for children of differing
ages and include ways to help these routines
move smoothly.

Separation

Godwin, L. J., Groves, M. M., & Horm-Wingerd, D. M.
(1994). "Don't leave me": Separation distress in
infants, toddlers, and parents. In K. M. Paciorek
& J. H. Munro (Eds.), *Early childhood education
94–95* (15th ed.). Guilford, CT: Dushkin. The
authors discuss separation problems encountered
at different developmental stages and include
practical advice about easing this sometimes difficult transition from home to school.

Nutrition

Cryer, D., Ray, A. R., & Harms, T. (1996). *Nutrition
activities for preschoolers.* Menlo Park, CA: Addison-Wesley. This sensible, attractively illustrated
book provides a wealth of ideas of ways to integrate information on food and nutrition into
just about every area of the curriculum.
Highly recommended.

Dietz, W. H., & Stern, L. (1999). *American Academy of
Pediatrics guide to your child's nutrition: Making
peace at the table and building healthy eating habits
for life.* New York: Villard. Sensible, accurate
advice on nutrition and eating is provided in a

professional yet chatty way—helpful for teachers
and for the parent bookshelf. *Highly recommended.*

Fuhr, J. E., & Barclay, K. H. (1998). The importance of
appropriate nutrition and nutrition education.
Young Children, 53(1), 74–80. The authors provide many practical examples of how to integrate
information about nutrition into many aspects of
the curriculum.

Tambourlane, W. V. (Ed.). (1997). *The Yale guide to children's nutrition.* New Haven, CT: Yale University
Press. The guide offers sensible advice on eating
and nutrition as it affects children of various ages.
It includes chapters on special circumstances—
for example, diabetes, cystic fibrosis, anorexia. A
good reference for the parent bookshelf.

Menu Planning

Dunkle, J. L., & Edwards, M. S. (1992). *The no leftovers
child care cookbook.* St. Paul, MN: Redleaf. The
authors explain the Child and Adult Care Food
Program of the U.S. Department of Agriculture
and offer useful quantity recipes for 6, 20, 25, or
100 children. Nice since it covers family child
care, as well as larger centers.

Edelstein, S. (1992). *Nutrition and meal planning in child-
care programs: A practical guide.* Chicago: American Dietetic Association. (Available from the
Association, 216 West Jackson Boulevard, Suite
800, Chicago 60606–6995) Edelstein bases her
recommendations on USDA guidelines, which
makes this book particularly helpful for centers
receiving federal nutrition grants. It highlights
important basic nutrition information and
endears itself to me because the menus take into
account cultural food preferences as diverse as
Hispanic, lacto-ovovegetarian, and Jewish menus.
Highly recommended.

Taking Cultural Food Preferences Into Account

Cox, B., & Jacobs, M. (1991). *Spirit of the harvest: North
American Indian cooking.* New York: Stewart,
Tabori, & Chang. This book features attractive
American Indian recipes classified according to
region. Overviews of Indian tribes and handsome
photographs of some recipes are included. Every
effort has been made to keep the material as
authentic and respectful as possible.

Crocker, B. (1993). *Betty Crocker's Mexican made easy.* Upper Saddle River, NJ: Prentice Hall. Reasonably authentic Mexican recipes are featured that use readily obtainable ingredients.

Parham, V. R. (1993). *The African American child's heritage cookbook.* South Pasadena, CA: Sandcastle. Parham provides a good array of recipes, including ones specifically identified as African, Creole, Jamaican, and soul food, and healthy ways to fix old favorites. A section is devoted to the legacy of George Washington Carver. *Highly recommended.*

Wilson, M. (1989). *The good-for-your-health all-Asian cookbook.* Washington, DC: Center for Science in the Public Interest. The book's 220 recipes are drawn from Korea, Indonesia, Malaysia, Pakistan, India, the Philippines, Singapore, Thailand, Vietnam, Japan, and China. Emphasis is on good nutrition, as well as on ethnic background.

Cooking with Children

Refer to The Pick of the Litter choice for this chapter

Lakeshore Learning Materials. (n.d.). *Multicultural cooking with kids.* Carson, CA: Lakeshore Equipment Company. This spiral-bound, plastic-coated book offers two or three recipes from each of several diverse cultures—Mexican, Japanese, and German, for instance—plus a cultural fact about each recipe.

Problems Related to Routines

Aronson, S. (1997, November/December). Food allergies can be fatal. *Child Care Information Exchange,* #118, 88–91. This is an important article filled with practical information about what to do when working with highly allergic youngsters.

Ferber, R. (1985). *Solve your child's sleep problems.* New York: Simon & Schuster. Ferber, who is director of the Center for Pediatric Sleep Disorders at Boston Children's Hospital, offers practical advice about this sometimes difficult problem.

Satter, E. (1987). *How to get your kid to eat . . . but not too much.* Palo Alto, CA: Bull. Satter provides sensible, expert advice on establishing normal feeding patterns for children, together with suggestions about what to do when the pattern is not normal. Helpful for teachers and indispensable to parents.

Schaefer, C. E. (1979). *Childhood encopresis and enuresis: Causes and therapy.* New York: Van Nostrand Reinhold. Schaefer reviews prominent theories about bowel movement retention and wetting and concludes with lists of practical recommendation.

For the Advanced Student

Bowlby, J. (1982). Attachment and loss: Retrospect and prospect. *American Journal of Orthopsychiatry,* 52(4), 664–678. This article summarizes how Bowlby, who did groundbreaking work on the effect of long-term separation of child from parent, developed his theory and supported it with research.

Center on Hunger, Poverty, and Nutrition Policy. (1998). *Statement on the link between nutrition and cognitive development in children.* Medford, MA: Tufts University, Center on Hunger, Poverty, and Nutrition Policy. This concise publication presents a summary of research documenting the serious consequences of undernutrition and its relationship to reducing growth and functioning of the brain. This very important information is available from the Center on Hunger, Poverty, and Nutrition Policy, Tufts University, 11 Curtis Avenue, Medford, MA 02155.

Powell, G. J. (1983). *The psychosocial development of minority group children.* New York: Brunner/Mazel. Powell offers information on specific nutrition problems of Black, Hispanic, and Indian children.

Journals and Organizations of Particular Interest

The Nutrition Action Healthletter is published by the Center for Science in the Public Interest, 1875 Connecticut Avenue, NW, Washington, DC 20009–5728. The center is an advocacy group favoring sound nutrition and safe food practices. *Highly recommended.*

chapter five

Development of the Physical Self

How to send a sick child home without hurting her feelings?

Whether it's really all right to admit a child to school whose parents are "going to get her her booster shots just as soon as they can"?

What in the world you can do to provide some variety and range to large muscle play?

. . . IF YOU HAVE, THE MATERIAL IN THE FOLLOWING PAGES WILL HELP YOU.

Birds gotta sing, fish gotta swim, and kids gotta MOVE AND TOUCH. Moving and touching are how children first learn about the world. Feeling the sun and grass on their skin, throwing and catching balls, stretching their arms to the ceiling, climbing jungle gyms, and running in great circles are examples of ways that children gain the important information they require to function well. Nature's plan is for young children to absorb sensory knowledge through their skin, muscles, and joints as a foundation for more complex learning.

Carol S. Kranowitz (1994, p. 37)

Good food, reasonable toilet procedures, and adequate rest are important factors in maintaining the physical and emotional well-being of young children. Additional factors that affect the physical development of children include health and safety and the provision of maximum opportunities for their bodies to grow and develop in the healthiest way.

PROMOTION OF HEALTH AND SAFETY IN THE CHILDREN'S CENTER

Providing Safe Transportation to School Is a Must!

As information continues to indicate that safety seats and seat belts help save lives, it becomes clear that teachers *must* encourage their consistent and correct use (Aronson, 1998). Preprimary teachers have a unique opportunity to foster automobile safety because they meet parents as they deliver their youngsters to school.

Many schools now insist that any child delivered to their premises be transported there "buckled up," and it is a policy that *every* school should institute. Since some children do not like these restraints, teachers should also support the parents' efforts by discussing the value of safety restraints during large-group times, explaining in a matter-of-fact, non-alarmist way how lucky we are that we have this practical way to keep us safe.

Basic Ways to Protect and Foster the Physical Health of Children

Beginning teachers who come from middle-class homes sometimes do not realize how necessary it is for early childhood centers to take the lead in making sure young children have adequate health care. Many families served by preschool centers have very low incomes but do not understand how to make use of free services available to them through Medicaid or other health facilities. Families from the lower middle-income bracket are often even more hard-pressed to find the money that medical care requires. Both these groups may need advice from the teacher about how to make use of free or inexpensive community health resources. Even the more well-to-do families need to be encouraged to make sure their children have health checkups and immunizations.

Since the first edition of this book, some encouraging progress has been made in the area of immunization, although much remains to be done. According to UNICEF (1999), about 2 million children worldwide under age 5 still die every year from six vaccine-preventable illnesses; diphtheria, measles, pertussis, polio, tuberculosis, and tetanus. We should count our blessings that in the United States recent federal legislation has made free vaccines more available than formerly so that by 1996 78% of American toddlers had actually received their full series of shots, as compared with 4 years previously, when only 55% had been immunized ("Child Immunizations," 1997). Even more encouraging is the news that, following an epidemic of measles in 1990, a special effort was made and now 91% of U.S. toddlers are immune to its potentially serious aftereffects ("Child Immunizations," 1997).

Despite this rise in child immunity it is still necessary to caution adults that *rubella* (often called 3-day *measles*) remains a menace to many women who were not protected from it during childhood–a circumstance that may have deadly implications for the fetus, should a woman become pregnant. In particular, teachers of young children must take special care that they are vaccinated against rubella as well as hepatitis A and B.

Although immunization shots are more available now, still not all states require vaccination checks at the preschool level. To make matters worse, even when these regulations exist they are often only laxly enforced. For these reasons all full- and half-day preschools and centers should establish their own policies and be *adamant about requiring up-to-date immunization records from parents.* Such certification protects not only the child in question but also all the other children and adults in the school. Anything short of full enforcement of this policy is inexcusable. (Appendix C provides a childhood immunization schedule recommended by the American Academy of Pediatrics.)

Physical Examinations Should Be Required Before the Child Enrolls

Because the preschool is often the first institution that comes into contact with families of young children in a formal way, it is particularly valuable for each school to require pre-entry physical examinations, as well as inoculations. Careful evaluation of potential vision and hearing problems should be a part of this process. Some states already make this requirement part of their licensing regulations for full-day centers; states that do not should be encouraged to add this rule to their regulations promptly.

The Teacher Should Be Prepared to Help Parents Find Health Care During the Year Whenever Possible

In addition to the free or low-cost health insurance now more available for low-income families throughout the Unites States ("Tobacco Settlement," 1999), a variety of other free health services and examinations are also available that teachers should be acquainted with so that they can refer families who need that help. These services are as varied as university-sponsored speech and hearing clinics and free asthma checkups. Sometimes arrangements can be made with training schools to supply health services in return for the opportunity to work with young children. Dental hygienists in training, for example, may be willing to clean children's teeth to obtain experience with preschoolers. A good way to locate information about such services is to contact the public health nurses in your community. These people are gold mines of practical information about sources of assistance.

The Teacher Should Act as a Health Screener

An alert teacher can often spot problems that have been overlooked by families and even by pediatricians, who though expert, lack the teacher's opportunity to see the child over an extended period of time. The teacher should particularly watch for children who do not seem to see or hear well, who are very awkward, who seldom talk, who are unusually apathetic, or who are excessively active. The behavior may be only an idiosyncrasy, or it may require professional help, and the sooner help is sought the better. (See chapters 9 and 16 for further details on identification of special problems.)

The teacher should make a health check of every child as she arrives at school each day. This ensures a personal greeting for each child and provides a quick once-over so that a child who is not feeling up to par may be sent home before her parent departs. Although some standard signs should be checked for, such as faces that are flushed or too pale or "sickly looking," rashes, and marked lethargy, the most important symptom to be aware of is any significant change in the child's appearance. Teachers who see the same children every day get to know how they usually look and behave and can often spot such variations promptly; then they can take the appropriate steps to avoid exposing other children in school to the condition. (See Appendix B for a list of common diseases, their symptoms and incubation periods.)

Providing care for sick children is a particularly difficult problem for families when both parents work outside the home. Centers and preschools need very clear, firm policies concerning contagious diseases and how they are handled and at the same time do everything they can to make compliance as easy as possible for the families. Since a youngster can seem perfectly healthy in the evening yet turn up green and pale the next morning, it is important to encourage parents to have backup care planned–relatives or a friendly neighbor to be relied on. Sometimes schools maintain lists of home caregivers who specialize in sick child care.

The Teacher Must Know What to Do When a Child Becomes Ill at School

No matter how careful the teacher and how conscientious the parent, an occasional child will come down with some illness during the day. Ideally the child should be sent home immediately, but in practice this can be very difficult to do (S. Cohen, 1998). Even when parents have been asked to make alternative arrangements for emergency care, these arrangements sometimes fall through, and the school and youngster have to make the best of it. Reputable schools try to keep children who are ill apart from the rest; usually the center office serves this purpose fairly well. The child should have a place to lie down located as close as possible to a bathroom, and she will need to be comforted and reassured so that she does not feel bereft and lonely.

Because sending a child home from school often embarrasses and angers the parent and hurts the child's feelings as well, it is desirable to be firm but gentle when doing this. Sending something home along with the youngster, such as a book, will help her feel less rejected and make her return to school easier when she is feeling better.

General Health Precautions Should Be Observed Consistently by Children and Staff

Blowing noses in disposable tissue, washing hands before handling food and after toileting, and not allowing children to share food, cups, or utensils they have had in their mouths are basic precautions that must always be observed. If teachers form the habit of washing their hands whenever they have children participate in that routine, it not only sets a good example but also helps maintain the teachers' good health (Kendrick et al., 1995). Another routine that should be maintained is regular toothbrushing. Surveys reveal that more than half the children in the United States between the ages of 5 and 17 have cavities. Minority children in particular tend to suffer from that condition and so deserve special attention ("National Briefs," 1993).

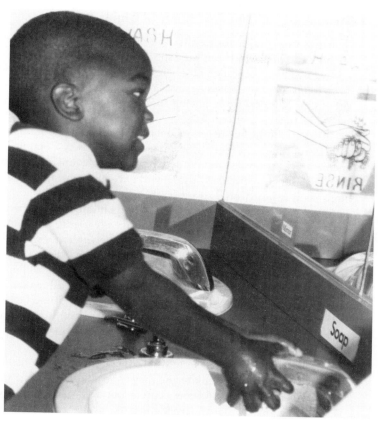

Washing hands before eating is an absolute must for children—and for teachers.

Sometimes when a youngster is well enough to return to school, she must still continue taking medicine during school hours. A word of warning is in order here: To avoid the possibility of lawsuits most schools make it a practice *never to administer any kind of medication* (*including aspirin*) without the express written request of the physician and parent (S. Cohen, 1998). Children who have been ill must also be watched carefully to make certain they do not become overtired and suffer a relapse of their illness when they return to school.

It is also important to be aware of the temperature of the day, to take the children's jackets off indoors, and to dress the children warmly enough outdoors, but not too warmly. Particularly in autumn mothers tend to weigh their children down with too much clothing, and the children may be so absorbed in their play that they can be dripping with sweat and not realize it. The teacher needs to remind them about staying comfortable and help them adjust their clothing to suit the temperature when necessary.

Maintaining the Physical Safety of Children

Teachers must never forget that the children in their care are not their own and that supervising them carries with it a special responsibility.

Even though insurance costs are high, it is very important for all schools to carry it both to protect themselves against lawsuits and to provide accident coverage for the children. One solution for financing such protection is to include a one-time insurance fee when the child is first enrolled.[1]

In addition, the entire school needs to be checked continually to make sure it is maintained in a safe condition (Consumer Product Safety Commission, 1997). Broken equipment such as tricycles without pedals and wobbly jungle gyms *must be removed or repaired promptly.* Sticks, particularly those with nails in them, should be discarded. Safety precautions such as using only swings with canvas seats should be observed. The danger area around swings must be clearly marked, and children should be taught to wait on the bottom step (which can be painted red to make it easier to identify) of the slide.

Disinfectants, ant poisons, scouring powders, bleaches, and antiseptics, which are all commonly found in centers and schools, should be kept on high shelves in the kitchen, where children are not permitted, or better yet in locked cabinets.

In chapter 1 it was suggested that inexperienced teachers stop an activity if it looks dangerous to them rather than permit an accident to happen. One other safety rule has proved to be generally helpful: The teacher should never lift a child onto a piece of play equipment if she cannot manage to get on it by herself (swings are an exception to this rule). Of course, youngsters sometimes climb up on something, feel marooned, and must be helped down; but that is different from lifting them onto the top of the jungle gym or boosting them onto a tippy gangplank before they are really able to cope with these situations.

A study of Atlanta child care centers found that accidents occurred most frequently at 11 a.m. and 4 p.m., that the accident rate was highest for 2-year-olds, and that the peak days for accidents were Mondays and Fridays (Sacks et al., 1989). It appears that these are times when teachers should be especially careful while supervising children.

It is particularly important to remember that high places such as slides and monkey bars are dangerous for young children. Of the 280,000 children treated during 1 year in hospital emergency rooms for playground injuries, two out of three were injured by falling from equipment, often onto hard surfaces ("Check Playgrounds for Safety," 1996). For this reason it is vital to maintain soft, deep surfaces such as sand, rubber, or bark mulch beneath such equipment. *Grass is not suitable* (Consumer Product Safety Commission, 1997).

The concern for safety has to be moderated by the teacher's good sense and self-control. Children must be protected, but they also need the chance to venture and try things out. This venturesomeness is a hallmark of 4-year-olds in particular. Occasional small catastrophes are to be expected, and teachers should not become so overly protective that they hover over the children and remonstrate with them constantly to be careful. Instead they should try to maintain a generally high level of safety combined with the opportunity for the children to experiment with the mild risks that build feelings of competence as they are met and mastered.

---

[1] *The reader may wish to check with the National Association for the Education of Young Children (NAEYC), as well as with other sources for information on insurance policies.*

Kids gotta move . . .

BASIC PRINCIPLES OF PHYSICAL DEVELOPMENT

Before reading about specific ways to foster psychomotor development, the student needs to understand some developmental principles that have important implications for education.

Development Occurs in Predictable Patterns and Sequences

Although some investigators have questioned the idea that chronological age should determine when children are taught various skills (Bruner, 1964; Gagné, 1968), it is still generally agreed that children progress through a predictable sequence of developmental stages (Gallahue & Ozmun, 1998). The examples provided in Table 5.1 illustrate this clearly. (Appendix D provides a chart of normal development from infancy to 6 years of age, organized according to the various selves.) This is as true of physical development as it is true of intellectual development (Piaget & Inhelder, 1967). Children usually sit before they stand, stand before they walk, and walk before they run. In addition specific skills such as running, jumping, and throwing and climbing progress through a series of sub-stages of competency before they emerge as mature physical abilities (Payne & Rink, 1997; Readdick & Park, 1998; Thelen, Ulrich, & Jensen, 1989).

Table 5.1
Age at which a given percentage of children perform locomotor skills

	25%	50%	75%	90%
Rolls over	2.3 mo	2.8 mo	3.8 mo	4.7 mo
Sits without support	4.8 mo	5.5 mo	6.5 mo	7.8 mo
Walks well	11.3 mo	12.1 mo	13.5 mo	14.3 mo
Kicks ball forward	15 mo	20 mo	22.3 mo	2 yr
Pedals trike	21 mo	23 mo	2.8 yr	3 yr
Balances on one foot 10 seconds	3 yr	4.5 yr	5 yr	5.9 yr
Hops on one foot	3 yr	3.4 yr	4 yr	4.9 yr
Catches bounced ball	3.5 yr	3.9 yr	4.9 yr	5.5 yr
Heel-to-toe walk	3.3 yr	3.6 yr	4.2 yr	5 yr

Source: From Developing Motor Behavior in Children: A Balanced Approach to Elementary Physical Education by D. D. Arnheim and R. A. Pestolesi, 1973, St. Louis: C. V. Mosby. Selected items from the Denver Developmental Screening Test by permission of William K. Frankenburg, M.D., and Josiah B. Dodds, Ph.D., University of Colorado Medical Center.

Teachers need to be able to recognize these stages of development so that they can adjust their curriculum offerings to provide a good balance between opportunities for practice to consolidate the skill and opportunities for accepting the challenge of a slightly more difficult activity to go on to next.

The Course of Development Moves from Head to Tail

That development moves from head to tail is the *cephalocaudal* principle. It means that children are able to control the region around their head and shoulders before they can control their hands and feet. This is an easy principle to remember if one recalls that babies can sit up and manipulate playthings long before they are able to stand on their feet and walk. Quite simply, children are able to reach, grasp, and use their hands with considerable skill before they are able to master the art of skipping or kicking accurately. The curriculum of the preschool should be planned accordingly.

The Course of Development Moves from Large to Fine Muscle Control

Large muscle activities include static balance, dynamic precision, gross body coordination, and flexibility. Examples of *fine muscle activities* include finger speed, arm steadiness, arm and hand precision, and finger and hand dexterity. Development from large to fine muscle control means that children gain control over their larger muscles first and then gradually attain control over the finer muscle groups. Thus a child is able to walk long before she is able to construct a tabletop house of small plastic bricks.

The educational implication of this developmental principle for early childhood teach-ers is that preschool children need ample opportunities to use their large muscles in vigor-ous, energetic, physical play. It can be torment for young children to remain confined too long at chairs and tables. Since the finer muscle, eye-hand skills are also developing during this period, activities that stimulate children to practice these skills should also be offered—but not overdone to the point that excessive demands are made on the children's self-control.

FOSTERING LARGE MUSCLE DEVELOPMENT IN YOUNG CHILDREN

Use of Apparatus to Promote Large Muscle Skills

In general the school should furnish a large assortment of big, sturdy, durable equipment that provides many opportunities for all kinds of physical activity. It should also provide a teacher who values vigorous large muscle play and encourages children to participate freely in this pleasure.

Equipment good for crawling through, climbing up, balancing on, and hanging from should be included. Children need things they can lift, haul, and shove around to test their strength and use to make discoveries about physical properties the equipment possesses. They need things they can use for construction, and they need equipment that provides opportunities for rhythmic activities, such as bouncing and jumping and swinging. In addition, they need places of generous size for carrying out the wonderful sensory experiences that involve mud, sand, and water. Finally they need plenty of space in which to simply move about.

I have been deliberately nonspecific about suggesting particular pieces of large muscle equipment in the hope that talking about children's activity requirements will encourage the teacher to consider afresh what might be used to meet these needs. For those who wish to pursue this question in detail, however, an excellent publication provides detailed lists of indoor and outdoor equipment and firms that manufacture it: *Selecting Educational Equipment and Materials for School and Home* (Moyer, 1995).

There is also a continuing and heartening trend toward designing play equipment that is novel, often beautiful, and occasionally less expensive than our more mundane playground furnishings (Greenman, 1993, 1998b; Talbot & Frost, 1989).

Equipment need not be expensive to provide sound play value. Several references that give suggestions about how to combine economy with beauty and ingenuity are included at the end of this chapter (Kelly & Kelly, 1997). It is wise to remember, though, that poorly constructed, cheap equipment can be the poorest kind of economy in the long run. Children are hard on things, and it does not pay to buy or make playthings that are flimsy—better to have a bake sale and raise money for better quality equipment than be stuck with buying two cheap swing sets 2 years in a row.

In general, the more movable and versatile the equipment is, the more stimulating and interesting it will remain for the children. Observations at many schools have convinced me that movable outdoor equipment is one of the items in shortest supply in the play yard, yet it is vital to have plenty of boards, sawhorses, large hollow blocks, ropes, rubber tires, and barrels lest the children feel starved when they cannot complete their more ambitious projects. Schools should budget for more of this kind of equipment every year; there is no such thing as owning too much of it.

However, before buying outdoor equipment, every teacher should read the discussion by Kritchevsky and Prescott (1977) about how to plan and develop play centers that will have maximum attractiveness and play value for young children. Material explaining the English concept of adventure playgrounds should also be investigated (Allen, 1968; Brett, Moore, & Provenzo, 1993). These wonderfully messy, casual-looking playgrounds place great emphasis on freedom to try out and explore.

Once the equipment has been acquired, it is important to maintain it carefully. Hollow blocks, which are very costly, should be used on grass or on outdoor, grass-type carpeting, not on cement or asphalt, where they will splinter badly when knocked down. Most wooden equipment has to be sanded and varnished every year to keep it smooth, and over a period of time this treatment can make it beautiful as well. Wooden items must be stored under cover at night. Metal items should be stored under cover when possible to avoid rust.

Of course, children's vigorous activities do not need to be restricted to the school yard. Children will be delighted with the chance to visit parks with large open spaces where they can run freely and roll down hills. Many communities have wading pools for preschoolers or special play areas set aside for younger children. Even a trike expedition around the block with a pause at an interesting long set of steps can offer challenges that should not be overlooked, particularly in a full-day program.

Role of the Teacher in Fostering Large Muscle Play

In addition to providing equipment to enhance large muscle play, teachers can do much to encourage this kind of activity. Probably the most important thing they can do is provide enough uninterrupted time for satisfying play to transpire. Children need time to develop their ideas and carry them through, and if they build something, they need time to use it after they build it.

Outdoor playtime at the preprimary level is not treated in the same way as teachers often handle recess in the elementary school. Preschool playtime at this level requires active involvement of the teacher with the children. She does not do this by participating as a companion in their play, but by observing and being alert to ways to make the play richer and by offering additional equipment or tactfully teaching an intrusive child how to make herself more welcome to the group. Because her function is to encourage the continuation of play, she tries to be as facilitative yet unobtrusive as possible. The Research Study for this chapter illustrates what a valuable contribution teacher planning and participation can make to the physical development of children.

It is especially important for teachers to be aware of children with special needs during outdoor playtime. According to Merle Karnes (1994), some ways in which teachers can help children with disabilities enjoy playtime include letting these children become familiar with the play area without having other children around to overwhelm them, making certain such youngsters understand outdoor safety rules, encouraging them to take part in large motor activities, encouraging them to play with or at least nearby other children, and encouraging them to try out things within their abilities while keeping a sensible balance between overprotection and poorly judged risk taking.

Can a Little Instruction Make a Big Difference?

Research Question: Can instruction in large muscle skills really make a significant difference in the way young children develop their physical motor abilities?

Research Method: In this two-part study, 14 college students majoring in physical education worked with 53 Head Start children. After all the children were assessed on a competency-based test of motor skills, half of them (Group A) worked with the physical education majors for 1 hour once a week, and half (Group B) did not. At the end of 10 weeks the children in both Group A and Group B were retested. During the second half of the study, Group B received physical training and Group A did not.

Research Results: The retest results clearly demonstrated that training in motor skills significantly improved the children's abilities. Statistical analysis revealed that "for Group A, scores for tests 2 and 3 were significantly higher than test 1 ($p = .0001$). For Group B the test 3 score was significantly higher than tests 1 and 2 ($p = .0001$)" (p. 81). Boys and girls showed similar gains in their skills.

Implications for Teaching: This study provides evidence that *as little as 1 hour a week of instruction in physical skills can make a real difference in what children are able to do.* When we consider the contributions to improved self-esteem and the foundations these skills lay for the development of more complex motor activities as the children grow, the value of providing carefully planned outdoor play opportunities becomes clear. Of course, this finding does not imply that every minute of outdoor play should be devoted to planned activities. It does, however, make a good case for the value of providing a range of large motor activities that help children gain command and satisfaction over what their bodies can do.

Source: From "Physical Education for Head Start Children: A Field-Based Study" by A. A. Ignico, 1991, Early Child Development and Care, 77, 77–82.

If the teacher keeps her eyes and mind open to possibilities, she can adapt outdoor equipment in many ways to make it accessible to everyone (Breath, DeMauro, & Snyder, 1997). For example, wide pathways paved with a relatively solid material such as crushed brick makes the use of wheelchairs simpler. Slides that have handrails for protection and are within reach of the teacher are safer, more enjoyable, and accessible to all the children. Straps or extra-thick pedals on tricycles allow more children to ride. If a portion of the sandbox is built waist-high, children with crutches or in wheelchairs can reach the sand more easily. The same is true for water tables. If a child with limited vision is attending the school, it may be necessary to add physical barriers around such areas as swings, to use brightly contrasting colors on equipment, and to provide a plentitude of rich opportunities for sensory play activities. Large muscle play also offers excellent opportunities for children with disabilities to play with the other children if equipment is included that requires two or more youngsters to make it work: Rocking boats, trikes with wagons, and round tire-swings can all help meet this need.

While the teacher needs to keep the environment safe, at the same time she should keep an open mind about the uses to which equipment can be put. If encouraged, children often come up with original or unconventional uses of materials that are not dangerous and that should be welcomed by the teacher since they are so creative and satisfying to the children. For example, one of our center children recently got together all the bean-bags to use as a pillow in the playhouse, and another youngster used the hose to make a worm tunnel in the sandbox. These harmless, innovative activities are all too easily squelched if the teacher is insensitive to their value or too conventional in her thinking.

Finally, the teacher should keep on the lookout for children who are at loose ends and involve them in activities before they begin to run wildly and aimlessly about. Teachers need to be comfortable with a good deal of noise, though, and welcome the vigorous activity so characteristic of 4-year-olds because they need this opportunity for vigorous assertion and movement to develop fully.

USE OF PERCEPTUAL-MOTOR ACTIVITIES TO ENHANCE PHYSICAL DEVELOPMENT

Reports concerning the general level of physical fitness in young children are not encouraging. One study that assessed activity patterns and fitness levels of children ages 6 to 9 years reported that schools do not offer enough scheduled physical education time and that recess times also provide inadequate physical education experience (Ross & Pate, 1987).

Overweight and its potential for incipient heart attacks is also increasing in young children. When the most recent national study of overweight preschoolers compared the number of 4- and 5-year-olds who were overweight in 1974 with the number in 1994, researchers found that the percentage of overweight preschoolers had doubled, from 5.8% to more than 10% (Association for Childhood Education International, 1997; Woolston, 1997).

Recent research has also made it clear that physical exercise is closely related to developing cognitive abilities since, among many other benefits, it increases the number and complexity of neural connections in the brain (Hannaford, 1995). In particular, children should be encouraged to participate in activities that use what is termed *cross-lateral movement*—movement that requires them to cross the midline off their bodies—where both arms are swung across the center line windmill style, or arms and legs from opposite sides are used together as in crawling.

Despite these studies that make the value of plentiful exercise so evident many preschool teachers are still inclined to turn the children loose during outdoor play and content themselves with just supplying an assortment of equipment such as swings and slides, hoping the children will seek out the experiences they need by using this apparatus in a variety of ways (Pica, 1997). But we now know that perceptual-motor activities should go beyond this without requiring children to be regimented and drilled. We really must offer them a broader selection of physically developmental activities than we formerly did if we wish to enhance the full range of their skills and developmental potential.

As we will see later in the chapter, creativity can be enhanced when creative movement activities stress thinking up a variety of ways to use the body, and emotional relief can be provided both by vigorous exercise and by relaxation experiences.

Physical fitness itself and the satisfaction that feeling of fitness provides must not be overlooked, either. Children should be encouraged to play vigorously and to *sustain* their efforts while avoiding overfatigue so that they increase their level of endurance while playing. Just as wholesome eating habits contribute to better lifelong health, so, too, does the establishment of healthy habits of exercise in early childhood (S. W. Sanders & Yongue, 1998).

The teacher can approach the area of planned perceptual-motor activities in two ways: The first is to provide opportunities for practice in specific skills; the second is to use physical activity to promote creative thought and self-expression. Both approaches have merit.

Planning for Specific Perceptual-Motor Activities

After considerable review of the literature I have concluded that a moderate program offering the clearest language combined with a structure easily understood by teachers and applicable to preschool children is the one first used by Arnheim and Sinclair in their

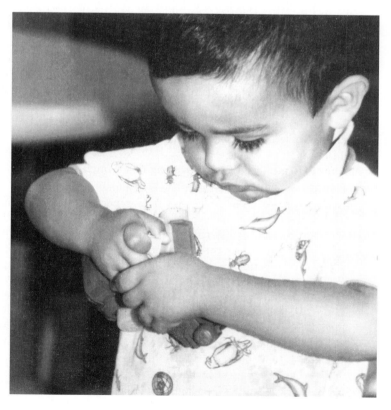

Fine muscle skills are absorbing but tiring for young children to pursue.

book *The Clumsy Child* (1979). This approach, which remains practical and simple today (S. W. Sanders, 1992), divides motor tasks into the following categories: locomotion, balance, body and space perception, rhythm and temporal awareness, rebound and airborne activities, projectile management, management of daily motor activities (including many fine muscle tasks), and tension releasers.

It is easy to think of motor activities in relation to these headings once they have been identified and to make certain that opportunities for repeated practice in each of the categories are included in curriculum plans. The trick lies in concocting ways of presenting them that appeal to children. Obstacle courses, simple want-to-try-this kind of noncompetitive games, and movement activities can all be used effectively if only the teacher will keep in mind the diversity of action that should be incorporated. Fortunately the mere challenge of having such possibilities available often provides attraction enough because youngsters are almost irresistibly drawn to physical activities that are just challenging enough without being too difficult. As a matter of fact, if children are encouraged to experiment, they will often develop the next hardest task for themselves following mastery of its simpler elements, a nice illustration, incidentally, of children moving toward the growing edge of their zone of proximal development (Vygotsky, 1978).

Fostering Fine Muscle Development (Daily Motor Activities)

Table 5.2 primarily stresses large muscle involvement, so a word is said here to remind the reader that fine muscle (eye-hand) skills are just as important. Examples of these skills are feeding oneself, buttoning sweaters, sewing, and working with pegboards, puzzles, beads, and put-together materials (often termed *manipulatives*). Block building (which taps stacking and balancing skills), pouring and spooning in their many forms, and manipulating art materials (most particularly pencils, brushes, scissors, and crayons) also require careful coordination of eye and hand, as does woodworking; it takes a good deal of skill to hit a nail with something as small as a hammerhead.

Things to Remember When Presenting Fine Muscle Activities

Offering a range of challenge in levels of difficulty is particularly important in a group of mixed ages, but even in a relatively homogeneous group of 3-year-olds provision must be made for the fact that the level of fine muscle skill—not to mention the amount of emotional control and ability to concentrate—will vary considerably from child to child. Rather than setting out three or four puzzles of 16 pieces each, the children's range of abilities will be better met if one or two inset puzzles and perhaps 7-, 15-, and 22-piece puzzles are set out and changed as they become boring.

Sometimes it adds interest to offer two levels of otherwise identical material. Large and small wooden beads make an interesting contrast, or occasionally puzzles that have the same picture but vary in the number of cut pieces can be purchased and made available for use. Children enjoy having access to both levels and like to put into words what makes the materials similar and what makes them different.

Fine muscle activities should be of reasonably short duration. It is difficult for young children to hold still for very long, much less sit and concentrate on a fine muscle task that requires considerable self-control. For this reason several activities should be avail-

Table 5.2
Categories of physical activities and some suggestions for providing practice of these skills at the preschool level

Category	Illustrative Activities	Comments
Locomotion		
Rolling	Roll over and over, sideways, both directions. Forward roll (somersault).	Nice to have tumbling mats, but not essential—rug, grass, or clean floor also works.
Crawling, creeping	Move by placing weight on elbows only, dragging feet. Use alternating arm/leg crawl or crawl using arm and leg in unison, on same side of body.	Works well to give these movements animal names such as "bear walk," "duck waddle." Emphasize cross-lateral movement.
Climbing	Apparatus valuable here—good to incorporate stretching, hanging, and reaching in this activity.	Necessary to be careful of safety.
Walking	Can vary with big, little steps, fast or slow. Encourage movement in different directions.	Good to do walking activities barefoot on contrasting surfaces for sensory input.
Stair climbing	Nice to use this during an excursion unless the school has a five- to six-step stairway.	This is an interesting indicator of developmental level: Younger children take steps one at a time, drawing second foot up to meet leading foot. Older children alternate feet in this task.
Jumping, hopping, and skipping	Children can jump over lines or very low obstacles, as well as jump down from blocks of various heights. Hopping is difficult for young children; it is a prelude to skipping. Encourage learning to hop on either foot and alternating feet. Skipping is often too difficult for nursery school youngsters. Valuable skill to ultimately acquire, because it involves crossing midline in a rhythmical alternating pattern.	Can use animal names here, too. Don't encourage running backward—young children often catch feet and trip themselves.
Running and leaping	Nice to find a large, grassy area for these kinds of activities; makes a nice field trip.	Often provides emotional relief, too. Gives marvelous feeling of freedom, power, and satisfaction.

Table 5.2 continued

Category	Illustrative Activities	Comments
Balance		
Static (balance while still)	Balance lying on side.	
	Balance standing on tiptoes.	
	Balance on one foot, then the other, for short periods of time.	
Dynamic (balance while moving)	Use balance beam many ways, or use large hollow blocks as stepping stones, or walk on lines.	A swinging clatter bridge of loosely joined boards to step on, if available, is a particularly challenging task; may overwhelm some children.
	Build a beam that tapers from wide to narrow for children to use.	
Balance using an object	Balance beanbags on hands, or back, or head.	
	Work with unbalanced objects—pole with weight on one end, for example, or an umbrella.	
Body and space perception	Movement education techniques apply to this category particularly well.	Helps to refer to other people's bodies, too; for example, "Where is Henry's elbow?"
	How big can you be? How little?	Listening, imitative actions such as "Simon says" are fun if not carried on too long.
	Can you make a sad face?	
	Can you fit inside this circle? Can you fill up this circle (a very big one)?	
	How much of you can you get in the air at once?	Can stress position in space—"over," "under," and so on; tedious if overdone.
	Use shadow dancing for effective awareness building.	
Rhythm and temporal awareness	Any moving in time to music or to a rhythmic beat.	Creative dance is the usual medium—"rhythm band" is a typical kindergarten-level activity, which is essentially conforming rather than creative. (See also material on dancing in chapter 14.)
	Can be varied in many ways—fast, slow, or with different rhythmic patterns. Important to keep patterns simple and clear with preschoolers.	
	Remember that many preschool level activities such as swinging and using rocking horses, also fit this category; fun to add music to these for a change.	

Activity	Description	Notes
Rebound and airborne activities	At preschool age these are generally thought of as "bouncing" activities; mattresses, bouncing boards, and large inner tubes offer various levels of difficulty. Swings and hand-over-hand bars are also, in a sense, airborne.	Do not use a trampoline; it requires extraordinarily careful supervision. Many insurance companies absolutely refuse to provide insurance for this piece of equipment.
Projectile management		
Throwing and catching	Throwing and catching usually require teacher participation. Children throw best using relatively small objects but catch best using large ones!	Use objects that move slowly and are harmless; Nerf balls, beanbags, large rubber balls, whiffle balls, and fleece balls meet this requirement.
	Can throw objects at a target such as a wall, or into a large box. Bean bags work well.	Need lots of beanbags; not much fun to have to run and pick them up every two or three throws.
	For catching, older children can use a pitchback net; useful for understanding effect of force in relation to throwing.	
Kicking	Begin with kicking a still ball, then go to a gently rolling one.	Children whose families are interested in soccer are particularly fond of this activity.
Striking	Hit balloons with hands and then with paddle.	Many teachers are nervous about striking activities, but these activities are challenging to children and worth the careful supervision and rule setting they require.
	Can hit a ball balanced on traffic cone with light plastic bat (whiffle ball good for this).	
Bouncing	Best with a large rubber ball; use two hands then go to one hand; bounce to other children.	
Daily motor activities (fine muscle activities)	Includes many self-help skills such as buttoning and even toothbrushing! Also includes use of almost all self-expressive materials and use of tools in carpentry and cooking.	Be careful of overfatigue.
	See discussion on fine muscle activities in text.	
Tension releasers and relaxation techniques	Refer to material in text.	

Source: Based on The Clumsy Child *(2nd ed.) by D. D. Arnheim and W. A. Sinclair, 1979, St. Louis: C. V. Mosby.*
Note: These activities are only a handful of a great many possibilities. For more extensive material see Hendrick (1998) and S. W. Sanders (1992).

able at the same time, and children should always be free to get up, move around, and shift to more or less taxing experiences as they feel the need. Quiet periods such as story hours or snack times should not be followed by additional quiet, fine muscle play but by more vigorous large muscle activity.

When children are using fine muscle materials, the teacher should watch out for signs of unusual frustration. I once had a little boy in my nursery school who participated with enthusiasm and happiness in almost everything we did, with one notable exception: Whenever he played with floor blocks, he would work for a while and then in a rage send them flying. Yet he was drawn to them as a moth to a flame. His mother and I were baffled; he seemed well adjusted and easygoing, with only this exception. The staff tried building his skills, investigated whether he was happy at home, and watched to see whether other children interfered with his work and made him angry, but we could find no satisfactory answer. Finally one day his mother arrived beaming at school with the following tale. Alan and his father had been looking out the window the week before, and he had said, "Oh, look Papa, see those two kitties!" But his father had looked and asked, "What two kitties?" since he could see only one. "Why, those two little black kitties right over there," said Al. Shortly thereafter, when his eyes were examined, the answer to his block problem became clear: He was slightly cross-eyed, just enough so that stacking small blocks was a particularly irritating problem for him to solve, and it was this condition that caused him to send them tumbling down when his self-control was exceeded by the difficulty of the task.

This story may help other teachers remember to be alert to activities that seem to provoke consistent frustrations in some children. Such a reaction can often be a symptom of a physical problem that warrants further investigation, since early remediation makes correction more likely.

Relaxation and Tension-Relieving Activities

Sometimes we do not think of relaxation as being a motor skill, but rather as the absence of one, because "all the child has to do is hold still!" However, the ability to relax and let go can be learned (J. H. Humphrey, 1998; Sutcliffe, 1997), and the ever-increasing stress of life as people mature in our culture makes acquiring these techniques invaluable. Moreover, since full-day centers invariably include naps as part of their routine, knowledge of relaxation techniques is doubly valuable there. Tension, of course, is intimately tied to emotional states, as well as to activity level. We all know that children who are emotionally overwrought find it more difficult to relax. It is worth taking extra time and pains with such youngsters to teach them relaxation skills because of the relief they experience when they can let down even a little.

When one is encouraging children to relax, reducing stimulation from the outside is a good principle to bear in mind. This is often done by darkening the room, playing quiet music, and providing regular, monotonous sensory experience such as rocking or gently rubbing backs.

Yawning, breathing slowly, shutting eyes, and lying somewhat apart from other children will make relaxation easier. The attitude of the teacher moving slowly about and talking quietly is a significant influence as well. Sometimes young children are able to use imagery and picture a quiet place they would like to be. For very young children it is usually necessary to suggest such places—perhaps rocking in their mothers' laps, or lying on a water bed, or resting on the grass on a warm, sleepy day.

During movement and dance activities, children should alternate between quiet and active activities. They can be encouraged to sense their own bodies and purposefully relax themselves by being floppy dolls or boiled noodles or melting ice cream. Relaxation should be contrasted with its opposite state of intense contraction. Even young children can learn to make their bodies stiff and hard and then become limp and soft, thereby applying Edmund Jacobson's techniques of progressive relaxation (1991). Stretching, holding the stretch, and then relaxing are also easily understood by children of preschool age, and it does feel wonderful. As we come to understand more about meditation, it becomes evident that some of these techniques can be used with children, too. An interesting example of such an application is *The Centering Book* (Hendricks & Wills, 1975), which lists many kinds of awareness and relaxation activities, some of which can be adapted for preschool children (J. H. Humphrey, 1998). Cherry's book *Think of Something Quiet* (1981) also provides many practical ideas of ways to help even very young children learn to attain at least a modicum of inner peace by using various relaxation and meditative techniques.

Even more fundamental than relaxation techniques, however, should be the goal of alleviating whatever is generating tension in the first place. There are numberless reasons why children or adults feel tense, ranging from suppressed anger to shyness, or that general feeling of apprehension commonly termed *anxiety*. Since methods of fostering emotional health and reducing anger are discussed in considerable detail later on, suffice it to say here that perhaps the most basic way to help people become less tense is to enable them to become more competent in as many areas of their lives as possible. This feeling of competency—being in command of oneself and one's life—is a highly effective, long-term antidote for tension.

Using Physical Activity to Promote Creative Thought and Self-Expression

Using Movement Exploration

An interesting aspect of creative physical education is termed *movement education* (Pica, 1995, 1998). It is a blend of physical activity and problem solving that can be considerable fun for children. The teacher may ask a youngster, "Is there some way you could get across the rug without using your feet?" and then, "Is there another way you could do that?" Or she might question, "What could you do with a ball with different parts of your feet?" or, "Can you hold a ball without using your hands?"

A nice example of how this kind of material can be presented is provided by Mimi Chenfield (1993):

> We stay very still. Now move just one part. Move another part. And another. The miracle of the moving parts. Now move two parts of you. Another two. Now three—four—five!
>
> We make Thumbelinas with our thumbs and watch them dance. We dance all the toys in the toy store: windup toys that spurt to action, then slow down; cars, trucks, trains, planes; limp rag dolls that leap into limp rag-doll dances; fluffy soft toys that make everyone feel wonderful.

We imagine the sounds our bodies would make as they move. We make the sounds of a finger wiggling, a head shaking, feet kicking, a back bending, arms waving.

We wear a "Happy-face" button and wonder how we would move if we were "Happy faces." How would a happy face move shoulders? Feet? How would a happy face dance? (p. 38)

Using Creative Dance as a Means of Self-Expression

Dancing can be the freest and most joyful of all large motor activities. For young children, dancing usually means moving rhythmically to music in a variety of relatively unstructured ways. The quandary beginning teachers often feel is just how unstructured this should be. On the one hand, it is rarely effective just to play a recording, no matter how appealing, and expect the children to "dance." On the other hand, the teacher who sets out to teach specific patterns, often in the guise of folk dances, surely limits the creative aspects of this experience. Besides that limitation, patterned dances are usually too complicated for young children to learn unless these are stripped to very simple levels.

What works best is to have an array of recordings on hand with which the teacher is very familiar and that provide a selection of moods and tempi. It is important also to have several fallback activities thought out in advance in case some activity does not go over well and to plan on participating with the children. Finally, as the session moves along, more and more ideas and movements can be drawn from the children themselves—an approach that makes the activity truly creative and satisfying for them.[2]

FOSTERING SENSORY EXPERIENCE

It has been maintained that 80% of everything we learn comes to us through our eyes, but it seems to me that our society encourages use of this one sense far more than is necessary. One has only to watch the deodorant and disinfectant advertisements on television to become aware of the tremendous emphasis on the desirability of smelling only a few choice fragrances. Children are continually admonished not to touch things, and as they mature, they are also taught not to touch other people except under carefully restricted circumstances. As for tasting, how many times have you heard a mother warn, "Don't put that in your mouth; it's dirty." The latest victim of the war against the senses appears to be the sense of hearing. In self-defense, people seem to be learning to tune out the continual piped-in music of the supermarket and the constant noise of the television set.

Teachers need to contend with this narrowing and restricting of the use of the senses by deliberately continuing to use *all* of them as avenues of learning. Children should be encouraged to make comparisons of substances by feeling them and smelling them, as well as by looking at them. Science areas should be explored by handling and manipulating, rather than by looking at bulletin board pictures or observing demonstrations carried out by the teacher. Stress should be placed on developing auditory discrimination skills (telling sounds apart), as well as on paying attention to what is said by the teacher. Learning through physical, sensory participation should be an important part of every preschool day.

---

[2] *Refer to chapter 14 for more detailed suggestions.*

The Sensory Experience of Close Physical Contact Is Important to Children

The recent handful of sensational court cases concerning sexual abuse in children's centers has made some teachers of young children uneasy about touching or cuddling youngsters lest they, too, be accused. They feel torn between the desire to protect themselves and the knowledge, well substantiated by practical experience, that young children require the reassurance and comfort of being patted, rocked, held, and hugged from time to time.

Research, as well as experience, supports the value of close physical contact. Montagu (1986) reviewed numerous studies illustrating the beneficial effect of being touched and the relationship of tactile experience to healthy physical and emotional development. Investigations documenting the link between touching and the development of attachment confirm those findings (Bernal, 1997).

Yet staff members must realize that parents are understandably concerned about the possibility of sexual abuse. Centers need to do everything they can to reassure them. No one, teachers included, wants children to be molested, and parents worry about this particularly when their children are away from home. To allay these fears, centers should have clearly stated policies encouraging parents to drop in for unannounced visits, and they should create opportunities for families and teachers to become well acquainted so that a climate of trust develops between them. If the center is staffed so that more than one person is with the children at all times, so much the better.

When such openness is the case, parents are reassured, and children and staff are more comfortable, too. In these circumstances the children will grow and thrive, and Cornelia Goldsmith's statement will prove as true today as when she said it 40 years ago: "The teacher's most important piece of equipment is her lap!"

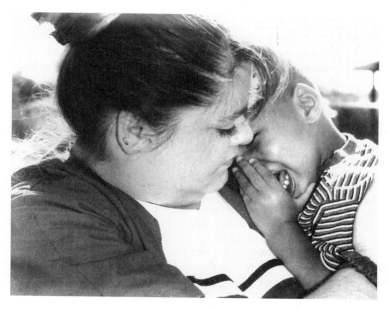

There's just no substitute for cuddling.

SUMMARY

The promotion of health and safety is vital to the physical well-being of young children. During the hours when children are at school, it is the teacher's responsibility to see that they follow good health practices and to keep the children as safe as possible without nagging them or being overprotective.

In addition, it is desirable to offer equipment and activities that foster large and fine muscle development. Attaining competence in these physical areas enhances children's self-esteem and provides opportunities for children to gain social expertise as they develop wholesome feelings of vigor and good health.

Equipment for large muscle activities should be versatile, sturdy, safe, and well maintained. The teacher can encourage active play by tuning in on what is happening and being alert to ways to add to its richness, rather than by regarding large muscle playtime as a recess period when she can sit down and relax.

Fine muscle activity is also valuable to offer, but it is important to provide an assortment of levels of difficulty and to be sure such activities do not continue for too long a time without relief.

Increasing knowledge of perceptual-motor development has made it necessary for preprimary teachers to broaden the range of activities offered to young children and so provide opportunities for practice in specific motor skills: locomotion, balance, body and space perception, rhythm and temporal awareness, rebound and airborne activities, projectile management, management of daily motor activities (fine muscle activities), and tension relievers. Movement activities that encourage creative thinking and self-expression should also be included.

Use of all the senses is important in education. Encourage children to touch, taste, and listen, as well as look to make the fullest use of these potential pathways for learning.

By using this comprehensive approach involving large and fine muscle skills and various sensory abilities, teachers can assure themselves that the physical development of the child is brought to its fullest potential.

Questions and Activities

1. *Predicament:* A little girl has just fallen out of a swing and is brought into the office, bleeding heavily from the mouth. Examination reveals that her front tooth is still whole but has cut entirely through her lower lip. As the teacher in charge, how would you handle this emergency? Remember to think about both short- and long-term aspects of the situation.

2. What conditions, if any, in the school where you are teaching are particularly well handled in terms of safety precautions? What possible hazards, if any, warrant attention?

3. Suppose you were beginning a new school and had a budget of $5,000 for large muscle equipment. In your opinion, what would be the most satisfactory way to invest this money? What would you buy and why?

4. What could be some advantages of putting children through a planned series of physical exercises on a regular basis? (This might not be calis-

thenics as such; it might be tumbling or learning ball skills.) What might be the disadvantages of this approach to physical education?

5. Some preprimary teachers, particularly male ones, appear to avoid physical contact with children. What do you think might be the reasons for this restraint? Is it always fear of being accused of sexual abuse, or could the teachers have other reasons for this behavior?

6. Describe some examples from your own experience in which you are aware that the use of every sense except vision is restricted or curtailed?

Self-Check Questions for Review

Content-Related Questions

1. Explain why it is so important for children's centers to insist that children be immunized and have a physical examination before attending school.

2. List some general health precautions teachers should follow when caring for children.

3. List three principles of physical development.

4. Name the categories of large muscle behaviors discussed in the text and give an example of an activity that fits each category.

5. Describe some possible adjustments that could be made to an outdoor play yard that would enable children with various kinds of disabilities to participate more fully.

6. What are some typical fine muscle activities offered to young children in preprimary schools? Why is it important not to keep children doing these activities for overly long periods of time?

7. Discuss some effective ways to help children learn to relax.

8. What are some effective policies that schools might follow to reassure parents their children are safe from sexual abuse?

Integrative Questions

1. *Predicament:* You are now the director of a child care center, and the annual visit by the licensing agency is due very soon. When you check the immunization records of the children in preparation for that visit, to your surprise you find that about one third of the children's immunizations are not up-to-date. You send parents a notice requesting they take their children to their physician to have the necessary shots. Three weeks

later, only two parents have turned in updated reports. What steps would you take next to ensure compliance with the regulations?

2. The teacher in the room next door is very interested in promoting physical fitness, so she usually organizes her 4-year-olds into teams and has them compete to see which team can get through an obstacle course fastest. Explain whether you would include that kind of activity in your plans for the children in your room. Be sure to include reasons why you would or would not do this.

3. An obstacle course that includes crawling through a concrete pipe; swinging across the grass, holding on to a rope with both hands; and walking along a narrow line drawn on the sidewalk has been planned for outdoor play. Which of the eight categories described in this chapter are included in this obstacle course? What categories are *not* included? Suggest activities to add to the obstacle course that would provide practice for two more categories.

4. A child with limited vision is in your 3-year-old group. She can tell light from dark and see coarse details of objects held close to her eyes, but her distance vision is almost nil. Explain what changes you will make in your playground to keep her safe and enable her to participate happily in many outdoor activities.

Coordinating Videotape

By leaps and bounds. Tape #2. The whole child: A caregiver's guide to the first five years. The Annenberg/CPB Collection, P.O. Box 2345, South Burlington, VT 05407–2345. *By Leaps and Bounds* surveys children's physical development, including large and fine muscle groups and motor skills, and provides instruction on good health practices, environmental safety, and appropriate developmental activities.

References for Further Reading

Pick of the Litter

Greenman, J. (1998b). *Caring spaces, learning places: Children's environments that work.* Redmond, WA: Exchange Press. Greenman provides wonderful ideas for anyone redesigning or designing space for children. The book is delightful to read—written with humor and experienced insight.

Overviews

Pica, R. (1997). Beyond physical development: Why young children need to move. *Young Children, 52*(6), 4–11. Pica explains how the development of the physical self affects the development of all the other selves.

Sanders, S. W., & Youngue, B. (1998). Challenging movement experiences for young children. *Dimensions of Early Childhood, 26*(1), 9–17. A good overview of how to present enhancing motor activities for preschool and kindergarten children is provided here.

Children's Health

Cohen, A. J. (1998). Caring for mildly ill children: Limiting your legal liability. *Child Care Information Exchange, #119,* 101–105. This practical article cites four ways centers and preschools can deal successfully with youngsters who are under the weather. *Highly recommended.*

Kendrick, A. S., Kaufmann, R., & Messenger, K. P. (Eds.). (1995). *Healthy young children: A manual for programs* (Rev. ed.). Washington, DC: National Association for the Education of Young Children. The authors cover topics as varied as nutrition, child abuse, and infectious diseases. The writing style is simple and practical. *Highly recommended.*

Activities

Griffin, C., & Rinn, B. (1998). Enhancing outdoor play with an obstacle course. *Young Children, 53*(3), 18–23. Don't let any obstacles stand in *your* way of reading this inspiring article— lavishly illustrated.

Kelly, N. T., & Kelly, B. J. (1997). *Physical education for preschool and primary grades.* Springfield, IL: Charles C Thomas. This is a good resource for times when you feel "dried up" on ideas for activities to stimulate specific aspects of development. Includes a good chapter on children with handicaps, and one on improvising inexpensive equipment.

Miller, K. (1989). *The outside play and learning book: Activities for young children.* Mt. Rainier, MD: Gryphon House. Many age-appropriate, attrac-tive, fresh suggestions for outdoor activities are included. Topics are as diverse as ideas for riding-toy play and snow and woodworking activities.

Pica, R. (1995). *Experiences in movement with music, activities, and theory.* Albany, NY: Delmar. This book is replete with ideas for activities based on developmental levels. It covers just about everything the teacher needs to know when presenting movement experiences and integrating them throughout the curriculum.

Sanders, S. W. (1992). *Designing preschool movement programs.* Champaign, IL: Human Kinetics. Readers of *The Whole Child* will find Sanders's book especially helpful because it follows the same outline of physical skills used in chapter 5. It offers lots of ideas for activities that are appropriate and stimulating.

Torbert, M., & Schneider, M. A. (1993). *Follow me too: A handbook of movement activities for three- to five-year-olds.* Menlo Park, CA: Addison-Wesley. Clear instructions and discussions of possible difficulties are included in this helpful activity book.

Including Children Who Have Special Physical Requirements

Block, M. (1994). *A teacher's guide to including students with disabilities in regular physical education.* Baltimore, MD: Paul H. Brookes. Two chapters in this book are particularly valuable for preschool teachers. One provides suggestions for adapting activities to specific disabilities. The other discusses how to draw preschool children with disabilities into active physical participation—and shows how to translate an individualized educational program (IEP) into actual activities. *Very practical.*

Breath, D., DeMauro, G. J., & Snyder, P. (1997). Adaptive sitting for young children with mild to moderate motor challenges: Basic guidelines. *Young Exceptional Children, 1*(1), 10–16. Sitting in as correct a position as possible makes a big difference in participation for some children with limited motor abilities. Here is the most helpful article I've ever come across about how to help them position themselves in a desirable way.

Sheldon, K. (1996). "Can I play too?" Adapting common classroom activities for young children with limited motor abilities. *Early Childhood Education*

Journal, 24(2), 115–120. The author provides many practical examples of ways to include opportunities for children with limited motor abilities to participate in satisfying activities at preschool.

Helping Children Learn to Relax

Humphrey, J. H. (1998). *Helping children manage stress: A guide for adults.* Washington, DC: Child and Family Press. Written by a foremost authority on stress, this plainly written book provides many suggestions for alleviating the physical manifestations of stress.

Sutcliffe J. (1997). *The complete book of relaxation techniques.* Allentown, PA: People's Medical Society. Although everyone may not subscribe to the value of some of the techniques included here, the reader is bound to find several helpful. Instructions and illustrations are clear and helpful.

Equipment and Environment

Moore, R. C., & Wong, H. H. (1997). *Natural learning: Creating environments for rediscovering nature's way of teaching: The life history of an environmental schoolyard.* Berkeley, CA: MIG Communications. The authors present an enchanting example of what a schoolyard environment *could* be, compared with the disheartening asphalt jungle it typically is. The approach demonstrates how the philosophy was—temporarily—transformed into practice by a group of dedicated people.

Moyer, J. (Ed.). (1995). *Selecting educational equipment and materials for school and home* (Rev. ed.). Wheaton, MD: Association for Childhood Education International. This book offers a particularly thorough list of psychomotor equipment divided according to children's ages.

For the Advanced Student

Allen, Lady of Hurtwood. (1968). *Planning for play.* Cambridge: MIT Press. Lady Allen, a progressive thinker, was among the first to advocate the development of adventure playgrounds. She describes the purpose of this book as being "to explore some of the ways of keeping alive and sustaining the innate curiosity and natural gaiety of children." It does that. A classic.

Brett, A., Moore, R. C., & Provenzo, E. B. (1993). *The complete playground book.* Syracuse, NY: Syracuse University. For a useful overview of playgrounds past and present, this is an excellent resource. Particular attention is paid to European playgrounds, and plentiful illustrations enrich the text.

Consumer Product Safety Commission. (1997). *Handbook for public playground safety.* Washington, DC: Author. This is the basic reference in the field for all playgrounds, preschool ones included. *Indispensable.*

Gallahue, D. L., & Ozmun, J. C. (1997). *Understanding motor development: Infants, children, adolescents, and adults* (4th ed.). New York: McGraw Hill. Replete with charts and illustrations this updated, clearly written book on physical development remains the Bible of motor development. *Highly recommended.*

Publications and Associations Having Related Interests

American Alliance for Health, Physical Education, Recreation, and Dance, 1900 Association Drive, Reston, VA 22091. The alliance offers many publications and media materials related to an astonishing range of physical activities.

Child Health Alert, P.O. Box 610228, Newton Highlands, MA 02461-0228. This 6-page, 10-a-year newsletter contains summaries of the latest findings on important child health care topics—a good, quick way to stay informed on health issues.

Child Health Talk, National Black Child Development Institute, 1463 Rhode Island Avenue, NW, Washington, DC 20005. *Child Health Talk* presents brief, basic information on various aspects of health care; a special emphasis on nutrition seems always to be included.

Division for Early Childhood of the Council for Exceptional Children, 1444 Wazee Street, Suite 230, Denver, CO 80202. The Early Childhood Division offers a relatively new publication entitled *Young Exceptional Children* that is an outstanding resource for all early childhood teachers. It provides information on ways to adapt teaching strategies that enable more children to fit in comfortably to the preschool environment.

part *III*

Nourishing and Maintaining Emotional Health

chapter six

Fostering Mental Health in Young Children

chapter seven

Developing Self-Esteem in Young Children

chapter eight

Tender Topics: Helping Children Master Emotional Crises

chapter nine

Welcoming Children Who Have Special Educational Requirements Into the Life of the School

Fostering Mental Health in Young Children

Have you ever wondered . . .

How to get a child to say what he's feeling instead of hitting somebody?

What to do for a child who just won't stop crying?

How to tell whether a child is mentally healthy?

. . . IF YOU HAVE, THE MATERIAL IN THE FOLLOWING PAGES WILL HELP YOU.

Children of all ages need an atmosphere of warmth in which to thrive, the warmth of close, honest human contacts. They need the feeling that adults, teachers, and parents like them, are interested in them, enjoy them, and feel ready to be responsible for them, to protect them even from themselves when occasion demands.

Barbara Biber (1984, p. 5)

Until your child can express her feelings in words, she doesn't really picture her feelings as you do. The idea is difficult for adults to grasp since we are all so familiar with feelings, but until your child has negotiated this stage she lives in an action- and body-oriented state. She experiences her feelings as impulses in her body—a sudden urge to strike out, for example, or a tightening in her chest that causes her to fall on the floor in tears. The sensation is concrete, as is the rest of her experience. Until she grows into the world of ideas, she doesn't have the capacity to understand the very abstract idea of feelings.

Stanley I. Greenspan and Serena Wieder (1998, p. 219)

The valuable contribution early childhood programs can make to fostering mental health was emphasized as long ago as 1970, when the Joint Commission on the Mental Health of Children repeatedly pointed out that day care centers, nursery schools, and compensatory programs present outstanding opportunities for carrying out preventive and remedial work in this area.

The potential value of these programs to children's mental health continues to be recognized today because the incidence of mental illness remains high (Koplow, 1996; Mash & Barley, 1998). The 1999 *Report on Mental Illness* by the surgeon general of the United States (Elias, 1999) summarizes thousands of studies of mental illness that document that one out of every five Americans experiences some type of mental disorder each year. The report agrees that some of these illnesses are the result of genetic factors but also emphasizes that some are the result of malign environments and life experiences.

It is in the latter area that preschool staff can be of real help—in part by providing information, support, and good examples for the children's families, and in part by providing wholesome, emotionally healthy environments while the children are at school. For this reason several chapters of this book are devoted to establishing general therapeutic policies, dealing with crisis situations, and building self-esteem, since these are all important aspects of developing emotional health. Additional aspects of mental health, covered under the development of the social self, include learning to care for other people, handling discipline and aggression, and valuing cross-cultural education. An ounce of prevention is worth thousands of dollars worth of remedial care.

IMPORTANCE OF DEVELOPING BASIC ATTITUDES OF TRUST, AUTONOMY, AND INITIATIVE IN YOUNG CHILDREN

The most fundamental thing the teacher can do to foster mental health in young children is to provide many opportunities for basic, healthy emotional attitudes to develop. Erikson (1959, 1963, 1982) has made a significant contribution to our understanding of what these basic attitudes are. He hypothesizes that during the life span an individual passes through a series of stages of emotional development wherein basic attitudes are formed. Early childhood encompasses three of these stages: trust versus mistrust, autonomy versus shame and doubt, and initiative versus guilt. Although children at the preprimary level are likely to be working on the second and third sets of attitudes, it is important to understand the implications of the first set, too, because Erikson theorizes that the resolution of each stage depends in part on the successful accomplishment of the previous one.

In the stage of *trust versus mistrust* the baby learns (or fails to learn) that other people can be depended on and that he can depend on himself to elicit needed responses from them. This development of trust is deeply related to the quality of care the mother provides and is often reflected in feeding practices, which, if handled in a manner that meets his needs, help assure the infant that he is valued and important. Although by the time he

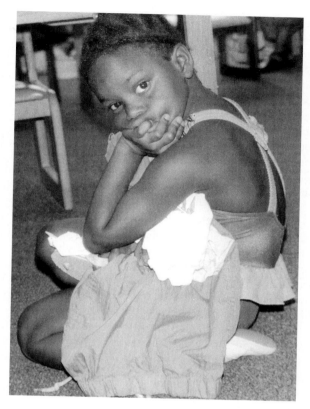

Not all feelings are happy ones.

enters child care the balance between trust and mistrust will have been tipped in favor of one attitude or the other, the need to experience trust and to have it reaffirmed remains with people throughout their lives. This is also true for the other attitudes as they develop.

Therefore it is vital that the basic climate of the center encourages the establishment of trust between everyone who is part of that community. If the teacher thinks of establishing trust in terms of letting the children know they can depend on him, it will be fairly easy for him to implement this goal. For example, consistent policies and regularity of events in the program obviously contribute to establishing a trustful climate. Being reasonable also makes it clear to the children that they can depend on the teacher. In addition, if he is sensitive to the individual needs of the children and meets these as they arise, the teacher can once again confirm the message that they are worthy of love and thus further strengthen trust and self-esteem.

In our society the attitudes of *autonomy versus shame and doubt* are formed during the same period in which toilet training takes place. During this time the child is acquiring the skills of holding on and letting go. This fundamental exercise in self-assertion and control is associated with the drive to become independent and to express this independence by making choices and decisions so often couched in the classic imperatives of the 2-year-old: No! Mine! and Me do it! Erikson maintains that children who are overregulated and deprived of the opportunity to establish independence and autonomy may become oppressed with feelings of shame and self-doubt, which result in losing self-esteem, being defiant, trying to get away with things, or in later life developing various forms of compulsive behavior.

The desirable way to handle this strong need for choice and self-assertion is to provide an environment at home and school that provides many opportunities for the child to do for himself and to make decisions. This is the fundamental reason why self-selection is an important principle in curriculum design. At the same time, the teacher must be able to establish decisive control when necessary since young children often show poor judgment and can be tyrannized by their own willfulness unless the teacher is willing to intervene.

Gradually, as the child develops the ability to act independently, he embarks on building the next set of basic attitudes. Around the age of 4 or 5 he becomes more interested in reaching out to the world around him, in doing things, and in being part of the group. At this stage he wants to think up things and try them out; he is interested in the effect his actions have on other people (witness his experimentation with profanity and "bad" language); he formulates concepts of appropriate sex roles; he enjoys imaginative play; and he becomes an avid seeker of information about the world around him. This is the stage Erikson has so aptly named *initiative versus guilt.*

To feel emotionally satisfied, a child of this age must be allowed to explore, to act, and to do. Preprimary schools are generally strong about meeting children's needs to explore and create, but they often underestimate the ability of older 4- and 5-year-olds to participate in making plans and decisions for their group or to attempt challenging projects. Of course, the teacher must make allowance for the fact that 4- and 5-year-olds are better planners and starters than they are finishers. Satisfaction in completing projects is more likely to be part of the developmental stage that follows this one: the stage of *industry versus inferiority,* which is characteristic of the child during the early years in primary school. But encouraging the ability to initiate plans and take action will enhance the child's feeling of self-worth and creativity, as well as his ability to be a self-starter—all highly desirable outcomes necessary for future development and happiness.

HALLMARKS OF AN EMOTIONALLY HEALTHY YOUNG CHILD

To determine whether the child is in good emotional health, the teacher should ask the following questions about him. If the majority of them can be answered affirmatively, chances are good that the child is emotionally healthy.

Is the Child Working on Emotional Tasks That Are Appropriate for His Age?

We have already talked about the fundamental need for planning a curriculum that provides many opportunities for children to exercise their autonomy and initiative. When looking at individual children, the teacher should consider whether they are taking advantage of these opportunities. He will find that the majority of them are achieving independence, choosing what they want to do, and generating their own ideas with zest and enthusiasm; but there will be a handful of youngsters who will need sensitive help to venture forth. This usually involves taking time to build a strong foundation of trust between child and teacher and then helping him advance to increased independence as his confidence grows (Balaban, 1989).

Is the Child Learning to Separate from His Family Without Undue Stress and to Form an Attachment with at Least One Other Adult at School?

In chapter 4 considerable space was devoted to handling separation anxiety in a constructive way because the ability to separate from significant others and form additional relationships is an important skill (Saarni, 1997; Thompson, 1998). The teacher should realize that most children, particularly shy ones and those who are very young, make friends with a teacher at school before they branch out to make friends with other children. This link between teacher and child is, of course, not so strong as the bond between parent and child (Godwin, Groves, & Horm-Wingerd, 1994). It seems reasonable to propose, however, that in a milder way a wholesome attachment between teacher and child encourages the youngster to explore and venture out in the center setting, just as it has been demonstrated by Ainsworth and her colleagues (Ainsworth, Blehar, Waters, & Wall, 1978; V. Wallach & Caulfield, 1998) that toddlers who are well attached to their mothers are more likely to venture and explore new experiences when that parent is present. The teacher who is aware that this is a typical and valuable pattern can relax and enjoy this process without fretting about the child's dependency since he has confidence that in time most children will leave his side in favor of being with other youngsters. This bond between teacher and child may not be so evident with socially able 4-year-olds as it is with younger children, but it should exist all the same. If the child has not formed a relationship with some adult after he has been at school for a while, he should be encouraged to do so. Being attached to the teacher makes it more probable that he will use the teacher as a model or come to that person for help when it is needed. Affection between teacher and child is also important because it is a fundamental ingredient of good discipline—but more about that later.

At the same time, the teacher has to be sensitive to the quality of the attachment. Oversolicitude for the child's feelings of loneliness or the teacher's own unmet needs for affection can occasionally create a form of dependency that is undesirable since it restricts the child's venturing out and making friends with his peers. This situation should, of course, be avoided. The teacher must learn to tell the difference between a youngster who genuinely needs the emotional support of a close relationship at first and the one who is using the teacher as an emotional crutch.

Is the Child Learning to Conform to Routines at School Without Undue Fuss?

Of course, conforming to routines varies with the age of the child and his temperament, and teachers anticipate some balkiness and noncompliance as being not only inevitable but healthy. Two-year-olds are particularly likely to be balky and at the same time insist that things should be done the same way every time. Self-assertiveness appears again rather prominently between the ages of 4 and 5. The quality of the behavior seems different though: The assertiveness of age 2 comes across as being more dogmatic and less logical, whereas the assertiveness of age 4 seems to be more of a deliberate challenge and trying out of the other person. However, consistent refusal to conform differs from these healthy behaviors because it goes beyond these norms. When this is the case, it should be regarded as a warning sign that the child needs help working through the behavior.

Is the Child Able to Involve Himself Deeply in Play?

One characteristic of severely disturbed children in mental institutions is that they cannot give themselves up to the experience of satisfying play. Indeed when they become able to do so, it is encouraging evidence that they are getting ready to be released from the hospital. Being able to play is also important for more typical children. The child's ability to enjoy participating in play by himself or with other children as he grows older not only is a hallmark of emotional health but also contributes to maintaining mental health.

Is the Child Developing the Ability to Settle Down and Concentrate?

Children may be distractible or restless for a variety of reasons, and no child is able to pay attention under all circumstances. Excitement, boredom, the need to go to the toilet, fatigue, interesting distractions, or not feeling well can all interfere from time to time with any child's ability to concentrate. But occasionally the teacher will come across a child who never seems to settle down: He flits continually from place to place and seems to give only surface attention to what he is doing. There are a multitude of reasons for this behavior, ranging from attention deficit/hyperactivity disorder (ADHD), subtle birth injuries, to just plain poor habits, but a common cause of distractibility that is often overlooked is tension or anxiety due to some family crisis.[1]

Is the Child Unusually Withdrawn or Aggressive for His Age?

One of the great advantages teachers have is that by becoming acquainted with hundreds of children over a period of time they are able to develop some norms for behavior that make it relatively easy to identify youngsters who behave in extreme ways. Very withdrawn behavior is more likely to be overlooked than aggressive behavior since it is much less troublesome to the teacher. She should be aware, however, that either response is a signal from the child that he is emotionally out of balance and needs some extra thought and plans devoted to helping him resolve whatever is causing him to cope in that manner.

---

[1]   *For further discussion of restless behavior possibly attributable to ADHD, refer to chapter 9, and to chapter 10 for dealing with family crises.*

Does the Child Have Access to the Full Range of His Feelings, and Is He Learning to Deal with Them in an Age-Appropriate Way?

Some children have already learned by the age of 3 or 4 to conceal or deny the existence of their feelings, rather than to accept and express them in a tolerable way. Early childhood teachers can help children stay in touch with the full repertoire of their emotions by showing them that they, too, have all sorts of feelings and that they understand that children have feelings as well, whether these be anger, sadness, or affection (Saarni, 1997). Healthy children should also begin to learn during their early years to express their feelings to the people who have actually caused the feelings and to do this in a way that does not harm themselves or others. Learning to do this successfully takes a long time but has its roots in early childhood.

PERSONAL QUALITIES THAT WILL HELP THE TEACHER ESTABLISH AN EMOTIONALLY POSITIVE CLIMATE IN THE CHILDREN'S CENTER[2]

Early childhood teachers should use their personal qualities, as well as what are commonly referred to as "teaching techniques," to foster a growth-enhancing climate for young children. Such a climate consistently favors the active development and maintenance of an atmosphere conducive to mental health. It frees people to develop to their fullest potential as balanced, happy individuals, and the personal qualities of the teacher have a lot to do with establishing this desirable climate. For this reason they are discussed next.

Consistency

One way to build a sense of trust between teacher and children is to behave in ways children can predict and to be consistent about maintaining guidelines and schedules—a very basic form of being "trustworthy" and dependable. Thus, the children know what to expect and do not live in fear of erratic or temperamental responses to what they do. For this reason, emotional stability is a highly desirable trait for teachers of young children to possess. Of course, consistency does not mean that rules must be inflexible, but their enforcement should not depend on the whim of the teacher or the manipulative power of various children.

Reasonableness

Coupled with the steadiness of consistency should go the trait of reasonableness, which I define as "expecting neither too much nor too little from children." One practical way to increase reasonableness is to learn the characteristics of the developmental stages when

---

[2] *The work in this section owes much to the humanistic philosophy of Carl Rogers and his client-centered approach to psychotherapy.*

these are discussed in child development courses. The brief developmental summaries presented in this book are intended to remind the student of general developmental characteristics. Knowledge of these characteristics prevents inexperienced teachers from setting their standards too high or too low. On the one hand, they do not expect a 2-year-old to have the self-control of a 4-year-old. On the other hand, when a 4-year-old starts making demands more typical of a 2-year-old, they know that he is regressing and that they must search for and alleviate the stresses causing his retreat.

Another excellent way to help children (and adults, too) see that the teacher is reasonable is to really listen when people try to tell you something. Walter Hodges (1987) describes this kind of active listening to perfection:

> Active listening requires giving undivided attention to children and accepting what they say without blame, shock, or solving their problems for them. Giving undivided attention is signaled by positioning squarely in front of a child, getting close to the child's eye level, and leaning forward without crowding. Active listening enables us to reflect the feelings of the child, respond appropriately, and check to see if we understand. Active listening communicates respect, warmth, and empathy. Children know that they are important and that they belong when they are heard. (p. 13)

I am indebted to one of my students for the following example of what can happen when one shuts out such information.

> We were in the playhouse corner and Heidi was wearing a coat while doing all her kitchen duties. Jennifer came in and stood beside me and said, "I want that coat!" I was about to see if maybe Heidi was wearing Jennifer's coat when a nearby student-teacher said it was Heidi's and that Jennifer had a sweater in her cubby.
> "Jennifer, why don't you get your sweater from your cubby?" I suggested.
> "But I want that coat!" she said, on the verge of tears.
> "I can see you want that coat very much, but I can't take it away from Heidi," I said.
> "But it's mine; I don't want a sweater."
> "Do you have a coat at home that looks like that? Is that why you think it's yours?" I asked.
> "Uh-huh. Give it to me!" she demanded (tears still there in the eyes).
> "I'm sorry, Jenny, I can see that you're very unhappy not to have your coat, but I can't take Heidi's," I said.
> "My mommy said I could have it!"
> By now I was finally suspicious, so I checked the coat Heidi was wearing. There, written across the collar, was the name, Jennifer!
> Heidi gave up the coat without a fuss, Jenny put it on, I apologized to her, and she went out to play!

The student concludes by commenting, "All I can say is that I would make sure next time of what I was talking about. It taught me, 'Look before you leap!' to which I would add the advice, 'Take time to listen; you may learn something important.'"

Courage and Strength of Character

Particularly when dealing with outbursts of anger, the student will find that courage and the strength of character commonly called "fortitude" are required to see such outbursts through. Understandably the embarrassment and insecurity of fearing that the scene may not turn out all right may make it easy to placate an angry child or, more usually, to allow him to run off or have his way. But the problem with allowing this to happen is that the child will repeat the behavior and feel contemptuous of the adult who permits it. Therefore being courageous and seeing a problem through are worth the struggle when coping with the strong emotional reactions so common in children at this age. (Refer to chapters 8, 11, and 12 and for more detailed discussions of how to do this.)

Trustful Confidence

Trustful confidence is the teacher's faith that the child wants to grow and develop in a healthy way. Interestingly psychoanalysts maintain that this ability to have trust or confidence in the good intentions of other people goes back to the individual's own experiences as an infant when he found he could or could not generally depend on his environment to be a nurturing one. Be that as it may, research bears out what many teachers and parents have determined empirically: Children respond to what is genuinely expected of them by the people who matter to them (Rosenthal & Jacobson, 1968). The teacher who optimistically trusts children to act in their own best behalf is likely to obtain this response from most children most of the time.

Congruence

The teacher also promotes trustful confidence between himself and the child by being honest with himself and with the youngster about his own feelings. This is what Rogers and Dymond (1954) call "congruence" and Patterson (1977) terms "genuineness." A congruent person attempts to recognize and accept his own feelings and be truthful about them to other people. Thus a teacher might level with one child by saying, "I don't want you to kick me again; I feel really angry with you when you do that to me," or with another by saying, "I'm glad to see you today. I've been looking forward to hearing about your new kittens."

However, a note of caution is in order. Rogers advocates revealing such feelings *when it is appropriate to do so*. Children should not be subjected to outbursts of temper or angry attacks by adults in the name of congruence. Uncontrolled outbursts are too disturbing to children because they know they are relatively helpless and at the mercy of the teacher.

Empathy

Empathy is the ability to feel as other people feel, to feel *with* them, rather than *for* them. Empathy is valuable not only because it allows teachers to put themselves in the child's place but also because it helps them identify and clarify for the child how he is feeling

Warmth

Warmth is so important and deserves special emphasis since its presence has been linked with the development of positive self-concepts in children (Rohner, 1986). The warm teacher lets the children and staff know that he likes them and thinks well of them. Both children and adults flourish in this climate of sincere approval and acceptance. But being warm and accepting does not mean the teacher just sits around and smiles at the children no matter what they do. There is a difference between expressing warmth and being indulgently permissive, and there are times when the teacher must exert control because a child is unable to. But when a teacher does this for a child, he must make it plain that he is taking control because he truly cares for the child and not because he wants to obtain power for its own sake or have the satisfaction of winning.

Interestingly a study by Stipek, Daniels, Galluzo, and Milburn (1992) indicates that the quality of teacher warmth is typically linked with the style of instruction provided by the teacher. They found that teachers who used a "didactic," teacher-directed approach stressing academic skills ranked low on subscales evaluating teacher warmth, child initiative, and positive control. Teachers who used a more child-centered approach, in contrast, scored high on those same subscales, thereby making the presence of a positive social climate more probable.

Appreciation

Teaching must be unbearable, or at least much less satisfying, for those who fail to take time to relish and enjoy the children in their care. What a shame it would be to overlook the comment, "Oh, see! That little cat is licking her sweater!" or not sense the impact for a 2-year-old who bids his mother adieu and then says stoutly, "I'm my own Mommy, now!" Such precious moments can be a major reward of teaching if only teachers take the time to savor and appreciate the children and their reactions.

I hope *appreciation* is not interpreted by the reader to mean "be amused by" the children. Appreciation is not the same thing as amusement. Appreciation is composed of perceptive understanding and empathy—with a dash of delight thrown in! When children sense this attitude, they blossom since they feel the approval it also implies. I suspect it feels to them as if a generous sun were shining in the room.

Good Health

The longer I teach and observe students teaching, the more firmly I become convinced it is necessary to emphasize the significance of valuing and taking care of oneself if one wishes to facilitate health in others.

We all experience times when we seem to have no other choice than to operate on the ragged edge of energy. Some teachers, however, appear to accept this as being a continuing, necessary style of life. Teachers who wish to do their best with children, as well as with their other personal relationships, need to recognize what their bodies and spirits need and make certain they honor these needs to remain physically and emotionally healthy. The prescription includes adequate rest, exercise, wholesome food, and someone to care about who cares in return. Providing oneself with these requisites should be viewed as being part of one's own basic self-respect, as well as being plain good sense.

Being warm and close with children is an important part of teaching.

Attaining These Qualities

Some of the aforementioned qualities such as consistency, fortitude, and reasonableness can be acquired through practice and experience. The others—empathy, trustful confidence, congruence, warmth, and the ability to appreciate others—can often be enhanced by participation in well-run group therapy or through psychological counseling if they do not seem to come naturally. Many teachers have found that such experiences have improved both their teaching abilities and their personal relationships.

PRACTICAL WAYS TO HELP YOUNG CHILDREN ACHIEVE HEALTHY EMOTIONAL DEVELOPMENT

Before turning to a discussion of more concrete things the teacher can do to contribute to a life-enhancing milieu, the student should remember two principles. The first principle is that young children respond with encouraging quickness to a change in atmosphere or approach. It is possible to quickly bring about positive changes in their feelings and behavior by using appropriate methods. The second principle has been mentioned before: Children are resilient (Rouse, 1998; Werner, 1999; Werner & Smith, 1992). They bounce back from their own and others' mistakes, and it is unlikely that a teacher's one imperfect handling of a situation will inflict permanent damage on a child. This is not said to sanction irresponsible actions by teachers, but rather to reassure beginners that when dealing with difficult situations they should not be unduly hesitant on the grounds they may injure the child. It is the repetition of procedures and the overall quality of the milieu, rather than the single episode, that are likely to enhance or damage.

Develop Friendly, Close Relationships with Each Family

Entrance to the children's center or preschool usually marks the occasion in the child's and parents' lives when the child leaves parental protection for the first time on a regular basis. If the school and family establish a feeling of closeness and a shared interest in the child's welfare, it is easier for him to make this transition because his world is thereby widened, rather than split into two pieces.

Teachers are quick to see the advantage of establishing a friendly, comfortable atmosphere since such an atmosphere means the family is more likely to seek advice from the school. But another advantage should not be overlooked: The teacher is also in a better position to accept advice and suggestions from parents when a caring-sharing atmosphere is established. This two-way respect fosters genuine mutuality and lays the basic foundation for emotional health at school.

Remember That Children Have Different Temperaments

As anyone who has ever visited a nursery of newborns can attest, children respond differently to their environment right from the moment of birth. This disposition to respond in a characteristic way or style is called *temperament*. Some babies wince at every loud noise; some are fretful; and some more placid. As children develop, temperamental differences become even more apparent. One child can be crushed by a look, whereas another seems impervious to all but the most explicit expression of displeasure from the grown-up. Some youngsters are excitable or lose their tempers easily. Some are so emotionally expressive that the teacher is rarely left in doubt about the child's feelings; others seem impassive, and feelings (which may be just as intense internally as that of the more outwardly expressive child) are not sensed as easily by the caregiver. And, of course, teachers have temperaments, too, and so may find they are more "in tune" with some children than they are with others.

This interplay and mix of temperaments is one reason that working with young children is so interesting—and so challenging. Although it would be much easier if only "one size fit all" and we could treat all children just alike, particularly when working with the emotional self we must remember to be sensitive to these variations and adjust our responses accordingly.

A valuable way to increase that sensitivity is to ask parents about their child: How do they see him, and what would they like you to know about him? What does he care about most intensely? What is most likely to hurt his feelings—or to bring him joy? How is he best comforted when feeling sad?

Another way to gain insight is to quiet oneself inside and be as open and receptive as possible to what a child might be feeling before jumping to conclusions. Wait a little and widen the frame of possibilities through which you can see the youngster; for example, what might that scowl on José's face mean: Is he angry? Or is he thinking very seriously about something? Or could he be squinting because he needs glasses?

Reduce Frustration for the Children When Possible

Children should not have to spend time waiting for things to happen when this can be prevented. Children's needs are *immediate, intense,* and *personal,* and the longer they are kept waiting the more irritable and out of hand they become. Snack should be available as the children sit down, and someone should be outside for supervision as the children are dressed and ready to go outdoors to play. Duplicates of equipment mean there is generally enough to go around; two or three toy trucks are much more satisfactory than just one. A good assortment of developmentally appropriate activities must be available so that 3-year-olds are not expected to stack tiny plastic blocks and 5-year-olds do not have to make do with eight-piece puzzles. The day should be planned so that few and moderate demands are made on children at points when they are likely to be tired and hungry.

Of course, the teacher cannot and should not seek to eliminate all frustrating circumstances. Children benefit from learning to cope successfully with such situations as long as these are not overwhelming in frequency or intensity. But so many interruptions and frustrations inevitably happen in even well-run preschools and centers that eliminating unnecessary sources of frustration makes sense.

Understand the Fundamental Principles of How the Brain Handles Strong Emotions

Since teachers and parents spend a good part of their lives teaching children to control what they do about their feelings, it is very helpful to understand the fundamentals of what happens in the brain that makes it likely children will sometimes act impulsively—seemingly "before they even think!"

Recent research reported by Goleman (1995) and Greenberg and Snell (1997) confirm that that is exactly what happens. Because of the way the brain responds, people sometimes *do* act before they think. When children (or adults) feel an emotion strongly (typically fear, love, anger, or sadness), two parts of the brain respond to that feeling. The first part is located in the limbic system and is called the *amygdala* (uh-mig´-duh-luh). It is a very valuable organ since the amygdala is the body's first line of defense, and it moves so quickly there is, literally, no time to think before it causes us to fearfully duck a foul ball or, if we are 2-years-old, perhaps to angrily bite a child who took a toy we wanted.

Fortunately, there is a second part of the brain related to emotion that is a more rational, thinking part. It is called the *neocortex*. Given enough time (only a split second) to act and the necessary learning to go with it, the neocortex provides the indispensable balance that can exert control over the first rush of emotion-based reaction coming from the amygdala. It protects us from acting too spontaneously when a more thoughtful response would be the wise thing to do.

As teachers and parents, then, it becomes clear that if we want children to gain control over their impulses, we should do all we can to strengthen the ability of the second part, the neocortex, to take action in all but the most dangerous circumstances. One of the most effective ways to involve the neocortex is to couple language with emotion whenever possible.

Learn to Couple Language with Emotion by Identifying and Describing Children's Feelings to Them and by Helping Them Express These Feelings to Relevant People in an Acceptable Way

In our society we seem to have reached the conclusion that it is dangerous to allow some emotions to be expressed. The assumption is that if they are expressed they will become stronger or the person will act the feeling out but that if we ignore them or deny their presence they will vanish. Actually, the opposite of this premise is psychologically true. The following stanza from William Blake's poem "A Poison Tree" puts this neatly:

> I was angry with my friend,
> I told my wrath, my wrath did end.
> I was angry with my foe,
> I told it not, my wrath did grow.

Research supports the principle that if negative emotions are recognized, accepted, and expressed they usually fade but that if they are not expressed they seem to generate pressure that ultimately causes the person to relieve them in a more explosive or veiled yet hostile way. Also if children are *not* provided with ways of telling someone else how they feel, they are almost inevitably driven to *show* how they feel by acting the feelings out (Eisenberg, Fabes, & Losoya, 1997).

It is not easy for such young children to put their feelings and impulsive intentions into words instead of actions. As we will see in chapters 11 and 12, learning to self-regulate aggression requires a lot of experience and practice, but teaching children to recognize what they are feeling inside and to say "outside" what that feeling is instead of acting it out is a crucial step toward acquiring self-regulation. As researchers Greenberg and Snell (1997) point out:

> Helping children develop awareness of emotional processes (both in themselves and in others), applying verbal labels to emotions, and encouraging perspective taking and empathetic identification with others are the first steps in developing these [i.e., the brain's] frontal lobe functions of interpersonal awareness and self-control. (p. 113)

Sometimes it helps to look at what can happen when feelings are ignored. A student submitted the following example and analysis when asked to submit an insensitive response that did *not* take the child's feelings into account.[3]

---

[3]   *Courtesy Paige Gregory, University of Oklahoma, Norman.*

One evening I was staying with Vickie, age 3, while her father visited her mother in the hospital. Grandmother had dropped by with a covered dish for supper and some sweetrolls for breakfast. Vickie hadn't eaten a very big dinner. She went over to the counter and tried to reach the rolls.

"Can I have a roll?"

"No, Vickie, those are for breakfast."

"But I need just one."

"You can have one for breakfast."

A few minutes later she said, "How about a roll?"

"No, Vickie." Later as I was cleaning the kitchen, Vickie was coloring at the table while Stephen, age 1½, watched. He snatched a crayon.

"No, Stevie, no!"

"Vickie, maybe we could let Stevie use a crayon."

"Well, I think maybe a roll would help."

"How about some cheese? Are you hungry? Would you like some cheese and bread?"

"Yes!"

Rather than giving Vickie reasons, next time I would try to look at the real problem first. I would have liked the scene to have gone more like this:

"Can I have a roll?"

"Those rolls look awfully good to you, don't they?"

"Yes! I want one—my tummy says so!"

"You really want one because you feel kind of empty inside! But there are just enough for breakfast. I can't give you a roll now."

"Oh!" (Vickie looks pensive.)

"How about some cheese?—you like that?"

"OK!"

(Then I'd pick her up and rock her while she ate it and talk about feeling empty since she was missing her mommy—and that her mother would be coming home on Sunday—I also realize, now, I should have put those rolls out of sight!)

In the following example the teacher, working with an older child, encourages him not only to express his feelings but also to deal with the person causing the unhappiness.

Jonathan arrives at the woodworking bench very excited by the box of new wood he has spied from across the play yard. He reaches for Henry's hammer as it is laid down and is really surprised when Henry snatches it back. The teacher tells Jonathan that all the hammers are in use and he will have to wait. Jonathan stands on one foot and then the other—his hand obviously itching to snatch Henry's hammer. At this point, rather than trying to redirect him to the swings, the teacher says to him, "It's hard to wait, isn't it? I can see how much you want that hammer." "Yes, it is. I wish old Henry'd hurry." "Well, tell him so. Tell him what you want." "Henry, you son of a bitch, I want that hammer when you're done." (The boys grin at each other.) The teacher suggests, "Why don't you saw some wood while you're waiting?" "Don't mind if I do," says Jonathan.

In these examples the teacher did not content herself with the simple statement "You feel angry" or "You're hungry" or "You feel impatient." Instead she tried to describe to the child what he or she felt like doing and to name the feeling because she was fairly sure she could identify it. Describing feelings or intended actions is particularly helpful when working with young children since they understand the statement "You want her to stay" or

"It's hard to wait" better than they grasp the label "angry" or "impatient." In addition, description stands a better chance of being correct, and it is always better to talk about what a person does, rather than what he is.

With a younger or less controlled child the teacher may need to go further and reassure him by saying, "It's OK to want to grab it as long as you don't really do it." Sometimes she will need to go even further than that and actually restrain him, saying, "I can see you want to hit Henry, but I won't let you hurt him. Tell him you feel like taking his hammer." It takes many experiences for a young child to reach the level of the children in our examples, but it can be done. The moral is *Feel what you want*, but *control what you do*.

Teach Children the Difference Between Verbal Attack and Self-Report

Note that in the examples presented the teacher neither moralized, "Of course you really love your mother," nor said, "If you'd eaten your dinner you wouldn't be hungry now!" nor offered the children an involved interpretation of the reasons behind their behavior. Instead she concentrated on letting the children know that she understood what they felt, that it was a good idea to talk about it, and that she would help them draw the line between feeling and acting if they needed that help.

When teaching children to express their feelings, we must teach them gradually to understand the difference between saying how one feels about something (self-report) and telling another person what she is (verbal attack). There's a big difference between allowing a child to attack by shouting, "You selfish pooh-pooh pants! You nerd! Gimme that shovel now or you can't come to my birthday party!" and teaching him to say instead, "I need that shovel now—I'm dying for it! I can't wait another minute!"

Admittedly this is a sophisticated concept for little children to grasp. Sad to say, even some adults seem unable to make this distinction and say something nasty about the other person, rather than explain their own feelings. Nevertheless self-report is such an extraordinarily valuable emotional and social skill to acquire that teachers should begin to model and teach children the rudiments of self-report very early. Acquisition of this skill will benefit them all their lives.

There are many many additional ways to express feelings through play and through the use of sublimative and expressive materials (which are discussed later on), but *the ability to recognize and acknowledge feelings openly* is the soundest and most fundamental therapeutic skill to use to foster mental health.

Remember That Putting Feelings Into Words Is Only Half the Solution

This chapter stresses the value of recognizing the full range of children's (and adults') feelings and channeling the resulting impulses into words rather than deeds because this is such a fundamental part of generating emotional health. But having the ability to do this is only half the self-regulation equation. The other half of the equation that adds up to self-regulation and control is having a repertoire of coping behaviors—practical things to do that help relieve or resolve those feelings (M. T. Greenberg & Snell, 1997).

For example, suppose Peidong and Emily are working in the block corner and Peidong wants the only tiger to put in her corral but Emily holds tight and won't give it to her.

Encouraged by the teacher, Peidong does a good job of putting her feelings into words by saying, "I've been waiting and waiting—and I—don't—want—to—wait—*any*—longer!" She scowls at Emily and *then* says, "Tell you what—"You can have the elephant and her baby if you'll do it."

Here we see that Peidong is adding together both parts of the self-regulation equation to get what she wants: *First* she says her feeling out loud, and *then* she copes by doing two additional things—she looks threatening and she also proposes a bargain.

Of course, there are all kinds of coping mechanisms—some more desirable (waiting a little, substituting something else, using equipment together, making a trade) and some less so (sulking, whining, telling fibs, and tattling, just to name a few). Peidong's striking a bargain is only one of many socially desirable coping strategies discussed at greater length in chapters 10 and 11.

Learn to Recognize Signs of Stress and Emotional Upset in Children

Children give many signals besides crying or fussing that indicate emotional stress. Reverting (regressing) to less mature behavior is a common signal. We are all familiar with

Never underestimate the comfort a well-placed thumb can deliver in times of stress.

the independent 4-year-old who suddenly wants to be babied while recovering from the flu or the child who wets his bed after the baby arrives.

Various nervous habits such as hair twisting, deep sighing, nail biting, or thumb sucking also reveal that the child is under stress. Increased irritability, sometimes to the point of tantrums, is another indicator, as are lethargy and withdrawing from activities. Sometimes children suddenly begin to challenge rules and routines; sometimes they cry a lot; sometimes expressions of tension or stress are subtler and conveyed only by a strained look about the eyes or a tightened mouth; and sometimes stress is expressed in the more obvious form of excessive activity and running about.

In addition to this knowledge of common symptoms, as the year progresses and the teacher gets to know the children well, he will have the additional advantage of knowing how each child usually behaves. This makes it easier for him to spot changes and identify children who are signaling for special help (J. H. Humphrey, 1998).

Know What to Do for Children Who Are Emotionally Upset

Emotional upsets have to be handled on a short-term basis and sometimes on a long-term basis as well. (See also chapter 9.)

Short-Term, Emergency Treatment

The first thing to do for a child who is upset to the point of tears is to comfort him. But the manner of comfort will vary from child to child: Some youngsters need to be held and rocked, whereas others do best when they are allowed to reduce themselves to hiccuping silence while the teacher putters about nearby. Children who are using emotional outbursts as a means of controlling the adult's behavior require still a third response—mildly ignoring them until they subside. When in doubt, it is better to err on the side of comfort than to ignore unhappiness.

No matter why a child is crying hard, it is a waste of energy to try to reason with him until he has calmed down. However, it can help soothe him to repeat something in a quieter and quieter tone of voice so that he gradually quiets himself to hear what is being said. This may be as simple a sentence as, "When you've stopped crying, we'll talk things over," or, "I'm waiting to help you when you've stopped crying." Occasionally it can also be helpful to remark matter-of-factly if the occasion warrants, "You know, I will keep on holding you, even when you've stopped crying."

As the child calms down, getting him a drink of water or wiping his eyes may also soothe him. It is often effective at this point to talk over the difficulty, but sometimes it is better to wait and discuss it in a casual way later in the day to clarify how he felt or why he broke down. Each situation has to be judged in its own context.

Finally the teacher should either help the child return and resolve the problem in the group or, if she deems it wiser, help the child get started on another satisfying activity. Activities that are particularly helpful at such times include swinging, water play, and messy activities such as finger painting or working with clay. Water play generally seems to be the best choice.

Long-Term Treatment

It is always wise, before deciding that an emotional upset represents a serious long-term difficulty, to wait and see whether the child is coming down with something; incipient illness is a frequent source of loss of emotional control. It is also wise to consider whether an approaching holiday could be causing the disturbance. Christmas and Halloween are notorious tension increasers, and we have found in our campus children's center that the weeks before and during college examinations are likely to be edgy ones, too. Many episodes of fighting, crying, and other exaggerated responses to minor crises will disappear after such times have passed.

If the symptoms of stress do not subside, it is necessary to find out more about what is causing tension in the child. The behavior may be caused by something going on at home or by something going on at school or by a combination of these circumstances.

One helpful way to locate the cause is to think back to the point when the signs of stress appeared and then to confer with the parent about what else changed in the child's life at about the same time. Perhaps the youngster was moved to another room at school, or his close friend was absent because of chicken pox; perhaps his grandfather died, or his father was away, or houseguests were visiting. Once the cause has been discovered, steps can be taken to help the youngster feel more at ease. Sometimes just recognizing the source helps a lot, without doing anything more.

Other signals of disturbance can be traced to continuing environmental situations. Perhaps discipline policies are erratic at home, or affection is lacking, or the child is excessively fatigued because he watches television until late at night. These are more difficult situations to deal with, but even they can often be resolved successfully by working together with the family.

If the situation is too complicated or difficult to be quickly eased by the teacher's intervention, he must encourage the family to seek counseling from a psychologist or psychiatrist. The area of guidance and referral is such an extensive one that it cannot be treated in detail here. The reader is invited to pursue the subject further in chapters 3, 8, and 9.

SUMMARY

Growth-enhancing child care seeks to create as many opportunities as possible for young children to develop their sense of autonomy and initiative in a setting that is reasonable, consistent, trustful, empathic, warm, and appreciative. Children who are mentally healthy are working on emotional tasks appropriate for their age. They are learning to separate from their families and to conform to school routines without undue stress. They can involve themselves deeply in play, and they are developing the ability to settle down and concentrate. Emotionally healthy children are not excessively withdrawn or aggressive; they have access to the full range of their feelings and are beginning to learn to deal with these feelings in appropriate ways.

Teachers can help the children in their care develop in emotionally healthy ways by forming good relationships with their families, reducing frustration for them when possible, identifying and describing the children's feelings for them and helping them express these to the relevant people, recognizing the signs of stress that signal that help is needed, and handling emotional problems on a short-term and long-term basis as necessary.

Questions and Activities

1. What are some matter-of-fact ways to express warmth and liking to young children?
2. Looking back on your own education, give an example of a teacher who had unreasonably high expectations of you as a pupil. What was the effect on your learning?
3. With other members of the class, set up some role-playing situations that provide opportunities for "children" to express their feelings and "teachers" to practice phrasing responses that would help each child identify how he feels and show that the teacher understands him. Practice this a lot!
4. Do you believe it is always wise to be forthright about your own feelings? On the one hand, what limitations might be helpful to remember? On the other hand, can you think of times when it would have been better to take the risk and be more open and frank in your response? What did you do instead of being direct? Do you think it was a satisfactory solution?
5. Describe some examples in which you have seen adults ignore, suppress, or mislabel a child's feelings. Could you see how the child was immediately affected by this kind of response? What would you predict might be the long-term effects of a child's experiencing many such responses to his feelings?

Self-Check Questions for Review

Content-Related Questions

1. What percentage of people in the United States are estimated to suffer from mental disorders severe enough to require special treatment?
2. Name the first three stages of emotional development identified by Erikson and list some actions early childhood teachers can take to foster the successful mastering of each stage.

3. Identify the hallmarks of an emotionally healthy child.
4. Select four personal qualities of teachers that would help foster emotional health in the children, and explain why each is important.
5. What common behaviors of children might alert you to the fact that they are experiencing stress?

Integrative Questions

1. What is the difference between feeling sympathy for someone and feeling empathy for him? Provide an example of an emotional situation with a child and explain what you would say if you were expressing sympathy and what you would say to show you were experiencing empathy.
2. Analyze the following gem contributed by a student and suggest what the adult might have said instead that would have described the children's feelings to them.[4]

I was baby-sitting two children in their backyard late in the afternoon. Robby is about 5 years old and Joel is about 3.

Robby: Hey, look at this rock I found!

Me: Make sure you don't throw it at somebody.

Joel: I'm gunna throw that rock at Jimmy's mean cat!

Me: You'd better not, young man.

Robby: I wanna throw rocks!

Me: Not now, Robby. It's time to go in and eat dinner, OK?

Both boys: No!

Me: Why don't you want to eat dinner?

Robby: I'm not hungry. I wanna stay out here and play.

---

[4] *Courtesy Sarah Strain, University of Oklahoma, Norman.*

Me: You've played long enough; now you need to get your vitamins.

Robby: Mom said I already have enough vitamins.

Me: You'll really like what we're having—meat loaf and baked potatoes, and spinach.

Joel: I hate spinach!

Me: You should eat it. It's good for you!

3. Analyze the following statements and categorize them according to whether they are examples of "self-report" or "verbal attack."

    "I feel pretty worried when you climb that high."

    "Let Ahmed have some crackers, too. Don't be so selfish!"

    "You're always so quick to criticize others!"

    Then change each statement into the opposite form. For example, if the original statement was "You're always making me do things I don't want to do," you might change it into "I just feel too shy to do that; please don't press me to try it."

Coordinating Videotapes

Dealing with feelings. Tape #4. The whole child: A caregiver's guide to the first five years. The Annenberg/CPB Collection, P.O. Box 2345, South Burlington, VT 05407–2345. *Dealing With Feelings* shows practical activities that promote a child's emotional health in areas including working with the child's family, encouraging self-expression, dealing with frustration, identifying stress, and managing short- and long-term emotional issues.

Babies are children, too. Tape #3. The whole child: A caregiver's guide to the first five years. The Annenberg/CPB Collection, P.O. Box 2345, South Burlington, VT 05407–2345. *Babies Are Children, Too* introduces students to the special concerns when caring for infants in groups and emphasizes the importance of providing nurturing care. The program reviews infant development and ways to foster growth in all areas.

References for Further Reading

Pick of the Litter

Koplow, L. (1996). *Unsmiling faces: How preschools can heal.* New York: Teachers College Press. This wonderful book is filled with examples of teach-

ers working and talking with children in emotionally enhancing ways. I cannot recommend it highly enough!

Overviews

Brazelton, T. B. (1992). *Touchpoints: The essential reference: Your child's emotional and behavioral development.* Reading, MA: Addison-Wesley. Brazelton's book is filled with understanding comments about children that are sensible, reassuring, and practical. It is a useful book both to recommend to parents and for use by the teacher. *Highly recommended.*

Goleman, D. (1995). *Emotional intelligence.* New York: Bantam Books. For an interesting, diverse book about emotions and their effects on children and adults this book is hard to beat. It has a particularly good, clear chapter about the anatomy of the brain as related to the emotional realm.

Greenspan, S. (1999). Six stages to a strong self-image. *Scholastic Early Childhood Today, 14*(1), 42–46. In this excerpt from his book *The Growth of the Mind,* Greenspan singles out six factors important for building emotional health. *Highly recommended.*

Hyson, M. C. (1994). *The emotional development of young children: Building an emotion-centered curriculum.* New York: Teachers College Press. Hyson presents a good review of recent research on emotional development. The second half of the book provides sound advice on ways to honor and support the role of emotions in the classroom.

Stages of Emotional Developmental and Emotional Needs of Children

Erikson, E. H. (1963). *Childhood and society* (2nd ed.). New York: Norton.

Erikson, E. H. (1971). A healthy personality for every child. In R. H. Anderson & H. G. Shane (Eds.), *As the twig is bent: Readings in early childhood education.* Boston: Houghton Mifflin.

Erikson, E. H. (1982). *The life cycle completed: A review.* New York: Norton. These publications contain original source material that explains in detail Erikson's concepts of the eight stages of man and the emotional attitudes of paramount importance at various stages of development.

Greenspan, S. I., & Greenspan, N. T. (1985). *First feelings: Milestones in the emotional development of your baby and child.* New York: Viking Press. The Greenspans propose six steps in emotional development occurring in the very early years. Interesting reading that also provides practical recommendations.

Building Sound Emotional Relationships with Children

Faber, A., & Mazlish, E. (1980). *How to talk so kids will listen, & listen so kids will talk.* New York: Avon Books. Numerous examples of describing and sharing feelings make this book a treasure trove of helpfulness.

Roemer, J. (1989). *Two to four from 9 to 5: The adventures of a daycare provider.* New York: Harper & Row. Insightful, sensitive encounters with children are a hallmark of this delightful reading. *Highly recommended.*

Rogers, C. R. (1961). *On becoming a person.* Boston: Houghton Mifflin. Rogers sets forth his philosophy that desirable emotional relationships between people are facilitated by the presence of warmth, congruence, and empathy.

Samalin, N., & Jablow, M. M. (1987). *Loving your child is not enough.* New York: Viking Press. The chapter on acknowledging feelings provides many examples of how to reflect and describe feelings to children. Helpful reading.

For the Advanced Student

Greenberg, M. T., & Snell, J. L. (1997). Brain development and emotional development: The role of teaching in organizing the frontal lobe. In P.

Salovey & D. J. Sluyter (Eds.), *Emotional development and emotional intelligence.* New York: Basic Books. The authors provide clear explanations of what is known about the areas of the brain involved in emotional functioning.

Greenspan , S. I., & Wieder, S. (1998). *The child with special needs: Encouraging intellectual and emotional growth.* Reading, MA: Addison-Wesley. Although this book focuses on youngsters with a variety of unique characteristics, the descriptions of how to form meaningful relationships with hard-to-reach children can be used with all children.

Mash, E. J., & Barkley, R. Q. (Eds.). (1989). *Treatment of childhood disorders* (2nd ed.). New York: Guilford Press. Another first-rate book, this one provides a thorough discussion of history, causes, and recommended treatments of children with a wide variety of serious emotional disorders such as extreme fears, obesity, encopresis, and autism.

Wenar, C. (1994). *Developmental psychopathology: From infancy to adolescence* (3rd ed.). New York: McGraw-Hill. The author offers a detailed overview of developmentally related emotionally based problems. The book includes a chapter on working with children from minority groups.

Journals of Continuing Interest

Zero to Three, 734 15th Street, Suite 1000, Washington, DC 20005–1013. *Zero to Three* is published by the National Center for Infants, Toddlers, and Families. It stresses emotional health and covers all kinds of topics relevant to working with the infant-toddler age-group, but the practices it advocates are sound to follow for older preschoolers as well. *Highly recommended.*

chapter seven

Developing Self-Esteem in Young Children

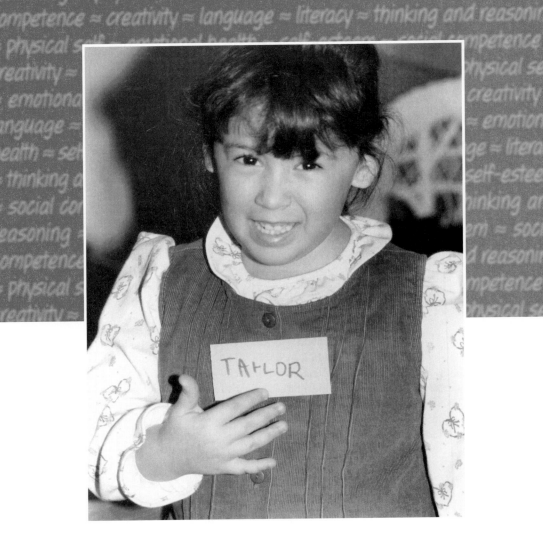

Have you ever wondered what to do about . . .

The child who habitually protests, "I can't—I know I can't—don't make me!"

Or the one who always wants to know, "Did I do it right?"

Or the youngster who says sadly, "Nobody likes me—nobody!"

. . . IF YOU HAVE, THE MATERIAL IN THE FOLLOWING PAGES WILL HELP YOU.

One of the greatest diseases is to be nobody to anybody.

Mother Teresa (1996, p. 65)

Self-esteem creates natural highs. Knowing that you're lovable helps you to love more. Knowing that you're important helps you to make a difference to others. Knowing that you are capable empowers you to create more. Knowing that you're valuable and that you have a special place in the universe is a serene spiritual joy in itself.

Louise Hart (1996, p. 83)

Perceiving oneself as a person who has something worthwhile to contribute to the life around one is such an important aspect of being emotionally healthy that it is necessary to devote an entire chapter to this concept. It is this feeling of internal worth I have in mind when describing individuals who possess positive self-esteem. People who feel like this are able to venture out into the world, work toward attaining what they hope for, and welcome life with pleasurable anticipation. As the Research Study in this chapter indicates, such people are also likely to get along more cooperatively with others.

On the other hand, individuals who suffer from low self-esteem fit, to varying degrees, the following description:

> The child with low self-worth focuses on failure instead of success, problems instead of challenges, difficulties instead of possibilities. A child with low self-esteem experiences the world as a dark and gloomy place, filled with danger and threat. (C. A. Smith, 1988, p. 5)

Moreover, an English study of young adolescents found that "individuals who were anxious, depressed, neurotic or *have poor self-esteem* [italics added] do tend to be more prejudiced than others. They have to a greater extent chosen the cultural symbols of racism as a means of protecting their identity, or enhancing their view of themselves. (Bagley, Verma, Mallick, & Young, 1979, p. 194)

It is clear from a perusal of these findings and others like them (Harter, 1998) that a good self-concept and adequate self-esteem are highly desirable qualities to foster in young children because no one wants children to suffer from the feelings and experiences just described. What teachers and parents need to understand more clearly is how to help children generate good feelings about themselves that are based on reality. These good feelings form the basis for healthy self-esteem.

RELATIONSHIP OF SELF-ESTEEM TO SELF-CONCEPT

Self-esteem and self-concept are closely related. *Self-concept* refers to an individual's idea of who she is, and *self-esteem* is a part of this since her feelings of self-esteem result from her reaction to what she judges herself to be and to her anticipation of being accepted or rejected (Harter, 1998; Kosnik, 1993). Thus a youngster who is well coordinated, who is sought after by her playmates, and who gets along well with her teacher will probably see herself as adequate and will possess good feelings of self-esteem, whereas an overweight high school girl suffering from a poor complexion and having few friends may come to think of herself as being unattractive and unlovable and as a result will hold herself in low esteem.

Is Positive Self-Esteem Related to Positive Social Behavior Toward Other People?

Research Question: Cauley and Tyler wanted to find out whether a child's positive self-concept was related to the prosocial behaviors of sharing, helping, and cooperating.

Research Method: To investigate this relationship, they studied 32 boys and 20 girls who were 4 and 5 years old. The majority of the children came from White, middle-class families.

The researchers used a combination of measures to find out about the children. They asked the children to assess themselves using the Purdue Self-Concept Scale for Preschool Children. This scale offers paired pictures showing a child being successful (e.g., running fast) or not being successful (e.g., not running fast) and asks the child to point to the picture that he feels best describes himself. They also used teacher evaluations of each youngster that ranked the frequency of helping, sharing, and cooperating behavior with other children and the teacher's perceptions of the child's self-concept.

In addition to the paper evaluations, trained observers recorded 20 minutes of observations of each child over several days' time. The observers recorded only instances of the prosocial behaviors included in the study: sharing, helping, and cooperating.

Results: Careful statistical analysis revealed that some factors such as gender, age, family size, and number of years in day care were not related to the prosocial behaviors selected for study.

When the researchers looked at the relationship between the presence of positive self-esteem and the three prosocial behaviors, only one of the three was found to be significantly related ($p < .01$)

to self-concept. This was the amount of cooperative behavior various children demonstrated during the observation periods. As the authors put it, "a child with a positive self-concept has less need to engage in competitive interactions with other children and is more willing to engage in cooperative behavior" (p. 57). They found that when cooperative prosocial behaviors were initiated *by the child,* the result was likely to be more effective than when the behavior was urged upon him from without. Finally the study revealed that teacher assessments of the child's self-concept and the child's self-assessment matched closely.

Implications for Teaching: In these days when so much of the world seems involved in tooth-and-nail competition, it is heartening to find information that suggests a practical way to foster cooperation rather than competition among children. Evidently when children think well of themselves, this frees them to relate more generously and less selfishly with their peers, particularly when the impulse to cooperate comes from within themselves rather than being teacher suggested.

The other finding of note is the correlation between teachers' knowledge of children's feelings about themselves and the feelings actually reported by the children. Apparently teachers should trust their judgment when assessing how children feel about themselves. That evaluation could alert teachers to the necessity of helping some children increase their self-esteem by applying the recommendations included in this chapter.

Source: From "The Relationship of Self-Concept to Prosocial Behavior in Children," by K. Cauley and B. Tyler, 1989, Early Childhood Research Quarterly, 4(1), 51–60.

SOURCES OF SELF-ESTEEM

Although individuals should ultimately develop *internal* resources for generating self-esteem, in the early stages of growth the child's feelings of self-esteem come from the people around her. Parents are very significant influences (Coopersmith, 1967; Stipek, Recchia, & McClintic, 1992a). As children move out into the larger world, the opinions of other adults such as teachers become important, too, as do the opinions of their peers. That society also has an impact is evident from studies indicating a higher percentage of people of minority groups possess low self-esteem than people of nonminorities do (Fitzgerald, Lester, & Zuckerman, 1999; Nieto, 1992). Because the unhappy effects of persistent prejudice on the self-image and self-esteem of minority children cannot be overestimated, an entire chapter is devoted to a discussion of ways to sustain or improve the self-image of such youngsters (chapter 13).

Since so many powerful factors influence the development of self-esteem, teachers should not believe that they can completely alter the way a child sees herself. The numerous research studies cited by Harter (1998), however, support the idea that in addition to the family, other adults such as teachers can establish policies in their classrooms that will help build a child's self-esteem, and they can meticulously avoid employing practices likely to have destructive side effects.

Regan's sense of self is much enhanced by this scrapbook that includes a page for every child in the group.

COMMON SCHOOL PRACTICES LIKELY TO REDUCE SELF-ESTEEM: SELF-ESTEEM IS LIKE A BALLOON

One way to think of self-esteem is to picture it as a balloon—a balloon that just a little prick of criticism will puncture and collapse. Unfortunately, teachers can prick these balloons in many ways every day, often when they do not intend to.

Using Comparison and Competition to Motivate Good Behavior

Although younger children seem unaffected (Stipek, Recchia, & McClintic, 1992b), competitiveness reaches a peak in children around the age of 4 to 5 years (Stott & Ball, 1957). It is all too easy for the teacher to use this fact to obtain quick results by asking, "I wonder who can get her coat on quickest today?" or by commenting, "See how carefully Shirley is putting her blocks away? Why can't you do it like that?" The trouble with motivating behavior by drawing such comparisons and setting up competitive situations is that only a few children "win" under this system. Even the child who turns out to be "best" and whose self-esteem has presumably been enhanced pays an unfortunate price because she has obtained that good feeling at the expense of the other children's well-being and may have earned their dislike in the process.

A more desirable way to use comparison is by invoking it in relation to the child's own past performance (Katz, 1994). This can be a true source of satisfaction for her when the teacher says, "My goodness, Ajeenah, you're learning to pump better and better every time you try!" or, "Remember the way you used to bite people? You haven't done that in a long time now. I'm proud of you!"

Overhelping and Overprotecting Children

Teachers may unintentionally lower a child's self-esteem by doing too much for her. Thus they rush in to carry the bucket of water so that it will not slop or without thinking put all the shoes and socks on the children following nap time. Helping in these ways has the virtues of saving time and ensuring that the job will be done properly, as well as keeping the teacher busy. But it is much more desirable to wait and let children do things for themselves since this allows them to experience the triumph of independence such achievements bring.

Judging Children Within Their Hearing

Children often develop ideas of who they are from hearing what other people say about them. Sometimes this happens in direct form, as when the teacher says impatiently, "Come along now; you're always so slow," or asks, "How can you be so selfish?" Other children are also prone to deliver pronouncements such as, "You pig! You never share anything," or, "Hazel is a pooh-pooh pants, Hazel is a pooh-pooh pants!" Labels such as these tend to stick; enough of them plastered on a child can convince her that she is neither liked nor worth much, so she might as well not try. This is one reason why teaching children to use self-report rather than verbal attack is so important. Verbal attacks are too destructive to other people's self-esteem.

Consider the difference in effect between the child who shouts, "I'm so mad I'd like to sock you! You gotta let me play!" and the one who sneers, "Aw, I don't like you anyway—you stink!"

Sometimes negative evaluations are not delivered directly to the child but are said over her head to someone else instead: "My, aren't we in a terrible temper today!" "I see she's having a hard day again!" "There's no point in asking *her*—she always holds on like grim death." Somehow overheard comments have a special, painful power to compel belief. Teachers should avoid making them not only for this reason but also because they may hurt a child's feelings and can strengthen a negative self-image. On a subtler level, talking over children's heads implies that they are not important enough to be included directly in the conversation (Katz, 1997).

POSITIVE METHODS OF ENHANCING SELF-ESTEEM

Unconditional Positive Regard

The most effective way to help a child build a basic feeling of self-esteem is, unfortunately, also the most elusive for some teachers to achieve: It is the ability to feel and project what Carl Rogers terms *unconditional positive regard.* This kind of fundamental acceptance and approval of each child is not contingent on her meeting the teacher's expectations of what she should be; it simply depends on her being alive, being herself, and being in the group. A good test of being accepting or not is to become aware of what one is usually thinking about when looking at the children. Ask yourself, "Am I taking time to enjoy the children, or am I looking at each one with a critical eye—noting mainly what behavior should be improved?" If you catch yourself habitually noting only what should be changed, then this is a sign you are losing sight of half the pleasure of teaching, which is to appreciate the children and enjoy who they are right now, at this particular moment in time—no strings attached.

This ability to be uncritical implies a kind of faith in the way the child will turn out, an attitude that subtly makes her aware that the teacher has confidence she will grow in sound directions. There is no substitute for these underlying feelings of trust and confidence in the child. Some teachers are fortunate enough to have developed optimism about people as a result of their own trust-building childhood experiences, some gain it from long experience with children themselves, and some acquire it by means of psychotherapeutic treatment, which helps restore their own confidence as well as their faith in others.

Acceptance of the child as she is also includes accepting her right to be different from the teacher and from other children. Here again, ethnic and cultural differences and various disabilities come particularly to mind. Teachers can make a significant contribution to increasing the self-esteem of such children by unconditionally valuing them and by using themselves as models to influence the attitude of the other children and their families.

Honest Recognition and Praise

Rewarding a child with praise is usually the first way teachers think of to build self-esteem. Unfortunately, sometimes praise is the *only* method they think of. Actually it is only one of several and perhaps not one of the better ways to enhance a child's feelings of self-worth (Damon, 1995).

Morgan (1984) lists more than 80 research projects that have been carried out on the effects such external rewards as praise or prizes have on motivating repeated behavior. These studies have asked the question "Do children work harder when they receive a reward?" (praise is one kind of reward) and the answer generally has been no!

Even the effects of praise vary quite a bit (Kohn, 1993). If you do use praise, remember that to be an effective esteem raiser and motivator, praise should include information about something specific a child has achieved; that is, praise should be based on performance. Used in that context, it can heighten the inner *intrinsic* satisfaction of the child. For example, it is better to say to a 4-year-old, "Thanks for letting Mary Lou play; it cheered her up," than to say, "You sure are a nice little boy!" Erikson is right when he says, "Children cannot be fooled by empty praise and condescending encouragement" (1963).

We must be wary of teachers who use praise continually as a means of reinforcing behavior and who often dole it out in such a mechanical way that it comes to have almost no meaning at all. On the other hand, some teachers hardly ever take time to comment favorably on what a child has done. They seem to feel that praise weakens character and that individuals should do things simply because it is right to do them. But praise that is merited should surely be given; everyone who has experienced it knows that honest recognition is sweet indeed.

Using encouragement rather than praise is another effective way of building self-esteem while recognizing what a child is accomplishing. Such comments as, "I bet you can do it if you try," or, "Look how much work you've done," or "Atta girl!" encourage children without passing judgment on what they've done.

Children also need to learn that failing at something is not the end of the world. For this reason it is also important to appreciate the effort of children when they have not been successful. They particularly need encouragement at this point since the reward inherent in successful accomplishment has not been realized. The teacher can say, "I see how hard you've worked on that," or, "I'm proud of you; you really tried," or, "It takes a while to learn to do that. You've really stuck with it; it's *hard* to learn things sometimes, isn't it?"

Then the teacher might follow up that comment by asking a question—coupled with an offer of support if needed—for example, "I guess that didn't work. How can we fix it?" or, "Want to try again? I'll stand here and see if I can help you balance," or, "Tell you what. Why don't I hold the box for you? Then I bet you could get all those crayons back in." Responses like these are worthwhile because they encourage the child to persist—to continue trying—and persistence is a valuable part of achieving mastery. Note also that these responses illustrate ways of encouraging a child to move closer to the growing edge of her abilities—à la the zone of proximal development so beloved by Vygotsky.

Respect

Respecting the child is such a high-minded phrase that examples of behavior must be provided in order to see how respect can be implemented when working with young children. One basic way to show respect is to abide by the child's decision when she has been given a valid choice (see also chapters 6 and 11). When a teacher does this, she is really saying, "What you want is important. I have confidence that you know yourself better than I do, and I count on you to choose what will enhance your existence most." Children also sense respect when the teacher asks their opinion and listens carefully to their replies. Even young children can answer "Do you think we should . . . " kinds of questions.

Another way to show respect and thus sustain the child's self-esteem is to avoid humiliating a child in front of other people. It is best to carry out disciplinary measures as unobtrusively as possible. Belittling a child's behavior at any time is, of course, fundamentally disrespectful as well as destructive of self-esteem.

A third valuable way to show respect is to pay the child the compliment of explaining the reason behind the rule. Coopersmith (1967), who carried out an extensive study of children possessing high self-esteem, found that parents of such youngsters were firm in their control of them but also took time to explain the reason for their actions. Such reasoning confers respect since it assumes that the child is important enough to be entitled to an explanation and intelligent enough to comprehend it.

Finally, we must never lose sight of the fact that children are intensely aware of how teachers feel about their families. Teachers who truly respect and value the child's family show this each day in the way they welcome them to the classroom, by the way they avoid making derogatory remarks about them, and by the way they really listen to a family member who has something to say.

HELPING THE CHILD ACHIEVE COMPETENCE

Positive regard, respect, and merited praise are sound in that they help build positive self-pictures for children, but they have one weakness in common: *They all depend on the goodwill of another person for implementation.* Yet the ultimate goal should be the internalization of esteem so that the individual will not remain permanently dependent on others to supply her feelings of self-worth.

But how can children be helped to shift from relying on external praise or other supports to experiencing *intrinsic* satisfaction from within themselves? The most effective answer is that helping children achieve competence is the surest way to instill internal feelings of self-worth. Every time a youngster does something that works out well, be it standing up for her rights in the trike area or pumping herself on the swing, the reward of success is inherent in the act, and the child feels competent because of what she *did*, not because of what someone said. This knowledge of capability makes children (and adults, too, for that matter) feel good about themselves, feel that they are worth something—*and in that knowledge lies the foundation of inner self-esteem* (J. Greenberg, Pysozynski, & Solomon, 1995).

Robert White (1968, 1976) summed this up when he pointed out that people have a continuing drive toward competence, which is a powerful motivating agent in their lives. He defined competence as "effectiveness in dealing with the environment." This sense of being effective builds the child's self-esteem internally. No one can take it away from her, and no one, as White comments, "can confer this experience. No one can give another person a sense of competence" (1976, p. 9). What teachers *can* do is provide many opportunities for children to *become* competent. A good place to begin is by asking oneself, at the start of every morning, "How can I help each child experience success today?" Once a child is able to do something well, be it practicing diplomacy in the housekeeping corner or using the brace and bit, she has gained a small portion of confidence in herself that does not require the plaudits of others to sustain it.

Allow Children to Experience Mastery by Making Their Own Choices and by Being as Independent as Possible

Making choices and being independent are two ways to encourage competence that have already been discussed. Maccoby (1980) speaks of this as keeping the *locus of control* as much within the hands of the child as possible. She cites several studies that support the value of encouraging children to feel that they are in control of their environment at least part of the time. Of course, this should not be interpreted as meaning that the teacher or parent should submit unquestioningly to every passing whim. Rather, it does mean that encouraging children to make choices and decisions and to do things for themselves is worth doing whenever reasonable and possible since granting them such "power" reduces their feelings of helplessness and increases their feelings of mastery by placing the locus of control within rather than outside themselves.

More recently Albert Bandura (1997) has called this development of autonomy *self-efficacy*. He defines *self-efficacy* as the individual's belief in her or his power to reach particular goals, and he presents a thorough and convincing explanation of how efficacy is attained and how it contributes to the individual's sense of competence and self-worth throughout the span of life.

Along with encouraging children to develop autonomy and a sense of efficacy by making decisions for themselves when appropriate goes establishing reasonable expectations of achievement by the teacher. For instance, a teacher who wishes to build self-esteem in a newly generous little boy appreciates his helpfulness when he volunteers to pass the snack but overlooks the fact that he has served himself the largest portion first, just as she thanks the child who has stuffed his boots away in his cubby but refrains from telling him to fix them so that the toes point out.

Provide Opportunities That Are Challenging but Not Excessively Difficult to Give Children the Chance to Test Themselves Against Difficulties

The derring-do of 4-year-olds is a prime example of this desire to make things a little bit harder every time they attempt them. (The reader may recall learning the game of jacks and its steady progression from Rolling Down Broadway to the more difficult game Around the World and finally on to Eggs-in-a-Basket and Shooting Star.) In general, children should always be allowed to attempt more difficult feats as they think of them unless it is evident they have not anticipated any serious dangers that may be involved.

Something else first-time teachers may forget is that it takes practice to acquire a new skill. I have seen students offer an activity once and assume that that would be sufficient opportunity for the children to learn how to do it. Be it using the scooter or cutting around a circle or playing lotto, other things being equal, repeated practice increases competence, so it is important to provide chances for children to do something more than once if you want them to become skillful.

Emphasize the Value of Building Cross-Sex Competencies of Various Kinds

It is still the case that girls often grow up unable to use power saws or drills or lacking even a rudimentary understanding of the combustion engine and that boys are sometimes described as limited in their ability to express emotion. Most women (and many men) have only to recall the last time they dealt with a garage mechanic to realize the sense of inferiority such incompetence produces. Methods of remedying these deficiencies are discussed at greater length in chapter 13, so it is only noted here that broader and more various educational experiences for both sexes should be encouraged.

Make Certain That Children with Disabilities Experience Opportunities to Build Competence, Too

Although opportunities to achieve success are important for all children, they are particularly important for children who have special difficulties they must overcome. It's so easy to underestimate and overhelp these youngsters with disabilities in the interests of kindness or, more realistically, saving time. Perhaps it is as simple a thing as handing the child a crayon instead of waiting for her to reach for it, or answering for her when another youngster asks her a question. It isn't just one tiny episode that makes a difference. It's when all three episodes are added together that the child gets the message she cannot be effective or competent. Then her fragile balloon of self-esteem begins to deflate.

Although we often speak of the *child who has special needs*, perhaps in these circumstances it would be better to think of the *teacher who has special needs* and identify what a few of these are if the child is to prosper. When working with such a youngster, some of the teacher's special needs that come to mind are the teacher needs to know what the child is able to do *and* what she can probably do next, she needs to feel and project confidence that the child wants to attempt something for herself, and she needs to have patience and wait that extra minute it may take for the child to experience success.

Provide Many Different Ways for Children to Experience Success

Sheer variety of activities is important here since one child may excel at assembling puzzles, whereas another's forte may be hanging by her heels on the jungle gym. It is important also not to be too hidebound when selecting curriculum activities because a youngster may possess a special skill not usually thought of as being age appropriate but that, when well used, can confer distinction on her and enrich the lives of the other children. Our center, for example, had a child attending who loved to embroider. She knew several stitches, and two or three of the older children relished learning them from her even though "everyone knows" that embroidery is too difficult for preschool children to carry out successfully.

Offer Many Opportunities to Accomplish Meaningful Work

One of the most effective yet often overlooked ways to generate feelings of mastery and self-worth is to provide many opportunities for children to do meaningful work. This work should not be limited to tedious chores such as putting all the blocks back on the shelves. Many jobs such as washing the finger-painting aprons, dying eggshells to crush for collage, or mixing paint are fun, not too difficult, and provide valuable opportunities to do something that helps the group. What's more, they all have tangible results—accomplishments that can be viewed with satisfaction and that help children see doing work in a positive light. This is a very healthy attitude to instill since working is a cornerstone of so much adult existence and satisfaction.

Doing meaningful work helps children feel valued and important.

Offer Creative Activities Because They Provide Excellent Opportunities for Experiencing Competence

There is so much latitude for individual abilities and differences to be expressed in creative activity areas that they must be singled out as avenues for building self-esteem. Indeed, as the work from Reggio Emilia demonstrates, the very essence of a child's ideas and being can be revealed through paint or clay or collages. What adult has not experienced the satisfaction and boost in self-esteem that came from attempting a new art or craft? Children feel the same way. It feels good to make something attractive generated by oneself. Therefore the value of creative self-expression is an avenue to building self-esteem that must not be overlooked.

In Addition to Competence in Activities and Motor Skills, Interpersonal Competence Is of Great Importance

The final vital source of positive self-esteem stems from the child's perception of how adequate she is in dealing with other people. The youngster who believes that she can get along with others, that she is liked by them, and that she generally manages to have her needs met is likely to feel socially competent and able to take care of herself. Chapters 10, 11, and 12 present more detailed discussions of how to help children gain these all-important skills and competencies in interpersonal relationships.

SUMMARY

When working with young children, practices such as using comparison and competition, being overprotective, and judging children within their hearing should be avoided since these tend to lower self-esteem.

Teachers who want to increase feelings of self-esteem in the children have many more effective ways of accomplishing this goal. These include the expression of unconditional positive regard, the provision of recognition and sincere praise, and the expression of genuine respect.

Finally the attainment of competence should be valued highly. The more opportunities children have to acquire instrumental and interpersonal skills, the more likely they are to acquire an inner conviction of their own ability to cope. This is particularly true for children who have disabilities. The inner conviction of basic competence is, in the long run, the most satisfactory builder of self-esteem.

Questions and Activities

1. Pick a school or family life situation (perhaps a trip to the grocery store) for role playing and include in it as many possible ways as you can think of to deflate and lower the self-esteem of the "children" who are involved.

2. Select a youngster in your school who seems to suffer from low self-esteem. As far as you can tell, what are some principal reasons for this self-image? What could you do to modify it in a more positive direction?

3. Many activities, even for college students, center on externalized sources of self-esteem. Grades are a prime example of external input. What college-related policies appear likely to produce internalized sources of positive self-esteem?

4. This chapter questions the value of using competition to motivate behavior because competition often reduces feelings of self-esteem. Is this necessarily true in all cases? Can competition ever be both satisfying and desirable?

5. Listen to yourself for several days while you are working with the children. Every day put 10 pennies into your pocket and whenever you hear yourself talking to someone else about a child in front of her, transfer a penny to your other pocket. Can you go an entire day without shifting any pennies?

6. Go down your roster and try to identify opportunities during the past week in which each child had the chance to gain competence in some activity. Did each youngster have a chance to accomplish this in some manner?

Self-Check Questions for Review

Content-Related Questions

1. Explain how low self-esteem and being prejudiced against other people are related.

2. Describe what methods Cauley and Tyler (1989) used to find out whether a relationship existed between positive self-esteem and the prosocial behaviors of helping, sharing, and cooperating with others. What would be the weakness of using only one of these approaches to study this subject?

3. What are three common things teachers might do that tend to lower the self-esteem of the children in their care?

4. Is praise the most effective way of increasing the self-esteem of a young child? Explain the reasoning behind your answer.

5. Why is competence such an effective builder of self-esteem?

6. What is the difference between extrinsic and intrinsic methods of increasing self-esteem? Which do I as the author think is more desirable, and why?

Integrative Questions

1. Suggest some reasons why having a strong sense of positive self-esteem might make a child more likely to cooperate with other children than she would be if she had a poor self-concept.

2. Imagine a new rule has been instituted at your school: You may not praise a child for anything during the day, and yet you must increase the child's self-esteem substantially. How would you go about implementing this rule?

3. Give an example, other than praise, of something that could be an *extrinsic* source of self-esteem for an adult and then give an example of something that could be an *intrinsic* source of self-esteem for an adult.

4. Briefly describe three children whom you know well and propose what you could do to help each of them gain a new skill.

5. How does building cross-sex competencies contribute to girls' sense of self-esteem? How does it contribute to boys' sense of self-esteem? Might it detract from boys' self-esteem? Explain your conclusions about that answer.

Coordinating Videotape

I'm glad I'm me. Tape #5. The whole child: A caregiver's guide to the first five years. The Annenberg/CPB Collection, P.O. Box 2345, South Burlington, VT 05407–2345. *I'm Glad I'm Me* shows how children internalize feelings of self-worth, identifies techniques for respecting and recognizing children's accomplishments, and teaches the importance of offering children opportunities for making individual choices.

References for Further Reading

Overviews

Hewitt, D., & Heideman, S. (1998). *The optimistic class-room: Creative ways to give children hope.* St. Paul, MN: Redleaf. Following a down-to-earth general discussion, the authors present many examples of activities that foster development of such skills as building empathy and reframing one's point of view to broaden understanding and acceptance of other people. Upbeat and practical.

Katz, L. (1997). *Fostering children's social competence: The teacher's role.* Washington, DC: National Association for the Education of Young Children. In her chapter "Creating the Context for Social Development," Katz describes an environment conducive to establishing healthy attitudes both toward others and toward the self. *Highly recommended.*

Owens, K. (1995). *Raising your child's inner self-esteem: The authoritative guide from infancy through the teen years.* New York: Plenum Press. This book provides a thorough discussion of the myriad ways our behavior with children can enhance or reduce their feelings of self-worth.

Developing Mastery

Eaton, M. (1997). Positive discipline: Fostering the self-esteem of young children. *Young Children, 52*(6), 43–46. Eaton explains the value of putting decision making for their behavior in the hands of children by providing opportunities for them to make choices in discipline situations.

Hauser-Cram, P. (1998). I think I can, I think I can: Understanding and encouraging mastery motivation in young Children. *Young Children, 53*(4), 67–71. This review of research emphasizes that mastery and the ensuing sense of achievement and competence are integral components of self-worth.

Katz, L. G. (1993). *Distinctions between self-esteem and narcissism: Implications for practice.* Urbana, IL: ERIC Clearinghouse on Elementary and Early Childhood Education. Katz delivers well-taken comments on ways to foster true self-esteem in children.

Kohn, A. (1993). *Punished by rewards: The trouble with gold stars, incentive plans, A's, praise, and other bribes.* Boston: Houghton Mifflin. Kohn makes a well-documented, impassioned plea against extrinsic rewards and urges the substitution of intrinsic rewards in their place.

Encouraging the Development of Self-Esteem in All Children

Andrew, C., & Tracy, N. (1996). First steps toward competence: Promoting self-esteem and confidence in young children with disabilities. In L. E. Powers, G. H. S. Singer, & J. Sowers (Eds.), *On the road to autonomy: Promoting self-competence in children and youth with disabilities.* Baltimore, MD: Paul H. Brookes. This chapter explains ways family and support staff can contribute to building independence and hence self-esteem in children with special needs. *Highly recommended.*

Hopkins, S., & Winerts, J. (1990). *Discover the world: Empowering children to value themselves, others, and the earth.* Philadelphia, PA: New Society. This unusual book offers numerous curriculum charts replete with ideas for integrating information about various cultures, friends, self-esteem, and so forth into the preschool day. Since it is published in cooperation with Concerned Educators Allied for Safe Environment (CEASE), the emphasis refreshingly is on conflict management and peace-related concerns. *Highly recommended.*

Meaningful Work

Jacobs, N. L., Changler, T. M., & Hausknecht, D. R. (1996). Unraveling the mystery of parents' work. *Early Childhood Education Journal, 24*(1), 61–64. The authors explain how to help children attach value to work by making their parents' jobs more real to them.

For the Advanced Student

Bandura, A. (1997). *Self-efficacy: The exercise of control.* New York: Freeman. The empowerment of people is the central theme running through this very long but readable book written by a distinguished psychologist.

Harter, S. (1998). The development of self-representation. In W. Damon & N. Eisenberg (Eds.), *Handbook of child psychology: Vol. 3. Social, emotional, and personality development.* New York: Wiley.

Harter provides a thorough, scholarly review of current and past theories and research about self-awareness. An indispensable reference for the serious student.

Rodgers, D. B. (1998). Supporting autonomy in young children. *Young Children, 53*(3), 75–80. Rodgers concisely summarizes recent research related to the value of developing the ability to be "governed by oneself."

Stipek, D., Recchia, S. A., & McClintic, S. (1992a). Self-evaluation in young children. *Monographs of the Society for Research in Child Development, 57*(1, Serial No. 226), 1–84. The results of these studies, which have to do with the expression of feelings and competitiveness, are well worth reviewing. The material is also valuable as an example of how to investigate interesting questions in age- and child-appropriate ways.

White, R. W. (1976). *The enterprise of living: A view of personal growth* (2nd ed.). New York: Holt, Rinehart & Winston. White's chapter on competence is a classic in the field. It discusses competence in relation to development, traces its growth through various stages, and talks about why the concept is significant. The entire book is superlative reading.

chapter eight

Tender Topics

Helping Children Master Emotional Crises[1]

H a v e   y o u   e v e r   w o n d e r e d . . .

What to advise a parent who asks whether he should tell his son that his grandfather is dying?

How to help a 3-year-old get ready to have a hernia repaired?

What you should do when you are helping a child undress for nap and find something that looks like a cigarette burn under his arm?

. . . IF YOU HAVE, THE MATERIAL IN THE FOLLOWING PAGES WILL HELP YOU.

I, a stranger and afraid
In a world I never made.

A. E. Housman (1922)

---

[1] *I am indebted to Donna Dempster (McClain) of Cornell University for suggesting that a chapter on "tender topics" be included in the revised edition of* The Whole Child.

Young children are as subject to stress and strain when a crisis strikes their families as adults are, but this may be difficult for the family to recognize who often hope that if nothing is said, the child will be unaware of the problem. Or they may be so overwhelmed by the crisis that they have little emotional reserve available to help the child through his troubles at the same time. But children are keen sensors of emotional climates, and they are aware of telephone conversations, comments by neighbors, and so forth. As Furman (1974) says, "Children are so observant of and sensitive to their parents moods and nuances of behavior that, in our experience, it is impossible to spare them from knowing or to deceive them about the true nature of events" (p. 18). Indeed the secrecy and avoidance often practiced by families when crises occur may serve only to deepen the child's anxiety. It is far better, then, to reduce this misery when we can by facing facts squarely and by providing as much stability as possible than to worsen the problem by failing to deal with it.

Moreover, the experience of crisis is not always undesirable in itself. It is important to realize that adverse circumstances do not always weaken children. In their book *Overcoming the Odds: High-Risk Children From Birth to Adulthood*, Werner and Smith (1992) trace the development of Hawaiian children living under the stressful conditions of chronic poverty from birth to adulthood. They found that even in the harshest circumstances, many children succeeded despite such adversity. In a comparison of these resilient children with their less successful peers, three clusters of protective factors were found to be significant: The child had (a) at least average intelligence and personality attributes that drew forth positive responses from other people (robustness, vigor, and a sociable temperament), (b) ties of affection with parent substitutes such as grandparents or siblings, and (c) an external support system such as a youth group, church, or school. Wang and Gordon (1994) also present evidence that some children can find purpose and hope in some of the most apparently hopeless situations.

So as we approach this discussion of the perils and problems that will confront many of the children we teach, we should remember what Werner and Smith (1982) say so well:

> The terrors of our nature and the world remind us forever how vulnerable we are. Hence biological and behavioral scientists have spent a great deal of time, energy, and resources exploring the roots of our aggression, alienation, disease, and unease. What is often overlooked, but seems more awesome and miraculous, is our resilience as a species. (p. 152)

Crisis *can* constitute "a dangerous opportunity" for growth if it is handled well. Needless to say, this is not always the case. Young children seem particularly vulnerable to potential disaster in part because they lack experience and in part because they are relatively powerless and helpless. If they are lucky, they have adults who can help them through these difficult times. Since preprimary teachers occasionally are confronted with such opportunities, the following material is included.

WHAT CONSTITUTES A CRISIS?

We usually think of a crisis as being something sudden, and surely death or illness or a trip to the emergency room all fall in this category. Other crises are of longer duration: the mental illness of a parent, a divorce, a new baby, physical abuse, moving to a new neighborhood, and even adjusting to child care outside the home.

Some crises are unhappy events—loss of a job, for example—and some are happier occasions—a marriage, perhaps, or the adoption of a child. The one thing all crises have in common, whether sudden or chronic, unhappy or joyful, is that they all involve change. These changes occur far more commonly than one would wish. For example, Schiono and Quinn (1994) report that "it is projected that nearly half of all babies born today will spend some time in a one-parent family which occurred as a result of single parenthood or divorce" (p. 15), and the Dougy Center for Grieving Children (1999) reports that 1 in 20 children will lose one or both parents by age 15.

Fortunately some effects of crises can be mitigated if families and teachers know where to turn and what to do. It is my hope that the following material will be useful in this regard. *Because of the nature and gravity of the crises presented, however, the reader should understand that this chapter represents only the barest minimum of information and that it is intended only as a starting point, not as a comprehensive guide.*

SOME GENERAL PRINCIPLES FOR HELPING FAMILIES DEAL WITH CRISES

There is no other time in life when the parent is more important to the child than during a time of crisis. Teachers, psychologists, social workers, and sometimes police officers may also offer meaningful aid, but the family is the most significant influence; for this reason the fundamental goal of the teacher should be to support the family as well as possible. There are a number of ways to accomplish this.

Make Certain the Parents Understand That It Is Better to Include the Child in the Situation Than to Exclude Him

Particularly in matters of death, serious parental illness, or job loss, adults may attempt to shield children from what is happening, but as mentioned before, children always know when something is wrong. Parents may not realize how frightened this can make youngsters when they are left to fantasize about the nature of the trouble or the reason for it. It is the primeval fear of the unknown. To remedy this, the teacher should encourage the family to explain in simple terms *but not gory detail* the nature of the emergency.

The same recommendation applies to expressing feelings: Children should be allowed to participate in feelings of concern or grief, rather than be excluded. Again I caution that this principle should be followed within reason. The point to get across to the family is that it is all right for children to understand that grown-ups sometimes feel sad or frightened or upset—as long as this is mingled with steady assurances from family members that the child will be taken care of and that life will continue.

Try Not to Overreact, No Matter What the Parent Tells You

Teachers can be of little help if they allow themselves to become as upset as the parents are over a crisis, although I cannot deny that crises such as suicide or the rape of a 4-year-old are deeply shocking to everyone. However, if teachers can present a model of relative calm as well as concern, they can influence the parents to behave in the same manner. By providing information on what will help the child, they can encourage the institution of rational steps in dealing with the situation.

Teachers should also guard themselves against being overcome with pity for a youngster or the parents since pity is not beneficial for the family, either. I recall one situation in which a little boy, returning to school after his mother died, was greeted by a teacher who threw her arms around him and burst into tears, saying, "Oh, you poor child! Whatever will you and your poor papa do now?" This unfortunate response overwhelmed the boy and froze him into an inexpressive state from which it was very difficult to retrieve him. One would think that an adult would have more sense, but crises do strange things to people.

Of course, pity is not always so obvious. It may manifest itself in the subtler forms of overindulgence or spoiling, and this is equally undesirable. Pity is a weakening experience for the person who is its object. It encourages feelings of despair, self-pity, and helplessness (C. Peterson, Maier, & Seligman, 1993)—the exact opposites of competence. It is far better to substitute compassionate understanding and to express quiet confidence that although the family and child feel bad right now, you are certain they will ultimately come through the experience all right and that you are there to do whatever you can to help them.

Do Not Violate the Privacy of the Family

Particularly when something sensational has happened, be it a car involved in an accident or a home burning to the ground, it can be tempting to participate in the tragedy by gossiping about it with other parents. It is impossible to avoid discussion of such events entirely when they are common knowledge in the community, but care should be taken to keep private details private. For one thing, any parents who hear the teacher repeat such personal details are bound to conclude that the teacher will gossip about their personal affairs, too. For another thing, behaving in this way is a breach of professional ethics.

Offer Yourself as a Resource

As chapter 3 emphasized, being a good listener is one way to offer yourself as a resource as long as parents do not come to feel that you are mainly interested in the sensational aspects of the crisis or that you cannot wait for them to stop talking so that you can offer advice. Remember also that sometimes families do not want any help; this desire must be respected, too.

Sometimes, after the emergency aspect has subsided, parents find it helpful when the teacher lends them a good reference book. If the resource center has a reserve of at least a few such basic books on hand, they can be instantly available when needed.

Finally the teacher can also be a resource for referral to other supporting agencies. This ticklish matter of referrals is discussed in greater detail in chapter 9, so I only comment here that it is necessary to be careful of offering referral resources too hastily lest the family interpret this as your wanting to get rid of them and their uncomfortable problem. Sometimes, however, it is better not to wait. Crises that result from a sudden deep shock or trauma, such as being in a severe automobile accident, experiencing rape, or witnessing a murder or suicide, require immediate psychological attention.

SOME GENERAL PRINCIPLES FOR HELPING THE CHILD DEAL WITH CRISES

Don't Ignore the Situation by Pretending It Hasn't Happened[2]

It takes a sensitive teacher to face a crisis with a child in a matter-of-fact way without overdoing it or rubbing it in. This is not to say that the teacher should imply that everything is fine and dandy and that getting over the disaster will be easy or that everything will be just as it was before. It is better to admit that it is not a happy time while making the point that it is not the end of the world, either.

It helps to be alert to clues that the child wants to talk about his feelings or that he has the problem on his mind. Sometimes this occurs long after the event in question. For example, one child in our center suffered a serious burn on her arm that caused her a good deal of misery. Although she seemed fully recovered, later events proved she had not come to terms with it completely at that time. Several months afterward, she happened to be part of a group of youngsters who went on a field trip to inspect the human skeleton in the biology department. She was very quiet while she surveyed the bones, and slipping her hand into the teacher's on the way home, she whispered to her, "But what happened to the skin?" To which the teacher responded, "Are you wondering if it got burned off?"— and all of Amy's concerns about skin and injuries came tumbling forth.

But it is best if the situation can be dealt with while it is happening. If the child is unable to bring the problem up, the teacher can provide play experiences for working through the event, or include a book on the subject at story time, or mention the problem casually when the opportunity for a quiet private interlude presents itself. Sometimes this can be done tactfully by saying, "I remember when I was little and had my tonsils out. I didn't know what was going to happen in the hospital. I wondered if my mother would stay, and if . . . [include a shrewd guess about what is troubling the particular child]. I wonder if you are wondering about that, too."

The focus of such discussions should be on what the child thinks and what he is worried about. Reassurance and explanation have their place in talking problems over with young children, but they are not nearly so helpful as listening and encouraging youngsters to express their worries through talk and, most valuably, through play (C. C. Norton & Norton, 1997).

---

[2]   For further discussion of coping with emotional disturbance in children, refer to chapter 9. Indications of disturbance are discussed in chapter 6.

Remember That It Is All Right for Children (and Adults) to Cry and to Feel Bad

We early childhood teachers do better than most other people at accepting children's rights to cry about everyday matters, but sometimes we find ourselves feeling very uncomfortable when children sob over more serious situations, such as the death of someone they love or a parent's going to jail. Perhaps this is because we know these griefs represent more serious situations, and so we feel more concerned and sorry that the child must go through those experiences. It is natural, when you care about someone, not to want the person to feel bad.

But it is important to remember that crying brings relief in serious situations, just as it does in more mundane ones and that this relief is valuable and helpful to the child. Therefore it is important for us not to cut off such a response because of our own discomfort and consequent need to comfort the child. Unfortunately feeling bad is a part of life, just as feeling joyful is. Teachers who realize this learn to endure and accept children's expressions of grief, rather than block them by providing too-swift reassurance, hastily distracting them, or telling them, "Don't feel bad . . . it's all right!"

This does not mean, of course, that one stands coldly by while a youngster sobs forlornly in a corner; supportive warmth and cuddling are appropriate comforts to provide for grieving children. It *does* mean that children should be encouraged to cry as well as to talk about their feelings if they feel the need to do so.

Provide Play Opportunities to Express and Clarify Feelings About the Crisis, and Try to Be on Hand to Help the Child Interpret Them

Imaginative play is a very satisfactory way for children to resolve their feelings about crises. Some kinds of play, such as hospital play, benefit children most if special equipment is provided. This might include a set of crutches, something that can substitute for shot needles (we use turkey basters for this purpose), aprons, surgical gowns, and masks. Hand puppets, little rubber dolls, dollhouse furniture, and a housekeeping corner well equipped with dolls and other paraphernalia of family life are props that can be used to express concerns related to the family situation.

An alert teacher can be aware of the turn the play is taking and help a troubled child ease his feelings. She might, for example, remain close enough to a housekeeping group to comment quietly to a 3-year-old pounding on a baby doll. "Gosh! You really want to show that baby she makes you mad! You want her to stop bothering you and crying so much. That's OK—it's OK to feel that way. You can pretend anything you want. Of course, we can't do that to the real baby even when we feel that way, but we can *pretend* anything we want. We can *feel* what we wish, but we must control what we do."

Play opportunities that permit the sublimated expression of feelings are also valuable (see chapter 12). Some materials are especially good as aggression relievers—dough and finger paint that can be pounded and squished, and simple hammering come to mind— and some are more relaxing and tension relieving—water play and swinging, for example. In general, unstructured materials that make few demands for "correct" performance are the most effective ones to use for such purposes.

Absolve the Child from Guilt

Young children are not good reasoners about cause and effect. Piaget has provided us with many examples in which children have reasoned that effect was the cause. (For instance, a child may see trees bending in the wind and conclude that trees bending make the wind blow!) Piaget also teaches us that young children are self-centered and see things mainly in relation to themselves. And finally we know children are prone to magical thinking, tending to believe that the wish has the same power as the act.

If we think about the implications of these developmental facts, it becomes easier to understand why children often conclude that they are the cause of the family's disaster— something usually so far from the actual truth it may not even occur to adults that the child is blaming himself for the trouble and feeling guilty and unhappy as a result (Dougy Center for Grieving Children, 1997; K. Miller, 1996). Warren (1977), in her excellent pamphlet *Caring*, suggests that the teacher can offer comfort in this kind of situation by helping the child separate adult from child business. For example, she suggests that the teacher might say:

> When your parents fight, that is very hard for you and sometimes makes you cry. But grown-ups' fighting is really grown-up business. Even if they are fighting about you, it is because they are mad at each other and not because of you or anything you did. (p. 22)

Maintain as Stable and Dependable an Atmosphere as Possible for the Child While in Your Care

When children are living through turmoil at home, the preschool or children's center provides a reassuring haven of safety for them because of the predictability of routines and consistent expectations for behavior. Knowing they can count on what to expect is vastly comforting to such youngsters.

The art of working with troubled preschoolers is knowing when to maintain that stability and when to make exceptions. These youngsters are emotionally needy and distressed, and the teacher should offer comfort and leniency when the child cannot eat, or is particularly irritable, or has trouble falling asleep, or frequently bursts into tears.

Sometimes teachers resist offering special comfort because they fear that it will make other children jealous or that giving special attention isn't "fair." It is true other children may comment, "How come he sits on your lap so much?" or, "You don't let me do that!" A helpful reply to these plaints can be, "Well, you know, in this school different people get different special things," followed by an example such as, "Remember when you bumped your chin on the slide and I held you and we put ice on it? Now it's Jamal's turn to have something special 'cuz he's feeling kind of sad today."

Help the Child Know What to Expect

Sometimes families know in advance that a crisis is approaching since they can generally anticipate such events as having a new baby, undergoing routine surgery, or moving to a new city. In such cases it is important not to build up unrealistic ideas of what such a change entails. The new baby will *not* be a wonderful little playmate for the preschooler as soon as she arrives, and ice cream is *not* going to taste wonderful after a tonsillectomy.

It is not necessary to be negative about changes and build undue apprehension. It just helps to talk over what will happen in advance to reduce the element of the unexpected. This is particularly true if the teacher and family talk with the youngster in terms of the plans being made for him—how his pet dog will get to the new house and where the family will have dinner on the day of the move. It is this kind of simple detail that children find reassuring and that adults sometimes forget to tell them because they already know the answers or consider them unimportant.

Help the Child Retain a Sense of Being in Control

During stormy times of crisis when children are upset, they often revert to less mature, more uncontrolled behavior. Therefore it may seem paradoxical to recommend they be given as many opportunities to control their lives as possible during such difficult periods, but there is sound reason for urging this strategy: Feeling "in charge" combats the sense of helplessness and panic the youngster must also contend with (Bandura, 1997).

Fortunately there are some age-appropriate, commonsense ways of helping even young children retain at least some confidence that they can control what is happening to them. For example, I have already alluded to the value of providing, when possible, appropriate information about what is going to happen. This frankness not only relieves the child of the burden of free-floating anxiety but also provides opportunities for him to ask questions and to make simple plans about how to cope with the change. "I hear you're going to your grandma's while Mommy's in the hospital. Have you thought about what you want to put in your suitcase?"

Opportunities to make simple choices and decisions also contribute to the child's sense of being in command. "Would you like to paint a picture to take to her, or would you rather make something else?"

Knowing what to do beforehand helps, too. For this reason, earthquake, fire, and tornado drills have value that goes beyond the commonsense one of improving safety. By helping children know how to protect themselves, such drills also increase their confidence and sense of control. This is an important alleviator of panic (Deskin & Steckler, 1996).

Finally it can restore a child's feelings of being in control if he is encouraged to do something for someone else; even such simple things as helping the teacher set out the cups or hammering in a nail can help a youngster retain his sense of being an able, effective person.

HELPING CHILDREN COPE WITH SPECIFIC CRISES

Adjusting to School and Dealing with the Parent Who Picks Up the Child Late

Ways of helping a child adjust to the center were already discussed in chapter 4, but it should be pointed out here, too, that coming to school can represent such a change in the child's life that it may be a real crisis from his point of view. Particularly if the adjustment is a difficult one, we should not underestimate the anguish he is experiencing when separated from his mother, and we should do all we can to alleviate it.

Moving from preschool to kindergarten is such a big change from the child's point of view that it, too, may constitute a crisis. Although we can alleviate the child's concern about this change in many sensible ways, studies continue to reveal a disheartening gulf between the two situations. For example, only 10% of primary schools reported systematic communication between kindergarten teachers and preschool teachers, and less than half of them had formal programs for visits by parents prior to enrollment. Worse yet, only 12% of primary schools used a curriculum designed to build on what the children had learned in preschool (Love & Logue, 1992).

In addition to deliberately increasing communication and coordination between the two situations—a process fraught with difficulties in many cases—there are some sensible, immediate actions everyone can take to ease the transition. Among these are scheduling a visit to the new school, talking over what will be expected of the child in the new setting without making him apprehensive, inviting parents to a come-to-school night in late summer, and generally following the procedures recommended in chapter 4 such as sending each child a special welcome letter.

Another part of attending school that can be a crisis to a child is a late pickup by his parent. I have known children to fly into a panic over this if it is not handled well by the teacher, so a few suggestions are in order. First, be careful to reassure the child that his parent *will* come and that you will stay with him until she does. It also is reassuring to say that you know some good reasons why she could be delayed (avoid speculating within the child's hearing about what various disasters may have befallen the parent along the way). Second, locate an alternative person to come as soon as possible. The entry record for each child should include the telephone numbers of at least three people to be contacted in case the child becomes ill during the day or the parent is late. However, do not let the child stand beside you as you dial number after number, getting no response! Remember, too, that *no child should ever be released to any adult who is not on the parent's list.*

Third, hold your temper and do not make the child pay for the parent's sins. It is really difficult at the end of a long day to wait and maybe miss the bus, but it is not the child's fault his parent is tardy. Some schools in which parents are consistently inconsiderate establish policies of charging extra for overtime care, or of not allowing the child to attend the next day, or of asking the parent to drive the teacher home if he missed the bus. These penalties should be avoided if possible since they breed ill will. It is usually sufficient to explain, when tempers have cooled, why the teacher prefers to leave on time and to ask the parent to be more considerate in the future.

Arrival of a New Baby

Parents who often go out of their way to prepare a youngster for a new baby during the 9-month wait somehow assume once the infant arrives that the preschooler will be delighted and certainly not jealous! But the reality of the mother's going to the hospital, possibly having someone unfamiliar take over at home meanwhile, and then seeing his world changed by the homecoming of the baby with all the extra demands on the parents' time and energy can turn out to be an unpleasant surprise to a preschooler.

These demands on parents' time that common sense and experience tell us are likely to take place have been measured in a study of firstborn children (Dunn & Kendrick, 1981). Researchers found that the arrival of the second child really *did* change the mother-firstborn relationship because the mother no longer spent as much time playing with the child or even beginning conversations with him. These changes were coupled (not surprisingly) with a significant rise in the number of negative confrontations that took place between them. No wonder the arrival of a baby constitutes a crisis in the lives of some youngsters!

Some simple remedies the teacher can apply to help alleviate these feelings of intrusion and jealousy are to not dwell on how wonderful it is to have a new baby in the family and to provide plenty of opportunities for the preschooler to act like a baby if he wants to. I recall one youngster who derived deep satisfaction from sitting in the privacy of my office being rocked and fed a bottle occasionally; she especially liked being burped!

It also helps to be realistic about the situation: Point out the things the baby *can't* do, as well as all the obvious privileges accruing to the preschooler. Help the older child find satisfaction in his own abilities and competencies that are related to being more mature and make it clear he will retain this advantage for a long time to come. After all, he will always be the older child.

Finally, if jealousy is interpreted to the parents as *the fear of being left out,* this may enable them to stop deploring or denying it and make plans that show the child he is definitely included. These can be as simple as reading to him by himself for a while before bedtime, or making a special time of going to the store together while the baby remains at home. When the baby begins to crawl, it is only fair to provide a safe place for the older child's belongings. Sometimes older children appreciate having a barrier they can hook across their doorways to keep the baby out. It is an interesting fact of human nature that the more protection of the child's rights the parent provides, the less protective the child will feel driven to be.

Hospitalization of the Child

Preparation in Advance

When surgery or other inpatient treatment for the child can be anticipated in advance, home and school have time to help the child grasp what will happen, and he is entitled to this information (K. Miller, 1996). After all it is his body that will, in a sense, be violated. Several good books for children about doctors and hospitals have been written, and a few bibliographies are included in the References for Further Reading at the end of this chapter. Hospital play and discussion of the forthcoming hospitalization will also help—not only to reassure the child himself but also to comfort his playmates. In these discussions I have found that using the word *fix* is helpful. Saying the doctor is going to fix a bad leg or the infected tonsils seems to be a concept that children can grasp and that they find comforting. Using hospital masks in dramatic play is also helpful since such masks are often one of the more frightening aspects of hospitalization (remember how upsetting masks are to some children at Halloween?).

Some hospitals permit children to visit before their stay. This possibility should be suggested to the parents even if it means they must ask the physician to make special

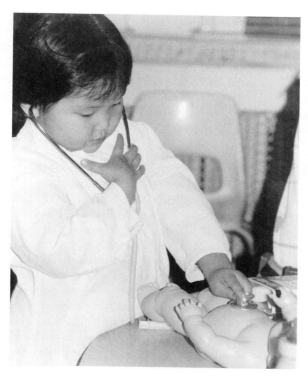

Hospital play helps children work through fears and misunderstandings.

arrangements. (I will never forget the relief of one of my own children, age 6, when she went for such a visit and discovered there would be a television set in her room, something that had not occurred to me to mention. Because she was not allowed to watch TV during the day at home, this was indeed a selling point for the hospital!)

Another encouraging trend is the policy of admitting children for minor surgery on a day basis only. Under these circumstances the youngster is admitted early in the morning before surgery and released to go home as soon as the effects of the anesthesia have worn off. This sensible procedure not only cuts hospital costs but also reduces the potential for misery and fright caused by parental separation.

When day surgery is out of the question, a longer stay is often mitigated by providing the child opportunities for play experiences during his stay in the hospital. Such opportunities help the child understand what is being done to him to get him well, puts him in temporary control of the situation, and allows him to express his concerns and anxieties (Lansdown, 1996).[3]

While the child is recovering and out of school, it is important to consider the feelings of his playmates, as well as the youngster himself, and to ask what they can do for their

---

[3]   *The professional people who offer these experiences are called* Child Life Specialists. *Training in early childhood education offers an excellent foundation for such a career.*

friend. Children often have very good ideas about this, such as baking something special or making a card with all their handprints on it.

Once again, on the child's return, more hospital play is definitely of value. This enables the child to work out his feelings and clarify them and helps inform the other children of what went on as well. Incidentally the mastery role of being doctor or nurse, as well as that of victim, is particularly satisfying to children who are struggling to overcome their feelings of angry helplessness often generated while under treatment. Many children find that giving pretend shots to someone else feels best of all.

Information for Parents

Parents should be encouraged to stay with their child as much of the time as possible while their youngster is hospitalized. Many hospitals today maintain open visiting privileges with no time limits for parents, but a few still do not. It is worthwhile becoming acquainted with the policies of various hospitals in your area so that you can inform parents about these in advance. Older 4- and 5-year-olds can also maintain contact with their families, particularly siblings, by talking with them on the telephone, and this should be encouraged.

Parents are usually cowed by hospitals and apprehensive of antagonizing staff. They do not know their rights, and they are also likely to be upset and worried. A chat beforehand can alleviate some of their concerns and enable them to insist on what is best for their child. Moreover they should be reassured that it is desirable for children to express their feelings. Indeed it is the quiet, passive child conforming unquestioningly to hospital routine who arouses the greatest concern among psychological consultants (Bowlby, 1973; Robertson & Robertson, 1989). Children should not be admonished ("Don't cry") or lied to ("This will just sting a little") or threatened ("You do it, or I'm going to go home!"). It is truly surprising that parents sometimes expect more of their children in these difficult and especially trying situations than they normally would dream of expecting at home.

Parents may also need to be prepared for the fact that children sometimes reject their mothers when they finally return home. This can come as a painful shock to families unless they have been prepared by an explanation of the reasons for the hostility. This reaction is thought to be an expression of the child's anger at being separated from his parents, particularly the mother, so in a way the hostility expressed by the child is a compliment to the family for the strength of their emotional bonds. But it can be a confusing compliment if it is misunderstood (Robertson & Robertson 1989).

The Emergency Room

One of the most trying crises for young children to experience is a visit to the emergency room. This is so because no advance preparation is possible, the parents are maximally upset, time is short, and the reason for being there is generally serious and painful. The prevalence of such emergencies is staggering: More than over 60,000 children seek emergency care every day in the United States ("Important Facts," 1993). It probably comes as no news to experienced parent-readers of these pages to learn that accidents are most likely to occur between 3 p.m. and 11 p.m. and that twice as many boys as girls require emergency care (Resnick & Hergenroeder, 1975).

One can make a very good parents' night out of offering a discussion of what to do in the emergency room to buffer the child from the worst shocks. Recommendations for parents include staying with the child as much as possible, staying as calm as possible, explaining very simply to the child what is going to happen next so that he is not taken completely by surprise when a physician suddenly materializes with a shot needle, and modeling fortitude by explaining with assurance that it may not feel good but that the doctor has to do whatever she is doing since it will help the child get well.

Hospitalization of Parents

A rare series of three studies reported by E. P. Rice, Ekdahl, and Miller (1971) reveals that emotional problems are likely to result for children whenever a parent is hospitalized for any length of time, be it for physical or mental illness. The impact of mental illness, particularly illness of the mother, causes the most marked difficulties. At least half the children studied gave evidence of such disturbance. This occurred because of several factors: (a) Unhappiness and family disorganization typically precede confinement in a mental institution; (b) families usually have no time to prepare children for the hospitalization; (c) child abuse or neglect may have taken place before hospitalization; and (d) confinement of the mother makes it more probable that the child will have to be cared for outside his home— often thereby losing the security of his familiar surroundings and friends as well.

Of course, the preschool or the center plays only one part in solving the overall problems of families involved in such difficulties, but it can be a significant one if the provision of child care means that the child can stay within the home and that he is provided a stable, understanding environment while at school. The general recommendations given at the beginning of this chapter capsulize what will help these children; here are four additional suggestions:

1. In such circumstances the school should make a special effort to coordinate its services with those of other agencies and be prepared to report undue distress to the social worker or psychologist, along with a request for help.

2. Young children are often particularly distressed over the unpredictability of the disturbed parent's behavior. Because of the possibility that angry encounters took place between parent and child or that a depressed parent may have been emotionally inaccessible by the child, it is of great importance to explain in simple terms to the youngster that he was not the reason that his mommy went to the hospital (K. Miller, 1996).

3. Despite the prehospitalization difficulties that may have troubled the child, remember that he is also feeling pain over separation and desertion. This produces deep feelings of loneliness, confusion, and *anger*.

4. Finally it is still true that many—perhaps the majority of—people regard mental illness as a shameful stigma and that being near former mental patients fills them with unease. The preschool teacher who can master this apprehension by behaving naturally with recovering patients offers a gift of acceptance much appreciated by the family (R. Carter, 1998).

Helping Children Through Divorce

Some useful facts to have in mind about divorce are that children's reactions to divorce vary widely in relation to their age, gender, emotional resources, subsequent life experience, and interpersonal relationships (Twaite, Silitsky, & Luchow, 1998). In general, boys appear to have more difficulty adjusting than girls do, younger children seem to cope more easily with the situation than older ones do, and children from divorced families are allowed more responsibility, independence, and decision-making opportunities than children of nondivorced families. Since 80% of men and 72% of women remarry following a divorce, it is probable that children will need to make a further adjustment joining a mingled family as part of that long-term divorce experience (Hetherington, 1992).

Occasionally teachers are aware in advance that families are having marital difficulties, but the announcement of an impending divorce often takes them as much by surprise as it does the child. Here are a few points to remember when this happens.

First, try not to take sides. This is difficult to avoid in part because blame assigning by friends and acquaintances seems to be part of the cultural pattern of divorce and in part because the parent who confides in the teacher tends, understandably, to present the other parent in a bad light. Second, the teacher should invite each parent to make appointments with her when it is time for parent-child conferences (Frieman, 1998). All too often the father is ignored by the school following a divorce, and yet the majority of men remain deeply concerned for their children and greatly appreciate being included. Third, be prepared for the fact that the child himself may exhibit irritability, regression, confusion, and anxiety during and after the divorce.

Still another difficulty that may be encountered by the center is related to custody. Occasionally members of the school staff are subpoenaed to testify in custody disputes. This is usually the case when one parent wishes to prove neglect by the other one. Here written records of attendance, written reports of parent conferences, and observational records of the child are valuable to have available for citation.

Potential custody problems constitute an additional reason for requiring written, signed lists of individuals to whom a child may be released when the parent is not picking up the youngster from school. Refusing release can create temporary inconvenience and bad feeling, but the school is legally responsible for the child while not in his parent's care. This explanation will usually appease irritated would-be helpers, and enforcement of the rule may protect the child from "parentnapping."

All parents should, of course, be welcome visitors at school, although once or twice I have found it necessary to make it clear they are welcome as long as the occasion remains a happy one for the youngster and is not used by parents to generate an upsetting scene.

When a parent remarries, it is equally important for the school to welcome the stepparent and additional siblings into the life of the school. Children in newly blended families often experience bewildering mixtures of feelings ranging from delight and relief to jealousy and insecurity about who is in charge. The teacher who is able to accept the child's positive and negative comments about the remarriage in a matter-of-fact, nonjudgmental way can hasten the child's adjustment to the changed situation (R. Berger, 1998).

Explaining the Divorce to the Child

Although most children ultimately adjust to this profound change in their family life, the effects of divorce on children have been found to be long lasting and painful (Hetherington, 1999a, 1999b). Wallerstein and Blakeslee (1989) maintain it is one of the severest stressors children can experience—even more severe than the death of a well-loved person since divorce carries with it an additional burden of uncertainty since it may not seem as final to the child as death does. The possibility of continuing and repeated tension between parents also complicates the situation.

Children are also confused because many parents give their children no explanation at all about the divorce, leaving them to concoct sad fantasies about the reasons for, and their own possible role in, the breakup. For these reasons, then, it is of *great* importance that parents be encouraged to provide children with truthful, clear information so that various misapprehensions and possible guilt may be allayed.

Kalter (1990) recommends that parents give simple explanations about the divorce—for example, "We aren't getting along anymore. When grown-ups who are married can't get along and don't love each other anymore, they need to stop being married and live in different homes" (p. 134). In addition to such clear, simple explanations, children need repeated reassurance that parents will keep right on loving *them* and that divorce is not the result of something the children have done.

Commonly seen behavioral changes include fear of separation in routine situations such as coming to the center or going to bed at night; sleep disturbances such as nightmares; being more tearful, irritable, or aggressive; and being more likely to be inhibited in play (Kalter, 1990).

But parents should also know that divorce is not always perceived as being unfortunate, even by young children. Youngsters are often well aware that their parents are unhappy and may experience real relief when the final separation takes place. Indeed a few studies indicate that children from frankly split homes generally do better than those from intact but unhappy households (Hetherington, 1999a).

If parents are advised to avoid degrading the other spouse within the child's hearing, the youngster will be less distressed. Children are usually feeling pain enough over divided loyalties anyway, and being party to the denigration of the other parent only complicates their emotional problems further. It is also of great value to explain to the child which parent he will be living with and to reassure him that he will (ideally) have many regular opportunities to be with the other parent as well (Twaite et al., 1998).

Divorce frequently means a move, often from a house to an apartment. For the child this may mean the loss of a beloved pet, a change of friends, and sometimes even a change of schools. It almost always includes financial hardship as well. His mother may be leaving the home for a full-time job for the first time, too. No wonder Mitchell (1985) likens the experience of divorce to death for young children—so many, often painful adjustments must transpire.

Building Sensitivity to Single-Parent Families Within the School

The teacher needs to be especially sensitive to single-parent children at school, not only because they may be unhappy or exhibit various kinds of emotional distress but also because so many activities typically revolve around family life. Contemporary teachers need to broaden their cultural awareness to include the many patterns of single parenting that now exist and must divest themselves of the tacit assumption that most children in the school undoubtedly belong to two-parent families. At least in day care this is not likely to be true.

Teachers may also need to divest themselves of ingrained prejudices against divorce and divorced people. Nothing is necessarily "wrong" with people who are no longer married or perhaps never have been. Indeed many single parents, men and women, should be admired for the extraordinary manner in which they have held their families together and continued to care for them. As Herzog and Sudia (1973) put it in their review of research on fatherless homes, "To focus only on problems and weaknesses [of fatherless homes] is to distort the picture and obscure some clues to ways of building on strengths" (p. 202). It is kinder also if the teacher learns to speak of "single-parent families" rather than "broken homes."

In terms of the curriculum, Mother's Day and Father's Day can take on a peculiar significance for single-parent children, as can vacations. Unless the teacher is careful, some children will be routinely expected to make gifts for parents they rarely or never see. Rather than have this happen it is better to be well acquainted with each youngster's living arrangements. It may be that he would prefer to make something for a grandparent or his baby-sitter or his mother's boyfriend.

The teacher also should take care in selecting books so that all kinds of family structures are represented. It is as unfortunate for some children to be continually confronted with stories of the happy, two-parent family going on a picnic as it was for African American children of the previous generations to be exposed only to "Dick and Jane."

Research on the relation of father absence to the establishment of adequate male and female role concepts remains inconclusive, but it is probably an especially good idea to employ male teachers in centers that serve single parents since divorce makes it more likely that children will be deprived of adult male companionship outside the school. Surely it is more desirable for children of both sexes to have some regular opportunities to relate to men rather than to be raised during their preschool years entirely by women.

Helping Children Understand Death

Although death remains a taboo subject for many people, the increasing frequency of publications and discussion about it provides evidence that at least a few people are no longer pretending that death does not exist. And even though we might prefer to deny it, we must face the fact that death is a part of life for young children, as well as for their elders. Children are also exposed to the deaths of grandparents, other family members, friends, and beloved animals, not to mention the continual accounts of death and murder reported endlessly on television. For these reasons it is necessary to learn how to help children cope with this subject even though we may be barely learning to talk about it ourselves.

What Can the Teacher Do?

It is heartening to learn that in the area of death education the early childhood teacher *can* be of real assistance to young children. Kliman (1968) terms this *psychological immu-*

nization and describes it as helping children acquire at least a modicum of "mastery in advance." By this he means it is helpful if the subject of death is included matter-of-factly as part of the curriculum to desensitize children by providing both information and mild experiences with it before a more emotionally laden death occurs. This can be accomplished in many ways.[4] Perhaps the most effective of them is based on the death of animals at school. Such a death should be followed by talking about how the animals have changed and what will become of them, as well as helping children carry out the simple burials that are of such intense interest to them. Books and discussions are also helpful, and some schools even advocate visiting cemeteries, which are, after all, quite beautiful places (Riley, 1989).

Reading stories related to death can also open that topic for discussion and help remove it from the realm of being unmentionable. Several references of appropriate books are included at the end of this chapter.

Helping the Child and the Family When Death Occurs

Kliman (1968) also points out that teachers and other nonmedical personnel, such as clergy, are more likely to be asked for help when a death occurs than physicians are, probably because families feel less hostile toward such people than they do toward the medical profession following bereavement. For this reason the teacher should be well prepared with some down-to-earth suggestions for helping the children by supplying resources for further information and by providing possible referral sources should these be requested.

Once again I repeat that the fact of a death should not be avoided by telling a child that his father has gone away on a long trip, or that Grandma will come back in the spring, or that Snowball is just asleep. Children need to be allowed to participate in the family's grief since it strengthens their feelings of belonging instead of feelings of isolation, and it helps them express their own sadness, too (Thomason, 1999).

As time passes, a child should be encouraged to reminisce about the absent parent or other loved ones. All too often once the initial crisis has passed, families and teachers hesitate to reawaken memories, but recall actually helps ventilate feelings so that the emotional wound can heal cleanly. It also helps the child retain his identification with and feelings of affection for people who have died. Family stories about "Do you remember when . . . ," photographs, and even movies and tapes have been found to be helpful.

Reliving old memories is also the second of three stages of mourning. The first stage is *the acceptance of loss*, the second is *remembering the past*, and the third is *substitution of a new relationship*.

Parents can do a better job if they also understand that the emotion of grief for children (and for adults as well) is not composed only of sadness. It also includes a component of anger (Bowlby, 1980; C. M. Sanders, 1999). Just as children feel a mixture of grief and anger when they are left at the center or preschool, so, too, they experience, to a much stronger degree, these same feelings when a parent abandons them in death. It is doubly important to understand this because young children often connect this anger back to some angry interlude before death and conclude they have caused the parent to

---

[4] *For a more complete discussion of teaching about death in the curriculum refer to Hendrick (1998, chap. 10, "Helping Children Understand and Value Life").*

(a)

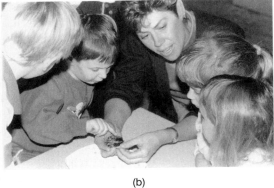

(b)

(c)

Although adults are often squeamish about dead animals, children find them deeply interesting. Here Deb Parkinson helps our 4-year-olds understand what being dead means, while also helping them appreciate the delicacy and wonder of the little chicken's feet.

die (just as they may believe this about divorce). They then may reason that the death is a punishment for their misbehavior—truly a terrible burden of guilt for a child to bear.

To counteract this misunderstanding, simple reasons for the death should be given ("Your father didn't want to leave us, but he was so sick the medicine couldn't help anymore"), combined with reassurances that the surviving parent and child are not likely to die for a long time yet (Dougy Center for Grieving Children, 1997). A child should also be told that the surviving parent will go right on taking care of him and be reminded that there are also Grandma, Grandpa, and Aunty Shawna, all of whom love him and care for him. The presence of siblings can provide an additional source of strength and family feeling, particularly among children who are older. The anger should be acknowledged by mentioning its presence and its naturalness. Statements such as, "I guess you feel mad your dad died and left us. . . . " "I see you feel like socking things a lot. . . . " and "We know he couldn't help dying, but it's hard to take sometimes, isn't it?" may relieve some of the hostile impulses.

Adults must also be cautioned against likening death to sleep. We surely do not want anxious children to guard themselves against sleep because they fear death may come while they are sleeping. Also, inexperienced young children tend to view death as being a temporary condition, one from which the person can be revived, and that belief can promote false hopes unless the child is confronted gently and persistently with the truth. It takes many repetitions of the facts to get such young children to accept that final reality (Goldman, 1996). The last reason for not equating death with sleep is that doing this is fundamentally untruthful. Why speak euphemistically of "sleep" and "slumber rooms" when what we mean is "death" and "a visiting room where people can view the body"? Why not face facts?

Finally, student-teachers often ask me about religious beliefs and children in relation to death. In general, writers on this subject maintain that talking about religion tends to be confusing to young children and should not be stressed when death occurs (Furman, 1982). Surely it is not the teacher's place to do this, anyway, although he may find it helpful to be conversant with the points of view of the major religions.

The question really raised by students, however, is what to do about children's statements with which they personally cannot agree. For example, a child may say, "My mommy says my puppy went to heaven, and now the angels are singing over him. Someday I'll see him up there." or, "You know what? My grandmother has it all fixed so she'll be froze solid when she dies. Then she can come alive again when she wants to."

Actually it is not necessary to agree or disagree with such statements. All one has to do is show that one respects the family's teaching by listening and then either ask the child what he thinks or say something that responds to the child's feelings, such as, "I can see you really miss him," or, "You'd like to see your puppy again, wouldn't you?" or at least say something noncommittal, such as, "So that's what your grandma is planning."

AIDS: A Continuing Crisis in the Lives of Children and Their Families

The issue of AIDS (acquired immunodeficiency syndrome) and young children is a terribly troublesome one. One related question is what if anything to tell children of preschool age about the condition, and another is what to do about admitting children with AIDS (also spoken of as "HIV" [human immunodeficiency virus]) to the preschool.

What Is Appropriate AIDS Education for Preschoolers?

Only a little has been written to date on the subject of AIDS education for preschools, and yet with the media constantly bombarding us with the word and precautionary recommendations, it seems impossible that it has entirely escaped young children's awareness.

Once again a matter-of-fact explanation is the best approach to take. When a youngster appears to be concerned, these explanations could include the information that AIDS can make people very sick, so sick they usually die; that it is very hard "to get"; that it is a grown-up sickness that doesn't usually afflict children; and that people can take care of themselves and protect themselves from becoming infected. Because of the emphasis on needles that is so prevalent in some anti-drug commercials, one or two mothers have reported to me that their 5-year-olds objected more strenuously than usual when they had injections. For this reason, it may also be helpful to realize that occasionally children may require additional reassurance that the needles the doctors are using are new ones, so nobody has to worry about getting sick from them.

For the more anxious child it may also be necessary to add, just as one does when discussing death, that particular people will always be around to take care of him—even if something did happen to Mother or Daddy—and reiterate, if he is worried, that there is almost no chance the child could become infected.

Of course, it is true that all these statements are only "mostly true," and tragic exceptions to them do occur. However, for most young children, they are still accurate.

Admitting HIV-Positive Children to the Preschool

According to the National Pediatric & Family HIV Resource Center (1999), AIDS is now the fifth leading cause of death in children ages 1 to 4 and seventh in young people ages 15 to 21. When you add to these statistics the estimate that for every child with AIDS, another 2 to 10 children are likely to be HIV positive, the seriousness of the problem becomes clear, and the probability that we early childhood teachers will encounter such children in our classes grows ever more likely.

Since that is true, it is important to know the basic facts about how HIV is transmitted (primarily through contact with semen or blood of infected people) and what the difference is between HIV-positive children and children with AIDS. When tested, HIV-positive children are found to be infected with the AIDS virus but do not necessarily exhibit other symptoms of that disease. The more unfortunate children are those youngsters whose bodies have been overwhelmed by the virus and have become deathly ill with AIDS (Kaiser & Raminsky, 1995).

Many myths surround this condition, even among people who understand the fundamental facts about transmission; for example, some early childhood staff and/or parents fear that biting will transmit this disease, however, no case of this happening has ever been reported (Black, 1999). As Black (1999) explains:

> To transmit HIV via biting, there must be an exchange of infected with uninfected blood. The infected child would have to have fresh blood in his or her mouth and break the skin of the uninfected child, mixing the infected blood directly with the uninfected blood. An uninfected child who bites an infected child would have to break the skin of the infected child, draw infected blood into his or her mouth, and have a blood-to-blood exchange. (p. 44)

Actually, no episodes have even been reported of children acquiring the infection from attending school with infected youngsters (Steglin, 1997). This is indeed fortunate because the Americans with Disabilities Act makes it illegal to refuse admission of such youngsters to child care centers (Child Care Law Center, 1994; Steglin, 1997).

Although it may be against the law to refuse admission to HIV-positive children, the fact remains that a great deal of uncertain and negative attitudes are expressed by both caregivers and parents about such admissions. The Research Study included in this chapter investigated just how widespread these feelings are, and research by Steglin, Atiles, and Smith (1996) continues to support these findings.

The research confirms that the problem of stigma remains a serious one; for this reason the issue of privacy and confidentiality remains important (Black, 1999; Christian, 1997). Parents are under no obligation to inform the school or center that their child or, for that matter, anyone else in their family is afflicted with the condition. Even when they have risked confiding to the staff, this does not mean the information is common knowledge. No matter whether one agrees with the ethics of this or not, when entrusted with that information the staff *must* treat it as confidential.

The fact that the issue of confidentiality may prevent the director's informing staff when an HIV child is attending their school emphasizes how important it is for everyone to follow the guidelines for taking *Universal Precautions* whenever any bleeding occurs, no matter how minor the accident may be to a child or, possibly, to an adult. Here is the list of recommended procedures as adapted for child care centers (Canadian Child Care Federation, 1999).

1. Wash your hands for 30 seconds after contact with blood and other body fluids contaminated with blood.
2. Wear disposable latex gloves when you encounter large amounts of blood, especially if you have open cuts or chapped skin. Wash your hands as soon as you remove your gloves.
3. Use disposable absorbent material like paper towels to stop bleeding.
4. Cover cuts or scratches with a bandage until healed.
5. Immediately clean up blood-soiled surfaces **and disinfect** with a fresh solution of one part bleach and nine parts water.
6. Discard blood-stained material in a sealed bag and place in a lined covered garbage container.
7. Put blood-stained laundry in sealed plastic bags. Machine-wash separately in hot soapy water.

Violence Against Children

It is a source of great sadness to me that this section of *The Whole Child* gets longer every time I revise the book. Now, in addition to discussing abuse and molestation, it is necessary to include a new aspect of that problem—violence in the community and its effects on children.

Research Study

Would You Do It?

Research Question: The investigators wanted to know how much children's center staff and parents know about the way AIDS is transmitted and how the staff really feel about having HIV-positive children in their day care center.

Research Method: Questionnaires were distributed to day care center providers working in 12 centers and to parents of children attending 4 centers. The questionnaires included questions assessing (a) knowledge of how HIV is transmitted and (b) attitudes about potential inclusion of infected children. The rate of questionnaires returned was exceptionally high. A total of 161 day care staff and 203 parents replied.

Extent of Knowledge About HIV Infections: Ninety-eight percent of adults knew sexual intercourse and sharing needles could transmit HIV, and 84% knew contact with blood from a cut could transmit it. Respondents showed a wide range of uncertainty, however, when it came to knowledge about other possible ways HIV could be transmitted. Almost half of both groups incorrectly thought tears, sharing food or utensils, changing diapers, vomit, and kissing could spread the disease. One in five of the adults thought toilet seats could spread the infection, and one in four thought coughing and sneezing could.

Attitudes About Child Inclusion: The questionnaires revealed that almost two thirds of parents surveyed would be either unwilling or unsure whether they would keep their child in a classroom with a child infected with AIDS. Of child care staff who responded, 86% said they would be either unwilling or at least uncertain whether they would care for a child infected with AIDS in their classrooms.

Another important finding of this study was that both staff and parents agreed they wanted to know whether an infected child was enrolled in the classroom.

Implications for Teaching: If we assume this careful study accurately reflects the opinions of parents and staff in typical child care centers, it becomes obvious that inclusion of HIV-infected children will require very careful and compassionate handling to be successful.

One part of effecting this success must be the provision of increased education and understanding about what constitutes safe contact between infected and noninfected people. Another aspect must be a continuing emphasis on consistent use of such universal health precautions as hand-washing and wearing gloves when coming in contact with anyone's blood. Still another is the need for immediate implementation of increased education and precautions so that they are in place *before* admission of a particular child is contemplated.

The high degree of agreement between parents and staff about wanting to know whether an infected child is attending their center calls into serious question whether the recommendations concerning confidentiality set forth by the American Academy of Pediatrics can possibly be followed. It is likely some sort of compromise will need to be worked out in this regard.

Source: From "Knowledge and Attitudes of Day Care Center Parents and Care Providers Regarding Children Infected with Human Immunodeficiency Virus," by A. L. Morrow, M. Benton, R. R. Reves, & L. K. Pickering, 1991, Pediatrics, 87(6), 876–883.

Coping with the Crisis of Community Violence

There is no doubt the problem of community violence is very serious. For example, the Children's Defense Fund (1998) reports that "an average of 14 children die each day from gunfire in America—approximately one every 100 minutes" (p. 78).

But it is not only these tragic children and their families who suffer from the effects of violence in their community. Every day we are faced with the saddening legacy of children who cannot be allowed outside to play because the neighborhood is too dangerous; children who are afraid to go to school because they fear what will happen to their families while they are away; children who have witnessed continuing violence in their own homes; and children who have watched their fathers shot or their siblings knifed on the street corner.

The truth is that no one is exempt. Even children who are fortunate enough to live in more sheltered circumstances are subject to endless examples of violence portrayed on television. Levin (1998) reports research revealing that children's cartoon shows average more than 20 acts of violence per hour and that, by the end of elementary school, children will have witnessed an average of 8,000 murders and 100,000 other violent acts. These figures do not include the gruesome reports relentlessly emphasized in daily news broadcasts.

The question that must be answered is, Can anything be done to stem this potentially overwhelming tide of violence? The answer is that *a lot of things can and are being done.* Among them are the following:

Begin with the Individual Child in Your Preschool Group   Teach children to reduce conflicts by controlling their aggressive impulses and also teach them many practical nonviolent ways to get what they want without hurting other people. Chapter 11, "Helping Young Children Establish Self-Discipline and Self-Control," and chapter 12, "Aggression: What to Do About It," offer considerable advice about how to accomplish this.

Be Sensitive and Alert to What Is Happening in the Community and to the Children's Responses to What Is Going On   Make certain the mental health principles advocated earlier in this chapter and in chapter 6 are put into practice. Remember that even very young children will benefit from talking about how they feel, as well as from playing out their feelings. Provide many opportunities for them to express their concerns by using self-expressive art materials, too.

Become Active in Your Community   Take a stand against the portrayal of violent acts on television, at least during peak viewing hours for children. Sensitize parents to the content of such programs and don't overlook the content of so-called news programs. If you personally don't like what you're seeing, protest to your local television stations—many of them are surprisingly sensitive to such criticism—and remember to commend them when they improve. The National Association for the Education of Young Children (NAEYC) publication *Remote Control Childhood? Combating the Hazards of Media Culture* (Levin, 1998) provides a valuable list of media-related resources available for contact.

Become Aware of Positive Steps Being Taken in Your Own Community to Make the Neighborhood a Safer Place for Everyone   Support churches, community leaders, and elected officials who are working hard to make that happen.

Child Abuse, Neglect, and Sexual Molestation

Child abuse constitutes one of the most terrible crises of childhood. The occurrence of such attacks is fundamentally repugnant to most people, and for a long time the subject went virtually ignored and uninvestigated. Statistics only began to accumulate as late as 1962, when Kempe initiated the first survey on the subject (Helfer & Kempe, 1987).

Prevent Child Abuse America ("Child Abuse," 1999) reports that between 1993 and 1997 although the nation's overall crime rate decreased 22%, the rate of child abuse and neglect increased 4%. For every 1,000 children there were 47 *reported* cases of abuse or neglect in 1997, and 15% per 1,000 were confirmed. (Many reported cases are never investigated at all—for a variety of reasons.) Perhaps the statistic to which we as teachers should pay most attention is that only 16% of all cases each year were reported by teachers and other school staff. The report concludes that much more training in identifying abuse is needed to teach school personnel how to identify signs of abuse and neglect as well as how to report it.

There are four kinds of abuse we must know about: (a) *physical abuse*, the most obvious kind; (b) *sexual abuse*, less obvious and very serious; (c) *neglect*; and (d) *psychological abuse*, the last two being the most difficult to identify with certainty and hence to prosecute. Although all kinds of abuse are worthy of scrutiny, preschool personnel should be particularly alert to signs of physical abuse since that kind of abuse happens most frequently to younger children, who are unable to defend themselves or put into words what happened to them. The average age of children experiencing major physical abuse is 5, and the average age of children who are fatally injured is about 2½ (Tzeng & Hanner, 1988).

What to Look For as Signs of Physical Abuse

Red wheals or strap marks should arouse suspicion, as most certainly should a black eye, cigarette burns, ear injuries where the ear has been twisted or is bleeding, sore areas of the scalp from having hair yanked or pulled out, and tender ribs or elbow joints. Bite marks are another fairly frequent sign of maltreatment (Green, 1997). If a child arrives at school smelling of alcohol or under the influence of drugs, this is also evidence of abuse—and this *does* happen.

A more general reason for concern exists when the parent's voluntary account of the accident does not match the kind or extent of the injury. The usual excuse for bruises is falling down stairs or out of a crib or bed (Weston, 1980), but common sense often tells the teacher that such an event could not possibly have caused the series of diagonal welts across the child's bottom. Still another cause for suspicion of abuse, or at least neglect, occurs when the child is subject to repeated injuries. The laughing comment by a mother that she "guesses her child is just accident prone" should not be repeatedly accepted by the teacher, particularly when the level of the child's physical coordination at school does not support this parental conclusion.

The emotional behavior of physically abused children may also reveal insecure attachments to the parents; mistrustful, "watchful' relationships with other adults; low self esteem; and inappropriate emotional affect ranging from overaggressiveness to emotionally flat unresponsiveness (Green, 1997; Kendrick et al., 1995).

Literature on the emotional symptomatology of these children describes their behavior as generally either very passive or very aggressive (Koralek, 1992; Mirandy, 1976). Mirandy (1976), reporting on the first 19 preschoolers admitted to Circle House Playschool (a center for abused young children), comments that most of them were very passive and inhibited, and she describes their behavior during their first months in school as being

> overly compliant, anxious to please, seeking out permission before initiating any new action. They were quite hypervigilant to the total environment of the preschool. None of the children demonstrated any separation anxiety in leaving mother, and they were indiscriminately and often physically affectionate with adult strangers. They were oblivious to peer interaction. There was often a hollow smile on a child's face and a complete void of emotions. . . . All lacked true joy. The children rarely expressed anger or pain, they had a poor sense of safety, frequently injuring themselves. Crying was either *highly* infrequent or continual. . . . Most abused children appeared compulsively neat. . . . Play was often noncreative and use of materials highly repetitive, the majority of such children appear to be lacking basic play skills. . . . Most have poor expressive language skills.
>
> It is crucial to stress that most of these traits, such as neatness, perseverance, quietness, compliance and politeness, are valued in the "normal" child and that if the teacher is not aware of the abused child's special needs, these traits may be further reinforced. An abused child has the ability to initially blend in too well and slip by unnoticed.[5]

Finally the teacher should be sensitive to some additional commonsense indications of possible abuse. Children who startle easily and cringe or duck if the teacher moves suddenly may be revealing that they are often struck at home. Then, too, it is sometimes evident in conversations with parents that they expect too much or are too dependent on their children or that they themselves know they get too angry and "do things they shouldn't" or "wish they hadn't." Such statements are really cries for help and should not be brushed aside on the grounds that everyone feels like that sometimes. These people often benefit from referrals to Parents Anonymous or to local child abuse hot lines.

Evidence of Sexual Molestation

Sexual abuse typically begins when the child is between 4 and 12 years old and includes such behaviors by the adult as fondling, voyeurism, child pornography, or rape. Because it can occur at such a young age, early childhood staff needs to be alert to the possibility of sexual abuse when young children complain they "hurt down there." According to Kendrick et al. (1995) additional physical indications might include difficulty in walking or sitting, underclothes with stains or blood on them, saying it hurts while urinating, or exhibiting bruises or bleeding in external genitalia, vaginal or anal areas, or mouth or throat. Behavioral indications include not wanting to have their clothes changed, holding themselves when not wet, fears or a strong dislike of someone or of going to some particu-

---

[5] *From "Preschool for Abused Children" by J. Mirandy, in* The Abused Child: A Multidisciplinary Approach to Developmental Issues and Treatment *(pp. 217–2128) by H. P. Martin (Ed.), 1976, Cambridge, MA: Ballinger. Copyright 1976 by Ballinger. Reprinted by permission.*

lar place, and other less specific symptoms of emotional disturbance such as those discussed in chapter 9. Although venereal disease may seem an unthinkable condition in children so young, we cannot afford to blot this possibility entirely from our minds because instances of this have also been reported.

Some sexual attacks are perpetrated by strangers, and these are deeply upsetting to families who nevertheless often prefer not to report them rather than risk notoriety for the child and endless rehashing of the event with authorities. Of course, if such attacks go unreported, the attacker is immune from arrest, but this can be a difficult and touchy situation to deal with. *Referral for psychological help for both parent and child is strongly recommended in such cases.*

However, the majority of sexual molestations are *not* perpetrated by strangers, but are carried out by people the child knows, such as older children or family members.

Children need to be empowered to protect themselves. They should be taught never to take anything (typically candy) from any stranger and never to get into a car with a stranger (even if a stranger knows the child's name). They need to understand the difference between "good touching," such as snuggling and hugging, and "bad touching" that doesn't feel right (behavior that is inappropriate). They should be assured that their bodies belong to themselves, that it's OK to say "No!" and that no matter the threat, they should tell their parents right away if anyone makes that kind of advance to them. In recent years some educational programs have become available that offer guidelines in such preventive kinds of instruction. In general they stress, "If an older, more powerful person touches you on any part of the body covered by a bathing suit, except for health reasons, say NO and tell someone." The success of these programs remains questionable, however (McLeod & Wright, 1996; Reppucci, Land, & Haugaard, 1998). It is certainly difficult to teach these principles in a way young children really understand without frightening them too much, so it is important to be definite but matter-of-fact to avoid arousing too much anxiety during such discussions.

What to Do When Abuse Is Suspected

Teachers who discover evidence of abuse are very upset about it. They may find it difficult to believe that such a "nice" family could do a thing like that and thus they deny it, or they may be so frightened for the child's safety that they do not think clearly and therefore act impulsively. For this reason, before going any further with this discussion, *I want to emphasize that handling such cases requires skill and delicacy* (National Association for the Education of Young Children [NAEYC], 1998f). The consequences of unsuccessful management may be so serious that we cannot risk jeopardizing such chances by acting in an ill-considered way. *Therefore teachers must not suddenly plunge into the problem by accusing the parents or even reveal suspicions by questioning them or the child too closely.* Instead if they suspect a case of abuse, they should contact whatever agency or individual in their community has the responsibility for handling such cases and report it. *They should ask these people for advice and do what they tell them, to the best of their ability.*

How to Find Help

The agency the teacher should seek out is whatever agency in the community is responsible for children's protective services. These agencies go by different names in different parts of the country: Department of Social Services, Social Rehabilitation Service, Bureau of Children and Family Services, and so forth. Still another way to locate protective services is to ask the public health nurse whom to call. If no such agency exists, as is sometimes the case in small or rural communities, a mental health clinic, a child psychologist or psychiatrist, or a knowledgeable pediatrician should be asked for help.

Action Should Be Prompt

Since abusers often repeat their behavior, prompt action is advisable; yet statistics reveal teachers sometimes hesitate to get involved. The teacher should realize that all states now have mandatory reporting laws and that many of these specifically identify teachers as being among those people *required* to report cases in which abuse is suspected (NAEYC, 1998b). Even when teachers are not specifically mentioned, the law is generally on the side of anyone reporting such a case "in good faith." Besides the necessity of conforming to the law, *reporting such cases is an ethical and moral responsibility the teacher must not overlook.*

Helping the Child's Family After the Referral Has Been Made

Even when teachers have taken the expert's advice and have handled the referral successfully, if the family is receiving help they must still deal with their feelings about the child and the parent or parents if they believe it is important to retain the child in the center. The relief to parents that such a respite provides, as well as the protection and education of the child it affords, means that continuing at school is important. Here we are confronted with a paradox. Teachers are more than likely experiencing feelings of revulsion and outrage over what the parents have done, and their impulse may be to judge and punish them. Yet experts tell us that what the parents need, among many other things, is understanding and acceptance—which they may have been woefully short on in their own childhoods. The question is, How can teachers possibly behave in an accepting, nurturing fashion toward people they regard with aversion?

Understanding the causes of child abuse as far as they are currently understood may help teachers master their feelings, or at least control them. It has become commonplace to assert that abusing adults were abused as children, and it is true that generational links may be ascribed in some instances. However, research now documents the fact that the great majority of abused children do *not* grow up to physically abuse their own youngsters (Milner, 1998).

Recent studies summarized by English (1998) and Milner (1998) emphasize that the causes of child abuse stem from a complex combination of factors, rather than from a single circumstance. These include such psychological factors as unreal parental expectations of the child's abilities, poor impulse control, low self-esteem and feelings of helplessness, inadequate knowledge of how to control children without using violence, and a past history of being abused themselves, combined with a terrible insensitivity to the child's needs and feelings. Social factors such as poverty (although child abuse occurs at all economic levels), lack of work, social isolation, and inadequate education also increase the likelihood of abuse. Several researchers have pointed out that some children particularly appear to elicit abuse, whereas others in the same family do not (Crosse, Kaye, & Ratnofsky, 1992). But the fact that the child is irritating can in no way be permitted to justify the behavior of an abusing parent.

The basic generalization that can be safely drawn at this point is that the causes of child abuse are rooted in a complex mixture of personality traits of parents and children, combined with various malign environmental influences. Disentangling this complicated web in order to reduce parental violence remains a serious challenge to everyone involved in working with young children.

What teachers *can* do is be aware of signs indicating there is a high risk that abuse or neglect *may* take place. Research reveals that the people at highest risk

> include parents who abuse drugs and alcohol, young parents who are ill-prepared for the parent-ing role, families experiencing great stress who have poor coping skills and have no one to turn to for support, and parents who have difficulty with or who have not developed an emotional bond with their infant. We need to be alert to these and other high-risk indicators and offer assistance, support, counseling, and/or parent education to these families *before* their children are harmed. (National Center on Child Abuse and Neglect, 1992, p. 11)

Teachers, who know so many of these families well are in a particularly advantageous posi-tion to help them in time.

When teachers are feeling upset about an abusive situation, it may also help them moderate their reactions to the parents if they realize that only a few of these people are estimated to suffer from serious psychotic disorders (Milner, 1998). It is more realistic to think of the majority of child abusers, not as "crazy people," but as people who are often deeply ashamed of their behavior, who have been unable to control it, and who are the products of their own childhoods and environments as perhaps their parents were before them. Many of them lack even rudimentary knowledge of practical, wholesome, child-rearing techniques. The statement "abusive parents care much for their children but do not care well" sums it up.

Finally, teachers will benefit by doing some thinking about the reasons why they them-selves are so angry over what these parents have done. Certainly part of the reaction stems from the ugly painfulness of seeing a child suffer and from the teacher's commit-ment to helping children, but it seems to me there is more to the anger than that. Perhaps some of the reaction comes because, more than most people, teachers have had to learn to control their own angry impulses toward children. Teachers who are honest with them-selves must admit that at times they, too, have felt rage toward a child surge within them. Their anger toward the abusive parent may turn to compassion if they realize that the dif-ference between themselves and those parents at that instant was that they were able to stop in time!

Helping the Child While His Family Is in Treatment

Most material having to do with the treatment of child abuse deals with the treatment of the adults or amelioration of the family's environment, but the child needs help, too—help that must go beyond the simple level of physical rescue. In addition to whatever may be prescribed in the way of receiving special therapies or attending nursery school, Head Start, preschool, or a children's center are frequently recommended, and Starr (1988) places considerable faith in what can be accomplished in those environments to help the child. The points he makes as being desirable ones in caring for abused children are those generally stressed throughout *The Whole Child* as being important in the care of all children.

In particular, it is important with such youngsters to emphasize the building of trust and warmth between them and their teachers; steadiness and consistency are invaluable elements of such trust building. The enhancement of self-esteem is also important to stress. Since developmental delays of various kinds appear to be characteristic of these children, a careful analysis of these deficits should be made and attention paid to remediating them when this can be done without undue pressure. (Both Martin [1976] and Mirandy [1976] comment particularly on apparent deficits in perceptual-motor development skills and expressive language ability.)

Above all, every effort should be made to retain the child in school; to maintain consistent, regular contact with the other people working with the family; and to be as patient and caring with both the child and his family as possible.

Protecting the Center from False Accusations of Abuse

As some recent cases have demonstrated, child care centers need to take sensible precautions to protect themselves, as well as the children, against abuse (Bordin, 1998; NAEYC, 1997; Strickland, 1999a, 1999b). Some recommendations offered by Bordin (1998) and Koralek (1992) that will reduce the possibility of false accusations include the following:

1. Conduct careful, thorough interviews of potential employees; complete with whatever background checks and references are legally permitted by the particular state.
2. Work to keep stress at a reasonable level for center staff—including adequate breaks, decent pay, and fair arrangements for special problems and circumstances.
3. Provide ongoing staff training, particularly in regard to working through discipline situations. Educate them about symptoms of child abuse in its various forms and explain the laws in your state concerning mandatory reporting of such evidence.
4. Have two adults present with the children whenever possible. Be careful about staff visiting children outside the center unless another adult will be present. This includes taking children home from the center.
5. Eliminate secluded, out-of-the-way places at the center where supervision may not be consistent. Bathroom areas in particular should be fully in view—with only half-high partitions.
6. Never allow new or volunteer people to be alone with the children.
7. Establish a well-publicized open-door visiting policy for parents. Create many occasions for staff-family contacts to build trust and respect between everyone.
8. Welcome each child as he arrives, take a careful look for obvious signs of injury before admitting him, and mention any you find to the parents.
9. Encourage the director to tour center rooms on a consistent but irregular basis.
10. Make certain the center's insurance policies cover court cases related to abuse.

SUMMARY

Practically all young children experience some form of crisis during their preschool years, and parents and teachers can do many things to help them come through these experiences in good condition and perhaps with added strengths. Teachers should encourage parents to *include* rather than exclude the child at such times. They should try not to overreact to the problem or violate the family's privacy and should offer themselves as a resource of information when the family needs such assistance.

The teacher can help the child and his family by facing the reality of the crisis with him, making certain he does not blame himself for situations he has not caused, keeping his life at school steady and calm, providing play opportunities for him that help him work through and understand his feelings, and helping him understand and anticipate what will happen next.

A discussion of various specific crises of particular concern to children concludes the chapter. Problems related to sending the child to the children's center, the arrival of a new baby, and hospitalization of either the child or one of his parents are some of these important crises. Additional crises discussed specifically include problems related to divorce, death, AIDS, and child abuse and molestation. Information and recommendations are provided to help teachers and families cope with each of these situations.

Questions and Activities

1. One youngster at your school has been scratching his head a lot, and on inspection you discover he has lice. How would you handle this minor but important crisis with the child and his family?

2. The pet rat at your preschool has been getting fatter and fatter, and it is obvious it has a tumor. The veterinarian pronounces it inoperable—what to do? How would you approach this matter with the children?

3. Keep a list for a month noting all the crises that happen to children and staff during this time. How many were there? How were they handled?

4. What crises, if any, should children *not* know about? How would you protect children from them?

5. Can you recall being jealous of a brother or sister? What did it feel like? Would you handle it as your parents did if you had a child in a similar situation?

6. *Predicament*: A child comes to school acting listless and looking pale and washed out. At nap time, when he undresses, you find several bruises on his chest and around his arms, and he complains that his neck hurts. On one previous occasion he arrived with a bump on his head and a black eye, which his mother said were a result of his falling down a flight of steps. Under these circumstances do you think it wiser to approach the parent with your concern, or should you explore alternative solutions? If the parent, in your judgment, should not be approached, what agencies in your own community would be the most appropriate and effective ones to contact?

7. How do you think you *ought* to feel and how would you *really* feel if your director came to you and told you she has admitted a child who is HIV positive and he will be in your class? What would you do about your feelings?

Self-Check Questions for Review
Content-Related Questions

1. Are crises always events that happen very suddenly?
2. Name four ways the teacher might help a family that was experiencing a crisis.
3. Explain why it is important to tell children the truth when a crisis occurs.
4. What are the basic principles teachers should remember when helping children work through a crisis?
5. Review the specific crises discussed in the chapter and explain, for each, what a teacher could do to help.
6. In this chapter, does the author recommend that the teacher confront the parents immediately if she suspects the child has been abused in some manner?

Integrative Questions

1. The chapter states that crises *can* strengthen people. Select from your personal experience or from history an individual who experienced a crisis and explain how it strengthened that person.
2. Granted that marrying and starting on a first job both represent a change in life, analyze other aspects of the two experiences that are similar.
3. A child arrives at school and tells you his father was in a car accident the night before. Give two examples of what you might say that would tend to deny his concerns about his father. What might you say that would reflect his concern?
4. Talk about the accident continues. The child tells you his brother socked him and he yelled and that's what made his father drive into a bridge. Predict how you think the child is feeling about his behavior. Then give an example of what you would reply and explain why you chose that particular reply.
5. One of the 4-year-olds caught her foot in a railroad tie, and it was crushed by a switching engine and later amputated. She is due back at school in a week. Basing your plans on recommendations from this chapter, explain how you would handle this situation with the other children in the group.
6. What are some ways the crises of death and divorce are similar, and how might the experiences differ?

7. Do you think preschool-age children with HIV should be admitted to child care? Why or why not? In your opinion should other parents be informed of that child's condition?

Coordinating Videotape

Listening to families. Tape #6. The whole child: A caregiver's guide to the first five years. The Annenberg/CPB Collection, P.O. Box 2345, South Burlington, VT 05407–2345. *Listening to Families* prepares caregivers to welcome families into the life of the children's center and then devotes considerable time to practical ways of helping them and their children work through life crises.

References for Further Reading
Pick of the Litter

Miller, K. (1996). *The crisis manual for early childhood teachers: How to handle the really difficult problems.* Beltsville, MD: Gryphon House. Following a general discussion, Miller singles out various crises and provides helpful advice on subjects as diverse as death and divorce and natural disasters. *Highly recommended.*

Alleviating Stress and Building Resilience in Children

Allen, J. S., & Klein, R. J. (1996). *Ready, set, relax: A research-based program of relaxation, learning, and self-esteem for children.* Watertown, WI: Inner Coaching. The authors provide clear discussions and "scripts" teachers can tell or read to induce relaxed states as children listen. *Highly recommended.*

Brazelton, T. B. (1992). *Touchpoints: The essential reference: Your child's emotional and behavioral development.* Reading, MA: Addison-Wesley. This book fits in so many chapters it's difficult to categorize it, but I place it here because of the sensible advice it provides about so many childhood crises.

Brohl, K. (1996). *Working with traumatized children: A handbook for healing.* Washington, DC: Child Welfare League of America. This pamphlet provides practical advice about dealing with the results of severe crises.

Deskin, G. D., & Steckler, G. (1996). *When nothing makes sense: Disaster, crises, and their effects on children.* Minneapolis, MN: Fairview Press. Written for families, this book discusses the value of advance preparation when possible and reactions to stress and how to cope. It includes true stories of how various families experienced and survived a variety of disasters. *Highly recommended.*

Hauser-Cram, P. (1998). I think I can, I think I can: Understanding and encouraging mastery motivation in young children. *Young Children, 53*(4), 67–71. This review of research emphasizes that mastery and the ensuing sense of achievement and competence are integral components of self-worth and feeling in control of oneself.

Oehlberg, B. (1996). *Making it better: Activities for children living in a stressful world.* St. Paul, MN: Redleaf. Oehlberg provides insightful discussions about the way children feel when confronted with traumatizing situations such as death, illness of family members, or moving. Although the activities may seem more suited to somewhat older children the discussion and recommended books are appropriate for use with younger ones.

Mental Illness

Carter, R. (with Golant, S.). (1998). *Helping someone with mental illness: A compassionate guide for family, friends, and caregivers.* New York: Random House. Is there a parent in your school, or a friend or relative diagnosed with mental illness? If so, this book, which includes clear descriptions of common mental illnesses and treatments, would be comforting since it does an exceptional job of dealing with the problem of social stigma. *Highly recommended.*

Effects of Divorce on Children

Carter, B. C., & McGoldrick, M. M. (Eds.). (1998). *The expanded family life cycle: Individual, family, and social perspectives* (3rd ed.). Boston: Allyn & Bacon. Four chapters on divorce, single parenting, and remarriage present a comprehensive analysis of these crises.

Frieman, B. B. (1998). What early childhood educators need to know about divorced fathers. *Early Childhood Education Journal, 25*(4), 239–241. The author provides succinct, sensible advice on this subject.

Thompson, R. (1994). The role of the father after divorce. *Future of Children: Children and Divorce, 4*(1), 210–235. This thoughtful article discusses questions related to custody, economics, and personal-social adjustment. *Highly recommended.*

Twaite, J. A., Silitsky, D., & Luchow, A. K. (1998). *Children of divorce: Adjustment, parental conflict, custody, remarriage, and recommendations for clinicians.* Northvale, NJ: Jason Aronson. This book provides a helpful summary chapter of recommendations for working with divorcing families that is based on extensive reviews of research.

Wassil-Grimm, C. (1994). *Where's Daddy? How divorced, single, and widowed mothers can provide what's missing when Dad's missing.* New York: Overlook Press. Title is self-explanatory.

Hospitalization

Lansdown, R. (1996). *Children in hospital: A guide for family and careers.* New York: Oxford University Press. The advantages of advance preparation and play therapy are cited as important ingredients in helping children cope with hospitalization. The author's suggestions are based on a combination of research findings and his own extensive practical experience—a valuable book on a hard-to-find subject.

Wallinga, D., & Skeen, P. (1996). Siblings of hospitalized and ill children: The teacher's role in helping these forgotten family members. *Young Children, 51*(6), 78–83A. This is a not-to-be-missed article helpful not only with siblings but also with youngsters adjusting to a sibling with a more permanent disability.

Death and Dying

Dougy Center for Grieving Children. (1997). *Helping children cope with death.* Portland, OR: Author. The sensible principles advocated here for helping children understand and begin to come to terms with dying can also be applied to many other crisis situations. A valuable pamphlet to have on hand before crises strike!

Goldman, L. E. (1996). We can help children grieve: A child-oriented model for memorializing. *Young*

Children, 51(6), 69–73. Goldman suggests tangible, concrete things young children can do to memorialize the death of someone they love.

Sanders, C. M. (1999). *Grief: The mourning after: Dealing with adult bereavement* (2nd ed.). New York: Wiley. This is a good, comprehensive survey of grief, and despite its title Sanders does include a helpful chapter on the impact of death in early childhood. *Highly recommended.*

Bibliographies of Crisis-Oriented Books for Children

Brohl, K. (1996). *Working with traumatized children: A handbook for healing.* Washington, DC: Child Welfare League of America. The chapter entitled "Metaphorical Storytelling" is filled with practical advice about how to use this indirect approach when helping children who are emotionally upset. *Highly recommended.*

Oehlberg, B. (1996). *Making it better: Activities for children living in a stressful world.* St. Paul, MN: Redleaf. Each topic such as death and family illness includes a good list of children's books appropriate for 4-year-olds and up.

Rudman, M. K., Gagne, K. D. M., & Bernstein, J. E. (1994). *Books to help children cope with separation and loss: An annotated bibliography.* New York: Bowker. Although this useful list is out of print, you can still find it at just about any library.

Thomason, N. C. (1999). "Our guinea pig is dead!" Young children cope with death. *Dimensions of Early Childhood, 27*(2), 26–29. A brief but appropriate bibliography of children's books is included in this excellent article.

For the Advanced Student

Berger, R. (1998). *Stepfamilies: A multidimensional perspective.* New York: Haworth. Berger explores the complexities if mingled families from a wide variety of aspects including chapters on immigrant, Black, and gay and lesbian stepfamilies. *Highly recommended.*

Black, S. M. (1999). HIV/AIDS in early childhood centers: The ethical dilemma of confidentiality versus disclosure. *Young Children, 54*(2), 39–45. Black explores problems related to privacy versus disclosure and who has the right to know or tell about it. General and specific guidelines for staff in these situations are proposed.

Bordin, J. (1998). An abuse allegation: Ten expectations for administrators. *Child Care Information Exchange, #124,* 65–67. This example of "crisis proofing" warns administrators in advance of what to anticipate when allegations are made. *Highly recommended.*

Crocker, A. C., Cohen, H. J., & Kastner, T. A. (Eds.). (1992). *HIV infection and developmental disabilities: A resource for service providers.* Baltimore, MD: Brookes. This entire book is devoted to the subject of children and AIDS and presents the most thorough treatment of the subject readily available to the lay public.

The future of children: Protecting children from abuse and neglect. (1998). *Future of Children, 1.* This issue covers many aspects of child maltreatment, with the primary focus on how to make child protective services more effective.

Hetherington, E. M. (1999a). *Coping with divorce, single-parenting, and remarriage: A risk and resiliency perspective.* Mahwah, NJ: Erlbaum. This is a collection of research-based, scholarly discussions on the topics listed in the subtitle. Valuable for the student with serious interests in these subjects.

Mikkelsen, E. J. (1997). Responding to allegations of sexual abuse in child care and early childhood education programs. *Young Children, 52*(3), 47–51. The author provides practical advice concerning ways to cope with accusations of abuse before and when such allegations occur.

National Association for the Education of Young Children (NAEYC). (1997). National Association for the Education of Young Children position statement on the prevention of child abuse in early childhood programs and the responsibilities of early childhood professionals to prevent child abuse. *Young Children, 52*(3), 42–46. Title is self-explanatory.

National Association for the Education of Young Children (NAEYC). (1998f). What would you do? Real-life ethical problems that early childhood professionals face. *Young Children, 53*(4), 52–54. This article relates the National Association for the Education of Young Children's *Code of Ethics* to real-life situations and concludes there are no easy answers.

Norton, C. C., & Norton, B. E. (1997). *Reaching children through play therapy: An experimental approach.* Denver, CO: Publishing Cooperative. Although written for therapists, this book would also be helpful for teachers as long as they are clear about the limits of their professional training. It makes an excellent case for the relieving possibilities of play and provides many examples of hearing at two levels of communication—what the child actually says and what the underlying message may be as well.

Rodgers, D. B. (1998). Supporting autonomy in young children. *Young Children, 53*(3), 75–80. Rodgers concisely summarizes recent research related the ability to be "governed by oneself."

Trickett, P. K., & Schellenbach, C. J. (Eds.). (1998). *Violence against children in the family and the community.* Washington, DC: American Psychological Association. This is a solid, up-to-date reference that includes a welcome section on prevention.

Wolchik, S. A., & Sandler, I. N. (Eds.). (1997). *Handbook of children's coping: Linking theory and intervention.* New York: Plenum Press. This comprehensive, scholarly book offers information on what is known about children's responses to crises and approaches to helping them through crises as diverse as divorce, maltreatment, and enduring painful medical procedures. *Highly recommended for the serious student.*

chapter nine

Welcoming Children Who Have Special Educational Requirements Into the Life of the School

physical self ≈ emotional health ≈ self-esteem ≈ social competence ≈ thinking and reasoning ≈ physical self ≈ emotional health ≈ self-esteem ≈ social competence ≈ creativity ≈ language ≈ literacy ≈ thinking and reasoning ≈ physical self ≈ emotional health ≈ self-esteem ≈ creativity ≈ language ≈ literacy ≈ emotional health ≈ self-esteem ≈ thinking and competence ≈ creativity ≈ language ≈ literacy ≈ thinking and ≈ physical self ≈ emotional health ≈ self-esteem ≈ social reasoning ≈ physical self ≈ emotional health ≈ self-esteem ≈ social competence ≈ creativity ≈ language ≈ literacy ≈ thinking and reasoning ≈ physical self ≈ emotional ≈ language ≈ literacy ≈ esteem ≈ thinking and ≈ social ≈ reasoning ≈ competence ≈ physical ≈ creativity

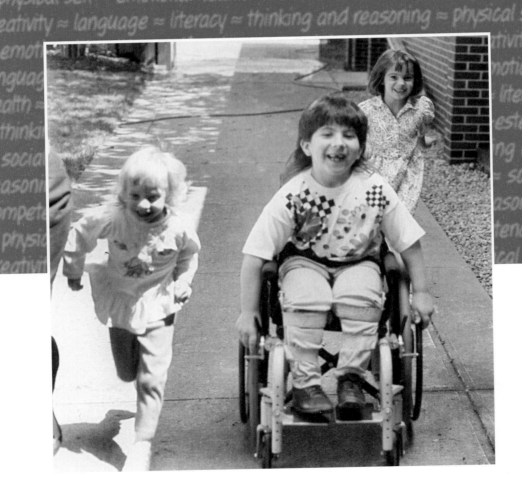

About a child who might need special help but were unsure what to say to the parent about it?

Whether you knew enough about a particular disability to admit a child with that condition to your class?

How to tell whether a child really needed help from a psychologist?

What to do with that exceptionally bright little girl who acts so bored when she comes to school?

. . . IF YOU HAVE, THE MATERIAL IN THE FOLLOWING PAGES WILL HELP YOU.

Whether they're handicapped or healthy, homeless or affluent, safe or at-risk, children need each other to grow. Children need to be together, in a safe, warm and caring environment—to play together, learn together. The rooted and the displaced, the graceful runner and the child who'll never walk, the sure-of-himself, easy smiler, and the child who's afraid to risk loving again all become part, each of the other.

Gretchen Buchenholz (in L. G. Johnson, Rogers, Johnson, & McMillan, 1993)

The moral test of government is how it treats those who are in the dawn of life, the children; those who are in the twilight of life, the aged; and those who are in the shadows of life, the sick, the needy, and the handicapped.

Hubert Humphrey (1977)

211

Although all children have special educational needs at one point or another in their lives, some children require specialized attention more consistently. This group includes a wide assortment of youngsters, including those who are physically challenged, who are emotionally disturbed, or whose intellectual development either lags behind or is markedly ahead of their peers. In short, the category of exceptionality covers children who deviate in at least one respect far enough from the typical that they are noticeable in the group because of this deviation.

The latest available report by the U. S. Department of Education (Sack, 1999) reveals that the number of children ages 3 to 21 years identified as having disabilities continues to rise. For example, in 1995–96 there was more than a 3% increase in identified children so that 1996 totals amounted to 5.62 million students with disabilities. This increasing attention to identifying and including children who have special educational requirements is the result of Congress enacting and revising the *Individuals with Disabilities Education Act* (IDEA) and the *Americans with Disabilities Act* (ADA) (Turnbull & Cilley, 1999). These laws mandate that such youngsters be educated in the most facilitative, least restrictive educational environments.

Perhaps the reader is thinking, "It's nice these laws exist, but what does that have to do with me?" The answer is threefold. First, passage of these laws means that help for young children with disabilities is more readily available than it was in the past. This is a wonderful comfort to teachers who still come across children who need help but have escaped the notice of other professionals before entering school. Second, it means that because of certain requirements in the laws, many more children who have disabilities are attending our "regular" public or independent early childhood centers, and each of them will come equipped with an *individualized educational program* (IEP) identifying specific skills the teacher and child are supposed to work on together. Finally, it means that we teachers are expected to become part of the treatment teams engaged in working with such children.

These circumstances make it increasingly important for teachers to have a practical, working knowledge of the commoner ways children deviate from the typical and also to understand how to work with such youngsters and the specialists who help them. Examples and resources are provided throughout *The Whole Child* in relevant chapters, but experience has taught me it is also helpful for students to have a concise source of information presented all together. That is the reason this chapter is included in the text. It is important to realize, however, that the subject of exceptionality is *huge*, and *so only an introduction can be offered here. I hope it will pave the way to further reading and education in this important area.*

IDENTIFYING CHILDREN WHO HAVE SPECIAL NEEDS AND FINDING HELP FOR THEM: THE PRESCHOOL TEACHER AS A SCREENING AGENT

One advantage teachers have that physicians do not is that they see the same children for extended periods of time, and this makes it possible to be aware of physical, emotional, and cognitive behavior that may indicate a serious underlying difficulty. It is a mistaken notion that such difficulties are always first noticed in the physician's office or by parents. Physicians see children for brief periods of time, often under conditions quite stressful to the child. In addition, they can be hampered by parents who either raise questions about insignificant symptoms, or paradoxically are too worried about something to bring it up, or who resist being told anything about their youngsters that may be upsetting. When physicians are caught in this kind of situation, it is only to be expected that occasional difficulties slip past without notice. These comments are not intended to imply that a highly trained medical specialist knows less than early childhood teachers do. Rather, teachers should keep their eyes open since they have the advantage of seeing the child in a natural setting for extended periods of time, and they have seen many youngsters of similar age and background. Thus it is possible that they may become aware of difficulties that should be drawn to the attention of the physician or psychologist.

The sooner such potential handicaps are identified, the sooner they may be ameliorated and further formation of undesirable habit patterns and emotional reactions reduced. Sometimes early diagnosis means a condition can be cleared up entirely (as when a child's hearing is restored following a tonsillectomy-adenoidectomy), and sometimes the effect of the condition can only be mitigated (as is often the case with youngsters who have cognitive delays). But *nothing* can be done until the child is identified as needing assistance and a referral has been successfully carried out. These are points at which the teacher's help is crucial because she is the person most likely to provide day-by-day linkage between the family and the services that can help them.

Referring Children for Special Help: Calling the Difficulty to the Parents' Attention

Calling a parent's attention to a special problem requires delicacy and tact on the part of the teacher since it is all too easy for parents to feel that they are being attacked or criticized and that they have failed to be good parents. This is particularly true if the teacher must raise the issue of a pronounced behavior problem. However, the teacher can do several things to reduce the strength of this understandable defensive reaction.

If Teachers Listen Carefully While Talking with the Parents, They May Find That the Parents Themselves Are Raising the Problem Very Tentatively

For example, the mother may ask nervously, "How did he do today?" or comment, "He's just like his older brother. Doesn't he ever sit still?" Many a teacher responds to such questions by just as nervously reassuring the parent, saying brightly, "Oh, he did just fine!" (while thinking wryly to herself, "Just fine, that is, if you don't count biting John, destroying Angelina's block tower, and refusing to come to story time"). Rather than being falsely reassuring, the teacher could use the opening the parent has provided by responding, "I'm glad you asked. He *is* having some difficulties at school. I'm beginning to think it's time to put our heads together and come up with some special ways to help him."

It Takes Time to Bring About a Referral

It is best to raise problems gradually with parents over a period of time because it takes a while for families to accustom themselves to the fact that their child may need special help. Even such an apparently simple thing as having an eye examination may loom as either a financial or emotional threat to particular families, and teachers should not expect instant acceptance and compliance with their recommendations just because they have finally worked up their courage to the point of mentioning a difficulty.

The Teacher Should Have the Reasons Why the Child Needs Special Help Clearly in Mind Before Raising the Issue with Parents

The recommendation of having the reasons for needing special help clearly in mind before talking with a child's parents is not intended to mean that teachers should confront parents with a long, unhappy list of grievances against the child. Rather, the reason is that they should be prepared to provide examples of the problem while explaining gently and clearly to the family the reason for their concern.

For example, while examining photographs I took for this book, the staff and I were surprised to notice that one child was looking at a seriation game with her eyes consistently "crossed." It was helpful to use these snapshots with the family when suggesting they have her eyes examined.

Usually, of course, one does not have anything as concrete as a picture to share, but episodes or examples of the problem can be described almost as well and are essential to have in mind when discussing such difficulties with parents. (See the photograph on p. 225.)

It Is Not the Teacher's Place to Diagnose

A particular behavior can have many different causes. For example, failure to pay attention in story hour may be the consequence of a hearing loss, inappropriate reading material, borderline intelligence, fatigue, poor eyesight, or simply needing to go to the toilet. The teacher's role is to recognize that a difficulty exists, do all she can to mitigate it in the group, inform the parent, and suggest a referral to an expert professional person for diagnosis and treatment when necessary.

Therefore, when she confers with the parent, the teacher should discuss the symptoms and express her concern but avoid giving the impression she knows for certain what the real cause of the problem may be. Instead she should ally herself with the parent in a joint quest to find the answer together.

Finding the Appropriate Referral Source

Teachers need to acquaint themselves with the variety of referral sources available in their community since it is both senseless and cruel to raise a problem with parents and have no suggestions about where they can go for help. When the problem appears to be serious, the foremost resource to seek out is whatever agency in your state administers IDEA. The names of these agencies vary widely; typical names are the State Health Department, Department of Human Services, or Office of Children, Youth, and Families.

Other resources include directories of community services, public health nurses, pediatricians, local children's hospitals, school counselors, county medical societies, and mental health clinics. The same resource and referral agency that provides lists of child care sources for parents and employers often know of appropriate referrals, as does the United Way. Whenever possible, it is always desirable to list three referral possibilities so that the family has the opportunity to select the one they think suits them best.

Observing Professional Ethics

I have already pointed out that the teacher should not assume the role of diagnostician. Often, however, he possesses information that is of value to the specialist to whom the child is referred. It can be a temptation to pick up the telephone and call this person without pausing to ask the parent's permission, but this is a violation of professional ethics. The teacher must obtain the parent's consent before he talks to the specialist. Some professional people even require that this permission be in writing before any information is exchanged. After permission is obtained, exchanges of information and suggestions from the specialist can be extraordinarily helpful and should be used whenever the opportunity presents itself.

Also when dealing with a special case, the teacher may be tempted to discuss it with people who are not entitled to know about it, because it is so interesting and perhaps makes the teacher feel important. This gossiping is an unforgivable violation of the family's privacy, and a teacher must never indulge her desire to do this.

INCLUDING CHILDREN WHO HAVE DISABILITIES

What the Laws Say

The truth is that long before Congress passed laws related to children who have disabilities, many nursery schools made it a point to welcome exceptional children into their groups (Moor, 1960; Northcutt, 1970), and their inclusion has usually worked out quite satisfactorily. The individualized, developmentally appropriate curriculum characteristic of nursery schools, children's centers, Head Start, and some kindergartens makes it relatively easy to incorporate a child and her IEP into the life of the school. Indeed, one would hope that every youngster in these schools already has at least an informal IEP developed for her and carried in the back of the teacher's mind.

As previously mentioned, this trend toward integration has been augmented by the passage of the two pieces of legislation mentioned at the beginning of this chapter: the Individuals with Disabilities Education Act (IDEA) [formerly known as the Education of the Handicapped Act (PL 91–142 and PL 94–457)] and the Americans with Disabilities Act (ADA).

What IDEA basically says is that every child (including infants and toddlers) with a disability is entitled to a free public education, that each of these youngsters shall be provided with an *individualized educational program* (IEP) or an *individualized family service plan* (IFSP) for the youngest children, and that she or he shall be educated in the least restrictive environment. Provisions are also included for parental input and protest opportunities to ensure that the intentions of the law are carried out in fact (Rab, Wood, & Taylor, 1995). A wide variety of disabilities ranging from cognitive or emotional disabilities to physical problems are covered, and many support services such as physical therapy and speech and language training are mandated. Emphasis is on service to families and fostering family autonomy and decision making.

The ADA legislation is sometimes spoken of as the "civil rights bill for people with handicaps." It states that people with disabilities are entitled to equal rights in employment, state and local public services, and public accommodations.

When Planning the IEP, It Is Essential to Have a Careful Assessment of the Child's Accomplishments and Abilities Available

The assessment is usually carried out by a team of professional people versed in the areas of development in which the child's difficulties lie. Working with the parents, the team does its best to identify the youngster's strengths and problem areas. Then it recommends things to do to help her develop as well as possible. As discussed in chapter 2, these assessments should involve a range of measures including naturalistic observations, parent reports, various standardized tests, a physical examination if it is warranted, and whatever special measures are appropriate to gain further insight into the individual youngster's disability (Hendrick, 1998; Raver, 1999).

Once the assessment has been accomplished, the information is pooled. A team is formed composed of whoever will be teaching the child, at least one of her parents, a representative of the school district, and if it is a first meeting, a member of the assessment team. During this conference the IEP is developed that outlines the most important learning goals and objectives for the child and suggested ways to achieve those goals.

For example, one child's IEP might include developing muscular dexterity and social independence by pushing the bar handle of the water tap while washing her hands, whereas another child's might include paying attention to hand gestures when the teacher uses sign language.[1] Follow-up meetings are scheduled to revise and update the IEP as needed.

Although IEPs may sound like a good deal of paperwork (and they are!), the clear intention of the law is to benefit children who have special needs and to protect their rights to a free, public education—a right sorely abused in prior times. They also have the virtue of protecting the family's right to privacy and their right to participate actively in planning what is best for their child's well-being and future.

LEARNING TO WORK AS A MEMBER OF THE TEAM

As more and more children with disabilities are placed in regular preschool settings, there is an additional reason to be grateful for IDEA: It requires that support services be provided to children who need them. This is a blessing since preprimary centers, though strong in offering a range of developmentally appropriate activities, are likely to be weak in providing the highly specialized educational strategies some children with special needs require. We desperately need the examples and advice such specialists can provide.

---

[1] *For a detailed description of this process see Cook, Tessier, and Klein (2000).*

Providing an extra set of crutches helped Jennifer understand John's problems when he was admitted to the school.

Currently the trend is to incorporate these special services into the setting right along with the child and to encourage the teacher and other specialists to combine their skills. This is called the *transdisciplinary approach* (Gallivan-Fenlon, 1994). It is a desirable change from former days when the speech therapist, for example, would arrive and take the child away to a quiet place where she drilled her on building language skills in isolation from ongoing classroom life. In addition to disrupting whatever the child was doing, the problem with this approach was getting the training to carry over into real-life situations.

Now physical therapists, speech pathologists, and other specialists are more likely to integrate their work into the ongoing school program—seizing opportunities for the child to practice desired skills as they arise during her play (Bricker & Cripe, 1992). This is particularly easy to do at the preschool and kindergarten level because the self-select, open-choice periods provide golden opportunities for practice to take place in a natural life setting.

The advantages of this activity-oriented approach are obvious, but it is up to the teacher and specialist to make it work, and this is not always easy! For example, the educational philosophies of the two people may differ considerably. Just as preschool teachers are well aware that many elementary school teachers do not understand or appreciate early childhood methods of instruction, so, too, are they aware that neither are many special education teachers—many of whom unfortunately have no background in early childhood. To these uninitiated people, self-select time may appear to be more like bedlam than the carefully planned array of educational opportunities the early childhood teacher perceives it as being. Nor do some of these people understand the value of play in the lives of all children.

Then, too, many special education specialists are devoted to the behavior modification approach to learning. In my opinion, there's no denying that approach has merit, particularly when one is working with certain kinds of severe disabilities. However, the early childhood teacher often finds the charts and reward systems this approach typically depends on to be repugnant.

Clearly both teacher and specialist will need to develop generous amounts of appreciation for each other's points of view and the unique strengths each brings to the children if the team effort is to succeed. Without that mutual appreciation, the specialist may feel so unwelcome and the teacher so irritated and threatened that the old, isolated approach to instruction will be reinstated. Unfortunately it is the child who pays the price in this ego-fraught situation (Bricker & Wilderstrom, 1996).

The best way to overcome prejudices and build respect is to make certain that *regular* times are scheduled for team members to talk together; *hurried conferences at the door when the children are present are not sufficient.* Sometimes these chats can fit in during the lunch break, or they can even take place over the phone. They present invaluable opportunities for teacher and specialist to exchange concerns and ideas and to coordinate strategies. This mutual approach to problem solving, *particularly when families are included,* maximizes the child's opportunities to thrive.

GETTING STARTED WITH A CHILD WHO HAS A DISABILITY

It Is Important to Make It Clear to the Family That the Staff Has Great Goodwill but Also Has Certain Limitations and Will Not Be Able to Work Miracles

Few early childhood teachers have much training in working with exceptional children. In addition it is unlikely that during the year they will be able to devote much extra time to studying this subject. They do, however, know a great deal about working with children in general and will bring to this particular child the benefit of these insights and practical, matter-of-fact treatment that emphasizes the normal rather than the exceptional.

The Staff Will Have to Come to Terms with How Much Extra Effort the Child Will Require Them to Expend Every Day

It is one thing to accept a child with mental retardation in a flush of helpfulness and sympathy, but it may turn out to be quite another when her pants have to be changed three or four times each morning. Some children with emotional disturbance may also require an inordinate amount of time and attention. The quandary for the staff is that they have obligations to all the children and that the time required to work with an exceptional child may eventually deprive the other youngsters of their due share of energy and concern.

Fortunately the rather extreme examples given above are the exception rather than the rule, but the possibility of overtaxing the staff must be taken into consideration when discussing an admission. However, experience has taught me that most exceptional children can and should be gathered in. Usually the amount of special care is considerable during the first few weeks but gradually declines as the child and staff make the adjustment.

It Will Be Necessary for the Staff to Examine Their Feelings About Why They Wish to Accept the Child

It is all too easy to succumb to a rescue fantasy and decide that what the youngster with a disability really needs is plenty of love and she will be all right. This is, of course, untrue. Children, whether exceptional or ordinary, require a great many other talents from their teachers besides the ability to express affection, and teachers should not delude themselves that affection can overcome all problems. If they intend to work with the child effectively, they must plan on learning the best ways to help her in addition to loving her.

Information garnered from the various specialists serving the child is, of course, invaluable, but never forget that the most valuable resource the teacher can call on is *the parents*.

Many Seemingly Insurmountable Problems Can Be Solved During the Trial Period if the Staff and Family Are Creatively Minded

How can seemingly insurmountable problems be overcome creatively? For example, a child who cannot negotiate a flight of stairs and who is too heavy to be carried can come to the center if her father builds a ramp over the stairs. A child who requires a good deal of extra physical care may be able to attend if she is accompanied in the beginning by her mother or, if the parent needs relief, by an aide who tends to the extra chores until the child becomes more self-sufficient (Rab et al., 1995).

There Are Several Ways to Ease Entry Pangs

The regular practice of asking the parent to stay with the child until she has made friends should be followed when welcoming a child with special needs into the group. Research has shown that this policy is of special importance for young children who are mentally retarded (Kessler, Gridth, & Smith, 1968).

Sometimes it also helps to begin with a short day and gradually extend the time the child attends as her skills and toleration of the group increase. The shorter day means she can go home while she is still experiencing success and has not been overwhelmed with fatigue. For example, in a half-day program it may be easiest if the child arrives in the middle of the morning and leaves when the other children do since this means she does not have to depart when everyone else is still having a good time.

A chat with the child's physician or other team members may also reassure the teacher and provide special guidelines that may be necessary for handling the newly admitted youngster. Children with heart conditions or asthma, for instance, occasionally require special treatment but sometimes arrive with firm instructions to let them alone so that they can pace themselves.

Many Disabilities Will Pass Unnoticed by Other Children in the Group, but Some Will Require Explanation

As the Research Study in this chapter reveals, children *do* notice differences and will conjure up their own explanations for the child's disability unless they are provided the correct one. Explanations need not be elaborate; they should avoid the condescension of pity and should stress matter-of-fact suggestions about how the children can get along with the child about whom they are asking (Derman-Sparks & ABC Task Force, 1989). It may be necessary, for example, to help the children understand that a particular child uses her ears and hands in place of her eyes because she cannot see, to coach them to stand in front of a child who is hard of hearing and catch her attention before speaking to her, or to explain that another youngster has to stand at the table sandbox to keep the grit out of her leg braces.

When our school recently included a child who had severe emotional problems, we found it helped the children and us a lot to discuss together what we could do to help him. It was heartening to see how our 4-year-olds, who were at first nonplussed by Stewart's behavior, came to ignore it in time and to brush off his panicky attacks. This was followed by a gradual shift to telling him he should "Stop it!" (which he often did, with staff assistance), and finally a gentle kind of pushing back and dogpiling took place while the children coached him about what to say. I recall one child saying, "Tell me to stop—*tell me to stop and I will!*" There is no denying that the therapy the child was undergoing concurrently had a very significant effect on his growth and development, but some credit must also go to the staff and children who worked together to understand, accept, and help Stewart.

GENERAL RECOMMENDATIONS FOR WORKING WITH CHILDREN WHO HAVE DISABILITIES

See Through the Exceptional to the Typical in Every Child

It can be easy to become so caught up in the differences of an exceptional child that the teacher loses sight of the fact that the child is largely like the other children in the group

Do Preschool Children Recognize Disabilities in Their Peers?

Research Question: Diamond wanted to know whether 4-year-old children without disabilities recognize the presence of a disability in their peers, and, if they do, how they explain the reasons for such a disability.

Research Method: Diamond questioned 28 4-year-old children without disabilities who participated with 14 preschool-age children with disabilities. These youngsters had played together during the free play period every day at their nursery school during the school year. The disabilities included mild-to-severe developmental delays such as cerebral palsy, Down syndrome, severe language delays, moderate-to-severe hearing loss, and developmental delay.

At the end of the school year the researcher asked the children without disabilities a series of questions. After a few get-acquainted questions she showed them photographs of each child in the class and asked them to tell her their names. Next she said, "Show me if there's anyone who (1) doesn't walk or run the way the other kids do, (2) doesn't talk as well, . . . (3) doesn't behave the way the other kids do—you know, they're silly or goofy." When a child was identified as fitting any one of these categories, she followed up by asking such questions as, "Why do you think he (or she) can't talk so well?" All the children's replies were then sorted into various categories.

Research Results: In all but 3 out of 196 opportunities the children who were questioned knew all the other children's names. Twenty-seven out of the 28 youngsters identified at least one child with a disability. The disabilities that were particularly noticed were obvious physical disabilities and mental retardation. Children with mild-to-moderate speech and language delays, however, were not selected as having a disability. Only eight children mentioned a child who had unusual behavior,

and interestingly enough all of those behavior nominations singled out boys who actually did not have disabilities.

Two thirds of the children gave reasons why the child was disabled according to a variety of causes. Most typically they explained why a peer couldn't walk or talk as being attributable to the child's age (e.g., "He's small," "She's a baby," "When she gets bigger, she can walk like everybody else"). Other explanations referred to the equipment the child used ("He's got a walker") or used a label ("She's handicapped"). The third kind of explanation was based on reasons such as accidents or trauma ("He broke his leg," or "He can't talk because he got hit in the mouth").

Implications for Teaching: Even though Diamond describes this as a preliminary study, it leaves no doubt that children as young as age 4 are aware of the more obvious forms of disability.

Since this is true, the policy followed by some teachers of just ignoring a disability so that the children will assume everyone is "the same" simply isn't effective. Just as we shall see in the chapter on multicultural education, children are well aware of many kinds of differences, and these differences must be acknowledged and dealt with if children are to acquire positive attitudes about them. *Ignorance is the handmaiden of prejudice.*

Because the explanations offered by the children indicate that many of them were not only aware of the differences but also had speculated about the reasons for them, the study also emphasizes the value of providing simple but correct explanations of causes to deepen the children's understanding of the disability.

Source: From "Preschool Children's Concepts of Disability in Their Peers," by K. E. Diamond, 1993, Early Education and Development, 4(2), 123–129.

and should be treated as much like them as possible. Feeling sorry for a child weakens her character and ultimately does her a terrible disservice. Many exceptional children have too many allowances made for them out of pity, misguided good intentions, and inexperience—and sometimes, where parents are concerned, as a consequence of guilt. The outcome is that the child may become a demanding and rather unpleasant person to have around. In other words, she becomes just plain spoiled.

Consistency, reasonable expectations, and sound policies are, if anything, *more important* to employ when dealing with exceptional children than when dealing with typical children. Teachers should feel comfortable about drawing on their common sense and considerable experience, but they should also be able to turn freely to experts for consultation when they feel puzzled and uncertain about how to proceed.

Try to Steer a Middle Course, Neither Overprotecting nor Overexpecting

The most common pitfall in working with an exceptional child is becoming so concerned for her safety and well-being that the child is stifled and deprived of the opportunity to be as normal as she might be were she not overprotected. In general the teacher should proceed on the assumption that the child should be encouraged to participate in every activity, with modifications provided only when necessary to ensure success. Thus a child who is behind her peers in intellectual development should be expected to participate in story hour but may enjoy it most if she sits with the youngest group.

On the other hand, some parents and teachers set their expectations unreasonably high and are unwilling to make any exceptions for the child with a handicap. This causes unnecessary strain and even despair for the youngster. Teachers can be helpful here by pointing out what is reasonable to expect of 3- or 4-year-olds in general and helping the parents understand what a reasonable expectation would be for their particular youngster. It is often helpful with such families to note each step as the child attains it and to discuss what the next stage of development will be so that the parents can see progress coming bit by bit. This may reduce the feeling of desperately driving toward a difficult distant goal.

Be Realistic

It is important to see the child as she is and to avoid false promises and unrealistic reassurances when talking with parents or the child herself. Everyone yearns for an exceptional child to "make it," and sometimes this yearning leads to unwitting self-deceptions, which can do the family and child a disservice by delaying acceptance of the disability or by encouraging them to make inadequate future plans. I once watched as a blind preschooler said to her teacher, "I can tell by feeling things with my hands what they are like; but when I grow up, then I will be able to see the colors, too, won't I?" The teacher replied, with tears in his eyes, "Yes, then everything will be all right."

Acceptance of the child's limitations, as well as capitalization on her strengths, is the balance to strive for and to model for the family. Some children will in time overcome a disability entirely, but others will not be able to do this. Helping the parents and the child accept this fact, as well as accepting it oneself, is difficult to do but valuable.

Keep Regular Records of the Child's Development

Since progress with all children, including exceptional ones, occurs a little at a time, it is easy to feel discouraged from time to time and to lose sight of how far the youngster has come. If teachers keep regular written records, however brief, an occasional review of that material can be encouraging.

It is particularly important to keep records on an exceptional youngster so that they may be summarized and referred to at the next IEP meeting or passed on to her next teacher to acquaint him with her interests and progress. The records should cover whatever incidents seem particularly important to the child, indications of growth or slipping backward, special interests and tastes, effective educational approaches, significant information contributed by the parents, physician, and other support personnel, and any possible questions that may have come up.

Occasionally the teacher may be asked to participate in an in-depth study of an emotionally disturbed youngster and may want to make more detailed written observations to be used in discussion and consultation. Although time-consuming, this kind of study can be helpful and revealing. The teacher can refer to references at the end of the chapter for models and suggestions about how to carry out such observations successfully.

Remain in Constant Contact with the Family

All parents are concerned about their children and need consistent contact with teachers, but parents of children who have special problems require this even more, and so do the teachers who have welcomed such youngsters to their group (W. H. Brown, 1997).

Parents can help the teacher with many details about child management. It may be as simple as explaining the easiest way to slip the arm of a child with cerebral palsy into her snowsuit or an offer of special equipment for pedals for a child with spina bifida who is dying to ride the tricycle. Moreover parents are often the intermediary between specialist and teacher, relaying information from one to the other.

Parents often hang on the teacher's words about how their exceptional child is getting along at school. For this reason teachers should choose their words with care while remaining sincere and truthful. As many opportunities as possible should be created for quick, friendly chats. Even notes sent home can help, but chatting is really to be preferred because of the direct person-to-person encounter it provides.

Do not limit your ideas of how families can help by thinking of them as only supplying physical labor. Always remember that parents are the foremost authorities on their child. They know the youngster in ways the specialists never can, and they can contribute an endless amount of advice and information if only the teacher will ask for it.

Moreover including the parents in discussions and plans makes consistency in expectations and handling at both home and school more probable. This consistency of approach is very valuable.

IDENTIFYING AND HELPING CHILDREN WHO HAVE PHYSICAL HANDICAPS

Some Specific Physical Conditions and Symptoms of Which the Teacher Should Be Aware

Speech and Hearing Problems

Various speech difficulties and symptoms of possible hearing impairment are reviewed in the chapter on language, so it is only noted here that speech and hearing problems are among the physical disorders that occur most frequently in childhood. Speech difficulties are likely to be noticed, but hearing loss may be overlooked as a possible cause of misbehavior, inattention, or lack of responsiveness. However, once hearing loss is suspected, it is a relatively simple matter to refer the child to an otolaryngologist for examination. Since such losses may be a result of infection, they can and should be treated promptly.

Difficulties of Vision

Another physical disability that may pass unnoticed but that occurs frequently is an inability to see clearly. The incidence of visual defects may run as high as one in four or five children of elementary school age (M. C. Reynolds & Birch, 1988). Although actual statistics on the incidence of vision defects in preschoolers could not be located, it seems probable that the incidence would be about the same. This means that in a group of 15 preprimary children as many as three or four youngsters may have some kind of difficulty with their eyes.

The presence of the following symptoms should alert the teacher to the possibility that the child needs to have her eyes examined (S. A. Kirk, 1972):

1. Strabismus (crossed eyes); nystagmus (involuntary, rapid movement of the eyeball)
2. How the child uses her eyes; tilting her head, holding objects close to her eyes, rubbing her eyes, squinting, displaying sensitivity to bright lights, and rolling her eyes
3. Inattention to visual objects or visual tasks such as looking at pictures or reading
4. Awkwardness in games requiring eye-hand coordination
5. Avoidance of tasks that require close eye work
6. Affinity for tasks that require distance vision
7. Any complaints about inability to see
8. Lack of normal curiosity in regard to visually appealing objects[2]

In addition to such symptoms, physiological ones include reddened or crusty eyelids, watery eyes, eyes that are discharging, excessive rubbing of eyes, shutting or covering one eye, squinting, blinking, frowning, and distorted facial expressions while doing close work (Cook et al., 2000).

One defect of vision in particular requires treatment during early childhood because later attempts at correction are not so effective (American Academy of Ophthalmology, 1993; Desrochers, 1999). This is *amblyopia*, sometimes called *lazy eye*, a condition in

---

[2]   *Samuel A. Kirk, EDUCATING EXCEPTIONAL CHILDREN, 2/ed. Copyright © 1972 by Houghton Mifflin Co. Reprinted by permission.*

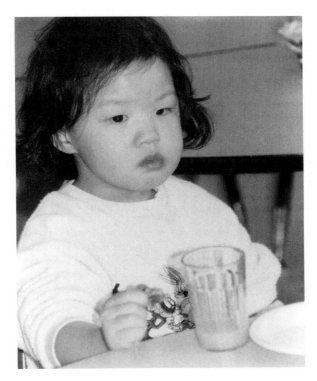

This youngster has the condition called lazy eye, or amblyopia. It is important for this condition to receive prompt medical attention.

which one eye is weaker than the other because of a muscle imbalance. Common signs of this condition include squinting with one eye or tilting the head to one side to see better, or having so-called crossed-eyes. Since early treatment of this condition is important, *if there is any possible way to incorporate visual screening tests into the school program it should be done*. Sometimes local ophthalmologic or optometric societies will sponsor this service; sometimes a public health nurse can be prevailed upon or an interested civic group will employ a trained nurse to visit centers and nursery schools and conduct such tests.

Screening is best done at school rather than at a central clinic because coverage of children attending the school is likely to be more complete and the environment in which testing takes place is familiar to the children, so they will be more at ease. Giving the children practice before the actual examination day in holding the E according to instructions will facilitate testing and help save the examiner's sanity. Central clinics should also be offered as a service to children who do not attend school.

It is important to remember that a screening test does only that—it screens for some of the more obvious vision disabilities. For this reason, even though a youngster may have passed the screening test with flying colors, if she continues to have difficulties she should be referred for further testing. Of course, when the screening test *does* pick up a possible problem, that youngster should be referred to an ophthalmologist or qualified optometrist for diagnosis and follow-up, too.

Attention Deficit Disorder

Attention deficit disorder (ADD) and its cousin *attention deficit hyperactivity disorder* (ADHD) are terms used by experts to describe a neurobiological disorder the general public labels *hyperactivity* (Aldridge, Eddowes, & Kuby, 1998). Because the hallmarks of this condition include impulsivity, inattention, and in some cases, overactivity, some school personnel and inexperienced parents have the tendency to misuse the term to describe every active, vigorous child. In the past this has occasionally led to overprescription of medication to control behavior that was actually within normal bounds.

As the following list makes clear, there is a tremendous difference between normal behavior and the behavior of youngsters who fit into this category:

1. Restlessness—the child appears to be a bundle of energy. The mother may come to feel that she can't take her eyes off him for a minute without his climbing on the refrigerator or running into the street. At nursery school, the child may be incessantly in motion except that he seems able to settle down when given one-to-one attention.
2. The child is easily distracted and has a short attention span. In nursery school he may rush from activity to activity and then seem at a loss for what to do. He may do as the teacher asks but forget quickly and revert to his former behavior.
3. The child demands attention insatiably—monopolizes conversations, teases, badgers, repeats annoying activities. May be emotionally unresponsive or undemonstrative.
4. Shows a weaker-than-average ability to control his impulses. Hard for him to wait, he may become upset rapidly, has many temper tantrums, acts on the spur of the moment—often with poor judgment. Parents may complain that the child is incontinent.
5. About half of these children exhibit difficulties in the coordination of fine muscle activities such as using scissors, coloring and so forth, or with problems of balance.
6. The child may have various kinds of interpersonal problems including resistance to social demands from parents and teachers, excessive independence, and a troublesome tendency to dominate the children he plays with, which makes him unlikable.
7. He may have various emotional problems including swings of mood, becoming excessively excited over pleasant activities, sometimes appearing to be insensitive to pain, demonstrating a low tolerance to frustration and overreaction to it when frustrated, and low self-esteem.
8. Some of these children have real difficulty tolerating change.[3]

Of course, most young children exhibit these kinds of behaviors from time to time. What sets the truly hyperactive child apart is the *intensity and consistency of the behavior.* Some, though not all, of these behaviors may appear to subside by adolescence, but the years of stress and the unhappy side effects of this condition have usually taken a painful toll by then (Fowler, 1994).

The most adequate referral is one made to a child psychiatrist or a pediatrician conversant with this disorder since medication often contributes to the successful management of this condition. A child psychologist or social worker can also provide valuable assis-

---

[3] *Taken from THE HYPERACTIVE CHILD. A Handbook for Parents by Paul H. Wender, M.D. © 1973 by Paul H. Wender. Used by permission of Crown Publishers, Inc.*

tance because behavior modification techniques may be helpful to use with some of these youngsters (Waslick & Greenhill, 1997).

Childhood Asthma

During the past few years the number of young children with asthma has increased alarmingly so that now it is the most prevalent of all chronic health-related disorders in childhood (De Mesquita & Fiorella, 1998; Phelps, 1998). Anyone who has ever seen the panic in a child's eyes as she wheezes and gasps desperately for breath knows how serious and frightening this condition can be. Although asthma can and does affect all kinds of children, research reveals it to be most prevalent among boys, African American youngsters, and children of the poor (Centers for Disease Control and Prevention, 1996).

During an attack three things happen: (a) The lining of the bronchial tubes become inflamed, thus constricting airflow, (b) the muscles around them become hypersensitive, restricting air flow even more, and (c) glands begin to secrete extra mucus, which clogs the airways even further. No wonder the asthmatic dreads these attacks. Unfortunately attacks are not always predictable, but some *triggers* such as heavy urban smog, cigarette smoke, various allergens, molds, furs, and dust mites are classic.

Although teachers can't do much about the presence of some triggers, there are some things they *can* do. Talking with the family and medical provider and being well informed about the particular youngster's condition and triggers is one of these. Doing everything possible to help the child feel that she can control what is happening to her is another, and the most effective way to accomplish this is to make certain she always has her inhaler with her, knows where it is, and knows how to use it. Many young children also know how to use a peak flow meter that can give early warning of an attack and so use the inhaler before the symptoms become severe. Since vigorous exercise in cold, dry air is a common trigger, the teacher should also encourage the child to wrap a scarf warmly around her nose and mouth before going outside; even then it's sometimes necessary to suggest something quiet like going down the slide rather than joining the others in the more active galloping around so dear to the hearts of many 4-year-olds.

Seizure Disorders

A condition that responds particularly well to medication is epilepsy. Indeed the *generalized tonic clonic seizures* (formerly termed *grand mal seizures*) in which the individual loses consciousness are now rarely witnessed in children's centers. Unless a major convulsive seizure occurs for the first time at school, teachers usually need not worry about referring such children because it is almost certain that they are already under treatment by their physician. Teachers should, however, report seizures to the family. The Epilepsy Foundation of America recommends that if an attack occurs at school, the following procedure be carried out:

1. Remain calm. Students will assume the same emotional reaction as their teacher. The seizure itself is painless to the child.
2. Do not try to restrain the child. Nothing can be done to stop a seizure once it has begun; it must run its course.
3. Clear the area around the student so that he does not injure himself on hard objects. Try not to interfere with his movements in any way.

4. Do not force anything between his teeth. If his mouth is already open, a soft object like a handkerchief may be placed between his side teeth.
5. It generally is not necessary to call a physician unless the attack is immediately followed by another major seizure or if the seizure lasts more than 10 minutes.
6. When the seizure is over, let the child rest if he needs to.[4]

The teacher will also need to explain to the other children, who may be either curious or distressed, what happened. The explanation should be simple and matter-of-fact to make it as easy as possible for the child to return to the group with little comment.

Epilepsy is not contagious, and people who have this condition do not have a mental illness or mental retardation (Needlman & Needlman, 1997). The seizures are the result of disturbances to the nervous system because of inappropriate electrical activity within the brain, but the causes of such activity are largely unknown at this time. Stress and fatigue may increase the probability of a seizure, but erratic use of prescribed medication is the most common cause of difficulty (Lectenberg, 1984). When medication is taken consistently, about 80% of all patients who have convulsive seizures experience good control (Michael, 1995).

The teacher needs to be more alert to the much milder form of convulsion, formerly called *petit mal* but now called *generalized absence* (pronounced to rhyme with *Alphonse*). It is important to pay particular attention to this kind of lighter seizure since it sometimes escapes the notice of the family, to whom it may seem to be a case of daydreaming or inattention.

According to Batshaw and Perret (1992), these brief episodes are characterized by the child having a glazed look, blinking, and being unaware of his surroundings. She may interrupt what she is saying and then pick up where she left off. Although this condition is uncommon, these seizures may occur hundreds of times a day and yet be undetected because they usually last less than 10 seconds. It is worthwhile to identify this behavior and refer the child for treatment to a pediatrician or neurologist since the probability of successful control by means of medication is high.

Excessive Awkwardness

The teacher should also notice children who are exceptionally clumsy. These are youngsters who, even though allowance has been made for their youthful age, are much more poorly coordinated than their peers. They may fall over their feet, run into things, knock things over, have trouble with climbing and balancing (and are often apprehensive about engaging in these activities), run consistently on their toes, or be unable to accomplish ordinary fine muscle tasks. This kind of behavior should not be "laughed off." Instead it should be drawn to the attention of the parent and referral to the pediatrician suggested. The causes of such symptoms are numerous, and many are amenable to treatment, but only if they are identified.

Sickle-Cell Anemia

I include here a discussion of sickle-cell anemia because it is both painful and serious for some children, and most teachers don't know much about it. It is a serious, chronic,

---

[4]   From "Epilepsy," published by the Epilepsy Foundation of America, 4351 Garden City Dr., Landover, MD 20785.

inherited condition. Although occurring mainly among African Americans (Morse & Shine, 1998), it also occurs in other populations—for example, some Turkish and Greek youngsters and those of Italian (primarily Sicilian) stock.

Since it confers immunity for certain types of malaria, possession of this condition has been a biological advantage for some African peoples, but in the United States, where malaria is not prevalent, the advantages are far outweighed by the disadvantages.

Teachers should understand the difference between having the sickle-cell trait and having sickle-cell anemia. Those who carry the trait as part of their genetic heritage do not necessarily experience this condition. Possession of the trait is harmless. It is only when a child inherits the trait from both parents that it becomes dominant and the anemia develops. In the United States it is estimated that 1 in 400 African American children is born with sickle-cell anemia (Gaston, 1990).

This serious disorder is not infectious and cannot be "caught." It is incurable at present and causes much pain and misery, but it *can* be treated. As with other anemias, the child may lack energy and tire easily. When people have this condition, their red blood cells become sickle-shaped, rather than remain round (hence the name), and painful episodes occur when these red cells stiffen because of lack of oxygen and stack up in small blood vessels. The plugging up of capillaries then deprives surrounding cellular tissues of oxygen. This is termed a *vaso-occlusive crisis,* and it may occur in various parts of the body. Depending on where it happens, the individual may have severe abdominal pain or an enlarged spleen, or the brain, liver, kidneys, lungs, or eyes may be affected. Children under age 3 are particularly likely to experience swollen hands and feet. Young children with this condition are often characterized by a barrel-shaped chest; an enlarged, protruding abdomen; and thin arms and legs. They have little ability to resist infections. Sometimes, for unknown reasons, production of red blood cells stops altogether (aplastic crisis). Symptoms of this include increased lethargy, rapid heart rate, weakness, fainting, and paleness of the lining of the eyelids (Morse & Shine, 1998). *(If an aplastic crisis occurs at school, the family and the physician should be notified promptly because this condition requires immediate medical attention.)*

Children who have been diagnosed as having sickle-cell anemia must be under regular care by a physician. The teacher can help by encouraging families to keep medical appointments and by carefully carrying out the physician's recommendations at school. These may include prohibiting vigorous exercise since lowered oxygen levels increase the likelihood of a vaso-occlusive attack. Such youngsters tend to drink more water than most children do and so may need to urinate more frequently. Careful, early attention should also be paid to cold symptoms because these youngsters are very vulnerable to pneumonia and influenza (Shirah & Brennan, 1990).

Since the condition is inherited, parents sometimes ask advice on whether they should have more children. This question is a ticklish one to answer and is best referred to their physician for discussion.

Other Physical Problems

In general, the teacher should watch for pronounced changes in the physical appearance of every child and, in particular, should take notice of children who are excessively pale or who convey a general air of exhaustion or lassitude. These conditions often develop so gradually that parents are unaware of the change. It is especially important to watch a child with care during the week or two after she has returned from a serious illness, such as measles, chicken pox, scarlet fever, or meningitis, because potentially serious problems occasionally develop following such infections.

Further Guidelines for Working with Children Who Have Physical Challenges

Since physical disabilities are as varied as blindness and cerebral palsy, it is, of course, impossible to discuss each condition in detail here. *Health-Related Disorders in Children and Adolescents* (Phelps, 1998), described at the end of this chapter, provides a wealth of information on particular problems when that is needed.

The suggestions already included apply to these children. A youngster who is physically challenged should be treated as typically as possible, and she should be neither overprotected nor underprotected. Conferences with her physician, physical therapist, or other specialist can help the staff ascertain the degree of protection and motivation that is necessary.

The teacher who bears these guidelines in mind and approaches each situation pragmatically will find it relatively simple to deal with children who have physical handicaps. Also parents are often gold mines of practical advice about how to help their child effectively, and their information, combined with the fresh point of view provided by the center staff, can usually solve problems if they arise.

IDENTIFYING AND HELPING CHILDREN WHO HAVE EMOTIONAL DIFFICULTIES

Signs of Emotional Disturbance That Indicate a Referral Is Needed

Deciding when referral for emotional disturbance is warranted and when it is unnecessary can be a difficult problem because transitory symptoms of emotional upset are common during early childhood. One study, for example, found that the typical child of nursery school age manifested between four and six "behavior" problems and that they seemed to appear and disappear over a period of time (Macfarlane, 1943). A good preprimary center environment can accomplish wonders with children who are emotionally upset, and many physicians routinely refer children who are having emotional difficulties to such centers because they have witnessed many happy results from such referrals.

However, the time may come when the staff begins to question whether the center environment, no matter how therapeutic, can offer sufficient help to a particular youngster. Perhaps after a reasonable period for adjustment and learning, she persists in "blowing her stack" over relatively inconsequential matters, or perhaps she insists on spending most of each morning hidden within the housekeeping corner or even crouched beneath a table. These behaviors, to name only two of a much wider list of possibilities, should arouse feelings of concern in the staff since they are examples of behavior that is *too extreme, happens too often,* and *persists too long.*

Strong feelings like this require prompt and sympathetic action from the teacher.

The teacher should also apply a fourth criterion when considering the necessity of a referral: whether the number and variety of symptoms manifested by the child at any one period are excessive. We have seen that signs of upset are common and often disappear either spontaneously or as a result of adequate handling by parents and teachers. Occasionally, though, a child will exhibit several reactions at the same time. She may begin to wet her bed again, be unable to fall asleep easily, insist on always having her blanket with her, cry a great deal, and refuse to play. When a cluster of these behaviors occur together, it is time for the staff to admit their limitations of time and training and to encourage the family to seek the advice of a qualified psychologist or psychiatrist.

Guidelines for Working with Children Who Have Emotional Disturbance

Even though teachers may not have a chronically disturbed youngster in their school, it is certain they will have to deal with children who are at least temporarily upset from time to time. These upsets may be as minor as a child who has occasional emotional outbursts or as major as a child who weeps frantically when she comes to school, refuses to eat anything, and is unable to lose herself in play.

The teacher should watch for any pronounced change in children's behavior, as well as for signs of withdrawal, inability to give or receive affection, reduced ability to play either by themselves or with other children, reduced interest in conversation, aggressive acting out, marked preoccupation with a particular activity or topic, and extreme emotional responses such as frequently bursting into tears or temper tantrums. She should also notice the usual signs of tension commonly seen in young children who are upset: whining, bedwetting, increased fretfulness and irritability, hair twisting, thumb sucking, stuttering, an increased dependence on security symbols such as blankets or toy animals, and so forth.

Teachers should realize that these behaviors are not reprehensible and that it is not desirable for them to concentrate their energy on removing these from the child's repertoire. The behaviors *are* signals that the child is suffering from some kind of stress either at home or school and that this should be looked into and mitigated.

Adults often discount the effect of important family crises on young children, either assuming that the children do not understand or that they simply are not aware of what is going on; but this is far from the truth. Children are sensitive to the emotional climate of the home, and although they may draw incorrect conclusions about the reasons for the unhappiness, they are almost always aware that something is going on and are likely to respond with a variety of coping mechanisms.

As noted in chapter 8, there are many causes of such disturbances, including hospitalization of the child or of a family member, desertion by one of the parents, a death in the family, divorce, the birth of a sibling, moving from one home to another, a mother going to work, a father losing his job, or chronic alcoholism or involvement with drugs by a family member. Even something as relatively innocuous as a long visit from a grandparent can be upsetting to the child if it becomes an occasion for disturbances in routine or for dissension.[5]

Short-Term Techniques

First, a note of caution is in order. When a child who has been getting along well at school suddenly falls apart, it is always best to consider whether the upset could be because of physical illness. Many an inexperienced teacher has spent a sleepless night over such a child only to have her mother call and report an illness the next morning.

Make a special point of offering tension-relieving activities to the youngster who is upset. The best of these is water play in a relaxed atmosphere in which the child can have her clothing well protected or can change afterward into something dry. Mud, dough, and soft clay can also be helpful, as are the sublimated activities listed in chapter 12, "Aggression: What to Do About It."

Relax standards somewhat to take stress off the child.   This does not mean that anything goes; it does mean that the teacher should ease the child's way through the day with only the more important demands enforced. In other words, she should take the pressure off when she can without creating additional insecurity by letting the child get away with murder.

---

[5]   *For a more detailed discussion of handling specific crisis situations, the reader is referred to chapter 8, "Tender Topics: Helping Children Master Emotional Crises."*

Talk things over with the family and work with them to identify what may be generating the upset in the child.   Discussing a child's emotional problems requires a delicate touch to avoid the impression the teacher is prying into personal matters that are none of her business, but the insight gained from such discussions can provide valuable information that enables the teacher to draw the child out and express in play or words what is troubling her. Increased understanding of the cause will help the teacher be more tolerant of the child's behavior. She may also be able to offer some helpful counseling resources for the family to explore or may sometimes offer help herself by listening and assisting the parents in clarifying alternative ways to solve the difficulty.

Help the child work through her feelings by furnishing opportunities to use dolls, puppets, and dramatic play to express her concern.   For example, a child who has been through a term of hospitalization may delight in using a doctor's kit and administering play shots to dolls or other children with spirited malevolence. When such play is combined with the teacher's perceptive comments that recognize how frightened and angry the child is, this activity can do a world of good.

Long-Term Techniques with More Severely Disturbed Youngsters

A few fortunate communities offer special preschool care for children categorized as chronically disturbed. Because such opportunities are still rare, however, and because many disturbed children profit from inclusion in at least a half-day school, it is desirable for preprimary teachers to offer this special service whenever they feel they can manage it. Apart from treating psychotic children, who generally require a specialized environment that allows more one-to-one contact combined with special expertise, nothing is particularly mysterious about providing care for more severely disturbed youngsters. What it really takes to make such a placement turn out successfully is common sense, patience, a steady temperament, determination, faith in oneself, and faith that the child and her family will be able to change.

Treat the chronically disturbed child as much like the other children as possible, and use her strengths to bring her into the life of the group.   In my school one boy who was unable to talk with either children or adults loved using the large push broom and spent many hours sweeping sand off the tricycle track. The first words he ever used at school grew out of this participation when, after weeks of sweeping, he yelled at one of the children who had bumped into his broom, "You just stay outta my way or I'll pop you one!" Once the sound barrier was broken, this youngster became increasingly verbal and was able to move on to kindergarten with reasonable success.

Anticipate that progress will be uneven.   Chronically disturbed children may move ahead in an encouraging way and then suddenly backslide. This should not be cause for despair. If she progressed once, she will do it again, and probably faster the second time. It is, of course, desirable to identify and ameliorate the reason for the regression if this can be discerned.

Provide support for those who are working with the child.   Staff members who make the decision to include a severely disturbed child will also require many opportunities to meet together and discuss the child's behavior. This is important so that consistency can be maintained in the way she is handled, so that everyone's insights and information can be pooled together, and so that group decisions can be made about what should be done next.

Working with such youngsters requires stamina and the ability to take a long-term perspective. It also requires enough staff so that someone can be spared as needed when the child flies off the handle. At the end of an exhausting day a touch of humor—but never in the sense of ridicule or denigration of the child—can help staff maintain perspective and provide the sense of camaraderie needed when people are under stress.

Draw on the advice of specialists and encourage the family to continue to do this.   A disturbed child often comes to school because she has been referred by a specialist. A regular arrangement for calling and reporting progress to the expert, invitations to him or her to come and visit the school, and perhaps some written reports during the year should be part of the teacher's professional obligation when she agrees to enroll a youngster with chronic disturbance. Needless to say the specialists who make such referrals should be willing to discharge their responsibilities by guiding the teacher when she requires their help.

Early Infantile Autism: A Special Case

From time to time the preschool teacher is still likely to come across children who seem truly out of the ordinary. A family may enroll a youngster who can generally be described in the following terms: She pays scant attention to other children or adults and seems emotionally distant and uninvolved; it is difficult or impossible to get her to look the person who is speaking to her in the eye; she may become very distressed when asked to change from one activity to another (e.g., she may fly into a panic when asked to stop swinging and go inside for snack); her speech may be minimal or nonexistent; she may repeat phrases in a meaningless way; and she may show a marked interest in things that spin or twirl, such as a tricycle wheel, which she may sit by and spin absorbedly, or a spoon, which she will twirl with great skill (Kanner, 1944; Tsai & Ghaziuddin, 1997). When several of these symptoms occur together, the youngster may be showing autistic behaviors. This condition, commonly called *infantile autism,* is rare, occurring in approximately 2 to 4 per 10,000 people (American Psychiatric Association, 1994), and serious.

With such unusual symptoms, it may be surprising that the teacher may be the first person who realizes how unusual the behaviors are. (In my 30 years of working with children, I have come across eight such youngsters—none previously identified as unusual except by their concerned parents, and sometimes not even by them.) Treatment is difficult, and *these youngsters need highly professional help as soon as they can get it.* Therefore, the family should be urged to seek help as soon as possible from a child psychiatrist or psychologist who specializes in treating this condition. Treatment is likely to include intensive work based on the principles of behavior modification possibly combined with medications to relieve specific symptoms such as anxiety behaviors and sleeplessness (Tsai & Ghaziuddin, 1997).

Parents and teachers wonder a good deal about the causes of this condition since the behavior can be so bizarre. Although included here in the category of emotional disturbance, research now indicates that the underlying cause of infantile autism is a disruption in the development of the brain. This has been traced to a variety of factors. Among these are rubella or other viral infections during pregnancy, phenylketonuria (PKU), genetically regulated disturbances, and many additional, yet-to-be-ascertained physiological insults or developmental anomalies (Cole & Arndt, 1998). This is valuable information to remember because it takes away a lot of the mystery and the possible tendency to blame parents. Much more remains to be learned about this unusual condition, and working with autistic children continues to be an exceedingly difficult challenge for their parents and teachers (Silver & Hagin, 1990).

IDENTIFYING AND HELPING CHILDREN WHO HAVE DELAYED OR ADVANCED MENTAL ABILITY

Children Who Have Developmental Lags

All teachers of young children need to know enough about developmental sequences and the ages at which behavioral milestones can be anticipated that they can tell when a child is developing normally, when she is lagging markedly behind her peers, or when she is exceptionally advanced for her age. Lists of developmental standards have been included in many chapters in this book, not with the intention of urging developmental conformity, but in the hope that they will help the teacher be tolerant of behaviors characteristic of various ages and also alert to children who are developing so far out of phase that they require special help. Appendix D also provides a chart of developmental guidelines.

Many preprimary teachers do not recognize cognitive delay when they see it. Being unaware of retardation can be an advantage in a way since it means a child is not stuck with a stereotyped reaction to her condition or burdened with an undesirable label. However, it may also mean that an undiagnosed, slow-learning 4-year-old who is actually operating at a 2½-year-old level may be expected to sit with the other 4-year-olds for long stories she does not comprehend or may be criticized and disciplined for refusing to share equipment when actually she is behaving in a way typical of her developmental but not chronological age. An adequate diagnosis would enable the teacher to match her expectations to the child's real level of ability.

Behavior that should be cause for concern includes a widespread pattern of delayed development that is a year or more behind the typical in physical, social, and intellectual areas. Such lags are usually accompanied by speech that is obviously immature for the child's chronological age.

The American Association on Mental Retardation characterizes mental retardation as being "significantly subaverage functioning," concurrently with related limitations in two or more of the following applicable adaptive skills areas: communnication, self-care, home living, social skills, community use, self-direction, health and safety, functional academics, leisure, and work. Mental retardation manifests before age 18 (Szymanski & Kaplan, 1997, p. 184).

Causes of the condition are numerous and range from physiological causes such as chromosomal disorders to pseudoretardation induced by environmental causes such as severe malnutrition or an insufficiently stimulating environment. It is often impossible even for specialists to determine why the child is developing slowly. For example, Weiss and Weisz (1986) state that "at present there are several hundred known causes of mental retardation; many professionals, however, believe this to be only a fraction of the total number of actual causes" (p. 357). Particularly, children whose retardation is due to physiological causes do not outgrow their condition or ultimately catch up with their more fortunate peers so it is necessary for teachers and parents to come to a relistic understanding of what can be reasonably expected of them. Knowledgeable specialists can provide many helpful, encouraging suggestions about how to maximize learning for these youngsters.

Guidelines for Working with Children Who Are Cognitively Delayed

Children who are mildly or moderately delayed are the best prospects for inclusion in children's centers. The mildly delayed child will probably fit so easily into a program serving a mixed age-group that no special recommendations are necessary other than reminding the teacher to see the child in terms of her actual developmental level, rather than of her chronological age.

Children who are moderately affected will also often fit comfortably into a mixed-age-group, but many teachers find it helpful to have a clear understanding of the most worthwhile educational goals for these children and of some simple principles for teaching them most effectively.

Basic learning goals for a preschool youngster with moderate delay should center on helping her be as independent as possible, which includes learning simple self-help skills, as well as learning to help other people by doing simple tasks; helping the child develop language skills; and helping her learn to get along with other children in an acceptable way.

These goals are only slightly different from those that are part of the regular curriculum. The only differences are that the child who is developing more slowly will be farther behind other children of her age and that she will need a simpler manner of instruction. Children who learn slowly should not be confused with a lot of talk and shadings of meaning. *They need concrete examples, definite rules, and consistent reinforcement of desirable behavior.* In general, the bywords with these children are *keep it concrete, keep it simple, keep it fun,* and *be patient.*

Some specific suggestions may also help the teacher:

1. As much as possible, treat the child as you would treat all children in the group, but exercise common sense so that you expect neither too much nor too little.
2. Know the developmental steps so that you understand what she should learn next as she progresses.
3. Remember that children with cognitive delays learn best what they repeat frequently. Be prepared to go over a simple rule or task many times until the child has it firmly in mind. (This need for patient repetition is one of the things inexperienced teachers may find most irritating, particularly when the child had appeared to grasp the idea just the day before. Don't give up hope; if the teaching is simple and concrete enough, she will eventually learn.)
4. Pick out behavior to teach that the child can use all her life; that is, try to teach ways of behaving that will be appropriate for an older as well as a younger child to use. For example, don't let her run and kiss everyone she meets, because this will

not be acceptable when she is just a little older. She has enough to do without having to unlearn old behavior (Odom, McConnell, & McEvory, 1992).

5. Take it easy. Give short directions, one point at a time.

6. Allow sufficient time for her to acquire a selected task. Complex things take longer; simpler things take less time.

7. Encourage the child to be persistent by keeping tasks simple and satisfying. This will encourage her to finish what she starts.

8. Remember that independence is an important goal. Make sure the child is not being overprotected.

9. Teach one thing at a time. For instance, teach her to feed herself, then to use a napkin, and then to pour her milk.

10. Provide lots of concrete experiences that use as many of the senses as possible.

11. Don't rely on talking as the primary means of instruction. Show the child what you mean whenever possible by modeling it.

12. Encourage the development of speech. Wait for at least some form of verbal reply whenever possible. Gently increase the demand for a "quality" response as her skills increase.

13. *Remember that these children are just as sensitive to the emotional climate around them as ordinary children are.* Therefore never talk about the child in front of her. It is likely that she will at least pick up the sense of what you are saying, and this may hurt her feelings badly.

14. Show the child that you are pleased with her and that you like her.

15. After a fair trial at learning something new, if she cannot seem to learn it, drop the activity without recrimination. Try it again in a few months; she may be ready to learn it by then.

Much can be said for the value of step-by-step, prescriptive teaching for children with cognitive delays in particular. This requires careful identification of the current level of the child's skills, as well as knowledge of the appropriate next step. Knowledge and application of behavior modification techniques can be very helpful when working with some of these youngsters (Singh, Osborne, & Huguenin, 1996).

Intellectually Gifted Children

Although the child who is slow to learn has received special attention for several decades, only during the past few years have preschoolers who are intellectually gifted received any attention at all. Currently still only a handful of special programs cater to their needs. In 1993, for example, only 51 preschool programs for gifted children were reported for the entire United States and its territories (Stile, Kitano, Kelley, & Lecrone, 1993), and this situation really hasn't changed markedly since then. Why this should be the case is hard to understand. Surely such promising children deserve the interest and support of their teachers. Perhaps they are overlooked since many of them fit smoothly into the center's curriculum (although it may present insufficient challenges for them), or perhaps most preschool teachers are uncertain about what kinds of behaviors indicate outstanding mental ability and thus fail to identify the children.

A child with exceptional mental ability usually exhibits a general pattern of advanced skills, but not always. Sometimes the pattern is quite spotty or its manifestations may vary from day to day (Piirto, 1999).

In general, a gifted child may exhibit some or all of the following skills: She learns quickly and easily; her language is more elaborate and extended than that of other children of the same age, and her vocabulary is likely to be large; her attention span may be longer if her interest is aroused; she grasps ideas easily; and she probably possesses an exceptional amount of general information, which is characterized not only by more variety but also by greater detail. She often has a very good memory. Gifted preschoolers like to pursue reasons for things, talk about cause-and-effect relationships, and compare and draw conclusions. They are particularly sensitive to social values and the behavior of those around them. They are often almost insatiably interested in special subjects that appeal to them. Some of them already know how to read. They may prefer the company of older children or adults.

Children who have disabilities and those who come from minority groups tend to be overlooked to an even greater extent than others as possibly being gifted children (Barclay & Benelli, 1994; Karnes & Johnson, 1991). Chicano children, according to Bernal (1978), may be identified as being gifted when they acquire English readily, demonstrate leadership skills (although this may be done in a subtle way), enjoy venturing and taking risks carefully, keep themselves busy (particularly by using imaginative play), assume responsibilities often the prerogative of older children, and know how to get along smoothly in the community in which they live. Additional characteristics described by Torrance (1977) that apply to various ethnic-cultural minorities include being able to express feelings through story telling, movement, and self-expressive activities, and being able to improvise, use rich imagery in informal talk, conceptualize problems in practical terms, have original ideas, adapt quickly to change, and be persistent in problem solving.

Teachers who do not build their curriculum and increase its complexity sufficiently during the year may find that gifted children become increasingly restless and gradually get into difficulties because they have lost interest in what is happening at school. Teachers who meet this challenge and deal with it satisfactorily modify the curriculum so that it meets the needs of these youngsters by adding more difficult and interesting learning activities. Some suggestions for accomplishing this are offered next.

Teaching Preschool Children Who Are Mentally Gifted

Although many interesting investigations have been conducted on intellectual giftedness and education, ranging from Terman, Baldwin, and Bronson (1925) to Piirto (1999), these have focused on older children and adults, and the possibility of educating intellectually gifted preschool children is just beginning to receive the attention it deserves, yet it is obvious that children of exceptional mental ability must be present in this portion of the population since they exist at an older age. However, it is still the case that when I raise the question of making special provision for such youngsters at the preschool level, many of my students and teaching colleagues appear bewildered at this possibility.[6]

---

[6]   *Giftedness, of course, is expressed in many forms (Karnes & Johnson, 1989), such as in the self-expressive giftedness of creative artists or the physical giftedness of talented athletes. Because ways of fostering such aspects of the child's abilities are covered in other chapters, this discussion is limited to the giftedness of the intellectually superior preschooler.*

Perhaps this is because we have fought a battle against undue intellectual pressure on young children for so long that we forget that gifted children thrive when provided additional stimulation and that we may be cheating them when we deprive them of it. Of course, gifted children should not be treated as precocious little adults or worshipped because of their special talents, but they should be provided stimulating things to learn while at the same time keeping their social and emotional life as natural and easy as possible.

The provision of an enriched curriculum does not necessarily mean that the teacher must teach the child to read, although Piirto (1999) states that one half to two thirds of gifted children read by age 5. I will never forget my surprise when one of the bright lights in my school wandered into my office, picked up a plain bound book from my desk, and commented, "Hmmmmm, this looks interesting—*All About Dinosaurs*. Can I borrow this?" (I let him.)

What the teacher *can* do is make sure such children have plenty of opportunities to pursue subjects that interest them in as much depth as they desire. It is important to avoid the trap of thinking to oneself, "Oh, well, *they* wouldn't be able to do *that*." It is astonishing what gifted children can do when given encouragement and materials. For example, I once had two young students, a boy and a girl, who were interested in the weather. They went from this to an interest in temperature and how heat makes thermometers work. Of course, all the children were interested in this subject to an extent, but these two youngsters, who later proved to be gifted, were truly absorbed. Their investigations included breaking open a thermometer to discover what it was made of, collecting different kinds of thermometers to see whether they all worked the same way and whether they all measured the same kinds of things, and even working out a number scale with drawings to show the range of temperatures measured by different instruments.

Intellectually gifted preschool children often love discussions that focus on "What would happen if . . . ?" or "How could we . . . ?" These questions require creative reasoning, as well as transforming old information into new solutions. Asking them to evaluate the potential results of these ideas, if done sensitively so that they do not feel crushed when an idea doesn't work out, will give them even wider scope for their talents.

Gifted children will also relish the more difficult activities suggested in the chapters on mental development since these activities can be adjusted to their level of ability and thus sustain their interest. Perhaps a few examples of specific ways of enriching the curriculum for them will best illustrate how to accomplish this.[7]

Investigate how things work, finding out either by close observation or by taking them apart and reassembling them.   A music box, a vacuum cleaner and all its parts, a Christmas tree stand, a flashlight, an old bicycle, and so forth can be offered. Ask the child to put into words her theory about what makes it work.

Build additional language skills.   Make a time to read the child books that are longer and have more detail in them than picture books do. After story time, have a special discussion with her. Encourage her to expound on the stories that were just read: Were they true? Has she ever had a similar or opposite experience? What did she like or dislike about the story? What would she have done differently if the main character had been she? Encourage the child to do most of the talking, and try to introduce new vocabulary. Select

---

[7] *My thanks to former nursery school majors at Santa Barbara City College for these suggestions.*

several pictures from the picture file, and ask the child to link them together by telling you a story about them—or allow her to select the pictures.

Offer more complex materials or advanced information.   A good example of this is the use of more difficult puzzles. Cube puzzles can be used to reproduce particular patterns, or jigsaw puzzles can be offered, rather than only the framed wooden ones typical of preschools. On a library trip take the child to the older children's section and help her find books on a particular subject in which she is interested.

Offer an enriched curriculum in the area of science.   Be prepared to allow for expanded scientific activities. For example, provide vinegar for testing for limestone in various materials such as tiles, building materials, and so forth. Or explore the concept of time. The child could learn to identify specific hours on the clock and take responsibility for telling the teacher when it is snack time. Talk about ways of keeping track of time; perhaps help the child make a simple sundial with a stick, letting her mark the spot where the shadow falls when it is group time or time to go home. See whether that spot stays at the same place over several weeks. Encourage the child to seek out people who speak different languages to tell her the names of different times of day in their own tongue. Visit a clock shop and write down for her all the kinds of clocks she sees there.

Note that language activities are particularly dear to preschoolers who are mentally gifted. They enjoy more advanced stories than average children do and also can put their superior ability to work by concocting tales of their own that are almost invariably complex, detailed, and advanced in vocabulary. An interesting example of this is the book *Barbara* (McCurdy, 1966), which begins with the writings of an intensely gifted 4-year-old and continues through her young adulthood. Discussion and conversation should be employed at every opportunity to allow these children to put their ideas into words and to test them against the ideas of other people.

Above all, the use of instructional methods that foster problem solving and encourage development of creative ideas should be employed (Smutny, Walker, & Meckstroth, 1997).   How can everyday items be put to new uses? How can old problems be solved in new ways? Here once again the value of asking pertinent questions and providing rich opportunities for children to propose answers and test them out to see whether they are correct, must be emphasized. I refer the reader to chapter 18, "Developing Thinking and Reasoning Skills: Using the Emergent Approach to Foster Creativity in Thought" for suggestions on how to go about doing this.

SUMMARY

Teachers who work with a preschool child with a special need must seek all the information they can on her particular condition if they really want to be effective teachers. This chapter can do no more than scratch the surface.

Increasing numbers of courses in exceptionality are being offered by schools of education, as in-service training, and by university extension units as the general trend toward including exceptional children in regular public school classes and early childhood centers gains ground. In addition to these courses, books are also available, and many are listed in the references at the end of this chapter.

Unfortunately the education of very young children with special needs is still only sparsely covered in the literature, but IDEA and ADA are gradually changing this situation for the better. These laws have made a difference to preschool teachers because their passage means that help for young children with disabilities is more readily available than it was in the past, many more children who have disabilities will be attending "regular" early childhood centers, and preschool teachers will become part of the treatment teams responsible for working with such children.

Preprimary teachers owe two main responsibilities to children who have special needs. First, they must serve as screening agents and help identify possible problems (physical, emotional, or mental) that have escaped the attention of the physician. Following identification of a difficulty, teachers should attempt to effect a referral to the appropriate specialist.

Second, they must do all they can to integrate these children into their group. This requires careful assessment before admission and flexibility of adjustment following entrance to school. It is vital that they treat the exceptional child as typically as possible and encourage her independence without demanding skills that lie beyond her ability. Specific suggestions for working with physically handicapped, emotionally disturbed, cognitively delayed, and intellectually gifted preschool children conclude the chapter.

Questions and Activities

1. Do you think it is generally wise to suggest medication as a means of controlling hyperactivity in children? Why or why not?

2. This chapter makes a strong case for the early identification of potentially handicapping disorders. What are the real disadvantages of labeling children as being *different*? What are some ways to obtain help for such youngsters without stigmatizing them at the same time?

3. What do you think accounts for the fact that very intelligent children are often overlooked at the preschool level? Might the provision of a special curriculum for them result in precocity and overintellectualization, thereby spoiling their childhood?

4. *Predicament:* A 4½-year-old girl attending your school is cognitively delayed and functions at about the 2½-year-old level. She hangs around the housekeeping corner and the blocks a lot, but the children push her aside. One of them in particular makes a point of saying, "She can't play here. Her nose is snotty, and she talks dumb." (There is more than a modicum of truth in this.) What would you do?

5. *Predicament:* A 4-year-old boy in your group has a heart condition. In addition to looking somewhat pale, he is not supposed to exert himself by climbing or other vigorous exercise, which, of course, he yearns to do. He is well liked by the other children, who invite him frequently to climb around and play with them. What would you do?

Self-Check Questions For Review

Content-Related Questions

1. List three reasons why the passage of IDEA and ADA are making a difference in what teachers of preschool children need to know and do.

2. What is one of the most important services preprimary teachers can provide for young children?

3. List some symptoms that should alert the teacher to the possibility that a child might need to have her eyes examined.

4. What basically sets the hyperactive child apart from other young children?

5. If a child had a *generalized tonic clonic seizure* in your classroom, what would you do to help her? What about the other children?

6. What is sickle-cell anemia? Is it contagious? What does the teacher need to know about when to call the physician? What symptoms should she be aware of?

7. What are the guidelines for deciding when to refer a child who seems to be emotionally disturbed for outside help? What behaviors might signal that the child has possible autistic tendencies? What are some guidelines teachers may use when working with children who are emotionally disturbed?

8. What kinds of behaviors might alert a teacher to the possibility that a child could be developing more slowly than normal? What are some practical pieces of information to remember when teaching such a child?

9. Describe some behaviors that might signal to a teacher that a 4-year-old is intellectually gifted. Suggest some ways the teacher could adjust the curriculum to meet the needs of that youngster.

10. Explain some important steps in making a referral when a child has a special problem.

11. What are IDEA and ADA? How do they affect the welfare of exceptional children?

12. What are some general principles for working with exceptional children?

Integrative Questions

1. How are IDEA and ADA different, and how are they the same?

2. The book states that teachers should "see through the exceptional to the typical in every child." Explain how doing this could be an antidote for either expecting too much or too little from the youngster with a disability.

3. It is important for teachers and parents of all children to remain in close contact. Using the example of a disability, give an example of something a parent might share with the teacher that would be helpful. Now give an example of something the teacher could share with the parent. Be as specific as possible.

4. *Predicament:* Jody, a 2½-year-old, has been in the next-door teacher's classroom for 3 months and does not talk at all. At lunch the teacher tells you he arranged a conference with the parents to tell them he thinks Jody is mentally retarded. Analyze all the elements of this situation and explain why you would or would not agree that the teacher has done the right thing.

5. Many people are confused about the difference between children who are termed *mentally ill* (emotionally disturbed) and those termed *mentally retarded*. Explain the similarities and differences between these conditions.

Coordinating Videotape

Everybody's special. Tape #7. The whole child: A caregiver's guide to the first five years. The Annenberg/CPB Collection, P.O. Box 2345, South Burlington, VT 05407–2345. *Everybody's Special* provides guidelines for working with families whose children have special educational needs. This program suggests what teachers can do to help parents identify problems and recommends ways to integrate children with special needs into the classroom. Viewers will see specific ways of working with children who have special educational requirements.

References for Further Reading

Picks of the Litter

Phelps, L. A. (Ed.). (1998). *Health-related disorders in children and adolescents.* Washington, DC: American Psychological Association. For quick, reasonably thorough information on a wide variety of disabilities this is the source to turn to—includes a list of annotated references and helpful organizations for each condition. *Highly recommended.*

Rab, V. Y., Wood, K. I., & Taylor, J. M. (1995). *Child care and the ADA.* Baltimore, MD: Brookes. This down-to-earth book is an excellent place to start learning about including children with disabilities in ordinary classrooms since it provides a discussion of implications of relevant laws and a discussion of practical aspects of child inclusion from the administrator's and staff's points of view. *Highly recommended.*

Overviews

Brown, W. H., & Conroy, M. A. (Eds.). (1997). *Including and supporting preschool children with developmental delays in early childhood programs.* Little Rock, AR: Southern Early Childhood Association. This publication covers the most important aspects of welcoming a child with developmental delays into the regular classroom. It includes a particularly valuable chapter on assistive technology.

Derman-Sparks, L., & ABC Task Force. (1989). *Antibias curriculum: Tools for empowering young children.* Washington, DC: National Association for the Education of Young Children. Bias, of course, occurs against children with disabilities, as well as in other situations. Derman-Sparks provides a practical approach to dealing with this problem at the preschool level.

Understanding Parents

Cook, R. E., Tessier, A., & Klein, M. D. (2000). *Adapting early childhood curricula for children in inclusive settings* (5th ed.). Upper Saddle River, NJ: Merrill/Prentice Hall. The authors provide a sound overview of how to relate effectively to parents of children with special needs, including advice about conducting interviews.

Strong, M. F. (1999). Serving mothers with disabilities in early childhood education programs. *Young Children, 54*(3), 10–17. For a change of viewpoint, refer to this helpful article about working with adults with various disabilities. *Highly recommended.*

Practical Advice About Interventions

Cook, R. E., Tessier, A., & Klein, M. D. (2000). *Adapting early childhood curricula for children in inclusive settings* (5th ed.). Upper Saddle River, NJ: Merrill/Prentice Hall. General, practical discussions of basic principles of early childhood education are followed by specific recommendations of strategies for children with relevant disabilities.

Raver, S. A. (1999). *Intervention strategies for infants and toddlers with special needs: A team approach* (2nd ed.) Upper Saddle River, NJ: Merrill/Prentice Hall. Although Raver's book emphasizes educational aspects of working with very young children, it also includes general information on a wide range of disabilities, together with practical recommendations that apply to the preschool level. The book provides rich examples of ways

team members can work together to benefit the child and her family.

Working with Team Members

Bricker, D., & Cripe, J. J. W. (1992). *An activity-based approach to early intervention.* Baltimore, MD: Brookes. Bricker and Cripe's book is replete with examples of ways practice in various skills can be integrated into the typical preschool day. Long-term advocates of this method, they suggest using a combination of child-initiated, teacher-planned, and routine activities for such instruction. *Highly recommended.*

Information About Specific Disabilities

Cohen, S. (1998). *Targeting autism: What we know, don't know, and can do to help young children with autism and related disorders.* Berkeley: University of California Press. This readable book provides a thoughtful discussion of the difficulties and approaches to treatment available for autistic children.

Cunningham, C. (1996). *Understanding Down syndrome: An introduction for parents.* Cambridge, MA: Brookline Books. Noteworthy for its sensitivity toward parents, this book, by an experienced physician, summarizes what is known about this common form of mental retardation.

Fowler, M. (1994). *Briefing paper: Attention-deficit/hyperactivity disorder.* Washington, DC: National Information Center for Children and Youth with Disabilities. After I reviewed numerous publications on this subject, this proved to be the more useful, concise source. *Highly recommended.*

Hill, S. A. (1996). Caregiving in African American families: Caring for children with sickle-cell disease. In S. L. Logan (Ed.), *The Black family: Strengths, self-help, and positive change.* Boulder, CO: Westview/HarperCollins. Hill explains what sickle-cell disease is, who tends to be affected, and how families cope with this condition in their children.

Michael, R. J. (1995). *The educator's guide to students with epilepsy.* Springfield, IL: Charles C Thomas. This straightforward book discusses everything from the law to practical ways of enhancing self-esteem—"must" reading for staff who have such a child in their care.

Smutny, J. G., Walker, S. Y., & Meckstroth, E. A. (1997). *Teaching young gifted children in the regular classroom: Identifying, nurturing, and challenging ages 4–9.* Minneapolis, MN: Free Spirit. Title is self explanatory.

Trief, E. (Ed.). (1998). *Working with visually impaired young students: A curriculum guide for 3-to-4-year-olds.* Springfield, IL: Charles C Thomas. This book offers many suggestions of how to enrich learning opportunities for children who can't see well—includes material on developing concepts, fostering mobility, art, music, and more.

For the Advanced Student

Jacobson, J. W., & Mulick, M. A. (Eds.). (1996). *Manual of diagnosis and professional practice in mental retardation.* Washington, DC: American Psychological Association. Definitely for the serious student, this book presents a comprehensive survey of what is currently known about mental retardation.

Tsai, L. Y., & Ghaziuddin, M. (1997). Autistic disorder. In J. M. Wiener (Ed.), *Textbook of child and adoles-cent psychiatry* (2nd ed.). Washington, DC: American Psychiatric Press. The article includes an excellent description of the condition and discussion of possible causes of the autistic disorder.

Waslick, B., & Greenhill, L. (1997). Attention-deficit/hyperactivity disorder. In J. M. Wiener (Ed.), *Textbook of child and adolescent psychiatry* (2nd ed.). Washington, DC: American Psychiatric Press. The authors provide a comprehensive, scholarly discussion of ADD—its nature, causes, and treatment. *Highly recommended.*

Organizations of Particular Interest

Council for Exceptional Children—Division for Early Childhood, 1444 Wazee Street, Suite 230, Denver, CO 80202. The division publishes *Young Exceptional Children* and sponsors an annual conference. It is a subsidiary of the Council for Exceptional Children, which also publishes journals of interest and provides an annual conference. Its address is 1920 Association Drive, Reston, VA 20191–1589.

Fostering Social Development

chapter ten

Developing Social Competence in Young Children

Have you ever . . .

Thought that young children were just naturally selfish and that nothing could be done about this?

Wondered whether children felt generous *inside* when *you* made them share and take turns?

Wanted to know how to get children to help each other and work together?

. . . IF YOU HAVE, THE MATERIAL IN THE FOLLOWING PAGES WILL HELP YOU.

This point was brought home to me by the comments of a distinguished Soviet psychologist, an expert on development during the preschool years. He had been observing in an American day-care center for children of working mothers. The center was conducted under university auspices and reflected modern outlooks and methods in early childhood education. It was therefore with some concern that I noted how upset my colleague was on his return.

"I wouldn't have believed it," he said, "if I hadn't seen it with my own eyes. There were four children sitting at a table, just as in our nurseries. But each was doing something different. What's more, I watched them for a whole ten minutes, and not once did any child help another one. They didn't even talk to each other. Each was busy in his own activity. You really are a nation of individualists."

Urie Bronfenbrenner (1969, p. 5)

Peer relations contribute substantially to both social and cognitive development and to the effectiveness with which we function as adults. Indeed, the single best childhood predictor of adult adaptation is not school grades, and not classroom behavior, but rather, the adequacy with which the child gets along with other children.

Willard W. Hartup (1992, p. 1)

Early childhood is a time that can be rich in social learnings; it is a dynamic period characterized by many beginnings but few completely attained learnings in the development of social skills and interactions. Although the home is profoundly influential in this area, early childhood teachers can also make a valuable contribution to social development. Before pursuing important social goals for the young children in their care, however, teachers should review the developmental theories of social growth discussed here to help them understand what social behavior to expect from the children.

DEVELOPMENTAL TRENDS IN SOCIAL GROWTH

In the past, many people tended to view young children as generally self-centered human beings who were insensitive and uncaring about others. However, recent research now supports a more encouraging view of young children's nature. Prosocial behavior—behavior intended to help or benefit someone else—begins at an early age (Eisenberg & Fabes, 1998). For example, one study by Rheingold (1982) found that all the 2-year-olds included in the research spontaneously helped their mothers complete at least one household chore within a 25-minute period. Another study found that although most helping behavior in the nursery school happened because the teacher asked for it, during the observations two thirds of the children also volunteered help of one sort or another (Eisenberg et al., 1987). Moreover, several longitudinal studies reveal that children who are prosocially inclined during their early years continue that behavior as they become older and that children who are helpful in one situation are often (though not always) likely to be helpful in other situations (Eisenberg & Mussen, 1989).

Tables 10.1 and 10.2 provide summarize of some of the many additional social behaviors characteristic of children at various ages.

How Do Children Become Socialized?

Although opinion remains divided about how children learn to be like other people in their society—that is, become *socialized*—most experts agree it is a complex process that depends on the interaction of numerous factors. Among these are biological, cultural and family influences, personality traits, intellectual ability, developmental level, and situational influences (Eisenberg & Fabes, 1998).

Not only are a great many factors involved, but there are also complex interactions that go on among them. For example, initial analyses of socialization stressed the influence of parents on children's behavior and paid scant attention to the way children influenced their parents' behavior, but we now understand that this is very much a two-way street (Parke & Buriel, 1998).

Several theories attempt to explain how factors achieve this influence. It is useful to understand the most important of these theories since each of them provides a helpful

Table 10.1

Progress indicators of social development, first 3 years

Behavior Item	Age Expected*
	Weeks
Responds to smiling and talking	6
Knows mother	12
Shows marked interest in father	14
Is sober with strangers	16
Withdraws from strangers	32
Responds to "bye-bye"	40
Responds to inhibitory words	52
Plays pat-a-cake	52
Waves "bye-bye"	52
	(Years, months)
Is no longer shy toward strangers	1, 3
Enjoys imitation of adult activities (smoking, etc.)	1, 3
Is interested in and treats another child like an object rather than a person	1, 6
Plays alone	1, 6
Brings things (slippers, etc.) to adult (father)	1, 6
Shows beginning of concept of private ownership	1, 9
Wishes to participate in household activities	1, 9
Has much interest in and watches other children	2
Begins parallel play	2
Is dependent and passive in relation to adults	2
Is shy toward strangers	2
Is not sociable; lacks social interest	2, 3
Is ritualistic in behavior	2, 6
Is imperious, domineering	2, 6
Begins to resist adult influence; wants to be independent	2, 6
Is self-assertive; difficult to handle	2, 6
Is in conflict with children of own age	2, 6
Refuses to share toys; ignores requests	2, 6
Begins to accept suggestions	3
Has "we" feeling with mother	3
Likes to relive babyhood	3
Is independent of mother at nursery school	3
Tends to establish social contacts with adults	3
Show imitative, "me too" tendency	3
Begins strong friendships with peer associates, with discrimination against others in group	3, 6

*As is true for all developmental charts, these ages should be regarded as approximate.

Source: Abridged from The Longitudinal Study of Individual Development, *by L. H. Stott, 1955, Detroit: Merrill-Palmer Institute.* © 1955 by the Merrill-Palmer Institute. Reprinted by permission.

Table 10.2
Progress indicators of social development, ages 4 through 10

Behavior Item	Age Expected (Years)
Is assertive, boastful	4
Has definite preference for peer mates	4
Tries to gain attention; shows off	4
Tends to be obedient, cooperative; desires to please	5
Seeks approval; avoids disapproval of adults	5
Shows preference for children of his own age	5
Shows protective mothering attitude toward younger sibling	5
Is sensitive to parents' and others' moods, facial expressions	6
Has strong desire to be with father and do things together (especially true of boys)	6
Insists on being "first" in everything with peers	6
Bosses, teases younger siblings	6
Has rich capacity to "pretend" in social play	6
Shows compliance in family relations	7
Desires to be "good"	7
Begins to discriminate between sexes	7
Forms close friendships with one of the same sex; the age of "bosom pals"	8
Sex cleavage is definite; girls giggle, whisper; boys wrestle, "roughhouse"	9
The age of "clubs"	9
Sex differences are pronounced: girls show more poise, more folk wisdom, more interest in family, marriage, etc., and in their own personal appearance	10

Source: Abridged from The Longitudinal Study of Individual Development, *by L. H. Stott, 1955, Detroit: Merrill-Palmer Institute. © 1955 by the Merrill-Palmer Institute. Reprinted by permission.*

way to think about how to foster positive social growth in young children. One of these is *social learning theory*. It proposes some matter-of-fact explanations of the way socialization comes about that are helpful for teachers to understand. That theory emphasizes that children learn to become like other people and to get along with them as a result of identifying with and imitating them and by experiencing reinforcement for desirable social behaviors.

Considerable evidence indicates that children do learn by observing grown-ups and other children and that, particularly if the person is nurturing and powerful, they will seek to be like the model and imitate his behavior (Bandura, 1986). Evidence also indicates that although children may be somewhat influenced by how people tell them they should behave, they are even more strongly influenced by actual modeling of desirable behavior (Eisenberg, 1992; Oliner & Oliner, 1988). So it behooves teachers to model the behavior they wish to encourage, rather than just talking about it or, worse yet, preaching something they don't do themselves.

Research indicates that children also learn socially acceptable responses as a result of reinforcement either by adults or by peers. This can be negative reinforcement in the form of punishment that may suppress behavior, or positive reinforcement in the form of recognition, praise, approval, admission to the group, or other positively reinforcing responses and satisfactions that come from without or within themselves. Although scholarly discussions of socialization processes currently pay scant attention to the value of this theory, it must be noted that adults who rely on punishment or gold stars to produce good behavior are continuing to rely on it and put it into daily practice.

A differing point of view about how children become socialized has been contributed by the developmental interactionists typified by Piaget (1948), DeVries and Zan (1996), and the sociocultural theorist Vygotsky (1978). Supporters of this theory contend that, to exist successfully in the social world, the intricacies of learning require explanations that go far beyond the simplicities of reinforcement and modeling theory. They maintain that social development occurs as a result of interaction between people. The cognitive, intellectual learnings that result from the experience of that interaction coupled with maturation produce the widening range of social knowledge and skills necessary for social survival (Corsaro, 1997).

It is not only interaction between adults and children, of course, that enhances such learning. Child-child interaction becomes of ever-increasing importance during the early years as groups of children make it clear to their members that they favor positive, friendly behavior and dislike aggression and selfishness. Such groups rate socially competent children highly, and these attitudes, which are often frankly expressed, help shape the behavior of the children in the group. Then, too, as children become 4 or 5 years old, they turn to their peers more frequently for help than they turn to adults for it (Hartup, 1992). This aid seeking promotes additional opportunities for positive social interactions and learning to take place.

The quality of emotional attachment between mother and child is an additional important influence on socialization. Children who are closely attached to their mothers tend to be more compliant—that is, conform more readily to the wishes and instructions of their families (Honig, 1985)—and are better liked and accepted by their peers (Sroufe, 1983). Securely attached children also tend to be more sensitive to other people's feelings (Ianotti, Zahn-Waxler, Cummings, & Milano, 1987).

Information about how socialization takes place continues to grow as new investigative techniques are employed to study this process. For example, an interesting addition to research strategies is being contributed by researchers taking the *ethnographic* approach. Rather than using questionnaires or doing experiments, ethnographers rely on observing and recording what is happening in a particular environment—a nursery school, for example (Corsaro, 1997; Lubeck, 1985). Then they analyze the total context of what they have seen to construct meaningful interpretations of what is going on.

An example of this approach is provided in the Research Study in this chapter to show how ethnography can shed new light on individual and group social dynamics.

Research Study

Learning the Secret Passwords for Group Inclusion

Research Question: Kantor, Elgas, and Fernie used the ethnographic approach to find out why some children are welcomed into a group and others are rejected. They asked, "What is the difference between these youngsters?" and "What did the children have to understand about the culture of the group—i.e., what cultural passwords did the children need to know—in order to be admitted to membership?"

Research Method: The investigators chose to look at the culture of a particular friendship group of children operating in the context of a laboratory nursery school to investigate why two children were included in the group and a third youngster was not. The children within that group they selected to study were Bob, the leader of the group; Lisa, the only girl member; and William, who yearned to belong but did not.

For three quarters of the year the investigators videotaped, took field notes, and used teachers' retrospective notes of free play episodes that involved the friendship group.

After all the information was collected, the next step in the analysis was *not* to look at how the

three children were behaving. Instead the play itself was analyzed to find out what basic elements or ingredients were essential parts of that play. What elements did the children have to know about and participate in to be included? The researchers identified six ingredients: (a) possession of certain objects (sticks and capes), (b) use of objects in certain ways (pretend weapons), (c) certain pretend roles (e.g., superhero, firefighter), (d) certain kinds of language (e.g., "I'm a bad guy"), (e) exclusion of teachers, and (f) mock intimidation of teachers.

After these essential cultural elements of the play were identified, participation by each of the three children was examined in relation to their incorporation of these elements in their play. This examination revealed that Bob, the leader, always used some of those elements. For example, he used object possession and use, role playing, and language appropriate for the play 100% of the time. Lisa's activity was similar to Bob's, particularly in regard to object possession and use, role playing, and appropriate language.

In contrast, William, the outsider, "rarely acted in tune with the group" (p. 139). He just did not

Implications for Teaching

As far as teachers of young children are concerned, social learning theory, developmental interactionist theory, and sociocultural theory have merit because they all make it plain that teachers need to do more than sit idly by while the children grow and develop. Since one way that children acquire social behaviors is by identifying with models and imitating their behavior, obviously teachers should provide good examples (Wittmer & Honig, 1994). In addition, the relationship between themselves and the child should be based on mutual liking and warmth to encourage imitation of positive behavior (Eisenberg, 1992). Because young boys may tend to imitate male models more readily than they do female ones, it is also desirable to include male teachers and volunteers in the center whenever possible.

= physical self = emotional health = self-esteem = social competence =

seem able to figure out what the group's sociocultural expectations were. For example, although he realized that having a cape was an important aspect of the play, he would choose to play firefighter when the group was playing superhero, or use language that didn't fit the role. Moreover, rather than excluding the teachers, he tried to use them to help him enter the play. In other words, he was unable to crack the social password code.

Results and Conclusions: From an ethnographic point of view, the investigators concluded that, to be socially competent, William would have needed to understand not only that offering a prized object such as the sticks or wearing a cape was a way of obtaining admission to the group but also how to use the sticks in play, how to act toward the teachers, and what to say while playing in order to be admitted.

Kantor et al. drew three, more general conclusions from their research: (a) To be socially competent a child must be able to read the entire ongoing cultural context of the group rather than rely on a single, partial strategy; (b) the child's personality and behavior influence his ability to make those assessments; and (c) ongoing interactions among the children form a pattern of expectations for the future; in this case, these ongoing interactions spelled continuing success for Bob and Lisa and failure for William.

Implications for Teaching: This approach to research reminds us that, as teachers, we need to look at the entire context of what is happening within a group, rather than single-mindedly focus only on individual children. Taking this wider view can be a source of refreshing and more perceptive insights.

It also emphasizes that social behavior is a complex tapestry woven of many different threads. This means that even when we do look at individual children, we should not be too quick to single out individual strands to work with; one simple remedy may not cure a social difficulty. Instead we need to look at the whole cloth, as well as the whole child, if we are truly to understand what is happening in the groups of children with whom we work.

Source: From "Cultural Knowledge and Social Competence Within a Preschool Peer Culture Group," by R. Kantor, P. M. Elgas, and D. E. Fernie, 1993, Early Childhood Research Quarterly, 8(2), 125–147.

Since children also learn as a result of positive reinforcement, teachers need to be sure that children receive satisfaction from acting in socially desirable ways. Sometimes this reinforcement will be in the form of a pleasant comment or expression of affection, but a more desirable approach is for the teacher to point out to the child that it feels good to help other people so that the pleasure stems from this inherent reward rather than from a calculated external one.

In addition to these teacher-child interactions, plentiful opportunities for the children to interact together must also be included during the day since so much social learning takes place during play. As Hartup (1977) puts it, "Children learn many things through

rough-and-tumble activity that would not be possible in adult-child relations" (p. 5). This, then, furnishes us with yet another reason for including ample opportunities in the center day for social learning to occur among children.

HELPING CHILDREN BECOME SOCIALLY COMPETENT: SUGGESTIONS FOR TEACHING APPROPRIATE SOCIAL SKILLS

When young children want something, be it attention, assistance, or possession of an article, *their need is immediate, intense, and personal.* Their reactions, therefore, to having to wait or to consider the rights of others can be very strong, and it takes patient teaching backed by fortitude to help them develop the ability to wait a little, to control their feelings to a degree, and to consider the rights and desires of others when necessary. All these skills are central to the process of getting along in a social world. If teachers remember to take into account the strength of these immediate, intense, and personal needs as they read about specific social learnings, they will gain an added appreciation for the magnitude of the child's task in learning to become a socialized human being.

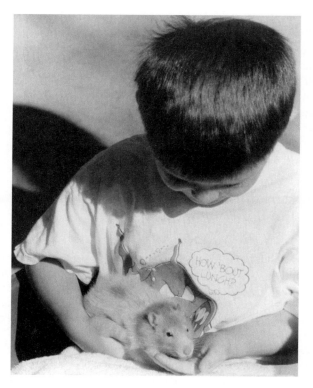

Taking care of animals can help children develop empathy.

It will, of course, take years and years for children to reach these goals in their maturest and most desirable form, but it is also true that socialization begins at the moment of birth as attachment develops between parents and children. Therefore early childhood is certainly not too early to begin instilling these important, positive values as long as they are worked on in an appropriate way. There are also many more social goals than the seven listed in this chapter. These particular goals have been chosen for discussion because they are frequently listed by teachers and families of young children in the United States as being important and as having long-term social value.

Goal I: Help Children Develop Empathy

Being able to feel what another person is feeling is a valuable social skill for many reasons. It helps us anticipate how someone will react to what we do, it helps us understand possible motives for other people's behavior, and it may encourage prosocial behavior (acting to benefit someone else when we realize how they feel).

Little children are just beginning to learn to separate themselves and their feelings from the feelings of other people. Indeed Piaget (1926, 1959) long maintained that young children are egocentric and unable to put themselves in the place of another. But research, as well as the experience of many early childhood teachers, indicates that this egocentrism is not an all-or-nothing condition. As children grow from age 2 to 5, they become increasingly able to assume roles and to perceive complex feelings (Zahn-Waxler, 1991). With training they can also become more sensitive to other people's feelings and to the effect their actions have on these feelings.

As children become more sensitive to those feelings, they can begin to feel concern for the person who expresses them. In one study (Zahn-Waxler, Radke-Yarrow, & King, 1979) a 17-month-old was reported comforting her mother when the mother began to cry. I recall my own 21-month-old daughter hugging me and patting my back after I shut the door on my finger, consoling me with tears in her eyes as she murmured, "Tired and hungry! Tired and hungry! We fix! We fix."

The interesting thing about Zahn-Waxler et al.'s (1979) study was the consistency of the style of empathic response displayed by youngsters as they developed. For example, a little boy who pushed one child aside to protect another child when he was 2 years old protected his grandmother when someone pushed ahead of her in line when he was 7 years old.

Encourage Role Playing

The teacher can do several things to increase the awareness of how it feels to be someone else. One of the most obvious of these is to provide many opportunities for dramatic and imaginative play involving taking roles about what people do. Most preprimary centers maintain housekeeping corners, which facilitate the role playing of family life so dear to 3- and 4-year-olds. We have seen that as children reach 4 and 5 years of age, their interest in the world around them increases and extends beyond the family and the school. For these youngsters enriched role opportunities can be offered with accessories for doctors and nurses, bus drivers, preschool teachers, or anyone else whose work is familiar to the children. The costumes need not be complete. Indeed it seems wise to leave some things out to exercise the children's imaginations. Hats are particularly fun, and it is good to have a variety of them representing different characters. For example, our Oklahoma children relish wearing the farm caps given away by seed and feed companies.

Help the Child Understand How the Other Person Feels

Teaching children how other people *feel*, in addition to what they *do*, is more difficult than simple role playing but is not impossible. One virtue of encouraging children to tell each other what they want or how they feel is that in addition to relieving the speaker's feelings, it informs the other child about someone else's emotions and desires. The other important reason for doing this, according to Piaget, is that children are freed of egocentrism by experiencing interactions with other people. He maintained that social conflict and discussion facilitate cognitive growth and the accompanying ability to put the self in another's place (Piaget, 1926).

Teachers can increase empathy for another's feelings by explaining how a child is feeling in terms that are personal to the observing child, relating the feeling to one they, too, have experienced. For example:

> Henry, who has just caught his finger in the door, is crying bitterly as the teacher holds him and comforts him. Frankie comes in and stands watching silently, his thumb in his mouth. He looks interested and worried, and as the teacher pats Henry on his back, she explains to Frankie, "Henry hurt his finger in the door. Remember when I rocked on your toe with the rocking chair?" Frankie nods. "Well, his finger feels like that." "It hurt," says Frankie. "It hurt a lot. But we put cold water on it and that made it stop. Let's put his finger in cold water." The teacher says, "That's a great idea! Henry, Frankie is telling you something." Frankie says, "Come on, Hennie, we'll put your finger in water; that will help." And off they go.

Here, the teacher related Henry's feelings directly to what Frankie already knew from his own experience. This helped make the feeling real to him and also encouraged him to use this insight to provide practical comfort for his friend.

During group time, showing pictures of people expressing strong emotions is yet another way to build awareness and sensitivity. Children can often identify the feeling (remember that it can be a positive as well as a negative one) and talk over what might have made that person happy or sad and how they might offer help or comfort if that is deemed necessary.

Goal II: Help Children Learn to Be Generous, Altruistic, and Able to Share Equipment, Experiences, and People with Other Children

It is worthwhile to do what we can to develop children's ability to feel empathy since it appears that this ability to sense someone else's feelings is related at least in younger children to a second prosocial skill as well (Eisenberg, McCreath, & Ahn, 1988): the development of altruistic behavior—behavior a person performs with the unselfish intention of making another person feel good or happy.

Research on social development indicates that when affection from the teacher is combined with verbal comments about what is happening, the greatest number of charitable responses is produced in children (Midlarsky & Bryan, 1967). Modeling generosity also increases this behavior (Grusec & Arnason, 1982; Rosenhan, 1972), and paternal nurturing facilitates generosity in boys of nursery school age (Rutherford & Mussen, 1968). Thus we again find support for the recommendation that *teaching a prosocial behavior is accomplished most effectively by a teacher who sets a good example and expresses affection while at the same time clarifying what is happening by discussing it with the children* (Corsaro, 1997; Eisenberg & Fabes, 1998).

Help Children Learn to Share Equipment

Teaching a specific aspect of generosity such as sharing (a social skill of real concern in children's centers and preschools) requires more than nurturing and setting a good example. It requires following through with clear-cut policies directed toward building the generous impulse within the child, rather than relying on externally enforced generosity supervised by the teacher. As one of my students put it, "I want him to share from his heart, not because I make him do it."

Many teachers try to teach sharing by regulating turn taking ("You can have it for 2 minutes, then he can have it for 2 minutes"). They seem to interpret sharing as meaning that the child has to hand over anything he is using almost as soon as another child says he wants it. Teachers who enforce taking turns on this basis find they are constantly required to monitor and referee the turn taking themselves. This not only is tiresome but also *puts the locus of control and decision making outside the child, rather than within him.* It also means that a child may not be permitted to have enough of an experience to be filled up and truly satisfied by it. Such deprivation builds a kind of watchful hunger and avarice that should be avoided. It is still true that one doesn't cure hunger by snatching away the bread.

Rather than struggling to institute the policelike control of the previous procedure, the teacher can establish a climate of generosity by making sure the child has enough of most experiences. Therefore she does not limit the child to two paintings or allow him to ride the trike around the course only three times because another child is waiting. Instead she follows the rule that the child may keep what he has or do what he is doing until he has had enough of it. This means that children do not have to be calculating and defensive about hanging on to things. It also makes settling arguments easier since it is relatively simple to base decisions on who was using it first and then to state the rule "Whoever had it first may keep it until he's done with it."

Once assured his own rights and desires will be protected, it becomes much easier for a child to share. When another child is waiting, the teacher can point this out, perhaps saying, "Dan, when you're done with the swing would you remember to tell Ashley? She'd like a turn when you're through." The final step in this process is recognizing when he *does* remember to tell Ashley he is through by commending him and pointing out, "Look how pleased she is that you remembered. She's really smiling at you. I guess you're her friend."

It helps in such situations to have enough equipment available so that children do not have to wait and wait. Several easels are better than one, and feeling free to improvise to meet peak demands will help, too. For example, if painting is suddenly very popular, setting out paint tables might help, or giving children cans of water and old brushes to paint the fence could satisfy their need and reduce waiting.

Help Children Learn to Share the Teacher

Children not only have to learn to share equipment, they also have to learn to share their teacher and her attention with other children. Again the best model is the generous one, in which each gets what he needs, rather than each getting an identical, metered amount. This may mean that only one child is rocked while several others play nearby in the block corner, rather than that every child is rocked a little. As long as each child receives comfort when he needs it, teachers do not have to worry about whether they are being "fair." They can explain to the children that different people get different special things according to what they need; to remind the children that this policy applies to everyone, teachers can cite examples of times when those children received special attention.

Sometimes individual satisfactions have to be put off because it is not possible for one child to monopolize the teacher's attention throughout lunch or story time. To handle such demands the teacher might say, "You know, lunch is for everyone to talk together, but I can see you really want to talk just to me. I promise we'll have time for that while I'm getting you ready for nap."

Goal III: Help Children Learn That Being Kind to Other People Feels Good

Helping Other People Is One Way of Expressing Kindness

I agree with the Soviet psychologist's implication at the beginning of this chapter that children in the United States are not encouraged to help their friends as much as they might be. Providing opportunities for children to experience the satisfaction and pleasure that come from helping someone else appears to be a sound way to generate willingness to take prosocial action since the resulting good feeling reinforces the behavior. Sometimes helping others takes the form of comforting another child; sometimes it is as simple as passing the cups at snack; sometimes it is as sophisticated as thinking of an excursion everyone will enjoy.

Children should be encouraged and expected to help each other. The teacher should emphasize that helping other people is a worthwhile, important thing to do. Here are some simple examples furnished by student-teachers[1] of how this can be clearly and consistently taught at the preschool level when teachers are sensitive to incorporating these values.

This episode took place in the hollow block area with some cardboard blocks that have foam packing glued to their insides. Janelle, Timothy, and Jenny were all climbing around on them.

Timothy:	Look, I can climb out of here by myself. (He proceeds to do so.)
Me:	Boy, Timothy, you sure can. I wonder if it's just as easy to climb in?
Timothy:	Yeah, I can. I got to put my leg over first. (He climbs in the box, accidentally putting his foot on Janelle's shoulder.)
Janelle:	Watch out, Timothy!
Me:	Whoops! He accidentally hit your shoulder, huh?
Janelle:	Yeah. Watch me hide in this corner. (She does so and almost gets stuck between the layers of foam. She finally gets herself out.) I almost got stuck!

---

[1] *My thanks to Mary Kashmar, Lauren Davis, Sandi Coe, and the children for the following episodes.*

Sometimes opportunities to help someone else come up unexpectedly.

Me:	Yeah, you finally slipped your way out.
Jenny:	(who has crammed herself in more firmly, shrieks) Help me, teacher. I can't get outta here!
Me:	Uh oh! Now Jenny's stuck in there. (Jenny continues to twist and struggle.) Janelle, do you remember how you got out?
Janelle:	Yeah! Here, Jenny, I'll help you. (With Janelle pulling and Jenny pushing, Jenny manages to get out.)
Me:	Good, you guys! She sure needed you, Janelle!
Jenny:	Yeah, I was stuck! I woulda spent the night in there! (She laughs.)

Or sometimes helping takes the form of one youngster's teaching another something.

Roe (age 4 years, 8 months) is washing and drying some toy animals when Yvonne (age 2 years, 3 months) walks up, takes up the other towel, and wants to play. Roe takes the towel away from Yvonne and looks at me.

Roe:	Will you dry?
Me:	Yvonne looks like she really wants to play. Why don't you ask her to dry them for you?

(Roe is agreeable to the suggestion.)

Roe: Yvonne, will you dry? (Yvonne nods her head yes. She begins to dry but is having difficulty.)

Roe: (snatching the towel away impatiently) She's too slow. You dry.

Me: I think you should give Yvonne a chance. Maybe you can show her how to do it.

Roe: Here, Yvonne, do it this way.

(Yvonne catches on quickly and squeals with delight.)

Roe: Wow, now she's waiting for me. I better hurry up.

Me: You girls work well together. Thanks, Roe.

(Soon all the toys are washed and dried.)

Or it takes the form of both comfort and help.

At the swings two children were playing and unhooked the seats from the chains. Anathea (playing in the cornmeal) looked over and saw this. "They broke it!" she cried. She seemed really upset by it.

Earon reached over and patted her on the back, saying, "It didn't break," and went on playing. Then he repeated this about three more times. "It didn't break, Anathea; it didn't break."

I said, "You're right, Earon, but can you tell Anathea what happened?"

"They didn't break it; they just took it off of there. See?" (He goes over and hooks them up.) Anathea smiled at him, and they both went back to playing in the cornmeal.

Note that it is necessary to handle these situations carefully to avoid the undesirable effect of comparing children with each other. For example, rather than saying, "Why don't you do it the way Alan does; he's a big boy," it is better to say, "Alan just learned how to zip his coat. Why don't you ask him to show you how it goes together?" Children are often generous about teaching such skills to each other as long as it does not take so much time that they lose patience.

The Presence of Children Who Have Handicaps Presents Special Opportunities for Children to Be Kind and Considerate

Although it is desirable to treat children who have handicaps as much as possible as we treat all the other children, it is also true that sometimes these youngsters require special consideration. For example, a child who is hard of hearing benefits from having those around him know at least some sign language (Antia, Kriemeyer, & Eldredge, 1994), just as a child who has Down syndrome benefits from frequent repetition and enforcement of simple social rules.

Experience has taught me that other children in the group can be quick to offer practical help in a kindly, matter-of-fact way if they are encouraged by the teacher to do so. The problem is helping them understand the difference between kindness and pity and the difference between offering help that empowers the child with the handicap to do all he can for himself and overwhelming him by being too solicitous or babying him. Although it is definitely worth encouraging such simple acts of thoughtfulness as moving the crayons within the reach of a child in a wheelchair, the best, kindest thing the children can do is include the child with the handicap in their play. The teacher cannot force them to do this, but she *can* encourage it by pointing out a practical way the youngster can participate and by subtly expressing approval when that takes place.

Not Doing Something Can Also Be a Way of Being Kind to Someone

Children also need to learn that kindness goes beyond doing something nice for somebody else. Sometimes it means *not* doing something you feel inclined to do. Although we cannot expect young children always to anticipate when their comments may be tactless or even hurtful, many times they know unequivocally that they are saying something with the intention of being mean. For example, the child who says with a sneer, "You can't come to my birthday party," or, "You talk funny," or, "Only guys with clean socks can come in," is saying those words with the deliberate intention of hurting the other youngster not only by excluding him but also by denigrating him.

The teacher should not tolerate this kind of deliberately hurtful behavior anymore than she would permit a child to hurt an animal. Instead, she should take the speaker aside and explain that what he said was unkind and made the other child feel bad. While acknowledging that nobody has to play with everybody, the teacher should tell the child that causing pain that way is not permitted in the group and that he is not to do it again. Then, of course, she must also deal with the feelings of the child who has been hurt. Perhaps she might say, "I'm sorry he was feeling mean and wanted to hurt your feelings. Everybody has stuff to learn at school, and he's just learning to be kind. Let's see what we can find that you'd like to do in case it doesn't work out for you to play here right now."

Goal IV: Teach Children That Everyone Has Rights and That These Rights Are Respected by All

I made the point earlier that children have individual needs and that teachers should not hesitate to meet these on an individual basis; that is, they should not interpret fairness as meaning that everyone gets exactly the same thing. But children do, in general, have to conform to the same rules. This impartiality of rule enforcement will help children gradually understand that everyone is respected as having equal rights.

Teach Children That Rules Apply to Everyone

A good example of this may be seen in handling sharing problems. At the beginning of the year there always seems to be one or two children who seize possession rather than asking and waiting for turns. Of course, the teacher often has to restrain such a youngster from doing this. It is particularly important with this kind of child that the teacher also watch carefully and almost ostentatiously protect the seizer's rights when someone tries to take his trike away, so that he sees that everyone, himself as well as others, has his rights of possession protected. This is an effective way to teach fairness and to help the child see what the rule is and that it applies to every child. The message is "You may not intrude on their rights, and they may not intrude on yours, either." As the year progresses and the child learns to know and apply these rules himself, he will become increasingly able to enforce them without the teacher's help and thus be able to stand up for himself in social interaction situations.

Teach Respect for Others' Rights by Honoring Personal Privacy

Children enjoy bringing things from home; it is a cheerful link between their families and the school. Because these items are their personal possessions, it should be their choice whether to share them or not. Even the teacher should ask, "May I see it?" before she reaches out to handle a personal possession.

When he does not choose to share something, the child should put it in his cubby. Keeping his possessions there provides an opportunity to teach privacy and personal rights if the rule is enforced that a child may go only in his own cubby, never in anyone else's without permission. Of course, there will be many transgressions of this rule, but the children will learn to honor this policy over a year's time, just as they will learn to stay out of the teacher's desk and out of the staff rest room if these rules are enforced.

Goal V: Emphasize the Value of Cooperation and Compromise Rather Than Stress Competition and Winning

Competition and winning are so much a part of American life that it hardly seems necessary to emphasize them with such young children, and yet many teachers do so since appealing to children's competitive instincts is such an easy way to get them to do what teachers want. It is particularly easy to employ competition as a manipulative device with 4- and 5-year-olds because rivalry increases around that time (Stott & Ball, 1957). Examples include, "Oh, look how well Joan's picking up the blocks; I bet you can't pick up as many as she can!" or, "It's time for lunch, children. Whoever gets to the bathroom first can sit by me. Now, remember, no running!" The trouble with these strategies is they reward children for triumphing over other children and neglect the chance to teach them the pleasure of accomplishing things together.

In Place of Fostering Competition, Model Cooperation and Helping Behavior Yourself

One effective way for the teacher to substitute cooperation for competition is to model it by helping the children herself. Thus when it is time to put away the blocks, the teacher warns in advance and then says, "It's time to put the blocks away. Come on, let's all pitch in. I guess I'll begin by picking up the biggest ones. Mike, would you like to drive the truck over here so we can load it up?" Mike may refuse, of course, but after a pause he will probably join in if the teacher continues to work with the group to complete the task, meanwhile thanking those who are helping.

Teach the Art of Compromise

Being able to compromise is another basic part of learning to cooperate. Four-year-olds love to strike bargains and are often able to appreciate the fact that everyone has gained some of what he wants when a fair bargain or agreement is reached. The following episode, which occurred at our children's center, is a good example of this.

> Jimmy has been pulling some blocks around the play area in the wagon. Finally, tiring of this, he asks the teacher to pull him instead. Just at this moment Alan arrives and wants the wagon. This is too much for Jimmy, who, dog-in-the-manger style, suddenly decides he wants to pull it after all. He says, "No, Alan! You can't have it! I'm using the wagon. I'm not done. I want to pull it! Get off!" "My gosh, Jimmy," says the teacher. "Weren't you just saying you wanted a ride? Here's your chance. Weren't you just asking for someone to pull you?" She pauses to let this sink in. "Maybe if you let Alan have a turn pulling the wagon, he would give you the ride

you want." She turns to Alan. "Would you do that, Alan?" She turns to Jimmy, "Would that be OK with you, Jimmy?"

Thus the teacher helped the boys strike a bargain whereby both got what they wanted.

As children become more socially experienced, the teacher could encourage the boys to think the situation through for themselves, rather than intervening so directly herself. Perhaps she might say at that point, "Jimmy, Alan is telling you he really wants to use the wagon, too. Isn't there some way you can both get something good out of this?" If the boys cannot conceive of any solution, then she can go on to the more obvious approach out-lined above.

Teach Children to Work Together

The teacher should also be on the lookout for opportunities for which it takes two chil-dren (or more) to accomplish what they want. Perhaps one youngster has to pull on the handle while the other shoves the wagon of sand from behind, or one must steady the juicer while the other squeezes. When these circumstances arise, encourage the children to help each other, rather than hurrying too quickly to help them yourself.

A few pieces of play equipment also require cooperation for success, and a point should be made of acquiring these. Double rocking horses, for example, just will not work if the children do not cooperate and coordinate their efforts; neither will tire swings that are hung horizontally. Some kinds of jump ropes also need at least two people participating for success, as does playing catch.

Goal VI: Help Children Discover the Pleasures of Friendship

Children become more and more interested in having friends as they grow older. By age 5 they are likely to spend more than half their playtime with other children (Valentine, 1956), and friendship bonds between particular children are generally much stronger at this age than they are in younger children (Hartup, 1992). By second grade it is almost intolerable to be without a friend.

As early as the preschool years, research reports that friendships occur typically between children of the same sex, race, age, and activity preference (Aboud & Mendel-son, 1996) and that those friendships persist over longer periods of time than was previ-ously thought. For example, some research by Howes and Phillipsen (1992), which stud-ied children in day care situations, reported that some friendships continued for as long as 3 years, although most of the children in the study also made new friends, separated from old friends, and ended friendships during that same time.

Ways of demonstrating friendship pass through developmental stages (Youniss, 1975), moving from a 6-year-old's interpretation of showing friendship by means of sharing toys and material items (Niffenegger & Willer, 1998), through the stage of playing together as a primary indication, and going on to showing friendship by offering psychological assis-tance such as giving comfort when needed.

One list compiled by a group of 4-year-olds at the Institute for Child Development at the University of Oklahoma included the following ways of showing friends they liked them: hug them, kiss them, play with them, have a party, celebrate Valentine's Day, run to them, mail them a letter, sing a song to them, tell a secret, give them a present, and let them spend the night.

Continuing a friendship depends on many variables, including similarity of age and interests, proximity, gender, and sociability, as well as the less readily analyzable qualities of personal attractiveness (Ramsey, 1991). Considerable variation also occurs in the capacity and need for close friendships at the preschool age.

Rubin (1980) reports a study by Lee that was carried out in a day nursery and that found some children were friendlier and better liked by other children even during the first 6 months of life (L. C. Lee, 1973). He reports another extensive study by Hartup, Glazer, and Charlesworth (1967) that found the most popular, sought-after children in nursery school were the ones who most often paid attention to other children, praised them, showed affection, and willingly acceded to their requests.

Other studies, in contrast, show that friendless preschoolers do not get along well in interactions with peers. They have difficulty initiating play with them and have fewer positive experiences (Newcomb & Bagwell, 1996). Older friendless youngsters were found to "display less adaptive social competencies . . . [were] less likely to show altruism and trust toward peers, . . . their play with peers was less coordinated and positive, and they had less mature conceptions of friendship relations" (Newcomb & Bagwell, 1996, p. 313).

It sometimes seems that the only friendships teachers are aware of are the ones they try to break up between older boys who egg each other on into trouble. Yet we must remember the many desirable relationships which should be noted and nurtured in the preschool. Having friends is important at every age.

Facilitate Friendliness by Using Reinforcement to Reduce Isolated Behavior

Social interaction between children can be increased by the judicious use of reinforcement. This is a particularly helpful technique to employ with shy, isolated children. Using this approach, the teacher provides some kind of social dividend whenever the child approaches a group or interacts with them but withholds such recognition when the child withdraws and plays by himself. (It is hoped that over a period of time the pleasure the youngster finds in being part of the group will replace this more calculated reward.) Note that this approach is just the opposite of the pattern that often occurs, in which the teacher tends to "try to draw the child out" when he retires from the group, thereby rewarding with attention the very behavior it is desirable to extinguish.

Increase the Social Skills of Friendless or Excluded Children

Another way to foster friendships among children is to teach less likable youngsters social skills that make them more acceptable to the other children.[2] For example, a child who has learned to ask for what he wants is generally more welcome than one who rushes in and grabs whatever appeals to him (Katz & McClellan, 1997).

As the Research Study in this chapter indicates, identifying just which skills a child needs in order to fit in with a group can require careful observation and analysis if it is to

---

[2] Refer to the discussion of teaching children alternative ways of getting what they want in the chapter on aggression (chapter 12).

be truly helpful. However, it is well worth the time and trouble it takes to do this. Research by Coie and Kupersmidt (1983) indicates that among the 20% of children who typically are rejected by their classmates, about half remain rejected from year to year. Such an experience can really dishearten and discourage a youngster, as well as have an unfortunate effect on his self-esteem unless someone lends an effective hand.

This kind of social instruction can sometimes be best accomplished on a one-to-one basis whereby children are coached by the teacher in more successful ways to behave. Sometimes, for example, it really clarifies the situation when the teacher simply points out, "You know, when you knock their blocks down, they don't like you. It makes Hank and Charley really mad, and then they won't let you play. Why don't you try building something near them next time? Then maybe they'll gradually let you join them and be your friends."

Particularly with 4-year-olds, simple small-group discussions of what works and what doesn't also help children learn techniques that foster friendly relations. It is, of course, important not to single out specific personalities during these discussions as being either "good" or "bad" examples.

Asher, Oden, and Gottman (1977) report two fascinating studies on the effect of teaching social skills by means of modeling (Evers & Schwarz, 1973; O'Connor, 1972), in which a film demonstrating successful methods of entering a group was shown to young children. Observation of their behavior following this film revealed marked and continued improvement in their use of these strategies.

Although such films are not readily available, other ways of presenting models can be developed easily. I recently observed two teachers acting out such situations in brief, simple skits for their 4-year-olds at group time. The children were delighted and readily talked the skits over afterward. When presenting such skits, remember that it is important to avoid the temptation to parody specific personalities in the group.

Pair Children Together

Pairing children sometimes helps them make friends. Coming to school in a car pool or going home from school to play together can cement a friendship, as can doing jobs together or sharing an interest in common. In the long run, though, it is up to the children to form the friendship; all the teacher can do is make such possibilities available to them.

Help Children When a Friend Departs or When They Are Rejected

Sometimes teachers underestimate what it means to a child when a friend moves away, or makes a new friend and rejects the former one, or is transferred to another room. Children often feel quite despondent and adrift when this occurs. Indeed in her study of friendships among children in day care, Howes (1988) found that "children who lost a high proportion of friends because the friends moved, and children who moved to new peer groups without familiar peers were less socially skilled than were children who stayed with friends" (p. 66).

When someone is transferring rooms or leaving school, everyone needs to be prepared for the change. This should include the child and his parents and the other children as well. When a child is transferring, we have often prepared everyone by inviting the child

It's hard when you lose a friend . . .

for a "visit" to the new room once or twice before making the total switch. And if we have warning, then we often serve a festive snack when a child is moving away. Allowing the departee to choose it and his friends to help make it adds to the fun.

As in working through any other kind of separation, the leaver's and the left-behinds' feelings of grief, apprehension, and sometimes anger need to be recognized and honored. There is no shame in feeling saddened when a friend has departed, and children should be allowed to mourn this without being ridiculed. They should also be assisted, in an unpushy way, to strike up a new friendship at the right moment.

Rejection by a former crony hurts, too, as does rejection by an entire group (Zakriski & Jacobs & Coie, 1997). Four-year-olds in particular can form tight little cliques, part of whose "joy" is excluding as well as including other children. Teachers of young children need to be on the lookout for these happenings and ease the ache of rejection when they can. Sometimes the exclusion is only temporary, but as the Research Study in this chapter reveals, sometimes the rejection is more lasting. When this happens, it takes sensitive analysis to determine the reason for the rejection and possible teaching of needed skills to both the rejectors and the rejectee. Sometimes the only alternative is to face reality, acknowledge the child's feelings, and encourage a new beginning with another friend or group.

Goal VII: Help Children with Special Needs Fit Into the Life of the Group

The primary advantage of including children with special needs in typical preprimary environments, often cited by proponents of inclusive early education, is that all the children derive social benefits from that inclusion, and research supports this suggestion if only to a limited degree (Guralnick, 1999)

This chapter has already pointed out that one of many social benefits typical children receive is learning matter-of-fact kindness from that experience, but there are other benefits as well. While learning to accept and adapt to those with special needs, the group also learns that all children are more alike than different and, ideally, to feel comfortable rather than uneasy around such youngsters.

The other side of the coin is that the child with the disability has the opportunity to learn to fit in with a group of ordinary peers and get along with them (Odom, McConnell, & McEvoy, 1992). He sees typical behavior modeled all around him, including various strategies the children employ for getting what they want and playing together. These can be emphasized quietly by the teacher, showing him how he, too, might use the same strategies.

Chapter 9, "Welcoming Children Who Have Special Educational Requirements Into the Life of the School," discusses many things the teacher can do to help all the children get along together, and many helpful resources are included at the end of that chapter. Therefore, I restrict myself here to reminding the reader how important it is to remember the 5 Ps when teaching social skills to children with special needs: *Don't* pity or overprotect these children. *Do* be patient, persistent, and practical.

SUMMARY

Social competence develops at a rapid rate during the years of early childhood, and several theories have evolved to explain how this complex process takes place. Children become socialized in part as a result of identifying with and emulating models they admire; in part as a consequence of reinforcement that encourages or suppresses various kinds of social behavior; and in part by other kinds of interactions among themselves and with adults that foster cognitive, intellectual learnings conducive to the development of social skills.

Although children begin to attain many social skills during this period, seven of them were selected in this chapter as being particularly important: (a) developing empathy, (b) learning to be generous, (c) understanding that everyone has rights that must be respected, (d) learning that it feels good to help other people, (e) discovering the value of cooperation and compromise rather than stressing competition, (f) discovering the joys of friendship, and (g) helping children with special needs fit into the life of the group.

Questions and Activities

1. *Predicament:* You are working as a teacher in a Head Start center. One volunteer is supervising the trike area and is firmly telling each child that he can ride his trike around the track three times and then must give a turn to the next child who is standing in line (several children are standing there already, making plaintive noises about wanting turns). What would you do to handle this situation on both a short- and long-term basis?

2. During the next week watch for situations in which a child could be helped to understand another person's feelings or point of view. Using the situations you observed, discuss possible ways that genuine feeling for another person could have been developed from these situations.

3. How much do you know about effective ways of entering a group? Make a list in class of strategies adults and children can employ for successful entrée.

4. Have you witnessed examples at your school of children seeking to comfort each other? Share the situation with the class and explain what the comforter did to help the other child.

5. *Predicament:* You agree with the author that children should have a special place of their own to keep their personal belongings while at school. Your school provides hooks for the children's hats and coats and a shelf above that for storage. What would you suggest could be done to provide private places for each youngster?

Self-Check Questions for Review

Content-Related Questions

1. What are some typical social behaviors of 2-year-olds? How does the social behavior of 3-year-olds differ from that of 4-year-olds?

2. After reviewing the processes by which children become socialized, discuss what the implications are for teachers. Basing your comments on what is known about the process of socialization, explain how teachers can apply that knowledge to further socialize the young children in their care.

3. Review the seven social learning goals and then list some practical pointers you would give a new teacher about how each of those goals might be accomplished.

Integrative Questions

1. Review the equipment in the school where you are teaching or have taught and identify which equipment facilitates social interaction between children. Do any items, for example, require two people using them at once to make them work effectively? Suggest additional activities you could offer that would be more successful if two or more children worked together to accomplish them.

2. The chapter discusses three theories about how children become socialized. What do these theories have in common, and how do they differ? Do these differences mean that only one of them is correct and the other is wrong?

3. Propose two or three brief skits or episodes the staff might act out that demonstrate social situations and/or social problems for the children to discuss. For example, two people might act out a problem at the snack table where two children both want to get refills. Be sure to think of at least one situation that demonstrates positive social interaction.

4. The woodworking table is very popular this morning; everyone wants to hammer and saw. Carpentry is offered several times a week. Which of the following solutions for regulating participation would you favor? Be sure to explain the pros and cons for following each of the four policies: (a) Allow each child to make one item and then let the next child have a turn; (b) have the teacher keep a list and have the children sign up for turns; (c) tell requesters the table is full right now and to please come back later; (d) suggest to children as they finish that they alert waiters there is space for them.

Coordinating Videotape

Getting along together. Tape #8. The whole child: A caregiver's guide to the first five years. The Annenberg/CPB Collection, P.O. Box 2345, South Burlington, VT 05407–2345. *Getting Along Together* traces the course of typical social development and stresses ways adults can enhance a child's social competence. It highlights the processes children use to develop empathy, generosity, respect, cooperation, compromise and friendship.

References for Further Reading

Pick of the Litter

Read, K. H. (1996). Initial support through guides to speech and action. In K. M. Paciorek & J. H. Munro (Eds.), *Sources: Notable selections in early childhood education.* Guilford, CT: Dushkin. I think this was the first material I ever read about working with young children, and this reprint is as sound today as it was 40 years ago! (It don't get no better than this!)

Overviews

Katz, L., & McClellan, D. E. (1997). *Fostering children's social competence: The teacher's role.* Washington, DC: National Association for the Education of Young Children. If you can read only one book about developing social competence, pick this one! Based on research, it is practical and obviously written by people who've "been there/done that." *Highly recommended.*

Kemple, K. M., & Hartle, L. (1997). Getting along: How teachers can support children's peer relationships. *Early Childhood Education Journal, 24*(3), 139–146. This very practical article outlines numerous ways teachers can facilitate positive relationships between young children.

Witmer, D. S., & Honig, A. S. (1996). Encouraging positive social development in young children. In K. M. Paciorek & J. H. Munro (Eds.), *Early childhood education 96/97.* Guilford, CT: Dushkin. A compendium of practical advice fostering positive social development is provided here. *Highly recommended.*

Direct Instruction About Social Skills

Beaty, J. J. (1995). *Converting conflicts in preschool.* New York: Harcourt Brace. Eight kinds of potential conflict situations are identified, together with practical suggestions for their alleviation. Beaty advocates fostering empathy, asking each child how the other one feels and what would make the other child feel happy as being a helpful way to settle these situations.

Mize, J., & Abell, E. (1996). Encouraging social skills in young children: Tips teachers can share with parents. *Dimensions of Early Childhood, 24*(3), 15–23.

The authors suggest six practical ways parents and teachers can influence the development of sound social relationships between children.

Forming Friendships

Wolf, C. P. (Ed.). (1986). *Connecting: Friendship in the lives of young children and their teachers.* Redmond, WA: Exchange. In a series of easy-to-read articles, this book offers an overview of the value of friendship to young children, along with comments on ways to enhance its flowering. *Highly recommended.*

Integrating Children with Disabilities Into the Life of the School

Conroy, M. A., Langenbrunner, M. R., & Burleson, R. B. (1996). Suggestions for enhancing the social behaviors of preschoolers with disabilities using developmentally appropriate practices. *Dimensions of Early Childhood, 24*(1), 9–15.

Guralnick, M. J. (1999). The nature and meaning of social integration for young children with mild developmental delays in inclusive settings. *Journal of Early Intervention, 22*(1), 70–86. A leading authority in the field of disabilities offers a clear-sighted assessment of current successes and limitations of integration.

For the Advanced Student

Adler, P. A., & Adler, P. (1988). The carpool: A socializing adjunct to the education experience. In G. Handel (Ed.), *Childhood socialization.* New York: Aldine De Gruyter. This delightful bit of research investigated the potential social learnings and contretemps available in the social life of the car pool. *Highly recommended.*

Bukowski, W. M., Newcomb, A. F., & Hartup, W. W. (Eds.). (1996). *The company they keep: Friendship in childhood and adolescence.* New York: Cambridge University Press. For the first time in 20 years this book summarizes in readable form the research about the complex and interesting questions of friendship—what it is (and definitions are not simple), how and why it occurs, and why it matters. This is research reporting at its best.

Corsaro, W. A. (1997). *The sociology of childhood.* Thousand Oaks, CA: Pine Forge Press. This is another interesting, research based book about social development with investigations reported at the preschool level.

Eisenberg, N. (Ed.). (1998). *Handbook of child psychology: Vol. 3. Social, emotional, and personality development.* New York: Wiley. This is *the* publication to review for serious students desiring a comprehensive review of research on social development. First rate but difficult.

Mize, J. (1995). Coaching preschool children in social skills: A cognitive-social learning curriculum. In G. Carledge & J. F. Milburn (Eds.), *Teaching social skills to children and youth* (3rd ed.). Boston: Allyn & Bacon. Mize provides a practical, clear description of a research study in which she deliberately taught prosocially inept preschoolers how to be more socially effective. *Highly recommended.*

Roopnarine, J. L., & Carter, D. B. (1992). *Parent-child socialization in diverse cultures: Annual advances in applied developmental psychology* (Vol. 5). Norwood, NJ: Ablex. Socialization in 13 cultures is discussed, including the influence of parents and schools. Very interesting reading.

chapter eleven

Helping Young Children Establish Self-Discipline and Self-Control

But What if She Won't Do What I Say?

How to help children control themselves instead of depending on other people to control them?

How to make it easier for children to behave in acceptable ways?

What to do when a child won't stop doing something she shouldn't be doing?

. . . IF YOU HAVE, THE MATERIAL IN THE FOLLOWING PAGES WILL HELP YOU.

In every discipline situation two people should learn something!

Alma Berg Green (1945)

It is insanity to believe that if we get children to feel bad, they will behave better.

Becky Bailey (1997, p. 73)

Since discipline worries beginning teachers the most, it is usually the subject they want to discuss first when they begin teaching. Sometimes this is because they fear physical aggression or that the children will not like them, but more frequently they fear losing control of a situation because they do not know what to do next. So when teachers say fervently that they want to discuss "discipline," what they usually have in mind is how to control the children or, as one forthright young student put it, "how to get the kids to do what I want."

TWO BASIC GOALS OF DISCIPLINE

Although "getting the kids to do what I want" is undeniably part of the package, should it be all that is encompassed by the concept of discipline? The teacher should also have in mind the higher goal of instilling inner self-controls in the child in place of teacher-maintained external ones. Therefore every discipline situation should not only achieve a workable solution to the current crisis (and this is discussed in the second part of the chapter) but also seek to interiorize self-control.

ESTABLISHING INNER CONTROLS: EGO STRENGTH AND MORAL DEVELOPMENT

Why Does Self-Control Matter?

Self- rather than "other"-control is desirable for numerous reasons. People who can control themselves are trustworthy and responsible. They can be counted on to do the right thing whether or not a police officer is standing on the corner watching to see if they run the red light. Since the control is internal, it is more consistent; and most valuably for mental health, the individual who is "inner controlled" makes choices on her own behalf. This is the opposite of the neurotic personality who feels powerless and unable to control what happens to herself and who sees herself as "done to" and in the power of others.

Granted that internalization of control is desirable, the questions that remain for parents and early childhood teachers to answer are, How can I begin to establish these inner controls in such young children? and How can I teach them not only to *know* what is right but to *do* what is right? Teachers must realize that this is a long process taking many years, and it rests on the gradual development of ego strength and moral judgment. A strong ego enables the child to control her impulses, and moral judgment (telling right from wrong) enables her to decide which impulses she must control.

Building Ego Strength

Fraiberg (1977) describes the ego as being the part of the personality that has to do with the executive and cognitive functions of the individual and that also regulates the drives and appetites. Obviously it is this part of the personality we want to strengthen to make it available to the child to help her control her impulses.

One Way to Do This Is to *Increase the Child's Feelings of Mastery by Giving Her Many Opportunities for Making Decisions*

The choices offered, however, must be appropriate and not too difficult. I recall a 4-year-old who was asked by her divorcing parents to decide which parent she wished to live with—an intolerably difficult choice for a child of that age to make.

Fortunately, the preschool day abounds with opportunities for decisions well within the ability of most 3- and 4-year-olds to handle. The catch is that *the teacher must be prepared to honor the choice once the child has made the decision.* Such questions as "Do you want dessert?" "Would you rather finger-paint or play with the blocks?" or "Would you like to pass the napkins today?" are examples of valid choices because it is all right if the child chooses to refuse. Unfortunately many teachers use "Would you like . . . ?" or "Would you please . . . ?" or "OK?" as a polite camouflage for conveying an order. Thus they inquire, "Let's get on the bus, OK?" or, "Would you like to put on your sweater?" Young children are likely to retort, "No!" when asked such questions, and then the teacher is really stuck. It is better not to ask, "Let's get on the bus, OK?" if the child has to get on the bus anyway, but to try saying, "The bus is here, and it's time to go home. Where do you want to sit?" or, "It's cold today. If you want to go out, you will need to put on your sweater." In short, honor choices when given, *but give no choice when there is no valid opportunity to make one.*

It is also important to see to it that the child experiences the consequences of her decisions. Perhaps the reader will recall the example in the chapter on routines (chapter 4) in which the child who elects to skip snack is not permitted to change her mind at the last minute. Abiding by decisions once they are made teaches youngsters to make responsible choices.

Increase the Child's Feelings of Being a Competent, Worthwhile Person

The feelings of self-esteem generated by competency also make the ego stronger. The child who thinks well of herself because she is competent is in a favorable position to assume command and control of herself because she sees herself as being effective and strong.

Unfortunately some children are noticed only when they do something wrong. This continual negative relationship with the teacher does not enhance the children's feelings of self-worth. Even the "worst" child in school does not misbehave all the time. A considerable part of her day is spent in acceptable activities. If her self-esteem and self-mastery are to remain intact, it is vital that she receive credit for her good behavior, as well as control for her transgressions.

However, as we saw in the chapter on self-esteem (chapter 7) the most desirable source of self-worth stems, not from the opinion of the teacher, but from the acquisition of skills. These may be as diverse as being able to walk the balance beam or knowing effective strategies for worming one's way into a play group. It does not really matter what the competency is as long as it contributes to the child's perception of herself as being an able person who is in command of herself.

Encouraging Moral Development: Fostering the Interiorization of Conscience

Another aspect of helping children establish inner controls has to do with the establishment of conscience and instilling a sense of what is right and wrong. *Conscience* (sometimes termed the *super-ego*) can be described as that inner voice that tells us what we should or should not do; that is, in very simple terms conscience enables us to tell right from wrong. Research in recent years is providing evidence that this ability to tell right from wrong begins much earlier than previously thought, and some of these experiments have been both ingenious and amusing because of their age appropriateness. For example, when trying to determine at what age children can tell right from wrong, Kochanska and colleagues (Kochanska, Casey, & Fukumoto, 1995) presented 2-to-3-year-olds with pairs of flawed objects—such as toy bears and Sesame Street cups, one of each pair being whole and the other being flawed in some way. Although intrigued with the flawed objects, the children invariably preferred the whole ones. This kind of concrete behavioral evidence coupled with other related experiments or observations (J. Kagan, 1981; Lamb, 1993) provides evidence that children have internalized standards of "rightness" or "correctness" at an age long before they can answer hypothetical questions about what would be the right thing to do in the moral dilemmas postulated by Kohlberg (1969).

Theoretical arguments continue over how this voice of conscience is instilled (Burman, 1999), but Hoffman's reviews of research on this subject (1970, 1975), which have been further supported by Edwards (1980) and refined by Kochanska and Thomson (1997), indicate that the growth of conscience is facilitated most strongly by the presence of two factors, both of which can be easily used by parents and teachers. One of these factors is the presence of affection and a nurturing relationship between the adult and the child—a condition that should generally pertain in school, as well as in the home. This factor was identified as being present in about half the studies reviewed by Hoffman.

The second factor, which appears to be even more potent since it was more consistently present in the reported studies, is the use of what is termed "induction techniques" (Honig & Lansburgh, 1994). In simple language this just means giving a child a reason why she should or should not do something. For example, one might say, "I can't let you hit Ginny with the block; it hurts her too much," or, "We always flush the toilet so it's fresh for the next person." Another more advanced example is, "We have to put the candy back. We didn't pay for it. We always have to give the clerk money when we take something. That's how people who work here get money to buy what *they* want." Surely such an explanation is preferable to the, "You're a bad, naughty girl for stealing that candy," that is so frequently heard.

The examples of reasons given in the preceding paragraph have something in common that also appears to help children grow toward moral maturity: Each example gives the child a particular *kind* of reason. Saying, "We flush the toilet because it leaves it fresh for the next person," rather than, "Remember the rule, flush the toilet," encourages children to think of other people's well-being. In other words it begins to teach them perspective taking—to take the *other person's point of view* into account, to feel empathy. Even though young children may not be very skilled at doing this, they can at least begin to learn such consideration. In any case giving a person-oriented reason for behavior certainly builds a better social foundation for internalizing morality than teaching blind obedience to a rule does.

Teachers often try to use this person-oriented–victim-oriented approach by saying to a child who has just tossed sand into another youngster's face, "Stop that! How would *you* like it if *you* were Maggie and someone threw sand into *your* eyes? How would *you* feel then?" This what-if-*you*-were-her approach may work with older children but is too complicated and involves too much role reversal for 3- or 4-year-olds to understand. It just leaves them bewildered.

The same lesson can be taught much more effectively by making a simple change in approach that is still other-person-oriented but related more directly to the sand-thrower's own experience. This teacher might begin by saying, "Stop that; keep the sand down! Throwing sand hurts too much when it gets in Maggie's eyes. Remember when Jim threw sand in *your* eyes? Remember how that hurt? Well, that's how Maggie's eyes feel now." This remember-when approach may not sound like a major difference from the what-if-you-were-her approach, but it is much easier for young children to understand. It really does help children learn to think about how their actions affect other people's feelings.

As children grow older, they continue to develop more mature concepts about what constitutes moral behavior. Buzzelli (1992) singles out two additional features as being important elements in developing more advanced moral understanding. First, as they mature, children gradually acquire knowledge of the social rules and standards of their particular culture just as they develop deeper understanding of how other people feel. The standards and rules they internalize stem from a variety of sources—the parents, teachers, and peers who are the transmitters of their society's cultural standards—and children become increasingly able to internalize them as they acquire linguistic and cognitive sophistication (Vygotsky, 1978). Second, their growing ability to feel empathy for others and their desire to become more like their parents and to attain feelings of mastery and competence also contribute to their understanding and desire to incorporate the social rules that govern reasonable behavior into their repertoire.

Buzzelli (1992) concludes that parents and teachers can facilitate the growth of moral understanding by valuing the growth of cognitive and language skills that form the foundation for moral understanding, setting clear and appropriate standards for the children's behavior so that they know what the rules are, and consistently pointing out how certain actions by the children affect other people in a positive or negative way.

PRACTICAL THINGS TO DO TO MAKE IT EASIER FOR CHILDREN TO BEHAVE IN ACCEPTABLE WAYS

It is evident from the foregoing discussion that establishing ego strength and conscience in young children is a complex and lengthy task that can only be begun in the early years. While this is in process, the teacher must be willing to assume control when necessary, always bearing in mind the ultimate goal of helping children achieve responsibility for themselves. There are many practical ways to go about doing this.

Long-Term Preventive Approaches to Discipline

Besides fostering ego strength and the development of conscience, teachers can do two other fundamental things to help young children behave in acceptable ways and to improve the ease and quality of discipline and control in the group. The first is to prevent discipline situations from generating when it is possible to do so. The second is to know what to do when a crisis occurs.

Some Practical Ways to Stop Discipline Situations Before They Start

Reward behavior you want to see continued; don't reward behavior you wish to discourage. Children (and adults) repeat behavior from which they obtain satisfaction. This reward does not necessarily come in the form of payoffs of chocolate chips or gold stars. Whether teachers realize it or not, they use rewards every time they say "thank you" or "that's a

Encourage the use of words, not deeds, to win arguments.

good job" or even when they smile at a child. The value of this technique, which is one form of behavior modification called *positive reinforcement*, has been well proved (Wolfgang, 1999). No doubt it is one of several effective strategies to use when dealing with recurring discipline and behavior problems. Therefore when undesirable behavior persists, it is a good idea to take a look at what reward the child is getting out of it. Preventing the payoff can help eliminate the behavior. It is also effective to note positive actions on the part of the child and to respond to them with pleasure since this positive reward, combined with the pleasure inherent in successful accomplishment, is a potent reinforcer.

It is *not* effective to "extinguish" aggressive behavior in young children by simply ignoring it. In my experience such behavior does not subside when ignored—apparently because children interpret this laissez-faire attitude as permission. Not only that, one cannot overlook the fact that there are inherent gratifications (payoffs) in attacking other children that are far more rewarding than the teacher's attention: these range from simply seizing what is desired to enjoying hitting someone; if you are angry, hitting somebody feels pretty good. For these reasons *it is important to take more assertive action and stop undesirable behavior*, rather than let it slip past on the grounds that it will go away if no attention is paid to it.

Be persistent.   When working with a child who repeats undesirable behavior, remember that in addition to analyzing and preventing the payoff, it takes time to change behavior. Sometimes teachers try something for a day, or even just once or twice during a day, and expect such a short-term change to work miracles. When it doesn't, they give up. Don't give up! Be consistent and persistent. It often takes repeated experience for learning to take place, but children can and *will* learn if you stick to your guns!

Consistently position yourself so that you are able to see a large area of the room or play yard at the same time.   All too often beginning teachers focus on only a small group of children at a time. This is partly because it is less scary to do so and partly because many teaching lab situations unintentionally encourage this by assigning specific areas to students for supervision. But no matter what the underlying reason is for such behavior, it is wise to teach oneself to avoid the kind of tunnel vision this practice promotes.

Learning to position yourself close to a wall or fence, for example, means you have a clear view of a larger area, just as sitting at a table so that you face most of the room makes it easier to scan the larger space (providing you remember to look up occasionally from what you are doing).

Teachers who circulate within the supervision area instead of remaining planted in one place are also more likely to be aware of what is going on. This awareness can help children avoid many unnecessary confrontations and misunderstandings by providing opportunities for timely interventions and positive teaching to take place instead of tears and fights.

When trouble repeats itself, analyze the situation and try changing it, rather than nagging the child.   When something happens over and over, in addition to checking up on payoffs, the teacher should think about changing the situation instead of the child. For example, instead of telling a restless youngster to be quiet all the time, it might be better to let her leave after hearing one story, to ask a volunteer to read to her alone, or even to let her play quietly nearby during story time until she becomes more interested and can be drawn gradually into the group.

Emphasize the positive rather than the negative; always tell the child the correct thing to do. This habit can be formed with a little practice. When using directions, rather than saying, "Don't get your feet wet," or, "Stay out of that puddle," say, "Walk around the puddle." Or say, "Put the sand in the dump truck," rather than, "Don't throw the sand." This technique is desirable not only because it reduces negative criticism but also because it directs the child toward something she can do that is acceptable.

Warn ahead of time to make transitions easier. The teacher should anticipate transitions with the children a few minutes before the activity is due to change. He might say, "It's going to be lunchtime pretty soon. I wonder what we're going to have?" Or he might warn, "There's just enough time for one more painting. Then you can help me wash the brushes, and we'll have a story." Warning ahead gives the children time to wind up what they are doing. Sometimes just walking around the yard and commenting here and there that soon it will be time to go in will serve this purpose. It takes the abruptness out of the situation and makes compliance with routines much easier for children.

Arrange the environment to promote positive interactions. Interest is continuing in studying the ecological relationship between children and their environments (Greenman, 1998d), and some of these findings about the interconnections are helpful to know when planning ways to prevent discipline situations from occurring.

Rohe and Patterson (1974) found that a combination of many children in a small space (a high density of children), combined with few resources, produced more aggression and more destructive and unoccupied behavior. In another study, Smith and Connolly (1980) found that reducing square footage per child to 15 square feet also produced more aggression, more parallel (rather than social) play, less friendly play, and less running (and even walking) activity. The conclusion from such studies seems obvious: If enough space is provided for the children to use, discipline problems will be reduced accordingly.[1]

The area illustrating this situation that comes most glaringly to my mind is the block area of many preschools. Although interest can run high in this activity, all too often blocks are cramped into a corner where there is no possibility for play to expand as interest dictates. Moreover unless they are encouraged to carry blocks a little distance away from the storage shelves, children tend to crowd as near the source of supply as possible. This combination of restricted space plus the crowding near the shelves at the beginning of a project promotes territorial struggles and consequent discipline situations.

In contrast, if the block area is planned to include room to spread out when enthusiasm mounts and if children are taught to start their projects 2 feet away from the shelves, the likelihood of positive interaction in play is enhanced.

Another matter-of-fact suggestion about room arrangement that decreases the necessity to restrain and discipline children is separating areas with high levels of activity from each other to provide protection. In one situation where I taught, only one large open area was available for block and large muscle activity. Noisy chaos was often the result in winter weather when children tried to use the same space for both activities at the same time. Students and staff dreaded working there.

---

[1] Note that these studies also have significant implications for licensing regulations: Adequate regulations can help promote desirable behavior.

With some rearranging, two widely separated areas were created. The result was that block play and the wonderful social-cognitive learnings that accompany it increased dramatically. The second area was then available for large muscle activities and for dance and group time. The entire tone of the group of 4-year-old children became calmer and more pleasant.

Attention to traffic patterns can also increase constructive participation and reduce problem behavior. When the large rooms frequently used in child care situations are broken up with dividers so that children are physically detoured around activity centers, the temptation to disrupt what other children are doing is reduced. Such dividers can be low bookcases, bulletin boards, or even a Japanese futon. Defining areas by using rugs for this purpose also helps guide children's feet away from trouble in a subtler way.

A final facet of environmental planning that will help reduce the need for discipline is the provision of quiet places to which children can retreat when they feel the need for such refreshment. We adults know that constantly being with large numbers of people is tiring, but we tend to forget that it is tiring for children, too. Cozy corners for books, a quiet retreat with some simple manipulative activity, or simply an area in which to stretch out and do nothing can meet this need and reduce the fatigue and irritability that so often lead to loss of self-control.

Have as few rules as possible, but make the ones you do have stick.　Unless the teacher is watchful, rules will grow up like a thicket around each experience. But if situations are reviewed from time to time, unnecessary restrictions can be weeded out.

Some rules are genuinely necessary, however, and their enforcement is desirable not only because research shows that establishing firm limits, coupled with warmth and a simple explanation of the reason behind the rule, enhances children's self-esteem (Coopersmith, 1967; Honig, 1985) but also (as we have seen earlier in the chapter) because it increases their ability to establish inner controls.

The problem is to decide, preferably in advance, which rules are really important. Students in particular seem to have trouble in this area—sometimes treating relatively minor infractions such as not saying "please" or "thank you" as though they were major transgressions, while dealing indecisively with more serious misbehavior such as tearing up picture books or running out the front door without an adult. In general the most serious infractions of rules are those related to *hurting other people, hurting oneself,* or *destroying another person's property.* If a reason for a rule is not easy to come up with, it may be a sign that the rule is not important and could be abandoned.

Although we adults regard following rules as being important, another interesting way to think about them is from the point of view of the child. In an amusing and enlightening analysis of that point of view, Corsaro (1988) selected several rules enforced in a nursery school he observed: Running was OK outdoors but not inside; guns and shooting were not permitted; bad language was not permitted; and everyone had to participate in cleaning up. Terming the children's evasion of these rules "the underlife of the nursery school," Corsaro identified common ploys such as pretending not to hear the cleanup time signal and continuing to play, or developing indoor games such as Policeman that required using guns and running to catch the bad people. He maintained that these responses of the children served more than one purpose. Obviously, they *did* provide ways of getting around rules, but they also fostered the children's ability to function in the culture of their peers. Although this bonhomie is inconvenient for the teacher, it is important to realize that being able to function in their peer group becomes of ever-increasing importance as children grow older. Mildly "beating the system" at nursery school is one way they learn to do this.

When supervising children, plan ahead.   Try to anticipate the point at which the children will lose interest or the play will fall apart; have alternatives ready to propose that will help the play continue to flourish. An insightful teacher might think, "Now, if I were she, what would I like to do next with those blocks and cars?" Perhaps it would be getting out the arches or the wood strips to make a garage, or maybe it would be constructing ramps for the cars to run down. Tactfully posing several possibilities to the children will serve to continue play and lengthen concentration, as well as keep the children happily occupied and out of trouble.

Keep the day interesting.   To combat idleness, the center day needs variety—not only variety of pace to avoid the fatigue that leads to misbehavior but also variety of activities to maintain interest and involve the children in productive ways. Accomplishing this requires planning and sensitivity, but it is well worth the investment of effort.

Short-Term Things to Do When a Crisis Occurs

Of course, the ideal to work toward even in crisis situations is to teach the children to solve their own problems, since in their adult lives they will not always have a teacher present to arbitrate differences. However, the situations discussed in the following sections are ones in which it is evident that the child has to have help to control herself and to be able to take action that is socially acceptable. Even in these situations the focus should never be on the God-like powers of the teacher to bring about justice, but rather on development of the child's ability to do this for herself.

Be decisive; know when to step in and control misbehavior.   Inexperienced teachers are often unsure of when they should interfere and when they should let children work the situation through between themselves. As I said earlier, the general rule of thumb is that children should not be allowed to hurt other people (either children or grown-ups), to hurt themselves, or to destroy property. This policy leaves considerable latitude for noninterference, but it also sets a clear line for intervention. An occasional teacher is particularly unsure about whether he should allow children to hit him or kick him as a means of "getting their feelings out." Children should not be allowed to attack adults anymore than adults should attack children. Aside from the fact that it hurts and cannot help making the teacher angry, permitting such attacks makes the child feel guilty and uncomfortable. She really knows she should not be allowed to do it.

In the unusual emergency situation in which it is necessary to prevent physical attack, the most effective thing to do is hoist the child on your hip, with her head forward and her feet stuck out behind. This unglamorous pose, known as the *football carry*, works very well to stave off attack and permit the teacher to carry the child someplace if he has to. Although it is rarely necessary to resort to such measures, it helps to know what to do in a real emergency.

When trouble brews, take action yourself before the child does.   Over and over again I have seen teachers sit on the sidelines and let a situation go from bad to worse until it explodes and then step in to pick up the pieces. If the situation is one that will have to be stopped at some point, *it is much more effective to step in before trouble starts*, rather than a minute after blood has been shed.

Prompt intervention makes it more probable that the teacher can use a rational approach with the children; indeed this is a better environment for teaching any skill. Intervening before the fight occurs also prevents either child from receiving gratification from the attack. For example, stepping in before one child bites another takes preternatural quickness but is vital to do since biting feels so good to the biter that no amount of punishment afterward detracts sufficiently from the satisfying reward of sinking teeth into unresisting flesh (Kinnell, 1998).

Accept the fact that physical restraint may be necessary.   We have already discussed using the football carry as an emergency means of fending off an attack by a child; but even when children are not attacking the teacher directly, it is often necessary in a crisis situation to move swiftly and take hold of a child before she can strike someone else again.

When doing this, it is important to be as gentle as possible and yet be firm enough that the child cannot slip away. Usually just catching an arm is enough, although sometimes it is necessary to put both arms around the obstreperous one. Unfortunately this often makes the child struggle harder against the restraint, but at least it prevents her from having the satisfaction of landing another blow on her victim. As soon as the child is calm

Sometimes it's necessary to use physical restraint.

physical self ~ emotional health ~ self-esteem ~ social competence

Research Study

Who's to Blame? Teachers' Reactions to Children's Misbehavior

Research Question: Scott-Little and Holloway wanted to find out what factors influence the way teachers respond to children's misbehavior.

Research Method: To investigate some factors that might cause teachers to respond more severely or less severely to children's misbehavior, the researchers observed the teachers and children together, noted episodes of misbehavior and the teacher's response to those episodes, and then questioned them afterward about the reasons why they had responded that particular way.

Forty head teachers from 34 different centers working in classrooms of predominantly 4-year-olds were selected. Their educational backgrounds ranged from high-school to master's degrees. They were each observed working with the children during a 2-hour period. The observers documented two examples of aggression or noncompliance by the children to which the teacher responded in some way; these were used as the database for the interviews later. The teachers' responses were classified as belonging to one of four types: (a) *non-power-assertive* (the

teacher might comfort the victim but do nothing about the aggressor), (b) *mildly power-assertive* (the child is asked to think about her behavior without the teacher making a direct attempt to exercise adult authority to correct it), (c) *moderately power-assertive* (the teacher takes action to assert his authority and correct the behavior), and (d) *highly power-assertive* (the teacher attempts to force the child to correct the behavior—perhaps by punishing the child).

At the interviews that followed, the teachers were asked to explain why they thought the child had misbehaved as she had—what did the teachers see as being the reasons (causes) for the misbehavior? These reasons were then classified according to whether the causes were external or internal, whether the child could or could not control the causes, and how consistent the child's response was.

Statistical analysis revealed that when the proportion of internal, controllable, and stable reasons (attributions) for the misbehavior were correlated with the power-assertion responses of the teach-

---

enough to hear what is being said to her, it will help bring the situation under control if the teacher says something on the order of, "As soon as you calm down, I can let go of you, and we can talk."

When a situation has deteriorated to the extent that physical restraint is needed, it is usually best to draw the child or children away from the group so that they do not continue to disrupt it. It is seldom necessary to take them out of the room, and it seems to me it is more desirable to remain where the other children can see that nothing too terrible happens to the offenders. Otherwise anxious children fantasize too much about what was done to the fighters.

When dealing with misbehavior, avoid using control strategies that are unnecessarily overwhelming. The way a teacher responds to a child's misbehavior depends on a lot of circumstances. Among these are the teacher's mood and energy on that particular day, how

= physical self = emotional health = self-esteem = social competence =

ers, it turned out that the teachers who rated children's behavior as being the result of their internal impulses and controllable by them used stronger power-assertion techniques in response to those behaviors than they did when they thought the reasons for the behavior were externally caused and uncontrollable by the children. In other words, teachers used more authority and punishing techniques when they blamed the child for her behavior than they did when they thought something or someone else was the cause of that behavior.

An interesting additional finding was that the amount of education/training the teachers had was not related to how much and what kind of power-assertive techniques they used to control the children.

Implications for Teaching: The investigators concluded that "adults who respond to children with more power assertion, or by asserting their authority over the child, seem not to facilitate children's development" (p. 603).

Scott-Little and Holloway suggest that one remedy for using too-strong power-assertion strategies is to train teachers to become more aware of external causes of misbehavior that lie beyond the child's ability to control. They reason that such insight would encourage teachers to use milder approaches. Evidently something needs to be changed about the way we educate teachers since the research indicates that at this point the degree of power-assertion does not correlate with the amount of education to which teachers have been exposed. Ideally, better education should provide teachers with more effective, less aggressive methods of controlling children.

The other contribution this research can make to fostering teachers' insights is that once our consciousness has been raised about the general tendency to come down hard on children who seem to be willfully misbehaving, we should be especially careful to put the responsibility for choosing more acceptable ways to behave squarely on the shoulders of the child instead of just punishing her. The six learning steps outlined in this chapter illustrate an effective way of stopping misbehavior by being firm but not punitive when coping with it.

Source: From "Child Care Providers' Reasoning About Misbehaviors: Relation to Classroom Control Strategies and Professional Training," by M. C. Scott-Little and S. D. Holloway, 1992, Early Childhood Research Quarterly, 7(4), 595–606.

many prior run-ins he has had with that youngster, how secure he feels when dealing with misbehavior, and a myriad of other imponderables. The research by Scott-Little and Holloway (1992) described in the Research Study in this chapter provides an additional and often unrecognized reason for the way teachers react in discipline situations.

When immediate control is necessary, follow the six steps for teaching children self-control. Since children do not always stop throwing sand or grabbing tricycles simply because the teacher tells them to or redirects them to another activity, it is necessary to know what to do when a child occasionally continues to misbehave. I call the approach I use the "six learning steps in discipline": (a) warning the child, (b) removing her, (c) recognizing and discussing feelings and rules, (d) waiting for her to decide when she is ready to return, (e) helping her return and be more successful, and (f) following through with losing the privilege when this is necessary.

Although all the steps are important parts of seeing a crisis through, if I had to select one of them as being the most important to remember to use, I would choose Step 4: Have the child take the responsibility of deciding for herself when she can control herself and return. Remember that the long-term goal of discipline is establishing *inner* self-control, so it is crucial that the child, not the teacher, make that decision.

1.   ***Warn the child and redirect her if she will accept such redirection.*** For example, you might warn a youngster that if she continues to throw sand, she will lose the privilege of staying in the sandbox; then suggest a few interesting things she could do with the sand instead of throwing it. It is important to make the child understand that *her behavior is up to her.* It is *her choice;* but if she chooses to continue, you will see to it that you carry out your warning.

2.   ***If necessary, remove the child promptly and keep her with you.*** Warn only once. If she persists in doing what she has been told not to do, act calmly and promptly. Remove her and insist that she sit beside you, telling her she has lost the privilege of playing in the sand. This is much more valuable than just letting her run off. Having her sit beside you interrupts what she wants to do, is a mildly unpleasant consequence of her act, and prevents her from substituting another activity she would enjoy or taunting you by running away.

Instead of keeping the child right beside them, many teachers send the child off to sit in a "time out" chair. Although this time-hallowed method is certainly an improvement over spanking or saying hurtful things, there are some drawbacks to its use that must be considered. Basically what is happening when the time-out chair is used is that the child is sent to the corner; all that is lacking is the old-fashioned dunce cap. Sent off by herself, the child is emotionally abandoned. Besides that, teacher and child frequently become involved in secondary struggles when the child tries to sneak away and the teacher catches her. Finally, as is pointed out, many time-out episodes go on way too long, either because it's such a relief to the teacher to have the child removed or because he forgets she's there. For all these reasons, despite its inconvenience, it is more desirable to keep the child nearby.

3.   ***Recognize and discuss feelings and rules after a reasonable degree of calm has prevailed.*** This is a very important part of handling a discipline crisis. Even if the child is saying such things as, "I hate you—you're mean! I'm going to tell my mother and I'm never coming back!" it is possible to show her you recognize her feelings by describing them to her; replying, "You're really mad at me because I made you stop grabbing the trike. [Pause] But the rule here is that people can keep something 'til they're done with it." If more than one child is involved, it is vital to put each child's feelings into words for them as well as you can. The virtue of doing this is that when children know you understand what they feel, even though you don't agree, they don't have to keep *showing* you how they feel.

Once feelings have been aired and everyone is calmer, this is also a good time to state whatever rules apply and discuss alternative ways of solving the difficulty. If the child is mature enough, she should be able to contribute her own ideas, as well as hearing what the teacher has to say.

4.   ***Have the child take the responsibility of deciding for herself when she can control herself and return.*** At this step many teachers say something on the order of, "Now you sit

here with me until lunch is ready," thus shifting the responsibility for the child's behavior to her own shoulders instead of putting the child in command of herself. But if the long-term goal of internalizing self-control is to be reached, it is much wiser to say, "Now tell me when you can control yourself, and then we will go back," or, more specifically, "When you've decided to keep the sand down, tell me, and then you can go back and play." Some children can actually say they are ready, but others will need help from the teacher, who can ask them when they look ready, "Are you ready to go back now?" (Perhaps she nods or just looks ready.) "Good, your eyes tell me you are. Let's make a plan. What would you like to do for fun there?"

5.   *It is important to go with the child and help her be successful when she does go back so that she has the experience of substituting acceptable for unacceptable behavior.* It will probably be necessary to take a few minutes and get her really interested. Be sure to congratulate the child when she has settled down, perhaps saying, "Now you're doing the right thing. I'm proud of you!"

6.   *Follow through with suspending the privilege if the child repeats the behavior.* Occasionally the teacher will come across a glibber customer who says hastily when removed from the sandbox, "I'll be good, I'll be good!" but then goes right back to throwing sand when she returns. At this point it is necessary to take firmer action. Have her sit beside you until she can think of something acceptable to do, but do not permit her to go back to the sandbox. You might say, "What you did [be explicit] shows me that you haven't decided to do the right thing; so you'll have to come and sit with me until you can think of somewhere else to play. You've lost the privilege of playing in the sandbox for now." Then when she decides, *go with her and take her to another teacher and tell him about her special need to get started on something productive.* Avoid sounding moralistic or "nasty-nice" while explaining the situation to the teacher, since this will just prolong bad feelings.

Keep your own emotions under control.   One way children learn attitudes is by observing models (Bandura, 1986). Teachers need to control their own tempers because by doing so they provide a model of self-control for the children to copy, as well as because intense anger frightens children. Also when discipline situations arise, it is not just one child and the teacher who are involved: Every child in the room is covertly watching what is happening and drawing conclusions from it. Therefore it is often valuable for the teacher to talk over what happened with various children afterward to help them deal with how they felt about it and to clarify and consolidate what they learned from it. For example, he might explain to a worried-looking 3-year-old, "Jacob was crying because he wanted that car, but Teddy had it first so Jacob had to let go. He was pretty upset, wasn't he? Did he scare you?"

Sometimes, of course, it is simpler to advocate self-control in the teacher than to achieve it (Samalin, 1991). Things that can help teachers retain control include remembering that one is dealing with a child, deliberately keeping control of oneself, and acknowledging the feeling and saying to the child, "Let's wait just a minute until we're both a little calmer. I feel pretty upset about what you did." The biggest help, though, comes from analyzing scenes and upsets after they have occurred and planning how best to handle them the next time they happen. This experience and analysis build skills and confidence, and confidence is the great strengthener of self-control. Children sense this

"Who had it first?" Who knows!

assurance in the teacher just the way dogs know who loves or fears them, and children become less challenging and more at ease when they believe the teacher knows how to cope and has every intention of doing so.

Remember that you don't have to make an instantaneous decision.   Not only does admitting to a child that you need time to control your feelings help you regain control of them, but it also models self-control and provides time to think about what to do next. In the heat of the moment it is easy to make a decision about punishment that the adult regrets later because it is inappropriate or too severe. For example, a child who has tried the teacher's patience all morning may be shoved into a chair with the statement, "You're gonna stay here 'til your mother comes, no matter what!" or a culprit who has smeared paint all over the sink will be told, "Well, you just can't use any more paint this week!"

Once the physical action has been halted, it is not necessary to render instant justice in this manner. Waiting a minute and thinking before speaking gives the teacher time to remember that he is going to have to keep that child sitting in that chair for an entire hour or decide it would be more effective to have the youngster wash the paint off the sink rather than deny her the privilege of using paints for 4 long days.

Knowing where your flash points are is helpful, too.   Different behaviors make different teachers (and parents) angry, and it is helpful to take time to analyze what your particular flash points are because this awareness can help you control your response to them.

Some examples of flash points students and staff provided to me recently included deliberate insolence, withdrawing and acting coy, intentionally hurting another child (particularly after the teacher has stopped the behavior a moment before), outright defiance, use of "bad" language, calculated ignoring of the teacher, and pouting or sulking and refusing to tell why.

No doubt all these behaviors are irritating to all teachers sometimes, but each of them had a special power to evoke anger in some particular member of our discussion group. The reasons that lie behind these specific vulnerabilities were as varied as the teacher's early upbringing or his lack of knowing how to respond effectively to a particular child's style. Sometimes, however, a teacher has no idea why he is sensitive to a particular behavior. Although knowing the origin can be helpful, it is not essential to understand why you become especially angry when such behavior occurs. Just *knowing* that you are vulnerable can be sufficient since the knowing can be linked to reminding yourself to make a special effort to keep your temper under control and be fair and reasonable when a child behaves in that particular way.

Settle fights by helping children express their feelings to each other.   In the chapter on mental health (chapter 6), considerable time was spent in explaining how to help children express their feelings verbally. Although this is fairly easy to accomplish when the teacher is dealing with only one child, it is considerably more difficult *but just as important* when dealing with more than one. When two children are involved in a hassle, it is a wonderful opportunity to help both of them develop this social skill, and the teacher should urge them to talk things over and to tell each other what they want and how they feel. Telling each other how they feel and knowing that these feelings have been heard often mean that children are no longer driven to act them out, and the way is opened for compromise.

It is also essential that teachers avoid being trapped into rendering judgments about situations they have not seen. Four-year-olds are particularly prone to tattle about the misdeeds of others. A polite name for this is *prosocial aggression;* it is a natural if unappealing stage in the development of conscience. Unless the reported activity is truly dangerous, the best course of action in the case of tattling is for the teacher to encourage the child to return with him and settle the matter. He should avoid taking sides or the word of one child, because George Washingtons are remarkably scarce in nursery school. When it is a case of who had what first, it may be necessary, if a compromise cannot be reached, to take whatever it is away from both youngsters for a while until they calm down. Remember that often the child who is crying the loudest began the fight, although she may appear to need comforting the most. The only thing to do in situations such as this is be fair and deal with both children in a firm but nonjudgmental way. Impartiality is the keynote.

When a fight develops, it can also be helpful to call a meeting of the nearby children to discuss ways of settling it. Some 3-year-olds and the majority of 4-year-olds are capable of offering practical remedies if the matter catches their interest. The point of such discussions is not to ask the witnesses who was to blame (remember that it takes two to make a fight), but rather to ask them for ideas and suggestions about how to arbitrate the difficulty. The fighters can often be prevailed upon to listen to what their peers have to suggest, and children often come up with surprisingly practical solutions, although these tend to be severe. It is fine experience for them to think about how to get along together and work out solutions based on real-life situations.

When a child has gone so far that she has hurt another youngster, she should be allowed to help remedy the injury. Perhaps she can put on the bandage or hold a cold towel on the bump. This constructive action helps her see the consequences of her act, relieve her guilty feelings, and show concern by doing something tangible. I do not believe that children should be asked to say they are sorry. Often they are not sorry, and even if they are, I fear teaching the lesson that glib apologies make everything all right. Moreover a replicated study by Irwin and Moore (1971) supports the idea that young children grasp the concept of restitution (doing something to right a "wrong") before they understand the true significance of apology, so making restitution by righting the wrong is a more developmentally appropriate approach.

Whenever possible, let the punishment fit the crime.   Preprimary teachers (and enlightened parents) avoid doling out punishment in its usual forms. Teachers do not spank children, shut them in closets, take away their television privileges, or deny them dessert because they have not been good. But they *do allow* another form of "punishment" to happen when it is appropriate: This is simply permitting the child to experience the natural consequences of her behavior (Samalin, 1991). Thus the child who refuses to come in for snack is permitted to miss the meal; the child who rebelliously tears a page from a book is expected to mend it; and the youngster who pulls all the blocks off the shelf must stay to help put them away. Even young children can appreciate the justice of a consequence that stems logically from the action. It is not necessary to be unpleasant or moralistic when any of these results transpire; it is the teacher's responsibility only to make certain that the child experiences the logical outcome of her behavior.

When the encounter is over, forgive and forget; don't hold a grudge.   Inexperienced teachers sometimes dread confrontations since they fear that the child will be hostile afterward or actively dislike them for keeping their word and enforcing their authority. However, such confrontations almost invariably build a closer bond between the teacher and the child, who usually seeks him out and makes it evident that she likes him after such encounters. Teachers are often surprised by this commonplace result. What I want to suggest here is that because children do not usually hold a grudge when disciplined fairly, teachers, too, should be willing to wipe the slate clean.

It is very important for a child's sense of self-esteem that she be seen in a generally positive light. If the teacher allows a few negative encounters to color his perception of the youngster so that she is seen as a "bad girl," it is difficult for her to overcome this image and establish a more positive relationship. For this reason, particularly with "difficult" children, teachers need to call upon all their reserves of generosity and maturity and make every effort to concentrate on the youngster's positive qualities (Katz & McClellan, 1997).

Most important, notice when children do the right thing, and comment favorably.   This entire chapter has been spent talking about preventing or coping with misbehavior. Fortunately most of the center day does not revolve around such episodes; many days go smoothly and the children get along happily. When the day is a good one, when the children are obviously making progress, when they mostly talk instead of hit each other, when they share generously and enjoy the opportunities to help each other, let them know that you are pleased with their good behavior. They will share your pleasure in their accomplishments, and this recognition will help perpetuate the growth and self-discipline they have displayed.

A Final Thought

No teacher (or parent, for that matter) in the world handles every discipline situation perfectly! When one of those less-than-perfect situations happens between you and a child, it is all too easy to spend energy on feeling guilty or regretful about how things went. Rather than doing that, it is wiser to think over what happened and learn from it, since every discipline situation provides opportunities for *two* people to learn something. When things have not turned out well, think about what the child learned and what you learned, and consider possible alternatives. Then resolve to use a different approach the next time a similar situation comes up. Perhaps it will be rearranging the environment, or perhaps stepping in sooner, or perhaps firmly seeing a struggle all the way through. Taking positive steps to analyze difficulties and improve your skills is infinitely more desirable than agonizing over past mistakes.

SUMMARY

Discipline should be more than just "getting the kids to do what I want." The real goal should be the development of self-control within the children. This is accomplished, in part, by strengthening the ego and by fostering the beginning of conscience. Two ego-strengthening experiences often used by early childhood teachers are offering appropriate choices to children to give them practice in decision making and helping children feel masterful through becoming competent. The growth of conscience is facilitated by the presence of warm, nurturing relationships between child and adult, as well as by the use of person-oriented induction (reason-giving) techniques.

Many desirable approaches can be subsumed under the general heading of (a) preventing discipline situations when possible and (b) knowing what to do when a crisis occurs. When all these preventive strategies are insufficient and a child continues to misbehave, it is important to take her through all six steps in learning self-control: (a) warning her, (b) removing her from the activity while keeping her with the teacher, (c) acknowledging feelings and stating rules, (d) waiting for her to make the decision to return to the activity, (e) helping her return and be more successful, and (f) following through with losing the privilege when that becomes necessary. Consistent use of this approach will be effective in helping children gain control of themselves, thus helping them become socially acceptable human beings.

Questions and Activities

1. Give three examples of choices you could encourage the children to make for themselves the next time you teach.

2. Have you ever had the experience of deciding, theoretically, how you would handle misbehavior and then found yourself doing something different when the occasion actually came up? How do you account for this discrepancy?

3. *Predicament:* A child is throwing sand in the sand-box, and you want her to stop. What should you say to put your statement in positive form, rather than tell her what not to do—that is, rather than saying, "Don't throw the sand"?

4. Select an activity, such as lunchtime, and list every rule, spoken and implicit, you expect children to observe in this situation. Could any be abandoned? Are any really for the teacher's convenience, rather than for the purpose of fostering the children's well-being?

5. Team up with another student and take 15-minute turns for an hour, keeping track of how many times you reinforced positive behavior of the children. Then keep track of how many opportunities for such reinforcement you overlooked.

6. *Predicament:* Elaine, who is 4½, is playing at the puzzle table and keeps slipping little pieces of puzzle into her pocket. No one except you sees her doing this. You have already told her twice to keep the puzzles on the table so the pieces won't get lost, but she continues to challenge you by slipping them into her pocket. What should you do next to handle this situation?

7. *Predicament:* As you enter the room, you see John and David hanging on to a truck, both shouting, "I had it first!" and, "I can keep it until I'm done with it!" How would you cope with this crisis?

Self-Check Questions for Review

Content-Related Questions

1. What are the two basic approaches advocated for reducing discipline problems in the classroom? In the long run, which is of greater value?

2. Is it true that someone who possesses ego strength is conceited? Explain your answer.

3. According to Hoffman's review of research (1970, 1975), what are the two most important factors involved in interiorizing conscience?

4. List and explain several principles teachers can follow that will help prevent discipline situations from developing.

5. Explain the six learning steps the child and teacher should go through when the child has done something she shouldn't have.

6. What two features did Buzzelli (1992) single out as being important elements in the development of moral understanding?

7. According to Scott-Little and Holloway (1992), how do teachers tend to react when they think a child is to blame for her misbehavior?

Integrative Questions

1. The book discusses self- versus "other"-controlled behavior. Using a college-age student as the example, explain how that student who is "other controlled" might behave, compared with one who has established inner controls. Give an example of potential behavior in a group social situation and one involving taking a class.

2. Give two examples of choices that are developmentally appropriate for a 4-year-old to make and two that are not developmentally appropriate.

3. *Predicament:* Jerry and Austin are squabbling over a sprinkling can in the garden, each wanting to water the radishes with it. Finally Austin tips it over and pours water on Jerry's shoes, and Jerry begins to cry. He seizes a shovel and whacks Austin's hand with it. Using this situation as the example, explain how you would use the six learning steps to control the boys' behavior. Next explain some longer term actions you might take to make it less likely that behavior would happen again.

4. Do you agree with the positive social values for nonconforming that Corsaro (1988) suggests in the discussion of the "underlife" of the nursery school? Explain your reasons for agreeing or disagreeing.

5. Is it necessarily a "bad" idea to use more power-assertive responses when a child has misbehaved by deliberately doing something she knows she should not have done? Why do you think teachers come on stronger in that kind of situation than in one in which they think the child was not at fault?

6. Using the Scott-Little and Holloway (1992) definition of degrees of power-assertive techniques, how would you rank the six steps for teaching children self-control?

Coordinating Videotape

Building inner controls. Tape #9. The whole child: A caregiver's guide to the first five years. The Annenberg/CPB Collection, P.O. Box 2345, South Burlington, VT 05407–2345. *Building Inner Con-*

trol provides the basis for helping young children learn to control themselves and to find acceptable ways of expressing their aggressive feelings. The program shows caregivers ways to internalize self-control. Discipline management and aggression prevention techniques are described.

References for Further Reading

Pick of the Litter

Hewitt, F. (1995). *So this is normal too?* St. Paul, MN: Redleaf. This is a really useful book that singles out 16 common behavior problems and suggests effective (and differing) things providers and parents can do to alleviate them. *Highly recommended.*

Overviews

Marion, M. (1998). *Guidance of young children* (5th ed.). Upper Saddle River, NJ: Merrill/Prentice Hall. Marion's book is filled with a sound combination of research, theory, and practical advice on this subject. *Highly recommended.*

Saifer, S. (1990). *Practical solutions to practically every problem: The early childhood teacher's manual.* St. Paul, MN: Toys 'n Things Press. My only problem with this book is where to place it in the references because it covers such a wide range of problems including gifted children, death, and biting, to name just a few. This is good, useful book.

Philosophies and Theories About Discipline

Bailey, B. (1997). *There's gotta be a better way: Discipline that works!* Oviedo, FL: Loving Guidance. Bailey discusses beliefs adults have about children and describes ways to use interactive discipline skills based on love and acceptance, rather than on fear and control.

Kohn, A. (1996). *Beyond discipline: From compliance to community.* Alexandria, VA: Association for Supervision and Curriculum Development. Kohn challenges widely held assumptions about class management and conflict, advocates shared deci-

sion making, and uses examples from real classrooms to invoke discussion.

McCadden, B. (1998). *It's hard to be good: Moral complexity, construction, and connection in a kindergarten classroom.* New York: Lang. This book argues that schooling is always an inherently moral activity that resides, not in the content of the curriculum, but in the everyday interactions between teachers and students.

Nelsen, J., Erwin, C., & Duffy, R. (1998). *Positive discipline for preschoolers: Raising children who are responsible, respectful, and resourceful* (2nd ed.). Rocklin, CA: Prima. This book is one of a series about positive parenting that is useful for parents and teachers. It is a clear, persuasive, practical advocate of proactive discipline. *Highly recommended.*

For the Advanced Student

Kochanska, G., & Thomson, R. A. (1997). The emergence and development of conscience in toddlerhood and early childhood. In J. Grusec & L. Kuczynsky (Eds.), *Parenting and children's internalization of values: A handbook of contemporary theory.* New York: Wiley. The authors provide sensible, research-supported insights about the developing roots of moral behavior at the preschool age. *Highly recommended.*

Shweder, R. A., Mahapatra, M., & Miller, J. G. (1987). Culture and moral development. In J. Kagan & S. Lamb (Eds.), *The emergence of morality in children.* Chicago: University of Chicago Press. This fascinating study contrasts Brahmin and Untouchable Indian ideas of morality with those of the American middle class.

Wolfgang, C. H. (1999). *Solving discipline problems: Methods and models for today's teachers* (4th ed.). Boston: Allyn & Bacon. Wolfgang presents a comprehensive overview of many approaches to maintaining control in the classroom. Although the material is targeted toward teachers of older children, a review of the approaches would help anyone identify and clarify the various strategies they are using to maintain control. *Highly recommended.*

chapter twelve

Aggression

What to Do About It[1]

What to do about a child who is particularly aggressive?

What to teach a youngster that would help him enter a group peacefully instead of by starting a fight?

What you could substitute in place of direct aggression that might still relieve an angry child's pent-up feelings?

. . . IF YOU HAVE, THE MATERIAL IN THE FOLLOWING PAGES WILL HELP YOU.

Punishing children does teach some lasting lessons, though. Take the use of violence to discipline children. Regardless of what we are trying to get across by spanking, paddling, or slapping them the messages that actually come through are these: "Violence is an acceptable way of expressing anger" and "If you are powerful enough you can get away with hurting someone."

Alfie Kohn (1993, p. 167)[2]

There is perhaps no psychological skill more fundamental than resisting impulse. It is the root of all emotional self-control, since all emotions, by their very nature, lead to one or another impulse to act. The root meaning of the word emotion, remember, is "to move."

Daniel Goleman (1995)

---

[1] *Adapted from "Aggression: What to Do About It" by J. B. Hendrick, 1968, Young Children, 23(5), pp. 298–305.*

[2] *Excerpt from PUNISHED BY REWARDS. Copyright © 1993 by Alfie Kohn. Reprinted by permission of Houghton Mifflin Co. All rights reserved.*

Now that the general subject of discipline has been discussed, it is time to talk about dealing with aggressive behavior in particular. When we work with young children, we must consider two kinds of aggression. The first, and by far the most common kind of aggression, is *instrumental aggression.* This aggression occurs without basic hostile intent. For example, a child reaches over and takes away another child's felt-tip pen because he wants to draw, or a 2-year-old pushes another child aside so that he can reach a book.

Although these actions may require arbitration, explanation, and protection of the second child's rights by the teacher, they differ from the hostile types of aggression toward other children discussed in this chapter. According to Mussen, Conger, and Kagen (1969) *hostile aggressive* behavior refers to "actions that are intended to cause injury or anxiety to others, including hitting, kicking, destroying property, quarreling, derogating others, attacking others verbally and resisting requests" (p. 370). Parke and Slaby (1983) emphasize that intended injury of some sort is the defining feature; they state that aggression is "behavior that is aimed at harming or injuring another person or persons" (p. 50), and Berkowitz (1993), a well-known authority on this subject, concurs, saying,

> Whatever other goals highly aroused persons may have, we must remember that they also want to hurt their targets. They may be gratified if they can assert their power or control over their victim, or maintain their values, but deep down—and at times more than anything else—they are trying to hurt the persons they are attacking. (p. 17)

Tavris (1982) points out that aggression is the result of anger—anger being the feeling, and aggression being the expression of that feeling.

At the preschool level we see examples of this kind of behavior manifested when children barge through the room, leaving a bedlam of smashed blocks or ravished housekeeping corners behind them, or when they spend most of their time whooping wildly about being tigers or monsters, or when they deliberately seek to injure other children by destroying what they are doing, teasing them, or physically hurting them. Such aggression differs from ordinary rough-and-tumble play because it is marked by angry frowns and unwillingness to stop until someone has been really hurt (Kostelnik, Whiren, & Stein, 1986).

UNDESIRABLE WAYS TO COPE WITH AGGRESSION

Teachers and parents deal with this acting-out behavior in both useful and not-so-useful ways. Descriptions of some of the more undesirable methods of responding to such behavior follow. When picturing the adults who fit these descriptions, it is helpful to think of how each category misuses power in some way. At one end of the continuum are the authoritarians who believe that exercising the maximum amount of power and control over children is essential to classroom management. At the other end are the overpermissive adults who use power weakly or not at all. In the middle range could be pictured the vacillators, the inconsistent adults who sometimes exercise power and sometimes don't.

The Authoritarian Teacher

Tightly controlling teachers, the *authoritarian teachers,* are similar to the authoritarian parents described by Baumrind (1989) in her studies of parenting styles. She describes authoritarian parents as intending to shape, control, and evaluate the way their children behave according to absolute standards of what is right. Such parents value obedience and favor taking punitive, forceful measures when children's behaviors conflict with those standards. Clearly these adults are pretty aggressive people themselves.

Authoritarian teachers also tend to respond to conflict between themselves and the children as if expressing their own aggressive tendencies, garbed in the disguise of authority and control, were the only way to cope with the problem. In forthright cases schools dominated by such teachers are likely to be riddled with many rules generally determined by what is convenient for the teacher: Don't run! Don't make noise! Sit down! Line up! Be quiet! Don't easel-paint with your fingers! Stay clean! Don't splash! Take turns! Tell him you're sorry!—and a thousand other tiresome injunctions are typical. Punishments used by such teachers are apt to be severe, occasionally to the point of being emotionally destructive or physically painful.

Sometimes beleaguered teachers feel that controls of this type are necessary because the classes are too large or too obstreperous for them to cope with in any other way. Sometimes they believe that this kind of control is what the parents expect and that they had better conform to this expectation or else the children will be withdrawn from school.

More than likely the real reason for the teachers' reaction runs deeper than this and has to do with strong patterns carrying over from their own childhoods, when little tolerance and freedom were granted to them by the adults in their lives and they were provided very authoritarian models. The frustration, resulting hostility, and covert aggression instilled by this treatment are particularly likely to be re-aroused when they are confronted by the challenge of a belligerent 4-year-old or a balky 2-year-old. Transgressions are often dealt with by stringent punishments, and contests of will are highly probable if these teachers cross swords with a genuinely spirited child.

What of the aggressive child who exists in this tightly controlled environment? What is the effect of overcontrol on him? For a few youngsters the bright edge of creative expression is dulled. Some children cannot afford to risk nonconforming (which is the essence of creativity) under these circumstances, and so most of their energy is used up holding on to themselves and "doing the right thing." These children have had their spirits broken. They conform—but at what a price!

There are almost bound to be other defiant young souls who continue to challenge or sneak past such teachers. Common examples of such underground, continued aggression are as varied as quietly pulling the fur off the guinea pig, being unable to settle down for stories, or consistently destroying other children's accomplishments at the puzzle table or in the block corner. Other children internalize the angry feelings generated by authoritarian restrictions and become resistant and sullen; still others settle for becoming openly defiant.

In such schools restlessness and tension seem to simmer in the air, and teachers work harder and harder to hold the line, an exhausting business for all concerned. They tend to operate on the assumption that stronger punishment will result in greater control of aggression, but this is not necessarily true. Overwhelming evidence from research studies indicates that strong punishment, particularly physical punishment, actually increases the amount of aggressive behavior (Kochanska & Thompson, 1997; Wolfgang, 1999). This finding holds particularly true for children who already show aggressive tendencies (G. R. Patterson, 1982). Such teachers also overlook the fact that there is a limit to how far they can go to enforce dicta. What will they do if matters persist in getting out of hand?

Unfortunately the next step for some of these teachers is resorting to corporal punishment. Although hitting and otherwise physically terrorizing young children at school may seem unthinkable to many readers, the fact is that such treatment does occur. In fact, as recently as 1992 it was still sanctioned in the public school systems of 33 states (Hyman, 1997).

The evil results of such an approach are well summed up by Moore (1982):

> Any parenting technique will work some of the time, but as a general rule, using harsh punishment to curb high levels of aggression does not work. Highly punitive parents (and we might equally well substitute the word *teachers* for *parents* here) not only provide their children with aggressive interpersonal models to emulate but they also risk undermining their child's sense of personal worth, frustrating and embittering the child, and orienting the child toward his own misery rather than to the plight of another. (p. 74)

The Overpermissive Teacher

At the other disciplinary extreme are teachers who believe that "anything goes." Such teachers are often confused about the difference between freedom and license, and they fail to see that true freedom means the child may do as he wishes *only as long as he does not interfere with the rights and freedom of other people.* This extremely permissive teacher is fairly rare in preprimary centers because the pandemonium that results quickly makes parents uneasy. Apparently the results of this kind of mishandling are more obvious to the unprofessional eye than are the results of overcontrol.

In response to overpermissiveness the children may display behavior similar to the response for overcontrol. They may destroy other children's accomplishments or unconcernedly take whatever appeals to them. Sometimes they seem driven to tyrannical desperation trying to find out where the limits are and just how far they must go before the teacher at last overcomes her apathy and stirs herself to action. A common example of children's behavior in these circumstances is defiant teasing and baiting of the teacher by being ostentatiously, provocatively "naughty."

What the children really learn in such overpermissive circumstances is that "might makes right." This is a vicious circle because the aggressor is often rewarded by getting what he wants and so is more likely to behave just as aggressively next time.

The Inconsistent Teacher

The third undesirable way to deal with aggressive behavior is to be inconsistent. Teachers may be inconsistent because they are unsure that it is really all right to control children, or they may be uncertain about how to control them, or they may be unaware that consistency is important; hence, they deal erratically with out-of-hand behavior, sometimes enforcing a rule when they think they can make it stick and other times sighing and letting the child run off or have his own way.

This approach creates deep unease in children and fosters attempts by them to manipulate, challenge, and bargain to gain special dispensations. Whining, nagging, wheedling, and implied threats by the youngsters are all likely to be prime ingredients in this environment. For example, a 4-year-old may threaten, "If you don't give me that trike right now, I'll have to cry very, very hard, and then I'll prob'ly throw up, and you will have to tell my mother!"

Inconsistent handling may sound merely weak; however, it may actually be the most undesirable approach of all because it has been found to increase aggressiveness in children (Hom & Hom, 1980; Parke & Slaby, 1983). The probable reason for this result is that the reward for aggressive behavior is intermittent rather than continuous. It has been effectively demonstrated that an intermittent reinforcement schedule is a powerful means of causing behavior to continue (Parke & Duer, 1972; Wolfgang, 1999), particularly when additional payoffs are involved such as having gotten what one wanted by grabbing it.

Conclusion

It is fairly easy to see that teachers who are overcontrolling (authoritarian) or undercontrolling (extremely permissive) or very inconsistent bring special difficulties upon themselves when dealing with aggressive behavior. It is less easy to determine what constitutes a reasonable balance between aggression and control and to decide how to handle this problem in an effective and healthy way. We want to harness and direct this energy, not abolish it. Teachers often feel confused about how and where to draw the line. They think it is important to relish the burgeoning vitality of young children, and so they want to provide vigorous, free, large muscle play, and plenty of it. But most teachers do not think large muscle activity should be permitted to be expressed in preschool as endless, aimless, wild running about or terrorization of the quieter children.

Many teachers can go along with the idea that the child has the right to destroy anything he has made so long as it is his own and not someone else's. However, they also believe that direct aggression in the form of throwing things at people, biting, hitting others with objects in hand, outright insolence, and defiance of basic rules are generally unacceptable.

The problem is how to channel the expression of hostile aggressive feelings into acceptable ways at school and in society. The remainder of this chapter provides some basic approaches that will help the teacher solve this problem.

DESIRABLE WAYS TO COPE WITH AGGRESSION

Assess the Underlying Causes of Aggression, and Ameliorate Them When Possible

First, it is helpful to remember that pronounced self-assertiveness is part of the developmental picture for 4-year-old boys and girls. Many boys show evidence of this by attempting feats of daring, being physically aggressive, and swaggering about with an air of brag-gadocio. Girls are more likely to express it by being bossy or tattling in a busybody way on the wrongdoings of other children. It is important to realize that this rather out-of-hand phase serves a healthy purpose for these youngsters who are busy finding out who they are by asserting their individuality (it is somewhat like adolescence in this regard).

Additional evidence that aggression should not be regarded as "all bad" is furnished by Lord (1982), who cites studies showing that "preschool children who are more aggressive than average often are also more friendly, empathetic, and willing to share materials than other children" (p. 237). *But she also stresses that this finding holds true only for preschoolers* and not for aggressive children who are older.

Besides the influence of the developmental stage, native temperament may have a lot to do with the expression of aggression (Soderman, 1985). Some children can stand more frustration than others can without exploding. Sex-linked characteristics also affect its expression. Maccoby and Jacklin (1980) summarize many studies indicating that in our culture more direct physical aggression is expressed by boys than by girls, and Feshbach and Feshbach (1972) have reported that girls are more likely to employ indirect means of expressing aggressive feelings. How much of this behavior is attributable to biological differences and how much to culturally instilled values, however, has yet to be determined (Coie & Dodge, 1998).

An impasse like this presents rich opportunities for the teacher to help children work things through.

In extreme cases of aggression, particularly when it is combined with hyperactivity, the possibility of brain damage should be considered because lack of impulse control may be indicative of such a condition. In these *unusual* circumstances medication can produce considerable improvement in such behavior for some acting-out youngsters.

Parental mishandling is the reason most frequently given by teachers as the cause of undue aggression in children; and it is true that rejection, particularly cold, permissive rejection by parents, is associated with aggressive behavior in children (Glueck & Glueck, 1950; McCord, McCord, & Howard, 1961; G. R. Patterson, DeBaryshe, & Ramsey, 1989). If such rejection appears to be the case, the teacher should encourage the parents to seek counseling.

It is all too easy for teachers to slough off their responsibility for aggression in a child by raising their eyebrows and muttering, "He sure must have had a tough morning at home. What do you suppose she did to him this time?" But it is more practical to ask oneself how the school environment might also be contributing to the child's belligerent behavior because this is the only area over which the teacher has any real control. Instead of blaming the parents, teachers should ask themselves, Am I teaching him alternative ways of getting what he wants, or am I just stopping his aggressive behavior? How frustrating is the center environment for this child? Take a look at him and assess how he is relating to the program. At what time of day does he misbehave? With whom? What circumstances bring on an outburst? Does he receive more criticism than positive recognition from the staff? Does he have to sit too long at story hour? Does he consistently arrive hungry and so need an early snack? Is the program geared to tastes of little girls and female teachers and lacking in areas that hold a boy's interests?

Do Not Permit Children to Tease or Bully the Other Children

It isn't only physical aggression that can hurt. Feelings can be hurt by aggression, too. This happens most frequently as the result of teasing and/or bullying. Whereas unkind remarks such as, "Your Mom sure drives a weird old car," can be unintentionally hurtful, deliberate teasing is always done on purpose and even if "between friends" still has an unkind edge to it. The child who chants, "Wish you had it! Wish you had it! Can't have it! Can't have it!" is saying something calculatedly mean in intent.

Bullying is even worse. It is defined by Olweus (1999) as being (a) aggressive behavior that does intentional harm (b), that is repeated, and (c) that is characterized by an imbalance of power. In recent years increased attention has been paid to this at the primary and secondary school level (P. K. Smith et al., 1999; P. K. Smith & Sharp, 1994), but many preschool and kindergarten teachers realize it also occurs with younger children. Some examples are flagrant: I recently saw a 4-year-old threaten, "Gimme that or I'm gonna sock you," and then he almost casually snatched the ball from the smaller boy and ran off. The teacher just shook her head and said, "Poor little Mikey. Kids pick on him all the time; he's such a pushover!"

It was unfortunate for both that bullying 4-year-old and for his victim that the teacher did not seem to think such behavior mattered very much—but it does! Studies reveal that consistent bullying has bad results for both victim and perpetrator: Children who are unduly aggressive as young children have been found to remain unduly aggressive as they mature and often get into trouble as a result (Coie & Dodge, 1998). Victims also pay a

physical self ~ emotional health ~ self-esteem ~ social competence

| Research Study |

What Kinds of Things Make Young Children Angry, and What Do They Do in Response?

Research Questions: Fabes and Eisenberg asked, How do young children cope with their feelings when they are angry with other children or with teachers? What is the relationship between their degree of social competence and popularity and the kind of anger-related responses they use? and Do boys and girls handle anger in different ways?

Research Method: Twelve research assistants observed 79 children (33 boys and 36 girls) who ranged in age from 42 to 71 months. The children were from English-speaking, White, middle-class families and were attending a university day care center. Aggressive situations in which they were involved were observed every school day for 3 months during the free play periods. Rather than observing individual children for a prescribed period of time, the observers rotated from one play area to the next on a regular basis, recording whatever angry episodes happened in that area during 10-minute periods.

Later each episode was classified according to what made the child angry. The causes were *physical* (e.g., the child was hit or kicked), *verbal* (the child was teased or insulted), *rejection* (the child was ignored or not allowed to play), *material disputes* (property or space was taken or destroyed), *compliance* (being asked or forced to do something such as teacher requests), and *other*.

Next, the way the angry child responded or coped was analyzed and classified. These categories included *revenge* (physical or verbal retaliation), *active resistance* (physical or verbal defense in nonaggressive ways such as telling the aggressor to return an item), *venting* (expressing angry feelings without taking direct action—crying, sulking,

tantrums), *avoidance* (leaving the area), *adult seeking* (tattling or seeking comfort), *expressing dislike* ("I don't like you" or "You can't play"), or *other*.

Research Results: The most common cause of anger turned out to be material disputes (fighting over possessions and territory), and the second most frequent cause was physical assault by another child.

Interestingly enough, the most common responses were not physical or verbal retaliation and revenge. Rather the most common responses to these provocations were venting and actively resisting the provocateur, although these responses differed somewhat according to gender. Boys most frequently responded by venting their angry feelings—not taking direct aggressive action but expressing feelings in such ways as sulking or crying. Girls most frequently defended themselves by actively resisting the aggressor in nonaggressive ways such as holding on.

Revenge and retaliation were most likely to occur when the initial aggressor had physically assaulted the youngster. But even when children were physically attacked, they only responded in kind 18% of the time.

Children who were identified by their teachers as socially competent and popular were not involved in angry conflicts as often as were children who were not well liked. The children's responses were also age related. Older youngsters used fewer avoidant strategies and were more likely to defend themselves in nonaggressive ways, rather than running off or going to the teacher for help.

Implications for Teaching: So little research is available on the subject of anger and young chil-

physical self = emotional health = self-esteem = social competence

dren that it is particularly useful to review Fabes and Eisenberg's pioneering study. Perhaps because physical and verbal vengefully aggressive responses attract so much attention when they *do* occur, it may surprise teachers to learn how relatively infrequent such responses actually are. It is indeed heartening to realize that nonviolent responses are used much of the time by even such young children.

One of the most useful features of this research for teachers is the categories it singles out for identification. For example, it is helpful when thinking about a child who always seems to be flying off the handle to keep track of which kinds of situations make him angry. Does he go to pieces when he's rejected, or does it happen when somebody takes something he's using? Once the type of situation is identified, the teacher has a clue about what to work on with him; it might be teaching him skills about how to accept rejection and work through it, for instance, or how to negotiate a mutually satisfactory cooperative sharing situation, or how to defend his rights without hitting back if it conflicts over material things that cause him the most difficulty.

The same suggestion holds true when considering the responses the children make to others' demands. It can broaden teachers' perspectives to consider the kind of response the child has selected. For example, an occasional teacher may dislike sulking so much that she categorically insists children never sulk, thereby losing sight of the fact that, unattractive as such behavior may be, it is certainly a more desirable response than biting or hitting someone else would be.

In closing I want to comment on another, more esoteric implication to draw from Fabes and Eisenberg's research. This particular study illustrates a practical way to sample and study a specific type of behavior in context—that is, in a natural setting. The result not only has been new insights about children's anger and how they respond to that feeling but also has demonstrated a reasonably rigorous approach to collecting that information—an approach that can be used to deepen our understanding even further in coming years.

Source: From "Young Children's Coping With Interpersonal Anger," by R. A. Fabes and N. Eisenberg, 1992, Child Development, 63, 116–128.

heavy price—often remaining diffident and unsure of themselves in later years (P. K. Smith et al., 1999). But we really do not need research to understand that outcome; many of us have only to recall episodes from our own childhood to understand the misery such treatment produces. For these reasons it is important to understand how to discourage teasing and stop bullying by using direct control when children act that way.

Use Direct Control of Aggression When Necessary, and Then Teach the Child to Find Alternative Ways to Get What He Desires

Nothing quite compares with the agonizing dread some beginning teachers experience because they fear they will be unable to control one or more children in their group. There is no denying that the problem of gaining confidence in control situations is one major hurdle students have to get over in the early days of their teaching. Reading about handling aggression will help to a degree, of course, but the truth is that, to learn to cope with aggressive children, you have to get in there and cope! It does not work to shrink away or to let your master teacher do it for you. Sooner or later every teacher must be willing to confront children and exercise direct control over them because doing this is an essential method of coping with children's aggressive behavior.

To recapitulate what was said in the previous chapter, a child must definitely be stopped from hurting himself or hurting another person or destroying property. It is important that the teacher step in *before* the child has experienced the gratification of seizing what he wants or of hurting someone. This is particularly true if it is unlikely that the child he has attacked will retaliate. It is also important to intervene promptly because this allows teachers to act before they are angry themselves, and it is highly desirable to present a model of self-control for an aggressive child to imitate (Hyman, 1997; Samalin, 1991).

Once the teacher has stopped the aggressive action, I cannot emphasize too strongly how important it is to go through the six steps for learning self-control outlined in chapter 11. In particular it is vital to emphasize recognizing and translating the child's feelings into words in place of actions and placing responsibility on the child to decide when to try again. These are essential steps in establishing *self*-control, rather than in eternally maintaining control from outside the child.

As a reminder, here are the six steps:

1. Warn the child and redirect him if he will accept such redirection.
2. If necessary, remove the child promptly and keep him with you.
3. Discuss feelings and rules after a reasonable degree of calm has prevailed.
4. Have the child take the responsibility of deciding for himself when he can control himself and return.
5. It is important to go with the child and help him be successful when he does go back so that he has the experience of substituting acceptable for unacceptable behavior.
6. Follow through with suspending the privilege and redirect the child to another activity if he repeats the behavior.

The encouraging thing to realize is how infrequently young children resort to the sort of aggression that requires use of these steps. The Research Study in this chapter reminds us that even very young children have many less-violent responses to aggression in their repertoire and that they use these much of the time.

Teach Children Alternative Ways of Getting What They Want

We cannot expect children simply to stop seizing what they want or to stop attacking other children when they are angry unless we teach them other effective ways of getting what they want in place of those behaviors. In previous chapters we have talked about helping children substitute words and talk about their own feelings in place of verbally or physically attacking other children.

The other important thing to teach is how to get what you want without hurting somebody else. The strategies teachers usually use are either trying to distract the "wanter" by redirecting him ("There's room at the easel. Let's see what colors we have today."), offering him something else as a substitute ("Here's another truck. Why don't you use it? See, it has a bell you can ring."), or telling him he has to wait for a turn ("Jerry's using it now. What's our rule?").

Although all of these strategies work some of the time, it is a shame for teachers to limit themselves and the children to so few alternatives. This is particularly true because none of these three strategies provide ways for the wanter to learn beginning negotiation skills.

Additional approaches that *do* encourage negotiation and interaction include coaching the wanter to play beside the group and, if possible, to begin to contribute to what they are doing in some way. (I urge the reader to recall the Research Study in chapter 10 on the importance of children learning to observe what is happening in the ongoing play and identifying the social passwords required to obtain entry.) Encouraging cooperation by pointing out to both children how doing something together can enhance the pleasure of the activity is yet another way to foster interaction ("If she holds the bowl while you whip the egg whites, it won't slide around so much"). Or sometimes the wanter can figure out how to strike a bargain to facilitate getting what he wants ("I'll let you see my sore knee if you'll let me be the patient").

Whatever alternative is employed, the teacher should make certain the child clearly understands that hurting others is not allowed but that this need not mean he must swallow his anger and knuckle under; instead he can use a variety of both effective and acceptable alternative ways to get what he wants.

Permit Reasonable Deviations from the Rules

Despite the fact that consistency is important and should generally prevail as a policy, there are exceptions to this rule. We have all seen timid children at school and have rejoiced when they finally ventured to shove back and stand up for their rights. It is important for such children to express these aggressive feelings in some form and come out of their shells as a first step; learning control can come later. Teachers simply have to use their knowledge of the children and their good judgment in these matters.

The teacher must also make allowances for children when they are under special stress. For example, standards should not be unreasonably high at 11:00 in the morning because lower blood sugar levels at that time usually mean less self-control. This is the time to practice adroit avoidance of confrontations since children cannot be expected to control themselves very well under such circumstances. The same thing holds true for children recovering from illnesses or experiencing family problems. They may require special allowances until they have regained their emotional balance.

Reduce Frustrating Circumstances When Possible

Although controversy continues over whether aggression is an inherent trait (Lorenz, 1966) or a learned behavior (Bandura, 1973, 1986), considerable evidence and common sense supports that frustration makes the expression of aggression more likely (Coie & Dodge, 1998). Thus it makes sense to reduce aggression by reducing frustration when it is possible to do so.

Frustration usually occurs when a child is thwarted or prevented from getting what he wants, be it the teacher's attention, going outdoors to play, the new fire engine, or even the blue sponge at the snack table. It is not possible to remove all frustrating circum-stances from the life of a child, and it would not be desirable to do so anyway because this would mean he never has a chance to learn to cope with these feelings. However, every-day life has so many restrictions and frustrations, that we really do not have to be con-cerned over the possibility of living in an environment without frustration.

As previously described, the most effective way to reduce frustration is to empower the child by helping him learn a variety of acceptable ways of getting what he wants. Another commonsense way to reduce frustration is to have a plentiful amount of play equipment available. The value of having sufficient equipment is borne out by a study done in Eng-land by Smith and Connolly (1980). They reported that the provision of plentiful equip-ment had several effects: Although children tended to play by themselves more frequently or to play in small groups, there was also less aggression, less competition, and less chasing and running about.

This finding supports the idea that it is desirable to have several tricycles, three or four swings, and numerous toy trucks and cars, sandbox shovels, and hammers. Young children cannot endure waiting very long, and enough play materials will reduce the agony of anticipation, which, if unassuaged, can lead to frustration and acting-out.

Still another way to reduce frustration is to keep rules to a minimum. Enforcement of the many petty rules cited in the discussion of the authoritarian teacher is one of the quickest ways to build anger in children. Such rules often go hand in hand with unreason-ably high expectations of behavior such as insisting that young children stand in line, sit for extended periods while waiting for something to happen, or never raise their voices.

Finally two other good frustration preventers, also previously mentioned, are follow-ing the policy of warning in advance so that children have the chance to prepare them-selves for a transition to a new activity and providing many opportunities for choices in order to reduce children's feelings of defiance by helping them feel they are masters of their environment.

Provide Substitute Opportunities for Socially Acceptable Expressions of Aggression

The cathartic (emotionally relieving) value of substituting socially acceptable but nonetheless aggressive activities has been questioned by some researchers who maintain that such activities do not drain off or relieve aggression but rather reinforce such behav-ior. Their arguments are persuasive, and I can only comment that my own experience and that of other early childhood teachers continue to convince me that offering substitute ways of working off steam does have value, cathartic or not, when working with aggressive children and children who have strong needs for high levels of physical activity. Such activities are obviously emotionally satisfying to children, they are safe for those around them, and they provide chances to be assertive in a harmless way for youngsters too immature to resist the need to express aggression in some physical form.

These activities are best offered, however, *before* the child reaches the boiling point. It is generally unsatisfactory to march a youngster over to a punching bag after he has hit someone and say, "It's all right to sock this!" By the time this happens or by the time he gets the boxing gloves on and the mock fight set up, a lot of the flavor has gone out of the

It's difficult sometimes to decide when it's rough-and-tumble and when someone's likely to get hurt.

experience. It is better to offer acceptable aggressive activities as part of each day, as well as to make sure they are available when the teacher anticipates that the day will be especially tense either for an individual child who is upset or for the entire group (e.g., on Halloween). Fortunately a great many activities will help. Remember, though, that these activities are substitutes for what the child would really prefer to do. When offering someone a substitute experience, be as free with it as possible, and supply plenty of material, plenty of time, and as few restrictions as you can tolerate.

In general, any kind of large muscle activity that does not have to be tightly controlled is valuable. Jumping on old mattresses spread out on the grass or jumping off jungle gyms or boxes onto mattresses works off energy harmlessly and satisfies a need to be daring as well.

Swinging is particularly effective because the rhythm is soothing and because it isolates the child from his companions and calms him at the same time. If the teacher has time to do some friendly pushing, the one-to-one relationship is easing, too.

Trike riding, climbing, and sliding, or, as a matter of fact, anything that works off energy harmlessly helps.

Some preschool teachers buy play equipment too small or flimsy to take the vigorous activity of 4- and 5-year-old children. It is always better to invest in sturdy, large equipment that will stand up to hard use, rather than to continually nag the children, "Don't shake the jungle gym, you'll break it," or, "Not too high, now!"

Activities that provide for vigorous use of the hands in an aggressive yet acceptable manner should also be included. If the teacher joins in with gusto from time to time and uses the material herself, the child will often participate with more spirit.

Beanbags are fine to use for this purpose, but rules should be established about where they are to be thrown. A large wall with a target marked on it is best, and the more bean-bags the better. It is no fun to have to stop and pick them up after every three throws. Thirty bags is about the right number.

Punching bags have some use, but it is hard for young children to coordinate really satisfying socks with the bag's tendency to rebound.

Inflatable clowns are somewhat useful, but there may be trouble with maintaining them in airtight condition.

Hammering and sawing and even smashing things such as old egg cartons, orange crates, or piano cases are appealing. Very young children can use knock-out peg benches for this same purpose.

Large quantities of dough (not tiny, unsatisfying dabs) are fine aggression expressers. We restrict the tools the children use with it (e.g., cookie cutters) and encourage the children to stand at the table so that they can work forcefully, using their hands to pound and squeeze and pinch and punish the dough to their heart's content.

In finger painting and other types of smearing techniques such as soap painting, emphasis should be placed on richness of color and lots of gooey paint base, be it liquid starch, wallpaper paste, or homemade, very thick, cooked starch.

Once in a while a particular child finds relief in tearing and crumpling paper or stomping on crumpled balls of it. Again large amounts are better than small amounts.

Noise is an excellent outlet for expressing aggression. The aggression-expressing possibilities of sheer noise (at least on the days when the teacher does not have a headache) should not be overlooked. It is wise to remember that noise has an infectious effect on the entire group and may accelerate activity too much. However, on the many occasions when things are in good order, I am all in favor of noise! Drums are an all-time, satisfying "best" for noise, but pounding on the piano is good, too. Real music and dancing can be added for those who enjoy it. Sitting on top of the slide and kicking one's heels hard makes a wonderful, satisfying noise. Yelling, playing loudly, and crying (the louder the better) also serve to express feelings harmlessly.

Opportunities for dramatic play can also help the child come to terms with aggressive feelings. Direct participation by dressing up and playing house will let youngsters work through situations that may be troubling them. Anyone who has ever watched an irate young "mama" wallop her "naughty" baby doll will understand the merit of providing this kind of play material as an aggression reliever. Dollhouse furniture and little dolls are useful, but more so for 4-year-olds than for 3-year-olds.

Sets of fairly large rubber wild animals and hand puppets lend themselves admirably to controlled aggressive play. Interestingly enough, the animal that produces the greatest amount of this play is not the lion or tiger but the hippopotamus. I have concluded that the open mouth and all those teeth bring this out. It makes me think how angry adults with toothy open mouths must appear to children, particularly since youngsters tend to look up and in!

The best thing for out-of-hand children to play with is water. It is deeply relaxing in any form. Washing doll clothes or plastic cars, playing with soap bubbles, or playing with water in the housekeeping area is beneficial. Even when it is squirted, it does no lasting harm.

Whenever weather permits, the best thing of all is a running hose and lots of sand and mud. This combination has led to some of the calmest, happiest days we have ever had in our school, but pouring and playing with water in tubs or basins can also be satisfying. At home a warm bath can work miracles.

Finally, encouraging very overactive youngsters to take time out to go to the toilet often simmers things down considerably.

Additional Techniques to Help Reduce the Amount of Aggressive Behavior

So much for the specifics. There are also some general techniques that the teacher may find helpful for handling aggression:

Provide kindly, one-to-one attention for acting-out children. A few minutes consistently invested every day with an aggressive child when he is doing positive things (before he gets into difficulties) often works wonders.

Teach children to use words in place of teeth and fists. Once more I want to remind the reader of the value of teaching children to tell other youngsters what they want and what their feelings are, instead of physically showing them what they feel.[3] Even as simple a sentence as "I want that!" or "Give it here!" is a step up from snatching what is desired. Of course, the other child may well refuse, but the teacher can support the requester by saying, "I'm sure glad to hear you asking him instead of just grabbing it." Then she can go on to teach the next step. "Jennie says you can't have it now. Why don't you ask her if you can have it when she's done with it. Say, 'Jennie, can I have a turn when you're done?' I bet she'll let you have it then!"

A more mature child can be encouraged to ask, and then add, "I really want that trike!" or, "Gosh, I wish you'd give it to me now!" Remember that these statements should *focus on what the child is feeling* and what he wants, not on calling the other child bad names or insulting or threatening him.

Stopping some activities before they start saves criticism and discipline later. I have learned, for example, to keep an eye out for "angry monster" games or Ninja Turtles or Power Rangers. When such a game gets too high pitched, the quickest way to bring it under control is to look for the ringleader and get him involved in something else he particularly likes to do.

Our staff discourages toy-gun play at our center because we believe that children should be encouraged to use more desirable play themes than killing each other. Moreover research by Watson and Peng (1992) has revealed that toy-gun play was one of the two strongest predictors of real aggression observed in the children's center. (The other predictor was the use of physical punishments by the parents.) Therefore, when toy guns are brought to school, our staff insists they be stored in the cubbies until it is time for the children to go home.

Be on the lookout for combinations of personalities that are currently poisonous, and do what you can to dilute them. Children who egg each other into trouble should not snack together or rest near each other, and other friendships for both children should be encouraged.

Finally, plan, plan, plan! Plan to provide interesting activities that children really like, and plan the daily program with specific children in mind. ("John is coming today; I'd better get out the hammers and saw.") The program must not make undue demands on their self-control and should include acceptable outlets for their energy. As a general principle,

---

[3] *For a more in-depth discussion of this principle, refer to chapter 6, "Fostering Mental Health in Young Children."*

"He did it!" Tattling is a typical form of prosocial aggression in 4-year-olds.

consistent opportunities that allow children to achieve mastery and competence in acceptable areas should be provided. Every time a youngster can do something well, whether it's building with blocks, doing meaningful work, creating a painting, or learning to pump on the swing, his aggression has been channeled into accomplishing something constructive.

Summary

Aggressive behavior is defined in this chapter as action intended to cause injury or anxiety to others. This kind of behavior needs careful handling and guidance so that children are not forced to suppress such feelings completely but learn instead to channel these impulses into socially acceptable activities.

Three approaches to coping with aggression in young children are particularly undesirable because they are all likely to increase aggressive responses in return. These are authoritarian, overpermissive, and inconsistent methods of dealing with such behavior.

On the more positive side, several approaches for working with acting-out children are effective in reducing and channeling such behavior. Among these are assessing the underlying causes of aggression and ameliorating them when possible, using direct control when necessary, and teaching the child to find alternative ways to get what he wants. Typical alternative approaches include distraction, redirection, and waiting. More desirable ones include learning social skills for entering the group, and negotiating by cooperating together, making bargains, or trading. In addition, permitting reasonable deviations from the rules in special cases and reducing frustrating circumstances when possible are helpful. Finally, substituting socially acceptable opportunities for expressing aggression can relieve the child's feelings without jeopardizing the safety and happiness of those around him.

Teachers who apply these principles when handling aggressive behavior will reduce tension within the child and themselves by preventing aggressive feelings from building up and will also help the child remain happier, more open, and more ready to welcome life with enthusiasm.

Questions and Activities

1. Everyone seems to have different "breaking points" in tolerating aggression. For example, one person sees red if a child is insolent, whereas another finds it more difficult to cope with a child who is cruel to animals or who deliberately hurts another child. Compare notes among the people in class about what they feel constitutes acceptable ways to express aggression, where their breaking points are, and what they do to control themselves when they reach that point.

2. Keep an eye out during the coming week and observe and briefly record several situations in which children or staff members appeared to be angry. Note what each individual did about this feeling. If the teacher was working with a child, what did she do to help the youngster recognize and express his feelings in an acceptable way?

3. Do any "discipline" situations in your school seem to recur? For example, are the children always being told not to run inside the building? Suggest several ways the situation could be changed instead of continuing to "teach the children to behave."

Self-Check Questions for Review

Content-Related Questions

1. Describe three styles of teaching that are likely to increase an aggressive response by some children.

2. Does aggression always stem from the same cause? If not, what are some circumstances that tend to generate such behavior?

3. List several alternative approaches children can be taught that will help them get what they want without hurting other people.

4. Suppose that a high-energy, aggressive child is in your group. Suggest several ways he or she could work off this energy without hurting other people.

5. Does the research by Fabes and Eisenberg (1992) support the idea that children usually solve physical aggression by hitting back when someone hits them?

Integrative Questions

1. This chapter suggests some reasons why a teacher might be too authoritarian. What are some reasons that might lie behind the behavior of the teacher who is too permissive?

2. The book defines *instrumental aggression* and *hostile aggression*. Give two examples of behavior that fit each kind of aggression.

3. If corporal punishment is such an undesirable way to discipline children, why, do you think is it still allowed in the public schools of 33 states? Select a reason and provide an argument that might convince an advocate of corporal punishment who supports that reason to change his or her mind.

4. *Predicament:* Four-year-old Sarah is reading a book, and Nancy tries to grab it. Sarah hits Nancy's hand away, and when she reaches again, Sarah pinches her very hard. Nancy begins to cry. You have worked through the first steps in the "learning self-control" sequence with both Nancy and Sarah, and now Nancy is ready to return to Sarah. Suggest at least two alternatives you could propose to her about how she might get a chance to look at the book she wants so badly to see. What alternatives might you suggest to Sarah about how to protect her rights without hitting or pinching?

5. *Predicament:* You have a 4-year-old named Billy in your group who is angry much of the time. For example, when children are building in the block corner and he arrives at school, he barges into the block corner, picks up some blocks, and begins to build. At that point the other children yell at him, saying, "We were here first. You can't play. Go away!" Billy begins to cry, and as the other children hold firm, he starts to knock down what they are building as the teacher intervenes. If you were a researcher using the categories that Fabes and Eisenberg (1992) used in their study, what category or categories of behavior would you use to describe the angry reaction by the children who found his intrusion to be unwelcome? What category or categories of behavior would you use to describe Billy's response to *their response?*

Coordinated Videotape

Building inner controls. Tape #9. The whole child: A caregiver's guide to the first five years. The Annenberg/CPB Collection, P.O. Box 2345, South Burlington, VT 05407–2345. *Building Inner Controls* provides the basis for guiding young children to control themselves and to find acceptable ways of expressing their aggressive feelings. Discipline management and aggression prevention techniques are described.

References for Further Reading
Pick of the Litter

Kinnell, G. (Ed.). (1998). *Addressing the biting dilemma: A resource for child care programs serving toddlers.* Syracuse, NY: Task Force on Biting, Child Care Council of Onondaga County. (3175 East Genesee St., Suite 5, Syracuse, NY 13224). This is selected as the Pick of the Litter because it is a rare and unusually helpful resource that discusses this perplexing problem in depth. *Highly recommended.*

Overviews

Carlsson-Paige, N., & Levin, D. E. (1998). *Before push comes to shove: Building conflict resolution skills with children.* St. Paul, MN: Redleaf. It is so difficult to find age-appropriate conflict resolution material that I particularly rejoiced when I came across this book. Brief, clear, and helpful, much of what the authors recommend should certainly work with 4-year-olds as well as with older children. *Highly recommended.*

Dealing with Anger

Marion, M. (1997). Research in review: Guiding young children's understanding and management of anger. *Young Children, 52*(7), 62–67. Several practical suggestions are included, together with emphasis on the value of using language to increase the child's understanding of his feelings.

Samalin, N. (1991). *Love and anger: The parental dilemma.* New York: Viking. Samalin discusses reasons for adult anger and outlines eight steps for controlling it effectively.

Dealing with Special Kinds of Aggression Problems

Bauer, K. L., & Dettore, E. (1997). Superhero play: What's a teacher to do? *Early Childhood Education Journal, 25*(1), 17–21. The authors make a case for the positive side of permitting superhero play in preschool.

Corporal Punishment

Hyman, I. A. (1997). *The case against spanking: How to discipline your child without hitting.* San Francisco: Jossey-Bass. Written primarily for parents of school-age youngsters, this very good book is filled with practical advice about controlling adult anger and aggression and instilling self control in children. *Highly recommended for teachers who teach younger children, too.*

Kaiser, B., & Rasminsky, J. S. (1999). *Meeting the challenge: Effective strategies for challenging behaviors in early childhood environments.* Ottawa, Ontario: Canadian Child Care Federation. This booklet is filled with plain talk and sensible advice about coping with acting-out children. *Highly recommended.*

Levin, D. E., & Carlsson-Paige, N. (1995). The Mighty Morphin Power Rangers: Teachers voice concern. *Young Children, 50*(6), 67–72. Levin and Carlsson-Paige make the case against violence and superhero play as portrayed in this television series.

Smith, P. K., & Sharp, S. (1994). *School bullying: Insights and perspectives.* London: Routledge. This book describes an actual program instituted in some British schools to reduce bullying. *Includes a chapter on bullying children with disabilities.*

For the Advanced Student

Baumrind, D. (1989). Rearing competent children. In W. Damon (Ed.), *Child development today and tomorrow.* San Francisco: Jossey-Bass. In this classic chapter Baumrind reviews her decades of research concerning long-term effects on children of authoritative, permissive, and rejecting parental styles.

Coie, J. D., & Dodge, K. A. (1998). Aggression and antisocial behavior. In N. Eisenberg (Series Ed.) & W. Damon (Vol. Ed.), *Handbook of child psychology: Vol. 3. Social, emotional, and personality development.* New York: Wiley. This is the definitive review of current theory and research on the subject of aggression. *Highly recommended for the serious student.*

National Association for the Education of Young Children (NAEYC). (1998e). *Violence in the lives of children: A position statement of the National Association for the Education of Young Children.* Washington, DC: Author. Title is self-explanatory.

Reguero de Atiles, J., Stegelin, D. A., & Long, J. K. (1997). Biting behaviors among preschools: A review of the literature and survey of practitioners. *Early Childhood Education Journal, 25*(2), 101–105. This investigation indicates not only how frequent biting is but also how infrequently centers have established policies for coping with it—something to think about!

Smith, P. K., Morita, Y., Junger-Tas, J., Olweus, D., Catalano, R., & Slee, P. (Eds.). (1999). *The nature of school bullying: A cross-national perspective.* London: Routledge. Evidently bullying in one form or another is widespread and serious. This book surveys countries as diverse as Japan, Sweden, United States, and Spain to determine its incidence and what is being done to curb it.

chapter thirteen

Providing Cross-Cultural, Nonsexist Education

What to say when a youngster says to a Mexican child, "I won't sit by you; your skin is dirty"?

What to do about name calling and racial insults?

How to help children value everyone, no matter what her or his race or color or gender?

What to tell a 4-year-old who asks where babies come from?

. . . IF YOU HAVE, THE MATERIAL IN THE FOLLOWING PAGES WILL HELP YOU.

I hear the train a comin',
A comin' round the curve.
She's using all her steam and brakes
And straining every nerve.
Get on board, little children,
Get on board, little children,
Get on board, little children,
There's room for many-a-more.
The fare is cheap and all can go,
The rich and poor are there.
No second class aboard this train,
No difference in the fare!
Get on board, little children,
Get on board, little children—
Get on board, little children!
There's room for many-a-more!

315

The wonderful lines of the old gospel tune,

> No second class aboard this train,
> No difference in the fare!

sum up what is meant by *equity in education* because in a well-presented cross-cultural, nonsexist curriculum there are no second-class children and surely no difference in what children must do or be in order to be allowed on the train with the other youngsters.

Perhaps the reader is thinking indignantly, "What does she mean! Of course there are no second-class children," but the truth is that sometimes teachers *do* treat some children as being second-class people.

EXAMPLES OF TEACHER PREJUDICE

Many examples of the way racist prejudice shows through in relations between teachers and students were presented by Leacock (1982), who reviewed studies of teacher attitudes toward low- and middle-income children who were African American or White. She reported that teachers not only spoke less frequently about curriculum matters to the African American children but also made many more critical and negative remarks to them, with poor African American children receiving the brunt of the negative comments. This was true even when teachers were African American themselves and when little difference in the children's behavior could be noted.

Boutte, LaPoint, and Davis (1993) report several episodes in which teachers either did nothing to protest the expression of prejudice by children in their classrooms or revealed their own negative feelings about certain youngsters who came from ethnic backgrounds different from their own.

Sexist prejudice shows through in the different ways some preschool teachers treat boys and girls. For example, Serbin, Connor, and Citron (1978) report that in one study boys were more likely to be reprimanded for aggression than girls were, that they received much more detailed instruction on how to solve problems than girls did, and that little girls had to be closer to the teacher than little boys did to be noticed by her. Or it can be expressed in subtler ways. For example, when Hendrick and Stange (1991) analyzed the conversational behavior of children and their teachers at the snack table, they found that not only did 4-year-old boys interrupt the teacher more than the girls were allowed to but also teachers interrupted the girls far more often than they interrupted the boys.

Can we deny, with such evidence before us, that many of us, however inadvertently, are actually relegating some children to second-class status?

CAN SUCH ATTITUDES BE CHANGED?

Fortunately the answer to this question is yes—at least to some degree. Although we must realize that attitudes and responses to groups, or individual representatives of certain groups, stem from long-ingrained habits and prejudices, teachers can change, and children can, too.

For many years attempts at changing racist and sexist attitudes at the preschool level seemed to concentrate on the more superficial aspects of differentness such as celebrating ethnic holidays and putting up pictures of female physicians and firefighters. Now a growing edge of work in the area of cross-cultural and nonsexist education is striving to reach beneath these surface manifestations of goodwill and to suggest ways to build deeper, more emotionally and socially meaningful relationships between people. For example, such vintage books as the earliest edition of *The Whole Child* (Hendrick, 1975)[1] and *The Anti-Bias Curriculum* (Derman-Sparks & ABC Task Force, 1989), and more recently *Teaching and Learning Anti-Racism* (Derman-Sparks & Phillips, 1997), *Beyond Heroes and Holidays* (E. Lee, Menkart, & Okazawa-Rey, 1998), and *Creating Culturally Responsive Classrooms* (B. J. Shade, Kelly, & Oberg, 1997) have provided practical ways to move toward more substantive changes in attitudes.

SUGGESTIONS FOR CONTROLLING AND OVERCOMING THE EXPRESSION OF PREJUDICE

Reality forces me to admit that, desirable as it may be, it is not always possible for people to overcome deeply held convictions about what other people are like. Everyone has negative opinions—prejudices—about someone. Some teachers may be genuinely unconcerned about skin color but find they are critical of unmarried or same-sex couples, or fat people, or how welfare recipients spend their money, or people who use profanity, or men who spit in public.

An important part of controlling the expression of that prejudice lies in honestly admitting to oneself that it exists, since once you recognize that the dislike or even hatred exists, you can begin to control expressing it. It is an interesting illustration of the principle "Feel what you wish, but (at least) control what you do about those feelings."

At the very least it is possible to monitor oneself and practice the mental hygiene rules advocated long ago by Clark (1963, p. 107):

---

[1] *It's instructive to remember that when the 1975 edition of* The Whole Child *was going to press, the editor called me and said, "Now, don't get mad; our review board just has one little question they want me to ask you: We want your book to sell all over the United States, including the South, and we just wonder about that chapter on cross-cultural education. How important do you really think it is to include it?" "Very important!" I replied. "Say no more," she said—"It's in!"*

Willow's hair ornaments were much admired by her friends, who often begged to borrow them.

1. As a beginning, find ways to become acquainted with at least one person or family of each racial and cultural group in your community.
2. Extend common courtesies and titles of address to persons of all groups, regardless of sinful community customs, regardless of their position, and regardless of however strange it may seem at first.
3. Learn the difference between paternalism (that is, loving down, loving in "their place") and true . . . respect of one human being for another.
4. Keep a close check on your thoughts and feelings. Watch out for any tendency to blame whole groups of people for what individuals do.
5. When you hear rumors that reflect on any group, demand proof. Do not repeat lies.
6. Never use hateful terms that slur any group. Show disapproval when others use them.
7. Do not tell stories, however funny, that reflect on any group. Do not laugh at them.
8. As a present or future employer, welcome new workers without regard to race or creed. Make very sure the boss does not refuse to hire people of some group because he imagines you would resent it. If you are seeking a new job, inquire among organizations where no such distinctions are made.
9. Request a policy of non-discrimination where you spend your money. (Remember, business firms may discriminate in employment and in serving customers since they imagine this pleases you. Make sure they know that it does not.)

10. Where there is a choice, take your patronage where there is the most democracy in every way. And let the proprietor know why.
11. ... When going with interracial groups to public places, always assume that you will be served. Many places will say "no" if you ask in advance, but will serve you when you come. It is good education for them to know you assume that they will serve you.
12. Watch out for the term "restricted." It generally means discrimination against someone.

The following pages contain many suggestions for ways to show that the teacher values the specialness of each child and every family background. Some suggestions are obvious such as planning a curriculum that includes everyone. Some, where human relationships are concerned, are more subtle.

But no matter what the teacher does or says, when you get right down to it, what matters most of all—what really sets the tone and what people sense almost instantly when they walk into the room—is the true character of the teacher. The teacher who practices a combination of decency, respect, and fairness toward himself and toward others is the person who by the very nature of his character establishes the climate of mutual positive regard so necessary for effective multicultural education.

Broaden Your Frame of Understanding and Acceptance; Find Out What People Are Really Like!

Of course, if acquiring information about the family viewpoints, values, and learning styles of Mexican American or Hopi children results in stereotyping (assuming that every Mexican American or Hopi child is a cookie-cutter replica of every other one) the value of such education is destroyed.

But if such information is used to further understanding of the children's and family's attitudes and behavior, that insight paves the way for liking and warmth to flourish. Indeed such information can even help the teacher overcome his own cultural deprivation. For example, the teacher who knows that owls are regarded as birds of ill omen and death by the Navajo will not include them in Halloween decorations, nor will a teacher feel embarrassed by the Japanese mother who brings a small gift each time she visits the school.

Ethnic studies programs and even some colleges of education offer a wealth of information on particular cultures, and teachers should take such courses whenever they can. Participation in ongoing discussion groups can also be extraordinarily helpful. Even just reading about the characteristics of various groups can build appreciation and sensitivity to variations in cultural style. Such resources not only broaden our frames of reference but may also help us avoid offending those we never intended to hurt.

A wonderful quotation from Tolstoy that comes to mind sums it all up: "Everyone thinks of changing the world, but no one thinks of changing himself." If we could only learn to understand and accept some differences as being just that, *differences*, without condemning them, it could be the beginning of changing ourselves and accepting a wider, warmer, more understanding view of the world and the children we care for.

Is Preschool Too Soon to Begin Cross-Cultural, Nonsexist Education?

Do such young children really notice the ethnic or gender differences of other children? If not, perhaps they are too young to require instruction. Might it not be better to ignore these issues and practice "color blindness," rather than make children self-conscious about such differences when they are so young?

Although some teachers might still prefer to answer yes to this question, research on the perception of differences in skin color shows that children as young as age 3 notice the skin color of African Americans and Mexican Americans (Derman-Sparks, 1993; Parrillo, 1985). Beuf (1977) has reported that this is also true for preschool-age Native American youngsters of Southwestern and Plains tribes. Moreover the number of these differentiating responses increases markedly from ages 3 to 5. A study by Derman-Sparks, Higa, and Sparks (1980) of the questions and comments by preschool children provides continuing evidence of their concern with and awareness of racial and cultural differences. These were as varied as "Is Mexican my color?" and "I didn't know that babies came out black."

Awareness of ethnic differences precedes the development of prejudice, so we must also ask, When do positive or negative *attitudes* toward ethnic differences begin to surface? After an extensive review of the literature, Aboud (1988) concluded:

> Ethnic attitudes are acquired by most children some time between the ages of 3 and 5 years. The age of 4 is probably a safe bet if one wanted to pick a single age at which children express negative reactions to certain ethnic members. Whether the negativity is directed toward their own or other ethnicities depends to a certain extent on the child's own ethnic membership. White children are consistently negative toward members of another group. Of the minority groups discussed here, only Native Indians were consistently more negative to their own group than to Whites. The other minority children—Blacks, Hispanics and Asians—were more heterogeneous in that some were initially more negative to their own ethnic members [than to Whites]. (p. 43)

Aboud goes on to say that as children approach ages 7 and 8, there is an increasing tendency for all groups to assign the most preferred rating to children who come from their own ethnic background.

Although research reports that at the earliest stage children depend on social cues such as hair or clothing to tell girls and boys apart (Bem, 1993), awareness of physiological differences begins as early as age 2, as any teacher of young children can attest, and children will comment freely on such differences unless they are suppressed (Coltrane, 1998; Fagot & Leinbach, 1993). One has only to listen during any toilet period in a children's center to hear such remarks as, "Why don't she have a hole in her pants?" or, "Don't you use that thing to wet on me!"

These kinds of comments and questions from children, as well as the more formal research already cited, make it clear that the children are indeed revealing a dawning awareness of ethnic and gender differences and developing feelings about these differences at a very early age. If we want them to learn at this same sensitive time that such differences are to be valued rather than scorned—that is, if we wish to combat the formation of bias and prejudice at the earliest possible moment—then we must conclude that early childhood is the time to begin.

WHAT DO CROSS-CULTURAL AND NONSEXIST EDUCATION HAVE IN COMMON?

Perhaps the reader has been startled to find cross-cultural and nonsexist topics linked together in one chapter even though it is now clear that the common problem of bias ties them together. They are linked together also because two underlying educational principles apply to both subjects. One principle is that we want children to value their *unique* identities in relation to both their ethnic background and gender role. The other principle is that we want children to learn that people of all races and both sexes have many *needs and abilities in common*, and we must recognize these held-in-common needs and abilities and encourage their satisfaction if we want to enable all children to make use of their potential.

In the following pages these principles are applied first to cross-cultural and then to nonsexist education.

PRINCIPLES OF CROSS-CULTURAL EDUCATION

Recognize and Honor Cultural and Ethnic Differences: Encourage Cultural Pluralism[2]

When weaving the cross-cultural strand into the curriculum, it is helpful to recall its two basic threads: (a) teaching that everyone has many unique and precious differences to be shared and appreciated and (b) teaching that all people have many basic needs in common. The first thread, honoring diversity, is sometimes termed *teaching cultural pluralism*. The emphasis in the following pages is placed primarily on that thread since it appears to be the area in which teachers need the most help.

---

[2]   *Since it is impossible to discuss each ethnic or cultural group in detail in a single chapter, in the following discussion I have used examples from as many individual cultures as possible. Of course, no one set of culture-based learning experiences is universally appropriate to all early childhood programs because each group of children has its own ethnically and socially unique composition (Mallory & New, 1993). Teachers who want to provide culturally responsive environments for the children in their particular group will find it helpful to peruse the references included at the end of this chapter for more detailed information on specific cultures. Fortunately there are also some general principles that can be applied in almost all circumstances.*

Valuing Individual Children for Their Special Qualities: Teaching Cultural Pluralism

A Reminder

Sometimes we get so wrapped up in thinking about children's cultural backgrounds that we temporarily forget all the other talents and quirks that make that youngster unique, but we must always remember that culture and gender aren't the only things that matter. The child's cheerful grin, her cleverness at block building, and her ready sympathy when someone cries are part of the child, too. In real life we must be careful not to dwell so much on only one or two characteristics—in this chapter, cultural/ethnic background and gender—that we lose sight of the whole child.

Most particularly we do not want any child ever to feel "on display" because she has been singled out for attention. Instead, the basic learning about cultural pluralism should be that everyone is worthwhile and that each child brings with her special things she has learned at home she can share for the benefit of the group.

Relate Cross-Cultural Learnings to the Here and Now

Just as other learnings are linked with reality, cross-cultural learnings should be linked with current experiences in which the children are actually involved. I don't know what leads otherwise sensible teachers to lose their heads and retreat to quaint pictures of little Dutch girls when they begin to talk about people of different cultures.

However, even when the people are real, the benefit in exposing young children to the concept of foreigners and foreign countries can still be limited. An incident that happened in my own school comes to mind that illustrates this point. The Institute of Child Development was visited by a delegation of Russian women touring the United States as part of the Peace Links group. Our families had, as usual, been informed of the impending visit, so on the following evening one of the fathers asked his little girl if she had enjoyed the visitors. "Oh, yes," she replied. "They were real nice grandmas!" "Ah," he said, "that's good, I'm glad you liked them. By the way, where did you say they came from?" "Oh," she replied, "they didn't say—" she paused, wrinkling her brow in thought, "but I think they were from some place out of town."

An interesting example of an effective way of helping children relate cross-cultural experiences to the here and now of their daily lives comes from some teachers at Pacific Oaks College who have been doing just that with considerable success. They are developing what is called "The Anti-Bias Curriculum" (Pacific Oaks College, 1985), and they define the purpose of that curriculum as being to "empower people to resist being oppressed or to resist oppressing others." The work includes dealing with concerns about bias against gender and disabilities, as well as about racial prejudice.

Although space does not permit a review of all their ideas here, I want to provide a taste of what they suggest in the hope that interested readers will pursue the matter further on their own (Derman-Sparks, 1993; Derman-Sparks & ABC Task Force, 1989; Derman-Sparks & Phillips, 1997). The curriculum, which emerges from day-to-day life experiences at the school, stresses the importance of fostering direct, open communication with children that helps them become aware of racially oppressive beliefs and learn that they can begin to counter these beliefs with positive action.

The teaching varies with the child's age, of course, in order for it to be developmentally appropriate. For example, they favor providing 2-year-olds with direct information about race, such as the fact that the brown color of skin does not wash off and is not dirty; whereas they encourage older 5-year-olds to participate in more activist possibilities. These have included helping the children recognize examples of unfair practices and take action to correct them. One instance involved the youngsters writing to an adhesive bandage company advocating the development of bandages not geared to pinkie-white skins, and another involved painting over a wall near their school that had been covered with racist graffiti.

How much more meaningful it is to children to offer such down-to-earth experiences that are closely related to their own lives and that include activities they can do and enjoy, rather than exposing the youngsters momentarily to people "from out of town"! The satisfaction they experience while participating in such real-life activities can build a foundation of positive attitudes toward other cultures on which we can build more advanced concepts at a later date.

Beginning Steps: Include Concrete, Visible Evidence of Cultural Diversity

Whenever possible, build bridges by using the child's dominant language. Someone should be available in every preschool room who can understand what the child has to say and who can make friends with her in her own language. Even such simple courtesies as learning to pronounce the child's name as her family does, rather than Anglicizing it, can make a dif-

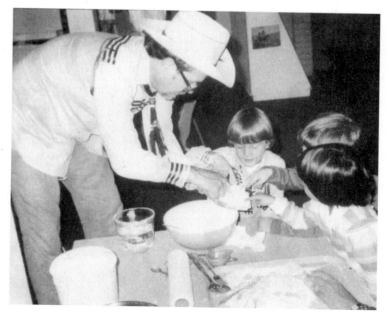

Mr. Duff is helping the children make fry bread. Contact with real Indian people can help children understand that they do not always wear feathers or dance around giving war whoops.

ference. Teaching English as a second language and the use of Black English are discussed more fully in chapter 16. I pause here only to comment that of course children need to learn to speak English but that a bicultural or multicultural program is a farce if we deny the child the right to also use her own dominant language or dialect.

Provide a cross-cultural link between home and school. The past 15 years have witnessed the publication of more authentic stories about African American, Indian, Mexican American, and Asian children (Tomlinson, 1998). Records and pictures are also available, but it is not necessary to depend on only commercial sources. Children often know rhymes and songs from their families, and the teacher can learn these with the parents' coaching and then help youngsters teach them to the group. Most homes have tapes or CDs, but this is a resource frequently ignored by teachers who may deem the music vulgar. However, many of the children's homes are saturated with rock or country music or Latin American rhythms, and using such music in school can draw children into movement and dance who spurn less colorful songs about little duckies waddling around the fish pond.

Stories brought from home, ethnically accurate and attractive dolls, and integrated pictures are also good choices. *Such cross-cultural materials should be available consistently, rather than presented as isolated units.* Dolls, pictures, books, and music from many cultures should be deliberately, though apparently casually, woven into the fabric of every preschool day.

Serve familiar food. This is another excellent way to honor particular backgrounds and to help children feel at home. Sometimes a shy child who appears to be a poor eater is actually just overwhelmed by the strangeness of the food served to her. Food in some day care centers still seems to be planned with the best of nutritional intentions but with total disregard of local food patterns and customs. This situation can be remedied by asking parents for suggestions about appropriate food, by using recipes from ethnic cookbooks (see the references following chapter 4), and by employing a cook who comes from a culture similar to that of the majority of the children.[3] Children can also be encouraged to bring recipes from home that they can cook at school, or mothers or grandmothers may have time to participate in this way. As the children feel more at ease, it can also be fun to branch out and visit local markets and delicatessens that specialize in various ethnic foods. For example, even in a community as small as my own, we have a Chinese market, several Mexican American tortilla factories, and German and Greek delicatessens. (Delicatessens are particularly good to visit because the food is ready, and it smells good and looks attractive.)

The special family customs of the children should be considered, too. For example, we discovered the reason why one Saudi Arabian child was not eating much lunch was that he had been taught it is good manners to refuse food the first time it is offered!

Holidays and other special occasions are also good times for children to share various customs. I recall one event in our group when a young boy lit Hanukkah candles and explained very clearly their purpose and the custom of gift giving. (It was especially fortunate that he was able to do this since he had recently experienced a severe burn, and the prestige of lighting the candles helped him overcome his fear of fire, as well as added enrichment to the life of our group.)

---

[3] *Refer also to Table 4.3 for suggestions of cultural food preferences of seven ethnic groups.*

A note of caution should be inserted here about the need to increase our sensitivity to the way some people feel about certain holidays. For example, some Indian groups have come to feel increasingly angry about the stereotyped presentation of Indians during the Thanksgiving season. All too often Indians in these circumstances are presented as wearing feathers in their hair and dancing around, war whooping as they go, and their real contribution toward helping the Pilgrims, as well as the way the White people ultimately responded, is overlooked. For this reason some Indian groups have gone so far as to observe Thanksgiving as a time of mourning for the Wampanoag Indians—the people who helped the Pilgrims so generously during those early days and who have almost completely disappeared (Derman-Sparks & ABC Task Force, 1989; Ramsey, 1979).

The backgrounds of each child may be savored by the group in many additional ways. Dress-up clothes that reflect the occupations of various parents or national costumes, when they can be spared, contribute much to the life of the school.

Suggestions That Foster Deeper Cross-Cultural Understanding

Building Good Human Relationships: Going Beyond Foods, Books, and Holidays

What worries me about listing such ideas as those above is that so many teachers seem to think this is all there is to multicultural education, whereas it is actually only the beginning. We must realize that the basic purpose of providing multicultural experience is *not* to teach the children facts about Puerto Rico or Japan or to prove to the community that the teacher is not prejudiced. *The purpose of a multicultural curriculum is to attach positive feelings to multicultural experiences so that each child will feel included and valued and will also feel friendly and respectful toward people from other ethnic and cultural groups.*

When you get right down to it, all the multiethnic pictures and recipes and books in the world will not make much difference if teachers, in their hearts, cannot appreciate the strong points of each child and his family and help the other children appreciate them, too.

Dealing with Racial Comments and Slurs at the Preschool Level

Preprimary teachers often ask me how they should reply when a 3- or 4-year-old comments on the difference in skin color of one of his classmates.

It seems to me there are two kinds of comments. The first is the kind of information-seeking question cited previously by Derman-Sparks and coworkers (Pacific Oaks College, 1985): "Will it rub off?" or "How come her backs [of hands] are brown but her fronts are pink?" Such comments should be welcomed (rather than brushed aside in an embarrassed way) because they provide opportunities to clear up confusions about skin color. Our African American head teacher has taught us all never to allow such opportunities to slip past. She is quick to explain and demonstrate that skin color does not wash off and that it is not dirty. She also points out that people may be different colors on the outside but that we are all the same color on the inside.

The second kind of comment is more difficult to handle. When 4-year-old Jan yells at Jamal, "You dirty nigger, get off my trike!" it is easy for teachers to feel so upset and angry they lose sight of the probable reason why such a young child resorts to such an ugly slur.

First, it is necessary to remember that 3- and 4-year-olds do not comprehend the full extent of the insult—just as they rarely comprehend the true meaning of *son-of-a-bitch.*

What they *do* know about these words is that they have a strong emotional power to hurt, and the children who use these words use them since they *are* angry and they *do* intend to hurt. This means the problem has to be dealt with in two parts.

The first part has to do with pointing out to both children the real reason why Jan is angry. She is angry because she does not want Jamal taking her trike, not because he is African American. It is important for Jamal to understand this to protect his self-esteem. It is important for Jan to realize that it is not the color of the person taking her trike that matters but the fact that she does not want *anyone* taking it at all. *She needs to learn to attach anger to its real cause, rather than displace it by substituting inaccurate or incorrect reasons.* This not only helps prevent the formation of prejudice but also is a basic principle of mental health everyone needs to learn and practice: *Always admit to yourself why you are really angry. Don't displace anger: Face facts.* Following this clear labeling of the reason for the fight, coupled with a brief description of each child's feelings ("I can see you're mad, and I can see you don't want to wait"), the argument has to be settled just as any other fight would have to be.

The second part of the problem, which is more likely to be mishandled, must also be faced. No one likes having her feelings hurt, and name calling of any sort is intended to and does hurt feelings. Although the usual advice about such matters is that if "bad" language is ignored it will go away, experience in the real world of day care has taught me that sometimes ignoring such words works but usually it does not. It is also true that some name calling hurts worse than others; when this is the case, it is essential for the teacher to be firm and clear with the children about what is acceptable and to stop what is not. Certainly racial insults must never be tolerated.

These standards of acceptability vary from school to school. My own level of tolerance is that although I can ignore many insults and bathroom words, I will not tolerate racial or sexist insults to myself or to anyone else. So after dealing with the social contretemps just described, I would take Jan aside for a quiet, firm talk about hurt feelings, reiterating the rule: "We do not use the word *nigger* because it hurts too much. When you're mad at Jamal, hold on to the trike and tell him, 'You can't have the trike—I'm using it now. You have to wait 'til I'm done,' *but we do not use the word* nigger *in our school.*"[4]

As the moment presents itself, I would also point out to Jamal that Jan was mad at him because he grabbed her trike and that she wanted to get even by calling him "nigger." Next time, he had better ask for the trike instead of just taking it. I would also make a big point with him that just because somebody says you're something or calls you a name doesn't make it true. *You* know who you are, and you don't have to let yourself be hurt by unkind people who are trying to make you feel bad. When someone calls you a bad name, remember that she or he is doing it to hurt you, so do your best to brush it off. Don't give that person that satisfaction.

It is important to understand that the problem of helping minority children deal with such attacks is a difficult one and could fill a book by itself. Geraldine Wilson (1980) suggests many ways that families can help African American children defend themselves against such attacks. She states that it is important for children to be able to respond with

---

[4] *I realize that in some African American circles* nigger *is no longer a derogatory term, but this is still untrue for the majority of the population.*

dignity and keep control of themselves. They might respond by saying, "Call me by my name!" or say, "Don't call me that again." She stresses that youngsters need a range of strategies that include ignoring the taunt, walking away and then returning with a reply, getting help from someone else, combining a response with getting help, and sharing the sadness at home, where she cautions parents that children should be allowed to cry about it if they feel like doing so and that they should be comforted. In addition it should be pointed out once again that providing the continuing countermeasure of building pride in ethnicity, which was discussed earlier in the chapter, is probably the strongest defense of all.

Involve and Honor All Parents When They Visit the Center

I recommended earlier that teachers should seek to acquaint themselves with various cultures by reading, taking courses, learning the language, and so forth, but I want to emphasize here that the most vigorous and lively source of ethnic learning is right on the school's doorstep—namely, the families themselves. In the long run cooperative sharing of themselves and their opinions and their skills will teach the teacher and the children the most about the personal strengths of family members. As a matter of fact, I do not see how one could conduct a multiethnic classroom without drawing on these resources.

Successful communication is vital. The teacher who is unafraid of parents and who genuinely likes them will communicate this without saying anything at all; there is really no substitute for this underlying attitude of goodwill and concern for the children. All parents appreciate the teacher who has the child's welfare genuinely at heart, and this mutual interest in the child is the best base on which to build a solid teacher-parent relationship. Since listening is so much more important than talking, teachers should particularly cultivate that ability in themselves.

Other facts about communication can help when speaking with the foreign born. A friend of mine to whom English is a foreign language suggests that teachers speak more slowly (but not more loudly!) and without condescension when talking with parents who are learning English. Sometimes writing words down in English also helps because some parents read English better than they understand the spoken word.

It is also worthwhile to go to the trouble of having a translator handy when necessary. This person may be another adult, but sometimes it can even be a 4- or 5-year-old who is bilingual. Notices sent home stand a much better chance of being read if they are written in the language of the home. Both languages should be printed side by side to avoid the implication that the one that comes first is better.

Welcome parent volunteers. The problem with making parents feel at ease and glad to participate in the school program is that they are always a little out of their element in the beginning. I have often thought it would be fair to require the teacher to visit and help out in the families' homes on a turnabout basis. If this were possible, it would certainly help teachers gain a better insight into how it feels to step into a strange situation in which the possibility of making fools of themselves is quite likely.

Over and over I have witnessed teachers asking mothers to wipe off tables or help in the kitchen, or letting them simply stand around, smiling a lot but knowing in their hearts their time is being wasted. Visitors may prefer simple tasks in the beginning because these are familiar, not threatening, and because they do not want to make waves or antagonize the teacher. Keeping them at such tasks is fundamentally denigrating, however, teaches the children that parents are not important at school, and deprives the children of the unique contribution such people can make when they are properly encouraged. For example, instead of setting up the tables for lunch, a mother might share with the children a book she has kept from her own childhood or bring pictures of her family's latest trip to India, or help the children make her child's favorite recipe, or bring the baby for a visit and let the children help bathe him (this presents an especially nice opportunity to teach about the universal similarities of human beings). Last fall one father in our group who is a member of the Wichita tribe helped the children make an authentic (and tasty) squash and cornmeal dessert. The children were delighted, and his son was ecstatic!

Remember that the fundamental purpose of providing these experiences is to create emotionally positive situations for the children and the adults who are involved. For this reason the teacher should concentrate on doing everything possible to help visitors feel comfortable and successful. It takes considerable planning, but the results are worth it.

Although it is not fair to put parents on the spot and ask them to control a group of children they do not know, it can be genuine fun and very helpful to have parent volunteers come along on field trips during which everyone can be together and everyone takes some responsibility. Families who are poor may latch on to such opportunities to get out and do things, and field trips can be a refreshing change for mothers who are homebound otherwise. For trips on which toddlers would be a burden, we have, from time to time, worked out arrangements whereby two mothers take over the little ones while others come on the trip, and then switch off child care for the next trip.

Families can often provide ideas for excursions, too. The children at our center greatly enjoyed a visit to a communal organic garden one spring, and they also loved a trip to a pizza parlor owned by one of the families.

Make visitors welcome for meals. One of the wisest policies of the Head Start program has been its welcoming, open attitude at mealtimes. I cannot recall working in a Head Start center where people were not spontaneously invited to share meals with the children, and it is true that breaking bread binds people together in basic friendliness. If possible, this is a good policy for all schools to follow. When finances cannot support this drain, visiting parents can order lunch a day in advance and pay a nominal fee to defray the cost.

Trust and use parent expertise on the advisory board. All programs receiving federal funds are required to have advisory boards that must have at least 50% parent representation to be legal. But many schools use such boards as rubber stamps and present parents with programs and plans literally for approval, rather than for consideration and modification—a policy that certainly does not make parents feel welcome or respected. A much better way to make plans is to trust the parents. It is unlikely they will suggest activities or policies detrimental to the children; and when differences arise, they can usually be settled by open discussion, which educates everyone.

Teachers who seek out parents' suggestions because they value their practical experience with their children will find that this approach reduces the parents' feelings of defensiveness when the teacher happens to be better educated or better paid. If meetings are held during times when child care is available, more board members are likely to attend. Attendance also increases when parents' suggestions are actually used and when parents are thanked sincerely for coming.

Increase the Number and Variety of Children in the School Who Come From Various Ethnic and Cultural Groups

As I commented earlier, some full-day centers and Head Start-type groups are luckier in the assortment of children who come naturally to their doors than some middle-class schools. Such multiethnic contacts can introduce children at an early age to the values of an integrated society. They can teach the basic fact that José's face is not brown because it is dirty and can couple this learning with the fact that José is fun to play with because he is the best block builder in the school.

Suggestions for Recruiting Children for Middle-Class Nursery Schools

Many middle-class center staff think racial isolation is undesirable and try to achieve a better ethnic balance through recruitment. The teacher who attempts this should realize that families understandably resent being used as tokens or being included only because of their color or poverty. The slightest trace of condescension or patronage will give offense, and it requires tact and genuine warmth to achieve participation by all.

Middle-class schools may do best when recruiting if they find three or four mothers who can come at the same time and therefore lend each other moral support. The fact that many states now allow their welfare departments to purchase child care from any licensed center also makes recruitment easier.

Of course, the closer the school is to the children it serves, the more likely it is that families will participate. Why should a mother of Mexican background trek her child halfway across town for the dubious privilege of placing her in an all-White children's center? It is hardly reasonable to accuse people of being standoffish under such circumstances; yet I have heard this conclusion drawn when such an invitation was refused.

Show Respect for People of Differing Ethnic Origins by Employing Them as Teachers

Cross-cultural learning in the children's center should be based on real ongoing experiences with real people whenever possible. This means, for example, that when we talk about how to emphasize that Mexican people are effective human beings, it is just not satisfactory at such an early level to use the historical examples recommended in many Hispanic curriculum guides. Historical figures are so remote and intangible that they do not mean much to preschoolers.

A much more effective way of teaching young children that people of all ethnic backgrounds are important is to employ them in positions of power. Many schools employ minority group members as aides. But this is far from enough. Children are quick to sense the power structure of the school, and they need to see people of all ethnic backgrounds employed in the most respected positions as teachers and directors. Unfortunately, Asian, Latino, and Indian teachers are still relatively rare. A study by the National Black Child Development Institute (1994) reports that although African Americans are well represented at the staff level, they remain seriously underrepresented at the leadership level of the profession, a problem the institute ascribes in part to lack of advanced educational qualifications.

Professional associations can and should help remedy these deficiencies by encouraging their local colleges to recruit heavily among ethnic groups other than Anglo, and they can also help by offering scholarships to sustain such students through college. Even a modest book scholarship may mean the difference for some young people between going to a community college or working in a fast-food outlet.

EMPHASIZING THE SIMILARITIES AS WELL AS VALUING THE UNIQUENESS OF PEOPLE

Not only do children and families need to have their cultural uniqueness welcomed and valued, but they also need to learn that all people have many things in common and that they are alike in some fundamental ways.

Teach the Commonality of Biological and Psychological Needs

One way to teach the similarities of all people is to emphasize the commonality of biological and psychological needs. Thus, when talking about the children's favorite food or what they traditionally eat for various holidays, the teacher can remind them that no matter what we like to eat best, everyone gets hungry and everyone likes to eat something, or she can point out at the right moment that it feels good to everyone to stretch and yawn or to snuggle down in something warm and cozy.

The same principle can be taught in relation to emotions: Everyone gets mad sometimes, everyone wants to belong to somebody, most people want to have friends, and most children feel a little lost when their mothers leave them at school.

In addition, the teacher can draw the children's attention to the fact that people often use individual, unique ways to reach a goal that most people enjoy. For example, Josie's father plays the guitar, whereas Heather's mother uses the zither; but they both use these different instruments for the pleasure of making music and singing together with the children.

Help Families Look Beyond Various Differences to Focus on Common Goals

Schools of various types can provide opportunities for friendships to form and thrive. Cooperatives are famous for doing this, of course, but it can also be accomplished in other groups. Advisory boards can draw families into projects that focus on the children and benefit everyone. This activity can take the form of a potluck dinner, with a slide show of what the children have been doing; it can be a series of discussions on topics chosen by the parents; it can be a workday combined with a picnic lunch for which everyone pitches in to clean and paint and tidy up. (There is nothing like scrubbing a kitchen floor together to generate a common bond.) It makes little difference what is chosen, as long as it results in the realization of a common goal and creates opportunities for everyone to be together in a meaningful, friendly way.

Keep Working Toward the Basic Goals of Socialization That Teach Children to Consider the Rights and Needs of Everyone

Finally the teacher should remember that working toward the goals of socialization discussed in chapter 10 will help children learn that everyone has the same basic rights and privileges and that everyone is respected and treated fairly at school. The social goals most important to emphasize in relation to cross-cultural education are (a) developing empathy for how other people feel, (b) learning that everyone has rights that are respected by all, and (c) gaining skill by cooperating, rather than achieving satisfaction by competing and winning over others. If these social skills are fostered, living in the group will be a good experience for all the children, and a healthy foundation will be laid for a more truly integrated society in the future.

CAN TEACHING ABOUT CULTURAL UNIQUENESS AND SIMILARITY OF NEEDS BE COMBINED?

There is at least one way to teach preschool children these two concepts—that people are enjoyably unique and that they have many similar needs in common at the same time. The staff at our day care center gradually evolved this approach after passing through two earlier stages.

During the first stage, in an effort to make experiences more real for the children, students and staff tended to bring in objects from other cultures for the children to pass around and look at during group time, or the items were displayed on a table, accompanied by books and pictures about the culture. This was basically a beginning attempt to honor cultural uniqueness. We now refer to this as "our museum period."

During the second stage we increased the here-and-now aspect by doing a lot of the sort of thing described in the first part of this chapter. We cooked ethnic foods together and enjoyed them, or we celebrated a holiday or made a piñata and talked about the many wonderful ways of satisfying hunger or having parties. We still continue to offer many of these stage-two experiences during the week, and the children continue to appreciate them.

However, the staff remained unsatisfied with these approaches. It just did not seem to us that we were helping the children grasp the reality and value of other cultures and appreciate the common humanity that binds us all. With such young children we thought we needed to link things together in more explicit and literal ways—ways they could really understand and enjoy.

To accomplish *this* goal we developed a third stage. In this current stage we are offering the children comparative experiences through which they can actually try out what it is like to sleep in a Czechoslovakian feather bed, a Guatemalan hammock, and our child-sized "American" bed, and we make these comparative play experiences available for a week at a time.

In another example we set up a comparison between Japanese and Western eating styles. On the Japanese side the children took their shoes off upon entering, sat on low cushions, and used bowls and chopsticks as they partook of ramen noodles and Japanese cookies. (Our Japanese children were gratifyingly proficient with chopsticks!) On the Western side they wiped their shoes on a mat, sat on low chairs, used plates and bowls, and had noodle soup and wheat crackers. In the offing is an experience comparing the different methods by which mothers carry their babies around, and one of our students has just finished a comparison of Navajo and Anglo weaving whereby the children tried out a Navajo-style loom.

Elaborate experiences like these are a lot of fun but are also a lot of work. Fortunately experiences do not have to be this fancy to get the point across. During a warm spring rain last year one student brought some banana leaves (often used in Thailand when it rains), and the children delighted in using them and comparing them with their more familiar umbrellas. Another easy comparison to offer is a simple tasting experience. For example, it is interesting to compare French bread, tortillas, matzo, and pita bread, or various cheeses, or fruits that come from different countries such as mangoes, oranges, and guavas. Or for a more extended experience grow Native American seeds such as amaranth, Hopi blue corn, Navaho watermelons, and Zapotec pleated tomatoes.

Once again, remember that families can make invaluable contributions of advice and resources if you decide to attempt stage-three activities, and it is most beneficial when these experiences are family related and based on the cultural backgrounds of children in the group.

Please understand that these more concentrated experiences do not constitute our entire approach to cross-cultural education. If they did, that would be too much like reverting to "Japanese Day" or "Cinco de Mayo." We continue to make certain that multiethnic materials such as books, pictures, puzzles, and other equipment are used throughout the school on a matter-of-fact, daily basis. The purpose of the stage-three activities is to accentuate that a human need can be met in more than one satisfactory way and, most important of all, that many of these ways are *fun*.

The most important element remains the teacher and the example of decency and respect she models every time she relates to a child in the classroom.

ENCOURAGING EQUITY BY PROVIDING A NONSEXIST EDUCATION AND HELPING CHILDREN VALUE THEIR OWN SEXUALITY

Today, when educational emphasis tends to be placed on the value of nonsexist education, it may be necessary to remind the reader that it is also important to teach children about reproduction and sexual differences and to help them value their femaleness or maleness.

Even though many of us want to enable children of both sexes to step beyond the narrowly restricted ideas of sex roles and stereotypes that currently exist, we must be careful to help them value their basic sexuality as well since that is an important and deeply elemental part of every individual's personality. If children grow up with the idea that sexuality is unimportant or not valued or, worse yet, that reproduction and sex are smutty topics to be snickered about and investigated in secret, we may have unwittingly undone much of what we hoped to accomplish by adding a nonsexist emphasis to teaching.

Teaching Simple Physiological Facts

The more open and matter-of-fact teachers and parents can be about differences in the anatomy of girls and boys, the more likely it is that children will not need to resort to "doctor" play or hiding in corners to investigate such differences "on the q.t." Open toileting has long been the rule in most preschool settings because when children use the same toilets, secrecy about sexual differences and toilet practices is avoided. This policy also generates opportunities for the teacher to supply answers to things young children wonder about such as why boys urinate standing up whereas girls urinate sitting down. The teacher makes simple statements about these matters: "Yes, boys and girls are made differently. Boys have penises, and so they stand up to urinate. Girls have vulvas, so they sit down to urinate." If little girls still want to know why they cannot urinate while standing up, the teacher can invite them to try it. There is no substitute for learning by experience! Casualness and answering the questions actually asked, rather than ones the teacher is nervously afraid the children will ask, should be the order of the day.

Sometimes it helps clarify matters if the adult replies to questions by asking the youngster what she thinks the answer is; this can provide a clue to how complicated the adult explanation should be. Sometimes, though, such a return question embarrasses an older 4-year-old who is sophisticated enough to suspect she should not be asking about such things anyway, and questioning in return can cause her to stop asking. So it takes a delicate perception of the child to know whether to respond with a question or just to answer as simply and clearly as possible. Of course, if you want to keep the line open for more questions, it is deadly to betray amusement at some of the naive answers you will receive.

Although the use of accurate words such as *vagina* or *penis* is more commonplace than it used to be, teachers and parents should note an interesting piece of research that points out grown-ups are more likely to use explicit terms when referring to boys' genitalia than when talking about the genitalia of girls. Koblinsky, Atkinson, and Davis (1980) surmise this is because boys' genitals are more visible. It seems that we adults need to learn from this research that we must make a special effort to remember to discuss the anatomy of little girls as well as that of little boys even though that part of the anatomy is not as apparent.

Since every child's self-concept is intimately tied to her or his sense of sexual worth, we must be careful to teach that each sex has an important role to play in reproduction. When grown, girls have the opportunity to carry and bear children, and boys, when grown, help start the baby growing. Then mothers and fathers work together to care for the baby following its birth (Lively & Lively, 1991).

Bear in mind when discussing the dual roles of parenting that it is necessary to think about the child's home situation. So many children in day care now come from single-parent homes that this has to be gently taken into account in such discussions so that the child does not feel "different" or peculiar because she has only one parent. And yet, it is these very children who may be least experienced with mother-father roles and who need the most help in understanding the ideal mutuality of the parenting relationship. It takes a combination of sensitivity and matter-of-factness without sentimentality or pity to deal with this problem successfully.

Once past the matter of simple anatomical differences, many adults still dread questions about reproduction and because of their discomfort either evade them (just as they

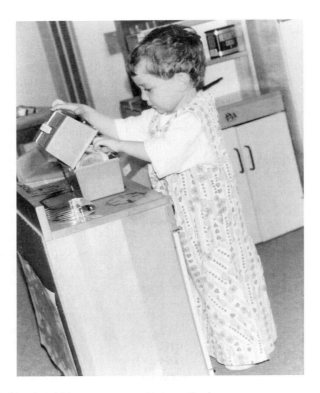

Both boys and girls should be encouraged to use the house corner.

avoid discussing race) or give such confused or elaborate replies that the children are bewildered. Therefore it can be reassuring to learn that the kind of question most preschool children are likely to ask is, "Where did the baby come from?" or "How will it get out?" This level of questioning, common to 3- to 5-year-olds, is termed the "geography level" by A. Bernstein in a delightful book called *The Flight of the Stork* (1994). Thinking of it as a "geography" question can make it reasonably unembarrassing to explain that a baby is growing inside the mother's uterus or that it will be born through a special hole women have between their legs, near where their urine comes out but not exactly the same place.

For the slightly older youngster who wants to know how the baby gets inside to start with, it is far better to tell her or him the truth rather than to talk about animals or seeds. This is because when children see animals mating, it really looks like fighting to them, or they may note an expression of resigned submission on the part of the female animal—attitudes we would rather not have children associate with human intercourse. The problem with the "planting seeds" idea is that it encourages them to think too literally about this concept in terms of what they already know about gardening. I was told of one little girl who queried after such a discussion, "Well, what I want to know is, when you picked out that seed, did it have my picture on it?"

To avoid such misconceptions, I suggest the teacher or parent explain that the mother and father start the baby growing in the mother by being very loving and close with each other and that when they are feeling this way, the father fits his penis inside the mother's vagina and a fluid passes into her that joins with the mother's egg and helps the baby start growing. I prefer this explanation because it is truthful and accurate and also because it mentions the role of warmth, caring, and mutual responsibility as being important parts of the experience.

Masturbation

Another aspect of helping children value their own sexuality deals with self-pleasuring masturbatory behavior so that children are not shamed by the teacher's reprimand and do not come to feel their sexual impulses are unclean or "bad."

Research indicates that masturbation is commonplace in adult males and females (Masters, Johnson, & Kilodny, 1994), and it is in children, too. Although the extent of such behavior is unknown in children, a Norwegian study found that 85% of kindergarten teachers who were interviewed reported that some children in their classes engaged in masturbation, although only 24% of teachers reported that such behavior happened "often" or "very often" (Gundersen, Melås, & Skår, 1981).

The question that confronts teachers once they admit the frequency and normality of the behavior is what to do about it, since it is still true that masturbating is not acceptable public behavior. It seems wisest to take the child aside and explain to her or him that you realize such behavior feels good but that it is something people do only in private.

Meeting the Special Needs of Boys in the Preschool

Still another aspect of helping children value their own sexuality has to do with recognizing the boys' needs for high-physical-energy activities and meeting their needs for role models in the children's center. Although it is difficult to talk about this without having it misinterpreted as advocating sexist practices, experience has taught me it is necessary to remind female teachers how important it is to provide young boys many experiences that fit their needs and that do not feminize them because the temptation is to approve of "female type" activities and reward those with positive attention.

Boys' physical activity needs appear to differ from those of girls. Research shows boys tend to engage in more rough-and-tumble play than girls do (J. E. Johnson & Roopnarine, 1983) and that they are more physically aggressive than girls are after age 2 (Jacklin & Baker, 1993; Ruble & Martin, 1998). But female teachers tend to suppress this vigor and energy since it is contrary to the teachers' own behavior patterns and also makes running a day care center more difficult. Although all children need opportunities for vigorous physical activity, boys do seem to need it especially, and we must provide for meeting that need. Their play requires large, sturdy equipment, plenty of space, and a teacher who genuinely welcomes such activity, rather than regards it as a threat to her ability to control the children.

Boys not only must be supplied with enough room to move and to let off steam but also must have the chance to form relationships with men who can serve as models for them.

In an age when the divorce rate remains high and many unmarried women are electing to raise their children rather than surrender them for adoption, many children in day care centers come from single-parent, mother-centered homes. The effect on boys' developing sense of masculinity in these mother-centered, father-absent homes varies according to age. Ruble and Martin (1998) report studies showing that "knowledge of gender-typed activities and occupations were higher among younger boys but not girls in father-present homes," whereas "older father-absent boys were *more* stereotypical in their overt behavior, particularly aggression" (p. 978).

Common sense, however, cannot help encouraging one to believe that the presence of a father facilitates sex role development at every age (although evidence also suggests that boys can develop normally without it). Girls also benefit from such experience because it probably helps them develop concepts of masculinity and femininity. For these reasons centers should do all they can to provide boys and girls consistent contacts with men who care about children.

Incidentally one of the continuing and unfortunate examples of sexism in our society is the fact that few men are employed as early childhood teachers. In 1997 the U.S. Department of Labor reported that 98.5% of people employed in child care occupations (including family child care providers, and prekindergarten and kindergarten teachers and aides) were women. This disparity is attributable in part to the perception that such work requires the nurturing qualities commonly attributed to females rather than to males, but it is also attributable to low pay combined with rising concerns about the potential for accusations of child abuse (King, 1998).

These difficulties mean that we will continue to need to think of ingenious ways to include men as participants in the preschool day. High school and college men can often be employed as aides, and occasionally warmhearted fathers will volunteer to show up regularly and spend time with the children. All the contacts, though admittedly not as satisfactory as a father's continuing presence in the home, will help both boys and girls formulate their concepts of what it means to be a man or woman in our society and ideally will help boys and girls grow up to be sturdy, attractive men and women themselves.

Suggestions for Providing a Nonsexist Curriculum

"Are boys really better than girls at analyzing problems?" "Are girls really better than boys at nurturing and comforting others?" Although research indicates that the answer to these questions is no, many teachers continue to act as if these myths were true and plan their curriculum and treat children accordingly. Jacklin and Baker (1993) report only two areas in which behavioral differences between boys and girls have been reliably established. These are that "boys are found to be more aggressive than girls, whereas girls' language development and verbal abilities exceed those of boys" (p. 42), but even these differences are not statistically pronounced. We may conclude, then, that there is really no prevailing *genetic* reason why both sexes cannot be equally interested in every activity offered at school. If we want this to happen, what must be changed is the culture in which attitudes toward sex roles are formed (Streitmatter, 1994).

Before embarking on approaches that may bring about changes in attitude, I want to remind the reader of the difference between children's ideas of sex roles and their feelings

Everybody needs the chance and the encouragement to try everything.

about sexuality and gender. In our zeal to provide all children with the widest possible range of activities and developmental experiences, we must also be careful to preserve children's deep, basic valuing of their own sexuality since that positive valuing is fundamental to their feelings of identity and being worthy people.

Does this valuing mean that teachers should not seek to change former, possibly sexist curricula? Of course not. We must do all we can to widen children's horizons to the rich possibilities heretofore unavailable to many of them.

One way that ideas about sex roles can be changed to be more equitable without undermining the child's pride in gender is by presenting an open curriculum that provides opportunities for both sexes to participate in all learning activities, rather than restricting children to obsolete sex role expectations. Teachers should work to develop wider competence and equal privileges for both sexes. Sprafkin, Serbin, Denir, and Connor (1983) demonstrated that providing 3½- to 4-year-old boys *and girls* opportunities to practice with "boy-preferred" toys such as blocks, dominoes, and building toys significantly improved the children's visual spatial ability—a skill on which boys typically score higher. This skill is fundamental to later achievements in such fields as architecture, mathematics, and engineering and so is one well worth fostering in children of both sexes.

Preschools are often the last chance children have to try out materials and activities that are contemptuously labeled in elementary school as "girl stuff" or "unfeminine." Surely activities such as woodworking and blocks should be freely available to girls, just as opportunities to enjoy dressing up or sewing should be available to boys. The chance to experience a full range of roles enriches the knowledge of each sex, does not produce sexual perverts, and, ideally, deepens understanding and empathy for the opposite sex.

Sprung and the Women's Action Alliance produced a landmark book (1975) replete with examples of how the nursery school curriculum can be presented so that all areas, whether blocks or the housekeeping corner, can attract both girls and boys. *Together and Equal* (Schlank & Metzger, 1997) offers many suggestions that could be used either with younger children directly or to raise the awareness of teachers who might otherwise use such phrases as "The girls can go first because . . . ," when they could easily say, "This table can go first," if they remember to take a moment to think before they speak.

It is, of course, important not only to offer wider opportunities to girls but also to offer them to boys. For example, opportunities for additional male roles should be included in homemaking such as scaled-to-comfortable-size men's clothing for workers of various kinds. These garments should be freely available for use by both sexes, and boys should be encouraged to join in formerly female-dominated activities such as cooking and caring for children (Marshall, Robeson, & Keefe, 1999).

Teachers may encounter a bit more resistance from boys when such cross-gender activities are first proposed than they will from girls. This is because girls are less criticized by their peers when they engage in "masculine preferred" activities than boys are. Fagot's research (1977, 1994) indicates that even when teachers encourage boys to cook or to engage in self-expressive art activity, other boys do criticize them for such behavior, so it is well to be on the lookout for such remarks by their peers and discourage them when possible.

Sylvia Greenberg (1985) presents a particularly interesting perspective on early childhood education. She points out that most of that curriculum stresses skills girls already possess but that boys often lack. These include emphasis on verbal activities (e.g., large-group time), small muscle activities (e.g., cutting, painting), and assistance in gaining impulse control. Participation in these activities, she maintains, is virtually obligatory.

However, much of the curriculum that might remediate deficiencies in little girls' education is left to "choice and chance." Participation in such activities as block play and large muscle activities that might also aid in developing spatial awareness are part of self-select time (as is selection of various science activities).

Basing her recommendations on research, Greenberg (1985) suggests teachers make a special effort to provide the following activities for girls:

1. Activities that require spatial exploration
2. Activities for practice in large muscle coordination and development of large motor skills (increase structured gym activities)
3. Equipment that enhances investigatory activity
4. Activities that permit learning from following directions
5. Tasks that require cooperative groups of three or more children for their accomplishment

6. Tasks that encourage distance from adults
7. Opportunities for experimenting with a wide range of future career options

Importance of Evaluating Educational Materials

Activities to be provided for boys include the following:

1. Activities that encourage listening, speaking, and conversing
2. Activities for small muscle coordination
3. Opportunities to learn from examples
4. Opportunities that encourage responsibility for others and to others
5. Opportunities for nurturing activities
6. Activities for helping boys develop flexible, effective self-management skills

All teachers should take a closer look at the materials they offer for educational activities. More nonsexist, multiracial materials in the form of puzzles, lotto games, and dolls are becoming available, but these materials are rarely sufficient for the needs of the preschool. Teachers should also expect to make many of their own items.

Although it remains necessary to search out adequate activity materials, the good news is that multicultural and nonsexist books are increasing in number (Ciancollo, 1997) and are quite readily available (see the Research Study in this chapter). *Children's Books From Other Countries* (Tomlinson, 1998) and *Great Books for African American Children* (Toussaint, 1999) are examples of annotated bibliographies of multicultural books, and *Together and Equal* (Schlank & Metzger, 1997) includes an extensive bibliography of nonsexist ones. Appendix E offers some helpful guidelines to follow when the supply of these materials ebbs and flows as the market dictates. Publishers print what the public will buy. If we want to have a continuing supply of good quality books that represent the cultures of all the children we teach, we have to write to publishers and make our desires known.

Importance of Attitude and Modeling

More basic than all the nonsexist curriculum in the world is the need to sensitize women and men to the negative consequences of unconsciously biased sexist teaching. What happens to the self-esteem of young boys who are criticized by female teachers for their high-energy, aggressive response to life? What effect does the constant use of such words as mail*man,* fire*man,* and police*man* have on young girls and their anticipation of future occupations?

Or on a positive note, what do children conclude when they see their female teacher confidently using the electric drill to install a new chalkboard or their male teacher matter-of-factly sewing a button on a child's shirt?

We do indeed have a long way to go in raising our awareness and control of the long-ingrained patterns of behavior and speech that perpetuate sexist and racist teaching, but we have come a long way, too. The danger to guard against is that complacency may permit us to become careless or to stop trying. Doing that opens the way to recapitulating the racist/sexist problem all over again.

Research Study

The Changing World of Picture Books

Research Question: Dellmann-Jenkins, Florjan-cic, and Swadener asked the question, Have the sex roles and cultural/ethnic themes and people included in children's picture books changed in recent years?

Research Method: To determine the answer, the investigators analyzed contemporary Calde-cott Award and Honor Books and compared these results with the findings from a study done 10 years earlier by Collins, Ingoldsby, and Dell-mann (1984).

To make the comparison between the studies valid, the current investigators analyzed their research by using the same methods used in the 1984 study and also extended the research design to check for androgyny and cultural diversity.

The characters in the 15 books awarded Calde-cott honors during the years 1989 to 1992 were assessed according to the characters' sex roles and kinds of participation in each story. Then ratios were calculated, comparing the number of male people and/or animals in titles and illustra-tions with the number of female people and/or animals in titles and illustrations. The ratio for nongendered animals was also calculated. The kinds of activities the characters participated in were analyzed according to whether they were active/passive and traditional/nontraditional. The androgynous quality of the characters' behavior and their cultural diversity were also assessed.

Results: When these factors were compared with the study done 10 years earlier by Collins et al., the researchers found a slight trend toward including more females in book titles and a statisti-cally significant trend (.001) toward including more females in illustrations. The most pro-nounced difference in sex roles was the increase in the number of nongendered animal illustrations. There was also a slight trend toward placing more females in central roles.

Defining *androgyny* as being "the state of possess-ing the best characteristics of masculinity and fem-ininity" (Kaplan, 1992, p. 432), the Dellmann-Jenkins et al. study found that 10 of the 15 books portrayed characters meeting this standard. They also found that 7 of the 15 books depicted people from nondominant cultures or minority groups.

Implications for Teaching: It is indeed encourag-ing to see that the award-winning books are becoming those that tend to be more balanced in their presentation of positive characteristics of an array of people. Whether this is happening because the results of the 1984 study and a similar study conducted in 1972 have become widely dis-seminated, thereby influencing the Caldecott judges to take a more gender-balanced approach to award giving, or whether it is simply the result of increased social consciousness is unknown. Whatever the reason, all of us should be thankful these high-quality, exquisitely illustrated books are available for us to share with children.

We cannot conclude, however, that this study reveals a prevailing trend throughout children's lit-erature. The Caldecott books represent the cream of the crop. One has only to read *Multieth-nic Children's Literature* (Ramirez & Ramirez, 1994) or *Books Without Bias: Through Indian Eyes* (Slapin & Seale, 1992) to be reminded that severe defi-ciencies are still present in many children's books that portray a variety of ethnic/cultural back-grounds. Since this is the case, adults who care about the effect books have on young children must continue to rigorously review every book and apply the standards listed in Appendix E to make certain it is truly a desirable book to share.

Source: From "Sex Roles and Cultural Diversity in Recent Award Winning Picture Books for Young Children," by M. Dellmann-Jenkins, L. Florjancic, and E. B. Swadener, 1993, Journal of Research in Early Childhood Education, 7(2), 74-82.

SUMMARY

Since children as young as age 2 differentiate between people of differing skin color and gender, it is important to begin a program of cross-cultural, nonsexist education as early as possible so that they learn that *different*, be it a difference in sex or race or culture, does not mean *inferior*.

Teaching this principle of equity can be achieved in several ways. First and fundamentally, we want to emphasize that every individual has the unique, treasurable gift of individuality to share with others. Second, no matter how unique the individual is, each person has some basic needs in common with the rest of the people in the world that can be satisfied in a variety of ways. Third and finally, every child of either sex or any color should be encouraged to explore the full range of her or his abilities and potential competencies.

Schools that incorporate such cross-cultural, nonsexist emphases in their programs help children learn to value the differences and similarities in themselves, their friends, and their teachers as being positive strengths. This positive valuing lies at the heart of equity in education.

Questions and Activities

1. Have you been with a young child when she commented on differences in skin color or other differences related to ethnic group membership? What did she say, and what would be an effective way to reply to her comments or questions?

2. Do you think it might be confusing or contradictory to teach children that people are alike and different at the same time?

3. It is the beginning of the year, and you hope to involve the many new parents in your group in participation. List some things you plan to do that will foster this participation. Also list some policies that would subtly discourage parents from wanting to be part of the life of the school.

4. Do you ever wonder whether perhaps you are unconsciously behaving in a prejudiced way by paying more attention to children from certain ethnic groups and less to members of other groups or favoring girls more than boys or vice versa? One way to check up on yourself is to ask a trusted colleague to keep track for various time periods of your contacts with the children over a week or more. All it takes is a list of the children's names and putting a check by each one for each contact made. If you wish to refine this strategy, plus and minus checks can be used, depending on the kind of encounter, whether it is disciplinary, showing positive interest, and so on. (A word of encouragement: This behavior is fairly easy to correct once the teacher is aware of it.)

5. Analyze the books in your center. Do some present both boys and girls as effective, active people? Do some appear to perpetuate stereotypes of little girl and little boy behavior? Are these books necessarily undesirable?

6. *Predicament:* You are working in a school that serves many single-parent families in which mothers have primary care of the children. Many of the children, therefore, have relatively little experience with men. Suggest some practical plans that would help alleviate this deficit for the children in your care.

7. Take a few minutes and make two columns headed "What I Am Good at Doing" and "What I Am Not Good at Doing" and then analyze why you are either good or not good at those particular activities. If you answer, "Well, I never learned that," identify what prevented you from learning it, whatever it was.

8. Is it really the responsibility of schools to provide information about reproduction and gender differences? If you think it is not, how would you handle such comments as, "What happened to her wee-wee—did they cut it off?" or (from a little boy), "When I grow up, I'm gonna have six children! There won't hardly be room in my stomach I'm gonna have so many!"

Self-Check Questions for Review

Content-Related Questions

1. When incorporating multicultural and nonsexist goals into the curriculum, what are the two fundamental principles we want children to learn?
2. Are preschool children too young to notice ethnic and gender differences? Cite some examples that support the accuracy of your answer.
3. Name five things you as an individual can do to control your own prejudices.
4. Are children's books about various ethnic groups increasing in quantity?
5. Are books representing sex role stereotypes increasing in quantity?
6. Provide several examples of ways multicultural experiences could be consistently included in an early childhood curriculum.
7. Provide several examples of ways nonsexist experiences could be consistently included in an early childhood curriculum.
8. Why is encouraging pride in sexuality an important part of nonsexist education?

Integrative Questions

1. Could some of Clark's (1963) mental hygiene rules for overcoming prejudice apply also to sexism? Which ones apply most directly in your opinion? Can you produce examples of sexism being expressed at the college level? At the preschool level?
2. Discuss the following quotation from William Blake's poem "The Little Black Boy" (1789/1978). Does this verse contain racist implications? Antiprejudice implications? If so, what are they?

My mother bore me in the Southern wild,
And I am black, but oh my soul is white.

White as an angel is the English child.
But I am black, as if bereft of light.

And how would you interpret these final verses of the same poem?

. . . And thus I say to little English boy:
When I from dark and he from white cloud free,
And round the tent of God like lambs we joy:
I'll shade him from the heat till he can bear
To lean in joy upon our father's knee
And then I'll stand and stroke his silver hair
And be like him and he will then love me.

3. Research shows that teachers interrupt girls more frequently than they do boys. How do you think this behavior might influence girls' concepts of their sex roles? How might the boys' sex role concepts also be influenced?
4. List some principles that cross-cultural and nonsexist education have in common.
5. A West African proverb says, "A log that lies in the river a long time does not become a crocodile." Do you think this proverb applies to cross-cultural education? If so, how?

Coordinating Videotape

Respecting diversity. Tape #10. *The whole child: A caregiver's guide to the first five years.* The Annenberg/CPB Collection, P.O. Box 2345, South Burlington, VT 05407–2345. *Respecting Diversity* examines how prejudice develops in both children and adults. It promotes the principle of equity in dealing with children and shows how to recognize and respect cultural differences, deal with racial insults at the preschool level, and honor both the similarities and uniqueness of individuals.

References for Further Reading

Note: Material on helping everyone overcome possible negative feelings toward individuals with disabilities is covered in chapter 9, "Welcoming Children Who May Have Special Educational Requirements Into the Life of the School."

Pick of the Litter

Lee, E., Menkart, D., & Okazawa-Rey, M. (Eds.). (1998). *Beyond heroes and holidays: A practical guide to K–12 anti-racist, multicultural education, and staff development.* Washington, DC: Network of Educators on the Americas. A rich assortment of articles about almost every aspect of racism and multicultural learning is included here. *Highly recommended.*

Overviews

Derman-Sparks, L. (1995). Children and diversity. *Scholastic Early Childhood Today, 10*(3), 42–45. The author reviews developmental stages of learning about racial identity and disabilities, providing examples of antibias activities to clarify intellectual misunderstandings that accompany those stages.

Derman-Sparks, L., & ABC Task Force. (1989). *Antibias curriculum: Tools for empowering young children.* Washington, DC: National Association for the Education of Young Children. This landmark book explains in practical terms how the anti-bias approach can be integrated into the early childhood curriculum. *Highly recommended.*

Head Start Bureau. (1992). *Multicultural principles for Head Start programs.* Washington, DC: U.S. Department of Health and Human Services. Title is self explanatory.

Marshall, N. L., Robeson, W. W., & Keefe, N. (1999). Gender equity in early childhood education. *Young Children, 54*(4), 9–13. The authors present what amounts to an Equity Bill of Rights to be observed in early childhood classrooms.

Shade, B. J., Kelly, C., & Oberg, M. (1997). *Creating culturally responsive classrooms.* Washington, DC: American Psychological Association. This outstanding publication discusses the impact of culture and variations in points of view of Mexican, Asian, African, and Native Americans. Although the classroom examples are from elementary schools, they are very interesting because they show how learning styles for different ethnic groups can be incorporated into classroom life. *Highly recommended.*

Wellhousen, K. (1996). Do's and don'ts for eliminating hidden bias. *Childhood Education, 73*(1), 36–39. Although this article focuses on reducing gender bias, it applies equally well to eliminating other forms of prejudice. *Highly recommended.*

York, S. (1992). *Roots and wings: Affirming culture in early childhood programs.* St. Paul, MN: Redleaf. This truly useful book includes discussions of what might generate prejudice, suggests age-appropriate activities, and includes an exceptional chapter illustrating how cultural standards are expressed in the child's experience, coupled with suggestions of ways to increase the comfort level between school and home points of view. *Highly recommended.*

Culture-Specific Information

Note: Information about bilingualism is included in chapter 16, "Fostering the Development of Language Skills."

Child Care Information Exchange. (1998a). Supporting multiracial children and families. *The Exchange, #122,* 53–62. This special focus section of *Child Care Information Exchange* presents several brief articles written by parents and/or children from biracial families. Most helpful is a list of recommendations for providing a healthy emotional environment for interracial children.

Mindel, C. H., Habenstein, R. W., & Wright, R. (Eds.). (1988). *Ethnic families in America: Patterns and variations.* Upper Saddle River, NJ: Prentice-Hall. For readers who wish to substitute accurate information about cultures in place of stereotypes, this collection of information about a wide variety of ethnic groups will be helpful. *Highly recommended.*

Education About Sexuality

Leight, L. (1988). *Raising sexually healthy children: A loving guide for parents, teachers, and caregivers.* New York: Avon. In this simply written book Leight presents a sensible discussion of developmentally appropriate approaches to sex education.

Lively, V., & Lively, E. (1991). *Sexual development of young children.* Albany, NY: Delmar. As the title implies, this book focuses on children up to age 8. It uses vignettes to introduce discussion of a wide array of sexual topics ranging from normal development to abuse and the impact of AIDS.

Coping with Puzzling Sexual Behavior by Children

Essa, E. L., & Murray, C. I. (1999). Sexual play: When should you be concerned? *Childhood Education, 75*(4), 231–234. Down-to-earth advice about potentially disturbing behavior is provided here.

Rothbaum, F., Grauer, A., & Rubin, D. J. (1997). Becoming sexual: Differences between child and adult sexuality. *Young Children, 52*(6), 22–30. This article cites actual comments and actions by young children that often nonplus adults. It includes sensible suggestions and is *highly recommended*.

Examples of Multicultural and Nonsexist Curriculum

Note: Some wonderful books of ethnic recipes are listed in chapter 4, "Handling Daily Routines."

Bisson, J. (1997). *Celebrate! An anti-bias guide to enjoying holidays in early childhood programs.* St. Paul, MN: Redleaf. Developmental suitability, purpose, diversity, and even meeting the needs of families who do not celebrate holidays are covered here.

Crawford, S. H. (1996). *Beyond dolls & guns: 101 ways to help children avoid gender bias.* Portsmouth, NH: Heinemann. Crawford includes up-to-date information on gender stereotypes and behavior, as well as suggesting many antibias, nonbias activities. Of particular note is a list of 15 ways to test for sexism. *Highly recommended.*

Schlank, C. H., & Metzger, B. (1997). *Together and equal: Fostering cooperative play and promoting gender equity in early childhood programs.* Boston: Allyn & Bacon. The authors begin by analyzing possible reader attitudes toward gender roles and next contribute a thorough discussion of activities and plans for creating gender equity environment. *Highly recommended.*

York, S. (1998). *Big as life: The everyday inclusive curriculum* (Vols. 1 & 2). St. Paul, MN: Redleaf. York takes various topics such as the more usual "bodies" and "feelings" and the more unusual ones like "money" and "work" and provides almost endless ideas of how each can be included in every aspect of the curriculum. What makes these books outstanding is the consistent inclusion of "affirming ourselves and one another" suggestions that touch on human rights, bias, diversity, and so forth in generally age-appropriate ways. *Highly recommended.*

Multicultural, Nonsexist Literature

Beaty, J. J. (1997). *Building bridges with multicultural picture books for children 3 to 5.* Upper Saddle River, NJ: Merrill/Prentice Hall. This volume presents multicultural books according to topics and shows how to integrate them into broader curriculum plans.

Isom, B. A., & Casteel, C. P. (1997/98). Hispanic literature: A fiesta for literacy instruction. *Childhood Education, 74*(2), 83–89. A bibliography of children's books follows this excellent discussion about presenting literature effectively.

Jalongo, M. R. (1997). Multicultural children's literature: Resources for teachers. *Early Childhood Education Journal, 25*(1), 51–51. Jalongo includes bibliographies of children's books and resources for presenting books effectively.

Kane/Miller Book Publishers. P.O. Box 8515, La Jolla, CA 92038. This publisher specializes in foreign children's books in English and in their native language, such as Spanish.

National Black Child Development Institute. (1995). *Young children and African American literature.* Washington, DC: National Association for the Education of Young Children. Title is self-explanatory.

Renck, M. A. (1997). Many people, many places, other times: An annotated bibliography of multicultural books for 3- to 8-year-olds. *Early Childhood Education Journal, 25*(1), 45–50. Title is largely self-explanatory, but of special note is the inclusion of books about Indian children.

Schlank, C. H., & Metzger, B. (1997). *Together and equal: Fostering cooperative play and promoting gender equity in early childhood programs.* Boston: Allyn & Bacon. Previously reviewed above, *Together and Equal* offers an exceptional list of annotated books related to the subject of equity—includes but is not limited to nonsexist books.

Tomlinson, C. M. (Ed.). (1998). *Children's books from other countries.* New York: Scarecrow Press. Books are categorized according to realistic, fantasy, or informational and according to appropriate age and country of origin. All books are in English.

For the Advanced Student

Boyd, A. (1999). *Guide to multicultural resources 1977–1998.* Atkinson, WI: Highsmith Press. This invaluable resource (which I'm told will be revised regularly) includes information on the major ethnic/cultural groups in the United States other than Anglo. For example, information on Hispanics includes demographics, festivals, associations, relevant colleges, radio stations, good videos about the culture, social service organizations, and more! *An indispensable resource.*

Coltrane, S. (1998). *Gender and families.* Thousand Oaks, CA: Pine Forge Press. Coltrane provides a review of current research and theory about how children are socialized into male/female roles.

Derman-Sparks, L., & Phillips, C. B. (1997). *Teaching/learning anti-racism: A developmental approach.* New York: Teachers College Press. The opening chapters present clear explanations of what racism is. This is followed by a description of a college-level course intended to broaden perspectives on intercultural, anti-racist understanding.

Johnson-Powell, G., & Yamamoto, J. (Eds.). (1997). *Transcultural child development: Psychological assessment and treatment.* New York: Wiley. Although the emphasis here is on psychological development and possible emotional difficulties, which conveys a somewhat negative tone to the book, it actually includes a great deal of additional information about a wide assortment of cultures, such as Hmong, Micronesians, African Americans, and Russian immigrants. The "problems" discussed are also helpful since they sensitize the reader to places where painful "glitches" may occur when one culture rubs against another.

King, J. R. (1998). *Uncommon caring: Learning from men who teach young children.* New York: Teachers College Press. The author reports a series of interviews of men actually teaching in the early primary grades and how they see their role and difficulties in that setting.

Leonhard, G. J. (Ed.). (1999). *The Asian Pacific American heritage: A companion to literature and arts.* New York: Garland. The wide variety of topics included here have one thing in common: They all focus on some aspect of life related to a specific Asian culture. All are interestingly written. *Highly recommended.*

Nakayama, T. K., & Martin, J. N. (Eds.). (1999). *Whiteness: The communication of social identity.* Thousand Oaks, CA: Sage. The increasing number of books on "whiteness" provide an interesting opportunity to consider race from a currently developing point of view. As one of the authors included states, "As in other Western nations, white children born in the United States inherit the moral predicament of living in a white supremacist society" (Marty, p. 51). Food for thought!

National Association for the Education of Young Children (NAEYC). (1995). *National Association for the Education of Young Children position statement: Responding to linguistic and cultural diversity: Recommendations for effective early childhood education.* Washington, DC: Author. The title is self-explanatory.

Phillips, C. B. (1998). Preparing teachers to use their voices for change. *Young Children, 53*(3), 55–60. Phillips emphasizes that teachers must start with examining and understanding their own possibly racist attitudes as they strive to present more emotionally wholesome environments for all children.

Quisenberry, M. L., & McIntyre, D. J. (Eds.). (1999). *Educators healing racism.* Reston, VA: Association of Teacher Educators. Various authors are explicit in their discussions of racism as it exists in U.S. schools and offer suggestions of what to do about it—basically, "We have met the enemy and it is us." *Highly recommended.*

Ruble, D. N., & Martin, C. L. (1998). Gender development. In N. Eisenberg (Series Ed.) & W. Damon (Vol. Ed.), *Handbook of child psychology: Vol. 3. Social, emotional, and personality development* (5th ed.). New York: Wiley. This well-written review of research about gender development should not be missed by anyone seriously interested in the subject. *Highly recommended.*

Szinovacz, M. E. (Ed.). (1998). *Handbook on grandparenthood.* Westport, CT: Greenwood. For a change

of pace, this book approaches cultural characteristics by describing differences in attitudes of
Black, Hispanic, and Asian grandparents, how
they vary according to gender, and how they are
treated and are expected to treat grandchildren.

Weber, S., & Mitchell, D. (1995). *That's funny, you don't
look like a teacher: Interrogating images and identity
in identity in popular culture.* London: Falmer Press.
Talk about stereotypes! This book documents the
effects of culture on how we see the role of the
teacher—amusing, informative reading.

Woodhead, M., Faulkner, D., & Littleton, K. (Eds.).
(1998). *Cultural worlds of early childhood.* London:
Routledge. Recent criticisms of developmentally
appropriate practice as seeing diverse children
through too narrow a cultural frame has produced
this attempt to widen the frame through which
we view child development. *Interesting reading.*

part V

Enhancing Creativity

chapter fourteen
**Fostering Creativity by Means
of Self-Expressive Materials**

chapter fifteen
Fostering Creativity in Play

Fostering Creativity by Means of Self-Expressive Materials

What to reply when a child whines, "Draw me a horse"?

How on earth you can vary easel painting today?

How to explain to parents why your school doesn't send home paper plates with little faces glued on them?

. . . IF YOU HAVE, THE MATERIAL IN THE FOLLOWING PAGES WILL HELP YOU.

Whatever an education is, it should make you a unique individual, not a conformist; it should furnish you with an original spirit with which to tackle the big challenges; it should allow you to find values which will be your road map throughout life; it should make you spiritually rich, a person who loves whatever you are doing, wherever you are, whomever you are with.

Teresa Amabile (1987)

The mind is focused through the fingertips.

Walter Drew (1997, p. 7)

Early childhood teachers have long valued creativity and sought to enhance it by fostering self-expression in the young children in their care. In the past we teachers have been particularly successful in presenting expressive materials and activities such as paint, clay, and dance in a manner that fosters unique personal responses from the children. But today as the schools of Reggio Emilia remind us (Hendrick, 1997), we are coming to realize that artistic creativeness represents only one facet of creative endeavor and that additional aspects of creativity in play and in divergence and originality of thought should be encouraged more fully. For this reason the discussion of creativity in this book does not stop with the presentation of expressive materials, but rather extends the concept in two additional chapters: "Fostering Creativity in Play" (chapter 15) and "Developing Thinking and Reasoning Skills: Using the Emergent Approach to Foster Creativity in Thought" (chapter 18).

DEFINITION OF CREATIVITY

Defining *creativity* where young children are concerned is rather difficult because the commonly accepted definitions include the requirement not only that the idea or product be novel but also that it be related to reality and stand the test of being worthwhile (Tardiff & Sternberg, 1988). However, a definition by Armstrong (1997) suits our needs well, since it fits young children's creative abilities more aptly. He defines creativity as being the "ability to see things in new ways and to make unconventional connections" (p. 32).

This "ability to see things in new ways and make unconventional connections" is a good description of what we hope young children will be able to do when they use self-expressive materials, play imaginatively, solve problems, and generate new ideas. It stresses originality and does not emphasize the quality of evaluation, which is less applicable to very young children, although as we shall see in chapter 18, even they can be encouraged to try out and talk over ideas, thereby going through reality testing and evaluation in an informal way.

The reader should also understand that creativity is not limited to a few gifted Rembrandts and Einsteins, nor is it necessarily associated with high intelligence (Piirto, 1999). The work of Getzels and Jackson (1962), Wallach and Kogan (1965), and Ward (1968) has demonstrated that high scores on creativity tests do not correlate strongly with high scores on academic tests of achievement or with high scores on standard measures of intelligence. This is because tests for creativity and intelligence measure at least two different abilities: Creativity tests typically measure divergent thinking skills, whereas intelligence tests measure other abilities, among them vocabulary comprehension, spatial abilities, and general information. Another finding of interest comes from a study by Margolin (1968), which indicates that teachers who deliberately foster uniqueness and originality of response in creative activities can actually increase the variety and diversity of such responses in young children.

These findings imply that we do not have to wait for that specifically gifted child to come along in order for creative behavior to take place in our groups. The ability to generate original ideas and to produce satisfying, freshly conceived products resides in many children; and because such behavior can be increased by appropriate responses from the teacher, it is worthwhile to learn how to do this.

IMPORTANCE OF CREATIVITY

The experience of being involved in creative activity satisfies people in ways that nothing else can, and the ability to be creative appears not only to reflect but also to foster emotional health. The act of creation enhances the child's feelings of self-esteem and self-worth. (The reader can test the validity of this statement by recalling the last time he or she produced something original—perhaps something as simple as a Christmas decoration or as complex as a set of bookshelves—and then recall the feeling of well-being that rose up inside when it was accomplished.) Something about creating a unique product or idea leaves people feeling good about themselves.

Creative experiences provide unparalleled opportunities for expressing emotions and, by gaining relief and understanding through such expression, for coming to terms with them (M. Cox, 1997). Because they have this strong affective component, they provide a balance for the emphasis on intellectual development which may overwhelm the rest of the program unless it is carefully managed.

While providing that balance, such activities also foster cognitive growth by providing endless opportunities for trying out ideas and putting them into practice, for ensuring many alternative ways to solve problems, and for encouraging use of symbols in place of "real" objects to represent ideas and feelings (Lowenfeld & Brittain, 1987; Weisberg, 1988). Incidental learning inevitably results from such experiences, too: Clay changes its form when water is added; sand feels gritty between the toes; paint runs down the same way water does.

Finally, creative activities offer an excellent opportunity to individualize teaching. Materials and activities that depend on open-ended replies permit uniqueness and diversity to flourish and allow each child to be himself, rather than requiring him to conform to closed-system, authority-centered learning.

STAGES OF DEVELOPMENT

One peak period for creative self-expression in our culture occurs between the ages of 4 and 6 (Schirrmacher, 1998). This stage correlates well with Erikson's developmental stage for this age, which he identifies as the stage of *initiative versus guilt.* Erikson's (1963) stage is characterized by reaching out, exploring, and experimenting and reflects an increase in creative behavior that is partially characterized by this same kind of activity.

As is true in other areas, children pass through general stages of development in the use of creative materials (M. Cox, 1997; Jalongo & Stamp, 1997). First, *they explore the material itself* and investigate its properties. Two- and 3-year-olds, for instance, spend many satisfactory hours in what appears to be mainly manipulation and exploration of paints and brushes or in relishing the mixing of play dough, and they employ all their senses to do this. Who has not seen such a youngster meticulously painting his hands up to the elbow, or beheld another squeezing the sponge in the paint bucket, or a third looking thoughtfully into the distance as he licks the back of the play dough spoon?

Once the qualities of the material have been explored and some skill has been gained in its manipulation, the child is likely to move on to what is called the *nonrepresentational stage*. Paintings at this stage, for example, seem to have more design and intention behind them, but the content is not readily recognizable by anyone but the painter. Because painting at this stage is not always done with the intention of depicting something in particular, the teacher must beware of asking, "What is it?" lest such a question unintentionally put the child on a spot.

Ultimately the youngster reaches the pictorial or *representational stage*, in which he quite deliberately sets out to reproduce or create something. He may paint a picture of

(a)

(b)

Variations on a theme—experimentation is the key to learning.

himself, or the sun in the sky, or a fascinating event such as a toilet overflowing or children going trick-or-treating. As the youngsters of Reggio Emilia have so amply demonstrated, some children attain this stage of representational art in preschool, but most children develop this ability during their year in kindergarten.

Brittain (1979), in a much more detailed study, has described similar stages for the evolution of drawing from scribbling. What is particularly interesting about Brittain's work is the finding that representations of a man done by a particular child at a particular age were very similar, no matter which medium the child employed—drawing, collage, or clay.

Implications for Preprimary Teachers

One implication to be drawn from these sequential stages of development is that teachers should permit children countless opportunities to experience and explore expressive materials because this learning is fundamental to the creative experience. The full knowledge gained through such exploration extends the ways a child may use the material, thereby enriching his creative opportunities; and the freedom to explore is also likely to keep alive his interest and openness to the medium (Amabile, 1996).

The second developmental implication is that young children, when using expressive materials, should not be expected to produce a finished product. Some 4-year-olds will do this, of course, but because many will not, the expectation of some sort of recognizable result is not a reasonable creative goal to set for children in their early years.

GENERAL RECOMMENDATIONS ABOUT CREATIVITY

I hope the reader will apply the general comments made here about fostering the child's creativity with self-expressive materials to all three chapters on creativity.

Be Aware of the Value of Nonconforming Behavior and of "Unattractive" Personality Characteristics

Torrance (1962, 1987), a long-time champion of creativity, frequently emphasized that the kind of behavior teachers identify as desirable in children does not always coincide with characteristics associated with the creative personality. For instance, teachers who think they value uniqueness may find they do not like creative exploration as much as they thought they did when a youngster has spilled his milk because he tried holding the cup with his teeth.

Not only can this lack of conformity be inconvenient, but the teacher should also realize that some creative individuals possess character traits she may not care for. Torrance (1962) cites 84 characteristics that differentiate the more creative person from the less creative one. Some of the less attractive qualities are stubbornness, finding fault with things, appearing haughty and self-satisfied, and being discontented—qualities often disliked by teachers. Yet it is easy to see how stubbornness might be a valuable quality to possess when carrying through a new idea, or how finding fault and being discontented could result in questioning and analyzing a situation before coming up with suggestions for improving it. In all fairness, we must admit that we do not know at present whether some of these less attractive attitudes lie at the root of creativity or whether some of them are only the result of squelching and mishandling by teachers, peers, and families as the child matures. On a more positive note, Torrance also found that creative children possessed many likable qualities such as determination, curiosity, intuition, a willingness to take risks, a preference for complex ideas, and a sense of humor.

The purpose of pointing out these possible problems of living with creative children is not to discourage teachers from fostering such behavior, but to enlighten them so that they will not subtly reject or discourage creative responses because they fail to recognize the positive side of such apparently undesirable behavior. Ideally such understanding will result in increased acceptance and valuing of creative endeavor.

Acceptance is vitally important because it will encourage children to develop these abilities further and because it will help balance the rejection and isolation to which people who dare to be different are often subjected. As long as we have creative youngsters in our care, we must help guard against rejection by recognizing and supporting originality in thought and deed.

Cultivate Three Teaching Skills in Yourself

Each creative area requires a specific teaching skill for its facilitation. The cultivation of these skills is discussed at greater length in the appropriate chapter, but they are listed here to provide the reader with a quick overview.

In fostering creativity by means of expressive materials, the teacher should make ample materials freely available and encourage children to explore and use them as their impulses and feelings require. When seeking to facilitate play, the teacher needs to be able to move with the children's imaginative ideas and respond to them by providing materials and support that keep the play ongoing and creative. When developing original thinking and attendant problem solving, the teacher must reinforce the children's production of ideas by carefully observing and listening to them, recognizing the value of what they suggest, and asking questions that encourage the further development of their ideas.

Do Your Best to Maintain an Emotionally Healthy Climate

In the chapters on handling routines (chapter 4), mental health (chapter 6), and discipline (chapter 11), considerable time was spent discussing ways to keep the center environment reasonable, consistent, and secure so that children will feel emotionally at ease. Such a stable, predictable climate is valuable for many reasons, but one outstanding reason is that it forms a sound base for the generation of creative activity, which in turn contributes to the development of emotional health. Children who feel secure are more likely to venture forth, try new experiences, and express themselves in creative ways than are children who are using up their energy by worrying or being frightened or anxious.

In addition some research supports the idea that highly structured classrooms in which preschool children are continually the focus of adult control and adult-designated activities appear to reduce the amount of creativity (Hirsch-Pasek, Hyson, & Rescorla, 1990), imaginative play (Dacey & Lennon, 1998), and curiosity and inventiveness (L. B. Miller & Dyer, 1975). The use of structured play materials, such as puzzles and coloring books, has also been shown to reduce divergent, creative responses to problem solving (Pepler, 1986). These findings provide yet another reason why teachers who wish to foster these creative traits should ensure an open structure to the program that provides many opportunities for children to think for themselves and to make choices and decisions within reasonable limits.

Foster an Appreciation of Beauty

In these days of grotesque cartoons, garish advertising, and urban squalor to which so many children are exposed it is more important than ever to make certain that the *children's* center—their special place—does not reflect that ugliness (Jalongo & Stamp, 1997).

Sometimes teachers are so caught up in the functional aspects of room arrangement and curriculum development they forget that the preschool center has an important influence on developing the children's concepts of what is beautiful. When the room—which is really the children's home away from home—is accented with pretty curtains, colorful pillows, well-proportioned furniture, and tastefully arranged activity centers, it has a significant influence on forming the children's taste—their aesthetic appreciation.

Children's creations should be included, too, because they add so much verve, joy, and loveliness to the surroundings. As the teachers in the schools in Reggio Emilia remind us, the children's contributions need not be limited to paintings, collage, and so forth, although displays of these abound in Reggio. They encourage us to go beyond those displays and include other evidence of what the children are doing. These might include typescripts of dialogues, stories and ideas the children are having about their activities, models of what they are figuring out, and photographs documenting their progress as they pursue a topic of particular interest to them (Hendrick, 1997).

Another way to draw the children's attention to beauty is to include it regularly in small-group time. The simplest way to do this is to share and pass around some lovely (fairly durable) object. It could be a stone Inuit carving of a whale, or a reproduction of a Gainsborough painting featuring one of the little dogs he so loved to include, or even a wonderfully leafy head of lettuce. (Remember that the purpose of such sharing is not to talk about how round or green the lettuce is or how it tastes, but rather to discuss the wonderfulness of the lettuce for its own sake—the way the light shines through its leaves and the astonishing way the leaves fold in together.) When you think about it for a moment, all sorts of possibilities come to mind. Any of these examples or others like them could draw the children's attention to the beauty that surrounds us if only we take time to see it.

Still another way to foster the development of aesthetic appreciation is to ask the children what they think about an object or picture—what is their opinion? With increasing practice they will be able to go beyond just describing it (think how many times we ask children for the names of things!!) and say whether they "like" it or perhaps whether they don't! A good follow-up question to that is, "How come you like (dislike) it?" Perhaps the colors are pretty together, or it feels good when they hold it in their hands, or they like puppies. Any of these reasons requires them to think about the content and quality of what they are viewing and to evaluate it, which is, of course, the beginning of aesthetic appreciation.

USE OF SELF-EXPRESSIVE MATERIALS TO FOSTER THE CREATIVE SELF

Expressive materials include such diverse media as painting, collage, dough and clay, woodworking, sewing, and dance. Although the materials themselves are different, some basic principles apply to all of them. (Suggested guidelines for use of specific materials are included later in the chapter.)

Value of Using Free-Form Materials

The most valuable quality that expressive materials have in common is there is no right thing to do with them or one right way to use them; so in a real sense these materials are failure-proof for the child. As long as the child observes a few basic rules, such as keeping the sand down and seeing that the dough stays on the table and off the floor, there is no way he can make a mistake with them. For this reason alone such materials are an invaluable addition to the curriculum.

Expressive materials are indispensable for additional reasons. Psychologists and experienced teachers agree that these experiences provide many opportunities for children to express their feelings and come to terms with them (Seefeldt, 1987). It can be fascinating to watch the development of a shy child who may begin finger painting by using only the middle of his paper and then see him gradually come to fill his paper with rich colors and swooping strokes of joy as he gains confidence during his months at school. Because each child is free to do as he wishes, these materials also represent the ultimate in an individualized curriculum. The youngster can express who he is and what he is as something within urges him to do; he is able to suit the material to himself in an intensely personal way.

In addition many values associated with creative materials lie in the social, sensory, and intellectual spheres. Children who are working side by side often develop a spirit of camaraderie. As a matter of fact, research by Torrance (1988) found that 5-year-olds were most willing to risk attempting difficult new tasks when working in pairs.

Using creative materials provides numerous opportunities for rich sensory input: Dough feels sticky and then firm; finger painting feels cool, gushy, and slippery; dance makes the child aware of his body as he moves in response to the music. Finally the amount of factual information children acquire about the substances they are using contributes to their intellectual growth: Red and yellow mixed together create orange, some woods are easier to saw than others, two small blocks equal one large one.

Although these social, sensory, and intellectual learnings are worthwhile, I still regard them as being like the frosting on the cake. The primary values of using expressive materials remain in the affective sphere. Expressive materials are fundamentally useful because they foster creativity, build self-esteem, and provide a safe, failure-proof experience. Most important they can be the source of open-ended opportunities for the child to be himself and for him to express and work through his individual feelings and ideas.

PRACTICAL WAYS TO ENCOURAGE THE CREATIVE ASPECT OF SELF-EXPRESSIVE MATERIALS

Interfere as Little as Possible

As I mentioned earlier, the most significant skill the teacher can cultivate in presenting self-expressive materials is the ability to let the child explore them as his impulses and feelings require, intervening only when needed. Brittain (1979), who studied various kinds of teacher interventions under such circumstances, found that, on the one hand, the more instruction the teacher offered, the less involved the child was likely to be in the project. On the other hand, teachers who stayed entirely on the sidelines also had children stay and paint for shorter periods of time. The children who stayed longest and who were judged to be the most involved were those whose teachers "played the role of an interested adult . . . who gave support and intervened only when the child seemed hesitant about either his own powers or the next direction to take in the project" (p. 160).

This problem of when to intervene and when to abstain from interfering can be a delicate one with which to come to terms. In recent years, as I have observed and talked with the teachers in the schools of Reggio Emilia, I have been interested to see how much more assistance they provide the children than we American teachers do. For example, whereas I, as an American teacher, might provide a child a brace and bit or a formless lump of clay and encourage the child to discover on his own how to make the bit work or the clay stick together, the Reggio teacher would not hesitate to tell the child to lean hard on the bit to make it bite into the wood or show him how to dampen the edges of the clay so that they will stick together. Whereas we often hesitate to teach such specific techniques because we fear such interference will crush the children's creativity, the Italian teachers maintain that deliberately teaching specific skills empowers the children to express their ideas more fully.

So which is the ideal approach? Where do we draw the line between support and interference? The answer to this quandary about how much is too much is that there is a great deal of difference between helping a child learn how to drill a hole and telling him where to make it and what he should do with it. This is where the Reggio teachers have something useful to share with us: They may intervene in an activity by offering instructional support, but they would never dream of interfering with the child's attempts to express his own ideas.

Of course, allowing children to explore self-expressive materials as their impulses and feelings require does not mean that they should be permitted to experiment with scissors by cutting off the doll's hair or that they should be allowed to smear clay all over the school chairs to "get their feelings out." It is as true here as in other situations that the teacher does not allow children to damage property or to do things that may hurt themselves or others.

Although inexperienced teachers occasionally allow destruction in the name of freedom, experience has taught me that the reverse circumstance is more likely to occur. Many teachers unthinkingly limit and control the use of expressive materials more than is necessary. Thus they may refuse to permit a child to use the indoor blocks on the table "because we always use them on the floor," or they may insist he use only one paintbrush at a time despite the fact that using two at once makes such interesting lines and patterns. These ideas are essentially harmless ones and should be encouraged because of their originality.

Never Provide a Model for the Children to Copy

A copy is not an original. When I was a little girl in kindergarten, the "creative" experiences offered consisted mainly of making things just the way the teacher did. I particularly recall sewing around the edges of paper plates to make letter holders and cutting out paper flowers to glue on sticks. I suppose that what was creative about these activities was that we got to pick which flowers to cut out and, as I remember, we could choose any color of yarn to sew with. Whatever educational merit such activities posses, creativity is not among them. Yet some child care centers persist in offering such experiences in the name of creativity. If the teacher really wishes to foster originality and the child's self-expression rather than her own, she will avoid models and make-alike activities and merely set out the materials and let the children go to it themselves.

Sometimes a child will attempt to lure the teacher into drawing something for him to copy by pleading, "Draw me a house," or, "Draw me a man so I can color him." Rather than complying, the wise teacher meets this request by recognizing the child's deeper request, which is for a one-to-one relationship; so she meets this need by talking with him, meanwhile encouraging him to make the picture herself.

Understand and Respect the Child's Developmental Level

I discussed earlier the stages through which children's drawings pass as youngsters become more mature. I am including here a developmental chart (Table 14.1) calling attention to the usual age at which children are able to copy various shapes, because some teachers do not understand that the ability to do this rests at least in part on maturation and so struggle endlessly to teach children at too early an age to draw squares and triangles when everyone's energies could surely be better expended teaching and learning more important things.

Understand That the Process, Not the Product, Matters Most to the Young Child

We live in such a work-oriented, product-centered culture that sometimes we lose sight of the simple pleasure of doing something for its own sake. For young children, however, getting there is more than half the fun. They savor the process and live for the moment. Therefore it is important not to hurry them toward finishing something or to overstress the final result. They will love to take their creations home, of course, and all such items should be carefully labeled, at least occasionally dated, and put in the children's cubbies so that this is possible, but the primary emphasis should remain on doing.

Table 14.1
Drawing and writing movements

Age (in years, months)	Behavior
0.1–1	Accidental and imitative scribbling.
1–1.6	Refinement of scribbles, vertical and horizontal lines, multiple line drawing, scribblings over visual stimuli.
2–3	Multiple loop drawing, spiral, crude circles. Simple diagrams evolve from scribblings by the end of the second year.
3	Figure reproduction to visually presented figures, circles, and crosses.
4	Laboriously reproduces squares, may attempt triangles but with little success.
4.6–5	Forms appear in combinations of two or more. Crude pictures appear (house, human form, sun). Can draw fair squares, crude rectangles and good circles, but has difficulty with triangles and diamonds.
6–7	Ability to draw geometric figures matures. By seven, can draw good circles, squares, rectangles, triangles, and fair diamonds.

Source: From Perceptual-Motor Efficiency in Children: The Measurement and Improvement of Movement Attributes *(p. 85) by B. J. Cratty & M. M. Martin (1969). Philadelphia: Lea & Febiger, © 1969 by Lea & Febiger. Reprinted by permission.*

Allow Plenty of Time and Opportunity for the Child to Use Materials So That His Experience Is Truly Satisfying

In the discussion about sharing I made the point that it is important for each child to have enough of an experience to be truly satisfied before giving up the place to someone else. This is particularly true when using expressive materials. One painting or one collage is just not enough. Children need the chance to work themselves into the experience and to develop their feelings and ideas as they go along. For this reason it is important to schedule time periods that allow for many children to move in and out of the expressive experience as their needs dictate. For real satisfaction this opportunity needs to be available for 60 to 90 minutes at a time.

Learn How to Make Comments That Enhance the Child's Creative Productivity

Making effective comments as the child creates will encourage him to continue and to involve himself ever more deeply in the activity. But it can be risky, as well as embarrassing, to be trapped into commenting on what the child is making either by trying to guess what it is or by asking him to name it. As mentioned previously, children often do not deliberately set out to represent anything in particular, and even if they do intend a representation, it may defy recognition by anyone else. An additional drawback to requesting that creations be labeled is that it places emphasis on the product rather than on the creative, dynamic aspect of the experience.

It is more enhancing to comment on the pleasure the child is feeling as he works or to ask him whether he would like to tell you about it. "You're having such a good time doing that!" or, "My goodness, you've worked on that a long time! Would you like to tell me about it?" or, "Do you need some more of . . . ?" These remarks show him that you are interested in and care for him, but they avoid the taint of passing judgment on the quality of what he has made or of emphasizing that the end is better than the means (Schirrmacher, 1998).

Grant the Child Who Is Dubious the Right to Refuse

Children benefit from the opportunity to stand and watch before they plunge into an activity more vigorously. Three-year-olds do a lot of this standing around, but older children who are shy or new to school may behave this way, too. This is a valid way to learn, and the teacher should respect the child who copes with new experiences in this manner. Usually after a few days he will want to try whatever it is he has been watching so intently.

A few children are extraordinarily concerned about getting painty or sticky. These youngsters are usually reassured if the teacher talks with the mother in their hearing and asks the mother to tell them that using paint and glue is all right at school. It can also help if "clean" materials, such as soap painting or snow, are offered as beginning messy activities. It should be made clear to such youngsters that water is instantly available should they feel the need to wash their hands and that the aprons will protect them and their clothes from undue contamination.

Remember to Make Self-Expressive Opportunities Available for Children with Disabilities

One has only to peruse the majority of textbooks about early childhood special education to realize the subject of self-expressive materials is rarely touched upon, and yet children with disabilities enjoy and need them just as much as other children do. Indeed offering them the chance to participate in these kinds of activities is of particular value to such youngsters because it provides them the sometimes rare opportunity to take control and make independent choices about what they are doing.

Although space does not permit an extensive list of suggestions, here are a few possibilities worth considering. For children who are poorly coordinated or movement restricted it is relatively easy to include movement education activities scaled to their abilities. This might mean modifications in the height of equipment, provision of additional handholds, or inclusion of safety mats. Herman and Smith (1992) devote an entire book to explaining how typical preschool activities can be adapted for use by children with a wide array of disabilities, and Spodek and Saracho (1994) provide a long list of large muscle activities appropriate for children with varied physical challenges. Children who are vision impaired will do best with art materials if the table is well lit and the materials are clearly contrasting in tone and texture. Light tables are particularly nice to use with them. Clay and other sensorily appealing modeling materials are worthwhile to offer. Children who are hearing impaired can be stimulated to try out all sorts of self-expressive materials if they are encouraged to come and see what is available for their delight. Children who are cognitively delayed will enjoy the same materials set out for the children who are more intellectually developed but will use the materials at a more exploratory level. They will benefit from clear, simple instructions about whatever limits are necessary in relation to the activity.

Some Comments on the Overall Presentation and Quality of the Materials

It is important to provide enough of whatever the children are using. Nothing is sadder than children making do with skimpy little fistfuls of dough when they need large, satisfying mounds to punch and squeeze. The same thing holds true for collage materials, woodworking, and painting. Children need plenty of material to work with, as well as the chance to make as many things as they wish.

Providing enough material for the children means that teachers must develop their scrounging and pack rat instincts to the ultimate degree. They not only must ferret out sources of free materials but also must find time and energy to pick them up regularly and produce a place to store them until they are needed. Parents can be helpful in collecting materials if the teacher takes the time to show them examples of what she needs. Any community has many sources of such materials. (Appendix F is included to inspire the beginner.)

Variety in materials is also crucial. Creative activity should not be limited to easel painting and paper collage. The reader will find examples of variations suggested for each of the materials, but to be quite clear, I want to remind the reader there is a difference between the use of self-expressive materials and many craft-type projects advocated for preschool children, even when these materials do not require making something just like the model.

Sometimes teachers justify such craft-type activities on the grounds that they have to do this because the parents expect it, but I have never had a parent protest the looser, freer treasures their children have borne home once they understood our goals of preserving the creative, less directive approach. Day care centers are particularly likely to be seduced by more structured crafts because of the need to provide variety and stimulation for the children to sustain their interest. Unfortunately the emphasis with these items is usually on learning to follow directions and on how clever the teacher was to think of doing it. The attraction for the teacher of sheer novelty tends to obscure the tendency of such crafts to be inappropriate to the ages and skills of the children, to require excessive teacher direction and control, to fail to allow for adequate emotional self-expression, and to emphasize conformity rather than creativity.

It is difficult to see what real benefits children gain from string painting, for example. The string is dipped in paint and then placed between a folded piece of paper and pulled out. The results are accidental, and although the colors may be pretty, this activity is not likely to be satisfying to the child unless he manages to turn the process into finger painting—which frequent observation has proved to me to be the common outcome unless the teacher prevents it! Fortunately several very good references currently available list innumerable and appropriate ways to present basic materials that also keep in sight the fundamental values of self-expression (Bos, 1982; Chenfield, 1995; Kohl, 1989; N. R. Smith, Fucigna, Kennedy, & Lord, 1993; Wilmes & Wilmes, (n.d.).

Finally, creative materials that will be used together should be selected with an eye to beauty. For instance, rather than simply setting out a hodgepodge, the teacher should choose collage materials that contrast interestingly and attractively in texture and color. Pieces of orange onion bags could be offered along with bits of dark cork, white Styrofoam, beige burlap, and dry seed pods; a black or bright yellow mat would be a good choice as a collage base for these items. Finger paint that makes a beautiful third color should be selected. For example, magenta and yellow combine to form a gorgeous shade of orange, but purple and yellow turn out dull gray.

PRESENTATION OF SPECIFIC MATERIALS

I have selected only the more common materials for the discussion in the following pages, but the reader can find additional suggestions in the references at the end of this chapter. I hope these suggestions will not be followed as gospel, but rather will serve to inspire the teacher to develop and carry out her own and the children's creative ideas.

Easel Painting

Easel painting is perhaps the one form of artistic endeavor offered by all children's centers, and it is an outstanding example of a creative material that is intensely satisfying to young children. In the fall, particularly with younger children and with newcomers, it is wise to begin with the basic experience of a few colors, one size of paintbrush, and the standard, *large-sized* paper; but as the year progresses and the children's skills increase, many interesting variations and degrees of complexity can be offered that will sustain interest and enhance the experience of easel painting for the more sophisticated young artists.

When looking at paintings or other expressive products, one can be tempted to play psychologist and read various interpretations into the children's work. Although it is perfectly all right to encourage a child to tell you about what he has painted if he wishes to do so, the interpretation of children's painting should be left to experts. Correct interpretation depends on a knowledge of the order in which paintings were produced, knowledge of the availability of colors, access to the case history, and a complete record of comments made by the child while the work was in progress. In addition, young children often overpaint, restructuring paintings two or three times as they work; this increases the likelihood of misinterpretation. Since all this information is required for understanding, it is easy to see why even professional psychologists may differ considerably about interpretations of such material, and it makes sense that teachers who have only a modicum of training in such matters should be circumspect about ascribing psychological meanings to children's art.

Suggested Variations

Offer a wide variety of colors, and ask children to select those they prefer; use a different size or shape of paper or one with a different texture such as corrugated cardboard or "oatmeal" paper. You may want the children to experiment by learning how to mix a new color from the ones you have presented. Try using the same color paint on the same color paper or several shades of just one color. Different sizes of brushes or different kinds of bristles in the same color paint make a nice contrast. Thinner brushes encourage children to add more detail to their work. You might want to try painting to music, painting woodworking, painting the fence with water, using watercolors, having several children paint on one large sheet to make a mural, or painting on a flat surface instead of an easel. Printing and stamping, using paint and sponges, can also be an interesting although not extraordinarily successful experiment to try. Cookie cutters are really more effective to use for stamping than sponges are. For further variations see Wilmes & Wilmes, 1997.

Finger Painting

Finger painting is one of the most tension-relieving and delicious creative experiences available. The brilliance of the colors and the general gushiness that characterizes successful participation make it both appealing and relaxing. It is particularly valuable because it is so messy, beautiful, and free and because it is a direct sensory experience for the children. It should be offered several times a week.

Joe has a wonderful ability to let himself experience paint fully.

Suggested Variations

Children may paint directly on the table, using a whipped soap mixture, either white or tinted with food coloring. Ivory Snow is most useful for this purpose. Remember that the children will enjoy helping beat this up. (Adding some vinegar to the wash water will make cleanup easier.) They may also finger paint directly on the table and take prints of their painting by pressing a piece of newsprint down on it. These prints are often stunning. Shaving cream offers another attractive way to vary finger painting. Painting can be done on textured papers, or different recipes can be used for variation in texture. Using cooked laundry starch or cornstarch in place of the liquid variety is always interesting because different thicknesses can be concocted, and it is also more economical.

Cornstarch Finger Paint

Dissolve ½ cup cornstarch in 1 cup of cold water and pour mixture into 3 cups boiling water, stir constantly until shiny and translucent. Allow to cool and use as a finger paint base, or ladle into jars and stir in tempera or food coloring.

If a thicker mixture is desired, be sure to add glycerin to reduce stickiness. Adding a little glycerin or talcum powder makes painting particularly slick. Scents such as oil of cloves may be used to add fragrance. Starch bases can be refrigerated and then offered as a contrast to warmed starch—perhaps one kind for each hand.

Collage and Assemblage

Collage is particularly useful because it fosters an appreciation of the ways different materials look when they are arranged together, thereby emphasizing the elements of design and composition. If collage is offered as recommended below, it also provides opportunities for deliberating over selections and making choices and provides many exposures to a wide variety of materials such as cotton balls, shells, and wood shavings. Also included might be bright bits of ribbon and yarn, coarse netting, sponge, aluminum foil, corks, and packing materials. Collage or assemblage lends itself nicely to carrying out nursery school themes or other matters of interest to the children. Using natural materials in this kind of work adds potential beauty and interest to the activity. For example, shells, seaweed, and sand are nice to use as collage ingredients after a trip to the beach. The teacher should remember that the intent is not to have the child make a picture of where he has been or to copy what the teacher has made, but rather to encourage the appreciation of contrast in texture and color and to foster pleasure in creating a design based on these differences.

Suggested Variations

Almost anything can be used as collage material, and it is pitiful to limit it to cutouts from magazines. This is one area in which good scroungers are in their element. Carpet scraps, pumpkin seeds, buttons, fur, and textured papers are all attractive ingredients. *Because food is so short in the world, our center no longer uses such items as macaroni, peas, and rice as collage materials.* The experience can be varied by using different mats and bases: Large pieces of old bark, heavy cardboard, or pieces of wood too hard to saw make interesting foundations. Food coloring can be used to tint the glue, or tempera can be added if a stronger, brighter colored glue base is desired. The variety can be endless and the satisfaction great (Honigman & Bhavnagri, 1998)!

An excellent way to recycle cardboard containers involves gluing boxes and cartons together to create interesting structures. These are particularly appealing if a mixture of cylinders and rectangular shapes is provided. The label advertisements add color and appeal, and children love painting over these once the glue has dried.

Dough and Clay

Dough and clay are alike because they both offer opportunities to be creative while using a three-dimensional medium. They also provide particularly satisfying opportunities to release aggression harmlessly by hitting, punching, and squeezing. In addition, these materials allow the child to enjoy smearing and general messiness, activities that many psychologists value because they believe it provides a sublimated substitute for handling feces. (Whether or not the readers agree with this theory or are repelled by it, they will certainly find, if they listen, that children often do talk with relish of "pooh-pooh" while they work with this kind of material.) For all these reasons, *dough and clay should usually be presented without cookie cutters, rolling pins, or other clutter* because these accessories detract from the more desirable virtues of thumping and whacking, as well as from making original creations.

Besides these general benefits, mixing dough helps the child learn about the transformation of materials and changes in texture. It also provides opportunities to learn facts about measuring and blending.

It is interesting to note that research has identified developmental stages in the use of clay just as such stages have been found in the use of other materials. Brittain (1979) comments that 2-year-olds beat, pull, and mush clay, whereas 3-year-olds form it into balls and roll it into snakes. Shotwell and colleagues (1979) identify the progression as moving from "product awareness" at 12 months to "elementary shaping" by age 3.

Suggested Variations

Allow the dough or clay objects made by the children to harden. Then paint and shellac the objects or dip painted clay objects into melted paraffin to give a "finish." *Occasionally* use dough and clay with accessories such as dull knives for smoothing or cookie cutters and rolling pins to alter form. Offer chilled dough as a contrast to the room temperature variety. Cookie and bread recipes are also dough experiences. Vary the dough experience by changing the recipe. The following are two of the best.[1]

Basic Play Dough

3 cups flour, ¼ cup salt, 6 tablespoons oil, enough dry tempera to color it, and about ¾ to 1 cup water. Encourage children to measure amounts of salt and flour and mix them together with the dry tempera. Add tempera before adding water. If using food coloring, mix a 3-ounce bottle with the water before combining it with the salt and flour. Combine oil with ¾ cup water and add to dry ingredients. Mix with fingers, adding as much water as necessary to make a workable but not sticky dough.

---

[1] *Both are from Hendrick (1998).*

Many basic recipes do not include oil, but using it makes dough softer and more pliable. It also makes it slightly greasy, and this helps protect skin from the effects of the salt. Dry tempera gives the brightest colors, but food coloring may be used instead if desired. Advantages of this recipe are that it can be totally made by the children because it requires no cooking, and that it is made from inexpensive ingredients usually on hand. This dough stores in the refrigerator fairly well. It gets sticky, but this can be corrected by adding more flour. This is a good, standard, all-purpose, reusable dough.

The following dough is lighter and more plastic than the first one; it feels lovely. It thickens as boiling water is poured in and cools rapidly, so children can finish mixing. It keeps exceptionally well in the refrigerator; oil does not settle out, and it does not become sticky—a paragon among doughs! Beautiful to use at Christmas if colored with white tempera.

Basic Play Dough II

Combine 3 cups self-rising flour, 1 cup salt, 5 tablespoons alum (can be purchased at drug stores) and 1 tablespoon dry tempera. Boil 1 and ¾ cups water, add ⅓ cup oil to it, and pour over flour mixture, stirring rapidly. Use.

Woodworking

Woodworking is a challenging and satisfying experience that should be available to the children at least two or three times every week. It requires unceasing supervision from the teacher, not so much because of possible hammered fingers or minor cuts from the saw, but because an occasional child may impulsively throw a hammer and injure someone. Although rare, this can happen in the twinkling of an eye, and the teacher must be alert so that she steps in before this occurs. *Never leave a carpentry table unsupervised.* The teacher should alleviate frustration by assisting children who are having difficulty getting the nail started or the groove made for the saw.

It is essential that the school purchase good-quality tools for the children to use. Tinny little hammers and toy saws are worthless. Adult tools, such as short plumbers' saws, regular hammers (not tack hammers, because their heads are too small), and braces and bits can all be used satisfactorily by boys and girls. Two real vises that can be fastened securely at either end of the woodworking table are essential to hold wood while the children saw through it. A sturdy, indestructible table is a necessity. It is vital for the teacher to learn how to distinguish hard wood such as walnut from soft wood such as pine: Hard woods are too difficult for children to saw through, so are best used in glue-and-paint constructions rather than in carpentry per se. Safety glasses are an additional necessary precaution.

One of woodworking's best qualities is the opportunity it offers for doing real work. Children can assist in fixing things while using tools or can make a variety of simple items *they have thought up.* These often include airplanes, boats, or just pieces of wood hammered together.

I particularly like offering carpentry because it is so easy to increase the challenge and difficulty of the experience as the year moves along. Children can begin with simple hammering, go on to using the saw, and finally enjoy the brace and bit. During the year they

This example of emergent curriculum developed in the space of just one morning at Starr King Parent/Child Workshop in Santa Barbara— It's a nice illustration of what can happen when adults work with children to implement a creative idea together.

When a parent arrived unexpectedly with a wealth of balloons, Hanne Sonquist's provocative question to the children was:

"Whatever shall we do with them?"

Hanne anticipated the children might want to play "Birthday Party" or have some kind of movement experience with the balloons— but the children's unexpected proposal was that they make the balloons into a balloon tree to take the place of a wonderful old tree destroyed by the recent flood.

Then the question was, "But how can we stand it up?"

That provocation was followed by, "How can we explain to other people why we needed the balloon tree? How will they know what happened to the old one?"

"This is a picture of how hard it rained," said Annie.

Another virtue of this emergent project was that it fostered discussion and cooperation among the children in order to get the signs up just right!

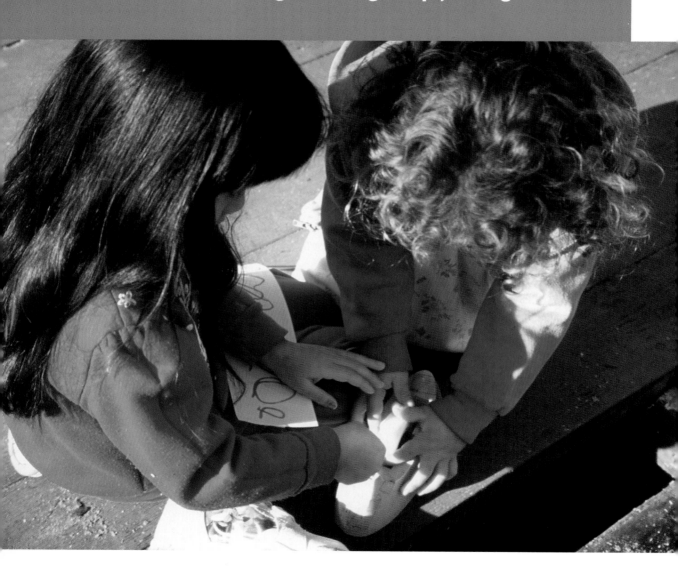

"Now everyone will know it," said the children.

And the interest and satisfaction continued the rest of the morning, including much discussion recalling what had become of the old tree and how the children had concocted a temporary replacement in its honor and memory.

can learn many kinds of tool-related skills and how to select the right tool for the right job. Carpentry is also an excellent way to develop eye-hand coordination. (But beware of the canny youngster who says, "Now, you hold the nail while I hit it!")

Finally, woodworking is a splendid way to harness intense energy and to sublimate anger. Hammering and sawing in particular are effective relievers of feelings.

Suggested Variations

Allow the children to take apart the brace and bit and the vise to find out how they work. Have various-sized bits available for making different-sized holes, and purchase dowels that will fit these holes when the wood is cut into pieces. Furnish different accessories for variety: Bottle caps, film-container lids, and jar lids make good wheels or decorations. String or roving cotton twisted among the nails is interesting. Unusual wood scraps that come from cabinet shops are nice. Wood gluing in place of nailing appeals to some youngsters and is a quicker form of wood construction. Many children enjoy going on to paint whatever they have made; this works well if it is done under another teacher's supervision at a separate table. Children will enjoy using a wide array of nails, ranging from flat, broad-headed roofing nails to tiny finishing nails, which for some reason they often like to hammer in all around the edges of boards. Sandpaper is occasionally interesting, particularly if several grades of it are available for comparison. An occasional child will also enjoy measuring and sawing to fit, although this activity is more typical of older children. Very young children will do best if soft plasterboard or even large pieces of Styrofoam packing are offered rather than wood (Andrews, 1999).

Dance and Creative Movement

Dancing has great potential for self-expression because it stimulates the child's imagination and offers many opportunities for emotional release. Moving to music can involve the child's entire body and draw satisfying expressions of emotion and pleasure from him that other creative experiences cannot tap.

There seem to be two extremes in presenting dance experiences that are not creative. At one extreme the teacher conceives the dance entirely beforehand and then puts the children through the paces. Folk dances, though desirable for cultural and ethnic reasons, are examples. This is simply providing a model for the children to copy. At the other extreme the teacher puts on some music and sits passively by while expecting the children to generate the entire experience for themselves. Children usually require more stimulation than this from the teacher to get a dance experience going. Beginning teachers often feel self-conscious about participating, but dancing with the children is essential for success. Taking a couple of modern dance classes in college frequently helps students feel more at ease with this medium.

It is helpful to have in mind a general plan that contains ideas about ways to begin and things to try that will vary the activity. Having in mind more activities than you can possibly use generates confidence, too. Also remember to use the children's suggestions and ideas whenever feasible. Be sure to mix quiet and more vigorous movement activities together to keep the situation pleasurable but not wild.

Following the children's suggestions encourages them to be more creative.

Suggested Variations

Accessories add a great deal to dancing and are helpful materials to use to get dance started. Scarves, long streamers, and balloons help focus the child's awareness away from himself and so reduce his self-consciousness at the beginning. Ethnic dance materials offer a rich resource for dance. Folk dance records and other rhythmic songs and melodies are delightful resources on which to draw. Current popular music is most likely of all to draw the children into movement. Using percussion instruments can also vary the experience. Dancing outdoors often attracts children who shun this activity in a more enclosed setting. Remember to include dance activities that appeal to boys as well as to girls. Moving like submarines, airplanes, seals, or bears helps take the stigma out of dance for boys, who may have already decided dancing is "sissy."

Using Rhythm Instruments

There are other ways to respond to music besides dancing, and participating with rhythm instruments is one of them. This activity is both somewhat creative and somewhat an exercise in conformity because children may respond imaginatively and individually with their instruments while doing something together at the same time. Participating in a musical experience basically will introduce children to the pleasures and delights of sound, rhythms, and melodies. If well handled, it should also teach children to care for instruments as objects of beauty and value and help them learn to listen to music and respond in a discriminating way.

Suggested Variations

Improvisations with musical instruments are a delight. Children can be encouraged to use them as the music makes them feel—to play soft or loud, fast or slow, together, or a few at a time. They can also make simple instruments of their own, such as sand blocks and shakers. Moving to music while using instruments (typically, marching) can also be a satisfying way of integrating this experience into a larger activity.

SUMMARY

Early childhood teachers have always valued the creative part of the child's self and have sought to enhance its development by fostering the use of self-expressive materials. Today we also seek to foster creativity in additional ways, which include generating creative play and encouraging originality of thought.

To accomplish these goals, teachers should cultivate three teaching skills in themselves: When presenting self-expressive materials, they must cultivate their ability to let children explore and use them as their impulses and feelings require. When seeking to facilitate play, they must learn to move with the children's imaginative ideas and support them. When working to develop originality in thought, they must be able to recognize the value of the children's ideas and to ask questions that will encourage further development of ideas.

Creativity is particularly valuable because it increases the child's feelings of self-esteem, facilitates self-expression and the expression of emotion, fosters an appreciation of beauty, provides a vital balance for the cognitive part of the program (while also promoting its growth), and helps teachers individualize their curriculum.

Teachers can foster creativity by understanding and accepting the creative child and by maintaining in their groups an environment that helps children feel secure so that they become willing to risk and venture. When presenting self-expressive materials for the children's use, teachers should avoid making models for them to copy, emphasize the process rather than the product, allow plenty of time and opportunity for the children to use the material, learn to make enhancing comments, and give reluctant children the right to refuse to participate. But the most important thing to do is to make the materials freely available and let the children explore them as their impulses and interests dictate.

Questions and Activities

1. If copying a model is really inhibiting to the development of creative self-expression, why do so many teachers persist in having children copy projects "just the way the teacher made it"?

2. Do you think of yourself as being artistic, or are you the sort of person who "can't even hold a paintbrush right-side up"? What attitudes in your previous teachers do you think contributed to your feelings of confidence or lack of confidence in this area?

3. *Predicament:* Irene is painting at the easel and gradually begins to spread paint off the paper onto the easel itself, then to paint her hands and arms up to the elbows, and then to flick drops of paint

onto a neighboring child and her painting. Should the teacher intervene and control any or all of this behavior, or should it be allowed to continue?

4. The variations of self-expressive activities listed at the end of each section represent only a few of numerous possibilities. What other activities have people in the class witnessed that could be added to these lists?

Self-Check Questions for Review
Content-Related Questions

1. Is it true that a person must be very intelligent to have creative ideas?
2. Identify several values the experience of creativity offers to the growing child.
3. List and define the stages children pass through when using a material that has creative potential.
4. Self-expressive materials are one avenue open to children for creative self-expression. What are the other two? What special skill is required of the teacher in relation to each of those avenues?
5. Discuss four or more practical suggestions for encouraging the creative use of the self-expressive materials introduced in the chapter.
6. Select one self-expressive material discussed in the chapter and pretend you are explaining to a newcomer how to present it effectively. What advice would you give her? Be sure to include suggestions for ways she could vary the experience.
7. Explain why it is valuable for children who have disabilities to participate in using self-expressive materials. Provide examples of ways materials might be adapted to make that participation more feasible.

Integrative Questions

1. A 4-year-old girl has just hammered together two pieces of wood and proudly announced she has made an airplane. In addition to noting the creative value of that experience, explain how woodworking might also benefit her physical, emotional, and cognitive selves. How might the experience also be used to benefit her social self?
2. It is the policy of some schools to allow each child to make just one painting or piece of wood gluing so that all the children have a chance to do the activity every time it is presented. What are the pros and cons of this approach in relation to fostering creativity?
3. The preschool teacher in the next room has had her 3-year-olds make caterpillars out of Styrofoam egg cartons and pipe cleaners. Each child was allowed to decide whether to use purple or red pipe cleaners for the legs and yellow or pink ones for the antennae. Her next project is showing the children how to glue artificial flowers onto pipe cleaner stems and stick them into balls of clay for Mother's Day. Evaluate these projects in terms of their potential creative benefit for the children. Be sure to explain why you think these projects would or would not enhance the children's creative selves.
4. Shana is a 4-year-old girl in your class who is new to school and is doing easel painting for the first time. She is distressed because the paint is runny and keeps dripping down the paper as she paints with it. Explain how an American preschool teacher devoted to the discovery approach might handle her predicament and compare it with the way a teacher from Reggio Emilia would be likely to handle it.

Coordinating Videotape

Creativity and play. Tape #11. The whole child: A caregiver's guide to the first five years. The Annenberg/CPB Collection, P.O. Box 2345, South Burlington, VT 05407–2345. *Creativity and Play* outlines the role of creativity in healthy child development by addressing its relationship to self-worth and self-expression. The program demonstrates how adults can encourage creativity with activities that promote self-expression. The value of play for healthy development is also emphasized.

References for Further Reading
Pick of the Litter

Ceppi, G., & Zini, M. (1998). *Children, spaces, relations: Metaproject for an environment for young children.* Reggio Emilia, Italy: Comune di Reggio Emilia/Ministero della Pubblica Istruzione. This book about school design as embodied by the Reggio philosophy is explained in essays and most enchantingly by a wealth of pictures. If only *all* children could learn in environments of such beauty! *Highly recommended.*

Overviews

Armstrong, T. (1997). Seeing things in new ways. *Scholastic Early Childhood Today, 11*(5), 32–35. Armstrong makes a persuasive case for the value of fostering creativity in the preschool classroom.

Chenfeld, M. B. (1995). *Creative activities for young children* (2nd ed.). Orlando, FL: Harcourt Brace. This is a very good book in which Chenfeld divides activities according to such topics as bodies and people we meet. She then suggests creative activities, including art, movement, and discussion activities, that could be related to the topic. Excellent bibliographies for children and adults complete each chapter.

Cox, M. (1997). *Drawings of people by the under-5's.* London: Falmer Press. Cox's book is replete with many, many examples of developmental stages. Of particular interest is her inclusion of a chapter of drawings by children with various disabilities.

Jalongo, M. R., & Stamp, L. N. (1997). *The arts in children's lives: Aesthetic education in early childhood.* Boston: Allyn & Bacon. This book covers the integration of various arts from birth through second grade—helpful to see the arts in relation to children's development in other areas.

Micklethwait, L. (1993). *A child's book of art: Great pictures with first words.* New York: Dorling Kindersly. In common with Montessori, I believe that one valuable approach to the arts is through aesthetic education, and this book is an excellent source of examples of fine art that appeal to young children. (My own grandchildren love this book!).

Schirrmacher, R. (1998). *Art and creative development for young children* (3rd ed.). Albany, NY: Delmar. Schirrmacher combines theoretical discussions with examples of developmentally appropriate self-expressive materials.

Interpreting the Reggio Approach in American Preschools

Dighe, J., Calomiris, Z., & Van Zutphen, C. (1998). Interpreting the Reggio approach in American preschools. *Young Children, 53*(1), 4–9. Inspired by a visit to Reggio Emilia, these teachers reveal ways they applied some of what they learned to their own teaching. *Highly recommended.*

Making Creative Experiences Available to Children with Disabilities

Herman, F., & Smith, J. C. (1992). *Creatability: Creative arts for preschool children with special needs.* Tucson, AZ: Communication Skill Builders. This book will be an inspiration to readers who have children with disabilities in their group. It is particularly strong in the chapters that provide general information about specific disabilities, followed by specific suggestions for how activities can be suitably adapted. I can't recommend this book highly enough.

Money Savers

MacDonald, S. (1996). *Squish, sort, paint & build: Over 200 easy learning center activities.* Beltsville, MD: Gryphon House. The strongest aspect of this book is the multitude of equipment and accessories teachers can make for almost no money which generate activities that provide variety and new experiences for the children—a superior example of creativity.

Information About Presenting Specific Self-Expressive Materials

Note: As I browsed through a considerable number of activity books that purported to present creative activities for children, I became increasingly depressed over the utter lack of creativity in evidence. Over and over these so-called creative activities were, in reality, tightly structured craft ideas that left almost nothing for the children to contribute in the way of their ideas or feelings. I encourage readers to look carefully at the values reflected in such activities before pawning them off on children as being creative. A handful of encouraging exceptions to this trend are listed below.

Andrews, T. (1999). Woodworking: Winning from the beginning. *Oklahoma Child Care, 1*, 28–33. The author includes very sound safety tips and discusses what children can learn while working with wood.

Gaines, L. (1998). Creative movement in the early childhood curriculum. *Scholastic Early Childhood Today, 12*(4), 45–47. Gaines provides practical suggestions about including creative movement ideas (not limited to dance) every day.

Honigman, J., & Bhavnagri, N. P. (1998). Painting with scissors: Art education beyond production. *Childhood Education, 74*(4), 205–212. Interesting ways to use and extend the concept of collage are included here.

Koster, J. B. (199). Clay for little fingers. *Young Children, 54*(2), 18–22. Everything the preschool teacher needs to know about presenting clay is included in these four pages.

Wilmes, L., & Wilmes, D. (1997). *Easel art.* Elgin, IL: Building Blocks. An almost infinite number of variations on painting are included by the authors.

For the Advanced Student

Amabile, T. M. (1996). *Creativity in context: Update to the social psychology of creativity.* Boulder, CO: Westview/HarperCollins. Written by one of the authorities in the field, this book endears itself by its own creative approach; namely, all the new research and ideas that have occurred since original publication in 1983 are identified by a special symbol. An indispensable reference that is *highly recommended.*

Csikszentmihalye, M. (1996). *Creativity: Flow and the psychology of discovery and invention.* New York: HarperCollins. This well-written book by an important theoretician uses examples of individual creative people to explain his concepts. The chapter "Enhancing Personal Creativity" is filled with sensible recommendations about how anyone can lead a more satisfying—ergo creative—life. *Highly recommended.*

Isenberg, J. P., & Jalongo, M. R. (1997). *Creative expression and play in early childhood* (2nd ed.). Upper Saddle River, NJ: Merrill/Prentice Hall. The authors present a lengthy, comprehensive discussion of the theoretical and practical aspects of creativity—best in the field.

Fostering Creativity in Play

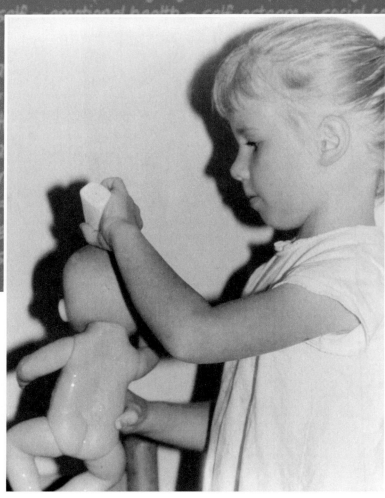

Whether play is as important as some people claim it is?

How to encourage play without dominating it?

Why some teachers think blocks are so important?

. . . IF YOU HAVE, THE MATERIAL IN THE FOLLOWING PAGES WILL HELP YOU.

Play is the purest, the most spiritual, product of man at this stage and is at once the prefiguration and imitation of the total human life—of the inner, secret, natural life in man and in all things. It produces, therefore, joy, freedom, satisfaction, repose within and without, and peace with the world. The springs of all good rest within it and go out from it.

Friedrich Froebel (1889, p. 25)

When the first edition of *The Whole Child* went to press in 1975, only a handful of citations was available concerned with research and the value of play. Twenty-five years later it is a happy fact that citations dealing with theory, research, and practice related to children's play abound (Fromberg & Bergen, 1998; Saracho & Spodek, 1998).

And yet, despite increasing evidence that play is the serious business of young children and that the opportunity to play freely is vital to their healthy development, early childhood teachers find that many administrators and parents continue to misunderstand and underestimate the importance of play in the lives of children.

It is difficult to say why some adults have undervalued play to such a degree. Perhaps it is a throwback to our Puritan ethic, which is suspicious of pleasure and self-enjoyment. Unfortunately as people advance through our educational system, they seem to conclude that any activity that generates delight must be viewed with suspicion: Learning can only be gained at the expense of suffering. But play is just the opposite of this. It is a pleasurable, absorbing activity indulged in for its own sake. The live-for-the-moment aspect of it, combined with the fact that play arises spontaneously from within the child and is not teacher determined, lends an air of frivolity to it that has led some work-oriented persons to assume it is not worthwhile.

Whatever the reason for that point of view, teachers of young children must be prepared all their lives to explain and defend the value of basing large parts of their curriculum on play. For this reason the following pages include an extensive analysis of the many contributions play makes to the development of the whole child.

PURPOSES OF PLAY

Before proceeding to an analysis of play's virtues, I want to point out that there is nothing wrong with providing consistent, lengthy opportunities for children to play together or by themselves simply because it is so satisfying and pleasurable to them. In a way it is a shame we must analyze and shred play's virtues to pieces to defend an activity that obviously has great intrinsic value for its participants. Yet it remains a fact that preprimary teachers must be forever prepared to defend and explain the worthwhile character of play to people who continue to attack it as being a trivial waste of time, time they contend would be better spent "really learning something."

Play Fosters Physical Development

Play fulfills a wide variety of purposes in the life of the child. On a very simple level it promotes the development of sensorimotor skills (Frost, 1992; Morrison, 1998). Children spend hours perfecting such abilities and increasing the level of difficulty to make the task ever more challenging. Anyone who has lived with a 1-year-old will recall the tireless persistence with which she pursues the acquisition of basic physical skills. In older children we often think of this repetitious physical activity as the central aspect of play because it is evident on playgrounds, where we see children swinging, climbing, or playing ball with fervor; but physical motor development actually represents only one purpose that play fulfills.

Play Fosters Intellectual Development

Both Piaget and Vygotsky assert that play is a major influence in cognitive growth (Saracho, 1998). Piaget (1962) maintains that imaginative, pretend play is one of the purest forms of symbolic thought available to the young child, and its use permits the child to assimilate reality in terms of her own interests and prior knowledge of the world. Vygotsky (1978) also extols the value of such fantasy play, arguing that during play children approach most closely the advanced edge of their zone of proximal development. Or to put it another way, Vygotsky believes that during episodes of fantasy, pretence play, when

This sand play illustrates a few of the many virtues associated with play: having creative ideas like using leaves for candles, playing cooperatively together, and an older youngster helping a younger child.

children are free to experiment, attempt, and try out possibilities, they are most able to reach a little above or beyond their usual level of abilities.

Another valuable aspect of pretend play, according to Vygotsky, is the opportunity it presents for children to self-regulate their behavior: Perhaps the child pretends to cry and then also pretends to stop crying, or agrees to accept a particular role in the play and then realizes she must remain in that role rather than assume another one "at whim" (Bedrova & Leong, 1998).

Play also offers opportunities for the child to acquire information that lays the foundation for additional learning. For example, through manipulating blocks she learns the concept of equivalence (two small blocks equal one larger one) (Jarrell, 1998). Through playing with water she acquires knowledge of volume, which leads ultimately to developing the concept of reversibility.

The pioneering work of Smilansky (1968) has offered additional support for the importance of play in relation to mental development. She points out that sociodramatic play develops the child's ability to abstract essential qualities of a social role and to generalize role concepts to a greater degree.

Saltz and Johnson (1977) found that 3-year-olds who received training in either thematic fantasy play or sociodramatic play performed significantly better on some tests of intellectual functioning than did children who only discussed fantasies (in this case, fairy tales) or who were not particularly encouraged to participate in fantasy or role playing.

Thus it is evident that imaginative, symbolic play contributes strongly to the child's intellectual development (Nourot, 1997). Indeed some investigators maintain that symbolic play is a necessary precursor of the development of language.

Language has been found to be stimulated when children engage in dramatic pretend play (C. Shore, 1998). Pellegrini (1986) found this to be particularly true in the housekeeping corner, where children tended to use more explicit, descriptive language in their play than they did when using blocks. For example, they used such phrases as "a very sick doll" or "a big, bad needle," in contrast with using "this," "that," and "those" when pointing to various blocks. (Could this be true because teachers do not teach children names for various sizes and shapes of blocks? We have no way of knowing.)

Research on the use of blocks as a means of representation (symbolization) further supports the value of play as an avenue for cognitive development (Jarrell, 1998; K. Weiss, 1997). Work by Reifel (1982), Reifel and Greenfield (1982), and Reifel and Yeatman (1991) demonstrating the developmental progression of complexity in symbolic play and by Goodson (1982) in her study of how children perceive the way models of blocks could be duplicated are only a sample of studies that show how play and thought are intertwined and illustrate the kinds of intellectual learnings that develop during children's play.

Indeed anytime children use one object to stand for or symbolize something else, be it blocks symbolizing a train track or a totally imaginary cup substituting for a real one, symbolic imagination is being used. This is a highly intellectual operation.

Play Enhances Social Development

One of the strongest benefits and satisfactions stemming from play is the way it enhances social development. Playful social interchange begins practically from the moment of birth, as the Research Study in this chapter demonstrates.

As children grow into toddlerhood and beyond, an even stronger social component becomes evident as more imaginative pretend play develops. Here again the methodological analysis provided by Smilansky and Shefatya (1990) is helpful. They speak of dramatic and sociodramatic play, differentiating between the two partially on the basis of the number of children involved in the activity. *Dramatic play* involves imitation and may be carried out alone, but the more advanced *sociodramatic play* entails verbal communication and interaction with two or more people, as well as imitative role playing, make-believe in regard to objects and actions and situations, and persistence in the play over a period of time.

Social play in particular has been found to be such a valuable avenue for learning that Rubin, who is conducting a rare, longitudinal study of the relationship of social play to later behavior, has concluded that "children who experience a consistent impoverished quality of social play and social interactions are at risk for later social maladjustment." (Coplan & Rubin, 1998, p. 374).

Sociodramatic play in particular also helps the child learn to put herself in another's place, thereby fostering the growth of empathy and consideration of others. It helps her define social roles: She learns by experiment what it is like to be the baby or the mother or the doctor or nurse. And it provides countless opportunities for acquiring social skills: how to enter a group and be accepted by them, how to balance power and bargain with other children so that everyone gets satisfaction from the play, and how to work out the social give-and-take that is the key to successful group interaction (G. Reynolds & Jones, 1997).

Play Contains Rich Emotional Values

The emotional value of play has been better accepted and understood than the intellectual or social value because therapists have long employed play as a medium for the expression and relief of feelings (Axline, 1969; Landreth & Homeyer, 1998). Children may be observed almost anyplace in the nursery center expressing their feelings about doctors by administering shots with relish or their jealousy of a new baby by walloping a doll, but play is not necessarily limited to the expression of negative feelings. The same doll that only a moment previously was being punished may next be seen being crooned to sleep in the rocking chair.

Omwake cites an additional emotional value of play (Moffitt & Omwake, n.d.). She points out that play offers "relief from the pressure to behave in unchildlike ways." In our society so much is expected of children and the emphasis on arranged learning can be so intense that play becomes indispensable as a balance to pressures to conform to adult standards that may otherwise become intolerable.

Finally play offers the child an opportunity to achieve mastery of her environment. When she plays, she is in command. She establishes the conditions of the experience by using her imagination, and she exercises her powers of choice and decision as the play progresses. The attendant opportunities for pretended and actual mastery foster the growth of ego strength in young children.

Play Develops the Creative Aspect of the Child's Personality

Play, which arises from within, expresses the child's personal, unique response to the environment. It is inherently a self-expressive activity that draws richly on the child's powers

physical self = emotional health = self-esteem = social competence

Research Study

Games Babies Play

Research Questions: As education coordinator for a Head Start program that was beginning a home-based parent education program for Chinese, Filipino, Mexican, and American mothers of European descent, Van Hoorn wanted to find out how to strengthen cultural understandings and links between the home visitors and the families they would be serving. To further that understanding and possibly have it serve as a starting point for home-visiting activities, she wanted to find answers to several questions about what mothers and babies play together. She asked the following research questions: What kinds of games do the mothers and babies play together? How do those games differ from culture to culture, and what, if anything, do they have in common? How do the games reflect the culture of the family?

Research Method: Information for the study was gathered in two ways. First, the interviewer made friends with the mother and asked her to describe the games she played with her baby. Then the interviewer asked the mother to show how she played the games with her child. The 152 interviews were conducted with mothers from four cultures: Chinese, Filipino, Mexican, and European-descent American. Assistants from the same culture as that of the mother were employed as interpreters when they were needed. Altogether the mothers demonstrated 450 games.

Chinese games included Count the Insects (pointing to body parts), a clapping game, a swinging game, and a rowing game in which mother and child row back and forth in synchrony. Filipino games included Open/Close Them, many variations on that theme, and tickling games. Mexican games were based on clapping, tickling, and rocking or swinging accompanied by rhymed verses. The most popular American games focused on disappearance and reappearance such as peeka-boo, followed by patty-cake (a clapping game).

Results and Conclusions: Van Hoorn concluded that in some ways "games do appear to reflect the specific culture. The most basic way . . . is

of imagination. Because imaginative play is also likely to contain elements of novelty, the creative aspect of this activity is readily apparent. As Nourot (1998) says, "The joyful engagement of children in social pretend play creates a kind of ecstasy that characterizes the creative process throughout life" (p. 383).

The freedom to experiment creatively with behavior in the low-risk situations typical of play is another virtue mentioned by Bruner (1974), who points out that play provides a situation in which the consequences of one's actions are minimized and there are many opportunities to try out combinations of behavior that under other circumstances could never be attempted. In addition, Sutton-Smith (1971) points out that play increases the child's repertoire of responses. Divergent thinking is characterized by the ability to produce more than one answer, and it is evident that play provides opportunities to develop alterna-

≈ physical self ≈ emotional health ≈ self-esteem ≈ social competence

that they transmit the language" (pp. 58–59). For example, she reported that most of the Chinese games involving words mentioned family relationships; many of the Filipino games were "didactic" and played in English—a fact the mothers ascribed to the influence of American missionaries; and several of the Mexican games reflected the hardships that pervaded their lives ("Tortillitas for Dad and Mom who are tired," "The carpenters of San Juan, they ask for bread and they don't give them any"). Although the Americans also used language in their games, they differed from the other groups by encouraging their babies to play more independently.

Besides these interesting differences, Van Hoorn found that the games had many elements in common no matter which culture she observed. Most games were traditional and had been handed down in families. These were action games based mainly on clapping, swinging, rocking, running, finger play, tickling, and appearance/disappearance. The games generally promoted the social values of mutuality, cooperation, and attachment, and mothers from various cultures signaled to babies that

this was play by smiling, exaggerating their facial expressions, and emphasizing rhythmic expression.

Implications: I know of no better example of research having to do with children that demonstrates so clearly the fact that people from a variety of cultures have some things in common and also differ in interesting ways. By identifying the elements held in common, this research holds out hope that it *is* possible to build bridges of understanding between people of differing backgrounds by using these commonalities as a foundation.

The study also demonstrates how valuable it is to make every effort to identify and understand what the differences are. This identification and appreciation of differences forms the rest of the foundation of understanding so indispensable when building bridges between cultures.

Source: From "Games That Babies and Mothers Play," by J. Van Hoorn. In P. Monighan-Nourot, B. J. Scales, and J. Van Hoorn (with M. Almy), 1987, Looking at Children's Play: A Bridge Between Theory and Practice. New York: Teachers College Press.

tive ways of reacting to similar situations. For example, when the children pretend that a fierce dog is breaking into their house, some may respond by screaming in mock terror, others by rushing to shut the door, and still others by attacking the "dog" or throwing water on it. The work of Lieberman (1968) provides added indications that playfulness and divergent thinking are related—although which comes first remains to be determined.

Another researcher interested in "pretend" play is Garvey (1977, 1979). She points out various ways children signal to each other that they are embarking on "pretend" play or have stopped pretending. These include *negation* (e.g., "Well, you're just Jon. You can't be a monster while we eat lunch"), *enactment of a role* (e.g., crying affectedly like a baby), or *stating the role or transformation that is taking place* (e.g., "This is the operating table—lie down, baby, so I can cut you up!").

Notice two things in this picture: For one thing, notice how cramped the play space is because the children started playing so close to the shelves; for another thing, notice how creatively stimulating it is when plentiful (yet relatively inexpensive) accessories are provided.

Conclusion

No matter what value the theoretician perceives in play, the fact remains that it is common to all cultures and that it is the lifeblood of childhood. Thus Russians may offer hollow blocks while reasoning that their size promotes cooperation, whereas Americans may offer the same hollow blocks on the grounds that their cumbersome qualities develop feelings of mastery. But the children continue to use blocks with satisfaction regardless of adult rationalizations, just as they continue to play house on the windswept tundras of the North and in the Wendy corners of the British Infant School.

DEVELOPMENTAL STAGES OF PLAY

As is true in so many other areas, children's play progresses through a series of stages. There are two widely accepted methods of classifying these developmental stages. A combination of the two is often used by researchers (Bergen, 1988; K. H. Rubin & Coplon, 1998) because the classifications concentrate on differing aspects of the activity.

"What was that you wanted, Dear?"

The first classification system used for identifying stages of play has its roots in Piaget (1962). In this theory, play is divided into stages according to the way children use play materials. Thus play begins at the *functional level* (simple, repetitive, exploratory activity—as simple as a baby playing with her toes or a 2-year-old squeezing dough through her fists). The second stage is *constructive play* (activity that has some purpose or goal, such as pouring water to fill a bucket), which develops into *dramatic play* (play involving pretend circumstances) and finally proceeds to the fourth stage, *games with rules*.

The two middle levels of play, constructive and dramatic (or fantasy) play, are of most interest to preschool teachers. According to Butler, Gotts, and Quisenberry (1978) constructive play is most frequently seen in children ages 2 to 4 years, and it is characterized by children learning the uses of simple or manageable play materials and then employing them to satisfy their own purposes. For example, a child might learn how to string beads and then make a necklace for herself. Dramatic play increases in frequency as children mature, and the golden age of sociodramatic role playing develops between ages 4 and 7, although we see the beginnings of this play in much younger children. At this level we see children assigning roles as varied as "teacher" or "baby" or "dog biter" to themselves and others around them.

The second commonly used system for identifying stages of play was developed by Parten (1932, 1933). It divides play according to the kind of social interaction that is taking place between children. In this system of classification play develops from *solitary* through *parallel play* (playing beside but not with another child); to *associative play* (playing together); and ultimately to *cooperative play* (playing together with role assigning and planning).

This division into steps is not a mutually exclusive one, however. For example, in an analysis of just one 30-minute observation of children at an easel, Reifel and Yeatman (1993) demonstrated that the children's play involved four levels or kinds of play (parallel, associative, cooperative, and pretend). While acknowledging that solitary play happens more frequently with younger children, research by Kenneth Rubin (1977) provides evidence of varying levels of sophistication in solitary play; that is, although some of that kind of play takes place at the functional level, some of it, as anyone who has watched a 4-year-old playing alone with a dollhouse can attest, uses a great deal of imaginative language, role assigning, and storytelling at a more mature, dramatic play level. Therefore the teacher should not assume that solitary play by older preschoolers is generally regressive and undesirable. It is particularly important to recognize the value of such individual playful preoccupation in day care centers, where children are almost relentlessly in contact with other people all day long. Children need the opportunities to think and develop their ideas through play by themselves, as well as while in the company of other children, and they need opportunities for privacy, too. Of course, if solitary play continues too long or is the only kind of play indulged in by a 4-year-old, it should be cause for concern (K. H. Rubin & Coplon, 1998), but some of this less social play is to be expected and even encouraged for most children attending preschool.

Parallel play also continues to have its uses even after group play has developed, and it is often used by 3-year-olds as an effective way to enter a group, the children first playing alongside and then with the group as they work their way into the stream of activities. Perhaps teachers could deliberately use this strategy with 3-year-olds, encouraging them to play beside the other youngsters as a stepping stone to more direct social encounters.

Educational Implications

Although preschool teachers are likely to see functional, constructive, and dramatic play, they will rarely come across the final Piagetian stage—games with rules—because this kind of play is the prerogative of older children. The child care center teacher should realize that organized, competitive games are developmentally inappropriate as well as uncreative for young children. Activities such as relay races, dodge ball, and kick the can are loved by second and third graders but do not belong in centers for younger children.

While hoping to foster originality and imagination in young children's play, we must realize that not every idea generated by the children will be new, no matter how supportive and encouraging the atmosphere of the school. Children's inspirations will be like flashes—touches here and there, embedded in a foundation of previously played activities. A lot of "old" will always be mixed in with a little "new."

Finally the teacher should be prepared for the somewhat chaotic quality of creative play because it is impossible to organize inspiration before it happens. But this chaos can be productive, and the teacher can maintain reasonable order by picking up unused materials and returning them to their place and by seeing that the play does not deteriorate into aimless running about.

FACTORS LIKELY TO FACILITATE CREATIVE PLAY

Avoid Dominating the Play

As is true with self-expressive materials, teachers should do their best to avoid dominating the play experience and seek instead to foster children's abilities to express themselves in their own unique ways. Such teachers help children base their play on their own inspirations because the teachers are convinced youngsters can be trusted to play productively without undue intervention and manipulation (G. Reynolds & Jones, 1997).

This freedom for children to generate their own ideas can be difficult for some teachers to allow, and the tension between enhancing self-expression and the temptation to use play to further adult goals is not new. As Nourot (1991) recognizes, "This paradox—balancing knowledge of the possibilities for learning inherent in play with total freedom for the child to play without adult intervention—plagued [even] the earliest early childhood educators" (p. 197). Indeed some teachers are so eager to use play as a medium for teaching that they cannot resist overmanipulating it in order to provide a "good learning experience." For example, I recently visited a teacher who had taken the children to the fire station for a visit. The next day, overwhelmed by the temptation to use play as an avenue for teaching, she set out all the hats, hoses, ladders, and pedal trucks she could muster, and as the children walked in the door, she pounced on them, announcing, "Boys and girls, I have the most wonderful idea. Remember when we went to the fire station yesterday? Well, why don't we play that here today? Jerry, you can be the chief. Now, who wants to hold the hose?"

Children may learn a good deal about fire engines this way, and if this is the real purpose, very well. However, the spontaneous, creative quality of the play will be greatly reduced by the teacher's using this approach. It is generally better to wait until the children express an interest and then to ask them how you can help and what they need.

However, there are some circumstances in which the teacher must assume a more direct, intervening role since, as mentioned earlier, some children come to the center with poorly developed play skills. This approach was first investigated by Smilansky (1968) when she examined differing methods teachers might use to stimulate increased sociodramatic play among children who came from families of the poor. In her more recent work, Smilansky has continued to be a strong advocate of deliberate intervention. In *Facilitating Play* (1990) Smilansky and Shefatya cite studies that indicate such intervention has produced rich dividends for these children, such as increased receptive and expressive language skills, higher intellectual competence, more innovation and imaginativeness, reduced aggression, better impulse control, and better emotional and social adjustment. Because of these benefits, sociodramatic, make-believe play should be included as a vital element in every preschool and kindergarten day, and during such play teachers should help the children gain social skills rather than focus on content or subject matter.

The problem with recommending consistent intervention in some children's play is that this can be tricky advice to give beginning teachers because many beginners have great difficulty maintaining the subtle blend of authority and playfulness required to sustain this role. Instead they either overmanage and overwhelm the children or reduce themselves to "being a pal"—approaches not at all what those authors had in mind. It is vital to remember that even when teaching children with special educational needs, *the purpose is not to dominate but to stimulate play.* The teacher should make interventions accordingly, stepping in only when necessary and withdrawing whenever possible. The following suggestions are intended to illustrate some effective ways of doing this.

SOME PRACTICAL WAYS TO STIMULATE AND EXTEND PLAY

I think about play as being like pulling taffy: The more it is stretched and extended, the better the result! To be most helpful to the children, it is important to pay attention to what they are playing and to think a little ahead of what is happening so that the teacher can encourage the play to continue *before* it languishes.

One way to do this is to ask the children what will happen next. For example, if they are playing "going to the market," the teacher might ask, "Now you've got all those big bags of groceries, I wonder how you're going to get them home?" or, "I see you've bought a lot of soup and crackers. Does your family have a pussycat, or an elephant? What do you suppose they'd like to eat?"

Suggesting additional roles for bystanders to fill can also extend play. Perhaps a child on the sidelines is yearning to join the others at the airplane/rocket site. A question such as, "Gee, how's that airplane going to fly without any gas?" [pause] "Perhaps Aahmed could use that hose and help you," or, "I see you all have such full grocery carts. Where could that checkout person be?"

It is also very important to provide enough time for play to develop (Christie & Wardle, 1992). When Johnsen and Peckover (1988) compared the kinds of play that took place among children during 15- and 30-minute play intervals, they found that the amount of group play, constructive play, and dramatic play increased substantially in the later portion of the 30-minute sessions. As they commented, it takes time for children to recruit other players, conceive and assign roles, and get the play under way. It seems to me that the play arena where this requirement of plenty of time is most apparent is the block corner, where construction requires much satisfying time before other sorts of playful interaction can begin.

And finally never forget the value of enriching and extending the play by the use of language—putting into words what the children are doing. Doing this while the play is going on, recapitulating it in large group, and recalling yesterday's or last week's play by means of pictures or discussion at the start of the next self-select period will delight the children, as well as increase their own ability to think about what they are doing or have accomplished already.

Make a Special Point of Including Children Who Have Disabilities in the Play

It can be an unfortunate fact that children who have various disabilities are often not included in the play of other children at school. This can be attributed to a variety of reasons including inexperience (on both sides), being at a different developmental level than other children are, or having limited communication skills because of restricted hearing abilities or vision problems. Then, too, sometimes these children have been overly sheltered from contact with other children or have spent an unusual amount of time in special education situations in which the emphasis has been on drill and practice, rather than in a more playful environment. Such youngsters in particular need the relief offered by play.

Whatever the reason for the limited participation, these children, like all other children, are entitled to and benefit from endless, rich opportunities to experience the joy of playful living. However, it may require more special attention from the teacher than is typically necessary to bring this about.

A variety of specific suggestions are incorporated throughout *The Whole Child* and more thoroughly in chapter 9, but a quick reminder is included here of a basic approach that will encourage play to develop. Remember to explain in matter-of-fact terms to the other children the nature of the child's disability and to suggest some appropriate ways they could include the youngster in the activity. Be careful always to include activities in the curriculum plan at which you know the child with the disability can be successful. (Linder's *Transdisciplinary Play-Based Intervention* [1993] and Spodek and Saracho's *Dealing with Individual Differences in the Early Childhood Classroom* [1994] are indispensable references for such activities.) Keep an attentive eye on what is happening in order to promote as much success as possible during the play experience and be sure to commend the children in a low-key way for that success when it is appropriate to do so.

Encourage Divergence of Ideas and Unusual Uses of Equipment

As in creative thought and self-expressive activities, the teacher seeks to remain open to originality of ideas in the children's play and to do everything possible to reinforce their production of imaginative ideas by giving them the satisfaction of trying out the ideas. For this reason the use of equipment is not overrestricted, and children are encouraged to use familiar equipment in original and unusual ways. Play materials are kept accessible so that they are instantly available when the children require them.

Sometimes such uses can be quite ingenious. An acquaintance told me an interesting instance of such an unconventional idea. His little boy was going through the stage of flipping light switches on, something he could just manage to do by standing on tiptoe and shoving up on the switch. The trouble was that he was too short to pull the switch down again, so his father always had to walk over and turn the light off for him. This went on for several days, and finally, as he said, "I reached my limit—I'd had it. He flipped the switch, and I was just too tired to get up and turn it off. I was really mad. So I said to him, 'All right, Joey, I've warned you and you did it anyway. Now *you* think up some way to turn it off, and you do it before I count to 10. No! You can't drag the chair over there; that scratches the floor.' And so," he continued, "I began to count one, two, three, four. Well, he just stood there for a minute and looked at the light and looked at me. Then he ran over to me, took my steel measuring tape out of my pocket, and hurried over to the switch. He extended the tape up to reach it, hooked the little metal lip over the switch, and pulled it down. I gotta hand it to that kid! Don't you think that was smart? After all, he's only 3!"

This incident is a particularly felicitous example of using familiar equipment in an original way, but teachers can have this kind of original thinking happen at preschool, too, if they do not overrestrict children and equipment. Many things children want to try out are unconventional but not seriously dangerous. I have seen various children try the following things, which though unusual, were reasonably safe.

- A child turned a dump truck upside down and pushed it along, making train noises.
- Another one extended the slide by hooking a board to the end of it. Then, finding that it slid off and dumped her on her bottom, she talked her crony into bracing it at the end to keep it from slipping.
- Another youngster used the half-moon plywood blocks to make a cradle for her doll.

None of these ideas worked perfectly or were earthshakingly different, but all of them had two cardinal advantages: They were original ideas that came from within the children, and they required a generous amount of imagination to make them be completely satisfactory.

And from another culture come these delightful examples collected by Spar and McAfee:

On the Navajo reservation when I was little, I tended my grandfather's sheep. I would search out areas where I could find soft clay. I would shape figures of men and women and sheep with the clay. I would find sand and press it in my hand and shape it into a small hogan. I pushed my finger into the side to make a door and stuck a small twig in the top to make a chimney. The clay figures of the sheep went in a small twig corral near the hogan, and the people would fit into the hogan.

There were many different colors of sandstone near our home. I spent hours pulverizing the sand and layering it in soft colors in an old canning jar.

We made corncob dolls. The ear of corn was the doll, the silk was the hair, and the leaves were draped around the corn as clothes.

We would fill the small milk-cartons our older brothers and sisters brought home from school with mud mixed with dried straw to make adobe brick. We built dollhouses with small tree twigs or branches.

We played a lot with mud and water, constructing roads, ditches, rivers and canals.

We molded mud-pies in empty flat cans.[1]

---

[1] From McAfee, O. (1976). "To make or buy." In M. D. Cohen & S. Hadley (Eds.), Selecting Educational Equipment and Materials for Home and School, p. 27. Wheaton, MD: Association for Childhood Education International. Reprinted by permission of Oralie McAfee and the Association for Childhood Education International, 11141 Georgia Ave., Ste. 200, Wheaton, MD. © 1976 by the Association.

Cast Yourself in the Role of Assistant to the Child as You Help Play Emerge

Fostering creative play demands that teachers add another skill to their repertoire: the ability to move with the child's play and support it as it develops. This does not mean they play with the children as their peers, anymore than it means they should sit on the sidelines being thankful the children are busy and not in trouble. Rather, teachers who are skilled in generating creative play sense what will enhance the play and remain ready to offer suggestions that might sustain or extend it should this become necessary. Such teachers cast themselves in the role of supporter or facilitator of the child; they imagine themselves inside her skin and see the child's play from that point of view. This gives them an empathic understanding that enables them to serve her play needs well. Sometimes this insight is expressed by as simple a thing as going to the shed and getting out a variety of ropes, chains, and hooks for a construction project. Sometimes it is evident on a subtler level as the decision is quietly made to delay snack so that play may build to a satisfying climax.

Some of this empathic ability may go back to remembering what it was like to be a child oneself, and some of it may be related to opening oneself to sensing the child and taking time to "hear" her. It is a skill well worth cultivating because it makes possible the perception of the child's play in terms of what she intends. This enables the teacher to nurture the play by sensitively offering the right help at the right moment.

Putting the child in command of the play situation is valuable not only because it fosters her creative ability but also because it strengthens her feelings of mastery. When the teacher becomes her assistant and helper and defers to her judgment, the child is freed to determine what will happen next in her play. She exercises her ability to make choices and decisions. As mentioned previously, Erikson (1963) maintains that becoming autonomous and taking the initiative are fundamental tasks of early childhood. Creative play presents one of the best opportunities available for developing these strengths.

A Rich Background of Actual Life Experience Is Fundamental to Developing Creative Play

Children build on the foundation of real experience in their play. The richer and more solid the background of experience that children accumulate, the more varied the play will become. Field trips, holidays, and experiences with many ethnic groups, as well as things brought into the school in the way of science experiments, books, and visitors, will increase the base of experience upon which they can build their play. There is no substitute for this background. In addition, play is thought to serve the function of clarifying and integrating such experiences (Piaget, 1962) as the child gains a greater understanding of reality through her recapitulation of it in make-believe.

Equipment Plays an Important Role in Facilitating Play

Buy Equipment That Encourages the Use of Imagination

The kinds of equipment the teacher provides have a considerable influence on the play that results. Research indicates that children younger than age 3 benefit from the use of realistic play props when involving themselves in pretend play (McLoyd, 1986). Then, as the children mature and their ability to represent reality through imagination increases, it becomes more desirable to offer them less realistic items to play with (Pellegrini & Boyd, 1993). Thus a young 2½-year-old may play house more freely, using actual cups and saucers, whereas a 4-year-old may simply pretend she is holding a cup in her hand with equal satisfaction.

Of course, I am not advocating that 3- and 4-year-olds should never have realistic playthings to enjoy. We all know that dolls, dress-up clothes, and little rubber animals are beloved at that age and act as powerful enhancers of play. I just mean that teachers should not go overboard on supplying every little thing. Some things are best left to the child's imagination.

Where larger pieces of equipment are concerned, however, teachers can make their money go further and enhance the potential variety of play experiences for the children by buying equipment that can be used in a variety of ways and that is not overly realistic (Chaillé & Young, 1980; Pepler, 1986). Boards, blocks, and ladders, for example, lend

Blocks provide endless opportunities to use the same items in a variety of ways. Isn't it wonderful that the teacher didn't interfere with a possibly budding architect?

themselves to a hundred possibilities, but a plywood train tends to be used mostly as a plywood train the children just sit in. A good question to ask before investing a lot of money is, How many ways could the children use this? If you can think of three or four rather different possibilities, that's a good indication the children will use their imaginations to think of many more.

Being able to use the same item in more than one way also cuts down on a needless proliferation of "stuff" that tends to crowd the children out and make the environment confusing if we are not careful. When carried to an extreme, Tobin's (1997a, 1997b) comments are worth thinking about:

> Consumer desire is reproduced by the material reality of our preschools. The variety of things and choices offered by [some] middle-class preschools is overwhelming to many children. We create overstimulating environments modeled on the excess of the shopping mall and the amusement park and then complain that children are hyperactive and unable to focus on what they are doing.
>
> . . . . Many parents select a preschool the way they settle on an amusement park, shopping mall, or resort; by counting the variety of choices available. (1997a, p. 16)

Select a Wide Variety of Basic Kinds of Equipment

When equipment is selected, choices should reflect a good range and balance. This means that careful attention must be paid to all areas of the curriculum, both indoors and outdoors. For example, puzzles should be chosen not only with varying numbers of pieces in mind but also in terms of different kinds of puzzles: Have they informative pictures in the frame behind the pieces? Are they printed on both sides to make them more complicated? Are they the three-dimensional kind? And outdoor, wheeled equipment should not be limited to only trikes and wagons. Instead, scooters, an Irish mail, and a wheelbarrow should be included.

Although equipment does and should vary from school to school, it is also helpful to refer to a basic list from time to time as a source of ideas and inspirations. One of the best is *Selecting Educational Equipment and Materials for School and Home* (Moyer, 1995). This reference is particularly useful for new centers because it sets priorities for purchases according to essential first-year items, suggests second- and third-year additions, and extends from infant through upper elementary levels.

Change Equipment Frequently

Rather than having everything available all the time, change accessories in the basic play areas such as the housekeeping area and the block corner. Changing attracts different children, keeps life fresh and interesting for them, and encourages them to play creatively. Adding boys' clothes or an old safety razor (minus the blade, of course) or bringing the guinea pig for a visit might break the monotony in the housekeeping corner. Using trains, rubber animals, dollhouse furniture, or the cubical counting blocks could provide variety in the block area. Moving play equipment to a new location is another fine way to vary play and foster creativity. Boys, for example, are more likely to play house if the stove and refrigerator are out on the grass or if the house is made of hollow blocks for a change. Different locations attract different customers.

Rearrange Equipment Frequently and Recombine It in Appealing and Complex Ways

Besides moving equipment to new places, it is also valuable to consider how it can be recombined. What if we moved the mattress to the base of the low wall? Would this attract (and protect) the 2-year-olds while they teeter along its edge or jump freely from it? What if the refrigerator box was moved near the climbing gym with boards, ladders, and sawhorses provided nearby? What if the pots and pans from the sandbox were included in this play? Or perhaps we might move the refrigerator carton over to the sandbox. What would happen then?

An important concept to understand here is the one presented by Kritchevsky and Prescott (1977) and Shipley (1993). They point out that *simple* play units such as swings or tricycles have low absorbing power; that is, each item soaks up only one child at a time for play. When two kinds of materials or equipment are combined, such as when digging equipment is added to the sandbox, the play unit becomes *complex*. This has stronger absorptive power for children than the simple units do. Better yet are the *super play units*. These units, which combine three or more kinds of equipment and materials at once (e.g., sand, digging tools, water), do an even more effective job of drawing groups of children into cooperative play for extended periods of time. Evidently if we wish to draw children into interactive, creative play, we should do all we can to concoct these superunits for their delight.

Of course, teachers do not have to produce all the ideas for recombining equipment and enriching play. If the children are encouraged and their ideas supported, they will contribute many fruitful ideas for such elaborations and recombinations on their own, thus providing an additional outlet for their creative ideas.

Store Equipment in Convenient, Easy-to-Reach Places

Besides purchasing equipment that will stimulate imagination and changing and recombining it to keep the play fresh and interesting, the teacher must also arrange adequate storage for these materials. This is often the place that nursery centers scrimp, but good storage will keep equipment available and save the teacher's sanity as well. Storage can actually make or break a play situation, so it is well worth the time, effort, and money involved to solve this problem adequately. Material should be conveniently arranged so that it can be reached easily, and, of course, it should be returned to the same place after use to expedite locating it the next time it is needed. Labeled shelves, racks, hooks, and storage closets that are large enough all help. In addition, storage should be located close at hand so that the teacher may continue to provide supervision while getting out something the children have requested.

Keep Play Areas Safe and Attractive

The general appearance and presentation of the play areas will inspire (or discourage) children to play there. All areas should be set up at the beginning of the day in a fresh, appealing way. New touches should be added here and there to spark interest and avoid dull repetition.

Play is also better encouraged if materials are not allowed to degenerate into a shambles during playtime. No one wants to wade through a welter of costumes on the floor or build in a chaos of blocks dumped and abandoned in that corner. Attractiveness fosters attraction, and the teacher is the person who bears the primary responsibility for creating and maintaining appealing play areas.

Moreover, when things are left scattered about, they not only lose their appeal, but they also become navigational hazards. Children (and sometimes teachers) rarely watch their feet as they hasten from one area to another, and loose pegs, little cars, and beads on the floor increase the likelihood that someone may fall and strike her head on the corner of a chair or table.

A Final Thought

One last reminder: Children need plenty of freedom, time, and materials if they are to become maximally involved in imaginative play. They need the freedom to move from one activity to another as their tastes dictate, they need uninterrupted time to build a play situation through to its satisfying completion, and they need enough materials to furnish a challenge and provide a feeling of sufficiency. Making these resources available is a good way to say to a child in tangible terms that there is enough of what she needs in the world and that she need not scheme and plot to get her fair share.

SPECIFIC ACTIVITIES TO ENCOURAGE CREATIVITY IN PLAY

Creative Dramatic Play—"Just Pretending"

In addition to the many virtues discussed earlier in the chapter, creative dramatic play such as dress-up, birthday party, and playing house provide unparalleled opportunities to use the imagination and play "as if" something were true. The potential for intellectual development that this implies cannot be overemphasized. Sometimes we fail to realize that pretending something is real—that it exists—when it actually does not is an amazing intellectual *tour de force,* and one whose mechanisms are not well understood at the present time (Lillard, 1998).

Pretend play also encourages children to think up ideas and try them out—all in the risk-free safety of "let's pretend." In this kind of setting divergent ideas and unusual uses of equipment and material can abound if the teacher acts as friendly supporter but not intruder.

Usually pretend play involves more than one child at a time and contains a lot of role assigning and role assuming ("Now, you be the mother and I'll be . . . "). Three-year-olds tend to play a simple version of "house," but 4-year-olds love to embellish the premises with dogs, cartoon characters, naughty children, and interesting domestic catastrophes. All these activities develop the use of language because the children will discuss and describe among themselves what is happening ("Let's get the babies and pretend they've been in that mud again"). Teachers should encourage this use of imaginative language whenever possible.

Dress-up clothes and props can enhance the play, but having unstructured materials available that may be used in many ways is even more desirable because it helps the children be inventive and use their imaginations. Thus a scarf may become a hat, an apron, a blanket, or even a child's wished-for long hair.

Suggested Variations

Some teachers enjoy assembling play kits for the children. This is all right as long as the teacher resists the tendency to supply every little thing or to offer such specific equipment that no room is left for developing a creative use for a familiar material. It is essential to vary dress-up clothes and housekeeping accessories regularly. Using different hats and costumes, pans, empty food packages, or a milk bottle holder and bottles can kindle new interest. Dress-up clothes for both sexes should be provided. Hats, vests, and old firefighters' jackets and boots will find favor with boys, but both sexes should be encouraged to try all kinds of garments. Ethnic costumes are a nice variation and often enhance the image of the child who lends them, but be sure these are not valuable, treasured mementos. Doctor play is always popular, partly because it represents thinly veiled concerns about sexual differences and partly because it offers invaluable chances for children to play out their fear of doctors, shots, and being hurt. The teacher should be available for interpretation and control when such play takes place. Additional variations in props that have found favor in our school include a modest amount of paraphernalia donated by a local fast-food chain, obsolete typewriters and other business equipment, a birthday party box, wedding veils and bouquets, backpacks and camping gear, and, always, cowboy/cowgirl accessories such as an old saddle and plenty of boots.

Blocks

Blocks, ranging from Froebel's (1889) "gifts" to the big hollow blocks designed by Hill (1942/1992), are one of the timeless, classic play materials that have withstood the many comings and goings of ideologies and theories of early childhood education. No matter what theory of learning is espoused by which educator, children have continued to play with blocks with concentrated devotion (Hirsch, 1996).

The sheer variety of kinds of blocks available for use in the preprimary school rooms attests to their appeal. These range from large hollow ones through unit blocks to the so-called cubical counting blocks (which have so many other wonderful uses besides counting!). In addition, well-designed types of interlocking blocks are available that foster the development of fine muscle abilities.

The quantity of blocks available is also an important point to consider. There is no such thing as having too many. This conclusion has been supported by Bender (1978), who found that increasing the supply of hollow blocks from 20 to 70 tripled the number of children participating, generated a great deal more conversation and role playing, reduced fighting significantly, and increased the amount of problem solving.

Unfortunately because of their initial expense, many schools stint on this kind of equipment, but there are ways around that problem (G. T. Moore, 1997). Initially cardboard blocks can serve as a reasonable substitute for the more expensive hollow ones, or someone with an electric saw can make an inexpensive but copious set of unit blocks from pine until the school can begin acquiring the longer lasting maple variety. Then every year additional blocks should be included without fail in the equipment budget.

Infants begin to stack objects (a primitive block-building skill) almost as soon as they are able to sit up, and children continue to use blocks with satisfaction throughout their elementary school years if they are given this opportunity. Blocks provide endless opportunities for the development of emerging perceptual-motor skills. Stacking, reaching, grasping, lifting, shoving, carrying, and balancing are only a few of the countless motor skills practiced in block play (see Figure 15.1).

Possibilities for emotional satisfactions abound as well. What teacher has not seen a shy child build herself a corral and seek safety within it, or a pent-up child send blocks toppling down, or two little girls construct block houses and establish families firmly within their confines?

Blocks lend themselves readily to achieving large effects quickly, thereby building ego-expanding structures of considerable height and large dimensions, which help the child feel strong and masterful, as well as provide opportunities for her to be creative.

Blocks provide unparalleled opportunities for understanding visual-spatial relationships. What does a structure look like when viewed from one side and then the other, or when seen from above or peered up at from underneath? They also provide opportunities for developing insight into mathematics and physics as the children struggle with cause-and-effect relationships when unbalanced towers topple down or roofs remain in place.

Blocks are also strong in their contribution to the child's learning the intellectual operations basic to Piagetian theory. They offer many opportunities for the child to grasp the principle that operations are reversible (when a tower falls, it returns to a prior form). They may be used to demonstrate conservation (four blocks can be piled into a variety of shapes and yet retain their quality of fourness), and they provide additional opportunities to demonstrate the principle of *transitivity* (four short blocks equal two longer ones, which in turn equal one very long one). Blocks have also been found to be very productive elicitors of language. For example, when Isbell and Raines (1991) compared the use of language in the block, housekeeping, and thematic centers, they found the children were "more verbally fluent, used more communication units and produced more diverse vocabulary" (p. 144) in the block center than in the other two locations.

Finally blocks foster the development of creative play. By nature they are unstructured and may be used to build anything that suits the child's fancy (Cartwright, 1988, 1990). Older children enjoy planning such structures in advance, but younger ones will content themselves with the experience of stacking and balancing for its own sake and perhaps assign a useful function to the construction at a later point in the building.

Suggested Variations

Accessories that may be offered to stimulate block play are legion and can add a lot of attractiveness to the area. However, teachers should not overlook the value and delight inherent in presenting block play with blocks alone. (I make this point because, from time to time, I have seen students at the Institute of Child Development become so dependent on accessories that they lose sight of the value of block construction combined with imagination and almost stifle the children with too many props.)

STAGE BY STAGE, BLOCK BY BLOCK

WHAT TO PUT IN THE BLOCK AREA	WHAT CHILDREN BUILD AND LEARN

AGE

0 to 2

Infants and toddlers use:

✔ foam blocks
✔ cardboard blocks
✔ nesting toys
✔ stacking toys
✔ medium-sized wooden blocks

Infants and toddlers will:

✔ stack, knock down, push, match drop, and eventually carry the blocks
✔ perform the same steps over and over again, and then move on to new experiments
✔ experiment with space, the nature of the materials, and object permanence

3 to 4

Threes and fours use:

✔ the basic set of unit blocks to explore the nature and potential of the material
✔ cylinders, arches, and ramps for their bold buildings
✔ color cubes to embellish their gravity-defying creations
✔ animals as they start to build enclosures that need something inside

Threes and fours will:

✔ make stacks, roads, enclosures, and lines of blocks placed end to end
✔ carry, push, and pile
✔ classify, sort, and match shapes and sizes
✔ start making elaborate and architecturally bold structures
✔ experiment with balance, symmetry, and problem solving
✔ make elaborate patterns
✔ begin to engage in dramatic play

5 to 6

Five and sixes use:

✔ cars, trucks, and boats as they build roads, highways, tunnels, and bridges
✔ people to inhabit the world they create
✔ paper, tape, and crayons to label their buildings
✔ new materials in new ways — film canisters make garbage cans, craft sticks make ladders, and cardboard tubes make tunnels and towers!

Five and sixes will:

✔ build with increasing complexity, often seriously considering what could be real
✔ create block structures specifically for dramatic-play scenarios that relate to their experiences
✔ build representations of various real-life items and places
✔ use a wide variety of materials, all of which they sort, match, classify, and arrange in patterns

Figure 15.1
Age-appropriate block play

Source: From SCHOLASTIC EARLY CHILDHOOD TODAY, *1997. Copyright © 1997 by Scholastic Inc. Reprinted by permission of Scholastic Inc.*

When accessories *are* used, the touches of color they can lend add beauty as well as stimulation to the play. Dollhouse furniture and rug samples, small rubber animals, and miniature people are all successful accoutrements. Variations in blocks themselves, such as gothic arches, flat "roofing" blocks, spools, and cubical counting blocks, add embellishment. Not all the blocks should be offered all the time; it is sound to save the arches, switches, or triangular blocks and ramps and offer them as interesting variations when the more common varieties begin to pall. The Skaneateles train is an incomparable block accessory; tracks and additional cars should be purchased every year because it seems to be impossible to own enough of these materials. It is also fun to build block pens for the rats and guinea pigs, although this requires careful supervision from the teacher for the animals' protection. Cars, trucks, derricks, boats, and airplanes are also delightful to use with block materials.

Outdoors the addition of boards, sawhorses, ladders, and old bedspreads and parachutes will extend large block play in a satisfactory way. Large, sturdy boxes and concrete pipes are additional accessories that make good combination units with blocks, and wagons and wheelbarrows are handy for carrying blocks about and delivering them to many locations in the yard.

It is also fascinating to combine large and small blocks indoors. Older children often enjoy using the small blocks as trimming on large-block constructions, and some creative and interesting structures can result from this merging of materials. If large blocks are moved close to where dramatic play is taking place, children will often incorporate them into the play in a way that facilitates and enlarges that activity. Moreover, Kinsman and Berk (1979) found that when these materials were combined (by simply removing a barrier that had been between them), sex-typed house and block play was reduced. Younger 4- and 3-year-olds in particular interacted more frequently with children of the opposite sex when this was done.

Water Play

Water play is one of the freest, finest play opportunities we can offer children. Although inexperienced teachers often dread it because they fear the children may become too wild or overstimulated, the opposite of this behavior is usually the case. Water play is absorbing and soothing; children will stay with it a long time and come away refreshed and relaxed if it is well presented. It is also valuable because it offers children many opportunities to work through conflicts resulting from the demands of toilet training (there is no better present for a newly trained 2-year-old than a sprinkling can!), it provides relief from pressures and tensions, and it stimulates social play. Sometimes children will play companionably with others while using water, even though they remain isolated the rest of the day.

Activities such as pouring and measuring help develop eye-hand coordination. Children also acquire intellectual concepts having to do with estimating quantity (how much will the cup really hold?), with Piagetian conservation (but it looks like more in the tall bottle!), and with physical properties of water (what became of the water when we poured it on the hot sidewalk?). Crosser (1994) provides a particularly comprehensive analysis of the many things children can learn while playing with water, and chapters 18 and 19 of this book illustrate how water might be used (along with ducks) to generate interesting curricula in depth.

Water play should be offered several times a week to provide maximum satisfaction for the children. In winter a large indoor bathroom with a drain in the floor is an invaluable asset. When water play is set up in such a location, spills run off quickly. Water can be offered in deep dishpans or sinks but is best offered in larger containers, such as galvanized laundry tubs, water tables, concrete-mixing tubs made of plastic, or even wading pools. At the Institute we put the containers at floor level when possible because this keeps the children's clothes drier as they kneel and play.

Suggested Variations

Too many schools limit this kind of play to hand-washing or dabbling in the sink. Although these activities are certainly better than not having water available at all, they stop far short of what children really require for this experience. Many variations can be employed for a change, although basic water play always remains a favorite. Running water from the hose is a fine thing to offer, although it is, of course, a warm weather activity. Water can be used in conjunction with a sandbox or mud pit with real pleasure. Apartments and manicured suburban gardens deprive children of the opportunity to play with such concoctions.

In addition water can be offered to use in sinking, floating, pouring, and quantifying experiments. Unbreakable bottles and containers, as well as various sizes of sieves and funnels, can be saved for this purpose. Ice is a fascinating variation to offer, or washing activities with dolls, doll clothes, preschool furniture, cars, or tricycles can be presented. Scrubbing vegetables, watering the garden, and washing dishes should not be overlooked as additional variations, which have the added appeal of participating in meaningful work. Making a variety of pipes and joints available for assembling and using with water is fascinating to children and teaches them some valuable concepts about cause and effect. Adding sponges, soap, or a little color will also change the appeal of the water and create additional interest.

Mud and Sand

Mud and sand have wonderful, messy, unstructured qualities that make them among the most popular creative play materials in preschool (E. W. Kirk & Stroud, 1997). They offer rich tactile sensory experiences and provide emotional relief as well: Messing and slopping through water and sand or mud are relaxing and are thought by some psychologists to provide relief from the stringent toilet training demands of our society. These materials also facilitate a lot of social interaction. Older children play imaginatively and cooperatively with each other while digging tunnels, constructing roads, and carrying on "bake-offs"; but sand and mud are also rewarding for younger children to use, and they often settle down to this activity in a particularly absorbed and satisfied way. In short, the chance to mix, stir, pour, measure, mold, and squish sand and mud is an indispensable component of the curriculum.

Since this experience is often restricted at home, it is particularly important to offer it consistently at the center, where it can be planned in advance and is relatively easy to clean up. It is good planning to locate the sandbox as far from the school door as possible, in the hope that some of the sand will shake off clothes on the way back inside, and it is also sound to check pants cuffs when the play has been especially vigorous, to reduce the likelihood of dumping the whole sandbox on the carpet. The sandbox should have a wide border around it so that children may sit on it and stay warm and dry when the weather is chilly. A waterproof chest beside it will make storage of commonly used equipment easier; plastic laundry baskets also make good containers because they allow the sand to fall back into the sandbox.

Mud is different from sand, and the school should provide chances for the children to play in both these materials. A mud hole and the opportunity to dig deep pits and trudge around in mud are interesting to children, so a place in the yard should be set aside for this purpose. (If the holes are deep, it will be necessary to fence them off for safety's sake.) Children will dig astonishingly deep pits if given room, good tools, time, and opportunity, and the satisfaction of doing this work is plain to see on their faces.

Suggested Variations

It is a shame to leave the same old buckets and shovels in the sandbox day after day when so many interesting variations may be employed. All kinds of baking and cooking utensils make excellent substitutes and may be readily and cheaply acquired at rummage sales. Toy trucks and cars are nice to add, too, particularly if they are wooden or sturdy plastic, since metal ones rust and deteriorate alarmingly quickly if they are used outdoors. Sturdy tools of various kinds are good to use. (Remember that when digging large holes, children need real shovels or clamming shovels—often sold in surplus or sporting goods stores—just as they need real hammers and saws at the woodworking table.)

Adding water to sand and mud is the best accessory of all. It can be offered in deep galvanized washtubs or buckets or as running water from hoses (having two hoses available at once will considerably reduce fighting and competition). Many children will enjoy having temporary low tables, constructed from sawhorses and planks, added to the sandbox. Such tables are particularly helpful to provide when the weather is cold and children should not get chilled.

Substitutes for sand and water may be offered when the real thing is unavailable. Cornmeal is good for pouring and measuring and may be presented in deep tubs or a sand table indoors, but the reader should realize that cornmeal makes floors slippery and is difficult to clean up. Cleanup is easier if a small, battery-operated vacuum is kept nearby. Some schools also use rice, dried peas, or wheat as a substitute in cold weather.

Gardening is another useful variation of digging and working with mud. Since digging is the best, most involved part of gardening from the children's point of view, several weeks of this experience should be offered to the children *before* seeds are planted. The other part of gardening that young children enjoy the most is watering. Although this can be done with a hose that has a sprinkling head attached, it is easier to control if sprinkling cans and a big tub of water for filling them are provided instead. This allows the children to water to their heart's content without washing the seeds away or creating undue runoff.

SUMMARY

Play serves many valuable purposes in the life of the child. It provides occasions for intense practice of sensorimotor skills; the symbolic nature of imaginative play fosters development of the intellect and generates increased understanding of events; play facilitates role playing and develops social skills; it furnishes opportunities to work through emotional problems and to experience the relief of acting like a child instead of an adult; and it provides many occasions for children to be creative by using their imaginations and abilities to think in divergent ways. Best of all, play provides endless opportunities to experience joy and delight.

Teachers who wish to foster the creative aspects of play will seek to extend it but avoid dominating it and will encourage children to try out original ways of using materials. They will purchase, plan, and arrange equipment so that creativity will be enhanced. But above all, teachers who wish to foster creativity in play will cast themselves in the role of assistant to the children, seeking to move with and support their play as it develops and to serve their play needs to the best of the teachers' ability.

Questions and Activities

1. *Predicament:* Suppose a parent comes to you after touring the school and says dubiously, "Well, it looks nice enough here, and I can see the children are happy; but don't they ever learn anything? Don't they ever do anything but play around here?" How would you reply?

2. Take time to make a brief record of the play of several children during the coming week. Can you find evidence in these observations that play is used symbolically by children to translate experience into a deeper understanding of events? Did you find evidence that children employ play to express emotions and work these through? Did you observe any instances in which the children generated new, divergent solutions to problems by trying them out in play?

3. What is the difference between overcontrolling play and acting in a supportive, fostering role that encourages it to develop in greater depth? Role-play the same play situation, demonstrating differences between these two approaches.

4. *Predicament:* It is wintertime, and you live in a northern city. The children play outdoors at your school, but water play cannot be offered outdoors for most of the year because it is too cold. Identify several ways it could be offered on a regular basis indoors.

5. Survey the play yard of your school. List the different play units around which activity occurs. Do some appear to generate more imaginative activities than others? Identify what properties these units possess in common. How are they alike?

6. Put all the housekeeping equipment away for a change and offer only hollow blocks in its place and some props such as pots and pans and dolls. Observe what happens to the children's play under these circumstances.

7. Try duplicating Bender's (1978) research by increasing the number of blocks available for the children to use (you may have to consolidate the supply of blocks from two or three rooms to accomplish this). What kinds of play did you see increase as a result of such consolidation? Did fighting increase or decrease? Do you think the results are valuable enough that it would be worthwhile to have more blocks for less time and pool the blocks permanently in this fashion so as to have a larger supply some of the time?

Self-Check Questions for Review

Content-Related Questions

1. Explain how play helps each of the five selves of the child (physical, intellectual, emotional, social, and creative) develop.
2. List and describe the four developmental stages of play as identified by Butler, Rubin, and Piaget and then list and describe the four stages of play identified by Parten. What is the difference between the two systems of classification?
3. What are three ways teachers can encourage creativity in play?
4. Describe how equipment may influence the play of children. Be sure to give several examples to illustrate your answer.
5. Pretend you are escorting a visiting parent around your center and compose an answer to her question, "Why do you have such a large block corner? Aren't they an awful lot of trouble to pick up all the time?" Be sure you explain the educational benefits of this material.
6. Now explain to that same parent why you make a point of offering water, sand, and mud play to the children.
7. In regard to the Van Hoorn (1987) study about games mothers played with their babies, give some examples of how the games differed among the four cultures studied. What points of similarity were found across the four cultures?

Coordinating Videotape

Creativity and play. Tape #11. The whole child: A caregiver's guide to the first five years. The Annenberg/CPB Collection, P.O. Box 2345, South Burlington, VT 05407–2345. *Creativity and Play* outlines the role of creativity in healthy child development, provides examples of how to encourage it, and devotes the second half of the tape to explaining why play is vital for healthy development and how to encourage it to flourish.

References for Further Reading

Pick of the Litter

Play, Policy, & Practice Caucus. (1999). *Play, Policy, & Practice CONNECTIONS.* This is the newsletter of the Play, Policy, & Practice Caucus of the National Association for the Education of Young Children (NAEYC). It comes out four times a year and is filled with current information and relevant articles useful as ammunition by anyone (all of us!) who needs to defend children's right and need to play. (Available from Lynn Cohen, 7 Browning Dr., Greenlawn, NY, 11740, $10/year.)

Overviews

Fromberg, D. P., & Bergen, D. (Eds.). (1998). *Play from birth to 12 and beyond: Contexts, perspectives, and meanings.* New York: Garland. This is a collection of more than 60 well-written articles covering play in its many aspects at all stages of life. *Highly recommended.*

Isenberg, J. P., & Jalon, M. R. (1997). *Creative expression and play in early childhood* (2nd ed.). Upper Saddle River, NJ: Merrill/ Prentice Hall. This book is filled with practical suggestions about incorporating play and self-expressive materials into the classroom. *Highly recommended.*

Landreth, G., & Homeyer, L. (1998). Play as the language of children's feelings. In D. P. Fromberg & D. Bergen (Eds.), *Play from birth to 12 and beyond: Contexts, perspectives, and meanings.* New York: Garland. Many actual examples of how children reveal their feelings through play are included here.

Reynolds, G., & Jones, E. (1997). *Master players: Learning from children at play.* New York: Teachers College Press. Replete with examples of how highly skilled children involve themselves and others in play, this book also contains four valuable chapters of advice for teachers about how to intervene and extend play in supportive ways. *Highly recommended.*

Encouraging Play by Children with Disabilities

Linder, T. W. (1993). *Transdisciplinary play-based intervention: Guidelines for developing a meaningful curriculum for young children.* Baltimore, MD: Brookes. If the reader can have only one book dealing with children who have special educational requirements, this is the one to get! In addition to many other subjects, Linder provides detailed information on play and play materials discussed in relation to developmental levels categorized according to cognitive, social-emotional, communication, and sensory-motor disabilities. *Highly recommended.*

Sheridan, M. K., Foley, G. M., & Radinski, S. H. (1995). *Using the supportive play model: Individualized intervention in early childhood practice.* New York: Teachers College Press. Another very practical book filled with specific suggestions about how to integrate children with disabilities into the life of the school through play. *Highly recommended.*

Practical Advice About Generating Various Kinds of Play

Brokering, L. (1989). *Resources for dramatic play.* Columbus, OH: Fearon. An outstanding opening chapter detailing the value of dramatic play is followed by a wealth of ideas about how to enhance it.

Crosser, S. (1994). Making the most of water play. *Young Children, 49*(5), 28–32. Crosser presents a detailed analysis of all the things children can learn from using this delightful substance. Also included is a list of 16 references elaborating even further on this subject. *Highly recommended.*

Hirsch, E. S. (Ed.). (1996). *The block book* (3rd ed.). Washington, DC: National Association for the Education of Young Children. *The Block Book* is the most comprehensive discussion of block play currently available. It does a satisfactory job of covering this subject in a helpful, thorough manner.

Kirk, E. W., & Stroud, J. E. (1997). Water, sand, and so much more. *Oklahoma Child care, 1, 14–20.* This article is bursting with ideas of ways to enjoy and embellish, sand, mud and water play. *Highly recommended.*

Moore, G. T. (1997). A place for block play. *Child Care Information Exchange, #115,* 73–77. Moore provides sensible recommendations for situating and setting up "the block corner."

Weiss, K. (1997). Let's build. *Scholastic Early Childhood Today, 12*(2), 30–43. This article provides practical advice about the value and presentation of block play at various developmental levels. *Highly recommended.*

Equipment

Greenman, J. (1998a). Can't find it, can't get to it, can't use it. In J. Greenman (Ed.), *Places for childhoods: Making quality happen in the real world.* Redmond, WA: Child Care Information Exchange. More cogent advice from Jim Greenman. *Highly recommended.*

Greenman, J. (1998c). A guide to equipping the developmentally appropriate center. In J. Greenman (Ed.), *Places for childhoods: Making quality happen in the real world.* Redmond, WA: Child Care Information Exchange. Cogent advice on selection is coupled with recommendations for appropriate equipment for children of differing ages.

Moyer, J. (Ed.). (1995). *Selecting educational equipment and materials for school and home* (Rev. ed.). Wheaton, MD: Association for Childhood Education International. Another very good list of proposed equipment is included in this publication—recommendations suggest first-, second-, and third-year purchases, which is very helpful.

For the Advanced Student

James, A., Jenks, C., & Prout, A. (1998). *Working children: Theorizing childhood.* New York: Teachers College Press. The chapter "Working Children" reminds us that all isn't play for children in various cultures—nor is work outside the home restricted to children in less affluent countries or children from low-income families in our own society. Interesting reading.

Nourot, P. M. (1997). Playing with play in four dimensions. In J. P. Isenberg & M. R. Jalongo (Eds.), *Major trends and issues in early childhood education: Challenges, controversies, and insights.* New York: Teachers College Press. The author succinctly reviews various theories of play and shows how they fit into a four-dimension paradigm.

Roopnarine, J. L., Johnson, J. E., & Hooper, F. H. (Eds.). (1994). *Children's play in diverse cultures.* Albany: State University of New York Press. The first in a series on play in society, this book covers eight cultures. Generally based on research studies, the chapters often include the school's attitude toward play, as well as that of the larger society. Interesting reading.

Saracho, O. N., & Spodek, B. (Eds.). (1998). *Multiple perspectives in early childhood education.* Albany: State University of New York Press. This collection of articles focuses on the growing edge of theory and research on play.

Other Resources of Continuing Interest

American Association for the Child's Right to Play. *IPA/Newsletter.* (Tom Reed, IPA/USA Membership, University of South Carolina: School of Education, 800 University Way, Spartenburg, SC 29303) This international association publishes various materials such as the *IPA/Newsletter* and conducts meetings that champion the child's right to play.

Developing Language Skills

chapter sixteen
Fostering the Development of Language Skills

chapter seventeen
Fostering the Emergence of Literacy

Fostering the Development of Language Skills

What are some practical things teachers can do to foster language development?

How to encourage children to talk with you and with other children?

Whether or not you should insist a Mexican American child speak English at school?

. . . IF YOU HAVE, THE MATERIAL IN THE FOLLOWING PAGES WILL HELP YOU.

The specifically human capacity for language enables children to provide for auxiliary tools in the solution of tasks, to overcome impulsive behavior, to plan a solution to a problem prior to its execution, and to master their own behavior.

Lev Vygotsky (1978, p. 28)

Learning a native language is an accomplishment within the grasp of any toddler, yet discovering how children do it has eluded generations of philosophers!

Jerome S. Bruner (1978)

In the past few years we have become increasingly aware of the value of developing language skills in early childhood. This emphasis is the result of research findings indicating that a close association exists between language competence and cognitive development (Bruner, 1978: Carroll, 1999), that differences exist between the speech of middle- and lower income children (B. Bernstein, 1960; B. Hart & Risley, 1995; J. R. Smith, Brooks-Gunn & Klebanov, 1997), and that most children acquire most of their language skills, though not most of their vocabulary, by age 4 or 5 at the latest (Holzman, 1997).

Well-documented findings such as these emphasize how crucial it is that we teachers and parents of preschool children do all we can to enhance language learning and use. We must do so because, whether one sees language as being related but separate from thought, as did Piaget (Piaget & Inhelder, 1969), or as ultimately bound together by means of social transmission, as did Vygotsky (1978), there is general agreement that the development of language abilities goes hand in hand with the development of mental ability (Bloom, 1998; Haslett & Sampter, 1997). For this reason we devote considerable attention to methods of fostering language development as we begin study of the child's intellectual self.

James (1990) has defined language as "a shared system of verbal symbols and rules that allow us to represent concepts and experiences and to communicate with others" (p. 2). She points out that language is also "arbitrary, creative, and learned" (p. 2). Of course, all these things are true, but this is indeed a bare-boned definition for preschool teachers, who must come to grips with the problem of how to foster language development to maximize the child's potential for both comprehension and expression. To bring this about, teachers must understand how the ability to use language is acquired and how it develops; above all, they must determine what they can do to foster its growth.

HOW LANGUAGE IS ACQUIRED

As Tabors (1997) points out, learning any language is a complicated business that involves putting together "a variety of interlocking pieces" (p. 7). Children (or other learners) must master five aspects to be successful: (a) the sounds of the language (*phonology*), (b) the words (*vocabulary*), (c) how the words are put together to make sentences (*grammar*), (d) how sentences are used for different purposes such as storytelling, giving directions, and asking for something (*discourse*), and (e) how language is used to affect other people's behavior (*pragmatics*).

The knowledge about how children manage to accomplish these tasks is increasing rapidly, and it behooves preprimary teachers to know as much as possible about the process so that they can apply this knowledge when teaching language skills. Currently we have considerable information on *what* happens and *when* it happens, but because we still do not understand completely *how* it happens, it is necessary to employ several theories that are, at best, only partial explanations of the process.

One school of thought emphasizes the role of inborn, innate mechanisms; the other theories dwell on the significance of environmental influences. Each of these theories has something to recommend it, although none of them offer a totally satisfactory explanation. The *nativist theory,* as described by Owens (1992) and originally championed by Chomsky (1968, 1981) and more recently by Maratsos (1998), maintains that human beings are born with an inherent, innate ability to formulate language, an ability that sets humans apart from almost all other animals. This ability or mechanism is then triggered into use by exposure to people speaking whatever language is specific to their culture. It remains difficult to either disprove or discount the existence of this unseen, intangible mechanism and to determine whether this mechanism, if it does exist, is language specific or is a more general, cognitive ability (Morford & GoldenMeadow, 1997).

At the other extreme is the *behaviorist approach,* which emphasizes the importance of imitation, modeling, and reinforcement as playing the most significant role in language acquisition (Bandura, 1977; R. Brown & Bellugi, 1964; Speidel & Nelson, 1989). Particularly in vogue during the heyday of behaviorism, this theory is currently criticized as offering insufficient explanations for how children are able to generate novel sentences they have never heard and therefore could not have learned by means of copying someone else (Holzman, 1997; Lightfoot, 1999). Still, reinforcement *does* play a significant role in language acquisition, and anyone who has lived through a child's learning to talk can cite numerous examples of mothers and babies imitating each other's speech, as well as many additional later episodes of imitation.

Like the purist behaviorist approach, the third theory or model, sometimes termed the *sociolinguistic* or *social communicative theory,* also emphasizes the role environment plays in how children learn to talk. These theorists (Bruner, 1983) believe that children learn about linguistic forms and rules by interacting with the people in the environment around them. Unlike the behaviorists, who see the child as being mainly acted upon by his environment, they picture the child as being an active participant in the learning process (Vygotsky, 1962, 1978). Many proponents of this point of view also acknowledge the possible existence of an inborn predisposing mechanism for language acquisition. As Haslett and Sampter (1997) comment, the current tendency appears to be that theorists are moving from more extreme positions favoring either nature or nurture toward a useful middle ground acknowledging the contributions of both.

Contributions by Adults to the Child's Acquisition of Language

Perhaps after even this brief review the reader is shaking his or her head over the complexity of the task of language acquisition. If so, it may be comforting to learn that adults make the child's work somewhat easier for him by using a special form or style of language when they speak to infants and very young children. Although this has been called *Motherese,* in actuality this adjustment of form is used by most adults and even older children when talking with little ones (Carroll, 1999). The style includes such characteristics as using a higher pitch and a wider range of pitch, speaking more slowly and distinctly, repeating words and phrases, using limited vocabulary, and coining words such as "goney-gone" and "tum-tum." Adults also tend to expand the briefer utterances of children and, most interesting of all, to adjust the level of communication difficulty to the child's increasing level of understanding as the youngster matures (George & Tomasello, 1984/85).

Maternal responsiveness—that is, how much attention a mother pays to her 1- and 2-year-old's attempts at talking—also makes a significant difference in the size of the youngster's vocabulary. The more responsive the mother, the greater the child's number of words (Olson, Bayles, & Bates, 1986). Surely this implies that teachers, too, should be careful to be attentive when children want to talk with them.

Contributions of Linguistics to Understanding the Process of Language Acquisition

From the practical point of view of the early childhood teacher, the most valuable contribution of linguistics so far is the information it is providing on the order in which various grammatical structures develop in the speech of children. Although *linguistic theory* is too advanced and complicated a subject to be presented in detail here, it can be defined as generally dealing with words and strings of words (Holzman, 1997). Two examples of the kinds of information this science is producing may help the beginning student gain an appreciation of the importance of this approach. For numerous examples of the current intricacies of linguistic research, the reader is referred to Carroll (1999) and Holzman (1997).

One early example of applied linguistics is the classic study by Menyuk (1963), who used the grammatical theory developed by Chomsky, a linguistic theorist in transformational grammar, to study the language of young children. Menyuk studied 3- and 6-year-olds and found few examples of restricted children's grammar at this level. Surprisingly most of the children's speech was similar to that of adults, and the children had gained a remarkable proficiency in structuring language correctly even by age 3. This is important information for we preschool teachers to possess because it implies that we need to stress the development of language function skills earlier than age 4—the point at which many preschool compensatory programs now begin. Obviously if grammatical structure has been largely acquired by this time, we should be building language skills in children between 18 months and 3½ years old to be maximally effective.

In another study Cazden (1970) also used transformational grammar to analyze the way children learn to pose questions. Briefly, she found that children first form questions by using inflection. Following that, questions become the yes-no kind, which depend on interchanging only two phrases. For example, "The boy can drive a car" would change to "Can the boy drive a car?" Next, children learn to perform a more difficult transformation, the "wh" question—"When can the boy drive a car?"—which involves two transformations. The next step involves forming negative questions: "Won't he be able to drive the car?" Finally comes the use of tag questions: "It's all right if he drives the car, isn't it?"

As more of these studies become available, it will be possible to outline sequential steps for many forms of grammatical structures. Then, following an analysis of a child's current level of ability, the teacher will be able to refer to these "maps" and know what step should be selected next for him and plan her teaching accordingly.

Contributions of Sociolinguistics to the Understanding of Language Development

Rather than focusing on how the structure of language is acquired, some researchers have become more interested in "the relation of language to social interaction" (Ervin-Tripp &

Gordon, 1986, p. 92); that is, they are interested in the way children use language to affect the behavior of other people. This is called the science of *pragmatics*. It stresses the interactional importance of the social and developmental aspects of language acquisition (Bloom, 1998; Bruner, 1974; Schiefelbusch, 1986; Snow, 1989). In this approach the *intention* of the child when speaking is accepted as being as important to consider as the form he uses while saying it. For example, a child who says, "Doggie!" might mean, "I want to pet the doggie," "Pick me up, I'm scared of that doggie," or "See the doggie!"

Pragmatics is particularly interesting to teachers of preschool-age children because it provides a helpful way to learn about various aspects of children's speech that may provide clues about what teachers can do to facilitate its development. For example, studies by Ervin-Tripp (Ervin-Tripp & Gordon, 1986) reveal how children gradually progress from making simple demands based on "more," "want," and "gimme" to phrasing requests as questions at age 3 ("Can I have a bite?") to using hints and indirect statements by age 4 such as a statement by one of my grandchildren, "I'm wondering if there's something in your pocket for this sweet little girl."

One large area of study included in pragmatics centers on what rules children must learn and follow to carry on a conversation—which Bruner (1978) defines as being the earliest experience in learning to take turns. Besides learning such conversational rules as that one person talks at a time and that the number of people involved in a conversation can vary (Holzman, 1997), children must also learn when and how to interrupt, how to introduce a subject into the conversation, and how to continue to talk about it over a period of time.

It's for you!

Another interesting area of investigation has to do with the way children change their conversational style to suit the people with whom they are talking (M. V. Cox, 1991). For example, 4-year-olds have been found to use much simpler instructions when talking with 2-year-olds than they use with peers or adults (Shatz & Gelman, 1973). Owens (1992) reports that children tend to be more directly demanding with their mothers than they are with other grown-ups and to use more imperatives with children their own age than they do when speaking with adults. Sometimes this adjustment has to do with how a particular culture defines politeness and/or appropriate social roles. For example, Ervin-Tripp points out that Italian families frown on children saying "I want" unless they soften that request in some way (Ervin-Tripp & Grodon, 1986). Still another kind of style or code switching is evident in the speech of children who use a dialect or even a second language when speaking with members of their gang and quite another style when talking with their teachers at school (Smitherman, 1994).

Conclusion

And so the debate on how the miracle of language comes about continues—with, it seems, an ever-widening range of things that affect its acquisition being considered. It is an exciting, fast-growing area of study and research that is particularly interesting because it has attracted the attention of people from a variety of academic disciplines who, by their diversity of approaches, have greatly increased the richness of our understanding (Bloom, 1998).

One may ask at this point, "Have we reached the point where these studies offer sufficient explanations of how language is acquired?" Surely the foregoing explanations are sensible and useful as far as they go, but the fact remains that although we are in the process of acquiring linguistic maps, although we are fairly certain that imitation and reinforcement combined with an innate ability play an important role in the acquisition of these forms, and although we acknowledge that context, development, and social interaction are important influences, we still cannot explain the fundamental magic of what happens in the child's mind that enables him to substitute symbol for object and to assemble these symbols into sentences he has never heard.

DEVELOPMENTAL MILESTONES

In addition to understanding that grammatical structure develops according to predictable rules, teachers should become acquainted with additional developmental milestones so that they can identify children who show marked developmental lags and so that they may have a clear idea of what is reasonable to aim for when establishing goals for language development. The teacher may find Table 16.1 ("Milestones in the Development of Language Ability in Young Children") quite helpful; but remember that the checkpoints represent averages and that children who are developing well may often be either ahead or behind the suggested time listed. The lag should be considered serious

Table 16.1

Milestones in the development of language ability in young children

Average Age	Question	Average Behavior
3–6 months	What does he do when you talk to him?	He awakens or quiets to the sound of his mother's voice.
	Does he react to your voice even when he cannot see you?	He typically turns eyes and head in the direction of the source of sound.
7–10 months	When he cannot see what is happening, what does he do when he hears familiar footsteps . . . the dog barking . . . the telephone ringing . . . candy paper rattling . . . someone's voice . . . his own name?	He turns his head and shoulders toward familiar sounds, even when he cannot see what is happening. Such sounds do not have to be loud to cause him to respond.
11–15 months	Can he point to or find familiar objects or people when he is asked to? *Example:* "Where is Jimmy? "Find the ball."	He shows his understanding of some words by appropriate behavior; for example, he points to or looks at familiar objects or people, on request.
	Does he respond differently to different sounds?	He jabbers in response to a human voice, is apt to cry when there is thunder, or may frown when he is scolded.
	Does he enjoy listening to some sounds and imitating them?	Imitation indicates that he can hear the sounds and match them with his own sound production.
1½ years	Can he point to parts of his body when you ask him to? *Example:* "Show me your eyes." "Show me your nose."	Some children begin to identify parts of the body. He should be able to show his nose or eyes.
	How many understandable words does he use—words you are sure *really* mean something?	He should be using a few single words. They are not complete or pronounced perfectly but are clearly meaningful.
2 years	Can he follow simple verbal commands when you are careful not to give him any help, such as looking at the object or pointing in the right direction? *Example:* "Johnny, get your hat and give it to Daddy." "Debby, bring me your ball."	He should be able to follow a few simple commands without visual clues.
	Does he enjoy being read to? Does he point out pictures of familiar objects in a book when asked to? *Example:* "Show me the baby." "Where's the rabbit?"	Most 2-year-olds enjoy being "read to" and shown simple pictures in a book or magazine, and will point out pictures when you ask them to.
	Does he use the names of familiar people and things such as *Mommy, milk, ball,* and *hat*?	He should be using a variety of everyday words heard in his home and neighborhood.
	What does he call himself?	He refers to himself by name.

Table 16.1 *continued*

Average Age	Question	Average Behavior
2 years (cont.)	Is he beginning to show interest in the sound of radio or TV commercials?	Many 2-year-olds do show such interest by word or action.
	Is he putting a few words together to make little "sentences"?	These "sentences" are not usually complete or grammatically correct.
	Example: "Go bye-bye car." "Milk all gone."	
2½ years	Does he know a few rhymes or songs? Does he enjoy hearing them?	Many children can say or sing short rhymes or songs and enjoy listening to records or to mother singing.
	What does he do when the ice cream man's bell rings, out of his sight, or when a car door or house door closes at a time when someone in the family usually comes home?	If a child has good hearing, and these are events that bring him pleasure, he usually reacts to the sound by running to look or telling someone what he hears.
3 years	Can he show that he understands the meaning of some words besides the names of things?	He should be able to understand and use some simple verbs, pronouns, prepositions, and adjectives, such as *go, me, in,* and *big.*
	Example: "Make the car go." "Give me your ball." "Put the block in your pocket." "Find the big doll."	
	Can he find you when you call him from another room?	He should be able to locate the source of a sound.
	Does he sometimes use complete sentences?	He should be using complete sentences some of the time.
4 years	Can he tell about events that have happened recently?	He should be able to give a connected account of some recent experiences.
	Can he carry out two directions, one after the other?	He should be able to carry out a sequence of two or three simple directions.
	Example: "Bobby, find Susie and tell her dinner's ready."	
5 years	Do neighbors and others outside the family understand most of what he says?	His speech should be intelligible, although some sounds may still be mispronounced.
	Can he carry on a conversation with other children or familiar grown-ups?	Most children of this age can carry on a conversation if the vocabulary is within their experience.
	Does he begin a sentence with "I" instead of "me," "he" instead of "him"?	He should use some pronouns correctly.
	Is his grammar almost as good as his parents'?	Most of the time, it should match the patterns of grammar used by the adults of his family and neighborhood.

Source: From Learning to Talk: Speech, Hearing, and Language Problems in the Preschool Child, *by National Institute of Neurological Diseases and Stroke, 1969, Washington, DC: U.S. Department of Health, Education and Welfare.*

enough to warrant concern only if the child is more than a few months behind on a particular measure.

Another quick rule of thumb for checking language development is sentence length, still thought to be one of the best indicators of verbal maturity. In general, sentence length increases as the child grows older. Schachter and Strage (1982) outline a pattern for the development of language in Table 16.2

When assessing language competence, the teachers in our center have also found it helpful to determine whether English or some other language, typically Spanish, is the child's dominant language and to determine whether he appears to possess what I term "the habit of verbalness." For whatever reason, be it temperament, age, level of intelligence, cultural pattern, or socioeconomic status, it is evident to our center teachers that some children use language to meet their needs more frequently than others do. We always try to note this behavior and use the techniques described in the following section to encourage the less verbally oriented children to increase their language abilities while attending the center.

Table 16.2
Development of language

Age in Months	Characteristics of Vocalization and Language
4	Coos and chuckles.
6–9	Babbles; duplicates common sounds; produces sounds such as "ma" or "da."
12–18	A small number of words; follows simple commands and responds to no; uses expressive jargon.
18–21	Vocabulary grows from about 20 words at 18 months to about 200 words at 21; points to many more objects; comprehends simple questions; forms 2-word phrases.
24–27	Vocabulary of 200 to 400 words; has 2- or 3-word phrases; uses prepositions and pronouns.
30–33	Fastest increase in vocabulary; three- to four-word sentences are common; word order, phrase structure, and grammatical agreement approximate the language of surroundings, but many utterances are unlike anything an adult would say.
36–39	Vocabulary of 1000 words or more; well-formed sentences using complex grammatical rules, although certain rules have not yet been fully mastered; grammatical mistakes are much less frequent; about 90 percent comprehensible.

Source: From "Adults' Talk and Children's Language Development" by F. F. Schachter and A. A. Strage. In S. G. Moore and C. R. Cooper (Eds.), The Young Child: Reviews of Research (Vol. 3), p. 83. (Adapted from Lenneberg [1966]). Reprinted by permission. © 1982, National Association for the Education of Young Children, 1509 16th St., NW, Washington, DC 20036–1426.

Basic Ways to Foster Language Development

I. Listen to the Children

Many adults, particularly women and most particularly nervous female teachers, are so busy talking themselves that they drown the children out. But children learn to talk by being heard. Paying attention to what they say and listening both to the surface content and to the message underneath offer the most valuable inducements to children to continue making the effort to communicate.

Of course, it is not always easy to understand what children have to say. If a comment is unintelligible, it is all right to ask a child to repeat it; and if the message is still unclear, it may be necessary to admit this and say, "I'm sorry, I just can't tell what you're saying. Could you show me what you mean?" At least this is honest communication and shows children that the teacher is really interested and is trying. Occasionally another child can be prevailed on to clarify what his companion is saying.

II. Give the Children Something Real to Talk About

Children's talk should be based on solid, real, lived-through experience. Sometimes inexperienced teachers want to begin at the other end and set up group experiences wherein the children are supposed to discuss planting seeds or thinking about what will sink and float before they have been exposed to the experience itself. This means they are expected to use words that have few actual associations for them and to talk about something vague and relatively meaningless. No wonder their attention wanders. It is much more satisfactory to provide the opportunity to live through the experience and to talk about what is happening while it is going on, as well as after it has been completed. At this point the child can really associate "sink" with "things that go down" and "sprout" with the pale green tip that poked its nose out of the bean.

Note also that talk and questioning are advocated as an accompaniment to experience. In former years some teachers of young children seemed to assume that mere exposure to interesting materials in the presence of a warm adult would automatically produce growth in language and mental ability. The work of Blank and Solomon (1968, 1969) has shown that unfocused attention in a rich environment is not enough. Children develop language best when they are required to use words to express concepts and thoughts about what is happening, has happened, or will happen; this kind of activity produces the greatest gains.

III. Encourage Conversation Between Children

As interest in the influence of social interaction on the development of speech increases, more attention is being paid to the importance of encouraging children to talk with each other. Of course, Piaget (1983) has long advocated such "discourse" and exchanges of opinion as an effective means of facilitating the acquisition of knowledge, and it is encouraging to see that currently the value of conversation between children as a facilitator of language development is once again receiving attention (Carroll, 1999; McTear, 1985; Vygotsky, 1978).

Talking about a book together is a great way to encourage conversation and to build vocabulary.

Encouraging children to talk with each other has many benefits as varied as teaching them to use words to negotiate disagreements in place of physical attacks and providing them with effective ways of entering a group. Besides these obvious advantages, as the children of Reggio Emilia consistently demonstrate, talking together can help children put ideas into words, increase their abilities to use language to explain to someone else what is happening, repeat an interesting experience, or make cheerful social contact with another youngster (Edwards, Gandini, & Forman, 1993, 1998). Most important of all, such encounters help persuade them that talking is satisfying and important—a valuable attitude to inculcate as a foundation for later interest in other language strategies related to literacy. (These strategies are discussed in more detail in chapter 17.)

Because talking *between* children is so valuable, the teacher should avoid making herself the constant center of attention, whether the situation is dramatic play or participating at the lunch table. Instead it is important to think of oneself as seeking to increase the amount of talk *among the children whenever possible.* Such comments as, "That's really interesting. Why don't you tell Blake about that?" or, "Have you talked that over with Pei Dong? She was talking about that just yesterday," provide openings for the children to relate to each other and focus attention on the relationships among them, rather than keeping attention focused on the teacher.

IV. Encourage Conversation and Dialogue Between Teachers and Children

Much more is involved in language development than teaching the child to name colors or objects on demand, although learning the names of things has undeniable value. The skills involved in discussion and conversation are vital, too, and the ability to conduct such dialogues develops rapidly throughout the preschool period (Bloom; 1998; S. L. James, 1990).

To develop these conversational interchanges, teachers must relax and stop seeing their role as one of instructor and admonisher. *Always supplying a fact or rendering an opinion in reply to a child's comment kills conversation very quickly.* Cazden (1972) quotes a perfect example of this. As she points out, the more frequent the prohibition in an adult's talk, the less the children reply.

Tape plays

Teacher:	Oh, you tease, Tom, what are you telling Winston?
Tom:	I tellin' him my brother Gary a bad, bad boy.
Teacher:	Oh, now that ain't nice.

After an analysis and discussion on this tape recording, the same teacher returns to the child, and the following conversation ensues.

Teacher:	Tom, what was you tellin' Winston this mornin' when you playin' with the ball?
Tom:	I tole him Gary my brother.
Teacher:	You like Gary?
Tom:	Yeah, I lahk him, but he bad.
Teacher:	Why's dat?
Tom:	'Cus he walked up and set with his friend when they was singin' 'bout Jesus and the preacher was preachin'.
Teacher:	Who whipped him?
Tom:	Daddy—he tuk him outside and whupped him with a red belt.
Teacher:	Did Gary cry?
Tom:	Oh, yeah, he got tears in his eyes. Mama wiped his eyes with a rag when he come back in. Then he popped his fingers. That boy can't never be quiet.[1]

The example brings out another important point to remember when building conversation. *Teachers should seek to prolong the interchange whenever they can.* Tossing the conversational ball back and forth is a sound way to build fluency and to establish the habit of being verbal.

The value of the one-to-one situation cannot be overestimated in this regard. It is not necessary to put this off and wait for a special moment; indeed this is impossible to do if the teacher wants to talk specially with every child every day. Instead of waiting the teacher can seize many little interludes to generate friendly talk between herself and a child or between two children. One teacher in our center maintains that some of her best opportunities for such chatting occur while she is helping children go to the toilet. Another capitalizes on brief moments while putting on shoes or while greeting children as they arrive at school.

---

[1]   *Adapted with permission of Prentice Hall Publishing Company from* The Devil Has Slippery Shoes: A Biased Biography of the Child Development Group of Mississippi *by Polly Greenberg. © 1970 by Polly Greenberg.*

Teachers should monitor themselves regularly to make certain they are not talking mainly to the most verbal children, because at least one research study shows that teachers talk most to children who are the best talkers to start with (Monaghan, 1971, as cited in Cazden, 1974). Some youngsters have a knack for striking up conversations with adults, whereas others do not. It is the children lacking this ability who are often overlooked and therefore receive the least practice in an area in which they need it the most. If teachers make a checklist of the children's names and review it faithfully, they will be able to recall which youngsters they have talked with and which they have not and then make a particular effort to include in conversation the ones who have been passed over.

Of course, a reasonable ratio of adults to children makes it more likely there will be time for such friendly encounters, but a good ratio is not the only thing that matters. A British study found that quality of conversation between child and adult is also increased if not too many very young children (under the age of 3) are included in the group. Stability of staff (low staff turnover) also increased the quality of interaction, as did staff feelings of autonomy (when staff were supervised very closely, they tended to be more aware of needing to please the supervisor than of the value of generating meaningful conversation with the children) (Tizard, Mortimore, & Burchell, 1983). Because all these qualities stem from good management and job satisfaction of the employees, it is evident that preprimary schools that wish to foster language and its accompanying opportunity for mental development must pay close attention to solving these management problems.

Besides these one-to-one conversations, two classic, larger group opportunities occur each day in the center when it is particularly possible to generate conversation. These occur at the snack or lunch table and during group time. (Group time conversation is discussed in the following chapter.) Indeed a study by Stone (1992) found that out of 81 narratives spontaneously produced by preschool children, the great majority occurred during lunchtime (73%). Stone concluded that the presence of an interested, attentive adult is crucial in developing this aspect of children's conversational ability.

Developing Conversation at Mealtimes

Gone are the days when children were expected to be seen and not heard at meals or when they had to clear their plates before they were allowed to talk. There are several practical ways the teacher can encourage conversation during meals.

Keep lunch and snack groups as small as possible.   It is worthwhile to keep the mealtime group down to five or six children if possible. Anyone who has ever sat at a banquet table knows how difficult it is to get conversation going under such circumstances, and yet an occasional children's center persists in seating 12 or 15 children all around one table. This kills interchange, as well as makes supervision difficult.

Adults need to plan their activities so that they are free to sit with the children during meals. Surprisingly often when I have visited day care centers at mealtime, I have seen staff roaming restlessly around, passing food, running back and forth to the kitchen, or leaning on counters, arms folded, simply waiting passively for the children to eat but not being part of the group at all. Good advance planning on food delivery should make it possible for staff to sit with the children, and a clearer understanding of the potential educational value of such participation should make them willing to do so. Sitting with the children fosters the feeling of family time that young children need and encourages the relaxed chatting that makes mealtime a pleasure.

It is wise, though, to avoid putting two adults together at one table. The temptation to carry on a grown-up conversation over the heads of the children can be too great when two adults eat lunch together. It is better to add more tables when more adults are present, thereby seizing this golden opportunity to reduce group size and making it more likely that individual children will join in the talk.

Think of good conservation starters.   Such questions as, "Did you see anything good on TV last night?" "Who's your favorite baby-sitter?" "What would you like for Christmas?" or, "Would you rather be a kitty or a dog?" will lead the children into talking about things that really interest them and that they can all share together. It is also fun to talk about brothers and sisters, new clothes, birthdays, what their parents' first names are and how old they are, what they call their grandfathers, or what they did over the weekend. In addition, their memories can be developed by asking them whether they can remember what they had for lunch yesterday or what they saw on the way to school.

It takes tact to ensure that one ardent talker does not monopolize the conversation under these circumstances. The teacher may need to make a deliberate effort to draw all the children into the discussion lest someone be consistently drowned out. But the half hour or so that lunch requires is really ample opportunity for everyone to converse.

Don't let the children get by with pointing to food they wish to have passed or with saying, "I want that."   Conversation, as such, is highly desirable to develop at the lunch table, but mealtime also provides many opportunities to build the children's vocabulary and concepts. All too often teachers permit pointing and saying "give me" to pass for language. This is just not enough. Children, particularly children from low-income families, need to acquire commonly used vocabulary, and mealtime is an effective place to teach this. It is easy for the teacher to make sure the child says the real name of the food he is requesting and then give it to him promptly. There is no quicker way to teach him that talking pays off!

If the child does not know the word, the teacher can say, "This red stuff is called Jell-O. Now you can tell *me*." When he does, the teacher should give it to him right away and tell him, "Good for you! You said the real name." Sometimes, however, the child refuses to reply. It is best to pass over such a response lightly without making a major issue of it, perhaps saying, "Well, maybe you'll want to tell me it's Jell-O next time."

Mealtimes are also good opportunities to teach certain concepts. For example, the teacher might start by talking about the food: "What are we having today? Did any of you look in the kitchen to see what dessert is?" She might then go on to ask, "What does this meat taste like? Is it hard or soft? Hot or cold? Tough or tender? Can you think of anything else that's like that?"

A word of warning is in order here. Mealtimes should remain basically social occasions in which verbal fluency and fun are the keynote, not opportunities for continuous dull inquisitions. Vocabulary and concept building should not be allowed to dominate the occasion, and such a delightful event as lunch should never be permitted to degenerate into a boring mechanical drill in which the talk centers on naming each food and discussing where it came from.

V. Use Questions and Answers That Generate Speech and Develop Language

Once again, the value of questions must be highlighted as we discuss effective ways of encouraging the development of language.

Ask Questions That Require More Than One-Word Answers

In chapter 18 asking questions that are open ended is advocated because doing this encourages children to see that many questions have more than one answer. Asking these kinds of questions has an additional virtue we should think about in this chapter: It also fosters language development by promoting conversation. Rogers, Perrin, and Waller (1987) conducted a series of observations of a teacher named Cathy that illustrates the value of doing this. This teacher had a particularly good relationship with the children in her care. When the researchers analyzed the reasons for this, they concluded she was adept at asking the children what she termed "true questions." These were questions for which she didn't have a preconceived answer in mind. (The opposite of a "true question" is a "known-answer" or fact question.)

For example, in one instance when the children had been building with bristle blocks, the following conversation took place:

Adam:	There's the chimney, see?
Cathy:	Oh-h-h. Do you have a woodstove in there? Or a fireplace?
Adam:	Uh-huh, a woodstove.
Cathy:	A woodstove.
Adam:	That's where the smoke comes out. Where my mom and dad live.
Cathy:	The what? (She leans closer to Adam.)
Adam:	It's our house.
Cathy:	Oh-h, and you built it for them, huh?
Adam:	Uh-huh, and we are living in it.
Cathy:	You're a good thing to have around. Does Nora live there, too? (Rogers et al., 1987, p. 21)

Clearly Cathy could not have known the answers in advance to the questions she asked; they reflect her genuine interest in what Adam was doing and what he had to say about it. That interest is an important element in generating true conversation.

When Replying to a Child's Questions or Statement, Elaborate

After the work of Roger Brown and Ursula Bellugi (1964) revealed that parents spend a good deal of their time reconstructing and expanding the limited sentences used by their young children, some teachers concluded that this technique of expansion would naturally be the most effective way to teach enriched language to all young children. Thus when a child commented, "Train, bye-bye," the teacher would dutifully reply, "Yes, the train is going bye-bye." It now appears that this technique may be most effective with children about 18 months to 3 years of age but that a different kind of reply was more effective with children over age 3 (Cazden, 1972). Rather than replying, "Yes, the train goes bye-bye," the teacher would respond to an older child by saying, "Yes, the engine is pulling the train out of the station. Good-bye, train. Good-bye, people." When working with older preschoolers, this kind of enrichment is superior to simple expansion in fostering language progress.

VI. When Necessary, Seek Professional Assistance Promptly

Every once in a while a teacher will come across a child who speaks rarely, if at all, or one who has a pronounced speech problem. These disabilities are discussed in more detail at the end of this chapter, but I want to emphasize here as a basic principle that it is important to seek professional help for these children promptly. Too often both teacher and parent let the year pass, hoping the child will somehow outgrow his difficulty. Although this does happen occasionally, it is generally wiser to refer such youngsters for professional help after 2 or 3 months at most. Children who have pronounced developmental lags or other speech disorders and who do not show signs of improvement by that time generally need consultation from a qualified speech therapist or psychologist, and a referral is definitely in order.

LANGUAGE AND DIALECTICAL DIFFERENCES

Which Language Should the Teacher Encourage?

In the chapter on cross-cultural education (chapter 13), a good deal of time was spent discussing ways to honor the cultural background the child brings with him from his home. Although there is no finer way to do this than by welcoming and encouraging him to use his native language or dialect at school, teachers are often torn between two directions on this question. On the one hand, they want to make the child welcome and to facilitate his learning in every possible way; this makes the use of his dominant language essential. On the other hand, the teacher cannot help looking ahead and knowing that as schools function today, each youngster will soon move on to elementary school, where he will have to speak Standard English, the dominant language of the middle-class world (Trueba, 1990).

This dilemma shows no signs of dissipating. Recent trends in population statistics make it plain that the question of bilingualism and dialects and what teachers should do about them will remain an important aspect of language education because the population of so-called minority groups is rising steadily. For example, in 1997 the U.S. Bureau of the Census reported that 1 in 10 residents in the United States had been born elsewhere and that that population was increasing at a 5% annual rate, whereas the national population's overall growth rate was 2% ("Nationaline," 1998). Another interesting statistic (attributed to the fact that the birthrate for African American families is declining) is that, for the first time in history, the number of Hispanic children has surpassed the number of non-Hispanic Black children by a small margin (L. Jacobson, 1998). And as Table 16.3 indicates, these shifts in the composition of cultural/ethnic groups are predicted to continue.

Statistics such as these are at least partially the reason for the storm of political controversy that arises from time to time over the value of bilingual education and the use of Ebonics in the classroom as pro-English advocates argue that all Americans should "melt in" and speak English. Perhaps as a result of our own typically inadequate foreign language instruction in the United States, these advocates seem to assume it is impossible to speak

Table 16.3
It is estimated by the U.S. Bureau of the Census that the racial/ethnic mix in the United States will be further transformed in the coming half century (Hall & Lynn, 1999).

American mix
Projected make-up of the U.S. population by Census racial or ethnic group over the next half century:

	2000	2050
White	82%	75%
Black	13%	15%
Native American	1%	1%
Asian/Pacific	4%	9%
Hispanic[1]	11%	25%

1 - May be of any race

Source: U.S. Bureau of the Census

two (or more!) languages with proficiency and therefore English must prevail entirely. Of course, common sense makes it plain it is essential that residents of this country be fluent in English, but it is also true that speaking English well need not obliterate the ability to speak another language, too. Indeed in recent years some college graduates are finding their job possibilities limited because they can communicate only in English.

Some resistance to providing a bilingual approach in classrooms also stems from early studies that concluded bilingualism has a negative effect on developing language and possibly mental development as well (Ellis, 1994; Imhoff, 1990). However, these results were complicated (confounded) by the presence of additional variables that we know affect learning and behavior, such as poverty. When such a mixture of possible causes is included in research findings, sorting the effects of one from another is next to impossible.

More sophisticated current studies suggest that when the effects of poverty are statistically controlled, bilingualism is not a deterrent to development (Soto, 1991). As Hakuta and Garcia (1989) document, *"all other things being equal,* higher degrees of bilingualism are associated with higher levels of cognitive attainment" (p. 375). Evidently learning a second language is not hampered by possession of the first language (McLaughlin, 1987). Indeed some research indicates that the acquisition rate for a second language is closely related to the proficiency level of the native language. The more proficient the child is in his first language, the more quickly he will be able to learn the second one (Hakuta, 1998).

As the Research Study in this chapter details, another continuing debate centers on when and how best to teach non-English-speaking children English (Garcia, 1990; Imhoff, 1990). Common sense argues against the folly of insisting that children try to learn important new concepts in a language they are only beginning to acquire. Imagine having to learn geometry by means of first-year French, which you are learning simultaneously—that's the stuff nightmares are made of. Yet in essence we expect this degree of expertise from a young semi-bilingual child when we teach him "all the important things" only in his second language (Areñas, 1978; Gonzalez-Mena, 1976). Children who are coming to school for the first time are undergoing a complicated enough set of adjustments without the teacher's expecting them to function entirely in a new language at the same time.

Research Study

Does Learning a Second Language Mean Losing the First One?

Research Question: What are the consequences of teaching English to non-English-speaking preschoolers? Is the resulting impact on their families necessarily desirable?

Research Method: The investigators prepared an interview form to be used with parents and translated it into many languages (e.g., Spanish, Japanese, Khmer, Vietnamese). The 45 questions focused on languages used in the home: Who spoke which language to various family members, what kinds of preschool programs their children attended, and whether there had been changes in the use of language at home as a result of the children's schooling. The interview form also asked about parental concerns over loss of the home language.

Next the researchers trained hundreds of volunteer interviewers, who contacted the families. (Wong Fillmore cautions that this was a "convenience" sample drawn from people the interviewers were acquainted with and not a "representative" sample of the language-minority families in the United States.) The results were divided into two groups. The first group included 690 returns from families whose children attended preschools in which English was used entirely or as part of a

bilingual program. That group included primarily Hispanic, Asian, and American Indian (mainly Navajo) families. The comparison group consisted of children enrolled in monolingual preschool programs in which only Spanish was spoken. The majority of the families in both groups had been in the United States for more than 10 years.

Results: The investigators caution that "it is not possible to determine (for certain) whether or not there is a causal relationship between language use in preschool programs and changes in patterns of language use in the home" (p. 332) because of other factors that also influence the use of English. They also point out, however, that when the data from the main (bilingual) sample were compared with the monolingual sample, the differences regarding language pattern and use and maintenance of that language in the home were "dramatic and highly significant" (p. 332).

Analysis revealed that 50% of the main sample reported a shift by the children from home language to English, compared with a 10% shift in the Spanish-only sample. This result was particularly strong in the families whose children attended English-only preschools (64% reported a shift).

Probably the best we can do at present, since children are expected to speak English in grade school and beyond, is to follow the bilingual model wherein young children are taught concepts first in their dominant language and then in English. This approach has been shown to be successful in some studies involving concept training or learning to read (Garcia & August, 1988; Hakuta, 1998; Macnamara, 1966; Orata, 1953; Spolsky, 1999). It has been effective with children speaking a variety of languages and coming from varied cultural backgrounds such as Mexican American and Irish. Moreover it has the virtue of helping maintain the child's ability to remain bilingual, rather than pushing toward proficiency only in English.

≈ physical self ≈ emotional health ≈ self-esteem ≈ social competence ≈

This language shift by the children also raises the question, What happens to parent-child communication when parents speak a language that differs from the one their child prefers to use? In the main sample, in which 97% of families originally had used their native tongue exclusively, the study found that only 78% of families did so following their children's experience in English-only or bilingual programs, whereas in the all-Spanish-speaking preschool comparison group, almost 94% of the parents continued to use their original home language.

Implications: It is my hope this study will cause the reader to question and think carefully about its implications. Depending on the reader's point of view, it is an interesting example of "Well, there's good news—and there's bad news!"

The conclusions drawn by the investigators emphasize the unfortunate bad-news effects losing their native language has on the children and their families: the lack of communication between generations, the loss of identity and sense of valuing their home culture, and the loss of a priceless communicative skill.

However, the research also indicates it really *is* effective to teach English at the preschool level. The good news is the children not only learn it but also use it. Many people unquestioningly accept this as a necessary and highly desirable goal for preschool education.

The research leaves us with as many questions as it answers. How dear a price must children and families pay for the benefits of assimilation into the "American" culture? What do children sacrifice in terms of closeness and communication with their parents as the gap between their English proficiency and that of their parents widens? What effect might it have on a child's self-image if he comes to see the value and usefulness of speaking English and compares it with the possibly more restricted usefulness of his first language? What about the children in the Spanish-only schools—how will they fare when they enter English-dominant kindergartens? How long should we wait before introducing English into the curriculum? Is it possible for children to reap the benefits from having the best of two language worlds? If we agree that achieving this would be desirable, what is the most effective way to make it become a reality? Currently the debate rages on as these and other equally knotty questions related to cultural and ethnic concerns continue to challenge us.

Source: From "When Learning a Second Language Means Losing the First," by L. Wong Fillmore, 1991, Early Childhood Research Quarterly, 6(3), 323–346.

Make It Clear to the Families That You Value the Child's Native Language and Cultural Background

In the following discussion I use Spanish and Mexico for the sake of brevity, but Navajo, French, Vietnamese, or any other language could be used to make the same points.

The most important thing for children to learn about school is that it is a place where they feel welcome and comfortable. Including songs and stories in Spanish, using multiethnic pictures, and observing Mexican customs honor the family by using the language and customs of the home at school. Asking children for the Spanish equivalents of English words will help clarify that there are two languages and, if done with respect and enthusiasm, emphasize that the Spanish-speaking child has a special ability and skill.

It is also valuable to form close bonds of mutual concern with the parents of the children (Areñas, 1978; Bowman, 1990). Not all parents want their children to continue to learn in Spanish. This attitude varies a good deal from family to family, and teachers should discuss this subject with them, help them weigh the pros and cons, and respect their preferences in every way they can. Most families are realistic about the value of learning English and are almost too eager to have their children gain this skill. It may even be necessary to explain why Spanish is being included as a major component in the curriculum. Other families, rarer in number, will welcome the bicultural emphasis to such an extent that they may be reluctant to include English at all. The research reported by Wong Fillmore (1991) points out some difficulties and questions that still exist concerning the pros and cons of teaching English to children during their preschool years.

Sometimes school values in language development run counter to deep-seated cultural values in the home. For example, it may be necessary to explain to parents the positive relationship between language competence and the maximum development of intelligence. Such explanations may encourage families to overcome their traditional view that children should be seen and not heard, and the parents may make greater efforts to encourage their children to talk more at home.

Sometimes, of course, the teacher, rather than the family, needs to make the cultural adjustment. Some teachers, for instance, in their eagerness to promote verbalness in the children, fall into the habit of allowing the children to interrupt adult conversations whenever they please. This is frowned on in Mexican American homes. In such cases the teacher would do well to change her policy and encourage participation by the children while seeing to it that they continue to observe the basic good manners taught by their own culture.

When Teaching Bilingual Children, Do Not Attribute All Verbal-Expressive, and Comprehension Difficulties to Bilingualism

Many children who come to school speaking only a little English are quite fluent in their mother tongue, and for them the transition to English is not too difficult. *It is very important to distinguish between these youngsters and those who do not talk very much in either language.* These nontalkers need all the help they can get in developing the habit of verbalness. For such youngsters the goal is to increase fluency and participation in whichever language they feel more at ease; teaching English to them is of secondary importance to gaining fluency and the habit of talking.

What to Do When You Do Not Speak a Child's Language

Although it's all very well and good to discuss bilingual education on a remote level, the problem that ordinarily confronts the preschool teacher is the young child who arrives at school unable to speak any English at all.

Despite the language barrier, somehow a bridge of understanding must be built between that child and the teacher. I never think about this situation without recalling the sage advice of my former head teacher, Clevonease Johnson. At that center we had many youngsters who came to us from Vietnam and Cambodia. There they would stand, alone and bewildered, struggling not to cry as their parent and the interpreter walked out the door.

Although it wasn't possible for the teacher to acquire the child's language (at one time Clevonease would have had to have known eight languages to meet that standard), there were two phrases she said it was essential for her to know, and she never allowed the interpreter to leave without writing these down in phonetic English. The first was "Your mother will be back soon" and the second was "Do you need to go to the bathroom?" With these phrases tucked in her pocket, combined with warm smiles and many gestures, Clev felt she could handle anything!

Actually, of course, we found many additional language-related strategies useful to employ when working with a child who spoke another language, and several suggestions are included below. Even more valuable than these strategies, however, is the overall attitude toward cultural differences that must prevail in the center. There is no substitute for providing the newcomer with the warm welcome and appreciation of his background advocated in chapter 13, "Providing Cross-Cultural, Nonsexist Education."

1. First of all, remember to talk to the child. Sometimes teachers give up speaking to him just because the child does not respond. However, it's obvious that if he isn't spoken to in English, he won't have much of a chance to learn it.

2. Encourage the child to say something right from the start if he is comfortable doing this, but remember that many children require a considerable "quiet period" before they are ready to venture into an unfamiliar tongue (Tabors, 1997). This hesitancy can sometimes be overcome if other children are encouraged to talk freely to the newcomer. Children are less shy talking with each other than with the teacher.

3. When possible, pair the child with another youngster who speaks the same language. This can help him feel he has someone to turn to when feeling blocked.

4. When speaking to the child, keep your voice natural and not too loud. Talking louder does not help children understand any better, and sometimes it makes them think you are angry with them.

5. Use the child's name when you speak to him, and take care to pronounce it as accurately as you can. Never deny the child his identity by giving him an "American" name instead.

6. If you can pick up a few basic, frequently used words in the child's language it will be helpful—words like *outside, jacket,* and *lunch.* Activity nouns like *blocks* and *tricycle* will help a lot in smoothing the child's way.

7. Be visually expressive. Use gestures, smiles, encouraging looks, and friendliness to help the child understand and feel at ease.

8. Demonstrate what you mean as you speak. For example, ask, "Would you like to paint?" Then pick up the brush, gesture toward the paper, and repeat, "Would you like to paint?"

9. Link language to objects and real experience whenever possible. Teach nouns and verbs first; they are some of the most meaningful and useful words (except for *yes* and *no*).

10. Don't try to teach too many words at once, and be careful to repeat words many times until they become familiar.
11. Offer some short, easily repeated rhymes and songs each day so that the child can join in with the group without being self-conscious about speaking out on her own.
12. Be careful not to overwhelm the child with attention. Too much pressure is as bad as no attention at all.
13. Encourage other children to include the newcomer in their play. Explain that he needs special help; encourage them to name things for him as they use them.
14. And, finally, be aware yourself of how limited you feel because you speak only one or perhaps two languages. Encourage the child's parents to help him retain his ability to be (ultimately) bilingual. In this way he will always retain the advantage we might lack—the advantage of being able to communicate in two languages.

What to Do About the Child Who Speaks a Dialect

It is also vital for the teacher who forms this language bridge to acquaint herself with research indicating that African American children who come from city ghettos speak a dialect whose value, before the work of Labov (1970), went largely unassessed and unappreciated. For example, White teachers often bemoan the lack of language skills of their African American students and yet are in total ignorance of verbal games such as "the dozens," which are played on street corners and depend on the ability to concoct elaborate and very funny insults—obviously a language-based skill of a high order (Folb, 1980; Heath, 1989; E. Smith, 1998). Moreover, middle-class teachers are often unable to grasp even the most common argot used by the African American families they serve. This ignorance causes them to look down on the verbal abilities of the children. The books by Folb (1980), Perry and Delpit (1998), and Smitherman (1994) described in the References for Further Reading section provide much information and actual examples of *Ebonics* (the term often used in place of the former *Black English*). As our understanding about it grows, it is becoming evident that its grammar has definite rules and that there is a real sophistication to its structure (Hecht, Collier, & Ribeau, 1993; Labov, 1970; Smitherman, 1977). Indeed some theorists are already asserting that the variation in language between social classes or ethnic groups may ultimately turn out to be more a question of difference than defect or deficit (Pflaum, 1986).

The best recommendation for working with Ebonics appears to be that the teacher should respect the African American child's lect[2] just as she respects the Mexican or Puerto Rican child's Spanish yet, while doing this, also make it possible for him to learn Standard English because many African American parents as well as teachers agree it is a valuable tool for the child to possess.

This ability to switch from one form of English or even from one style of address to another is termed *code switching*. It may turn out that the most desirable skill to teach children is facility in being able to shift from one lect to another as the situation warrants, just as speakers of Spanish, German, or French learn to code-switch from their language

---

[2] *The word* lect *is currently the term preferred by many students in place of* dialect.

to English to make themselves understood. While acquiring this skill, it is hoped that the child has the opportunity to learn Standard English in an atmosphere that values and appreciates his already present linguistic strengths, rather than in one that smacks of condescension and noblesse oblige.

CHILDREN WHO HAVE SPECIAL DISABILITIES RELATED TO SPEECH AND HEARING

Several kinds of speech and hearing disabilities are seen quite commonly in the preprimary classroom. Indeed the teacher may find that she is the first person to be aware that the child has a speech problem, because the parent may be too accustomed to it to notice or too inexperienced to identify it as deviating markedly from normal speech. The four problems the teacher is most likely to come across are articulation disorders, delayed speech, hearing disorders, and stuttering.

With all these conditions, if the difficulty is pronounced or continues without positive change for 2 or 3 months after the child enters the center, the teacher should talk the problem over with the parents and encourage them to seek professional evaluation and help. Such referrals usually require both time (for the parents to become used to the idea that their child needs extra help) and tact (so that they do not feel blamed or accused of neglecting him). (For more information on how to make a successful referral, refer to chapter 9, "Welcoming Children Who Have Special Educational Requirements Into the Life of the School.")

What are some appropriate referral resources for such children? Colleges and universities often maintain speech and hearing clinics supervised by highly trained professionals. Moreover often little or no cost is involved because the clinics also serve as training experiences for beginning speech clinicians. Children's hospitals usually have speech clinicians on their staffs, and public schools almost always have a speech therapist available. These people are always glad to suggest appropriate referrals for speech therapy if the youngster does not qualify for help directly from the hospital or school.

Children with Disorders of Articulation

The teacher's problem with articulation disorders is deciding which ones are serious and which ones should be overlooked. To make this decision, the most important thing the teacher must know is that children do not acquire accuracy in pronouncing certain sounds until they are in the first or second grade. The information included in Figure 16.1 will be helpful in determining whether a child who is mispronouncing certain sounds should be referred to a speech pathologist for help. At the preschool level, therefore, many distortions, substitutions, and omissions can be treated with a combination of auditory training and benign neglect. *Referral is warranted, however, when the child's speech is generally unintelligible and the child is older than 3 or 3½,* because it is probable that he will need special help from a professionally trained clinician to learn to speak more plainly.

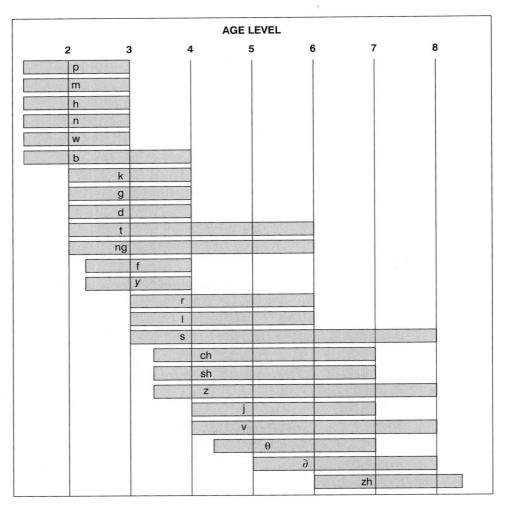

Figure 16.1
Average age estimates and upper age limits of customary consonant production. The solid bar corresponding to each sound starts at the median age of customary articulation; it stops at an age level at which 90% of all children are customarily producing the sound.

Source: From "When Are Speech Sounds Learned?" by E. K. Sander, 1972, Journal of Speech and Hearing Disorders, *37(1), p. 62. © 1972 by the American Speech and Hearing Association. Reprinted by permission.*

The only unfortunate outcome of such a referral is that the therapist might decide the child does not need special help after all. This can be mildly embarrassing to the teacher, but it is better to take this risk if the child's speech seems seriously impaired than to let his poor speech habits continue until he reaches kindergarten.

Besides knowing when to refer and when to overlook the articulation disorder, the teacher should realize there is a lot more to correcting an articulation problem than just reminding the child, "Don't say 'wed,' say 'red.'" Traditional speech therapists usually proceed by (a) using auditory discrimination games to help the child hear the error and tell it apart from other sounds, (b) eliminating the cause of the disorder if possible (e.g., encouraging the parents to raise their speech standards at home so that the child no longer gets by with infantile speech patterns), (c) teaching him to make the correct sound by itself, and (d) finally incorporating it into familiar words (Hegde & Davis, 1995).

The problem with this kind of isolated work is getting it to carry over into everyday speech (Gerber, 1993; Van Riper & Erickson, 1996). To make carryover more likely, newer approaches are coming into use (Gerber, 1993). Rather than pulling the child out of his usual environment, taking him off to a quiet place, providing isolated practice in particular skills, and then restoring him to the classroom, these therapists work right in the classroom along with the regular staff. They do their best to seize on opportunities for meaningful practice that occur as the child is involved in ongoing activities. This procedure means not only that the needed language skill is integrated into the child's ordinary life but also that the staff has the chance to observe and learn how to provide continued practice in those skills when the therapist is not present (Patrick, 1993). (Refer to chapter 9 for a more detailed discussion of how this interdisciplinary approach works.)

It is in this regard that the preschool staff can be the most help—not by nagging the child but by encouraging conversation. During such talk an occasional puzzled look of not understanding what the child is saying followed by pleased comprehension if he repeats the word more clearly will encourage better articulation habits. Of course, all the children will benefit from consistent auditory discrimination activities included in group time, just as they will from the many other means of developing language ability discussed earlier in this chapter. (Appendix G provides a list of auditory discrimination activities.)

Children with Delayed Speech

Although articulation disorders are encountered with greater frequency, the teacher is more likely to notice the child who does not talk or who talks very little. Such youngsters are often referred to preschools and children's centers by pediatricians and in certain cases can be helped effectively by that teacher.

Causes of Delayed Speech

Causes of delayed speech are myriad and range from the child's being hard of hearing to having a neuromuscular disorder such as cerebral palsy. Low intelligence is another common cause of delayed speech; being unfamiliar with English, and negativism or extreme shyness also take their toll. Lack of sufficient environmental stimulation or low parental expectations may also mean a child has not developed to his full verbal potential.

In such cases the teacher needs to take a keen, continuing look at the child to try to determine what lies behind the lack of speech. Making a home visit can help ascertain whether he just does not talk at school or whether his nonverbal behavior is consistent in all situations.

It is often difficult or impossible for someone who is not specially trained to spot the cause of lags in speech development. Contrary to general opinion, children who are slow learners do not necessarily look different from their peers. I have known several instances in which youngsters with mild or even moderate cognitive delays were denied help and appropriate teaching because the cardinal symptom of delayed speech went unquestioned by an inexperienced teacher because the child "looked normal." The services of a competent psychologist can be enlisted to identify the slow learner if the child is referred to her. Neuromuscular disorders do not always manifest themselves in obvious ways either; so when such a condition appears to be a likely possibility, a referral to the child's pediatrician is a sound approach to take.

Children who restrict themselves from talking because they are overwhelmed by the newness of school, who speak a different language, or who do not talk because they appear to have been deprived of sufficient speech stimulation or too low expectations at home are the ones with the brightest prognosis. In these cases the teacher can gently draw them forth and elicit more speech by responding positively to their venturings. Many of these children will make a heartening gain in fluency during the year or two they spend at the center if the methods described in the previous section on developing language skills are applied to them (Greenspan, 1998).

Children with Disorders of Hearing

Another useful way teachers can help the children in their care is to be on the lookout for those who do not hear well. This is a surprisingly common disorder, yet it often goes by unnoticed.

Studies show that as many as *one out of every three young children has some form of hearing loss* (Teele, Klein, & Rosner, 1989), and more than 80% of children suffer an ear infection by age 3 (Schering-Plough & *Scholastic Early Childhood Today*, n.d.). Ironically the most common kind of loss, a conductive hearing loss resulting from trouble in the middle ear and often the result of infection, is not usually picked up in screening tests; thus many youngsters who have had their hearing tested slip through the testing screen with this disability not identified. This is particularly unfortunate because middle-ear-type losses account for about 90% of all hearing losses in children and are also most amenable to cure or correction once detected. For these reasons it is important to educate parents that they should request a test for conductive hearing loss called a *tympanometric test,* as well as a pure tone audiometer test, when having their children's hearing evaluated.

Children attending centers are particularly likely to get these middle-ear infections (*otitis media*) because they are exposed to more colds and upper respiratory diseases, which often lead to infections and loss of hearing acuity in the middle ear (Bray & Khele, 1998). If left untreated, these infections can last for months and make a real difference in how well the youngster hears what is said and ultimately in how clearly he speaks. Families tend to adjust to this condition without realizing their children's hearing has diminished, so it is particularly important for teachers to be alert to the sometimes rather subtle symptoms of hearing loss (Watt, Roberts, & Zeisel, 1993).

A child with the following behaviors or conditions should alert the teacher to the possibility that he may be hard of hearing:

■ The child who does not talk

■ The child who watches you intently but often "just doesn't seem to understand"

- The child who does not respond or turn around when the teacher speaks to him in a normal tone of voice from behind him

- The child who consistently pays little attention during story hour or who always wants to sit right in front of the teacher

- The child whose speech is indistinct and difficult to understand, most particularly if high-frequency sounds such as *f* and *s* are missing from his speech

- The child who talks more softly or loudly than most of the other children

- The child whose attention you have to catch by touching him on the shoulder

- The child who often asks you to repeat sentences for him or says, "Huh?" a lot

- The child who has a perpetual cold, runny nose, frequent earaches, or usually breathes through his mouth

- The child who consistently ignores you unless you get right down and look him in the eye as you talk to him

- Any child who has recently recovered from measles, meningitis, scarlet fever, or a severe head injury

Such youngsters are prime candidates for audiometric testing. Of course, it is also true that children talk indistinctly, want to sit close to the teacher, or fail to pay attention for reasons other than hearing loss. But *particularly if more than one of these symptoms describe his usual behavior,* the possibility of a hearing deficit is worth investigating. Referrals may be made to an otolaryngologist (a doctor who treats ear and throat disorders) or to the child's pediatrician, who will send him to the best place to receive help.

Hearing losses can result from many causes besides otitis media. Sometimes the loss can be remedied through surgery; but if the loss is permanent, continued professional guidance will be necessary. Although hearing aids do not alleviate all forms of deafness, they can be effective in many cases. Hearing aids combined with speech therapy and auditory training are helpful for many children who have loss of hearing.

Children Who Stutter

Although we do know that an easy, unself-conscious form of repetitive speech is often observed in children under age 5, we do not yet understand why this should be the case. This first stage of repetitive speech differs markedly from the strained, emotion-laden hesitancies and repetitions of the confirmed stutterer and is more than likely liable to vanish *if teachers and family do not react to it with concern and tension.*

Teachers can play an effective role in helping parents deal with their concern over this potential problem. First, they should encourage parents to relax and not to direct attention to the behavior. This includes *not* saying to the child, "Now, just slow down; I'll wait 'til you're ready," or, "Don't talk so fast," or, "Your ideas just get ahead of your tongue; take it easy" (Hulit, 1996). They should also reassure the family by explaining that this behavior is common in young children who are undergoing the stress of learning to talk. The goal here is to encourage parents to relax and reduce stressful situations in the home so that the child will not become concerned about his speech.

Since stuttering increases when the child is undergoing stress, it can be helpful to avoid hurrying him when possible, to allow plenty of time for him to speak, to speak a little slowly when carrying on conversations with him, to provide him your full but relaxed attention when he speaks to you, and to avoid putting him on the spot by asking direct questions or by urging him to talk in front of others during group time (Bray & Kehle, 1998).

It is also wise to inquire of the family whether something is currently making life more difficult for the child at home. Do what you can to relieve that situation. Examples of stressful events are a visit from a critical grandparent, a new baby-sitter, a move to a new home, the arrival of a baby, being held to unreasonably high standards of behavior, or a death or divorce in the family. Tension-relieving activities such as dramatic play, water play, and various forms of sublimated aggressive activities can be provided that may reduce some of the child's tensions and attendant stuttering.

As with other speech disorders, it is also necessary to have some rule of thumb for referral when working with a child who stutters. At the preprimary level it seems wise to refer the family for further help if they are reacting strongly to the behavior and are unable to control their signs of concern, if they seem unable to reduce the tension-generating situations without outside help, or if the stuttering persists.

SUMMARY

The development of language skills in preschool children has become of cardinal interest to their teachers as evidence mounts that linguistic competence and mental ability go hand in hand.

Children appear to acquire language partially as a result of an inborn ability to do so and partially in response to environmental stimulation and conditioning. Much remains to be learned in this area, and a complete explanation of how language is acquired remains one of the tantalizing mysteries of human development.

In recent years the science of pragmatics, which stresses the interactional importance of the social and developmental aspects of language acquisition, has come increasingly to the fore. In this area studies relating to the way children learn to use conversation have been of particular interest to early childhood teachers.

Teachers of young children can do many things to facilitate children's language acquisition:

- Listen carefully to what children have to say.
- Provide a meaningful base of experience to talk about.
- Encourage conversation among children.
- Talk to the children themselves.
- Use questions to generate speech and develop language.
- When necessary, seek professional assistance for children who require it.

In this chapter the questions of bilingualism and the use of Ebonics in the preschool were also discussed, and some suggestions were included about teaching English as a second language.

Finally four common disorders of speech and hearing were identified: disorders of articulation, delayed speech, deficient hearing, and stuttering. Recommendations were made for classroom treatment and remediation of these disorders, and suggestions for referral were included.

Questions and Activities

1. Identify some factors in the school where you teach that encourage the development of conversation between children and adults. What are some things that discourage conversation between them?

2. List some additional conversation starters you have found useful in getting young children involved in talking with the teacher or with other children.

3. *Predicament:* A mother calls and says her pediatrician has suggested that she place Silas in your center because he has been a little slow in learning to talk. As you become acquainted with Silas, it does appear to you that his speech is slow to develop. He is 3 years old and still communicates mainly by grunting, nodding his head, or pointing when he wants something. List some possible reasons why his speech might be developing so slowly. How would you go about determining which cause is the most likely one? Propose a course of action that would be most appropriate for each probable cause.

4. Do you believe that teachers have the right to change something as personal to the child as his dialect or dominant language? Under what circumstances do you think doing this is warranted or unwarranted?

5. Do you advocate setting up schools that use only the child's native tongue or dialect? What would be the strong points of doing this? What might be the drawbacks?

Self-Check Questions for Review

Content-Related Questions

1. Describe three theories that attempt to explain the process by which children learn to talk.

2. On what aspects of language acquisition do people who study pragmatics concentrate?

3. Describe what Wong Fillmore (1991) found out about how language use changed when children attended bilingual or English-only preschools and compare it with how language use changed when children attended Spanish-only preschools.

4. About how many words should a child have at his command by the age of 1? By the age of 2?

5. Give some examples of what a teacher might say to encourage conversation between children.

6. List some important principles the teacher should remember for encouraging conversation between herself and the children.

7. Suppose you had a child in your room who did not speak any English. How could you help him feel comfortable and gradually learn a second language?

8. What are the four most common types of speech and language disorders in young children, and what might be the symptoms for each of these that the teacher should look for?

9. Should teachers and parents always be concerned when children repeat words several times when speaking?

Integrative Questions

1. Which theory—the nativist or the behaviorist—offers more hope to a teacher who has a 3-year-old child in her class who isn't talking yet? Explain why you selected that theory.
2. As a teacher of young children, do you think it is more valuable to understand the theories of how language is acquired or to understand the effects pragmatics has on language development? Be sure to explain why you have selected one or the other.
3. A friend has brought a nanny goat to visit your group of 4-year-olds at school and is milking her. Sarah Lee says, "Bubbles. See the bubbles!" Give an example of what you would reply if Sarah were 2½ years old and how you would change your reply if she were 4 years old.
4. The teacher in the room next door says to you, "I certainly admire you for taking that Spanish class so you can talk to Miguel and Angelica, but if I were you I wouldn't bother. After all, this is America, and if they want to be American, they'd better learn to talk English! You go on speaking Spanish to them, it'll just slow them down." What would be your response to her?
5. According to the findings in the Wong Fillmore (1991) study, what are the advantages and disadvantages of teaching English as a second language in the preschool? In your opinion, do the advantages outweigh the disadvantages or vice versa? Be sure to provide reasons for your decision.

Coordinating Videotape

Let's talk about it. Tape #12. The whole child: A caregiver's guide to the first five years. The Annenberg/CPB Collection, P.O. Box 2345, South Burlington, VT 05407–2345. *Let's Talk About It* reviews the process of language acquisition and demonstrates methods for increasing language competence in young children including those with special language or hearing problems, bilingual children, and children who speak a language unfamiliar to the teacher.

References for Further Reading
Pick of the Litter

Tabors, P. O. (1997). *One child, two languages: A guide for preschool educators of children learning English as a second language.* Baltimore, MD: Brookes. This book is selected as *Pick of the Litter* not only because it is filled with examples and useful advice about helping children who have a dominant language other than English but also because it is an outstanding example of how to translate well-done research into practice. *Highly recommended.*

Overviews

Carroll, D. W. (1999). *Psychology of language* (3rd ed.). Pacific Grove, CA: Brooks/Cole. This is a good, general text that discusses many aspects of language, including development.

Holzman, M. (1997). *The language of children* (2nd ed.). London: Blackwell. Generally well written, *The Language of Children* includes a very good chapter on early language development. *Highly recommended.*

Rice, M. L., & Wilcox, K. A. (Eds.). (1995). *Building a language-focused curriculum for the preschool classroom: Vol. 1. A foundation for lifelong communication.* Baltimore, MD: Brookes. This book and its companion volume by B. H. Bunce (1995)—*Building a language-focused curriculum for the preschool classroom: Vol. 2. A planning guide* (Baltimore, MD: Brookes)—are filled with sensible advice and examples of ways to incorporate a rich infusion of language stimulation into an otherwise "typical" children's center. The material is based on the Language Acquisition Preschool at the University of Kansas. *Highly recommended.*

Bilingualism and Ebonics

Hakuta, K. (1998). Improving education for all children: Meeting the needs of language minority children. In D. Clark (Moderator), *Education and the development of American youth.* Washington, DC: Aspen Institute. Hakuta sums up research about bilingual education in a succinct paper. *Highly recommended.*

Perry, T., & Delpit, L. (1998). *The real Ebonics debate: Power, language, and the education of African American children.* Boston: Beacon Press. Written shortly after the controversy over Ebonics erupted in Oakland, this book provides a reasoned explanation of the value of Ebonics as a means of communication.

Smitherman, G. (1994). *Black talk: Words and phrases from the hood to the AMEN corner.* Boston: Houghton Mifflin. This is primarily a dictionary of current usage but also includes a helpful introductory essay. *Highly recommended.*

Language Disabilities

Blasi, M. J., & Priestley, L. (1998). A child with severe hearing loss joins our learning community. *Young Children, 53*(2), 44–49. This description of an actual situation provides useful reminders about incorporating any child with a disability into a group.

Greenspan, S. (1998). Recognizing and responding to language delays. *Scholastic Early Childhood Today, 13*(1), 67–69. Common examples of delayed speech, the cause, and practical responses to the conditions are discussed here.

Hulit, L. M. (1996). *Straight talk on stuttering: Information, encouragement, and counsel for stutterers, caregivers, and speech-language clinicians.* Springfield, IL: Charles C Thomas. Lots of information and practical advice is provided here. *Highly recommended.*

Oyer, H. J., & Hall, B. J. (1994). *Speech, language, and hearing disorders: A guide for the teacher.* Boston: College Hill. This is a clear, quick-reading, concise book that offers practical recommendations for what the classroom teacher can do to facilitate good language habits. *Highly recommended.*

For the Advanced Student

Bloom, L. (1998). Language acquisition in its developmental context. In D. Kuhn & R. S. Siegler (Eds.), *Handbook of child psychology* (5th ed.): Vol. *2. Cognition, perception, and language.* New York: Wiley. A careful, comprehensive description of how language develops is provided by an authority on the subject. Indispensable for the serious student.

Fishman, J. A. (Ed.). (1999). *Handbook of language and ethnic identity.* New York: Oxford University Press. This book focuses on the complex relationship between the use or revival of a language and attitudes toward it—a readable introduction to this aspect of bilingualism.

Garcia, E. E., & McLaughlin, B. (1995). *Meeting the challenge of linguistic and cultural diversity in early childhood education.* New York: Teachers College Press. This book focuses almost entirely on bilingual Mexican children. It covers subjects as diverse as assessment and social development.

Hart, B., & Risley, T. R. (1995). *Meaningful differences in the everyday experience of young American children.* Baltimore, MD: Brookes. This landmark study identifies factors that influence the quality of language development in children's families of different economic levels.

Rodriguez, J. L., Diaz, R. M., Duran, D., & Espinosa, L. (1995). The impact of bilingual preschool education on the language development of Spanish-speaking children. *Early Childhood Research Quarterly, 10*(4), 475–490. This is a well considered reply and follow-up to the Wong Fillmore research discussed on pages 424–425. It presents evidence that children do not lose Spanish proficiency while learning English. It does not address the effect learning English may have on parent/child relations.

chapter seventeen

Fostering the Emergence of Literacy

What to say to parents when they suggest you teach the 4-year-olds to read?

What people are talking about when they mention *emergent literacy*?

How you can get wiggly Matilda to hold still during group time?

. . . IF YOU HAVE, THE MATERIAL ON THE FOLLOWING PAGES WILL HELP YOU.

Children at every age possess certain literacy skills, although these skills are not fully developed or conventional, as we recognize mature reading and writing to be. Emergent literacy acknowledges as rudimentary writing a child's scribble marks on a page, even if not one letter is discernible. The child who knows the difference between such scribbles and drawings certainly has some sense of the difference between writing and illustration. Similarly, when a child narrates a familiar storybook while looking at the pictures and print and gives the impression of reading, we acknowledge the activity as legitimate literacy behavior.

Lesley M. Morrow (1997, p. 131)

A current concern of many preprimary teachers is the pressure some parents and school districts are putting on them to present a highly structured reading program in the preschool.

Rather than just deploring the effects such pressure would have on the children because such expectations are developmentally inappropriate, as the opening quotation makes clear, it is wiser to understand what parents (and, hence, school districts) want and then to understand how to reassure them while protecting the children from unreasonable expectations.

Parents are not ogres; they simply want what's best for their children. They see the world as a difficult place to grow up in, they see technology advancing at a frightening pace, and they want their children to be successful, competent grown-ups who can cope with that world. They know that intellectual competence is one key to effective functioning in that world, and they think of the ABCs and reading as being cognitive skills that will provide their children with that competence. After all, this is what they were taught when they went to school, so it is only reasonable that they think of "real learning" as consisting of that kind of instruction.

What teachers should do is conduct a careful educational campaign with the children's parents to inform them about what the children are learning at the center. The teachers should explain that what they are doing *is* appropriate for the children's ages and developmental stages and that it paves the way for learning to read more easily later on.

Part of this information will inevitably involve explaining how children learn from play; all the benefits children derive from being involved in such preschool activities as blocks, sand, and water; and how they help form the foundation upon which later skills are built. But it should also include clear-cut descriptions of the various reasoning and problem-solving skills that are incorporated into the curriculum each day, accompanied by explanations of how these abilities underlie later competence in school. These skills are discussed in detail in chapters 18 and 19.

In addition to these explanations the teacher needs to add information about all the language development activities that are part and parcel of a good preschool curriculum (L. M. Morrow, 1997; Schickendanz, 1999). He needs to emphasize that these activities construct the foundation upon which reading is later built (refer to chapter 16). These range from learning new words to telling a coherent story about what happened on the way to school. They include using language in conversation or using it to make the child's desires known, as well as learning that books can be a source of fascinating pleasure at group time.

Activities such as these form the foundation for later reading and writing. Parents need to understand that learning to read is a lengthy process and that much preparation and maturation must take place before it can be accomplished successfully (Fields & Spangler, 2000). Once parents realize the teacher knows what he is doing and that he is "really teaching the children something" that will form a solid foundation for later learning at the elementary school level, they generally stop asking about reading per se and become supportive of what is provided at the preschool level.

DOES FOSTERING LITERACY MEAN TEACHING READING?

From one point of view it is unnecessary to discuss implementing literacy in the preschool classroom since children have been doing it for years, anyway! Every time a child singles out her name tag and puts it on, or finds the book she has been hunting for, or supplies the phrase the gingerbread boy says as he runs from his potential captors, or counts the number of spoonfuls needed pictured on a recipe card, she is using literacy-related skills. Every time she substitutes a pretend spoon for a real one, or tells what's happening in a picture, or uses language in any form, then, too, she is engaged in emerging literacy activities because all these activities and hundreds like them are examples of the array of skills that underlie the ultimate skills of reading and writing.

This understanding of what constitutes true literacy makes it clear that its development entails far more than learning skills such as handwriting, decoding the printed word, and spelling. As McLane and McNamee (1990) point out, "Literacy development consists of mastering a complex set of attitudes, expectations, feelings, behaviors, and skills related to the written language. This collection of attitudes and skills constitutes what has been called 'emergent literacy'" (p. 4).

And yet the idea of fostering reading and writing strategies continues to make many preschool teachers feel uncomfortable and concerned. This resistance is not without reason. As the guardians of children's right to be children and to learn in developmentally appropriate ways and at suitable levels, we teachers of very young children have had to resist the pressures of inappropriate expectations and methods and watered-down elemen-

Loving books is an important aspect of motivating the desire to attain literacy.

tary curricula for more years than we like to remember. If literacy means teaching the ABCs and phonics to 3- and 4-year-olds, then we must continue our resistance.

However, *emergent literacy* does not advocate such approaches. It does *not* mean we are going to teach the children to read—far from it. Research has shown time and time again that the arts of reading and writing (for the two must go together) rely on the prior acquisition of a great many foundation concepts and strategies—strategies that teachers of young children have been encouraging children to develop for many years. Figure 17.1 lists many activities that are basic to helping children develop literacy. Note that all of them down through scribbling in item 5 are frequently part of the preschool curriculum.

SOME FUNDAMENTAL PRINCIPLES TO KEEP IN MIND

The majority of the basics listed in Figure 17.1 have been discussed in previous chapters, so only the most fundamental principles are reviewed here.

Encourage Families to Read to the Children at Home

When concerned parents ask teachers, "When are the children really going to learn something?" what they often have in mind is the alphabet and similar skills. Rather than brushing aside these well-meant requests, it is more productive to think of them as providing a wonderful opportunity not only to explain the foundation reading skills incorporated in the preschool curriculum but also to enlist the parents' cooperation in reading to their children at home.

Admittedly getting parents to read to their children is not always easy to do. For a variety of reasons as varied as exhaustion and illiteracy, some children rarely or never see their parents read anything. This does not mean, however, that teachers should not do all they can to encourage reading at home; experience has taught me that some families are always willing to "give it a try" once they understand how important it is to take an active part in their children's learning to read. Perhaps it is reading the funny papers to their youngster, or perhaps it is leafing through a picture book lent from the center and talking about the pictures, or reading the directions on a lottery ticket: Just about anything that emphasizes the value of the written word is worth encouraging.

Of course, some kinds of reading are more desirable than others. If the preschool provides a lending library of inexpensive, good-quality paperback picture books such as the ones made available by Scholastic[1] and Gryphon House,[2] the children's enthusiasm makes it likely these will go home to be enjoyed. Talking with parents about finding a regular time to read to their children is also worth encouraging. Once this part of the program is going well, some of the parents will be interested in learning how to make their book time even more effective by getting the child to comment about the book, too—and, the ultimate of ultimates, tell the story back to the parent. Although this may seem to be expect-

---

[1] *Scholastic, Inc., 555 Broadway, New York, NY 10012.*
[2] *Gryphon House, P. O. Box 207, Beltsville, MD 20704–0207.*

Figure 17.1

Foundations of literacy

Source: From Let's begin reading right: Developmentally appropriate beginning literacy *(3rd ed., p. 104), by M. V. Fields and K. S. Spangler, 1995, Upper Saddle River, NJ: Prentice Hall. Used by permission.*

Literacy Basics

1. A print-rich environment
   - adults who read for their own purposes
   - adults who write for their own purposes
   - frequent story time experiences
   - dictation experiences
   - high-quality literature
   - contextualized print
   - functional print
   - answers to questions about print

2. A rich oral language environment
   - adult language models
   - adults who listen to children
   - free exploration of oral language
     - peer conversation
     - dramatic play roles
   - experiences for vocabulary enrichment
   - vocabulary information as requested

3. Firsthand experiences of interest
   - play
   - daily living
   - field trips
   - nature exploration

4. Symbolic representation experiences
   - dramatic play
   - drawing and painting
   - music and dance

5. Pressure-free experimentation with writing
   - drawing
   - scribbling
   - nonphonetic writing
   - invented spelling

6. Pressure-free exploration of reading
   - reading from memory
   - reading with context clues
   - matching print to oral language

physical self ≈ emotional health ≈ self-esteem ≈ social competence

| Research Study |

Promoting Literacy in a Developmentally Appropriate Way

Research Questions: Morrow wanted to find out whether children's voluntary literacy behaviors could be increased during play by altering the design and equipment of the dramatic play areas. She also wanted to find out what effect teacher guidance during play would have on the amount of literacy behavior.

Research Method: The middle-class suburban sample consisted of 13 preschool classrooms with a total of 170 children, half of each sex. The staff for each room was composed of a cooperating teacher and a student-teacher. Prior to the experiment, literacy materials had not been incorporated into the dramatic play areas of any of the classrooms.

The classrooms were divided into four groups, with the three experimental groups (E1, E2, E3) receiving the same literacy materials: paper of various sizes, a stapler, blank booklets, books, magazines, and writing materials such as pencils, crayons, and felt pens. The differences in the three experimental groups had to do with whether the teacher guided the play by suggesting possible literacy-based activities at the beginning of each play period (E1, E2) and whether a specific theme was used in the play (E2, E3).

C1—*the control group* in which nothing was changed

E1—*nonthematic guided play* with literacy materials placed in the housekeeping area

E2—*thematic nonguided play* with literacy materials using the theme of a veterinary office

E3—*thematic guided play* with literacy materials using the theme of a veterinary office

All four groups were observed several times before the experiment began in order to establish a baseline and determine the amount of literacy activity before changes were introduced.

After that the literacy materials were introduced into the experimental classrooms. Observations of the children's play in the control and experimental settings were made for 3 weeks and then, after 1 month's lapse, for 3 more weeks.

The resulting data were sorted into four categories of literacy behavior: paper handling, attempted writing, attempted reading, and combined scores for the three behaviors.

Results: Morrow found that changing the physical design definitely did increase the amount of voluntary literacy behaviors for some of the children (the investigator notes that the use of the materials was "limited to only a few children per classroom" [p. 549]). The children who participated in all three experimental groups included more literacy behaviors during their play than did the control group. The two groups that experienced teacher guidance along with the addition of the literacy materials used the materials more than the group that did not have teacher guidance. Moreover the introduction of the theme of the veterinarian's office produced more total literacy behaviors and more interactive play than did the nonthematic housekeeping setting. The final interesting result was that the literacy behavior continued over a rather long period of time (3 weeks of observation, 1 month interim, plus 3 more weeks of observation time).

Implications for Teaching: It is clear from this research that teachers who want their preschool

physical self ≈ emotional health ≈ self-esteem ≈ social competence ≈

children to participate in voluntary literacy activities can encourage that behavior in several ways: They can add literacy materials to various dramatic play areas for the children to use as they see fit; they can provide specific play themes that encourage the use of attempted writing and reading; and they can provide ideas and guidance about how these materials might be used by the children during their play.

In closing, some cautionary notes must be added as reminders. On the one hand, it is evident that this activity appealed to only a handful of children in each classroom, so we should not conclude that all children will benefit from having this opportunity provided to them. On the other hand, the amount of time and satisfaction obviously present for some of the children points to the value of

making such materials consistently available for those who are ready for them. Another thing to remember—which Morrow stresses—is that although the play was enhanced by the presence of the materials, provision of a theme, and teacher suggestions, the play that resulted was *voluntary* and produced by the children themselves; it was not the result of teacher domination. This is an important point to remember. When offering guidance, teachers must remain exquisitely sensitive to what is happening and stop short of the point at which play becomes manipulation by the teacher and loses its vital quality of spontaneity and delight.

Source: From "Preparing the Classroom Environment to Promote Literacy During Play," by L. M. Morrow, 1990, Early Childhood Research Quarterly, 5(4), 537–554.

ing too much, research by Lonigan and Whitehurst (1998) does reveal that such dialogues between adults and children, rather than only reading aloud, make a significant difference in the development of oral language skills. Offering a program on parents night with a catchy title such as "Teaching Your Kids to Read—Let's Begin Now!" and demonstrating how to have fun with a book and engage the children in conversation makes it much easier to understand. (We had a hilarious time last year with the staff and some volunteer parents acting as the children while a mildly harassed director acted as the teacher; several parents said later they'd gone home and let their children respond more as they read to them as a result of that evening program.)

Teachers Should Make It Plain That They Value the Wonderful World of Books

Teachers can show that they value books if they clearly enjoy the good books they read aloud as much as the children do. There is no substitute for this infectious enthusiasm.

Since children's literary and aesthetic tastes are being formed every time they come in contact with a book, it is important to select books with great care. There's really no excuse for offering children "cute" but essentially worthless books when all it takes is a trip to the library to find wonderful, beautifully illustrated ones. *Story Stretchers* and *More Story Stretchers* (Raines & Canady, 1989, 1991) are helpful resources for choosing such books. Additional resources are included at the end of this chapter.

The high value the teacher places on good books is also shown in subtler ways by the care that everyone in the room takes of them. Books belong in people's laps or enjoyed in the rocking chair—not left on the floor to be trampled. Old favorites should be promptly mended and torn pages carefully taped with the children's help.

Teachers Should Emphasize How Useful the Written Word Can Be

As an example of how teachers can emphasize the usefulness of the written word, the shared experience of writing a note to the janitor asking her to leave up their block construction can make this usefulness obvious to the block builders. Empowering children by encouraging them to follow an illustrated recipe on their own provides the satisfaction of accomplishment for independent 4-year-olds. "You didn't even have to tell me nothin'!" chortled one of the Institute youngsters the other day. "I read it all!"—and he had. Labeling containers and activity areas also helps tie together the idea that written words stand for real objects.

Opportunities that encourage children to incorporate various forms of language into their play are yet another effective way to foster emerging literacy skills. For example, Schickendanz (1999) suggests that the housekeeping corner could include a telephone book, cookbooks, coupons, marketing list materials, play money, and calendars, just to name a few possibilities. Office play could use envelopes, telephone message pads, magazines, and, of course, paper, pencils, an old typewriter or perhaps a computer, stamps, and a stamp pad. In recent years several studies, exemplified by the Research Study in this chapter, have demonstrated how the use of such materials can positively affect children's literacy behavior.

EVEN VERY YOUNG CHILDREN CAN AND SHOULD BE INVOLVED IN PRODUCING THE WRITTEN WORD

It is helpful to think about children's writing from two aspects. The first aspect focuses on the children's attempts to write for themselves. The second is dictating what they want to say to someone else.

Writing on Their Own

A surprising number of children have little or no practice writing at home—either because materials are not available, or parents do not realize beginning scribbles may be early attempts at writing, or they think pencils are dangerous, or they don't want the children to mark up walls, tables, or so forth.

Whatever the reason for the inexperience, the teacher who wants to encourage the link between spoken language and the printed page needs to provide many opportunities for children to "do writing" on their own. Having materials available for them to use, such as felt pens, crayons, soft pencils, interesting paper, and old envelopes, nicely sorted and attractively arranged, is essential.

Using stamps to write your name is a nice step on the path toward attaining literacy.

Just as essential as having materials consistently available is showing respect for the children's efforts. These efforts, of course, won't look like much to start with. Over time they will gradually advance through a series of steps progressing from wavy lines, dots, and scribbles all the way through to consistent, reasonably accurate printing in primary school (Soderman, Gregory, & O'Neill, 1999). Such comments as, "Look at all that writing you're working on!" and, "It looks to me like you're saying something there" [pause, expectant glance at child to see whether she wants to tell you what she intends] will encourage the children to make further attempts.

Having Someone Write for Them

Another way children can experience turning language into written text is by dictating stories, letters, or ideas for the teacher to write down. Doing this emphasizes the relationship between reading and writing while empowering the child to express her ideas more completely and freely.

Pitcher and Prelinger (1963) studied more than 300 stories told by children ages 2 to about 6 years. They found that as the children matured, their stories included an increasing use and mastery of space, a less clear differentiation of main characters, more happenings that affect the characters, and a significant increase in the use of fantasy and imagi-nation. Therefore, when pursuing creative stories with preschool-age children, the teacher should be prepared for considerable literalness in stories by younger children and a greater use of fantasy and imagination by older ones. But since the stories are personal descriptions and reflections of the children's feelings and perceptions, they may also be considered self-expressive and hence creative.

The following two examples of dictated stories are both factual and quite expressive of feelings.

The Doctor and the Nurse
Marice

When I got the cast off, we used an electric saw and I had something on my ears. The saw was very sharp and looked just like the sun.

The thing I had on my ears was round. I couldn't hear the electric saw, but the other doctors could. It played music very loud, as loud as the saw.

The doctor held my hand because he didn't think I could walk by myself. He's not a very good doctor, and I don't like him either—the first doctor I'm talking about.

The nurse clipped the cast off. She went out after that. I needed my privacy, anyways.

My House Story
Angelique

This first page will be about my dog. His name is Toulouse. Sometimes I can't play with him because he goes to dog school. At dog school, somebody makes him fetch sticks and makes him beg. Then he comes home and he shows me what he has learned. I also have a cat. His name is Goya, named after a painter. We always name our animals after painters.

Now about my grandmother and grandfather. My grandmother goes to Weight Watchers. They weigh her there without her shoes on.

Now about my grandfather. He drives a car. It's a red Datsun wagon pickup.

My house is white with a white picket fence. My grandma, grandpa, mommy, and me all live in the house.

My grandfather went to the hospital the day before yesterday. He had his operation yesterday. I don't like to have him in the hospital. He's not here to read me a bedtime story.

I miss him.

These stories mattered a lot to the children who wrote them. At that time the teachers were using little handmade books for recording the stories so that the children were free to illustrate them if they wished. This provided an additional way to work off their feelings and be creative. But it is not necessary to make story telling that elaborate an occasion. Taking the story down as the child dictates it often provides sufficient encouragement for the young storyteller. Pitcher (Pitcher & Prelinger, 1963) collected her stories by waiting until a child was either sitting quietly by herself or playing alone and then by saying, "Tell me a story. What would your story be about?" This is a good way to get started. Of course, children sometimes do not want to participate. In this case the teacher just says, "Well, I expect you'll want to do it another time. I'll ask you then."

As with other creative materials, the teacher should scrupulously avoid suggesting what the story should be about or what might happen next. But it does encourage the creator to ask, "Then what happened?" "Then what did she do?" or, "Do you want to tell me anything else?" These questions will help sweep the child along into the narrative.

Creative stories can also be stimulated by providing hand puppets (Burn, 1989) or flannel board materials, which can be set out for the children to use as they feel the need or used at group time for this purpose. Rubber dolls and toy animals offer another medium for imaginative stories and play. Creative stories can also be stimulated by providing pictures, which may be used as starting points for discussion.

Besides dictating and telling stories, children can learn to value written language by chanting along with the teacher, "I think I can, I think I can, I think I can," as he points to the words while reading the beloved *Little Engine That Could* (Piper, 1980). They can listen as the teacher reads aloud to them the note he is sending home to their families, and they can mail their letters at the post office before Valentine's Day. If attractive writing materials are assembled in a convenient spot, the children can elaborate on their scribbles and enclose the messages in old envelopes.

Although these literacy activities and others like them should be spread throughout the curriculum, just as *whole language* is integrated into the curriculum of many elementary schools, there is one particular experience during the day that provides an outstanding opportunity to foster emergent literacy. This is the experience of group time.

SUGGESTIONS FOR PRESENTING A LANGUAGE-RICH GROUP TIME EXPERIENCE

A well-planned group time can be a high spot of the day for teachers and children, or it can become a dreaded encounter between them as the children thrash about and the teacher struggles to maintain a semblance of order.

Successful group times depend on careful advance planning by the teacher that takes into consideration such things as including enough variety, making certain the material is interesting, providing opportunities for the children to interact with the teacher, and knowing how to pace activities so that they sustain the children's interest. The primary goal, of course, is to provide wonderfully enriching opportunities for the use of language and the development of emergent literacy.

Include a Variety of Activities

Unfortunately, a survey by McAfee (1985) reveals that only one out of every three teachers actually took the trouble to plan for group time at all! The same study showed that out of 14 potential activities mentioned by teachers as being likely ingredients for group time, only a handful were actually included. Of these the ones most frequently presented were books and music-related items.

It is not only the McAfee study that reveals such limited use of large group time. While revising *The Whole Child* this time, I examined three of the foremost texts on literacy. I found that although they presented some sage advice about cozy library corners and reading aloud at group time, not one of them mentioned other language-related activities—

not even singing or poetry—thereby allowing priceless opportunities to slip through teachers' fingers.

Of course, books, particularly nonsexist and multicultural ones, are an essential ingredient of group time, but it is a pity to restrict this potentially rich language experience to only a book and, if luck is with us, a song, when the group can do together so many other interesting language-related activities. Poetry (only mentioned three times by teachers in the McAfee (1985) study as a possibility); fingerplays; auditory discrimination skills activities; and chances for discussions that involve problem solving, thinking, and reasoning skills are additional activities that merit inclusion at least once a week, and more often than that, if possible.

Some Specific Suggestions About Materials to Include

Do Include a Book and Poetry

The selection of a fine children's book is usually the best place to begin when planning the time together, and many good lists of books are available (D. Norton, 1999; Zeece, 1999). Poetry should also be offered on a daily basis. Like the books, this should be good-quality poetry, rather than the nondescript examples generally included in so-called activity books.

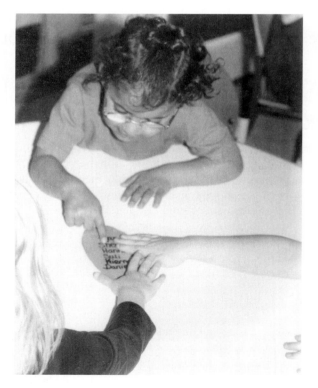

There's my name!

Incidentally, the only way I have ever been able to use really fine poetry successfully has been to make a poetry file. This involves taking time to paw through some poetry anthologies and duplicate a large variety of appropriate poems, mounting them on stiff cardboard to preserve them and keep them from getting lost, and then filing them according to topic. This arrangement has meant that when we suddenly need a poem about rain, all we have to do is look under that topic heading in the file and pull out poems on that subject.

Music and Fingerplays Are Important, Too

Singing has its merits because it fosters language, memory, musical development, and pleasure. It takes a good deal of repetition for children to learn a new song; teachers should be prepared to sing one or two verses with them three or four times and then repeat the same song for several group times so that children can learn it well enough to sing it with verve (Moomaw, 1997).

Jalongo and Collins (1985) remind us that children of different ages respond differently to songs presented by the teacher. By age 2 to 3, children can sing an average of five different notes, join in on certain phrases of familiar songs, and show interest in records and rhythm instruments. By age 3 to 4, children have better voice control and mastery of song lyrics. They are able to combine creative drama with singing and possess basic musical concepts such as loud-soft and fast-slow. By age 4 to 5, children can sing an average of 10 different musical notes, as well as sing complete songs from memory. At that age they form the concepts of high-low and long-short tones.

Fingerplays are another fine ingredient to include during groups. Again, experience has taught me that 2- and 3-year-olds are likely to be able to do just the actions at first and then later will add the words. But you should not be discouraged. If you persevere long enough, keep the pace slow enough, and the material brief enough, then they will eventually be able to put words and actions together, which they do love to do.

Auditory Training Should Also Be Provided

A well-planned group time includes at least two additional kinds of activities besides those previously listed. The first of these is some activity that provides for auditory training and discrimination. Sometimes this can be included as part of a fingerplay or poem, and sometimes it needs to be a special activity. Children need work on learning to tell sounds apart and to tell when they are the same, and group time provides a fine chance to practice this skill. It is a valuable activity since it may be a helpful introduction to phonics, and it is definitely helpful for teaching children to discriminate among sounds so that they speak more clearly.

Perhaps during a song they could sing as loud as they can and then as soft as they can; or listen to high and low notes on the autoharp, standing up when they hear a high one, and sitting down when they hear a low one; or perhaps half the children can clap their hands when they hear the sound "eee" and the other half listen for "iii."

Some other examples of activities include matching the sounds of shakers, some of which have been filled with sand, some with beans, and some with rice; everyone shutting their eyes and opening them when a particular sound is heard; listening for words left out of familiar nursery rhymes; or having the children signal when they hear sentences that do not make sense, such as "When I went to the market, I bought a camelope"—a game that appeals strongly to 4-year-olds.

Many speech correction texts (Patrick, 1993) contain numerous suggestions for such activities that may be adapted for preschool children. Appendix G lists some ideas, too.

Group Time Is an Ideal Time to Provide Practice in Cognitive Skills

The second kind of activity that should be but is only rarely included in group time is one that provides practice in thinking and reasoning (such activities are described in more detail in chapters 18 and 19). These include practice in the midlevel mental ability skills, such as matching and temporal ordering, and also practice in the higher level skills of talking problems over and discussing how the group might solve them. Offering these activities during group time ensures that all the children are receiving practice in these vital skills.

Group Time Should Provide Multiracial, Nonsexist Subject Matter

Two additional ingredients should also be woven into group time. Every group should contain some multiethnic or nonsexist material, or both, and conversely should not contain material that is sexist or racist. This means the teacher will have to appraise carefully the material in songs, books, and poetry before presenting them and either discard those that possess objectionable material or draw it to the children's attention and discuss it.

For example, should the teacher choose to read a book about going to the hospital, where all the doctors are white males and the nurses white females, a discussion should ensue about whether there are women doctors and male nurses and whether only white people can work at such jobs. (Refer to chapter 13, "Providing Cross-Cultural, Nonsexist Education," for additional suggestions and for lists of multiethnic and nonsexist books.)

Management Suggestions to Help Group Time Go More Smoothly

It Is Always Wise to Plan More Activities Than You Are Likely to Use

Particularly for inexperienced teachers, it is difficult to know in advance which activities will go well and which will not. It is also difficult to estimate the amount of time a particular activity will absorb. So it is better to be safe and have extra reserves than to be caught short and run out of things to do. You can always use them next time.

Make Certain the Children Talk, Too

Include opportunities for children to respond to the teacher. During group time children should be encouraged to think, reason, and guess (hypothesize) about what is being discussed: "What would you do if you were Peter and Mr. MacGregor chased you into the potting shed?" "What *is* a potting shed, anyway?" "Do you think Peter was really sick when he got home?" "Was that the best punishment his mother could do, to put him to bed without dinner?" "What does *your* mother do when you're naughty?" and so forth. These opportunities for discussion are an invaluable part of the group experience.

Table 17.1 (see p. 454–455) presents an example of one student's plan and evaluation of a group time for 4-year-olds. During this time the children were interested in "families."

Make Certain the Material Is Interesting

Part of the secret of making sure the material is interesting is to read the material first yourself. If you don't think it's interesting, it's a sure thing the children won't either. It helps a lot to select books the children genuinely enjoy. Unfortunately the world abounds in dull books designed to improve children's minds but not lift their spirits. When books of such charm as *Mary Betty Lizzie McNutt's Birthday* (Bond, 1983) and *The Tabitha Stories* (A. N. Wilson, 1997), of such humor as *Gregory the Terrible Eater* (Sharmat, 1980), *Silly Goose* (Kent, 1983), and *Tops and Bottoms* (Stevens, 1995), and of such sound social values as *A Chair for My Mother* (V. B. Williams, 1982), *The Gardener* (Steward, 1978), *The Goat in the Rug* (Blood & Link, 1980), *Alejandro's Gift* (Albert, 1994), and *Owl Moon* (Yolen, 1987) exist, there's really no excuse for boredom. The teacher who selects stories like these will enjoy them right along with the children, and they will arouse much comment and discussion from everyone. Remember that when a book is dull and the children are not interested, it is not necessary to read grimly through to its end; it is better simply to set it aside and go on to a more attractive choice.

Think, too, about how to present material so that it captures the children's attention. Using visual aids such as flannel boards helps, as does simply telling a story rather than reading it (M. Carter, 1994; Trelease, 1995). I have seen children absolutely enraptured by this activity, and telling stories lets the teacher look at the children all the time and be more responsive to them as they listen. Using a hand puppet also increases appeal.

Read with verve and enthusiasm. Remember that using different voices for different characters when reading *The Three Bears* (Galdone, 1985), suiting your tone of voice to the mood of the material (e.g., sounding anxious and wistful when being the little bird that inquires, "Are *you* my mother?"; Eastman, 1960), or building suspense during *The Three Billy Goats Gruff* (Galdone, 1981) as the children wait for the troll to appear all contribute to the fun for everyone.

Keep the Tempo of Group Time Upbeat

Pace has a lot to do with sustaining interest. Some teachers are so nervous and afraid of losing control that they rush the children through the experience, ignoring children's comments and wiping out the potential richness of interchange between themselves and the children. A relaxed but definite tempo is a better pace to strive for to hold the children's attention while not making them feel harassed.

At the same time it is important not to drag things out. This is why it is deadly in a preschool group to go all around in the circle and have each child say something. When this happens, attention lags among the other youngsters and restlessness rises like a tide. Far better to include children spontaneously as the opportunity presents itself—a few adding suggestions to the story, others putting figures on the flannel board, and the entire group participating in a fingerplay.

Assess the difficulty of what the children will be learning and present anything that is new or potentially difficult to understand *early* in the group time, while the children are still feeling rested. A new mental ability activity, for instance, should follow the opening songs, rather than come at the very end of the time together.

Table 17.1
Plan and evaluation of a group time for 4-year-olds who were interested in families

Area	Materials	Reason for Inclusion	Was It Used?	Evaluation
Story	Radlaver, *Father Is Big* (Bowman Publishing, 1967)	Many children today do not have a father figure. This book was not sexist; it just stated facts. Example: "His hand feels big around mine." There were actual photos that gave realistic quality.	Yes	The children seemed to enjoy the book. I got lots of comments about "my daddy." However, there seemed to be some competition as to whose daddy was biggest. This might have been bad for a child without a father. So, next time, to avoid any negative side effects, I would have used another book to read aloud (about daddies) and left this book out for individual utilization.
Poetry and fingerplays	Fingerplay: Grandmother's Glasses	This provided a good way to include the third generation in my large group. This fingerplay also incorporated poetry (rhyming words) and gave the children some form of a guided activity since they were to make the actions follow the words of the fingerplay.	Yes	The children were familiar with this fingerplay, and I received some advice on "how to do it." So, although I intended this activity to be teacher directed, the children felt free to give suggestions. I thought that this was good. Next time, I would probably do this fingerplay two times in a row—as one time went so quickly, and the children did enjoy themselves.
Auditory training	Tape recorder. Identify sound of family members on a tape recorder. Example: baby, mom, dad, child, dog, and older persons. Also could include some household sounds. Example: washing dishes, raking leaves, TV, doorbell. Ask the children, "Who is making these noises?"	It would be interesting to see if the children could identify different family members' voices. The household sounds tape could lead to good discussions of whose jobs are whose responsibilities; also, to find out if the children help at home. Would hope to encourage nonsexist ways of thinking.	No	I did not use this activity, but if I did I would try to steer the activity in a nonsexist way. Example: "Daddies can wash dishes, too."

Song	"This is the Way," (sung to Mulberry Bush)	I wanted to get the children to realize all the duties that go into making a household work. I also wanted to have more movement in the large group time.	Yes	This activity did not work well. I started a verse and demonstrated the actions, but I found that some of the children just sat and watched me. So I encouraged them to get up and asked them how we would move to the next verse—raking leaves. This helped a little bit, but still not all the children had stood up before I started. Also, I might ask individual children to move to each verse, or ask them to suggest work that members of their family do around the house.
Cognitive game	Pictures of families or members of family cut from magazines. Asked the children, "What do you think is happening here?"	I wanted to hear the children's suggestions about what was going on in the pictures. I thought that this activity might give good insight into what the children's families were like. I tried to include nonsexist and multiethnic pictures.	Yes	This activity went much better than I had expected. The children seemed really interested in looking at the pictures, and I got lots of feedback. Next time, however, I would allow more time—as I feel that I quit while the children were still interested.
Discussion	See ideas for topics throughout outline.	Wanted children to realize that there are many kinds of families and all are equally good. I wanted some feedback, would mostly try to give information, new terms, etc., would hope to increase the children's positive feelings about their own families.	No	I did not include this activity because I felt it would take too much time, and I wanted to include the other areas.
Multiethnic and nonsexist area	I would probably normally end the large-group session by having some "stereotyped" activities that both boys and girls could use (woodshop area, cooking area, housekeeping, etc.) and encourage everyone to use those activities.	I would use this activity in hope of encouraging the children to be involved in nonsexist type play. Also, I think that sometimes teachers "forget" to incorporate this into everyday activities.	No	Since this was not possible on this particular day, I tried to incorporate nonsexist and multiethnic material in all my other activities. Example: In a picture I showed a father cooking with his son and talked about how everyone can be a good cook.

Source: Courtesy Erika Miller, Institute of Child Development, University of Oklahoma, Norman.

Opportunities for the group to move around a bit also provide a needed change of pace. Singing a song during which children get up and down answers the need for large muscle activity, just as fingerplays about the "eensy weensy spider" harness the energy inherent in wiggly fingers.

Some Advice About Starting and Stopping

Start as soon as the children begin to gather, and quit while you're ahead. It is not necessary to wait until all the children have arrived to begin group activities. The children who have come promptly need something to do other than just sit and wait for stragglers. A good action song or fingerplay is a fine way to begin. It catches the group's attention and involves them immediately, and it is easy for latecomers to join in unobtrusively while this is going on. If such late arrivals are welcomed with a quick smile rather than a reproachful look, they will want to arrive more quickly next time.

Closing a group time well is equally important. Some teachers do this by ending with the same song every time to give the children a sense of finishing or completion. Children love the sense of ceremony this conveys. Others just anticipate its ending by saying something like "Well, we certainly did a lot of interesting things in group today, didn't we?" and then summarizing what was done. Still others just move smoothly into some sort of dismissal routine: "Everyone who is wearing blue jeans can go first today" (or everyone who has spotted socks, or who has freckles, or who ate oatmeal for breakfast). Children enjoy this sort of thing, and it has the advantage of not sending the entire herd off at once in a thundering way.

The most important points about finishing group time are that the children have a clear idea of what they are expected to do next and that group time ends before the youngsters are so exhausted that the experience has degenerated into a struggle to maintain order. *Finishing a group time while the children are still interested and attentive makes it more likely they will want to return because they recall group time as being a satisfying experience they enjoyed.*

What to Do About Undesirable Behavior

The McAfee (1985) survey also points out that when teachers were asked to explain why certain group times or activities were not successful, 75% of the time they cited conditions beyond their control. These conditions included such things as the children's developmental levels, their emotional or behavior problems, home backgrounds, and classroom conditions, such as too large a group or too wide an age span. It is certainly true that all of these conditions can and do cause problems. What is distressing is that so few teachers saw themselves as generating some of the difficulties. Yet teachers *can* control some of the aforementioned variables.

For example, it is important for everyone's sanity that the material is geared to the age of the children. The younger the children, the shorter the books, poetry, and songs should be and the more opportunities should be provided for moving around. Whatever the age of the children, the teacher must remain sensitive to the group—tuned in—so that he can sense when a shift of material is necessary to hold their attention. Of course, no group is completely attentive at any time. Even during a very high interest activity, McAfee reported, several children were not attentive. So another thing to remember is not to expect perfection from children who are, after all, very young.

To obtain maximum benefit from such experiences, groups should be kept as small as possible. Larger groups almost always produce behavior problems because of lack of involvement and inattention. What typically happens is that assistant teachers spend their time admonishing some children, patting others on the back, and holding still other unwilling participants on their laps. A far better solution, when a second teacher is available, is to split the group in half so that each staff member works with a smaller number of children. Under these circumstances there can be a better balance between teacher-dominated activities and conversation and discussions, and the children will pay closer attention and develop their language skills more richly.

But these recommendations do not deal with the problem of what to do about the child who is punching her neighbor, rolling over and over on the floor, or continually drifting away from the group to play in the housekeeping area.

The teacher can deal with this situation in several ways. Making certain the material is interesting is the first thing to consider. Sometimes it is effective to have the acting-out youngster sit beside you as you read, turning the pages or doing other helpful things. Sometimes it is enough just to separate her from her boon companion. Sometimes calling the child by name and drawing her attention back to what the group is doing is helpful, although I avoid doing this as a reproach. Sometimes the behavior can be overlooked. And as a final resort sometimes the child loses the privilege of staying in the group and must be sent away. The problem with this method is that an adult really has to go with her to prevent her from getting into further mischief.

Remember that almost all children who misbehave at the beginning of the year can learn to conform to the requirements of the group if they are provided patient teaching. Hold them only to reasonable expectations. Be persistent and don't give up hope. It can be helpful to talk with the youngster privately at some time other than group time, *pointing out when she has done well*, and arranging with her in advance that she does not have to stay the entire time. Perhaps she will just try to stay for the first song and poem, or for the story, and then, *before she loses control* she can go off with the staff member and do something quiet and not very interesting until group time is over. The time in the group can be gradually extended as the child's ability to control her behavior increases.

When a child has consistent difficulties enjoying group time, we should take a careful look at possible reasons within the child for this behavior because, if most of the children are enjoying the activity, there may be some special reason why this particular child is not. Possibilities to consider when this is the case include hearing and vision difficulties. These are common but frequently overlooked reasons for inattentiveness. The other common reason is immaturity. If the material being presented is above the child's level, she won't pay attention. Any of these conditions require sensitive discussion with the family, as well as special diagnosis by an appropriate professional person. (For a discussion of how to make an effective referral, refer to the chapters on exceptionality [chapter 9] and parenting [chapter 3].)

USING THE COMPUTER AS A METHOD OF PRESCHOOL INSTRUCTION

Much has been learned about the appropriate use of computers since the 1980s, when they first began to wend their way into preschool classrooms. At that time many well-taken objections to their use were expressed, and some of those objections and drawbacks remain today. One of the most serious is the question of quality—not only whether skills are age appropriate but also, even more seriously, whether programs actively involve the children in thinking and offer content that is worthwhile (Haugland, 1999; Haugland & Wright, 1997). Even when the programs are adequate, all too often I have visited a room where a child is quite obviously just interested in randomly and monotonously tapping keys.

Another potential difficulty is that the majority of teaching staff are inexperienced not only in using computers themselves but also in knowing the most desirable ways to encourage their use by the children. Finally there is the problem of expense and obsolescence. Even the most moderately priced computers remain well beyond the reach of most preschool programs, in which increasing meager salaries must still take priority. If only the most affluent schools can afford this equipment, might it mean that children from the more well-to-do families will have the benefit of becoming computer literate while the other youngsters are left behind? Perhaps we are indeed in danger of "replicating inequities," as Healey (1998) suggests, when we add this equipment to some classrooms and not to others. Finally Healy, a well-known authority on the brain and mental development in young children, has recently raised questions about the potentially serious consequences of too much radiation, undesirable effects on vision, and other possible neurological ills yet to be determined that may result from overexposure to computer monitors and programs. Although it is easy to scoff at such warnings, perhaps we should ask ourselves, What if some of these predictions turn out to be correct? Surely such cautions warrant our attention.

Many of these objections, of course, can be overcome as supporters of computers quite correctly maintain. The quality of some software is gradually improving. Staff can certainly learn to use and present computer activities in appropriate ways, and possibilities for money-raising schemes to purchase the equipment are numerous.

The tide is gradually turning in favor of including computers in preschool classrooms. For example, Head Start reversed itself in 1990 and authorized their addition to their classrooms, although the supply for those programs is still inadequate (Thouvenelle, 1994). In 1994 the National Association for the Education of Young Children published a book favoring their appropriate use with young children (Wright & Shade, 1994). Some arguments that have helped turn that tide include the following: (a) Computers are nonjudgmental and do not scold or disapprove of "wrong" answers; (b) programs can be suited to the level of the learner; (c) at the preschool level, research has revealed that computers often foster children working and talking together as they use the equipment; (d) computers can be a source of empowerment for youngsters with such disabilities as cerebral palsy or other physically limiting disabilities; and (e) computers prepare children for later literacy, and their early use prevents children from becoming "computer shy" (Haugland & Wright, 1997; D. D. Shade & Davis, 1997).

Gee! How come it did that?

However, despite their charms we must also remember that computers are, by nature, a highly symbolic, visually based activity. As such their value in the education of young children is bound to be somewhat limited. We must never allow them to preempt time best used for other activities (as television is now preempting real-life experiences at home). And yet my guess is that despite their limitations, computers will continue to make a significant place for themselves in the preschool classroom as time goes on, as more appropriate programs are written for them, and as teachers of young children become better informed about how to present them effectively by linking them closely to real experience.

SUMMARY

The current approach to preparing children for learning the later skills of reading and writing is termed *emergent literacy*. This term includes the underlying concepts and strategies related to developing all aspects of literacy, whether written or oral.

This chapter stresses that teachers should make it plain they value good books and emphasize the usefulness of the written word by providing ways for children to use written literacy materials in their play, by writing down children's dictated stories, by including carefully planned group time experiences, and by encouraging the judicious use of computers.

Group time presents a particularly rich opportunity for fostering emergent literacy, and the chapter includes practical suggestions for making that experience satisfying for both children and teachers.

Questions and Activities

1. *Predicament:* The mother of a child in your group glows as she tells you her 3-year-old is so smart— she knows all her ABCs and her father is drilling her every night with flash cards to help her learn to read. What, if anything, do you think you should do about this?
2. Role-play a story hour in which the teacher seems to do everything possible to prevent the children from talking.
3. For the sake of variety and to extend your language-building skills with the children, resolve not to use books at all during group time for a month! What will you offer instead that will enhance the language abilities of the children?
4. Make up blank paper "books" and invite the children to dictate stories to you on any relevant subject. Many youngsters will relish adding illustrations to these tales if they are encouraged to do so.

Self-Check Questions for Review

Content-Related Questions

1. Give three examples of emergent literacy activities a 3-year-old might participate in with pleasure.
2. What are three fundamental principles for developing literacy that teachers should keep in mind?
3. Name three additional kinds of language activities besides songs and stories that should be regularly included in group time.
4. You have a beginning student-teacher working with you in your class of 3-year-olds. She reads to them in a steady monotone, never looking up and never smiling. What advice would you give her that would help her hold the children's attention?
5. Discuss some possible ways teachers can reduce misbehavior during group time.

6. In the research by L. M. Morrow (1997) on including literacy materials in children's play, what factors did she identify as increasing the use of those materials most strongly?

Integrative Questions

1. The teacher next door who works with 4-year-olds complains to you that he has a terrible time during group because the children keep interrupting him. Explain why you would or would not agree that this is undesirable behavior on the children's part.
2. Picture in your mind's eye one book you most enjoy reading to children. Propose three questions based on that book that would promote discussion between you and them.
3. Then, using that book as the central idea or theme, suggest a poem, an auditory discrimination activity, and a nonsexist or multicultural idea you could use along with the book during a group time for 3- or 4-year-olds.
4. L. M. Morrow's (1997) research points out that the addition of teacher guidance increased the amount of literacy-related play by the children. Using "playing birthday party" as an example, describe how a teacher might manipulate the play to such an extent that he takes the qualities of spontaneity and delight away from it.

Coordinating Videotape

Let's talk about it. Tape #12. The whole child: A caregiver's guide to the first five years. The Annenberg/CPB Collection, P.O. Box 2345, South Burlington, VT 05407–2345. *Let's Talk About It* first reviews language acquisition and then explains the "emergent literacy" approach to reading and writing.

References for Further Reading

Pick of the Litter

Ballinger, C. (1999). *Teaching other people's children: Literacy and learning in a bilingual classroom.* New York: Teachers College Press. I know, I know! The Pick of the Litter for the language chapter was bicultural, too, but I cannot pass up recommending this treasure, which is about teaching Haitian children and the effect their culture had on what the teacher did. Only 99 pages long, it is worth reading every sentence.

Overviews

Fields, M., & Spangler, K. L. (2000). *Let's begin reading right: Developmentally appropriate beginning literacy* (4th ed.). Upper Saddle River, NJ: Merrill/Prentice Hall. This book discusses the underpinnings of literacy and then discusses the development of reading and writing with older youngsters. *Highly recommended.*

Morrow, L. M. (1997). *Literacy development in the early years: Helping children read and write* (3rd ed.). Boston: Allyn & Bacon. Although most of this standard text is more appropriate for use with older children, several early chapters on language development and learning centers are helpful at the preschool level.

Schickendanz, J. A. (1999). *Much more than the ABC's: The early stages of reading and writing.* Washington, DC: National Association for the Education of Young Children. The author explains the long journey children must make before reaching the ability to read independently. Includes a particularly interesting chapter on children's beginning writing. *Highly recommended.*

Grouptime and Reading Aloud

Note: Refer to chapter 13 for many references listing multicultural books.

Briggs, D. (1993). *Toddler storytime programs.* Lanham, MD: Scarecrow Press. This book is a godsend for teachers who want to use flannel boards with stories, poems, and music yet feel limited by their self-perceived inability to draw. Patterns galore accompany a large assortment of language possibilities to use with the often neglected 2-year-old set.

Charner, K. (1996). *The giant encyclopedia of circle time and group activities for children 3 to 6: Over 600 favorite circle time activities created by teachers for teachers.* Beltsville, MD: Gryphon House. Countless alternatives to "only reading a book" are described here.

Jalongo, M. R. (1988). *Young children and picture books: Literature from infancy to six.* Washington, DC: National Association for the Education of Young Children. The joy of really good picture books is captured here. The author explains how to select quality books and how to present them so effectively that children will fall in love with them and with reading, too. *Highly recommended.*

Norton, D. (1999). *Through the eyes of a child: An introduction to children's literature* (3rd ed.). Upper Saddle River, NJ: Merrill/Prentice Hall. Norton provides a welcome exception to the general absence of poetry discussions by providing an entire chapter of advice on presenting this valuable literature. It also includes a good, annotated bibliography of quality children's books.

Trelease, J. (1995). *The new read-aloud handbook* (4th ed.). New York: Penguin Books. This sensible, easy-to-read paperback is filled with good advice for parents and teachers on enjoying books with children. Excellent bibliography.

Children's Literature

Note: Refer to chapter 13 for many references listing multicultural books.

Raines, S. C., & Canady, R. J. (1989). *Story s-t-r-e-t-c-h-e-r-s: Activities to expand children's favorite books.* Mount Rainier, MD: Gryphon House.

Raines, S. C., & Canady, R. J. (1991). *More story s-t-r-e-t-c-h-e-r-s: More activities to expand children's favorite books.* Mt. Rainier, MD: Gryphon House. In these two books the authors provide a wonderful selection of really *good* books and offer extensive ideas of ways to tie them to other activity areas. *Highly recommended.*

Raines, S., & Isbell, R. (1994). *Stories: Children's literature in early education.* Albany, NY: Delmar. This book reviews literature for children from birth to age 8 and includes many examples of teachers trying different techniques. Replete with practical suggestions, it features an outstanding selection of books; multicultural books are integrated throughout the text.

Poetry and Fingerplays

Arbuthnot, M. H., & Root, S. L. (1968). *Time for poetry* (3rd ed.). Glenview, IL: Scott, Foresman. This book is a treasure. It is filled with poetry (most of which can be used at the preschool level) arranged by topic, and it also contains a valuable chapter on sharing poetry with children. Although out of print, this is worth getting from the library.

Dowell, R. I. (1987). *Move over, Mother Goose: Finger plays, action verses, & funny rhymes.* Mount Rainier, MD: Gryphon House. This nice mix of materials is divided into topics such as animals and family.

Livingston, M. C. (1994). *Animals, vegetables, minerals: Poems about small things.* New York: HarperCollins. Myra Cohn Livingston writes delightful, brief poems for young children. *Highly recommended.*

Prelutsky, C. (Ed.). (1986). *Read-aloud rhymes for the very young.* New York: Knopf. Charmingly illustrated, these poems *are* simple. They are also arranged somewhat according to subject.

Redleaf, R. (1993). *Busy fingers, growing minds: Fingerplays, verses, and activities for whole language learning.* St. Paul, MN: Redleaf. Simple, brief, relevant verses and group time activities contributed by a very experienced teacher are included.

Music

Moomaw, S. (1997). *More than singing: Discovering music in preschool and kindergarten.* St. Paul, MN: Redleaf. If it weren't for the Ballinger book, this would have been Pick of the Litter. It is an excellent, practical book that explains ways to include music throughout the day and contains advice on helping children enjoy singing and incorporate other musical experiences during group time. *Highly recommended.*

Computers

Haugland, S. (1999). Computers and young children: The newest software that meets the developmental needs of young children. *Early Childhood Education Journal, 26*(4), 245–254. Haugland describes winners of the Developmental Software Awards for 1999—an invaluable reference for anyone wondering what to buy and what standards should be applied before purchase.

Healy, J. M. (1998). *Failure to connect: How computers affect our children's minds—for better or worse.* New York: Simon & Schuster. This well-reasoned evaluation by a specialist in mental development covers what is known about how computers interact with young children. The author is no longer as strongly in favor of using them as she once was. Valuable cautionary reading for the computer enthusiast.

McNamme, G. D. (1990) Learning to read and write in an inner-city setting: A longitudinal study of community change. In L. C. Moll (Ed.), *Vygotsky and education: Instructional implications and applications of sociohistorical psychology.* New York: Cambridge University Press. I hope readers will not be put off by the title. Actually the chapter is a delightful account of how Head Start staff and community people worked with an adviser to increase developmentally appropriate literacy activities in their centers. *Highly recommended.*

Shade, D. D., & Davis, B. S. (1997). The role of computer technology in early childhood education. In J. P. Isenberg, & M. R. Jalongo (Eds.), *Major trends and issues in early childhood education: Challenges, controversies, and insights.* New York: Teachers College Press. These authors enthusiastically refute various objections to the use of computers with young children.

For the Advanced Student

De Oliveira, M. K., & Valsiner, J. (Eds.). (1998). *Literacy in human development.* Stamford, CT: Ablex. This book has many interesting chapters related to literacy and illiteracy in older children and adults. Of particular interest is the chapter "Illiterate Adults in Literate Societies." *Highly recommended.*

Zeece, P. D. (1999). And the winner is: Children's literature awards and accolades. *Early Childhood Education Journal, 26*(4), 233–239. If you are interested in the best new books for children, locate this article and copy it for reference. It explains current awards, their standards, gives Web addresses, and, of course, the current winners. *Highly recommended.*

Developing Thinking and Reasoning Skills

Using the Emergent Approach to Foster Creativity in Thought

He who learns with pleasure gathers honey like a bee.

Romanian Proverb

Experience shapes the brain.

Daniel Siegel (1999)

Whether there's a better way to develop thinking skills than teaching children the names of shapes and colors?

Just who this Vygotsky person is that everyone seems to be talking about?

How to help children really think up ideas for themselves?

. . . . IF YOU HAVE, THE MATERIAL IN THE FOLLOWING PAGES WILL HELP YOU.

NEW KNOWLEDGE ABOUT BRAIN DEVELOPMENT SUPPORTS THE VITAL ROLE EARLY CHILDHOOD EXPERIENCES PLAY IN FOSTERING ITS GROWTH

During the past few years a wealth of research-based information about early brain development has become available (Goleman, 1995; R. Shore, 1997; D. J. Siegel, 1999). It is gratifying that, at last, biological science now supports what early childhood people and child psychologists have known for a long time—that what happens to children when they are very young has permanent implications for how they turn out as adults.

For the first time, technology has made it possible to study what is happening inside the brain while it is occurring. Such equipment as MRIs (magnetic resonance imaging) and PETs (positron emission tomography) allows us to see how, where, and how much energy various areas of the brain are using at different times, and to do this without harm. This means we can tell when development and/or activity is taking place within the brain and therefore when children are able to acquire and use particular abilities. For example, skills related to developing perception and vision have a "prime learning time" (sometimes called a *critical period*) of under age 4, and language, including learning a second language, is best acquired by age 10 (D. J. Siegel, 1999).

Although space does not permit a discussion of all the fascinating findings and implications of brain research, some of the most relevant ones are discussed here. For further information the reader should consult the references at the end of the chapter.

How Does the Brain Work?

Although much remains to be learned, we do know that the brain is composed of billions of specialized nerve cells called *neurons*. These special cells are present at birth. What is not present are most of the connections between the cells; these connections (*synapses*) develop as the result of electrochemical impulses that "spark" across little tendrils (*axons* and *dendrites*) reaching out from the neurons. These connections are essential because they form networks that transmit impulses between and beyond them to additional neurons located in different areas of the brain where different functions are situated. The more connections made between the neurons (and one neuron can have thousands of connections!), the greater the ability of the brain becomes to generate a variety of responses to the environment. For example, most of the hearing function is located in one area of the brain, the language function in another, and higher mental functioning in yet another. The more connections generated between these areas, the richer the potential for learning to use language and have ideas becomes.

Why Is the Period of Early Childhood Especially Important?

It may be easier to remember three of the most important findings about the brain and early childhood if we think of them as the three "E's"—*experience, earliness,* and *emotion.* We know that *experience* stimulates formation of those all-important connections between neurons. So parents and teachers need to make certain plentiful amounts of experience are provided for that stimulation. It is important, of course, that the stimulation be developmentally appropriate so that the brain has developed sufficiently to make use of that experience. It is also important to use as many sensory channels to carry the information as possible. This is why concrete manipulation and use of objects is desirable. Manipulation uses several sensory pathways such as touch, taste, and smell, as well as vision and hearing. Tying in language adds vital enrichment to connections, too. The more sensory channels used, the richer the learning will be. *Experience generates connections; repetition strengthens them.*

Earliness—as in *early* childhood—is the second important "E" to remember because biological research now confirms that although learning continues throughout life, the first 10 years are absolutely vital for learning. After age 10 the brain prunes (discards) neurons that have not been used; in other words the old adage "*Use it or lose it*" holds true in regard to developing mental capacity.

The third "E" is *emotion.* Something else early childhood people already knew from experience and from psychological research is that attachment—the positive emotional bonding between infants and children with adults—is an important ingredient in fostering emotional stability and growth and that secure attachment can reduce the ill effects of prolonged stress (Cassidy & Shaver, 1999). We also knew that too much emotional stress interferes with the ability to learn. Now neuroscience has provided the biological explanation for what happens in the body when too much stress occurs. When stress occurs, the body produces a hormone called *cortisol.* Careful study of its effect on the neural connections has found that too much of it weakens or destroys some connections between neurons, thereby reducing the ability to learn. Fortunately it has also been determined that strong emotional attachment promotes and protects connections and insulates neurons, at least to a degree, from the malign effects of increased cortisol (Gunnar, 1996). *Warm, consistent, responsive caregiving really matters because this kind of caregiving generates the wonderful insulation of attachment.*

SELECTING VALUES AND PRIORITIES IN THE COGNITIVE REALM

Since biological and psychological research, as well as our own observations and common sense, now confirms how much the work of families and early childhood teachers matters in the early years—even more than some of us may have realized—it certainly behooves us to think carefully about what we are providing in the way of experiences and how we are providing them as we think about planning curriculum for the cognitive self. Which learnings are more important, and which less so?

As priorities are ranked, it is desirable to consider them in terms of their *relative* merit, rather than as being "good guys" and "bad guys." For example, is it more important that the child experience joy and verve when learning or that he learn to sit quietly and not interrupt the teacher? Is it more significant that he speak fluently and spontaneously, or that he speak Standard English? Is it more valuable that he be able to think about problems and feel confident about his ability to solve them or that he be able to pick out all the things in the room that are shaped like squares?

It is not that any of these values are reprehensible or should not receive attention: It *is* a question of deciding which goals should receive *primary* emphasis because the teacher who elects to foster joy and verve is likely to employ a different teaching style from one who believes that quietly paying attention is vital to classroom success.

Thus we must begin by asking ourselves, What are the most important things we want children to learn in the cognitive sphere? and Which goals should have first priority? Once these are identified, we must understand what practical, day-by-day things teachers can do to emphasize those priorities as they work with the children.

WHAT ARE THE MOST VALUABLE PRIORITIES?

Priority I: Maintain the Child's Sense of Wonder and Curiosity

As teachers of young children know, most youngsters come to school wondering about many things. They want to know where the water goes when the toilet flushes, why the dog died, and what makes their stomachs gurgle.

The age of 4 is particularly appealing in this respect. Four-year-olds are avid gatherers of facts and are interested in everything. For this reason it is a delight to build a cognitive curriculum for them. But 3-year-olds, too, are seeking and questioning. They are more concerned with the manipulation of materials and with finding out what everyday things and people close to them are like. This kind of investigation, though different in focus from that of the 4-year-olds, may also be used to make a rich contribution to mental development.

The most obvious way to maintain children's sense of curiosity is by encouraging them to continue to ask questions and by making it possible for them to find out the answers. But underlying the teacher's willingness to encourage investigation lies something deeper: the teacher's basic point of view about what children are capable of achieving. The teacher whose image of children is that they are richly endowed, strong, competent people conveys this sense of worthiness to the children. She sees her role as empowering children—enabling them *to do for themselves,* rather than doing for or to them.

In this atmosphere of respect, autonomy and the willingness to venture flourishes best. It is a climate in which there is a balance of reasonableness, choice, trust, protection, spontaneity, moderate control, and challenge. Given the security of respect combined with encouragement, children sense they have a firm base from which to explore when the impulse moves them to do so, and connection building flourishes.

Another way the teacher can help is by presenting materials that are fascinating and by modeling curiosity and wonder herself. Asking simple questions about cause and effect or wondering together what will happen next often captures children's interest and starts them observing, wondering, and thinking for themselves. Thus the teacher might discuss with the children whether the mother rabbit will do anything to get ready for her babies now that she is growing so fat and full of them, or she might ask the children whether they think it would be better to keep the ice in the sun or shade until it is time to make the ice cream and how they might find out which is better.

Priority II: Let Cognitive Learning Be a Source of Genuine Pleasure for Children and Teacher

If we agree with the behaviorists that people tend to repeat activity that is rewarded in some way, it follows that if we want to strengthen connections, we should do everything in our power to attach pleasure to cognitive learning. We want children to want to think and learn, and they are more likely to continue to do so if they experience pleasure while they are involved in learning. Therefore the second most important priority that we should consider when planning a cognitive curriculum is presenting it so that it is a genuine source of pleasure. This can be accomplished in numerous ways.

Keep It Age Appropriate.   Nothing is more disheartening to a youngster than being confronted with material that is too difficult. To foster pleasure in learning, it is necessary to match the child's learning opportunities with his developmental level. This means, on the one hand, learning opportunities must be challenging but not so difficult that they are beyond the child's grasp.

On the other hand, learning opportunities should be challenging enough that the bright 4-year-olds in the class are not bored by too much repetition at the same ability level all year. Teachers must walk a delicate tightrope of sensitivity—not allowing themselves to be held prisoner by the concept of developmental stages, yet at the same time taking their knowledge of those stages into account so that they expect neither too much nor too little from the youngsters.

Keep Curriculum Real and Relevant.   *Real and relevant* means we want to tie learning to actual concrete experience as much as possible because, as we have seen documented by neuroscience, the more avenues of sensory input we employ, the thicker and more numerous the connections will be.

Relevant in the usual sense of the word means basing curriculum on the children's interests and what they want to know. A curriculum that does not accomplish this goal breeds disinterested, dissatisfied learners, no matter what their age. Yet even preschool teachers often lay out a year's curriculum in advance, formulated at best on knowledge of what other children in previous years have cared about. Thus a schedule will show that in September the school will be building experiences around the family, in December around holidays, and in the spring around baby animals. Although this approach has the value of convenience and reduced effort, the danger of such extremely long-range planning is that teachers may become so tied to it that they are unable to respond to the interests of the children who are now in their room, thereby deadening some of their pleasure and motivation for learning. This does not mean the curriculum should be completely unpredictable; it does mean the subject matter should be drawn from the current interests of the group.

Perhaps one year the children are most concerned about disasters, as were children in Oklahoma in 1999 because of violent tornadoes that drove many of them from their homes. Or perhaps they are particularly interested in a fantasy character from a new movie, or what to do with the baby bird that has fallen from its nest. These interests should not be ignored, but considered as possible starting points for developing a curriculum for the cognitive self and possibly for the social and emotional selves as well.

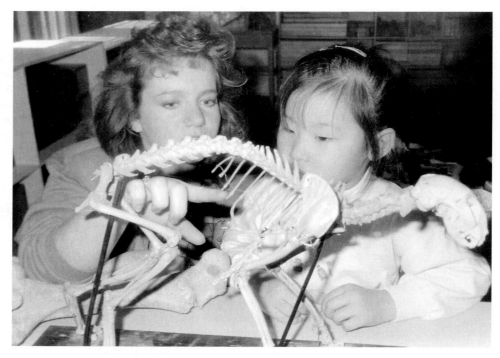

Wondering together stimulates everyone's curiosity.

Once they have been identified, it is the teacher's responsibility to respond to the children's interests in several ways. She is constantly on the lookout for opportunities for using the children's interest to foster higher order mental abilities related to solving problems of various kinds. She also supplies the children with information and vocabulary about subjects that matter to them and that they cannot find out about by themselves. She employs the interest as a medium for teaching basic midlevel mental ability skills, such as matching and grouping, that she wants them to acquire.

Relevant has another meaning we should remember as well—since it means *related*. Curriculum not only should be related to the children's interests but, to make it easier to understand and remember, also needs to be related, linked, to something they already know. This is so because neuroscience demonstrates it is easier to learn and remember something when it is tied to an existing neuronic structure (Goleman, 1995). (For example, I was baffled when I had to take a course in chemistry. The subject was entirely new to me, and I recall my father saying thoughtfully, "Well, you know, Honey, the trouble is, you have to know chemistry to understand chemistry." That sums it up in a nutshell.) This linking ideas together is why the teaching strategy of webbing makes sense. As we shall see in the discussion of creating learning pathways, however, it is important to keep the links closely related, rather than just branching out in a multitude of far-fetched associations.

Keep Cognitive Learning Brief and Unstressful.   Thinking is hard work. The episodes should be brief enough that the children do not feel strained from working too long. It is always better to stop before stress and boredom set in, since stopping at the right moment makes it more likely the child will want to return the next time.

The teacher must learn to recognize common signs of stress in children because these behaviors are an indication that it is past time to stop or that the activity needs to be modified to a more attractive and appropriate level. These signs include thumb sucking, wiggling, inattention, restlessness, hair twisting, constantly trying to change the subject, asking to leave or just departing, picking fights, and creating disturbances.

Enjoy the Experience with the Children.   The final way to sustain children's pleasure in learning is by enjoying it with them. Cognitive learning should not be a sober-sided, no-nonsense business. It is a fine time for experiences that include humor, fun, and discovery when the teacher enjoys the activity along with the children. The use of a relevant, emergent curriculum definitely enhances that pleasure. When teachers and children share learning together, everyone experiences satisfaction.

Priority III: Bind Cognitive Learning to Affective Experience Whenever Possible

Other emotions in addition to pleasure are bound to be involved in cognitive learning since such learning does not take place in an emotional vacuum. Feelings and social experience should be a fundamental part of cognitive learning. *Good education recognizes, accepts, and deals with feelings as they arise;* it does not ignore them or push them aside until later because now it is time to learn about baby animals or study the weather.

In particular the effect too much anxiety and stress have on learning must be taken into account. Children who are unduly stressed because of poverty, illness, unreasonable expectations, or families in turmoil need extra security, understanding, and affection to build the attachments that will help protect them as much as possible from the ill effects of too much cortisol.

The same principle holds true for social skills. Many opportunities for understanding and getting along with others will arise during experiences primarily intended to enhance the cognitive self. These windows of opportunity for social learning should be kept open and used as they occur.

Priority IV: Accompany Cognitive Learning with Language Whenever Possible

The word *accompany* is crucial here since language should be an integral part of, rather than a predecessor of, cognitive learning. One of the most common errors of beginning teachers seems to be that they depend too much on using language by itself when approaching cognitive development. Mere discussion about roots, petals, and stems is largely worthless for children unless they are able to tie that new vocabulary to the real experience of beans, earth, water, and sunlight.

Spoken language should not be thought of as the only way children have of communicating ideas and feelings. Besides oral language, children also use body posture, gestures, and expressions to communicate. As they reach the age of 3½ or 4, they become increasingly adept at using a variety of graphic materials to consolidate their ideas and explain them to other people. For example, they might use pieces of colored paper tinted from darkest red to palest pink to stand for (symbolize) the lowest to highest notes on a scale, or they might draw squares of various sizes to stand for those same notes. The Hundred Languages of Children exhibit now touring the United States is rich with illustrations of the graphic materials Reggio children use to express their ideas. These include examples of dialogues, drawings and paintings, punched paper, cutouts, shadow plays, bent wire, and objects modeled from clay, to name only a few of their 100 ways of making visible what they know.

PUTTING THESE BASIC PRINCIPLES INTO PRACTICE: TWO APPROACHES TO LEARNING

Once we have identified the basic priorities of maintaining the child's sense of wonder and curiosity, keeping cognitive learning a source of genuine pleasure, binding it to affective experience whenever possible, and enriching it with language, the next step is deciding how to provide a comprehensive program while integrating these principles into the life of the school. There are two ways of doing this, both of which are useful.

The first approach is best used as the overall framework for presenting learning. It is often called the *emergent, constructivist approach.* When teachers use this approach, they draw subject matter from the interests of the children and encourage them to construct their understanding and learning based on those interests. As we shall see, the value of this approach is that it provides structure while also allowing teachers and children to surge forward spontaneously as they use higher order thinking skills to think through and solve problems.

The second approach, which is discussed in the concluding chapter, is the more traditional, *conventional approach* to fostering cognitive learning. It identifies certain basic midlevel mental ability skills such as matching or grouping. These skills are then interwoven into themes or topics, hopefully but not necessarily, stemming from the children's interests. These themes are then used by the teacher to plan activities in advance that provide many opportunities for practicing those skills.

IMPLEMENTING THE EMERGENT CURRICULUM

Sometimes novice teachers assume the term *emergent* means that every idea must emerge from the children and that the curriculum must be entirely unplanned and spontaneous to fulfill the criteria of emerging. This is not what I have in mind when using the term. In this book *emergent* means that the direction a topic takes develops as the children and teachers investigate it together—each contributing her or his own ideas and possibilities as they evolve, in somewhat the same way the children and teachers at Reggio Emilia do. The teachers do make plans in advance and have ideas for possible topics, just as the children do, but as Rinaldi (1994) puts it so well, "these plans are viewed as a compass not a train schedule."

This image of a curriculum plan serving as a compass indicating direction and intention rather than being a predetermined schedule is particularly helpful to keep in mind when using the emergent approach. After all, if the curriculum is seen as gradually emerging, it really cannot be completely scheduled in advance, but it certainly does require a sense of direction and purpose.

If we carry the image of a compass a little further, it also clarifies why I, like Loris Malaguzzi (1992), the founder and architect of the Reggio Emilia preschools, prefer to use the word *pathway*, rather than *project*, to describe the development of a topic. *Pathway* conveys the sense of a continuing journey, rather than a unit that has a preplanned end or goal in mind from the start. As teachers and children venture down the pathway together, learning stems from the social interaction and collaboration that takes place along the way.

As this idea of a collaborative, learning-together approach has gained impetus, interest has also grown in the works of a Russian psychologist named Lev Vygotsky because of his emphasis on the value of the child and a more knowledgeable person working in collaboration together. Therefore it makes sense to take a moment to consider some of his most basic ideas.

SOME BASIC CONCEPTS OF VYGOTSKIAN PSYCHOLOGY

During his brief life (he died at age 37 from tuberculosis) Vygotsky contributed some insightful ideas about cognitive development and how it takes place. He maintained that language and cognitive ability do not appear automatically as the child passes through landmark stages, but rather that they develop in part because of interaction with other people—other peers, adults, and even imaginary companions as the child grows. As the title of his book *Mind in Society* (1978) emphasizes, the mind develops as the result of society's action on it. Since mental development cannot be separated from the social context in which it takes place, this theory about children's mental development is often spoken of as a sociocultural or sociohistorical theory. All this means is that society (and its past development—hence historical) and the culture it generates have great influence on what the child learns and the means by which he learns it.

Perhaps the most familiar Vygotskian concept is the idea of the *zone of proximal development (ZPD)*. Vygotsky (1978) defines this as "the distance between the actual development level [of the child] as determined by independent problem solving and the level of potential development as determined through problem solving under adult guidance in collaboration with more capable peers" (p. 86). Vygotsky points out that with the assistance of a more knowledgeable person, the child can advance closer to the farther edge of his potential ability. Another way of saying this is that there's a difference between the current or actual level of development and the child's potential level of development. The

Going Down the Road to Learning—Which Path Is Best to Take?

Preamble: The research reported here is a continuation of a study begun in 1986 that was initially intended to follow a group of children from their preschool experience through the first grade. It was initiated in the District of Columbia schools because of the unacceptably high rate of retention that was occurring when the children entered the formal school system. Since the results of that study turned out to be so clear and important, the research was later extended to find out how the children were faring through the fourth and fifth grades. It is that part of the research with which we are most concerned here.

However, to understand the second study, it is first necessary to review the results of the original one. The findings of the original research were based on studying a group of low-income children participating in three kinds of preschool models. These were characterized as being (a) academic, teacher-directed models, (b) child-initiated active learning models, or (c) middle-of-the-road models.

The results of that 3-year study revealed that the children in the middle-of-the-road model did poorest of all the groups in first grade, "scoring significantly lower in language, social, and motor development and also in overall adaptive function-

ing and mastery of basic skills (Marcon, 1994a, p. 11). Evidently it is better to believe consistently in anything rather than in an inconsistent hodge-podge. But the questions remained, "Since preparation for academic success is so important in later school years, how did the children turn out who were in the academic, teacher-directed programs compared with the ones in the child-initiated active learning model?" "Did academic instruction in the preschool produce superior academic gains later on in elementary school?" The answer is that, at the first-grade level, the children from the academic programs didn't turn out so well. In fact the youngsters in the child-initiated model "actually mastered more basic skills than did the youngsters in the academic one" (Marcon, 1994a, p. 11). More ominous, still, was another trend that seemed to be appearing: Along with their lower scores in first-grade reading and math, the social development scores of the children in the academically directed models were declining.

When the study was repeated the following year with a second, different group of children, the results were the same. This provided an even stronger reason to continue to follow the children as they advanced in school.

---

possibility of maximum advancement depends on the assistance lent to the learner by a more knowledgeable person—either an adult or another child.

This concept of the ZPD, as it is affectionately called, has encouraged teachers striving to put the emergent curriculum into practice to see their role as first beginning at the child's level of ability and then collaborating with him—by offering questions and cues, as well as more tangible assistance, that may enable him to extend his mental abilities a bit beyond what he was previously able to do.

The peril involved in using this approach at the preschool level is that it may become so teacher dominated and developmentally inappropriate that the child becomes a puppet—manipulated into parroting ideas beyond his understanding in order to please the adult. The best protection against this happening is careful sensitivity to the child's responses. That sensitivity must be the result of continual observation not only of what the child says but also of what he does. Does his physical behavior reveal underlying stress

The Follow-Up Study

Research Question: * Marcon asked, "How are the children in the academically directed and child-initiated preschool models turning out as they make the sometimes cognitively difficult transition from third to fourth and fourth to fifth grades?" "Which program has the most positive impact?"

Research Method: Information was available for 372 children who had participated in the academic or child-initiated models at the preschool level. Ninety-seven percent of the children were African American, and most of them came from low-income families. Data about the children in the fourth grade were gathered from a variety of sources, such as standardized tests, progress reports, and measures of social skills. The results were sorted according to whether the children had attended academic preschools or child-initiated programs. The findings from the groups were analyzed and compared.

Results: Marcon (1994b, p. ix) reported that "the negative impact on achievement and social development of overly academic early childhood programs was clearly apparent by age nine. By fourth grade, children who had attended academically directed pre-K programs had noticeably lower grades and were passing fewer fourth-grade read-

ing and mathematics objectives. By fourth and fifth grades, children from academic pre-K programs were developmentally behind peers and *displayed notably higher levels of maladaptive behavior* [italics added]" (1994b, pp. ix–x). In short, she concludes that "children who attend programs that focus on academic preparation (at the expense of other aspects of development) are more likely to develop social and scholastic problems by fourth grade" (1994b, p. 16).

Implications for Teaching: The findings of this study offer strong evidence of how important it is to provide child-initiated, active learning environments. This is true not only because it facilitates later intellectual ability *but also because it facilitates more positive social behavior.* In an era when violence is rising and life seems increasingly difficult, this may ultimately be the most significant reason of all for providing child-initiated active education.

* **This study has many more facets than the material reported here can cover. Because of space limitations, only the findings related to the children attending preschool classes are summarized. Readers who desire further information should refer to Marcon 1992, 1994a, and 1994b.**

Source: From "Doing the Right Thing for Children: Linking Research and Policy Reform in the District of Columbia Public Schools," by R. A. Marcon, 1994a, Young Children, 50(1), 8–20.

and tension? For example, is he wiggling, twisting his feet around chair legs, grimacing, twisting his hair, gnawing on fingernails, making excuses, and not wanting to participate—just to name a few common ways of relieving tension?

The other aspect of Vygotsky's theory of particular importance to preschool teachers is his emphasis on the significance of spoken language as the mediator between the world, the child's mind, and his ability to express, understand, and explain to other people what he knows. Vygotsky theorizes that by using the tool of language, children are able to master themselves and gain independence and self-control of behavior and thought. It is certainly true that many of us who work with 2-year-olds have heard examples of their attempts to use language to regulate behavior which support this contention. Who has not witnessed a child of that age say to himself, "No! No! Baby!" as he reaches simultaneously for the scissors?—or dealt with a 4-year-old reporting prissily on another's misdeeds in the sandbox?

Once again a peril must be noted concerning the use of language with young children: While acknowledging its indispensable value, teachers must also remember not to substitute it for real experiences. For language to have meaning, it must be tied to the concrete world, and for the world to acquire meaning, the child must have language.

GETTING STARTED WITH EMERGENT CURRICULUM

Many teachers, particularly early childhood teachers, are very attracted to this idea of the curriculum unfolding and developing as the children's interest grows. Yet when actually thinking about putting the approach into practice, they feel baffled and unsure about where to begin.

It is really not so difficult once the approach is analyzed into its various aspects and some fundamental concepts are grasped. One of the most important of these is that it is valuable for children to be able to generate their own ideas, figure out answers for themselves, and try out a variety of solutions until they find one that works—in other words, to make connections for themselves.

Moreover this "child activated" approach is gaining documentation and support from the research community. For example, the research studies reported by Marcon (1994a) (see the Research Study in this chapter) provide valuable evidence that using a child-initiated active learning model produces a variety of more desirable, long-term results than a more teacher dominated, academically oriented one does.

SOME BASIC PRINCIPLES TO REMEMBER WHEN USING THE EMERGENT APPROACH

Foster the Children's Ability to Generate Their Own Creative Ideas

Armstrong's (1997) definition of creativity as the "ability to see things in new ways and make unconventional connections" (p. 32) applies as well to cognitive activity as to play and the use of expressive materials because the ability to put past experiences together to connect in new ways is crucial to developing creative thinking. Of course, sometimes building on past knowledge produces unexpected and delightful results. I recall hearing of two young friends who were eating lunch together when the following dialogue took place.

> Henry: "Well, you know, Andrew, I'm black! I'm black all over—from my head right down to inside my shoes!"

There is a pause while this information is digested in silence by his friend Andrew.

Henry continues, "But that's OK! 'Cuz my Mother says, 'Black is beautiful!'"

Andrew continues to eye Henry speculatively while Henry somewhat complacently spoons up his Jell-O. There is silence around the table.

"Well," says Andrew, putting down his spoon and looking thoughtfully at Henry, "I guess being black's OK, all right—it's OK with *me*—but you know, Henry, if you wuz green, you could hide in the trees!"

Using prior information as Andrew did to produce new possibilities is just one kind of creative thinking. Children are also thinking creatively when they produce more than one answer to a question, or conceive of new uses for familiar materials, or generate uniquely descriptive language and self-expressive stories. To do these things, they need a wealth of experience to draw upon, and they need the help and expertise of the teacher to encourage them.

One person who has helped us understand the difference between the kind of thinking processes in which only one answer is correct and the thinking processes in which many answers might be correct is Paul Guilford (1981). He named the uncreative one-correct-answer sort of thinking *convergent* and the creative many-possible-answers kind of thinking *divergent*.

Convergent thinking is elicited by such questions as, "What color is this?" "Can you tell me the name of this shape?" and, "What must we always do before we cross the street?" Nothing is wrong with this kind of mental activity; children need a variety of commonly known facts at their fingertips. But teaching that stops at the fact-asking information level fails to draw out the child's own ideas. Children who are trained like robots to produce facts when the right button is pushed are unlikely to grow up to produce the new ideas desperately needed in science, medicine, and human relationships.

Unfortunately most teaching is still geared to convergent, one-answer learning. Zimmerman and Bergen (1971) found even as early as first grade what they termed "an inordinate emphasis placed on factual knowledge questions." They reported that only about 2% of questions asked by first-grade teachers were structured to draw forth divergent replies. Honig (1982) has also studied question-asking behavior and reports similar discouraging findings. The children she studied averaged around 27 months of age, and of the nearly 800 questions she observed being asked by caregivers, "15% were requests, 4% were reproofs, and 81% were true questions" (p. 65). This sounds encouraging until one reads that only 20% of those "true" questions were divergent and that fewer than 1% offered these children any choices!

But just because this has been true of teaching in the past does not mean it must continue. The following examples of ways to encourage children to generate emerging ideas of their own may encourage teachers to produce more divergent thinking in the children in their groups. Doing this is fun, it is interesting, and it can be exciting for both children and teachers when presented in the right manner. All it takes is practice.

Base the Curriculum on the Interests of the Children as Their Ideas Develop

When I dwell on the value of basing topics on the children's interests, the question of a former student always comes to mind. She asked most desperately and sincerely, "But what if the children don't have any ideas? What do I do then?"

My answer to this is that the ideas are always there if the teacher asks the right questions, waits for answers, and *listens closely enough*. Even when beginning with a potential topic generated by the teachers, note in the following example how the Reggio staff listened to the children and changed direction according to the interests of the 3-year-olds.

In this particular project described by Gambetti (1993), the teachers initiated the investigation because they thought it would be interesting to find out how the 3-year-olds viewed seasonal events, with late autumn as a particular focus. They began the study by

(a)

(b)

I took these pictures during one self-select period as the children investigated what the scale could do. Just think of how many different possibilities for curriculum might stem from this hour's investigation if the teacher observed and listened closely enough to what the children were doing and saying. The use of the airplane was especially interesting; note that Wong has his hand on the needle. He actually was using the needle as a spring that, when released, shot the plane into the air—a truly unanticipated, creative use of equipment.

talking with the children and asking them questions such as, "According to you, what is a season?" (To which one of the children replied, "Something that passes by!")

As they listened closely to what the children said, it became clear to the teachers that the children were more interested in clouds and what they do than they were in seasons. So they dropped the idea of seasons and decided to follow that lead. Over a considerable period of time a variety of experiences with clouds ensued—some suggested by the teachers and others by the children. These included looking at clouds at different times, observing frost in the morning and how the children's breath made clouds, projecting images of ice and clouds on the shadow screen, making cloud forms for screen shadows from materials suggested by the children, and drawing clouds—filled with whatever the children thought should be inside them. Finally the children decided they wanted to make "real" clouds of their own based on what they had learned about them and journeyed around the school looking for materials from which to form the clouds and materials with which to fill them. These ingredients, which were intended to represent raindrops and snowflakes, were as varied as wedged paper, lace, Styrofoam, bits of mirrors, and actual water. During the investigation the children were challenged (or *provoked*, as they say in Reggio) to produce various hypotheses about clouds and how they work and also to

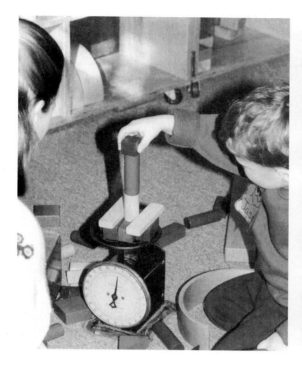

(c)　　　　　　　　　　　　　　　　　(d)

solve some problems. For example, they hypothesized about what's inside clouds, and they solved the problem of how to represent that content and the mechanics of how to hang the clouds up in the classroom "near the sky." All required solutions (unfortunately my notes don't say what they did about the water!).

Careful recordings and pictures were made of what the children said as they worked on this project over many days. Their conclusions and explanations of what they did and why they did it were encouraged and written down, and all this information was transcribed onto documentation boards for the children, teachers, and families to review as the pathway developed.

Remember to Keep the Pathway Focused:
Don't Let It Branch Off in Too Many Directions

Although it is all very well and good to pay attention to the children's interests, it is the teacher who must provide continuing direction to the pathway lest the group lose its way. Only the teacher has the vision to keep the entire forest in view while not losing sight of the individual trees.

Take the example of ducklings, for instance (see Table 18.1). Without consistent direction, interests might spread to barnyard animals in general, baby animals, raising a kitten, how animals swim, how people swim, what comes out of eggs, going duck hunting (remember that many children live in families in which family members hunt as a pastime), what's alive and what's dead, Easter customs from other lands, and so forth.

Table 18.1
Example of how a pathway might emerge based on the children's interests using the emergent approach to cognitive development

Children's Original Concerns and Interests	Adults' Visions of Possible Pathways to Explore	Children's Choices	Adult "Provocations"
[Children actually hatched eggs . . . have cared for ducklings & realized they've outgrown current cage]	Provide some way for ducks to go swimming	Make a pond for the ducks to enjoy	What could we use or make for pond? How can we keep the water in?
During a discussion, they say they want the ducks to feel happy—			
1. Find their mother			How could the ducks get into or out of the water?
2. Take them swimming			How can we fill the pond with water?
3. Make them a shower			Could we make a shower for them?
4. Let them play outside			
5. Fix them a bigger house	Build an outdoor shelter and pen	Maybe later—let's do the pond first . . . that will make them *most* happy	
6. Feed them stuff ducks really like to eat			
	Investigate relationship of form to function: web feet vs. claws vs. fingers & so forth	Children not interested when topic is brought up	

Children's Proposed Solutions	Examples of Higher Order Thinking Skills Tapped Using this Emergent Approach	Companion Midlevel Mental Abilities that Could Be Added by Teacher
Dish pan Galvanized tub Children's pool Dig hole, fill with water	Use imagination to solve problems. (What kind of things hold water?) Anticipate outcomes of proposed solutions and/or try them out.	Refer to Chapter 18 Refer to Chapter 19
Make them a ramp Build stairs from blocks Lift them ourselves (but we have to catch them first!)	Think of alternatives. (What to do when hole is dug and water seeps away) Estimate future size of ducks. (Find out how to find how big ducks grow) Apply concept of measurement. (How long does the hose need to be to reach the pond?)	
Add pipes on to end of hose Use bucket Squirt hose very hard Move pool	Gain understanding of some principles of physics related to force and pressure. (How can you make water run up hill?)	
Hold watering can up and sprinkle ducks Tie hose to top of slide Use pipes, screw on flexible dish rinsing hose from kitchen on pipe's end Squirt hose	Value other people's ideas when something doesn't work. (What if the cook needs to use the dish rinsing hose herself?)	

Such a far-ranging mixture of subjects will most likely provide the children with what Katz (1991) terms "smatterings" of information—mostly factual learning only loosely related to the children's core of interest. How much stronger it would be to focus clearly on a particular aspect of ducklings as is illustrated in Table 18.1 and to pursue the learning possibilities of that subject in more depth.

The Number of Children's Ideas Will Be Increased If the Teacher Recognizes Their Value and Responds to Them in a Positive Way

It is easy to go on doing things the same old way or to establish a set of procedures that have become so sanctified by custom that no one considers deviating from the established formula. But an open-minded teacher who keeps on the lookout for spontaneous ideas and suggestions will find she can frequently go along with variations in approach and changes in procedure when they are suggested by the children. The teacher who is willing to let the children put their ideas into practice offers strong positive reinforcement for this behavior, which will nourish problem solving talent in the children, and she will find herself blessed with ever more interesting, fresh contributions from the youngsters in her group.

Sometimes these ideas can be very simple. For example, I remember the time we offered a cooking project that involved slicing bananas for Jell-O. The inexperienced young student in charge thought she could watch only two children working with paring knives at once and therefore sensibly limited the activity to two children at a time. A third little boy hung around and watched, badly wanting to have a chance with the bananas; but the student truthfully explained she was so new that she thought she just couldn't supervise more than two knives at once. Then he said to her, "I tell you what—I could use one of the scissors for the bananas. I know how to do that. I *never* cut myself with scissors." She immediately saw the value of his suggestion and let him snip up as many pieces as he liked.

Another independently minded 2½-year-old was going through a streak of wanting to get into the swing by herself. Since she was short and the swing was high, she struggled and wriggled, doggedly refusing assistance. Finally she rushed away and returned with a large hollow block, which she put under the swing and used successfully as a mounting block.

Use Language Consistently Along with More Tangible Ways of Trying Out Ideas

Although there are perils in overintellectualizing discussions, it is important to remember that language is of genuine value in the development of ideas. Just remember that conversation must not be allowed to take the place of actual involvement with real things.

The staff at Reggio Emilia make a particular point of valuing language in such interesting ways that these warrant special discussion here. They use tape recordings as well as videotapes and photographs to capture children's comments about topics. These recordings are then transcribed so that staff can review and talk them over together—searching for clues about what the children know and what turn a pathway might take next.

Transcriptions, though time-consuming to do, have so many uses that they are well worth the extra work. Besides being used for the teachers to study, some of them are used to review events and ideas with the children—allowing the youngsters to revisit (re-cognize) what they have been doing and thinking about.

In addition transcriptions often become part of "documentation boards" assembled as the investigations continue. These boards, which combine written and pictorial documentation, are used for the children's direct benefit and to keep the parents informed about what is going on. Ultimately the documentation boards and transcriptions, together with other records, provide concrete evidence of accomplishment that can be very useful for assessment purposes (Cadwell, 1997).

Use Questions in Ways That "Provoke" the Children Into Thinking for Themselves as Ideas Emerge

Sort Out the Different Kinds of Teacher-Generated Questions: Understand the Difference Between Using Fact and Thought Questions. We have already noted that all questions are not alike because some elicit convergent and others divergent replies. This is easiest to understand if one thinks of questions related to mental development as being of three kinds: (a) *convergent fact questions*, which request the child to reply with one right answer; (b) *figuring-out questions*, which require the child to apply a concept such as grouping or common relations to arrive at one or more right answers; and (c) *open-end questions*, which elicit an original idea (hypothesis) or solution from the youngster.

Fact questions are the simplest and, regrettably, most frequently used kind of question. They can usually be spotted because they request information ("Do you make cookies in the oven or in the broiler?" "You're right! It *is* a rabbit. What else do you know about rabbits?"), request labeling or naming ("Let's see, I have some things in this bag, and I wonder if you can tell me what they are."), or request the child to recall something from memory ("How about telling us what happened when you went to the pet store? Did you buy rabbit food?"). All these questions are "closed" or convergent questions because they anticipate simple, correct-answer replies.

Figuring-out questions, which we deal with more fully in chapter 19, are a big step up from fact questions, but in the final analysis they are still going to produce right (convergent) answers. They are more advanced than fact questions because, to answer the question, the child must be able to apply a concept to a situation and reason out the reply. For example, to select the pictures that are the same (e.g., playing Bingo), a youngster must understand the concept of sameness and then be able to apply it by matching the pictures that are identical. Or if he is asked how birds are not the same as butterflies, he must analyze what is the same about them and what is different. Even though there would be several differences to identify, and even though more analysis and insight is involved than is required just to say, "It's called a butterfly," the final result is the production of closed-end, correct answers. These midlevel intellectual skills are useful because they form part of the foundation for verbal and mathematical literacy later on, but they do not provide children opportunities to express the full range of what they know and to produce unique solutions.

Open-end questions, in contrast, foster the production of original, divergent ideas and solutions. They are termed *open-end* because the questioner does not know what the answer will turn out to be. This chapter concentrates on using these kinds of questions because these are the ones most needed when using the emergent approach.

Fortunately, producing open-end questions is really easy if you think of it as coming in three types: *opinions, reasons for the opinions,* and *possible ways to try out the opinions to see whether they are sound.*

For example, with the first type, *asking-for-opinion-questions,* the teacher might ask, [In your opinion] "What could we do to help the ducks feel happy?" or, "Oh, oh! We've got the tub over in the shade, but how in the world can we get enough water over there to fill it," or, "What do you think we should feed them?" or, "But what if we can't find their mothers?"

Examples of the second type, *asking-for-reasons-for-opinion-questions,* are, "Why'd you choose the bucket, Alvin?" or, "How come you think they'd like the lettuce best?" or, "Why do you think the hose is better to use than the bucket?"

The third type, *asking-how-can-we-find-out-questions,* typically encourage the children to think up ways to try out their type one opinions. "Now let's think about this. Sharon thinks we should feed them hot dogs, Willie is voting for lettuce, and Alvin thinks peanuts would be just right. How are we going to find out which the ducks like best?"

When just beginning, it helps to think up actual topic-related questions in advance to pose to the children such as, "How could we get the water to their pond?" or, "Suppose we couldn't use a pipe; is there something else we could use instead?" These are the kinds of questions that encourage children to do creative thinking in return.

Wait for Answers and Ask Only a Few Questions at a Time.   One of the most important things about asking questions is learning to *wait* for an answer. This is surprisingly hard to do. Many teachers ask excellent questions but then plunge right ahead and answer them themselves. In one study of "wait time," Rowe (1974) found that teachers only waited, on the average, 1 *second* before answering their own questions. Perhaps this is because teachers are afraid of silence or of the children's failing. But children, like adults, need time to collect their thoughts and formulate their replies. Pausing allows them to do this.

Something else to beware of is asking too many questions. The plaintive little song by Hap Palmer puts this neatly when he inquires,

> Questions, questions, askin' me endlessly
> How many more must I answer today?
> Questions, questions, don't drive me crazy, please,
> How much more can I say?[1]

In our zeal to help children think, we must remember that most young children are not highly verbal and that they do not enjoy long, drawn-out intellectual dialogues. To prevent questions from becoming burdensome, it is best to weave them into general discussions while the actual experience is going on, as well as to provide all possible opportunities for children to put their suggestions into practice promptly.

---

[1] *Source: From "Feelin' Free," a recording by Hap Palmer made for Educational Activities, Freeport, NY 11520 (AR 516). Some nice creative questions are also on this same record.*

Resist the Impulse to Always Answer the Children's Questions Yourself.   Asking opinion-type questions and waiting for the children to answer them is only half of what teachers need to know about the inquiry approach. The other half is knowing how to respond when children ask *them* questions.

Of course, many times teachers can help children make satisfying progress by supplying information they couldn't figure out for themselves, but *just as often* the children can figure things out on their own if teachers do not rush in and furnish the fact immediately. The easiest and most effective response (and yet the hardest one for many teachers to give) is just to wait a little while and see what happens next (and waiting has an additional advantage—it provides time for the teacher to think up a question in reply that will assist the child to figure out the answer if that cue becomes necessary).

When other children can be drawn into the discussion and encouraged to add their suggestions, comments, and evaluations, even more learning will take place—providing this can be done in a friendly and not a destructive way.

Encourage the Child or the Group to Produce More Than One Answer.   Since more than one correct answer is possible in divergent thinking, teachers need to learn how to encourage children to propose more than one possible solution to a problem. Making sure the children's ideas are not criticized will help generate many answers, whereas the negative experience of criticism will make sensitive children clam up and refuse to take the risk of confiding a second thought (Kline, 1988). If the goal is to encourage children to mention their ideas, it makes simple good sense to welcome the suggestions and ask for more rather than to submit each one to instant critical appraisal or, worse yet, amused laughter.

The kinds of questions that often lead children to generate more ideas related to creative problem solving are sometimes called "what-else?" and "what-if?" questions (Campbell & Arnold, 1988). Questions such as "What else could you do?" or "Is there another way?" will stimulate many suggestions from the children. For example, Aline and Franklin, both 4-year-olds, are trying to get the rat's cage open to feed him. As they work, the teacher jokes with them a little and asks them, "I wonder what we'd do if the gate were really stuck and we *couldn't* get it open. How could we feed the rat then?" "We could poke it through the lines [bars]," says Franklin. "Sure we could. That's a good idea, Franklin, but let's suppose we couldn't get it through the bars—what then?" "We could teach him to reach out," says Franklin. "Yes, he likes to reach; but if he couldn't do that, what then?" There is a long silence while the children consider. "But he *can*," answers practical Franklin. "But let's imagine, just pretend for fun, that he can't. Could we feed him another way, or would he just get hungry?" Suddenly Aline brightens visibly and says, "We could slide the tray out and feed him from the cellar?" (She means from underneath.) "Yes, we could," says the teacher. "My goodness, Franklin, you and Aline sure have a lot of ideas. I guess we'll be able to feed our rat after all." The children laugh with her.

This kind of elementary brainstorming can be done quite successfully with preschool children in a playful way. It encourages them to see that questions can have several right answers and to develop the habit of looking for more than one solution to a problem.

What-if? questions encourage even freer and more creative answers than what-else? questions do. Sometimes with older 4- and 5-year-olds this approach can be presented as a guessing game during group or lunch time. A problem can be postulated, such as, "What if we didn't have any blankets at nap; how could we keep warm?" Then all kinds of possibilities can be suggested. (One of our little boys replied, "Grow fur."). Four-year-olds often delight in thinking up nonsensical solutions whose funniness adds delight to this process and exercises their sense of humor as well.

Asking the children to consider a nonsensical possibility by using a variation of what-if? questions provides good practice and lots of fun, too. This just-suppose approach stimulates many imaginative replies.

For example, one might ask the children to just suppose something were true and then consider what would happen as a result. Just suppose bean vines never stopped growing, dogs could talk to cats, mice had wings, you were only as big as your thumb, or all your wishes would come true. It is clear that some of the most interesting fairy tales and folktales such as "Jack and the Beanstalk," "Tom Thumb," and "Why the Sea Is Salt" are based on exactly these kinds of interesting, fantastical possibilities.

When two of our 4-year-olds, Carolina and Katie, were asked what they would wish for if their wishes could come true they composed the following poem.

> I wish it could be snowy every day, and I could play in it
> I wish I had a long dress with a matching hat and purse
> I wish I was a big person
> I wish I had a house you could go out on the roof of
> I wish I had a crystal star

Enable the Children to Translate Their Ideas Into Concrete, Tangible Experience

The real joy and satisfaction of using the emergent approach must not be thought of as stopping at the idea stage. The real satisfaction comes from putting the proposals for solving problems into practice: trying out possible containers for water, determining what works and what lets the water soak through, seeing whether the ducks can manage the steps or really need a ramp to get in and out, and so forth.

This aspect of learning can stretch out over weeks as the children think of what could be done and put their ideas to the test of practicality. It is important to relax and allow plenty of time and an unhurried pace if the children are to obtain maximum value from the experience.

Of course, creative ideas and experiments do not always work, and adults, who have a much better grasp of cause and effect, as well as more experience than children have, can often foresee problems and difficulties associated with ideas produced by young thinkers. But if the situation is reasonably safe, the children should be allowed to try out their ideas even if the adult knows they will not work. Children are entitled to the right to fail, as well as to the right to succeed. The sensitive teacher will be matter-of-fact and low-key about such ineffective trials. She might say, "I'm sorry that didn't work out just right, but it was worth a try," or simply, "I can see you're really disgusted. Can I help?" or, "Well, what do you want to try next?"

"You're right!" he said. "That darn stuff just won't run up hill."

   Children can learn as much from experiencing failures as they can from successes. Sometimes they are able to modify the idea and turn it into a later triumph, sometimes not. More important than being successful is learning to accept the experience of failure as part of life while going on to try out other possible solutions.

Make Certain the Children Use Some Form of Expressive Medium to Explain to Other People What They Have Found Out.   The most obvious way children can communicate what they've learned is to explain it to the teacher as she writes it down for them, but there are many additional avenues for such explanations. For example, a typical Reggio approach, along with the consistent use of documentation boards, would be to have a party and show the parents the pool and the sprinkler and how much the ducks are enjoying them. Drawing pictures, no matter how unfathomable they are to the adult eye, is still another form of explanation, as is making a model of the ducks, pool, and sprinkler from clay. Or the children themselves might make a video record of how their ideas developed—what they tried along the way and how the completed duck pond turned out.

An Example of How American Teachers Collaborated with the Children to Develop an Emergent Pathway Using the School's Ducklings for Inspiration

Making a Map or Plan the Investigatory Pathway *Might* Follow Is Essential

Table 18.1, on pages 480–481, contains several important points for the reader to note: The original interest stemmed from the ducklings the children already cared about. The teachers, recognizing that interest, hypothesized possible investigatory directions the pathways might take. Further discussions with the children caused everyone to settle on an aspect of ducklings of interest to them all (the children wanted the ducks to be happy, and the teachers were dying to get the ducks outside). This in-depth concentration of ideas produced a lot of worthwhile collaborative problem solving. In addition the process empowered the children to do something kindly and considerate for animals, and (not the least of the advantages!) it moved the ducklings, who were becoming smelly and rather large, out of the classroom.

Summary

New biological research about the development of the brain confirms the crucial influence parents and teachers have during the early years of childhood. This is because the environmental stimulation we provide fosters the proliferation of connections between neurons that are so important for learning.

To determine the most desirable ways to foster learning, the priorities of maintaining the child's sense of wonder and curiosity, letting cognitive learning be a source of genuine pleasure, binding it to affective experience whenever possible, and accompanying it with meaningful language are important to consider. Once these priorities are acknowledged, two approaches can be used together to put them into practice. The first is the emergent, *constructivist approach* discussed in this chapter. The second, discussed in the concluding chapter, is the more *conventional approach,* which provides practice in midlevel mental ability skills.

Vygotsky's concepts of the zone of proximal development, and the vital role other people play in the development of the child's mental ability, coupled with his emphasis on the importance of language as the mediator of social experience, have gained prominence during the past few years as exemplars of how teachers can extend children's learning.

Vygotsky's ideas fit comfortably with the philosophy of the emergent curriculum exemplified by the preschools of Reggio Emilia. These schools, and others that foster the emergent approach, encourage the use of divergent, creative thinking by the children. To foster such thinking, teachers should learn to use open-end questions in ways that provoke children into thinking for themselves. They should ask only a few questions at a time, wait for answers, respond to the children's ideas in a positive way, and encourage production of more than one answer.

Questions and Activities

1. The next time you have to solve some sort of problem, take a few minutes and just for fun list all the ways, both silly and practical, that the problem might be solved. Try not to evaluate the merit of the ideas as you produce them, but just play around with many possibilities. Then evaluate them. Is a fresh one included that might be a good, new, though perhaps unconventional, way to solve the problem?

2. Might it be possible that preprimary teachers are depriving children of the right to learn the things that would help them succeed best in elementary school when we stress play, creativity, and mental health, rather than emphasizing such skills as learning the alphabet and counting? What might be the case for placing greater emphasis on academic learning at the preschool level?

3. In your opinion which is more important for mental development: the neurons that develop before birth or the connections that form afterward? Be sure to supply reasons why you have selected one or the other.

4. *Predicament:* You have in your room a little boy about 3 years old who asks a lot of questions. For example, he might ask, "Why are we going in now?" When dutifully provided with the reasons, he then asks, "But why do we have to do that?" When answered, he asks, "But why?" If you were his teacher, would you think this type of inquiry should be encouraged? How would you handle it?

5. Isn't it a waste of time to let children try things out that obviously won't work? Might it not be better just to lead a discussion with them about the proposed solutions, rather than go to the trouble of actually trying out something only to experience failure?

6. You have been reading about the emergent curriculum approach and are very eager to teach that way in your classroom of 4-year-olds, but you feel a little baffled about how to begin. The teacher next door is starting the year by focusing on bears. She plans to have the children bring teddy bears from home, reward them with little bear stickers when they're good, and tell the story of Goldilocks at group time. Explain why this

approach is *not* emergent and suggest some things you and the children might do concerning bears that would reflect the emergent approach more adequately.

Self-Check Questions for Review

Content-Related Questions

1. Describe some things teachers can do that will help cognitive learning be a source of genuine pleasure to the children.

2. Does work on cognitive learning mean the teacher should ignore what is going on emotionally and socially among the children.

3. List the four priorities that are most important to consider when developing a curriculum for the cognitive self.

4. In recent years what has happened in biological research that has made it possible to find out more about how the brain develops?

5. Explain what each of the three "E's"—experience, earliness, and emotion—has to do with how the brain develops.

6. Name at least two basic concepts of Vygotskian psychological theory.

7. Explain the difference between *divergent* and *convergent* thinking and why each is an important aspect of thought.

8. Numerous important strategies can be used when asking questions and dealing with answers that encourage children to develop ideas of their own. List several of these and explain why each is valuable. Does *emergent* mean the teacher should avoid planning the cognitive curriculum in advance? Be sure to explain your answer fully.

Integrative Questions

1. On a snowy day the children are fascinated with the snow itself because it's the first snow of winter. What are some activities you could do with them that would provide some learning while remaining real fun for the children? Be sure to identify what the children would be learning and why you think they will enjoy the experiences.

2. If a teacher was "held captive by the concept of developmental stages," what might be the implications for the way she would plan the social or cognitive curriculum for the children?

3. Why does Vygotsky's concept of the zone of proximal development fit so comfortably with the role of the teacher—the way the teacher is supposed to teach—when using the emergent curriculum?

4. Select a learning experience based on a natural science subject (e.g., ants) and make up a list of questions on this subject that will require convergent, fact-based answers. Now modify the questions so that they will be more likely to require children to do some creative thinking using opinions, reasons, and (possibly) trying out opinions to answer them.

5. It is your first year teaching in a classroom of 3-year-olds. You would like to add dishes to the housekeeping area, but the budget has no money for new ones. Propose three what-else-could-you-use-instead-of-new-ones? solutions.

6. Sort the following questions into their appropriate convergent or divergent categories.

"What did you watch on television last night?" After reading the book *If You Give a Mouse a Cookie* (Numeroff, 1987): "According to this story, *is* it a good idea to give a mouse a cookie?" "It looks like only two pieces of cheese are left, but everyone wants them. What do you think we should do?" "But what if Peter hadn't caught the wolf, what then?" "Who remembers the name of the little monkey in this book?"

Finally, add another example of your own to each category.

7. The duckling example uses experiences with water to show how children and teachers might collaborate to develop an emergent curriculum. Think of another duck-related possibility they might pursue that would allow further opportunities for even more ideas to emerge. Suggest what some of those opportunities might be.

Coordinating Videotape

Growing minds. Tape #13. *The whole child: A caregiver's guide to the first five years.* The Annenberg/CPB Collection, P.O. Box 2345, South Burlington, VT 05407–2345. *Growing Minds* describes two approaches to developing mental ability. The program offers basic ways teachers can encourage young children to think creatively by using emergent curriculum with an emphasis on the inquiry method as a means of stimulating thought. It also touches on the more conventional approach as teachers set up activities that provide practice in specific mental abilities such as matching and grouping.

References for Further Reading

Pick of the Litter

Note: I couldn't choose between Shore and Cadwell, so I picked them both.

Cadwell, L. B. (1997). *Bringing Reggio Emilia home: An innovative approach to early childhood education.* New York: Teachers College Press. The sense of fresh adventure and inspiration conveyed by this book should inspire all of us to translate some of that inspiration into our own school environments.

Shore, R. (1997). *Rethinking the brain: New insights into early development.* New York: Families and Work Institute. Also available from the National Association for the Education of Young Children, this landmark book is one of the first to make new information about brain development available to early childhood people in practical, usable, readable form. An indispensable reference.

Overviews

Jones, E., & Nimmo, J. (1994). *Emergent curriculum.* Washington, DC: National Association for the Education of Young Children. In a truthful and searching way, the authors recount their efforts to follow the principles of emergent curriculum over a year's time. *Highly recommended.*

Katz, L., & Chard, S. C. (1991). *Engaging children's minds: The project approach.* Norwood, NJ: Ablex. Katz and Chard provide practical suggestions of ways to shift from what they term "systematic instruction" to more flexible project work. Very helpful reading.

Information About the Brain

Goleman, D. (1995). *Emotional intelligence*. New York: Bantam Books. Goleman includes the best chapter I have found on the anatomy of the brain and the role it plays in development. *Highly recommended.*

Fostering Creativity and Problem Solving

Baum, S. E., & Cray-Andrews, M. (1983). *Creativity 1, 2, 3*. New York: Trillium Press. After toiling through many books *with creative* in their titles and finding them filled with do-it-this-way activities, it was a joy to find this small treasure, which really *is* about how to foster ideas generated by the children. Even better, it is still in print. *Highly recommended.*

Gelb, M. J. (1998). *How to think like Leonardo da Vinci*. New York: Delacourt Press. For those of us who may be wishing for fresh inspiration and encouragement for ourselves, this book is a welcome pick-me-up of suggestions for revitalizing thinking. *Highly recommended.*

Wien, C. A. (1995). *Developmentally appropriate practice in "real life": Stories of teacher practical knowledge*. New York: Teachers College Press. These descriptions of five teachers and their varying attempts to incorporate developmentally appropriate practice remind us how difficult it can be to make changes in our approaches to curriculum. Food for thought!

Information About Reggio Emilia Schools

Hendrick, J. (Ed.). (1997). *First steps toward teaching the Reggio way*. Upper Saddle River, NJ: Merrill/Prentice Hall. This collection of chapters first describes the philosophy of the Reggio approach and then provides many examples, written by actual participants, of ways they are attempting to use it in the United States.

Information About Vygotsky

Berk, L. E., & Winsler, A. (1995). *Scaffolding children's learning: Vygotsky and early childhood education*. Washington, DC: National Association for the Education of Young Children. This readable book clearly explains the basic principles of the theory, cites recent research related to it, and explains how it can be applied to preschool and early elementary school. *Highly recommended.*

For the Advanced Student

Dacey, J. S., & Lennon, K. H. (1998). *Understanding creativity: The interplay of biological, psychological, and social factors*. San Francisco: Jossey-Bass. In this very interesting book the authors review previous theories and research about creativity and add contributions of their own. The emphasis is on *creative problem solving*, rather than on self expressive materials. *Highly recommended.*

Edwards, C., Gandini, L., & Foreman, G. (Eds.). (1993). *The hundred languages of children: The Reggio Emilia approach to early childhood education*. Norwood, NJ: Ablex. Although the entire book is valuable, the several chapters describing actual projects may be most helpful for teachers striving to implement the emergent approach in their own classrooms.

Edwards, C., Gandini, L., & Foreman, G. (1998). *The hundred languages of children: The Reggio Emilia approach to early childhood education—Advanced reflections*. Greenwich, CT: Ablex. This revised and expanded edition is the comprehensive resource that explains the philosophy and implementation of the Reggio approach in its homeland and in the United States. *Highly recommended.*

Piirto, J. (1999). *Talented children and adults: Their development and education* (2nd ed.). Upper Saddle River, NJ: Merrill/Prentice Hall. Piirto includes a chapter discussing the relationship between creativity and intellectual giftedness.

Siegel, D. J. (1999). *The developing mind: Toward a neurobiology of interpersonal experience*. New York: Guilford Press. This is a detailed, carefully integrated account of how the mind functions. It is filled with gems of information for the advanced student.

Vygotsky, L. (1978). *Mind in society: The development of higher psychological processes* (M. Cole, V. John-Steiner, S. Scribner, & E. Souberman, Eds.). Cambridge, MA: Harvard University Press. Vygotsky sets forth his basic theory in this very readable book.

Additional Resources of Particular Interest

Innovations in Early Education: The International Reggio Exchange. Merrill-Palmer Institute: Wayne State University, 71–A East Ferry Ave., Detroit, MI 48202 ($20/year). This quarterly newsletter encourages the exchange of ideas from around the world that are related to the Reggio approach. Includes information on conferences and the Hundred Languages of Children exhibit. *Highly recommended.*

Rechild: The Reggio Children Newsletter. Reggio Children srl, Via G. DaCastello, 12 Piazza Della Vittoria, 6 42100 Reggio Emilia, Italy. Published three times a year, this bilingual newsletter from Reggio Emilia itself provides information about various aspects of the municipal schools of Reggio Emilia. *Highly recommended.*

Developing Thinking and Reasoning Skills

Using the Conventional Approach to Build Midlevel Mental Abilities

Why studying Piaget is so important?

What specific mental abilities could be worked on at the preschool level that would build a foundation for later success in primary school?

How to include practice in these abilities and keep it fun, too?

. . . IF YOU HAVE, THE MATERIAL IN THE FOLLOWING PAGES WILL HELP YOU.

In classrooms that encourage natural, spontaneous, lively, intense curiosity in an environment of interesting and challenging materials, children will gain experiences needed for developing both linguistic and mathematical concepts. For example, by using dough, they may experience that which is alike (one dough ball is like another). In using sand, they understand things that are not alike (wet sand is not like dry sand). The environment can yield other experiences: objects that are patterned (a brick wall is patterned, children's chants are patterned); events that follow a sequence (story comes after snack); parts and wholes (cutting apples, oranges, and bananas for salad); things that have direction (a pulley lifts the pail up); objects that have size, weight, texture.

Nancy Balaban (1984, p. 9)

Now that we understand how to provide an overall structure or framework of emergent curriculum that develops as teacher's and children's interests generate together, it is time to discuss the second approach. This approach is important to include because it provides practice in certain midlevel mental abilities that underlie the development of later academic skills. Therefore we need to understand what these skills are, why they are important, and how to embed them in the emergent approach.

Table 19.1 shows how the role of the teacher and child is quite different for each of the approaches, but this should not imply that one role should be selected and the other ignored. Skillful teachers combine the approaches to present a truly balanced curriculum for the children's cognitive selves.

The main difference between the conventional and the emergent approaches is the degree of responsibility assumed by the teacher. When a teacher is using the conventional approach to work on midlevel reasoning skills, the curriculum is predetermined to a greater extent by him. Although experienced teachers also seize spontaneous opportunities for practicing specific abilities as these arise, the majority of the learning materials are typically generated in advance and presented to the children for their pleasure and practice as *fait accomplis*. For example, to provide practice in common relations the teacher might make up pairs of animals and their feet and ask the children which feet belong to the ducks, which to the robins, ostriches, and so on. The children are expected to apply the concept of common relations by pairing feet and animal bodies together, thereby obtaining practice in common relations and the mathematical concept of one-to-one correspondence.

In contrast, when one is working with the emergent, problem-solving approach, the curriculum must be more fluid because the teacher cannot predict in advance what solutions the children may propose and what direction the investigatory pathway may take. Of course, *planning and direction remain necessary*, but they are done on a more ongoing basis. The result in the emergent approach is that learning becomes less teacher dominated and more of a mutual, collaborative experience as teacher and children share their ideas together.

This chapter concentrates on developmentally appropriate ways to use the more conventional approach by presenting activities that provide practice in the midlevel reasoning skills. In days gone by it was difficult to identify which of these skills were significant and which developmental level fit different ages of childhood. Fortunately in the past few years some aspects of these problems have been resolved by the work of Jean Piaget.

BASIC CONCEPTS OF PIAGETIAN PSYCHOLOGY

Although it is not within the scope of this book to attempt a comprehensive summary of Piaget's work, any discussion of the thought processes of young children must begin with at least a brief review of his work because he devoted a lifetime to studying the mental development and characteristics of young children (Piaget, 1926, 1950, 1962, 1963, 1965, 1983; Piaget & Inhelder, 1967, 1969). He was primarily interested in how people come to know what they know—the origins of knowledge—and his work has important implica-

Table 19.1
A comparison of learning opportunities using the conventional or the emergent creative approach

	Information Approach	Emergent Constructivist Approach for Teaching Creative Thinking and Problem Solving	Conventional Approach for Teaching Midlevel Abilities
Value of approach	Provides information base needed as foundation for midlevel and problem solving skills. Widens knowledge of world.	Allows children to develop full range of mental powers. Encourages application of prior knowledge to solving new problems. Empowers children to try out ideas and explain what they know to other children and adults.	Provides diversified practice in applying specific mental ability skills (concepts), which are valuable beginning literacy and beginning mathematical skills.
Examples of kinds of mental ability skills developed by approach	Pay attention. Process information. Retain information. Recall information. Reconstruct information.	Generate ideas on own. Form hypotheses (reasons) why something happens and try them out. Assess and evaluate possibilities. Pursue interests in depth.	Apply specific concepts such as matching, grouping, perceiving common relations, seriated and temporal ordering, cause-and-effect relationships, and conserving. May use children as source to determine interest around which to build a theme.
Teacher's role	Supply information to children and/or help them find information for themselves.	Listen to children; follow their lead to select pathway to investigate. Plan curriculum ahead but alter and adjust plans as pathways develop direction. Encourage generation of ideas by "provoking" children to consider problems and solve them. Develop opportunities with children to try out their ideas.	Plan ahead to think up and present activities and experiences for children that provide opportunities for practice and application of specific concepts.
Child's role	Soak up interesting information and store it in memory. Be able to recall, reconstruct and repeat information when needed.	Collaborate (toss ball of ideas back and forth) with teacher to pursue interests. Think up ways to express ideas and solve problems. Try ideas out. Express ideas and what is found out through language, graphics, and child-constructed models.	Participate in learning activities provided by teacher, thereby practicing various midlevel mental ability skills. Acquire mental ability concepts and apply them by reasoning. Express what the child knows by manipulating teacher-provided materials.

tions for teachers interested in the cognitive development of the children in their care because he provided evidence that children really *do* think differently than adults do.

Many of Piaget's ideas are bound to sound both familiar and comfortable to the contemporary student since a good deal of what he said for 60 years has been practiced in nursery schools and preschool centers during the same period and is similar in part to the philosophy of Dewey and Montessori (because of its emphasis on the value of experience). For a variety of reasons, however, his work passed largely unnoticed in the United States until the 1960s, and only since then has it been deliberately implemented in the preschool classroom by such investigators as Almy (Almy, Chittenden, & Miller, 1966), DeVries (DeVries & Kohlberg, 1990), Forman and Hill (1980), Kamii (1975, 1982, 1985), Lavatelli (1970a, 1970b), Saunders and Bingham-Newman (1984), and Weikart (Hohmann & Weikart, 1995).

Although his own realm of investigation was primarily in the cognitive area, Piaget agreed that affective, social, and cognitive components go hand in hand (Piaget, 1981; Wadsworth, 1989). Because these components are interdependent, it is evident that a school in which good mental health policies are practiced and sound social learning is encouraged will also be one in which mental growth is more likely to occur.

Piagetian Categories of Knowledge

Piaget theorized that children acquire three kinds of knowledge as they grow. *Social-conventional knowledge* is the first kind. This is information that society has agreed on and that is often learned through direct social transmission. For example, English-speaking people agree that the word *table* stands for a flat object supported by four legs. Rules that define what acceptable behavior is provide another example of socially transmitted knowledge.

The second kind of knowledge is *physical knowledge*. It is information children gain by acting on objects in the real world. Information about the quality of things and what they do are examples of physical knowledge.

The third kind of knowledge is less tangible because it cannot be directly observed. It is knowledge developed (constructed) in the mind of the child as she thinks about objects. Piaget calls this *logico-mathematical knowledge*. The development of logico-mathematical thought, which we might also think of as being the ability to reason, ultimately enables children to develop ideas of relationships between objects. When they can grasp what it is that items in a group have in common, for instance, they are able to assign a common name to that group, thereby classifying or grouping the things together. For example, the children might divide a set of pictures, sorting them into things you can wear and things you can eat, and name the groups "clothing" and "food." As Kamii (1985) points out, this idea of a common property exists only in the mind. It is not inherent in the pictures themselves; it is an *idea*, not a physical property. It is important to remember that reasoning knowledge is closely tied to physical knowledge since reasoning usually requires a foundation of factual information, but it also differs from factual information.

This gradual development of logico-mathematical ability frees children from being tied to concrete experience because it enables them to think with symbols and to deal with abstractions. However, it takes many years for children to reach that level of maturity. To attain it, Piaget and colleagues identified a series of stages through which children must pass as they develop. These stages are outlined in Table 19.2.

Table 19.2
Summary of the Piagetian model

Basic Stages in Developing the Ability to Think Logically	Behavior Commonly Associated with the Stage
Sensorimotor Stage (0–2 years)* Understanding the present and real	Composed of six substages that move from reflex to intentional activity, involving cause-effect behavior Involves direct interactions with the environment
Preoperational Stage (2–7 years) Symbolic representation of the present and real Preparation for understanding concrete operations (this is a tremendous period of transition)	Overt action is transformed into mental action. Child uses signifiers: mental images, imitation, symbolic play, drawing, and language to deal with experience. Understands verbal communication. Uses play to assimilate reality into herself. Believes what she sees; is "locked into" the perceptual world. Sees things from her own point of view, only one way at a time ("centering") and is learning to decenter. Thinking is not reversible. Intensely curious about the world. Busy laying foundations for understanding at the later concrete operations stage, which involves grasping concepts of *conservation, transitivity, classification, seriation,* and *reversibility.*
Concrete Operational Stage (7–11 years) Attainment of and organization of concrete operations Learns to apply logical thought to concrete problems	Has probably acquired the following concepts: *conservation, reversibility, transitivity, seriation,* and *classification*; that is, now believes that length, mass, weight, and number remain constant; understands relational terms such as *larger than* and *smaller than*; is able to arrange items in order from greatest amount to least amount; can group things according to more than one principle; can manipulate things in her mind, but these things are real objects. Becomes interested in following rules; games are important.
Formal Operational Stage (11–15 years) Hypothesis-making testing possible Masters logical reasoning	Age of abstract thinking; logical reasoning. Able to consider alternative possibilities and solutions. Can consider "fanciful," hypothetical possibilities as a basis for theoretical problem solving; abstract thinking, can make logical deductions and generalizations; can think about thinking.

*Note that the ages represent the *average* age of acquisition. This means that there is considerable variability in the time different children acquire the ability.

Research conducted over a period of more than 60 years convinced Piaget that the order of the stages through which children progress cannot be changed, although the age at which the stage occurs may vary. He demonstrated this convincingly in his detailed reports of investigations he conducted in which he presented problems to children and then asked them questions about their answers.

Piagetian Stages of Development

Of greatest interest to early childhood teachers is the *preoperational stage,* which extends roughly from age 2 to age 7. During this stage children make the profound transition from depending on the way things appear to depending on logic and reasoning when making a decision. They become able to keep two ideas in their minds at once. In other words children acquire the ability to think back to the original starting point and at the same time compare it in their minds with a current situation. Piaget calls this mental operation *reversibility,* and it is a good example of what is meant when we say the child is freed from concrete experience, since she performs this logico-mathematical reasoning process in her mind.

But young children in the preoperational stage do not possess this ability. Because they cannot consider two possibilities at once, they are unable to *conserve;* that is, they do not understand that quantity stays the same despite a change in appearance. This is because they cannot keep one idea in their minds while considering a second one. Thus they are likely to believe that a taller jar contains more water than a shorter jar does, even though they have previously been shown that the quantity was the same before pouring. For preoperational children, seeing is believing.

At this stage children may also have difficulty shifting objects into more than one kind of category (e.g., sorting according to size and then shifting to color), taking two attributes into account at the same time (e.g., sorting large pink circles and pink squares, small blue circles and blue squares into separate categories), or arranging a long series of graduated cylinders in regularly ascending order. Adults, however, no longer have difficulty grasping these concepts. This difference in the way children and adults think illustrates an important Piagetian principle: The thinking of children and adults differs in kind from each other. Children reason differently from the way adults do and thus often reach different conclusions.

Additional Basic Concepts of Value

Although Piaget has been criticized on such grounds as inconsistency of theory, obscure terminology, and poor scientific rigor, and although his work is consistently subjected to further critical evaluation and testing (Gardner, 1986; I. E. Siegel & Brainerd, 1978; Thomas, 1999; Wood, 1998), there is little doubt that despite these weaknesses he made many significant contributions to our understanding of the growth of children's mental abilities. Among these contributions is the idea that mental development is a dynamic process that results from the interaction of the child with her environment. The child acts on her own world, and by means of interaction with it she constructs her own knowledge (DeVries & Kohlberg, 1990). This is why Piaget favored the saying that "construction is superior to instruction" (Siegler, 1998). This close observer of children maintained that they use language and play to represent reality, and for this reason Piaget (1932) emphasized the extraordinary value of play as a basic avenue through which young children learn. Finally he stressed the importance of actual involvement of children with materials (as compared with observation and teacher explanation) and the significance of experience as a medium for learning.

Currently it appears that in addition to his general theoretical ideas, Piaget's identification of significant cognitive concepts and the steps and means by which they develop may be the most helpful contribution he has made to our understanding of the cognitive self. Siegler (1998) sums this up well when he concludes that despite recent clarifications and contradictions provided by more recent research, Piaget's theory remains valuable since "it provides us with a good feel for what children's thinking is like at different points in development" (p. 51.) This understanding makes it possible for teachers to generate a curriculum for stimulating the growth of certain cognitive abilities, rather than to merely teach children an endless array of facts.

From a Piagetian Perspective, What Can Teachers Do to Help Children Develop Fully at Each Cognitive Stage?

Of course, it is neither desirable nor even possible to accelerate children markedly through the stages of cognitive development. This practice of overpressure is called *hothousing* and robs children of their childhood (Elkind, 1987; Sigel, 1987). What teachers should do instead is assist children to develop richly and fully at each stage, thereby paving the way for successful attainment of the next stage at the appropriate time.

Piaget maintained that four factors work together to promote cognitive growth: *maturation, experience, socialization*, and *equilibration*. The thoughtful teacher can make a helpful contribution to each of these factors as he leads children through the day.

For example, first, physical maturation underlies cognitive maturation, and the good health practices followed by children's centers can make a definite contribution to physical development by providing the sound nutrition, rest, and physical activity so necessary for the child's growing body and particularly her brain to thrive.

Second, the provision of real experience with the physical world so stressed by Piaget is an essential cornerstone of early childhood education (C. K. Williams & Kamii, 1986). These experiences should include many opportunities for children to arrange things in order, to return substances to their prior state, and to group them according to their common properties *as well as the chance to talk about why they have put them in particular configurations.* Opportunities for exploring other relationships such as cause and effect, as well as the basic skill of telling same from different, should also be included. (The remainder of this chapter presents many examples of ways such experiences may be integrated into the daily life of the school.)

Third, socialization, too, is something most early childhood teachers know a good deal about. However, here a special point requires emphasis when discussing cognition from a Piagetian point of view. Whereas preschool teachers often think of socialization as lying in the realm of teaching children how to get along together or teaching them language (a profoundly useful social skill), Piaget thought of socialization as having another important facet. He maintained that interaction between children, particularly discussion, which he termed *argument*, is of extraordinary importance. Through such exchanges of ideas children test and modify what they think. And these modifications of what they think lead to the fourth factor that influences cognitive growth—equilibration.

Equilibration is the mechanism that brings maturation, experience, and social interaction into balance. It is the mechanism by which the child regulates her ideas (Wadsworth, 1989) and "puts things all together."

So if the teacher wishes to strengthen cognitive growth, in addition to providing optimum opportunities for physical maturation and real experience, he should also encourage dialogue *among* the children (as well as carrying out discussions between himself and the children). The result will be that children figure out more things for themselves. This enables them to coordinate their existing knowledge with their newly acquired knowledge by exercising the faculty of equilibration.

Thus when the children complain it's no fun to swing because their feet drag on the ground, instead of obligingly shortening the swing, the teacher might ask the children to propose what might be done to change that situation. Could they make their legs shorter? Could they stand up in the swing instead? Could someone push them so that they could hold their legs out straight? Or . . . ? Children can think up and debate many possibilities once provided the chance to do so. Such discussions and proposed solutions enable children to construct knowledge for themselves, construction that is so much more valuable than instruction.

How Is Piagetian Theory Linked with Such Midlevel Skills as Matching and Grouping?

We can see that Piaget's concept of equilibration fits nicely with the inquiry, discovery strategies associated with the emergent curriculum discussed in the previous chapter. In addition to more encompassing ideas such as equilibration, Piaget (1983) was also interested in how children develop their ability to perform more specific mental operations including classification, seriation, cause and effect, and conserving quantity (understanding that the amount remains the same despite changes in appearance).

The beginning levels of these skills are what preschool teachers term *matching, grouping, common relations, graduated ordering, cause and effect relationships,* and *initial understanding of the principles of conservation of quantity.* These skills are valuable not only because they are the precursors of later, more sophisticated Piagetian mental operations but also because, as Table 19.3 illustrates, they are vital foundation stones for building later academic skills related to reading and mathematical understanding.

For example, *matching* (being able to tell whether things are the same or different) is an important prerequisite for being able to read. If one cannot tell the difference between *d* and *b*, how can one tell the difference between *dog* and *bog*? *Grouping* (identifying the common property of several nonidentical items) underlies the concept of class inclusion, which is necessary for understanding set theory. Grouping is also an essential element of such sciences as botany, in which classification is very important. *Seriation* (arranging things in regular, graduated order) gives real meaning to enumeration. Finally, *common relations* (the ability to identify pairs of items associated together) helps children learn to

Table 19.3

Links between basic mental abilities and later school-related skills

Ability	Value
Matching: Can identify which things are the same and which things are different *Basic question:* Can you find the pair that is exactly the same?	The ability to discriminate is crucial to development of other mental abilities. An important aspect of gaining literacy: discriminate between letters (such as *m* and *w*). Promotes understanding of equality. Encourages skill in figure/ground perception (separating a significant figure from the background).
Grouping: Can identify the common property that forms a group or class *Basic question:* Can you show me the things that belong to the same family?	Fosters mathematical understanding: set theory and equivalency. Children must discriminate, reason, analyze, and select in order to formulate groups. Regrouping encourages flexibility of thought. Depending on manner of presentation, may foster divergent thinking—more than one way to group items. Requires use of accommodation and assimilation. Classification is a basic aspect of life sciences: allows people to organize knowledge.
Common relations: Can identify common property or relationship between a *nonidentical pair* *Basic question:* Which thing goes most closely with what other thing?	Fosters mathematical understanding: one-to-one correspondence. Fosters diversity of understanding concepts: many kinds of pairs (opposites, cause-effect, congruent). Can teach use of analogies and riddles.
Cause and effect: Can determine what makes something else happen: a special case of common relations *Basic question:* What makes something else happen?	Basis for scientific investigations. Conveys sense of order of world. Conveys sense of individual's ability to be effective: act on his world and produce results, make things happen. Encourages use of prediction and generation of hypotheses. Introduces child to elementary understanding of the scientific method.
Seriation: Can identify what comes next in a graduated series *Basic question:* What comes next?	Fosters mathematical understanding. Relationship between quantities: counting (enumeration) with understanding, one-to-one correspondence, equivalency, estimation. If teacher presents series going from left to right, fosters basic reading skill.
Temporal ordering: Can identify logical order of events occurring in time *Basic question:* What comes next?	Fosters mathematical understanding. Conveys a sense of order and a sense of time and its effect. Relationship between things: cause-and-effect and other relationships. Prediction. Requires memory: what happened first, then what happened?
Conservation: Can understand that a substance can return to its prior state and that quantity is not affected by mere changes in appearance *Basic question:* Are they still the same quantity?	Idea of constancy (reversibility) is fundamental as a foundation for logical reasoning, basic for scientific understanding; it is also the basis for mathematical calculations involving length, volume, area, and so forth.

draw analogies. This fascinating ability to move from one known relationship to a second by perceiving parallels in the two sets involves transferring ideas and making such linkages. It is surely an indispensable element in creative thought.

Each of these concepts develops over time by building on lower level concepts. One teacher presents this explanation of progression as follows:

> Thus, grouping begins with an understanding of the concepts of same and different and the ability to match identical objects, followed by the ability to see similarities across different objects. Gradually children develop the awareness that one object may belong to several possible groups (red, round, and big) and thus can begin to understand matrices (for example, arranging objects in rows by color and in columns by shape). Not until elementary school do they fully comprehend hierarchical classification (dogs and cats are animals; animals, people and trees are living things) and class inclusion (all dogs are animals, but not all animals are dogs).
>
> Seriation requires, first of all, an understanding of absolute size (big and small), followed by relative size concepts and the ability to compare sizes (this is bigger than that). As with grouping, children must learn that an object can have multiple size designations (bigger than some things and smaller than others). This leads to the ability to seriate, first by trial and error and with a few objects, and then without hesitation, with any number of objects. Awareness of these developmental progressions can help a teacher assess where children are in their thinking and what activities would be appropriate for them.[1]

Practice in these abilities entails the use of and practice in some additional mental skills that must be so generally employed that they apply to all the abilities. These are listed here rather than being repeated in Table 19.3. They include the abilities to pay attention, observe carefully, make comparisons, and use symbols (representations) in place of actual objects. The symbols might consist of models, pictures, language, or simply imaginary items as is done in play.

HOW TO PROVIDE OPPORTUNITIES FOR PRACTICING CONCEPT FORMATION SKILLS

Develop Needed Materials

There are two ways to obtain materials to use for teaching these midlevel skills. The easiest, most expensive, and most obvious way is to rely on commercially developed tabletop activities. Many such materials are available, particularly in the areas of matching and seriation. The trouble with them is that they often are not related closely to curriculum topics, and they generally use only pictures as the medium of instruction. (Montessori materials are a welcome exception to this trend.) The advantages of purchased materials is that they are readily available and convenient and can be self-selected and monitored by the children. The most significant danger to guard against is offering only commercially

---

[1] I thank Jean Phinney of California State University at Los Angeles for contributing this explanation of developmental progressions.

This memory game gives children more sophisticated practice in matching and is fun besides.

developed activities for concept development. This results in too narrow, sensorily limited, and dull a presentation to be fully effective.

The second way to introduce opportunities for this kind of concept development is to embed them directly in the curriculum. This is likely to be more work for the teacher, who will have to develop materials for the children's use, but it is also more satisfying since it gives him a chance to be creative and to use a much wider variety of materials and activities. Best of all, teacher-developed experiences mean the activities can be directly related to and coordinated with the topics that have interested the children. It is not difficult to generate such ideas. Interested readers will find many suggestions for such activities in *Workjobs* (Barata-Lorton, 1986), *Planning Around Children's Interests: The Teacher's Idea Book 2* (Graves, 1998), *Educating Young Children* (Hohmann & Weikart, 1995), *More Than Counting* (Moomaw & Hieronymus, 1995), and *The Piaget Handbook for Teachers and Parents* (R. Peterson & Felton-Collins, 1986).

Provide Consistent Opportunities for Practice

It is necessary to provide repeated opportunities for experience and practice (Hendrick, 1973). One or two repetitions to practice grouping, matching, or ordering are not sufficient. To build strong connections between neurons and to understand these concepts fully and richly, children need to practice them consistently, using many materials and moving from simpler to more difficult activities as their skills increase.

Above All, Make Certain the Activities Are Fun

Every year the students in my college classes devise and construct a great many activities to stimulate mental development, and every year I am struck by the attractiveness of these materials. Indeed if children happen to be passing by the door, it is all we can do to shoo them out while we are discussing what the teachers have made. Teachers seem to have a much better basic grasp of how to devise appealing materials than most manufacturers do. The teacher-made activities are so much more colorful, and they reflect a real familiarity with what young children really care about.

Pleasure is also increased for the children when the activities are at the right developmental level. As Vygotsky maintains, the satisfaction of meeting the challenge of an activity that is just a little bit but not too much harder than what the child has already mastered is obviously gratifying. Suggestions are included with the discussions of specific abilities showing how the levels of difficulty of various abilities can be increased, so strategies will only be summarized here that might be used with any of the abilities to increase the challenge. These include adding more choices, asking whether there is another way to do it, asking the children to put what they are doing into words, using a different sensory mode in place of vision (e.g., using only touch or only hearing), using memory, asking the children to tell you something in reverse order, or using items that are less familiar. A word of caution: We have had children in our center, usually 5-year-olds, who enjoyed being challenged in all these ways; however, the key word here is *enjoyed*. The purpose is not to make things so difficult that children sweat and struggle over them. The foregoing list is included merely to provide an idea of possibilities to go on to.

Another caution I want to add is the *undesirability* of resorting to competition and comparison to generate "fun." Setting up activities with the aim of seeing who can do something quickest or "best" takes a lot of fun out of it for the losers. It is fairly easy to substitute something like suspense in place of competition to sustain interest. Suspense strategies can be as simple as having children pull things out of a mystery bag and then decide where they should go, or asking them to choose from one hand or the other when the teacher holds two things behind his back.

SOME PRACTICAL SUGGESTIONS ABOUT PRESENTING MIDLEVEL THINKING AND REASONING SKILLS IN THE CURRICULUM

Before embarking on a detailed discussion of specific reasoning abilities, I want to stress once again that the purpose of including the following material is not to foster precocity in young children. It is included because experience has taught me that hardly any preprimary teachers possess a framework that identifies significant mental abilities or that explains how to go about fostering these skills in an appropriate and interesting way.

Although teachers may use a few lotto games that give practice in matching or grouping, or talk from time to time about the order in which something has happened, offering these activities seems to be haphazard and fortuitous, rather than part of a deliberate, coordinated plan. This may be all right for middle-class children who seem to absorb skills through their pores, but it is unforgivable for the large group of preschool youngsters who, though possessing other strengths, apparently lack experience with these aspects of learning in their daily lives. Teachers need to get their own heads together on the subject of cognitive development so that they can systematically and regularly provide opportunities for practice of these abilities, as well as of the broader problem-solving skills discussed in the previous chapter. (Incidentally, all the activities suggested in the following sections have been used over and over with preschool-age children at the Institute of Child Development, as well as by children in other preschools, so we know they are not too difficult.[2]) It is my hope that regular exposure to these kinds of activities will furnish all youngsters with beginning skills that will stand them in good stead as they move on to the next stage of intellectual development.

Note that the following descriptions of activities include suggestions for children who are less advanced, as well as suggestions for those who are more mature. They also stress that a diversity of experiences should be offered, *including large muscle activities.* All too often this kind of curriculum is limited to small muscle, tabletop experiences, which is most unfortunate.

Matching

Matching is the ability to perceive that two items are *identical,* and it depends on the child's grasping the concept of sameness and differentness. At our center we have found this to be one of the easier concepts for young children to acquire. Even 2- and 3-year-olds will work at this occupation with interest and diligence if the materials are attractive and not too detailed.

Many commercial materials are available that may be used to provide practice in matching. These range from simple, obvious pictures with few details to quite elaborate discrimination tasks that contain a great deal of detail and subtle differences. Lotto and bingo games are probably the most prevalent examples of such materials. But matching should not be limited to these kinds of activities. Younger children can grasp this concept by matching buttons (a perennial favorite), matching animal stamps or stickers, or playing simple picture dominoes. Fabric swatches and wallpaper samples are also fun to use for this purpose and can be surprisingly difficult. Incidentally, putting blocks back so that all of one kind go in the same place is a matching—*not* grouping—exercise, since the blocks are identical.

Matching experiences need not be limited to the sense of vision, of course. Children will also enjoy matching by touch (for texture and thickness), by hearing (duplicating sim-

---

2   *For a more detailed discussion of research projects dealing with teaching some of these abilities, see Hendrick (1973) or Safford (1978). The research of Meeker, Sexton, and Richardson (1970) also contains many specific examples of teaching strategies, although these focus on elementary-age children.*

ple sounds, rhythms, or melodies), and by taste and smell (it is interesting to cut up a variety of white fruits and vegetables, for instance, and ask the children to taste bits of them and find the ones that are the same). Imitation can also be thought of as an attempt to match actions; shadow or mirror dancing, Follow the Leader, and Simon Says may be employed for this purpose. Large muscle activities may be further incorporated by setting out two or three pictures and choosing a youngster to walk over to match one of them with the picture in her hand. (She then has the privilege of picking the next child to do this.) Children who are proficient at pumping may be asked whether they can match the arc of their swings with that of the child beside them.

When asking children to complete a match, the teacher should use sentences such as, "Show me the one that matches," or, "Find me one that's just the same," rather than, "Show me two that are just alike," because an occasional child is misled by the term *alike* and will blithely select something to show the teacher, saying, "Here, I like this one best!" Once she has acquired this verbal misconception of what the teacher means, it can be difficult to get her to change her mind; so talking about *same* rather than *alike* is the more effective choice of language.

As the child becomes more skilled, matching tasks may be increased in difficulty by making the matches more complex and difficult to analyze. This is usually accomplished by increasing the number of details that must be inspected in each picture and by increasing the number of items to be compared. Ultimately the material shifts from depending on pictorially meaningful content to more symbolic form. This leads, finally, to using the symbols of the alphabet and numbers.

Grouping

I use the word *grouping* here in place of *classification* to remind the reader that we are discussing an elementary form of the more sophisticated skill described by Piaget (1965) wherein older children can form hierarchical classes or classify items according to more than one property at the same time. Preschool children perform at a simpler level than classification, but 4- and 5-year-olds in particular are able to sort objects or pictures into categories meaningful to them. For example, I recall what happened when we were using companion animals as our focus for the week and invited the children to bring their pets to visit. When I asked Millie what kind of dog she had brought, she paused for a moment in thought and then replied, "Well, she's half collie—and half female."

Other examples of meaningful categorizing are placing dollhouse furniture into rooms according to their function (e.g., kitchen equipment in the kitchen) and sorting shells according to whether they are clams or mussels or pectins, rough or smooth, large or small. Teachers encourage categorizing every time they ask children, "Are airplanes birds? Why not?" or say, "Show me all the buttons that belong together." In these instances the child is being asked to determine what it is that various items have in common—to determine the common property that defines the class—and then she is usually expected to decide whether an additional item also possesses this property and can be included.

In essence such material may be presented in three ways. First, the child can be confronted with an assembled group and be asked to choose things to add to it (perhaps it is pictures of clothing such as a sweater, dress, and shirt, and the additional pictures might be a doll, a pair of pants, and an ice cream cone). Second, she can be presented with an assembled group and be asked to remove items that do not belong (e.g., "Everyone who isn't wearing a plaid top, sit down."). Finally, she can be given a melange of articles or pictures and be asked to sort them according to whatever criteria *she* establishes. *This third kind of presentation permits more divergent thinking* than the first two do and has the additional advantage of making regrouping according to different criteria more feasible.

Four-year-olds are rarely able to put their reasons for forming such groups into words at the beginning of the learning experience, although they can indicate by the sorting activity itself that they do perceive common properties. At our center we have found that many of them gradually learn to explain why particular items go together as they practice, or they become able to name the class or group they have in mind (Hendrick, 1973). Thus a child who is inarticulate in the fall may by spring put a toy frog, turtle, and fish together and be able to tell us that she did this since they all like water or because "they're swimmy things."

Even though many children will at first be unable to put into words the reason for grouping particular things together, the category may be obvious to the onlooker. If a child is unable to formulate a reply after she has assembled a group, the teacher can help by saying, "Hmmmm, it looks to me as though you are putting all the red ones here and the blue ones here. Is that what you're doing?" This assists the child in translating her actions into words.

Using a "secret" box adds suspense to mental ability activities.

It is wise to encourage the child to determine the categories for herself whenever possible. If the teacher hands a child a box of little animals and tells her to "pick out all the red ones" or to "pick out all the ones we saw at the zoo," he has done most of the thinking for her before she goes to work. But if he says, "Show me which ones you think belong together," and follows this with, "How come you put those together?" the child must do more of the thinking for herself. This is quite different from and more valuable than expecting the child to "discover" the category the teacher has thought up.

Of course, it is not necessary to limit "grouping" activities to small muscle experiences. Every time children are asked to show how many different ways they can run or to choose what equipment they need to play house with in the sandbox, they are essentially thinking of things that fit a particular category or class just as they are determining categories when the teacher asks them, "Do you think the wheelbarrow should be kept with the wagons and scooters or with the garden equipment?" Additional practice is also provided by asking older 4- and young 5-year-olds to select three or four children from the group who are wearing something similar—boots, perhaps, or plaid clothing—and then have the rest of the children guess what it is they have in common.

Piaget noted that younger children will change categories as they sort. This is a natural phenomenon and does not mean they are unintelligent. Maturation combined with opportunities to practice and talk about grouping will help the children learn to maintain consistent criteria.

Occasionally teachers become confused and attempt to teach grouping by using identical items for this purpose. Although being able to pick out things that are exactly the same and to tell them apart from those that are different is a useful literacy skill, it is not grouping; it is simple matching. *To teach grouping, it is necessary to use materials that possess common properties but are not identical.*

The easiest form of grouping is sorting that requires simple responses to a prominent sensory quality such as color (Lavatelli, 1970a, 1970b). Some children at the center will need to begin at this level, but this is only the beginning. The task may be made more difficult by asking the children to think of a way the materials can be regrouped, by using more complex materials, by increasing the emphasis on verbalization, or by asking them to group materials according to several properties at the same time.

Perceiving Common Relations

The basic skill required in developing the concept of common relations is the ability to identify and *pair* items that are usually associated together but that are *not* identical. The activity of perceiving common relations is similar to grouping because it depends on the identification of a common property or bond. It differs from grouping because it involves *pairing* such items, rather than working with larger numbers of them. It is useful to cultivate because it probably forms the basis for the later understanding and formulation of analogies (e.g., ring is to finger as belt is to . . . waist, buckle, or sash?). Because these combinations are usually culturally based (salt and pepper, shoes and socks, hat and head), it is important to know the home backgrounds of the children to be able to develop pairs likely to be familiar to them.

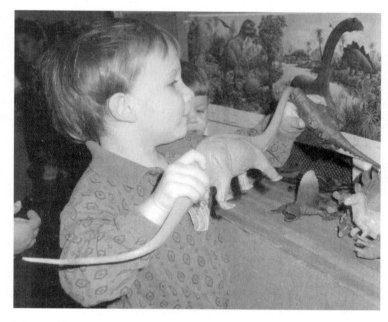

Pairing objects with pictures is a good example of a common relations activity.

Opposites can also be included in this activity since there is also a true relationship between them. Thus hot can be contrasted with cold, up with down, and thick with thin.

We have found that 3- and 4-year-olds enjoy practicing this conceptual task a great deal. It has the kind of appeal that riddles generally have, and the children relish pairing up an assortment of items that are either presented all together in a box or in more game-like form in which several items are set out and their related members are drawn out of a bag one by one. Some commercial materials on the market are useful for this purpose, such as two-piece puzzles linking animals with their homes, or occupations with appropriate tools. (We call these *congruent relationships*.) It is also helpful to acquire many pairs of real objects or models of them that belong together and to keep a reserve of these handy to be brought out from time to time for the fun of it.

When the teacher is working with these combinations, it is usually effective for him to ask the child to pick out the thing that *goes most closely* with a selected item or that *belongs best* with it. This is language that the children understand and that is clear enough for them to be able to follow the directions.

Perceiving common relations may be made more difficult for more mature children by including less familiar combinations, by increasing the number of choices, or by setting up true analogies in which the child has to ascertain the quality common to both pairs of items.

Understanding the Relationship Between Simple Cause and Effect

Although it takes children a long time to develop clear ideas of physical causality (Piaget, 1963), they can begin to acquire this concept while attending the center. Indeed good discipline often depends on teaching exactly this kind of relationship between action and outcome because letting the punishment fit the crime usually results in allowing the child to experience the logical consequence of her behavior. Thus the child who pulls all the blocks off the shelf is expected to help restack them, and the youngster who dumps her milk on the table must get the sponge and wipe it up herself.

In addition to understanding cause and effect in terms of social consequences, 4-year-olds can often handle cause-related questions that are phrased as "What would happen if . . . ?" or "What do you think made (something) happen?" These questions are sound to use since they do not require children to apply or explain scientific principles that lie beyond their understanding but depend instead on what they can see happen with their own eyes or on what they can deduce from their own experience.

Following are some examples of successful questions:

- What will happen if we add some sugar to the dough?
- What will happen to your shoes if you go out in the rain without your boots on?
- How come Brittany dropped the hot pan so fast?
- What made the kittens mew when mama cat got up?
- What made the egg get hard?

Finding the answers to these questions can be accomplished by setting up simple experiments to identify the most probable causes. These experiments enable the children to try out suggested causes, compare results, and then draw conclusions about the most likely reason for something happening, thereby introducing them to the scientific method.

For example, to determine what makes plants grow, the children might think of possibilities such as roots, water, and sunshine and then think of ways they could find out whether their ideas are correct. They might think of cutting the roots off a marigold or of putting one plant in the dark and another in the sunlight while watering both. Or they might try growing plants with and without water. Of course, doing experiments like this may involve wasting and breaking or destroying some things, but the teacher really cannot allow a misguided idea of thrift to stand in the way of letting the children figure something out. Four-year-olds in particular enjoy carrying out this kind of investigation, although they will need help figuring out how to set up the experiment. Remember it is much more valuable for children to propose possibilities, make predictions, and try them out than for teachers to guide them to thinking of possibilities the teachers have thought up already.

Teaching about simple cause-and-effect relations presents one of the most interesting educational opportunities available to the preprimary teacher, and both natural history and physical science offer rich possibilities that can be used for this purpose. For this reason several references on science for young children are listed at the end of this chapter.

Of course, cause-and-effect experiences need not be elaborate, full-blown experiments. Here is a partial list of simple cause-and-effect experiences identified by students in various classes: using a squirt gun, flashlight, or garlic press with dough or clay; blowing soap bubbles; turning on a light; blowing up a balloon and pricking it with a pin; using all sorts of windup toys such as hopping frogs, little cars, and paddle boats; blowing a whistle; using grinders and graters; making butter; using scales (weighing heavy and light things for contrast); listening to children's hearts after they have been sitting, walking, or running; using a bank made like a doghouse (when a penny goes in the front, the dog comes out and grabs the money); turning a kaleidoscope; painting the sidewalk with water in sun and shade; striking a match; mixing paint to obtain different colors; pushing a button to make the clown move; and stretching rubber bands between various nails on a board, different tensions producing sounds of different pitches.

Any of these experiences can generate good learning opportunities if the teacher encourages the children to do some predicting in advance or to explain in simple terms to each other what made the action happen.

Ordering

Ordering means arranging objects or events in logical order. The two kinds of ordering that appear to be most useful are (a) arranging a variety of items according to a graduated seriated scale (spatial ordering, the beginning of Piagetian seriation) and (b) arranging events as they occur in time (temporal ordering). The basic question the child must be able to answer when dealing with either of these concepts is, What comes next? Many interesting activities require a child to answer this question and to infer the logical order of either a spatial or temporal series.

Spatial Seriated Ordering
Almost any kind of item that comes in graduated sizes may be used for the purpose of teaching spatial, or seriated, ordering: various sizes of bolts and nuts, sets of measuring cups or spoons, nested mixing bowls, and empty tin cans of assorted sizes. Many commercial materials are also made for the purpose of practicing seriation. Montessori cylinders are excellent for this purpose, and an examination of equipment catalogs will reveal many additional possibilities as varied as nesting blocks and flannel board materials. Hardwood blocks, of course, present classic opportunities for becoming acquainted with the relationship between varying lengths, as well as for studying the regular relationships of equivalency that occur in block construction, because blocks may vary in length but generally are of the same width and depth.

I also favor including variations on seriation that teach gradations in quality. Grades of sandpaper can be provided so that children have opportunities to arrange them in order from rough to smooth; flavors can be provided that range from sweet to sour; tone bells can be arranged from high pitch to low pitch. Large muscle experiences that will draw the children's attention to graduated sizes might include having the children arrange themselves from shortest to tallest. (This can be fun to do if everyone lies down side by side and their heights are marked on a big roll of paper and then the same paper is used again later in the year to measure their growth.) Or they can be given a set of four or five boxes and allowed to throw beanbags into them when they have been arranged in correct order.

The easiest kinds of seriation problems are ones in which the youngster is asked to choose which items should be added to a chain of two or three to continue an upward or downward trend (L. S. Siegel, 1972). Preschool children manage well using three, four, and even five and six items at a time as they become more experienced. Very young children often grasp this principle best if it is presented in terms of "This is the daddy, and this is the mommy; now show me what comes next." The activity may be made more difficult by increasing the number of objects to be arranged, and even more difficult by asking the child to arrange a series and then giving her one or two items that must be inserted somewhere in the middle to make the series more complete. Finally the challenge can be increased even more by asking the child to arrange two sets of objects in corresponding order or, more difficult yet, in contrasting order—for example, going from low to high for one set and high to low on a parallel set. This is *very* difficult! Nuts and bolts make particularly nice items to use for this purpose, as do padlocks and various sizes of keys and paper dolls with appropriately sized clothing.

Temporal Ordering

Recalling or anticipating the order of events as they occur in time is called *temporal ordering*. A child can be asked to recount the order in which she got ready that morning: "First you got up, and then you went to the bathroom, and then . . . " Flannel board stories are another fine way to help children visualize the order in which things happen, and some social occasions also make excellent topics for discussion and pictures. Birthday parties, for example, often run quite true to form: First the guests arrive, then the birthday child opens her presents, and so forth. Recipes, too, can be set out with the ingredients arranged in the order in which they will be needed. Many of these orderly events can be played through as well as discussed; recapitulation through play is a most valuable way to rehearse the order in which events take place. Growth sequences based on human, plant, and animal development fit in here very naturally as a topic of study, as does the excellent series of sequenced puzzles generally available.

Although even 2-year-olds are keenly aware of the order in which daily events occur and are sticklers for maintaining that order, as many a mother will attest, older preschoolers also need continuing practice with this concept. The level of difficulty for these more sophisticated children can be increased by adding more episodes to each event, asking the child to arrange a series of pictures and then to interpolate additional ones after the series has been formulated, asking her to arrange the events in reverse, or asking her to consider what might happen if something occurred out of order ("What if you got in the bathtub and then took your clothes off?" To which one child replied, "Nothing, as long as I don't turn the water on!") Asking children to plan an activity step by step in advance also provides practice in temporal ordering. I recall doing some serious planning with one group about how to proceed with giving my springer spaniel a bath. All went well until Lady shook herself vigorously. "We didn't plan on that!" said one 4-year-old, looking with disgust at her dripping clothes.

Conserving

Perhaps no mental ability has come under more investigation than the ability to conserve quantity (Siegler, 1998). When a child possesses this ability, she is able to recognize that the amount of the substance remains the same despite changes in its appearance. Before that time, when she is too young to be able to conserve (typically in our culture before age 6 or 7), the child is deceived by appearances into reasoning that the quantity has increased or decreased because a change in shape has made the material look like more or less. For instance, two glasses of water that have been judged equivalent will then be judged unequal when one is poured into a squat, low dish and another into a tall, thin cylinder and the two are compared again, or two balls of clay previously demonstrated to be the same amount will be judged different in quantity when one has been mashed flat or divided into many little balls.

Considerable interest has centered on whether children can be taught this skill before the time they would typically acquire it, but the findings have been mixed and appear to be affected by several factors. For example, Inhelder (1968) reports that the amount children improve in their ability to conserve is always related to their prior level of development. Bruner (1966) reports that modifying the way materials are presented affects the children's answers to conservation problems. The age of acquisition of most conservation skills has also been shown to vary according to culture. Reporting on a survey of cross-cultural studies, Ashton (1975), for example, concluded that "acquisition of most conservation skills is delayed in non-Western cultures" (p. 481). Generally it appears that children who are on the verge of comprehending conservation may be pushed on to the next step in this process if they receive adequate instruction. The value of doing this, of course, remains open to debate.

Acceleration, however, is less important than making sure the child has ample opportunity to develop richly and fully at every level as she passes through it. This opportunity is particularly significant for children who come from lower socioeconomic levels, since evidence is mounting that such youngsters often lag behind their middle-class peers in developing such abilities (Almy et al., 1966; Sigel & McBane, 1967) and that additional experience and opportunities to practice may help them catch up.

Therefore preprimary teachers should see to it that the children in their groups have many occasions to try out and experiment with the results of pouring liquids back and forth into containers of various shapes to learn that shape does not alter quantity. Blocks present outstanding opportunities to demonstrate conservation of mass since it is relatively simple to see that a tower of four contains the same number of units as does a two-by-two stack. Clay and dough also lend themselves well to providing opportunities for youngsters to acquire this concept. In short, any material, whether liquid or solid, that can be divided and put together again may be used to investigate the principle of conservation.

It is also worthwhile to provide opportunities for measuring to demonstrate equality or inequality. Scales are useful in this regard, and yardsticks and measuring tapes are also valuable. Or children can create their own units of measure, using cutouts of feet or paper clips or Popsicle sticks. However, the teacher must realize that despite these aids, children who are too immature to grasp the principle of conservation will continue to insist that what their eyes tell them to be true is true.

Melissa is developing a concrete and meaningful idea of just how many 100 really is.

The teacher's role in this area lies in providing many opportunities for the children to manipulate materials and experiment with changing their forms and with returning them to their prior state (reversing the reaction). In addition to supplying experiences, they should make a point of talking with the children and drawing their attention to the unchanging nature of quantity as they manipulate the materials. This is also an excellent time to build related vocabulary, such as *more than, less than,* and *equal to.* Finally besides talking with the children themselves, teachers should foster discussion and "argument" among the children about the nature of conservation, since research (Murray, 1972; Smedslund, 1966) supports Piaget's contention (1926) that such interaction among children will help them reach correct conclusions.

It is unlikely that children of prekindergarten age will do more than begin to grasp the principle of conservation, but it may be of interest to know how problems could be increased in difficulty should they do so. Conservation problems can be made more difficult by making the contrasts in form more extreme—that is, by making one cylinder taller and thinner or the balls of clay more numerous. (This principle is easy to remember if the reader recalls that even adults can be seduced into believing that tall, thin cereal boxes are a better buy than thick, squat ones of the same weight.) The more pronounced the apparent contrast between the two quantities, the more likely the child will be misled by appearance and forget that the quantity is actually equal.

AN EXAMPLE OF HOW MIDLEVEL MENTAL ABILITY SKILLS CAN BE INCLUDED AS PART OF AN EMERGENT APPROACH

As we saw earlier in this chapter, it is not necessary or even desirable to rely exclusively on only one of the two approaches to fostering cognitive development in young children, because both the emergent and conventional approaches have merit. The most desirable strategy is to use the emergent approach as the fundamental foundation for fostering thinking ability and then to enrich it with specific practice in midlevel skills as well. Table 19.4 illustrates how a teacher could use this combination approach to provide maximum benefits for the children in his care.

SUMMARY

Piaget made many significant contributions to our understanding of cognition. Among these are his identification of various categories of knowledge and stages of intellectual development. He maintained that mental development is a dynamic process that results from the child's actions on her environment, that play is an important avenue of learning, and that children construct their own knowledge base.

The chapter concludes with detailed discussions of some basic thinking and reasoning skills that form the foundation for later, more sophisticated cognitive abilities and academic learning. These include matching, grouping, perceiving common relations, temporal and seriated ordering, conservation, and understanding elementary cause-and-effect relationships. A table illustrating how these skills might be incorporated into the curriculum is found at the end of the chapter.

Table 19.4

Example of how a pathway might emerge based on the children's interests using the emergent and midlevel approaches to cognitive development

Children's Original Concerns and Interests	Adults' Visions of Possible Pathways to Explore	Children's Choices	Adult "Provocations"
[Children actually hatched eggs . . . have cared for ducklings & realized they've outgrown current cage]	Provide some way for ducks to go swimming	Make a pond for the ducks to enjoy	What could we use or make for pond? How can we keep the water in?
During a discussion, they say they want the ducks to feel happy—			How could the ducks get into or out of the water?
1. Find their mother			
2. Take them swimming			How can we fill the pond with water?
3. Make them a shower			Could we make a shower for them?
4. Let them play outside			
5. Fix them a bigger house	Build an outdoor shelter and pen	Maybe later—let's do the pond first . . . that will make them *most* happy	
6. Feed them stuff ducks really like to eat			
	Investigate relationship of form to function: web feet vs. claws vs. fingers & so forth	Children not interested when topic is brought up	

Children's Proposed Solutions	Examples of Higher Order Thinking Skills Tapped Using this Emergent Approach	Companion Midlevel Mental Abilities that Could Be Added by Teacher
Dish pan Galvanized tub Children's pool Dig hole, fill with water	Use imagination to solve problems. What kind of things hold water?) Anticipate outcomes of proposed solutions and/or try them out.	*Matching* Get out spring lotto game made of "Easter" stickers of ducks, chickens, etc. *Grouping* Provide plastic animals for children to sort according to categories—include ducks, fish, farm animals, birds, etc.
Make them a ramp Build stairs from blocks Lift them ourselves (but we have to catch them first!)	Think of alternatives. (What to do when hole is dug and water seeps away) Estimate future size of ducks. (Find out how to find how big ducks grow) Apply concept of measurement. (How long does the hose need to be to reach the pond?)	*Common Relations* Pair different pictures of feet with animals they belong to (ducks and others) *Temporal Ordering* Take photos of ducklings as they grow and arrange them in order of developmental stages
Add pipes on to end of hose Use bucket Squirt hose very hard Move pool	Gain understanding of some principles of physics related to force and pressure. (How can you make water run up hill?)	*Graduated (seriated) Ordering* Measure height of ducklings as they grow Make graph comparing growth rate with growth rate of gerbils
Hold watering can up and sprinkle ducks Tie hose to top of slide Use pipes, screw on flexible dish rinsing hose from kitchen on pipe's end Squirt hose	Value other people's ideas when something doesn't work. (What if the cook needs to use the dish rinsing hose herself?)	*Cause and Effect* Were the ducks happier when they had the new pond? What made the water come out of the hose faster or slower?

Questions and Activities

1. Pick up on a current interest of the children in your group and propose some midlevel thinking activities that could be based on that interest.
2. Concoct activities that fit the various mental abilities, such as ordering and grouping, and try them out with the children. Then add variations to the activities that make them easier or more difficult in order to suit the needs of individual children in the group. Set aside some shelves in your school where these materials can be accumulated.
3. Review the activities related to mental ability in the school where you teach and identify the ones that foster literacy skills that lead to reading later on.

Self-Check Questions for Review

Content-Related Questions

1. Piaget identified three kinds of knowledge involved in children's thought. What are they?
2. List at least four important ideas Piaget contributed to cognitive education.
3. From a Piagetian point of view, explain what teachers can do to assist the cognitive development of young children.
4. This chapter discusses seven thinking and reasoning skills. Explain how these are related to later school-related skills.
5. Identify each of the reasoning skills, define them, and provide examples of how they could be included in the curriculum.
6. What is the main difference between the teaching style needed to teach the midlevel mental abilities and the teaching style needed for the problem-solving approach?

Integrative Questions

1. Explain why *matching* and *perceiving common relations* are examples of logico-mathematical knowledge.
2. Which of the following mental abilities is most likely to foster mathematical understanding: (a) matching, (b) seriation, or (c) cause and effect? Explain why you selected the answer you did.
3. How are *common relations* and *grouping* the same? How do they differ?
4. How do *matching* and *grouping* differ?
5. What is the *scientific method,* and how is *cause-and-effect reasoning* related to it?
6. How are *seriated* and *temporal ordering* alike? How do they differ?
7. Compare the two approaches to cognitive learning described in this chapter. What might be the strengths and weaknesses of each approach?

Coordinating Videotape

Growing minds. Tape #13. The whole child: A caregiver's guide to the first five years. The Annenberg/CPB Collection, P.O. Box 2345, South Burlington, VT 05407–2345. *Growing Minds* describes two approaches to developing mental ability. In the conventional approach, teachers set up activities that help children develop specific mental skills such as matching, grouping, and cause and effect. Basic ways teachers can encourage young children to think creatively by using the emergent approach are also illustrated with emphasis on using the inquiry method as a means of stimulating thought.

References for Further Reading

Pick of the Litter

DeVries, R., & Zan, B. (1994). *Moral children, moral classrooms: Creating a constructivist atmosphere in early education.* New York: Teachers College Press. The authors illustrate how constructivist theory can be generalized from cognitive development per se to make classroom management consistent with Piagetian theory. *Highly recommended.*

Overviews

Bybee, R. W., & Sund, R. B. (1990). *Piaget for educators* (2nd ed.). Prospect Heights, IL: Waveland Press. It is delightful to welcome this useful book back into print. It is filled with clear explanations of Piaget's theory combined with many examples of Piagetian tasks.

Singer, D. G., & Revenson, T. A. (1997). *A Piaget primer: How a child thinks* (Rev. ed.). Madison, CT: International Universities Press. The authors clarify explanations of the essential elements of Piaget's theory by tying them to examples of behavior from familiar literature. *Highly recommended.*

Wadsworth, B. J. (1996). *Piaget's theory of cognitive and affective development* (5th ed.). Reading, MA: Addison Wesley. This is a good, clearly written introduction to Piaget that also deals with implications for teaching.

Curriculum Suggestions for Developing Midlevel Thinking Skills

Barata-Lorton, M. (1987). *Workjobs: Activity-centered learning for early childhood education.* Reading, MA: Addison-Wesley. Photographs accompany every suggested activity, showing how a wide variety of cognitive materials can be made by the teacher. Also included are ideas for presentations of the materials and recommendations for follow-up discussions.

Graves, M. (1989). *The teacher's idea book: Daily planning around the key experiences.* Ypsilanti, MI: High/Scope.

Graves, M. (1998). *Planning around children's interests: The teacher's idea book 2.* Ypsilanti, MI: High/Scope. These two books offer many examples of ways classification, seriation, and other mental abilities can be included on a daily basis.

Hohmann, M., & Weikart, D. P. (1995). *Educating young children: Active learning practices for preschool and child care programs.* Ypsilanti, MI: High/Scope. This revision is a comprehensive description of the Piaget-based program that places emphasis on advance planning by child and teacher and includes helpful information on such key experiences as classification and seriation.

Moomaw, S., & Hieronymus, B. (1995). *More than counting: Whole math activities for preschool and kindergarten.* St. Paul, MN: Redleaf. This book has a nice emphasis on teacher-made materials and includes activities for grouping, counting, and matching.

Schiller, P., & Peterson, L. (1997). *Count on math: Activities for small hands and lively minds.* Beltsville, MD: Gryphon House. Some activities included provide practice in grouping, seriation, and temporal ordering. It also offers suggestions for related children's books and home activities.

For the Advanced Student

Flavell, J. H., Miller, P. H., & Miller, S. A. (1993). *Cognitive development* (3rd ed.). Upper Saddle River, NJ: Merrill/Prentice Hall. This book is filled with citations of research and examples—a readable book on a potentially difficult subject that is *highly recommended.*

Fosnot, C. T. (Ed.). (1996). *Constructivism: Theory, perspectives, and practice.* New York: Teachers College Press. This book presents a nice combination of theory accompanied by practical examples illustrating how Piagetian theory can be translated into practical classroom teaching.

Piaget, J. (1983). Piaget's theory. In P. H. Mussen (Series Ed.) & W. Kessen (Vol. Ed.), *Handbook of child psychology* (4th ed.): *Vol. 1. History, theory, and methods.* New York: Wiley. This work by the master himself is a reprint from *Carmichael's Manual of Child Psychology,* 1970 edition. A classic.

Siegler, R. W. (1998). *Children's thinking* (3rd ed.). Upper Saddle River, NJ: Merrill/Prentice Hall. Siegler presents a balanced discussion and criticism of Piaget's theories, complete with descriptions of contemporary experiments challenging some of his findings.

Thomas, R. M. (1999). *Comparing theories of child development* (5th ed.). Monterey, CA: Brooks/Cole. You can't beat Thomas for clear, well written explanations of developmental theories. *Highly recommended.*

Code of Ethical Conduct and Statement of Commitment

A position statement of the National Association for the Education of Young Children
Revised November 1997

Preamble

NAEYC recognizes that many daily decisions required of those who work with young children are of a moral and ethical nature. The NAEYC Code of Ethical Conduct offers guidelines for responsible behavior and sets forth a common basis for resolving the principal ethical dilemmas encountered in early childhood education. The primary focus is on daily practice with children and their families in programs for children from birth through 8 years of age, such as infant/toddler programs, preschools, child care centers, family child care homes, kindergartens, and primary classrooms. Many of the provisions also apply to specialists who do not work directly with children, including program administrators, parent and vocational educators, college professors, and child care licensing specialists.

Core values

Standards of ethical behavior in early childhood care and education are based on commitment to core values that are deeply rooted in the history of our field. We have committed ourselves to

- Appreciating childhood as a unique and valuable stage of the human life cycle

- Basing our work with children on knowledge of child development

- Appreciating and supporting the close ties between the child and family

- Recognizing that children are best understood and supported in the context of family, culture, community, and society

- Respecting the dignity, worth, and uniqueness of each individual (child, family member, and colleague)

- Helping children and adults achieve their full potential in the context of relationships that are based on trust, respect, and positive regard

Conceptual framework

The Code sets forth a conception of our professional responsibilities in four sections, each addressing an arena of professional relationships: (1) children, (2) families, (3) colleagues, and (4) community and society. Each section includes an introduction to the primary responsibilities of the early childhood practitioner in that arena; a set of ideals pointing in the direction of exemplary professional practice; and a set of principles defining practices that are required, prohibited, and permitted.

The **ideals** reflect the aspirations of practitioners. The **principles** are intended to guide conduct and assist practitioners in resolving ethical dilemmas encountered in the field. There is not necessarily a corresponding principle for each ideal. Both ideals and principles are intended to direct practitioners to those questions which, when responsibly answered, will provide the basis for conscientious decisionmaking. While the Code provides specific direction and suggestions for addressing some ethical dilemmas, many others will require the practitioner to combine the guidance of the Code with sound professional judgment.

The ideals and principles in this Code present a shared conception of professional responsibility that affirms our commitment to the core values of our field. The Code publicly acknowledges the responsibilities that we in the field have assumed and in so doing supports ethical behavior in our work. Practitioners who face ethical dilemmas are urged to seek guidance in the applicable parts of this Code and in the spirit that informs the whole.

Ethical dilemmas always exist

Often, "the right answer"—the best ethical course of action to take—is not obvious. There may be no readily apparent, positive way to handle a situation. One important value may contradict another. When we are caught "on the horns of a dilemma," it is our professional responsibility to consult with all relevant parties in seeking the most ethical course of action to take.

Section I: Ethical responsibilities to children

Childhood is a unique and valuable stage in the life cycle. Our paramount responsibility is to provide safe, healthy, nurturing, and responsive settings for children. We are committed to support children's development; respect individual differences; help children learn to live and work cooperatively; and promote health, self-awareness, competence, self-worth, and resiliency.

Ideals

I-1.1   To be familiar with the knowledge base of early childhood care and education and to keep current through continuing education and in-service training.

I-1.2   To base program practices upon current knowledge in the field of child development and related disciplines and upon particular knowledge of each child.

I-1.3   To recognize and respect the uniqueness and the potential of each child.

I-1.4   To appreciate the special vulnerability of children.

I-1.5   To create and maintain safe and healthy settings that foster children's social, emo-

tional, intellectual, and physical development and that respect their dignity and their contributions.

I-1.6   To support the right of each child to play and learn in inclusive early childhood programs to the fullest extent consistent with the best interests of all involved. As with adults who are disabled in the larger community, children with disabilities are ideally served in the same settings in which they would participate if they did not have a disability.

I-1.7   To ensure that children with disabilities have access to appropriate and convenient support services and to advocate for the resources necessary to provide the most appropriate settings for all children.

Principles

P-1.1   Above all, we shall not harm children. We shall not participate in practices that are disrespectful, degrading, dangerous, exploitative, intimidating, emotionally damaging, or physically harmful to children. This principle has precedence over all others in this Code.

P-1.2   We shall not participate in practices that discriminate against children by denying benefits, giving special advantages, or excluding them from programs or activities on the basis of their race, ethnicity, religion, sex, national origin, language, ability, or the status, behavior, or beliefs of their parents. (This principle does not apply to programs that have a lawful mandate to provide services to a particular population of children.)

P-1.3   We shall involve all of those with relevant knowledge (including staff and parents) in decisions concerning a child.

P-1.4   For every child we shall implement adaptations in teaching strategies, learning environment, and curricula, consult with the family, and seek recommendations from appropriate specialists to maximize the potential of the child to benefit from the program. If, after these efforts have been made to work with a child and family, the child still does not appear to be benefiting from a program, or the child is seriously jeopardizing the ability of other children to benefit from the program, we shall communicate with the family and appropriate specialists to determine the child's current needs; identify the setting and services most suited to meeting these needs; and assist the family in placing the child in an appropriate setting.

P-1.5 We shall be familiar with the symptoms of child abuse, including physical sexual, verbal, and emotional abuse, and neglect. We shall know and follow state laws and community procedures that protect children against abuse and neglect.

P-1.6 When we have reasonable cause to suspect child abuse or neglect, we shall report it to the appropriate community agency and follow up to ensure that appropriate action has been taken. When appropriate, parents or guardians will be informed that the referral has been made.

P-1.7 When another person tells us of a suspicion that a child is being abused or neglected, we shall assist that person in taking appropriate action to protect the child.

P-1.8 When a child protective agency fails to provide adequate protection for abused or neglected children, we acknowledge a collective ethical responsibility to work toward improvement of these services.

P-1.9 When we become aware of a practice or situation that endangers the health or safety of children, but has not been previously known to do so, we have an ethical responsibility to inform those who can remedy the situation and who can protect children from similar danger.

Section II: Ethical responsibilities to families

Families are of primary importance in children's development. (The term *family* may include others, besides parents, who are responsibly involved with the child.) Because the family and the early childhood practitioner have a common interest in the child's welfare, we acknowledge a primary responsibility to bring about collaboration between the home and school in ways that enhance the child's development.

Ideals

I-2.1 To develop relationships of mutual trust with families we serve.

I-2.2 To acknowledge and build upon strengths and competencies as we support families in their task of nurturing children.

I-2.3 To respect the dignity of each family and its culture, customs, and beliefs.

I-2.4 To respect families' childrearing values and their right to make decisions for their children.

I-2.5 To interpret each child's progress to parents within the framework of a developmental perspective and to help families understand and appreciate the value of developmentally appropriate early childhood practices.

I-2.6 To help family members improve their understanding of their children and to enhance their skills as parents.

I-2.7 To participate in building support networks for families by providing them with opportunities to interact with program staff, other families, community resources, and professional services.

Principles

P-2.1 We shall not deny family members access to their child's classroom or program setting.

P-2.2 We shall inform families of program philosophy, policies, and personnel qualifications, and explain why we teach as we do—which should be in accordance with our ethical responsibilities to children (see Section I).

P-2.3 We shall inform families of and, when appropriate, involve them in policy decisions.

P-2.4 We shall inform families of significant decisions affecting their child.

P-2.5 We shall inform the family of accidents involving their child, of risks such as exposures to contagious disease that may result in infection, and of occurrences that might result in emotional stress.

P-2.6 To improve the quality of early childhood care and education, we shall not cooperate with qualified child development researchers. Families shall be fully informed of any proposed research projects involving their children and shall have the opportunity to give or withhold consent without penalty. We shall not permit or participate in research that could in any way hinder the education, development, or well-being of children.

P-2.7 We shall not engage in or support exploitation of families. We shall not use our relationship with a family for private advantage or personal gain, or enter into relationships with family members that might impair our effectiveness in working with children.

P-2.8 We shall develop written policies for the protection of confidentiality and the disclosure of children's records. These policy documents shall be made available to all program personnel and families. Disclosure of children's records beyond family members, program personnel, and consultants having an obligation of confidentiality shall require familial consent (except in cases of abuse or neglect).

P-2.9 We shall maintain confidentiality and shall respect the family's right to privacy, refraining from disclosure of confidential information and intrusion into family life. However, when we have reason to believe that a child's welfare is at risk, it is permissible to share confidential information with agencies and individuals who may be able to intervene in the child's interest.

P-2.10 In cases where family members are in conflict, we shall work openly, sharing our observations of the child, to help all parties involved make informed decisions. We shall refrain from becoming an advocate for one party.

P-2.11 We shall be familiar with and appropriately use community resources and professional services that support families. After a referral has been made, we shall follow up to ensure that services have been appropriately provided.

Section III: Ethical responsibilities to colleagues

In a caring, cooperative work place, human dignity is respected, professional satisfaction is promoted, and positive relationships are modeled. Based upon our core values, our primary responsibility in this arena is to establish and maintain settings and relationships that support productive work and meet professional needs. The same ideals that apply to children are inherent in our responsibilities to adults.

A—Responsibilities to co-workers
Ideals

I-3A.1 To establish and maintain relationships of respect, trust, and cooperation with co-workers.

I-3A.2 To share resources and information with co-workers.

I-3A.3 To support co-workers in meeting their professional needs and in their professional development.

I-3A.4 To accord co-workers due recognition of professional achievement.

Principles

P-3A.1 When we have concern about the professional behavior of a co-worker, we shall first let that person know of our concern, in a way that shows respect for personal dignity and for the diversity to be found among staff members, and then attempt to resolve the matter collegially.

P-3A.2 We shall exercise care in expressing views regarding the personal attributes or professional conduct of co-workers. Statements should be based on firsthand knowledge and relevant to the interests of children and programs.

B—Responsibilities of employers
Ideals

I-3B.1 To assist the program in providing the highest quality of service.

I-3B.2 To do nothing that diminishes the reputation of the program in which we work unless it is violating laws and regulations designed to protect children or the provisions of this Code.

Principles

P-3B.1 When we do not agree with program policies, we shall first attempt to effect change through constructive action within the organization.

P-3B.2 We shall speak or act on behalf of an organization only when authorized. We shall take care to acknowledge when we are speaking for the organization and when we are expressing a personal judgment.

P-3B.3 We shall not violate laws or regulations designed to protect children and shall take appropriate action consistent with this Code when aware of such violations.

C—Responsibilities to employees
Ideals

I-3C.1 To promote policies and working conditions that foster mutual respect, competence, well-being, and positive self-esteem in staff members.

I-3C.2 To create a climate of trust and candor that will enable staff to speak and act in the best interests of children, families, and the field of early childhood care and education.

I-3C.3 To strive to secure equitable compensation (salary and benefits) for those who work with or on behalf of young children.

Principles

P-3C.1 In decisions concerning children and programs, we shall appropriately utilize the education, training, experience, and expertise of staff members.

P-3C.2 We shall provide staff members with safe and supportive working conditions that permit them to carry out their responsibilities, timely and nonthreatening evaluation procedures, written grievance procedures, constructive feedback, and opportunities for continuing professional development and advancement.

P-3C.3 We shall develop and maintain comprehensive written personnel policies that define program standards and, when applicable, that specify the extent to which employees are accountable for their conduct outside the work place. These policies shall be given to new staff members and shall be available for review by all staff members.

P-3C.4 Employees who do not meet program standards shall be informed of areas of concern and, when possible, assisted in improving their performance.

P-3C.5 Employees who are dismissed shall be informed of the reasons for their termination. When a dismissal is for cause, justification must be based on evidence of inadequate or inappropriate behavior that is accurately documented, current, and available for the employee to review.

P-3C.6 In making evaluations and recommendations, judgments shall be based on fact and relevant to the interests of children and programs.

P-3C.7 Hiring and promotion shall be based solely on a person's record of accomplishment and ability to carry out the responsibilities of the position.

P-3C.8 In hiring, promotion, and provision of training, we shall not participate in any form of discrimination based on race, ethnicity, religion, gender, national origin, culture, disability, age, or sexual preference. We shall be familiar with and observe laws and regulations that pertain to employment discrimination.

Section IV: Ethical responsibilities to community and society

Early childhood programs operate within a context of an immediate community made up of families and other institutions concerned with children's welfare. Our responsibilities to the community are to provide programs that meet its needs, to cooperate with agencies and professions that share responsibility for children, and to develop needed programs that are not currently available. Because the larger society has a measure of responsibility for the welfare and protection of children, and because of our specialized expertise in child development, we acknowledge an obligation to serve as a voice for children everywhere.

Ideals

I-4.1   To provide the community with high-quality (age and individually appropriate, and culturally and socially sensitive) education/care programs and services.

I-4.2   To promote cooperation among agencies and interdisciplinary collaboration among professions concerned with the welfare of young children, their families, and their teachers.

I-4.3   To work, through education, research, and advocacy, toward an environmentally safe world in which all children receive adequate health care, food, and shelter, are nurtured, and live free from violence.

I-4.4   To work, through education, research, and advocacy, toward a society in which all young children have access to high-quality education/care programs.

I-4.5   To promote knowledge and understanding of young children and their needs. To work toward greater social acknowledgment of children's rights and greater social acceptance of responsibility for their well-being.

I-4.6   To support policies and laws that promote the well-being of children and families, and to oppose those that impair their well-being. To participate in developing policies and laws that are needed, and to cooperate with other individuals and groups in these efforts.

I-4.7   To further the professional development of the field of early childhood care and education and to strengthen its commitment to realizing its core values as reflected in this Code.

Principles

P-4.1   We shall communicate openly and truthfully about the nature and extent of services that we provide.

P-4.2   We shall not accept or continue to work in positions for which we are personally unsuited or professionally unqualified. We shall not offer services that we do not have the competence, qualifications, or resources to provide.

P-4.3 We shall be objective and accurate in reporting the knowledge upon which we base our program practices.

P-4.4 We shall cooperate with other professionals who work with children and their families.

P-4.5 We shall not hire or recommend for employment any person whose competence, qualifications, or character makes him or her unsuited for the position.

P-4.6 We shall report the unethical or incompetent behavior of a colleague to a supervisor when informal resolution is not effective.

P-4.7 We shall be familiar with laws and regulations that serve to protect the children in our programs.

P-4.8 We shall not participate in practices which are in violation of laws and regulations that protect the children in our programs.

P-4.9 When we have evidence that an early childhood program is violating laws or regulations protecting children, we shall report it to persons responsible for the program. If compliance is not accomplished within a reasonable time, we will report the violation to appropriate authorities who can be expected to remedy the situation.

P-4.10 When we have evidence that an agency or a professional charged with providing services to children, families, or teachers is failing to meet its obligations, we acknowledge a collective ethical responsibility to report the problem to appropriate authorities or to the public.

P-4.11 When a program violates or requires its employees to violate this Code, it is permissible, after fair assessment of the evidence, to disclose the identity of that program.

Statement of commitment

As an individual who works with young children, I commit myself to furthering the values of early childhood education as they are reflected in the NAEYC Code of Ethical Conduct.

To the best of my ability I will

- Ensure that programs for young children are based on current knowledge of child development and early childhood education.

- Respect and support families in their task of nurturing children.

- Respect colleagues in early childhood education and support them in maintaining the NAEYC Code of Ethical Conduct.

- Serve as an advocate for children, their families, and their teachers in community and society.

- Maintain high standards of professional conduct.

- Recognize how personal values, opinions, and biases can affect professional judgment.

- Be open to new ideas and be willing to learn from the suggestions of others.

- Continue to learn, grow, and contribute as a professional.

- Honor the ideals and principles of the NAEYC Code of Ethical Conduct.

Source: This Code of Ethical Conduct and Statement of Commitment was prepared under the auspices of the Ethics Commission of the National Association for the Education of Young Children. The Commission members were Stephanie Feeney (Chairperson), Bettye Caldwell, Sally Cartwright, Carrie Cheek, Josué Cruz, Jr., Anne G. Dorsey, Dorothy M. Hill, Lilian G. Katz, Pamm Mattick, Shirley A. Norris, and Sue Spayth Riley. Reprinted with permission from the National Association for the Education of Young Children, © 1997.

appendix   *B*

Summary of Communicable Diseases

Disease	Agent	Incubation	Communicable Period	Transmission	Symptoms	Remarks
Chickenpox (Herpes Zoster; Varicella; Shingles)	Virus	2–3 weeks	1–5 days before rash; no more than 6 days after first vesicles	Direct contact with vesicle fluid, soiled articles, or droplets from respiratory tract	Sudden onset; slight fever; malaise; mild constitutional symptoms, followed by eruption of lesions; followed by fluid filled blisters for 3–4 days; ending with scab	Very communicable; lesions, blisters and scabbed sores can exist at the same time; lesions are most common on covered parts of the body
Conjunctivitis (Pink Eye)	Bacteria	24–72 hours	Throughout course of infection	Contact with discharge from conjunctiva or upper respiratory tract, or objects contaminated by those discharges	Tearing and irritation of conjunctiva; lid swelling, discharge; sensitivity to light	Most common in preschoolers
Cytomegalovirus (CMV)	Virus	May be acquired during birth, but show no symptoms for up to 3 months after delivery	Virus may be excreted for 5–6 years	Direct/indirect contact with membranes or secretions; blood; urine	Usually no symptoms; may show signs of severe infection of central nervous system or liver	Most serious in early infancy; many apparently healthy children in day care have CMV in urine or saliva; *potentially serious for pregnant women*
Giardiasis	Protozoa (a cyst in the inactive form)	5–25 days	Entire period of infection	Hand to mouth transfer of cysts from stools of infected person	Chronic pale, greasy diarrhea; abdominal cramping; fatigue; weight loss	Frequently found in day care centers; carriers may be asymptomatic

Disease	Cause	Incubation	Communicability	Transmission	Symptoms	Comments
Hepatitis	Several viruses	Hepatitis A: 15–50 days; Hepatitis B: 45–180 days	Hepatitis A: A week before infection to one week after appearance of jaundice. Hepatitis B: From several weeks before symptoms until weeks after symptoms; may be a carrier for years	Hepatitis A: Fecal/oral route; direct contact. Hepatitis B: Contact with infected blood; saliva, and vaginal fluids; semen	Hepatitis A: sudden onset with fever, lack of appetite, nausea, abdominal pain; jaundice follows in a few days. Hepatitis B: Lack of appetite; nausea, vomiting, and later jaundice	Hepatitis A: Common in day care; severity increases with age; infections in infants may be asymptomatic. Hepatitis B: May be present but asymptomatic in young children; HB vaccine available to prevent this type of hepatitis
Measles (Hard measles; red measles)	Virus	1–2 weeks before rash to 4 days after the rash appears	Communicable from before fever to 4 days after rash	Direct contact with nasal or throat secretions or freshly contaminated objects	Fever, conjunctivitis, cough, Koplik spots; rash appears on 3rd day—usually starting on face	Easily spread; very common in preschool populations; immunization available; potentially serious for ill or young children
Meningitis (Viral)	Several viruses	Incubation varies by specific virus	Communicability varies with specific virus	Direct contact with respiratory droplets or excretions of infected person, or objects contaminated by these secretions	Symptoms vary by specific type of virus; usually sudden fever and central nervous system symptoms; may have rash	Symptoms last 10 days with residual symptoms for a year or more

Disease	Agent	Incubation	Communicable Period	Transmission	Symptoms	Remarks
Meningitis (Bacterial)	Various bacteria	2–10 days	Until organisms are not found in discharge	Direct contact with respiratory droplets or excretions of an infected person or objects contaminated by these secretions	Sudden onset of fever; severe headache; stiff neck; rash	Early detection and treatment necessary to prevent death
Mumps	Virus	2–3 weeks	6 days before until 9 days after onset of illness	Direct contact with respiratory droplets or saliva of infected person	Fever, swelling and tenderness of one or more salivary glands	Meningitis occurs frequently; Vaccine available
Pediatric AIDS	Virus	Unknown	Unknown	Contact with blood and blood contaminated fluids and objects; sexual contact with semen and vaginal fluids	Early symptoms are nonspecific: loss of appetite; chronic diarrhea; fatigue; symptoms progress to opportunistic infections and central nervous system symptoms	Use universal precautions
Pediculosis (Lice)	Lice Adult, (larvae or nits)	Eggs hatch in a week; sexual maturity is reached 8–10 days after hatching	Communicable as long as eggs and lice are alive on person or clothing	Direct contact with infected person or indirect contact with contaminated objects	Itching and excoriation of infected head and body parts	Common in school children; Check with physician regarding use of over-the-counter products; some are not recommended for infants and young children

Ringworm	Fungus	4–10 days	Until lesions are gone and fungus is no longer on contaminated objects	Direct or indirect contact with infected persons or contaminated objects	Lesions appear flat, spreading, and ring shaped; outer ring may be filled with pus or fluid; inside may be dry and scaly or moist and crusty	Infected children should be excluded from common swimming pools
Rubella (three-day measles)	Virus	2–3 weeks	From one week before to one week after onset of rash	Droplet spread or direct/indirect contact with objects soiled with nasal secretions, blood, urine or feces	Symptoms may range from no symptoms to cold-like symptoms such as low grade fever, malaise, and runny nose; not all infections have a rash; if it does exist, it usually starts on the face and spreads to trunk and extremities	Easily spread; high incidence in pre-school populations; immunizations available; resembles measles; *potentially serious for pregnant women*
Scabies	Mite	2–6 weeks in person with no exposure; 1–4 days after re-exposure	Until mites and eggs are killed; usually 1–2 courses of treatment, one week apart	Skin to skin contact, or contact with recently infected undergarments or bed clothes	Intense itching of head, neck, palms, soles in infants; may also involve other body creases	In persons with reduced resistance, infection will be generalized; check with physician prior to use of over-the-counter medications, because some are not recommended for infants and young children

Source: *From Preschool Children With Special Needs (pp. 179–182), by M. T. Urbano, 1992, San Diego: Singular Publishing Group. Reprinted with permission.*

Recommended Childhood Immunization Schedule
United States, January–December 1999

Vaccines are listed under routinely recommended ages. ☐Bars☐ indicate range of recommended ages for immunization. Any dose not given at the recommended age should be given as a "catch-up" immunization at any subsequent visit when indicated and feasible. ⬭Ovals⬭ indicate vaccines to be given if previously recommended doses were missed or given earlier than the recommended minimum age.

Age ▶ Vaccine ▼	Birth	1 mo	2 mos	4 mos	6 mos	12 mos	15 mos	18 mos	4–6 yrs	11–12 yrs	14–16 yrs
Hepatitis B[2]	Hep B	Hep B	Hep B		Hep B					Hep B	
Diphtheria, Tetanus Pertussis[3]			DTaP	DTaP	DTaP		DTaP[3]		DTaP	Td	
H. influenzae type b[4]			Hib	Hib	Hib	Hib					
Polio[5]			IPV	IPV	Polio[5]				Polio		
Rotavirus[6]			Rv[6]	Rv[6]	Rv[6]						
Measles, Mumps, Rubella[7]						MMR			MMR[7]	MMR[7]	
Varicella[8]						Var				Var[8]	

Approved by the Advisory Committee on Immunization Practices (ACIP), the American Academy of Pediatrics (AAP), and the American Academy of Family Physicians (AAFP).
(For necessary footnotes and important information, see the following pages.)

1. This schedule indicates the recommended ages for routine administration of currently licensed childhood vaccines. Combination vaccines may be used whenever any components of the combination are indicated and its other components are not contraindicated. Providers should consult the manufacturers' package inserts for detailed recommendations.

2. *Infants born to HbsAg-negative mothers* should receive the 2nd dose of hepatitis B vaccine at least 1 month after the 1st dose. The 3rd dose should be administered at least 4 months after the 1st dose and at least 2 months after the 2nd dose, but not before 6 months of age for infants.

   Infants born to HBsAg—positive mothers should receive hepatitis B vaccine and 0.5 mL hepatitis B immune globulin (HBIG) within 12 hours of birth at separate sites. The 2nd dose is recommended at 1–2 months of age and the 3rd dose at 6 months of age.

   Infants born to mothers whose HBsAg status is unknown should receive hepatitis B vaccine within 12 hours of birth. Maternal blood should be drawn at the time of delivery to determine the mother's HBsAg status; if the HBsAg test is positive, the infant should receive HBIG as soon as possible (no later than 1 week of age).

   All children and adolescents (through 18 years of age) who have not been immunized against hepatitis B may begin the series during any visit. Special efforts should be made to immunize children who were born in or whose parents were born in areas of the world with moderate or high endemicity of HBV infection.

3. DTaP (diphtheria and tetanus toxoids and acellular pertussis vaccine) is the preferred vaccine for all doses in the immunization series, including completion of the series in children who have received 1 or more doses of whole-cell DTP vaccine. Whole-cell DTP is an acceptable alternative to DTaP. The 4th dose (DTP or DTaP) may be administered as early as 12 months of age, provided 6 months have elapsed since the 3rd dose and if the child is unlikely to return at age 15–18 months. Td (tetanus and diphtheria toxoids) is recommended at 11–12 years of age if at least 5 years have elapsed since the last dose of DTP, DTaP, or DT. Subsequent routine Td boosters are recommended every 10 years.

4. Three *H. influenzae* type b (Hib) conjugate vaccines are licensed for infant use. If PRP-OMP (PedvaxHIB and COMVAX [Merck]) is administered at 2 and 4 months of age, a dose at 6 months is not required. Because clinical studies in infants have demonstrated that using some combination products may induce a lower immune response to the Hib vaccine component, DTaP/Hib combination products should not be used for primary immunization in infants at 2, 4, or 6 months of age, unless FDA-approved for these ages.

5. Two poliovirus vaccines currently are licensed in the United States: inactivated poliovirus vaccine (IPV) and oral poliovirus vaccine (OPV).

   The ACIP, AAP, and AAFP now recommend that the first two doses of poliovirus vaccine should be IPV. The ACIP continues to recommend a sequential schedule of two doses of IPV administered at ages 2 and 4 months, followed by two doses of OPV at 12–18 months and 4–6 years. Use of IPV for all doses also is acceptable and is recommended for immunocompromised persons and their household contacts.

   OPV is no longer recommended for the first two doses of the schedule and is acceptable only for special circumstances such as: children of parents who do not accept the recommended number of injections, late initiation of immunization which would require an unacceptable number of injections, and imminent travel to polio-endemic areas. OPV remains the vaccine of choice for mass immunization campaigns to control outbreaks due to wild poliovirus.

6. Rotavirus (Rv) vaccine is shaded and italicized to indicate: 1) health care providers may require time and resources to incorporate this new vaccine into practice; and 2) the AAFP feels that the decision to use rotavirus vaccine should be made by the parent or guardian in consultation with their physician or other health care provider. The first dose of Rv vaccine should not be administered before 6 weeks of age, and the minimum interval between doses is 3 weeks. The Rv vaccine series should not be initiated at 7 months of age or older, and all doses should be completed by the first birthday.

7. The 2nd dose of measles, mumps, and rubella vaccine (MMR) is recommended routinely at 4–6 year of age but may be administered during any visit, provided at least 4 weeks have elapsed since receipt of the 1st dose and that both doses are administered beginning at or after 12 months of age. Those who have not previously received the second dose should complete the schedule by the 11- to 12-year-old visit.

8. Varicella vaccine is recommended at any visit on or after the first birthday for susceptible children, i.e., those who lack a reliable history of chickenpox (as judged by a health care provider) and who have not been immunized. Susceptible persons 13 years of age or older should receive 2 doses, given at least 4 weeks apart.

Immunization Protects Children

Regular checkups at your pediatrician's office or local health clinic are an important way to keep children healthy.

By making sure that your child gets immunized on time, you can provide the best available defense against many dangerous childhood diseases. Immunizations protect children against: hepatitis B, polio, measles, mumps, rubella (German measles), pertussis (whooping cough), diphtheria, tetanus (lockjaw), *Haemophilus influenzae* type b, chickenpox, and rotavirus. All of these immunizations need to be given before children are 2 years old in order for them to be protected during their most vulnerable period. Are your child's immunizations up-to-date?

The chart on the other side of this fact sheet includes immunization recommendations from the American Academy of Pediatrics. Remember to keep track of your child's immunizations—it's the only way you can be sure your child is up-to-date. Also, check with your pediatrician or health clinic at each visit to find out if your child needs any booster shots or if any new vaccines have been recommended since this schedule was prepared.

If you don't have a pediatrician, call your local health department. Public health clinics usually have supplies of vaccine and may give shots free. American Academy of Pediatrics

The information contained in this publication should not be used as a substitute for the medical care and advice of your pediatrician. There may be variations in treatment that your pediatrician may recommend based on individual facts and circumstances.

Chart of Normal Development

Infancy to 6 Years of Age

The chart of normal development on the next few pages presents children's achievements from infancy to 6 years of age in five areas:

Motor skills (gross and fine motor)

Cognitive skills

Self-help skills

Social skills

Communication skills (understanding and speaking language)

In each skill area, the age at which each milestone is reached *on the average* is also presented. This information is useful if you have a child in your class who you suspect is seriously delayed in one or more skill areas.

However, it is important to remember that these milestones are only average. From the moment of birth, each child is a distinct individual and develops in his or her unique manner. No two children have ever reached all the same developmental milestones at the exact same ages. The examples that follow show what we mean.

By nine months of age Gi Lin had spent much of her time scooting around on her hands and tummy, making no effort to crawl. After about a week of pulling herself up on chairs and table legs, she let go and started to walk on her own. Gi Lin skipped the crawling stage entirely and scarcely said more than a few sounds until she was 15 months old. But she walked with ease and skill by 9½ months.

Marcus learned to crawl on all fours very early, and continued crawling until he was nearly 18 months old, when he started to walk. However, he said single words and used two-word phrases meaningfully before his first birthday. A talking, crawling baby is quite a sight!

Molly worried her parents by saying scarcely a word, although she managed to make her needs known with sounds and gestures. Shortly after her second birthday, Molly suddenly began talking in two- to four-word phrases and sentences. She was never again a quiet child.

All three children were healthy and normal. By the time they were three years old, there were no major differences among them in walking or talking. They had simply developed in their own ways and at their own rates. Some children seem to concentrate on one thing at a time—learning to crawl, to walk, or to talk. Other children develop across areas at a more even rate.

As you read the chart of normal development, remember that children don't read child development books. They don't know they're supposed to be able to point out Daddy when they are a year old or copy a circle in their third year. And even if they could read these baby books, they probably wouldn't follow them! Age-related developmental milestones are obtained by averaging out what many children do at various ages. No child is "average" in all areas. Each child is a unique person.

One final word of caution. As children grow, their abilities are shaped by the opportunities they have for learning. For example, although many 5-year-olds can repeat songs and rhymes, the child who has not heard songs and rhymes many times cannot be expected to repeat them. All areas of development and learning are influenced by the child's experiences as well as by the abilities they are born with.

Table D–1
Chart of normal development

0–12 Months	12–24 Months	24–36 Months	36–48 Months	48–60 Months	60–72 Months
MOTOR SKILLS **Gross motor skills**					
Sits without support	Walks alone	Runs forward well	Runs around obstacles	Walks backward toe-heel	Runs lightly on toes
Crawls	Walks backward	Jumps in place, two feet together	Walks on a line	Jumps forward 10 times, without falling	Walks on balance beam
Pulls self to standing and stands unaided	Picks up toys from floor without falling	Stands on one foot, with aid	Balances on one foot for 10 seconds	Walks up and down stairs alone, alternating feet	Can cover 2 m (6'6") hopping
Walks with aid	Pulls toy, pushes toy	Walks on tiptoe	Hops on one foot	Turns somersault	Skips on alternate feet
Rolls a ball in imitation of adult	Seats self in child's chair	Kicks ball forward	Pushes, pulls, steers wheeled toys		Jumps rope
	Walks up and down stairs (hand-held)		Rides (that is, steers and pedals) tricycle		Skates
	Moves to music		Uses slide without assistance		
			Jumps over 15 cm (6") high object, landing on both feet together		
			Throws ball overhand		
			Catches ball bounced to him or her		
Fine motor skills					
Reaches, grasps, puts object in mouth	Builds tower of three small blocks	Strings four large beads	Builds tower of nine small blocks	Cuts on line continuously	Cuts out simple shapes
Picks things up with thumb and one finger (pincer grasp)	Puts four rings on stick	Turns pages singly	Drives nails and pegs	Copies cross	Copies triangle
Transfers object from one hand to other hand	Places five pegs in pegboard	Snips with scissors	Copies circle	Copies square	Traces diamond
Drops and picks up toy	Turns pages two or three at a time	Holds crayon with thumb and fingers, not fist	Imitates cross	Prints a few capital letters	Copies first name
	Scribbles	Uses one hand consistently in most activities	Manipulates clay materials (for example, rolls balls, snakes, cookies)		Prints numerals 1 to 5
	Turns knobs				Colors within lines
	Throws small ball				Has adult grasp of pencil

Paints with whole arm movement, shifts hands, makes strokes

Imitates circular, vertical, horizontal strokes

Paints with some wrist action; makes dots, lines, circular strokes

Rolls, pounds, squeezes, and pulls clay

Has handedness well established (that is, child is left- or right-handed)

Pastes and glues appropriately

COMMUNICATION SKILLS
Understanding language

Responds to speech by looking at speaker

Responds differently to aspects of speaker's voice (for example, friendly or unfriendly, male or female)

Turns to source of sound

Responds with gesture to *hi*, *bye-bye*, and *up* when these words are accompanied by appropriate gesture

Stops ongoing action when told *no* (when negative is accompanied by appropriate gesture and tone)

Responds correctly when asked *where* (when question is accompanied by gesture)

Understands prepositions *on*, *in*, and *under*

Follows request to bring familiar object from another room

Understands simple phrases with key words (for example: *Open the door. Get the ball.*)

Follows a series of two simple but related directions

Points to pictures of common objects when they are named

Can identify objects when told their use

Understands question forms *what* and *where*

Understands negatives *no*, *not*, *can't*, and *don't*

Enjoys listening to simple storybooks and requests them again

Begins to understand sentences involving time concepts (for example, *We are going to the zoo tomorrow*)

Understands size comparatives such as *big* and *bigger*

Understands relationships expressed by *if-then* or *because* sentences

Carries out a series of two to four related directions

Understands when told *Let's pretend*

Follows three unrelated commands in proper order

Understands comparatives like *pretty*, *prettier*, and *prettiest*

Listens to long stories but often misinterprets the facts

Incorporates verbal directions into play activities

Understands sequencing of events when told them (for example, *First we have to go to the store, then we can make the cake and tomorrow we will eat it.*)

Demonstrates preacademic skills

0–12 Months	12–24 Months	24–36 Months	36–48 Months	48–60 Months	60–72 Months
Spoken Language					
Makes crying and noncrying sounds	Says first meaningful word	Joins vocabulary words together in two-word phrases	Talks in sentences of three or more words, which take the form agent-action-object (*I see the ball*) or agent-action-location (*Daddy sit on chair*)	Asks *when, how,* and *why* questions	There are few obvious differences between child's grammar and adult's grammar
Repeats some vowel and consonant sounds (babbles) when alone or spoken to	Uses single words plus a gesture to ask for objects	Gives first and last name	Tells about past experiences	Uses models like *can, will, shall, should,* and *might*	Still needs to learn such things as subject-verb agreement, and some irregular past tense verbs
Interacts with others by vocalizing after adult	Says successive single words to describe an event	Asks *what* and *where* questions	Uses *s* on nouns to indicate plurals	Joins sentences together (for example, *I like chocolate chip cookies and milk.*)	Can take appropriate turns in a conversation
Communicates meaning through intonation	Refers to self by name	Makes negative statements (for example, *Can't open it*)	Uses *ed* on verbs to indicate past tense	Talks about causality by using *because* and *so*	Gives and receives information
Attempts to imitate sounds	Uses *my* or *mine* to indicate possession	Shows frustration at not being understood	Refers to self using pronouns *I* or *me*	Tells the content of a story but may confuse facts	Communicates well with family, friends, or strangers
	Has vocabulary of about 50 words for important people, common objects, and the existence, non-existence, and recurrence of objects and events (for example, *more* and *all gone*)		Repeats at least one nursery rhyme and can sing a song		
			Speech is understandable to strangers, but there are still some sound errors.		

COGNITIVE SKILLS

Follows moving object with eyes

Recognizes differences among people; responds to strangers by crying or staring

Responds to and imitates facial expressions of others

Responds to very simple directions (for example, raises arms when someone says *Come* and turns head when asked *Where is Daddy?*)

Imitates gestures and actions (for example, shakes head no, plays peek-a-boo, waves bye-bye)

Puts small objects in and out of container with intention

Imitates actions and words of adults

Responds to words or commands with appropriate action (for example, *Stop that, Get down.*)

Looks at story-book pictures with an adult, naming or pointing to familiar objects on request (for example, *What is that? Point to the baby.*)

Recognizes difference between *you* and *me*

Has very limited attention span

Accomplishes primary learning through own exploration

Responds to simple directions (for example, *Give me the ball and the block. Get your shoes and socks.*)

Selects and looks at picture books, names pictured objects, and identifies several objects within one picture

Is able to match two similar objects

Matches and uses objects meaningfully (for example, given cup, saucer, and bead, puts cup and saucer together)

Stacks rings on peg in order of size

Recognizes self in mirror, saying *baby* or own name

Can talk briefly about what he or she is doing

Imitates adult actions (for example, housekeeping play)

Recognizes and matches six colors

Intentionally stacks blocks or rings in order of size

Draws somewhat recognizable picture that is meaningful to child, if not to adult; names and briefly explains picture

Asks questions for information (*why* and *how* questions requiring simple answers)

Knows own age

Knows own last name

Has short attention span

Learns through observing and imitating adults, and by adult instruction and explanation; is very easily distracted

Has increased understanding of concepts of the functions and groupings of objects (for example, can put doll house furniture in correct rooms), and part-whole (for example, can identify pictures of hand and foot as parts of body)

Begins to be aware of past and present (for example, *Yesterday we went to the park. Today we go to the library.*)

Plays with words (creates own rhyming words; says or makes up words having similar sounds)

Points to and names four to six colors

Matches pictures of familiar objects (for example, shoe, sock, foot; apple, orange, banana)

Draws a person with two to six recognizable parts, such as head, arms, legs; can name or match drawn parts to own body

Draws, names, and describes recognizable picture

Rote counts to 5, imitating adults

Knows own street and town

Retells story from picture book with reasonable accuracy

Names some letters and numerals

Rote counts to 10

Sorts objects by single characteristics (for example, by color, shape, or size if the difference is obvious)

Is beginning to use accurately time concepts of *tomorrow* and *yesterday*

Uses classroom tools (such as scissors and paints) meaningfully and purposefully

Begins to relate clock time to daily schedule

Attention span increases noticeably; learns through adult instruction; when interested, can ignore distractions.

0–12 Months	12–24 Months	24–36 Months	36–48 Months	48–60 Months	60–72 Months
COGNITIVE SKILLS, *Continued*					
		Has limited attention span; learning is through exploration and adult direction (as in reading of picture stories) Is beginning to understand functional concepts of familiar objects (for example, that a spoon is used for eating) and part-whole concepts (for example, parts of the body)		Has more extended attention span; learns through observation and listening to adults as well as through exploration; is easily distracted Has increased understanding of concepts of function, time, part-whole relationships; function or use of objects may be stated in addition to names of objects Time concepts are expanding. The child can talk about yesterday or last week (a long time ago), about today, and about what will happen tomorrow.	Concepts of function increase as well as understanding of why things happen. Time concepts are expanding into an understanding of the future in terms of major events (for example, *Christmas will come after two weekends*).

SELF-HELP SKILLS

Feeds self cracker	Uses spoon, spilling little	Uses spoon, little spilling	Pours well from small pitcher	Cuts easy foods with a knife (for example, hamburger patty, tomato slice)	Dresses self completely
Holds cup with two hands; drinks with assistance	Drinks from cup, one hand, unassisted	Gets drink from fountain or faucet unassisted	Spreads soft butter with knife	Laces shoes	Ties bow
Holds out arms and legs while being dressed	Chews food	Opens door by turning handle	Buttons and unbuttons large buttons		Brushes teeth unassisted
	Removes shoes, socks, pants, sweater	Takes off coat	Washes hands unassisted		Crosses street safely
	Unzips large zipper	Puts on coat with assistance	Blows nose when reminded		
	Indicates toilet needs	Washes and dries hands with assistance			

SOCIAL SKILLS

Smiles spontaneously	Recognizes self in mirror or picture	Plays near other children	Joins in play with other children; begins to interact	Plays and interacts with other children	Chooses own friend(s)
Responds differently to strangers than to familiar people	Refers to self by name	Watches other children, joins briefly in their play	Shares toys; takes turns with assistance	Dramatic play is closer to reality, with attention paid to detail, time, and space	Plays simple table games
Pays attention to own name	Plays by self, initiates own play	Defends own possessions	Begins dramatic play, acting out whole scenes (for example, traveling, playing house, pretending to be animals)	Plays dress-up	Plays competitive games
Responds to *no*	Imitates adult behaviors in play	Begins to play house		Shows interest in exploring sex differences	Engages with other children in cooperative play involving group decisions, role assignments, fair play
Copies simple actions of others	Helps put things away	Symbolically uses objects, self in play			
		Participates in simple group activity (for example, sings, claps, dances)			
		Knows gender identify			

Source: *From Mainstreaming Preschoolers: Children with Health Impairments by A. Healy, P. McAreavey, C. S. Von-Hippel, and S. H. Jones, 1978, Washington, DC: U.S. Department of Health, Education and Welfare, Office of Human Development Services, Administration for Children, Youth and Families, Head Start Bureau.*

10 Quick Ways to Analyze Children's Books for Racism and Sexism

Both in school and out, young children are exposed to racist and sexist attitudes. These attitudes—expressed over and over in books and in other media—gradually distort their perceptions until stereotypes and myths about minorities and women are accepted as reality. It is difficult for a librarian or teacher to convince children to question society's attitudes. But if a child can be shown how to detect racism and sexism in a book, the child can proceed to transfer the perception to wider areas. The following 10 guidelines are offered as a starting point in evaluating children's books from this perspective.

1. Check the Illustrations

Look for stereotypes. A stereotype is an oversimplified generalization about a particular group, race, or sex, which usually carries derogatory implications. Some infamous (overt) stereotypes of Blacks are the happy-go-lucky water-melon-eating Sambo and the fat, eye-rolling "mammy"; of Chicanos, the sombrero-wearing peon or fiesta-loving, macho bandito; of Asian Americans, the inscrutable, slant-eyed "Oriental"; of Native Americans, the naked savage or "primitive" craftsman and his squaw; of Puerto Ricans, the switchblade-toting teenage gang member; of women, the completely domesticated mother, the demure, doll-loving little girl, or the wicked stepmother. While you may not always find stereotypes in the blatant forms described, look for variations which in any way demean or ridicule characters because of their race or sex.

Look for tokenism. If there are non-White characters in the illustrations, do they look just like Whites except for being tinted or colored in? Do all minority faces look stereotypically alike, or are they depicted as genuine individuals with distinctive features?

Who's doing what? Do the illustrations depict minorities in subservient and passive roles or in leadership and action roles? Are males the active "doers" and females the inactive observers?

2. Check the Story Line

The Civil Rights Movement has led publishers to weed out many insulting passages, particularly from stories with Black themes, but the attitudes still find expression in less obvious ways. The following checklist suggests some of the subtle (covert) forms of bias to watch for.

Standard for success. Does it take "White" behavior standards for a minority person to "get ahead"? Is "making it" in the dominant White society projected as the only ideal? To gain acceptance and approval, do non-White persons have to exhibit extraordinary qualities—excel in sports, get A's, etc.? In friendships between White and non-White children, is it the non-white who does most of the understanding and forgiving?

Resolution of problems. How are problems presented, conceived, and resolved in the story? Are minority people considered to be "the problem"? Are the oppressions faced by minorities and women represented as casually related to an unjust society? Are the reasons for poverty and oppression explained, or are they accepted as inevitable? Does the story line encourage passive acceptance or active resistance? Is a particular problem that is faced by a minority person resolved through the benevolent intervention of a White person?

Role of women. Are the achievements of girls and women based on their own initiative and intelligence, or are they due to their good looks or to their relationship with boys? Are sex roles incidental or critical to characterization and plot? Could the same story be told if the sex roles were reversed?

3. Look at the Lifestyles

Are minority persons and their setting depicted in such a way that they contrast unfavorably with the unstated norm of White middle-class suburbia? If the minority group in question is depicted as "different," are negative value judgments implied? Are minorities depicted exclusively in ghettos, barrios, or migrant camps? If the illustrations and text attempt to depict another culture, do they go beyond oversimplifications and offer genuine insights into another lifestyle? Look for inaccuracy and inappropriateness in the depiction of other cultures. Watch for instances of the "quaint-natives-in-costume" syndrome (most noticeable in areas like costume and custom, but extending to behavior and personality traits as well).

4. Weigh the Relationships Between People

Do the Whites in the story possess the power, take the leadership, and make the important decisions? Do non-Whites and females function in essentially supporting roles?

How are family relationships depicted? In Black families, is the mother always dominant? In Hispanic families, are there always lots and lots of children? If the family is separated, are societal conditions—unemployment, poverty—cited among the reasons for the separation?

5. Note the Heroes and Heroines

For many years, books showed only "safe" minority heroes and heroines—those who avoided serious conflict with the White establishment of their time. Minority groups today are insisting on the right to define their own heroes and heroines based on their own concepts and struggles for justice.

When minority heroes and heroines do appear, are they admired for the same qualities that have made White heroes and heroines famous or because what they have done has benefitted White people? Ask this question: Whose interest is a particular figure really serving?

6. Consider the Effects on a Child's Self-Image

Are norms established that limit the child's aspirations and self-concepts? What effect can it have on Black children to be continuously bombarded with images of the color white as the ultimate in beauty, cleanliness, virtue, etc., and the color black as evil, dirty, menacing, etc.? Does the book counteract or reinforce this positive association with the color white and negative association with black?

What happens to a girl's self-image when she reads that boys perform all of the brave and important deeds? What about a girl's self-esteem if she is not "fair" of skin and slim of body?

In a particular story, is there one or more persons with whom a minority child can readily identify to a positive and constructive end?

7. Consider the Author's or Illustrator's Background

Analyze the biographical material on the jacket flap or the back of the book. If a story deals with a minority theme, what qualifies the author or illustrator to deal with the subject? If the author and illustrator are not members of the minority being written about, is there anything in their background that would specifically recommend them as the creators of this book?

Similarly, a book that deals with the feelings and insights of women should be more carefully examined if it is written by a man—unless the book's avowed purpose is to present a strictly male perspective.

8. Check Out the Author's Perspective

No author can be wholly objective. All authors write out of a cultural as well as a personal context. Children's books in the past have traditionally come from authors who are White and who are members of the middle class, with one result being that a single ethnocentric perspective has dominated American children's literature. With the book in question, look carefully to determine whether the direction of the author's perspective substantially weakens or strengthens the value of his/her written book. Are omissions and distortions central to the overall character or "message" of the book?

9. Watch for Loaded Words

A word is loaded when it has insulting overtones. Examples of loaded adjectives (usually racist) are savage, primitive, conniving, lazy, superstitious, treacherous, wily, crafty, inscrutable, docile, and backward.

Look for sexist language and adjectives that exclude or ridicule women. Look for use of the male pronoun to refer to both males and females. While the generic use of the word "man" was accepted in the past, its use today is outmoded. The following examples show how sexist language can be avoided: ancestors instead of forefathers; chairperson instead of chairman; community instead of brotherhood; firefighters instead of firemen; manufactured instead of manmade; the human family instead of the family of man.

10. Look at the Copyright Date

Books on minority themes—usually hastily conceived—suddenly began appearing in the mid-1960s. There followed a growing number of "minority experience" books to meet the new market demand, but most of these were still written by White authors, edited by White editors, and published by White publishers. They therefore reflected a White point of view. Only in the late 1960s and early 1970s did the children's book world begin to even remotely reflect the realities of a multi-racial society. And it has just begun to reflect feminists' concerns.

The copyright dates, therefore, can be a clue as to how likely the book is to be overtly racist or sexist, although a recent copyright date, of course, is no guarantee of a book's relevance or sensitivity. The copyright date only means the year the book was published. It usually takes a minimum of one year—and often much more than that—from the time a manuscript is submitted to the publisher to the time it is actually printed and put on the market. This time lag meant very little in the past, but in a time of rapid change and changing consciousness, when children's book publishing is attempting to be "relevant," it is becoming increasingly significant.

Source: Reprinted with permission from the Bulletin *of the Council on Interracial Books for Children, Inc.*

A Beginning List of Free and Recyclable Materials

Material	Sources	Suggested Uses
Cardboard rolls	Gift-wrapping section of department stores for empty ribbon rolls; paper towel and toilet paper rolls	Tape two together beside each other, add string, and use as binoculars
		Put beans, rice, etc., inside, tape closed, and use as shakers.
		Use as a base for puppets, by adding decorative scraps of material.
		Tape several together lengthwise and use as tunnels for small vehicles.
		Punch holes 2 in. apart, secure wax paper over one end with a rubber band, and you have a flute.
Wood shavings and scraps	Building scrap piles, carpentry shops	
Material remnants	Interior design stores, upholsterers, clothing manufacturers	
Suede and leather scraps	Leather goods stores	
Pieces of styrofoam	Throwaways from drug stores, variety stores, radio and TV stores	Buy a supply of plastic colored golf tees, to be hammered easily into styrofoam chunks—a perfect activity for beginning carpenters.
		Poke sticks, straws, etc., into styrofoam chunks to make a 3-D collage.
Computer paper used on one side	Almost anywhere computers are used	

Material	Sources	Suggested Uses
Used envelopes	Offices, schools, junk mail	Use large envelopes for safe storage of special projects.
		Cut the bottom corners off old envelopes and decorate each as a different finger puppet.
Small boxes	Variety stores, hearing-aid stores, department and stationery stores	Stuff with newspaper and tape shut to make building blocks.
		Cut ⅔ of one side of a flat box (e.g., pudding box), decorate, and fill with scrap paper cut to fit, to make an ideal notepaper holder.
Large boxes	Appliance stores, supermarkets, department stores	Decorate boxes for use as "Treasure Boxes" to store artistic creations.
		Tie boxes together to make a train; large boxes also can turn into houses, cars, boats, etc.
		Use a series of large boxes for making an obstacle course or continuous tunnel.
Plastic lids and containers	Home throwaways	Cut shapes in the lids to use as shape sorters (make shapes from other household "junk").
		Use different sized containers for stacking and nesting toys.
		Add a wooden spoon to a large empty container, with lid, to make a perfect drum.
		Cut interesting shapes in lids and use as stencils for painting or coloring.
Meat trays and aluminum pie plates	Home throwaways	Use as a base for paintings and collages, Christmas ornaments, or table decorations.
		Put them in the bathtub or swimming pool to use as boats in water play.
		Equip older children with a dull needle and yarn to sew color patterns on meat trays.
Milk cartons	Home throwaways	Cut an opening in one side, hang it up, and use as a bird feeder.
		Cut the top off, add a handle, and decorate with ribbon for a springtime basket.

Material	Sources	Suggested Uses
Egg cartons	Home throwaways	Sort small objects into each egg pocket by size, texture, color, etc.
		Fill each egg pocket with earth, plant seeds (e.g., beans), and watch them grow.
		Decorate individual egg pockets and hang upside down for simple but effective bells.
		In the springtime, use separate egg pockets to house chicks made out of cotton balls painted yellow.
		Cut lengthwise and add paint and pipe cleaner legs for a cute caterpillar.
Wide-mouth jars	Home throwaways, recycling centers	Make a mini-terrarium by layering charcoal, potting soil, and humus, dampening the soil, and adding small plants; put the lid in place, but open weekly if too much moisture builds up.
		Glue a 3-D scene to the lid, fill jar with water and sparkles, put lid on, and turn upside down.
Pebbles, leaves, cones, feathers, seed pods, etc.	These natural materials abound; bird refuge for unusual feathers.	Make collages.
		Decorate other items.
Wallpaper sample books	Wallpaper stores	Decorate play areas or dollhouses.
Rug scraps	Carpet and department stores	Decorate dollhouses.
Burlap	Horse-boarding barns	Various art projects
Ticker tape and newsprint rolls and ends	Local newspaper office	
5-gallon ice cream containers	Drive-ins and ice cream stores	
Art papers of various sizes and colors	Print shops	
1- or 2-day animal loans	Local pet shops	

Source: Some materials and sources suggested by the Principles and Practices class, 1972, of Santa Barbara City College, CA; other materials and suggested uses from the resource sheet "Recycling for Fun: Creating Toys and Activities for Children from 'Beautiful Junk'" by the Canadian Child Day Care Federation and the Canadian Association of Toy Libraries and Parent Resource Centres, and from the author's experience.

Activities to Develop Auditory Discrimination

Have the children put their heads down on the table. Display on a nearby shelf or table various instruments: xylophone, cymbals, tambourine, bells, and so forth. While they have their heads down, play one instrument. Children can take turns making the sounds for others to identify.

I was in the kitchen at the sink, and D. was standing at the kitchen gate. He was swinging the gate back and forth so that it would bang against the stopper. As it got louder and louder I was about to tell him to stop when I decided to use this situation for auditory discrimination. We were promptly joined by two other children. First we listened to how loud the gate could bang shut. Then I asked them if they could make it very quiet so that there was not any noise. We did these two opposites several times. Then we started very quietly and got louder and louder and louder. We tried this with our feet stamping on the floor and also clapping our hands. First we did it loud then quiet, then quiet and louder, and then as loud as we could.

Under the table I made different sounds and asked the children to identify them. I used a bell, sandpaper rubbed together, two blocks hit together, scissors opening and closing, and tearing paper. Then I asked one child to make his own sound and let the rest of the children guess what it was.

Using one sound, have the children shut their eyes while you move about the room, and ask the children to point to where you are. Then let the children be the sound makers.

Record on a tape recorder familiar sounds such as a car starting, water running, a train, a door

shutting, a refrigerator door opening or closing, or a toilet flushing (if you use this last one, do it at the end, as it tends to break up the group). Stop at each sound and have the children identify it. For older children play a series of sounds, and see how many they can remember.

I put several things in a box, one at a time, and had the children listen to the sounds: a tennis ball, toothbrush, piece of metal, and a comb. Then I put the box behind my back, put one of the objects in the box, brought it in front of me and rattled it. The children guessed what made the noise.

With my children we listened to the sounds around us when we were outside. We heard the leaves blowing, other children yelling, a car going by, and sand falling. It was fun and made the children really aware of the sounds around them.

I used a triangle with a wooden stick and a metal one. The children listened while I showed them the sticks; then I had them close their eyes and tell me which stick I had used.

Using a xylophone, strike a middle note, then play other notes and ask the children if the new note is higher or lower than the middle one. Also, for degree of loudness, strike the notes hard or lightly and ask the children if the sound is loud or soft.

Material. Cans with tops, small nails, rice, beans, salt. I made up two cans of each material. I had all the cans on the table and went around and asked the children to pick one and shake it. Then I asked them to try and find one that sounded exactly the same. Then we opened the cans to see if the cans really did contain the same ingredient.

The children enjoyed playing this and wanted to have many turns.

Material. Six bottles, same size; one spoon; water. Take two bottles and put the same volume of water in them, then two other bottles with the same volume of water, and finally two more. I covered the bottles with Contact paper so the children would not see how much water each bottle held. Taking turns, the children tried to pick out sounds that matched by hitting the bottle with the spoon. If we were in doubt that the tones matched, we poured the water out and measured it.

In a small group, have one child turn his back and then have the teacher or a selected child point to someone in the group who says something. The child with his back turned guesses who has spoken; then the speaker takes his turn guessing, and the former guesser picks the next speaker.

I let each child draw out an animal picture from the "secret" box, and then they listened to me while I made various animal noises. They brought me the picture when they heard the noise that belonged to their animal. For variety, we played a tape recording of the sounds and had each child wave his card in the air when he heard "his" sound.

An activity for 4-year-olds that fosters auditory discrimination is to take different flannel board pictures in which the words rhyme, for instance, *cat/hat, mouse/house, rug/bug,* and so on. Either put up a few at a time and ask children to pair the ones that rhyme, or have groups of three pictured words and ask the children to remove the one that doesn't rhyme.

For older 4-year-olds, have children stand in a circle and close their eyes. One child moves around the outside of the circle several times and then stops behind one of the children, who guesses whether the child was hopping, jumping, tiptoeing, and so forth.

Source: Suggested by the Language and Cognitive Development classes, 1973, 1976, and 1978, of Santa Barbara City College.

Educational Organizations, Newsletters, and Journals Associated With Early Childhood

Educational Organizations

AAHPER
American Alliance for Health, Physical Education, and Recreation
1201 16th St., NW
Washington, DC 20036

ACEI
Association for Childhood Education International
17904 Georgia Ave., Suite 215
Olney, MD 20832

CCCF
Canadian Child Care Federation/Federation Canadienne des services de garde à l'enfance
30 Rosemont, Suite 100
Ottawa, Ontario K1Y 1P4 Canada

CEC
Council for Exceptional Children
1920 Association Dr.
Reston, VA 22091

Council for Exceptional Children: Division of Early Childhood
1444 Wazee St., Suite 230
Denver, CO 80202

CDF
Children's Defense Fund
1509 16th St., NW
Washington, DC 20036

CWLA
Child Welfare League of America, Inc.
440 First St., NW, Suite 310
Washington, DC 20001

ERIC/ECE
Educational Resources Information Center on Early Childhood Education
805 W. Pennsylvania Ave.
Urbana, IL 61801

NAEYC
National Association for the Education of Young Children
1509 16th St., NW
Washington, DC 20036

OMEP
Organisation Mondiale pour l'Éducation Préscolaire
L. Adams
M. School of Education
East Michigan State University
Ann Harbor, MI 48105

SECA
Southern Early Childhood Association
P.O. Box 55930
Little Rock, AR 72215

Newsletters

The Black Child Advocate
Black Child Development Institute
1023 15th St., NW, Suite 600
Washington, DC 20005

Child Health Alert
P.O. Box 338
Newton Highlands, MA 02161

Journals

Bulletin: Zero to Three
National Center for Infants, Toddlers,
and Families
734 15th St., NW, Suite 1000
Washington, DC 20005

Child Care Information Exchange
17916 NE 103rd Court
Redmond, WA 98032

Child Development
University of Chicago Press
5801 Ellis Ave.
Chicago, IL 60637

Childhood Education
ACEI
17902 Georgia Ave., Suite 215
Olney, MD 20832

Dimensions of Early Childhood
Southern Early Childhood Association
P.O. Box 55930
Little Rock, AR 72215

Early Childhood Education Journal
Human Sciences Press
238 Spring St.
New York, NY 10013

Early Childhood Research Quarterly
National Association for the Education of
Young Children
Ablex Publishing Company
100 Prospect St.
Stamford, CT 06901

Exceptional Children
Council for Exceptional Children
1920 Association Dr.
Reston, VA 22091

The Future of Children
Center for the Future of Children
300 Second St., Suite 102
Los Altos, CA 94022

Journal of Early Childhood Teacher Education
Ablex Publishing Company
100 Prospect St.
Stamford, CT 06901

Journal of Early Intervention
Council for Exceptional Children
1920 Association Dr.
Reston VA 22091

Journal of Research in Childhood Education
Association for Childhood Education International
17904 Georgia Ave., Suite 215
Olney, MD 20832

Nutrition Action
Center for Science in the Public Interest
1875 Connecticut Ave. NW, Suite 300
Washington, DC 20009

Scholastic Early Childhood Today
555 Broadway
New York, NY 10012

Young Children
National Association for the Education of
Young Children
1509 16th St., NW
Washington, DC 20036

Young Exceptional Children
Council for Exceptional Children:
Division for Early Childhood
1444 Wazee St., Suite 230
Denver, CO 80202

Aboud, F. (1988). *Children and prejudice.* Oxford, UK: Basil Blackwell.

Aboud, F. E., & Mendelson, M. J. (1996). Determinants of friendship selection and quality: Developmental perspectives. In W. M. Bukowski, A. F. Newcomb, & W. W. Hartup (Eds.), *The company they keep: Friendship in childhood and adolescence.* New York: Cambridge University Press.

Adler, P. A., & Adler, P. (1988). The carpool: A socializing adjunct to the education experience. In G. Handel (Ed.), *Childhood socialization.* Hawthorne, NY: Aldine.

Ainsworth, M., Blehar, M. C., Waters, E., & Wall, S. (1978). *Patterns of attachment.* Mahwah, NJ: Erlbaum.

Albert, R. E. (1994). *Alejandro's gift.* San Francisco: Chronicle Books.

Aldridge, J., Eddowes, E. A., & Kuby, P. (1998). *No easy answers: Helping children with attention and activity level differences.* Olney, MD: Association for Childhood Education International.

Allen, D. (1998). Trends in demand for center-based child care and early education. *Child Care Information Exchange. #123,* 8–11.

Allen, J. S., & Klein, R. J. (1996). *Ready, set, relax: A research-based program of relaxation, learning, and self-esteem for children.* Watertown, WI: Inner Coaching.

Allen, K. E., & Marotz, L. (1990). *Developmental profiles: Birth to six.* Albany, NY: Delmar.

Allen, Lady of Hurtwood. (1968). *Planning for play.* Cambridge: MIT Press.

Almy, M., Chittenden, E., & Miller, P. (1966). *Young children's thinking.* New York: Teachers College Press.

Amabile, T. (1987). The motivation to be creative. In S. G. K. Isaksen (Ed.), *Frontiers of creative research: Beyond the basics.* Buffalo, NY: Bearly.

Amabile, T. M. (1996). *Creativity in context: Update to The Social Psychology of Creativity.* Boulder, CO: Westview/HarperCollins.

American Academy of Ophthalmology. (1993). *Amblyopia.* San Francisco: Author.

American Psychiatric Association. (1994). *Diagnostic and statistical manual of mental disorders* (4th ed.). Washington, DC: Author.

Andrew, C., & Tracy, N. (1996). First steps toward competence: Promoting self-esteem and confidence in young children with disabilities. In L. E. Powers, G. H. S. Singer, & J. Sowers (Eds.), *On the road to autonomy: Promoting self-competence in children and youth with disabilities.* Baltimore, MD: Brookes.

Andrews, T. (1999). Woodworking: Winning from the beginning. *Oklahoma Child Care, 1,* 28–33.

Antia, S. D., Kriemeyer, K. H., & Eldredge, N. (1994). Promoting social interaction between young children with hearing impairments and their peers. *Exceptional Children, 60*(3), 262–275.

Arbuthnot, M. H., & Root, S. L. (1968). *Time for poetry* (3rd ed.). Glenview, IL: Scott, Foresman.

Areñas, S. (1978). Bilingual/bicultural programs for preschool children. *Children Today, 7*(4), 2–6.

Armstrong, T. (1997). Seeing things in new ways. *Scholastic Early Childhood Today, 11*(5), 32–35.

Arnheim, D. C., & Pestolesi, R. A. (1973). *Developing motor behavior in children: A balanced approach to elementary physical education.* St. Louis, MO: C. V. Mosby.

Arnheim, D. C., & Sinclair, W. A. (1979). *The clumsy child: A program of motor therapy.* St. Louis, MO: C. V. Mosby.

Aronson, S. (1997). Food allergies can be fatal. *Child Care Information Exchange, #118,* 88–91.

Aronson, S. (Ed.). (1998). Child passenger safety: Protecting children and reducing liability in child care. *Child Care Information Exchange, #124,* 86–89.

Aronson, S., & Smith, H. (1993). *Model child care health policies.* Washington, DC: National Association for the Education of Young Children/American Academy of Pediatrics, Pennsylvania Chapter.

Asher, S. R., Oden, S. L., & Gottman, J. M. (1977). Children's friendships in school settings. In L. G. Katz (Ed.), *Current topics in early childhood education* (Vol. 1). Norwood, NJ: Ablex.

Ashton, P. T. (1975). Cross-cultural Piagetian research: An experimental perspective. *Harvard Educational Review, 45*(4), 475–506.

Association for Childhood Education International. (1997). Government study finds more 4- and 5-year-olds overweight. *ACEI Focus on Early Childhood, 9*(4), 3.

Axline, V. (1969). *Play therapy* (Rev. ed.). New York: Ballantine Books.

Ayers, W. (1989). *The good preschool teacher: Six teachers reflect on their lives.* New York: Teachers College Press.

Bagley, C., Verma, G. K., Mallick, K., & Young, L. (1979). *Personality, self-esteem, and prejudice.* Westmead, Farnborough, Hants, UK: Saxon House.

Bailey, B. (1997). *There's gotta be a better way: Discipline that works.* Oviedo, FL: Loving Guidance.

Bailey, B. Z. (1992). "Mommy don't leave me!" Helping toddlers and parents deal with separation. *Dimensions, 20*(3), 25–27, 29.

Bailey, D. B., & Wolery, M. (1992). *Teaching infants and preschoolers*

with disabilities (2nd ed.). Upper Saddle River, NJ: Merrill/Prentice Hall.

Baker, J. L., Piotrkowski, C. S., & Brooks-Gunn, J. (1998). The effects of the Home Instruction Program for Preschool Youngsters (HIPPY) on children's school performance at the end of the program and one year later. *Early Childhood Research Quarterly, 13*(4), 571–588.

Balaban, N. (1984). What do young children teach themselves? In *Early childhood: Reconsidering the research: A collection of papers.* New York: Bank Street College.

Balaban, N. (1989). Trust: Just a matter of time. In J. S. McKee & K. M. Paciorek (Eds.), *Early childhood: 89/90.* Guilford, CT: Dushkin.

Baldwin, S. (1996). *Livesavers: Tips for success and sanity for early childhood managers.* Stillwater, MN: Insights Training and Consulting.

Ballinger, C. (1999). *Teaching other people's children: Literacy and learning in a bilingual classroom.* New York: Teachers College Press.

Bandura, A. (1973). *Aggression: A social learning analysis.* Upper Saddle River, NJ: Merrill/Prentice Hall.

Bandura, A. (1986). *Social learning theory.* Upper Saddle River, NJ: Merrill/Prentice Hall.

Bandura, A. (1997). *Self-efficacy: The exercise of control.* New York: Freeman.

Barata-Lorton, M. (1987). *Workjobs: Activity-centered learning for early childhood education.* Reading, MA: Addison-Wesley.

Barclay, K., & Benelli, C. (1994). Are labels determining practice? Programming for preschool gifted children. *Childhood Education, 70*(3), 25–50.

Barnett, W. S. (1995). Long-term effects of early childhood programs on cognitive and school outcomes. *Future of Children, 5*(3), 25–50.

Barnett, W. S., & Boocock, S. S. (1998). *Early care and education for children in poverty: Promises, programs, and long-term results.* Albany: State University of New York.

Barnett, W. S., & Escobar, C. M. (1990). Economic costs and benefits of early intervention. In S. J. Meisels & J. P. Shonkoff (Eds.), *Handbook of early childhood intervention.* New York: Cambridge University Press.

Batshaw, M. L., & Perret, Y. M. (1992). *Children with disabilities: A medical primer* (3rd ed.). Baltimore, MD: Brookes.

Bauer, K. L., & Dettore, E. (1997). Superhero play: What's a teacher to do? *Early Childhood Education Journal, 25*(1), 17–21.

Baum, S. E., & Cray-Andrews, M. (1983). *Creativity 1, 2, 3.* New York: Trillium Press.

Baumrind, D. (1989). Rearing competent children. In W. Damon (Ed.), *Child development today and tomorrow.* San Francisco: Jossey-Bass.

Beardsley, L. (1990). *Good day bad day: The child's experience of child care.* New York: Teachers College Press.

Beatty, B. (1995). *Preschool education in America: The culture of young children from the colonial era to the present*. New Haven, CT: Yale University Press.

Beaty, J. J. (1995). *Converting conflicts in preschool*. New York: Harcourt Brace.

Beaty, J. J. (1997). *Building bridges with multicultural picture books for children 3–5*. Upper Saddle River, NJ: Merrill/Prentice Hall.

Bedrova, E., & Leong, D. J. (1998). Development of dramatic play in young children and its effects on self-regulation: The Vygotskian approach. *Journal of Early Childhood Teacher Education. 19*(2), 155–124.

Behrman, R. E. (Ed.). (1999). Home visiting: Recent programs evaluation. *Future of Children, 9*(1), entire issue.

Bellenir, K. (Ed.). (1996). *Mental health disorders sourcebook*. Detroit: Omnigraphics.

Bem, S. L. (1993). *The lenses of gender*. New Haven, CT: Yale University Press.

Bender, J. (1978). Large hollow blocks: Relationship of quantity to block building behaviors. *Young Children, 33*(6), 17–23.

Bergen, D. (1988). *Play as a medium for learning and development: A handbook of theory and practice*. Portsmouth, NH: Heinemann.

Berger, E. H. (2000). *Parents as partners in education: Families and schools working together* (5th ed.). Upper Saddle River, NJ: Merrill/Prentice Hall.

Berger, R. (1998). *Stepfamilies: A multi-dimensional perspective*. New York: Haworth.

Berk, L., & Winsler, A. (1995). *Scaffolding children's learning: Vygotsky and early childhood education*. Washington, DC:

National Association for the Education of Young Children.

Berk, L. E. (1976). How well do classroom practices reflect teacher goals? *Young Children, 32*(1), 64–81.

Berkowitz, L. (1993). *Aggression: Its causes, consequences, and control*. Philadelphia: Temple University Press.

Berkson, G. (1993). *Children with handicaps: A review of behavioral research*. Mahwah, NJ: Erlbaum.

Berman, C., & Fromer, J. (1991a). *Meals without squeals*. Palo Alto, CA: Bull.

Berman, C., & Fromer, J. (1991b). *Teaching children about food: A teaching guide and activities guide*. Palo Alto, CA: Bull.

Bernal, E. M., Jr. (1978). The identification of gifted Chicano children. In A. Y. Baldwin, G. H. Gear, & L. J. Lucito (Eds.), *Educational planning for the gifted*. Reston, VA: Council for Exceptional Children.

Bernal, G. R. (1997). How to calm children through massage. *Childhood Education, 74*(1), 9–14.

Bernstein, A. (1994). *The flight of the stork: What children think (and when) about sex and family building*. Indianapolis, IN: Perspectives Press.

Bernstein, B. (1960). Language and social class. *British Journal of Sociology, 11*, 271–276.

Beuf, A. H. (1974). Doctor, lawyer, household drudge. *Journal of Communications, 24*, 142–145.

Beuf, A. H. (1977). *Red children in White America*. Philadelphia: University of Pennsylvania Press.

Beyer, E. (1968). *Teaching young children*. New York: Western.

Biber, B. (1981). The evolution of the developmental-interaction view. In E. K. Shapiro & E. Weber (Eds.), *Cognitive and affective growth: Developmental interaction*. Mahwah, NJ: Erlbaum.

Biber, B. (1984). *Early education and psychological development*. New Haven, CT: Yale University Press.

Birch, L. L. (1980). Effects of peer models' food choices and eating behaviors on preschoolers' food preferences. *Child Development, 51*, 489–496.

Birch, L. L., Johnson, S. L., & Fisher, J. A. (1995). Children's eating: The development of food-acceptance patterns. *Young Children, 50*(2), 71–78.

Birchinal, M., Lee, M., & Ramey, C. (1989). Type of day-care and preschool intellectual development in disadvantaged children. *Child Development, 60*(1), 128–137.

Bisson, J. (1997). *Celebrate! An antibias guide to enjoying holidays in early childhood programs*. St. Paul, MN: Redleaf.

Black, S. M. (1999). HIV/AIDS in early childhood centers: The ethical dilemma of confidentiality versus disclosure. *Young Children, 54*(2), 39–45.

Blake, W. (1978). "The Little Black Boy": Songs of innocence. In G. E. Bentley, Jr., (Ed.), *William Blake's writing* (Vol. 1). Oxford: Clarendon Press. (Original work published 1789)

Blanchard, K. (1992). *The one minute manager*. New York: Berkley Books.

Blank, M., & Solomon, F. A. (1968). A tutorial language program to develop abstract thinking in socially disadvantaged preschool children. *Child Development, 39*(1), 379–390.

Blank, M., & Solomon, F. A. (1969). How shall the disadvantaged child be taught? *Child Development, 40*(1), 48–61.

Blasi, M. J., & Priestley, L. (1998). A child with severe hearing loss joins our learning community. *Young Children, 53*(2), 44–49.

Blecher-Sass, H. (1997). Good-byes can build trust. *Young Children, 52*(7), 12–114.

Block, M. (1994). *A teacher's guide to including students with disabilities in regular physical education.* Baltimore, MD: Brookes.

Blood, C. L., & Link, M. (1980). *The goat in the rug.* New York: Four Winds Press.

Bloom L. (1998). Language acquisition in its developmental context. In D. Kuhn, & R. S. Siegler (Eds.), *Handbook of child psychology* (5th ed.): Vol. 2. *Cognition, perception, and language.* New York: Wiley.

Bond, F. (1983). *Mary Betty Lizzie McNutt's birthday.* New York: Crowell.

Bordin, J. (1998). An abuse allegation: Ten expectations for administrators. *Child Care Information Exchange, #124*, 65–67.

Bos, J. B. (1982). *Please don't move the muffin tins: A hands-off guide to art for the young child.* Carmichael, CA: Burton Gallery.

Boutte, G. S., LaPoint, S., & Davis, B. (1993). Racial issues in education: Real or imagined? *Young Children, 49*(1), 19–23.

Bowlby, J. (1973). *Attachment and loss: Vol. 1. Separation.* New York: Basic Books.

Bowlby, J. (1980). *Loss: Sadness and depression.* New York: Basic Books.

Bowlby, J. (1982). Attachment and loss: Retrospect and prospect. *American Journal of Orthopsychiatry, 52*(4), 664–678.

Bowman, B. T. (1990). Educating language minority children. *ERIC Digest: ERIC Clearinghouse on Elementary and Early Childhood Education* (EDO–PS–90–1).

Boyd, A. (1999). *Guide to multicultural resources 1997–1998.* Atkinson, WI: Highsmith Press.

Bradburn, E. (1989). *Margaret McMillan: Portrait of a pioneer.* London: Routledge.

Bray, M. A., & Kehle, T. J. (1998). Stuttering. In L. A. Phelps (Ed.), *Health-related disorders in children and adolescents.* Washington, DC: American Psychological Association.

Brazelton, T. B. (1992). *Touchpoints: The essential reference: Your child's emotional and behavioral development.* Reading, MA: Addison-Wesley.

Breath, D., DeMauro, G. J., & Snyder, P. (1997). Adaptive sitting for young children with mild to moderate motor challenges: Basic guidelines. *Young Exceptional Children, 1*(1), 10–16.

Bredekamp, S., & Copple, C. (Eds.). (1997). *Developmentally appropriate practice in early childhood* (Rev. ed.). Washington, DC: National Association for the Education of Young Children.

Brett, A., Moore, R. C., & Provenzo, E. B. (1993). *The complete playground book.* Syracuse, NY: Syracuse University Press.

Bricker, D., & Cripe, J. J. W. (1992). *An activity-based approach to early intervention.* Baltimore, MD: Brookes.

Bricker, D., & Widerstrom, A. (Eds.). (1996). *Preparing personnel to work with infants and young children and their families: A team approach.* Baltimore, MD: Brookes.

Briggs, D. (1993). *Toddler storytime programs.* Lanham, MD: Scarecrow Press.

Brittain, W. L. (1979). *Creativity, art, and the young child.* New York: Macmillan.

Brohl, K. (1996). *Working with traumatized children: A handbook for healing.* Washington, DC: Child Welfare League of America.

Brokering, L. (1989). *Resources for dramatic play.* Columbus, OH: Fearon.

Bronfenbrenner, U. (1969). Preface. In H. Chauncey (Ed.), *Soviet preschool education: Vol. 2. Teacher's commentary.* New York: Holt, Rinehart & Winston.

Bronfenbrenner, U. (1979). *The ecology of human development.* Cambridge, MA: Harvard University Press.

Brosterman, N. (1997). *Inventing kindergarten.* New York: Abrams.

Brown, R., & Bellugi, U. (1964). Three processes in the child's acquisition of syntax. *Harvard Educational Review, 34*, 133–151.

Brown, W. H. (1997). Family-centered practices and inclusive early childhood programs. In W. H. Brown & M. A. Conroy (Eds.), *Including and supporting preschool children with development delays in early childhood pro-*

grams. Little Rock, AR: Southern Early Childhood Association.

Brown, W. H., & Conroy, M. A. (Eds.). (1997). *Including and supporting preschool children with developmental delays in early childhood programs.* Little Rock, AR: Southern Early Childhood Association.

Bruner, J. (1983). *Child's talk: Learning to use language.* Oxford, UK: Oxford University Press.

Bruner, J. S. (1964). The course of cognitive growth. *American Psychologist, 19,* 1–15.

Bruner, J. S. (1966). On the conservation of liquids. In J. S. Bruner, R. R. Olver, P. M. Greenfield, et al. (Eds.), *Studies in cognitive growth.* New York: Wiley.

Bruner, J. S. (1978). Learning the mother tongue. *Human Nature, 1*(9), 42–49.

Bugental, D. B., & Goodnow, J. J. (1998). Socialization processes. In W. Damon (Series Ed.) & N. Eisenberg (Vol. Ed.), *Handbook of child psychology* (5th ed.): *Vol. 3. Social, emotional, and personality development.* New York: Wiley.

Bukowski, W. M., Newcomb, A. F., & Hartup, W. W. (Eds.). (1996). *The company they keep: Friendship in childhood and adolescence.* New York: Cambridge University Press.

Bunce, B. H. (1995). *Building a language-focused curriculum for the preschool classroom: Vol. 2. A planning guide.* Baltimore, MD: Brookes.

Burman, E. (1999). Morality and the goals of development. In M. Woodhead, D. Faulkner, & K. Littleton (Eds.), *Making sense of social development.* New York: Routledge.

Burn, J. R. (1989). Express it with puppetry—an international language. In S. Hoffman & L. L. Lamme (Eds.), *Learning from the inside out: The expressive arts.* Wheaton, MD: Association for Childhood Education International.

Butler, A. L., Gotts, E. E., & Quisenberry, N. L. (1978). *Play as development.* Upper Saddle River, NJ: Merrill/Prentice Hall.

Buzzelli, C. (1992). Young children's moral understanding: Learning about right and wrong. *Young Children, 47*(6), 47–83.

Bybee, R. W., & Sund, R. B. (1990). *Piaget for educators* (2nd ed.). Prospect Heights, IL: Waveland Press.

Cadwell, L. B. (1997). *Bringing Reggio Emilia home: An innovative approach to early childhood education.* New York: Teachers College Press.

Campbell, K. C., & Arnold, F. D. (1988). Stimulating thinking and communicating skills. *Dimensions of Early Childhood, 16*(2), 11–13.

Canadian Child Care Federation. (1999). Universal precautions. *Young Children, 54*(2), 40.

Carlsson-Paige, N., & Levin, D. E. (1998). *Before push comes to shove: Building conflict resolution skills with children.* St. Paul, MN: Redleaf.

Carnegie Corporation. (1994). *Starting points: Meeting the needs of our youngest children.* New York: Author.

Carroll, D. W. (1999). *Psychology of language* (3rd ed.). Pacific Grove, CA: Brooks/Cole.

Carta, J. J., Greenwood, C. R., & Atwater, J. B. (1986). *ESCAPE:*

Ecobehavioral system for complex assessments of preschool environments. Unpublished coding manual for observational systems. Kansas City, KS: Juniper Gardens Children's Project.

Carter, B. C., & McGoldrick, M. M. (Eds.). (1999). *The expanded family life cycle: Individual, family, and social perspectives* (3rd ed.). Boston: Allyn & Bacon.

Carter, M. (1994). Finding our voices: The power of telling stories. *Child Care Information Exchange, #98,* 47–50.

Carter, M., & Curtis, D. (1996). *Spreading the news: Sharing the stories of early childhood education.* Beltsville, MD: Gryphon House.

Carter, R. (with Golant, S.). (1998). *Helping someone with mental illness: A compassionate guide for family, friends, and caregivers.* New York: Random House.

Cartwright, S. (1988). Play can be the building blocks of learning. *Young Children, 43*(5), 44–47.

Cassidy, J. C. & Shaver, P. R. (1999). *Handbook of attachment: Theory, research, and clinical applications.* New York: Guilford.

Cauley, K., & Tyler, B. (1989). The relationship of self-concept to prosocial behavior in children. *Early Childhood Research Quarterly, 41,* 51–60.

Cazden, C. (1970). Children's questions: Their forms, functions, and roles in education. *Young Children, 25*(4), 202–220.

Cazden, C. (1972). *Child language and education.* New York: Holt, Rinehart & Winston.

Cazden, C. B. (1974). Paradoxes of language structure. In K. Connolly & J. Bruner (Eds.). *The growth of competence.* San Diego: Academic Press.

Center on Hunger, Poverty, and Nutrition Policy. (1998). *Statement on the link between nutrition and cognitive development in children.* Medford, MA: Center on Hunger, Poverty, and Nutrition Policy & Tufts University.

Centers for Disease Control and Prevention (CDC). (1996). Asthma mortality and hospitalization among children and young adults. *Morbidity and Mortality Weekly Report, 45,* 350–353.

Ceppi, G., & Zini, M. (1998). *Children, spaces, relations: Metaproject for an environment for young children.* Reggio Emilia, Italy: Comune di Reggio Emilia/Ministero della Pubblica Istruzione.

Chaillé, C., & Young, P. (1980). Some issues linking research on children's play and education: Are they "only playing"? *International Journal of Early Childhood, 12*(2), 53–55.

Charner, K. (1996). *The giant encyclopedia of circle time and group activities for children 3 to 6: Over 600 favorite circle time activities created by teachers for teachers.* Beltsville, MD: Gryphon House.

Check playgrounds for safety. (1996). *Oklahoma Child Care, 3,* 18-19.

Chenfield, M. B. (1993). *Teaching in the key of life.* Washington, DC: National Association for the Education of Young Children.

Chenfield, M. B. (1995). *Creative activities for young children* (2nd ed.). Fort Worth, TX: Harcourt Brace.

Cherry, C. (1981). *Think of something quiet: A guide for achieving serenity in early childhood classrooms.* Belmont, CA: Pitman Learning.

Child abuse. (1999, April). *Education Week,* p. 6.

Child Care Information Exchange. (1998a). Supporting multiracial children and families. *Child Care Information Exchange, #122,* 53–62.

Child Care Information Exchange. (1998b). Trends in federal support for child care. *Child Care Information Exchange: Insider's Report #6.*

Child Care Information Exchange. (1998c). Update on for-profit child care. *Child Care Information Exchange: Inside Child Care Report #2.*

Child Care Law Center. (1994). *Caring for children with special needs: The Americans with Disabilities Act and child care.* San Francisco: Author.

Child immunizations hit all-time high. (1997). *CDF Reports, 18*(11), 10–11.

Children's Defense Fund. (1998). *The state of America's children: Yearbook, 1998.* Washington, DC: Author.

Children's Defense Fund. (1999). *Psst—Good news for the children you care for! Your state now offers free or low-cost health insurance for children!* Washington, DC: Author.

Chomsky, N. (1968). *Language and mind.* New York: Harcourt Brace.

Chomsky, N. (1981). *Lectures on government and binding.* Dordrect, The Netherlands: Foris.

Christian, L. G. (1997). Children and death. *Young Children, 52*(4), 76–80.

Christie, J. F., & Wardle, F. (1992). How much time is needed for play? *Young Children, 47*(3), 28–32.

Ciancollo, P. J. (1997). *Picture books for children* (4th ed.). New York: American Library Association.

Cicerelli, V. G., Evans, J. W., & Schiller, J. S. (1969). *The impact of Head Start on children's cognitive and affective development: Preliminary report* (PB 184). Washington, DC: Office of Economic Opportunity.

Clark, K. B. (1963). *Prejudice and your child* (2nd ed.). Boston: Beacon Press.

Clifford, R. M. (1998). Who's in charge? *Young Children, 53*(3), 2–3.

Cochran, M. (Ed.). (1993). *International handbook of child care policies and programs.* Westport, CT: Greenwood Press.

Cohen, A. J. (1996). A brief history of federal financing for child care in the United States. *Future of Children, 6*(2), 26–40.

Cohen, A. J. (1998). Caring for mildly ill children: Limiting your legal liability. *Child Care Information Exchange, #119,* 101–105.

Cohen, S. (1998). *Targeting autism: What we know, don't know, and can do to help young children with autism and related disorders.* Berkeley: University of California Press.

Coie, J. D., & Kupersmidt, J. A. (1983). A behavioral analysis of emerging social status in boys groups. *Child Development, 54,* 1400–1416.

Coie, J. D. & Dodge, K. A. (1998). Aggression and antisocial behavior. In W. Damon (Series Ed.) &

N. Eisenberg (Vol. Ed.), *Handbook of child psychology* (5th ed.): *Vol. 3. Social, emotional, and personality development*. New York: Wiley.

Cole, C. L., & Arndt, K. (1998). Autism. In L. A. Phelps (Ed.), *Health-related disorders in children and adolescents*. Washington, DC: American Psychological Association.

Coll, C. G., Surrey, J. L., & Weingarten, K. (1998). *Mothering against the odds: Diverse voices of contemporary mothers*. New York: Guilford.

Collins, L., Ingoldsby, B., & Dellmann, M. (1984). Sex role stereotyping in children's literature: A change from the past. *Childhood Education, 60,* 278–285.

Coltrane, S. (1998). *Gender and families*. Thousand Oaks, CA: Pine Forge Press.

Consumer Product Safety Commission. (1997). *A handbook for public playground safety*. Washington, DC: Author.

Cook, R. E., Tessier, A., & Klein, M. D. (2000). *Adapting early childhood curricula for children with special needs* (5th ed.). Upper Saddle River, NJ: Merrill/Prentice Hall.

Conroy, M. A., Langenbrunner, M. R., & Burleson, R. B. (1996). Suggestions for enhancing the social behaviors of preschoolers with disabilities using developmentally appropriate practices. *Dimensions of Early Childhood, 24*(1), 9–15.

Coopersmith, S. (1967). *The antecedents of self-esteem*. San Francisco: Freeman.

Coopersmith, S. (1975). Building self-esteem in the classroom. In S. Coopersmith (Ed.), *Developing motivation in young children*. San Francisco: Albion.

Copeland, M. L., & McCreedy, B. S. (1997). Creating family-friendly policies. *Child Care Information Exchange, #113,* 7–12.

Coplan, R. J., & Rubin, K. H. (1998). Social play. In D. P. Fromberg, & D. Bergen (Eds.), *Play from birth to twelve and beyond: Contexts, perspectives, and meanings*. New York: Garland.

Corsaro, W. A. (1988). Children's conception and reaction to adult rules: The underlife of the nursery school. In G. Handel (Ed.), *Childhood socialization*. Hawthorne, NY: Aldine.

Cosaro, W. A. (1997). *The sociology of childhood*. Thousand Oaks, CA: Pine Forge Press.

Council for Early Childhood Professional Recognition. (1997). *The Child Development Associate national credentialing program: Making a difference in the early care and education of young children: General information*. Washington, DC: Author.

Cox, B., & Jacobs, M. (1991). *Spirit of the harvest: North American Indian cooking*. New York: Stewart, Tabori & Chang.

Cox, F. N., & Campbell, D. (1968). Young children in a new situation, with and without their mothers. *Child Development, 39,* 123–131.

Cox, M. (1997). *Drawings of people by the under-5's*. London: Falmer Press.

Cox, M. V. (1991). *The child's point of view: The development of cogni-*

tion and language (2nd ed.). New York: Guilford.

Cratty, B. J., & Martin, M. M. (1969). *Perceptual-motor efficiency in children: The measurement and improvement of movement attributes*. Philadelphia: Lea & Febiger.

Crocker, A. C., Cohen, H. J., & Kastner, T. A. (Eds.). (1992). *HIV infection and developmental disabilities: A resource for service providers*. Baltimore, MD: Brookes.

Crocker, B. (1993). *Betty Crocker's Mexican made easy*. Upper Saddle River, NJ: Prentice Hall.

Crosse, S. B., Kaye, E., & Ranofsky, A. C. (1992). *A report on the maltreatment of children with disabilities*. Washington, DC: U.S. Department of Health and Human Services, Administration on Children, Youth and Family, National Center on Child Abuse and Neglect.

Crosser, S. (1994). Making the most of water play. *Young Children, 49*(5), 28–32.

Cryer, D., Ray, A. R., & Harms, T. (1996). *Nutrition activities for preschoolers*. Menlo Park, CA: Addison-Wesley.

Csikszentmihalye, M. (1996). *Creativity: Flow and the psychology of discovery and invention*. New York: HarperCollins.

Cunningham, B. (1999). Men in child care, Part 2: Hiring and retaining male staff. *Child Care Information Exchange, #125,* 66–69.

Cunningham, C. (1996). *Understanding Down syndrome: An introduction for parents*. Cambridge, MA; Brookline Books.

Curtis, D., & Carter, M. (1996). *Reflecting children's lives: A handbook for planning child-centered curriculum.* St. Paul, MN: Redleaf.

Dacey, J. S., & Lennon, K. H. (1998). *Understanding creativity: The interplay of biological, psychological, and social factors.* San Francisco: Jossey-Bass.

Dahl, K. (1998). Why cooking in the classroom? *Young Children, 53*(1), 81–83.

Damon, W. (1995). *Greater expectations: Overcoming the culture of indulgence in America's homes and schools.* New York: Free Press.

Daniel, J. E. (1998). A modern mother's place is wherever her children are: Facilitating infants and toddlers mothers' transitions in child care. *Young Children, 53*(6), 4–12.

Davidson, J. (1996). *Emergent literacy and dramatic play in early education.* Albany, NY: Delmar.

Davis, C. (1939). Results of the self-selection of diets by young children. *Canadian Medical Association Journal, 4,* 257–261.

Davis, L., & Keyser, J. (1997). *Becoming the parent you want to be: A sourcebook of strategies for the first five years.* New York: Broadway Books.

Davis, M., Eshelman, E. R., & McKay, M. (1995). *The relaxation and stress reduction workbook* (4th ed.). Oakland, CA: New Harbinger.

Dellmann-Jenkins, M., Florjancic, L., & Swadener, E. B. (1993). Sex roles and cultural diversity in recent award winning picture books for young children. *Journal of Research in Childhood Education, 7*(2), 74–82.

De Mesquita, P. B., & Fiorella, C. A. (1998). Asthma (childhood). In L. A. Phelps (Ed.), *Health-related disorders in children and adolescents.* Washington, DC: American Psychological Association.

Dennis, R. E., & Giangreco, M. G. (1996). Creating conversation: Reflections on cultural sensitivity in family interviewing. *Exceptional Children, 63*(1), 103–116.

Dennis, W. (1960). Causes of retardation among institutional children: Iran. *Journal of Genetic Psychology, 96,* 47–59.

De Oliveira, M. K., & Valsiner, J. (1998). *Literacy in human development.* Norwood, NJ: Ablex.

Derman-Sparks, L. (1993/1994). Empowering children to create a caring culture in a world of differences. *Childhood Education, 70*(2), 66–71.

Derman-Sparks, L. (1995). Children and diversity. *Scholastic Early Childhood Today, 10*(3), 42–45.

Derman-Sparks, L., & ABC Task Force. (1989). *Anti-bias curriculum: Tools for empowering young children.* Washington, DC: National Association for the Education of Young Children.

Derman-Sparks, L., Higa, C. T., & Sparks, B. (1980). Children, race, and racism: How race awareness develops. *Interracial Books for Children Bulletin, 11*(3/4), 3–9.

Derman-Sparks, L., & Phillips, C. B. (1997). *Teaching/learning antiracism: A developmental approach.* New York: Teachers College Press.

Deskin, G. D., & Steckler, G. (1996). *When nothing makes sense: Disaster, crisis, and their effects on children.* Minneapolis, MN: Fairview Press.

Desrochers, J. (1999). Vision problems: How teachers can help. *Young Children, 54*(2), 36–38.

DeVilliers, P. A., & DeVilliers, J. G. (1992). Language development. In M. H. Bornstein & M. E. Lamb (Eds.), *Developmental psychology: An advanced textbook* (3rd ed.). Mahwah, NJ: Erlbaum.

DeVries, R., & Kohlberg, L. (1990). *Constructivist early education: Overview and comparison with other programs.* Washington, DC: National Association for the Education of Young Children.

DeVries, R., & Zan, B. (1994). *Moral children, moral classrooms: Creating a constructivist atmosphere in early education.* New York: Teachers College Press.

DeVries, R., & Zan, B. (1996). A constructivist perspective on the role of the sociomoral atmosphere in promoting children's development. In C. T. Fosnot (Ed.), *Constructivism: Theory, perspectives, and practice.* New York: Teachers College Press.

Diamond, K. E. (1993). Preschool children's concepts of disability in their peers. *Early Education and Development, 4*(2), 123–129.

Diamond, K. E., Hestenes, L. L. & O'Connor, C. E. (1994). Research in review: Integrating young children with disabilities in preschool: Problems and promise. *Young Children, 49*(2), 68–75.

Dietz, W. H., & Stern, L. (1999). *American Academy of Pediatrics guide to your child's nutrition: Making peace at the table and building healthy eating habits for life.* New York: Villard.

Diffily, D., & Morrison, K. (Eds.). (1996). *Family friendly communication for early childhood programs.* Washington, DC: National Association for the Education of Young Children.

Dighe, J., Calomiris, Z., & Van Zutphen, C. (1998). Interpreting the Reggio approach in American preschools. *Young Children, 53*(1), 4–9

Dougy Center for Grieving Children. (1997). *Helping children cope with death.* Portland, OR: Author.

Dougy Center for Grieving Children. (1999, April 18). *Norman Oklahoma Transcript.*

Dowell, R. I. (1987). *Move over, Mother Goose: Finger plays, action verses, and funny rhymes.* Beltsville, MD: Gryphon House.

Drew, E. (1997, Spring). From the guest editor. *Play, Policy & Practice Connections, 6,* 7.

Duncan, G. J., & Brooks-Gunn, J. (Eds.). (1997). *Consequences of growing up poor.* New York: Russell Sage Foundation.

Dunkle, J. L., & Edwards, M. S. (1992). *The no-leftovers child care cookbook.* St. Paul, MN: Redleaf.

Dunn, J., & Kendrick, C. (1981). The arrival of a sibling: Changes in patterns of interaction between mother and first-born children. In S. Chess & A. Thomas (Eds.), *Annual progress in child psychiatry and child development 1981.* New York: Brunner/Mazel.

Dunst, C. (1995). *Key characteristics and features of community-based family support.* Chicago: Family Resource Coalition.

Eastman, P. D. (1960). *Are you my mother?* New York: Random House.

Eaton, M. (1997). Positive discipline: Fostering the self-esteem of young children. *Young Children, 52*(6) 43–46.

Edelstein, S. (1992). *Nutrition and meal planning in child-care programs: A practical guide.* Chicago: American Dietetic Association.

Edwards, C., Gandini, L., & Forman, G. (Eds.). (1993). *The hundred languages of children: The Reggio Emilia approach to early childhood education.* Norwood, NJ: Ablex.

Edwards, C., Gandini, L., & Forman, G. (Eds.). (1998). *The hundred languages of children: The Reggio Emilia approach— Advanced reflections.* Norwood, NJ: Ablex.

Edwards, C. P. (1980). The comparative study of the development of moral judgment and reasoning. In R. L. Munroe, R. Munroe, & B. B. Whiting (Eds.), *Handbook of cross-cultural human development.* New York: Garland.

Eisenberg, N. (1992). *The caring child.* Cambridge, MA: Harvard University Press.

Eisenberg, N. (Ed.). (1998). *Handbook of child psychology: Vol. 3. Social, emotional, and personality development.* New York: Wiley.

Eisenberg, N., & Fabes, R. A. (1998). Prosocial development. In W. Damon (Series Ed.) & N. Eisenberg (Vol. Ed.), *Handbook of child psychology* (5th ed.): *Vol. 3. Social, emotional, and personality development.* New York: Wiley.

Eisenberg, N., Fabes, R. A., & Losoya, S. (1997). Emotional responding: Regulation, social correlates, and socialization. In P. Salovey & S. D. J. Sluyter (Eds.), *Emotional development and emotional intelligence: Educational implications.* New York: Basic Books.

Eisenberg, N., McCreath, H., & Ahn, R. (1988). Vicarious emotional responsiveness and prosocial behavior: Their interrelations in young children. *Personality and Social Psychology Bulletin, 19,* 848–855.

Eisenberg, N., & Mussen, P. (1989). *The roots of prosocial behavior in children.* New York: Cambridge University Press.

Eisenberg, N., Shell, R., Pasternack, J., Lennon, R., Beller, R., & Mathy, R. M. (1987). Prosocial development in middle childhood: A longitudinal study. *Developmental Psychology, 23,* 712–718.

Elias, M. (1999, December 14). Surgeon general finds many barriers to treatment. *USA Today.*

Elkind, D. (1987). *Miseducation: Preschoolers at risk.* New York: Knopf.

Ellis, R. (1994). *The study of second language acquisition.* New York: Oxford University Press.

Ellsworth, J., & Ames, L. J. (1998). *Critical perspectives on Head Start.* Albany: State University of New York.

Emery, R. E., & Forehand, R. (1994). Parental divorce and children's well-being: A focus on resilience. In R. J. Haggerty, L. R. Sherrod, N. Garmezy, & M. Rutter (Eds.), *Stress, risk, and resilience in children and adolescents: Processes, mechanisms, and interventions.* New York: Cambridge University Press.

Endres, J. B., & Rockwell, R. E. (1993). *Food, nutrition, and the young child* (4th ed.). Upper Saddle River, NJ: Merrill/Prentice Hall.

English, D. J. (1998). The extent and consequences of child maltreatment. *Future of Children,* 8(1), 39–53.

Epilepsy Foundation of America. (n.d.). *Epilepsy.* Landover, MD: Author.

Erikson, E. (1950). *Childhood and society.* New York: Norton.

Erikson, E. (1963). *Childhood and society* (2nd ed.). New York: Norton.

Erikson, E. (1958). *The good man Luther.* New York: Norton.

Erikson, E. H. (1959). Identity and the life cycle. *Psychological Issues,* 1(1), Monograph 1.

Erikson, E. H. (1971). A healthy personality for every child. In R. H. Anderson & H. G. Shane (Eds.), *As the twig is bent: Readings in early childhood education.* Boston: Houghton Mifflin.

Erikson, E. H. (1982). *The life cycle completed: A review.* New York: Norton.

Ervin-Tripp, S., & Gordon, D. (1986). The development of requests. In R. L. Schiefelbusch (Ed.), *Language competence: Assessment and intervention.* San Diego: College Hill Press.

Essa, E. L., & Murray, C. I. (1999). Sexual play: When should you be concerned? *Childhood Education,* 75(4), 231–234.

Evers, W. L., & Schwarz, J. C. (1973). Modifying social withdrawal in preschoolers: The effects of filmed modeling and teacher praise. *Journal of Abnormal Child Psychology, 1,* 248–256.

Faber, A., & Mazlish, E. (1980). *How to talk so kids will listen, & listen so kids will talk.* New York: Avon Books.

Fabes, R. A., & Eisenberg, N. (1992). Young children's coping with interpersonal anger. *Child Development, 63,* 116–128.

Fagot, B. I. (1977). Consequences of moderate cross-gender behavior in preschool children. *Child Development, 48,* 902–907.

Fagot, B. I. (1994). Peer relations and the development of competence in boys and girls. *New Directions for Child Development, 65,* 53–65.

Fagot, B. I., & Leinbach, M. D. (1993). Gender-role development in young children: From discrimination to labeling. *Developmental Review, 13,* 205–224.

Feeney, S., & Freeman, N. K. (1999). *Ethics and the early childhood educator: Using the NAEYC code.* Washington, DC: National Association for the Education of Young Children.

Fenichel, E. (Ed.). (1997). Some kids have dads and some don't, right? Wrong. *Zero to Three, 18*(1), entire issue.

Ferber, R. (1985). *Solve your child's sleep problems.* New York: Simon & Schuster.

Feshbach, N., & Feshbach, S. (1972). Children's aggression. In W. W. Hartup (Ed.), *The young child: Reviews of research* (Vol. 2). Washington, DC: National Association for the Education of Young Children.

Fields, M., & Spangler, K. L. (2000). *Let's begin reading right: Developmentally appropriate beginning literacy* (4th ed.). Upper Saddle River, NJ: Merrill/Prentice Hall.

Fishman, J. A. (Ed.). (1999). *Handbook of language and ethnic identity.* New York: Oxford University Press.

Fitzgerald, H. E., Lester, B. M., & Zuckerman, B. S. (Eds.). (1999). *Children of color: Research, health, and policy issues.* New York: Garland.

Flack, M. (1932). *Ask Mr. Bear.* New York: Simon & Schuster.

Flavell, J. H., Miller, P. H., & Miller, S. A. (1993). *Cognitive development* (3rd ed.). Upper Saddle River, NJ: Merrill/Prentice Hall.

Folb, E. A. (1980). *Runnin' down some lines: The language and culture of black teenagers.* Cambridge, MA: Harvard University Press.

Fontana, V. J., & Besharov, D. J. (1996). *The maltreated child: The maltreatment syndrome in children: A medical, legal, and social guide* (5th ed.). Springfield, IL: Charles C Thomas.

Forman, G. E., & Hill, F. (1980). *Constructive play: Applying Piaget in the preschool.* Monterey, CA: Brooks/Cole.

Fosnot, C. T. (Ed.). (1996). *Constructivism: Theory, perspectives, and practice.* New York: Teachers College Press.

Fowler, M. (1994). *Briefing paper: Attention-deficit/hyperactivity disorder.* Washington, DC: National Information Center for Children and Youth with Disabilities.

Fraiberg, S. (1977). *Insights from the blind.* New York: Basic Books.

Frieman, B. B. (1998). What early childhood educators need to know about divorced fathers. *Early Childhood Education Journal, 25*(4), 239–241.

Froebel, F. (1889). *Autobiography of Friedrich Froebel* (E. Michaelis & K. Moore, Trans.). Syracuse, NY: Bardeen.

Fromberg, D. P. (1997). What's new in play research? *Child Care Information Exchange, #118,* 53–56.

Fromberg, D. P., & Bergen, D. (1998). *Play from birth to twelve and beyond: Contexts, perspectives, and meanings.* New York: Garland.

Frost, J. (1992). *Play and playscapes.* Albany, NY: Delmar.

Fuhr, J. E., & Barclay, K. H. (1998). The importance of appropriate nutrition and nutrition education. *Young Children, 53*(1), 74–80.

Fuller, M. L., & Olsen, G. (Eds.). (1998). *Home-school relations: Working successfully with parents and families.* Boston: Allyn & Bacon.

Furman, E. (1974). *A child's parent dies: Studies in childhood bereavement.* New Haven, CT: Yale University Press.

Furman, E. (1982). Helping children cope with death. In J. M. Brown (Ed.), *Curriculum planning for young children.* Washington, DC: National Association for the Education of Young Children.

Future of Children. (1995). 5(3), entire issue.

The future of children: Financing child care. (1996). *Future of Children, 6*(2), entire issue.

The future of children: Protecting children from abuse and neglect. (1998). *Future of Children, 4*(1), entire issue.

Gagné, R. (1968). Contributions of learning to human development. *Psychological Review, 73*(3), 177–185.

Gaines, L. (1998). Creative movement in the early childhood curriculum. *Scholastic Early Childhood Today, 12*(4), 45–47.

Galdone, P. (1981). *Three billy goats gruff.* New York: Ticknor & Fields.

Galdone, P. (1985). *The three bears.* New York: Ticknor & Fields.

Gallahue, D. H., & Ozmun, J. C. (1998). *Understanding motor development: Infants, children, adolescents and adults* (4th ed.). New York: McGraw-Hill.

Gallivan-Fenlon, A. (1994). Integrated interdisciplinary teams. *Teaching Exceptional Children, 26*(3), 16–20.

Gambetti, A. (1993). *The cloud project.* Conference at Wayne State University, Traverse City, MI.

Garcia, E. E. (1990, Fall). Bilingualism, cognition, and academic performance: The educational debate. *Houghton Mifflin/Educator's Forum,* 6–7.

Garcia, E. E., & August, D. (1988). The education of language minority students. Springfield, IL: Charles C Thomas.

Garcia, E. E., & McLaughlin, B. (1995). *Meeting the challenge of linguistic and cultural diversity in early childhood education.* New York: Teachers College Press.

Gardner, H. (1986). Notes on cognitive development: Recent trends, new directions. In S. L. Friedman, K. A. Klivington, & R. W. Peterson (Eds.), *The brain, cognition, and education.* San Diego: Academic Press.

Garvey, C. (1977). *Play.* Cambridge, MA: Harvard University Press.

Garvey, C. (1979). Communicational controls in social play. In B. Sutton-Smith (Ed.), *Play and learning.* New York: Gardner Press.

Gaston, M. (1990). *Sickle cell anemia* (#90–3058). Washington, DC: National Institutes of Health, Clinical Center Communications.

Gelb, M. J. (1998). *How to think like Leonardo da Vinci.* New York: Delacourt Press.

George, B., & Tomasello, M. (1984/85). The effect of variation in sentence length on young children's attention and comprehension. *First Language, 5,* 115–128.

Gerber, A. (1993). *Language-related learning disabilities: Their nature and treatment.* Baltimore, MD: Brookes.

Gesell, A., Halverson, H. M., Thompson, H., & Ilg, F. (1940). *The first five years of life: A guide to the study of the preschool child.* New York: Harper & Row.

Getzels, J. W., & Jackson, P. W. (1962). *Creativity and intelligence.* New York: Wiley.

Ghazvini, A. S., & Readdick, C. A. (1994). Parent-caregiver communication and quality of care in diverse child care settings. *Early Childhood Research Quarterly, 9*(2), 207–222.

Glueck, S., & Glueck, E. (1950). *Unraveling juvenile delinquency.* Cambridge, MA: Harvard University Press.

Godwin, L. J., Groves, M. M., & Horm-Wingerd, D. M. (1994). Don't leave me! Separation distress in infants, toddlers, and parents. In K. M. Paciorek & J.

H. Munro (Eds.), *Early childhood education 94/95* (15th ed.). Guilford, CT: Dushkin.

Goffin, S. G. (1994). *Curriculum models and early childhood education: Appraising the relationship.* Upper Saddle River, NJ: Merrill/Prentice Hall.

Goldman, L. E. (1996). We can help children grieve: A child-oriented model for memorializing. *Young Children, 51*(6), 69–73.

Goleman, D. (1995). *Emotional intelligence.* New York: Bantam Books.

Gonzalez-Mena, J. (1976). English as a second language for preschool children. *Young Children, 32*(1), 14–19.

Gonzalez-Mena, J. (1998). *The child in family and community* (2nd ed.). Upper Saddle River, NJ: Merrill/Prentice Hall.

Goodson, B. D. (1982). The development of hierarchic organization: The reproduction, planning, and perception of multiarch block structures. In G. E. Forman (Ed.), *Action and thought: From sensorimotor schemes to symbolic operations.* San Diego: Academic Press.

Goodwin, C. J. (1999). *A history of modern psychology.* New York: Wiley.

Gordon, S. A. M., Thomas, J. M., Pfeil, D. K., Guerra, F. A., Stephens, K., & Neugebauer, B. (1997). Beginnings workshop: "Mealtimes." *Child Care Information Exchange, #115,* 39–58.

Graves, M. (1989). *The teacher's idea book: Daily planning around the key experiences.* Ypsilanti, MI: High/Scope.

Graves, M. (1998). *Planning around children's interests: The teacher's idea book 2.* Ypsilanti, MI: High/Scope.

Gray, S. W., Ramsey, B. K., & Klaus, R. A. (1982). *From 3 to 20: The Early Training Project.* Baltimore, MD: University Park Press.

Green, A. B. (1997). Personal communication. In B. Bailey, *There's gotta be a better way: Discipline that works.* Oviedo, FL: Loving Guidance.

Green, A. B. (1997). Physical abuse of children. In J. M. Wiener (Ed.), *Textbook of child and adolescent psychiatry* (2nd ed.). Washington, DC: American Psychiatric Press.

Greenberg, J., Pyszcynski, T., & Solomon, S. (1995). Toward a dual-motive depth psychology of self and social behavior. In M. H. Kernis (Ed.), *Efficacy, agency, and self-esteem.* New York: Plenum Press.

Greenberg, M. T., & Snell, J. L. (1997). Brain development and emotional development: The role of teaching in organizing the frontal lobe. In P. Salovey & D. J. Sluyter (Eds.), *Emotional development and emotional intelligence.* New York: Basic Books.

Greenberg, P. (1992). *The devil has slippery shoes: A biased biography of the Child Development Group of Mississippi.* Washington, DC: Youth Policy Institute. (Original work published 1970)

Greenberg, S. (1985). Educational equity in early education environments. In S. S. Klein (Ed.), *Handbook for achieving sex equity through education.* Baltimore, MD: Johns Hopkins University Press.

Greenman, J. (1993). It ain't easy being green. *Child Care Information Exchange, #91,* 36–40.

Greenman, J. (1998a). Can't find it, can't get to it, can't use it. In J. Greenman (Ed.), *Places for childhoods: Making quality happen in the real world.* Redmond, WA: Child Care Information Exchange.

Greenman, J. (1998b). *Caring spaces, learning places: Children's environments that work.* Redmond, WA: Exchange Press.

Greenman, J. (1998c). A guide to equipping the developmentally appropriate center. In J. Greenman (Ed.), *Places for childhoods: Making quality happen in the real world.* Redmond, WA: Child Care Information Exchange.

Greenman, J. (1998d). *Places for childhoods: Making quality happen in the real world.* Redmond, WA: Child Care Information Exchange.

Greenspan, S. (1998). Recognizing and responding to language delays. *Scholastic Early Childhood Today, 13*(1), 67–69.

Greenspan, S. (1999). Six stages to a strong self-image. *Scholastic Early Childhood Today, 14*(1), 42–46.

Greenspan, S. I., & Greenspan, N. T. (1985). *First feelings: Milestones in the emotional development of your baby and child.* New York: Viking.

Greenspan, S. I., & Wieder, S. (1998). *The child with special needs: Encouraging intellectual and emotional growth.* Reading, MA: Addison-Wesley.

Griffin, A. (1998). Infant/toddler sleep in the child care context: Patterns, problems, and relationships. *Zero to Three Bulletin: Babies, Parents and Sleep, 19*(2), 24–29.

Griffin, C., & Rinn, B. (1998). Enhancing outdoor plan with an obstacle course. *Young Children, 53*(3), 18–23.

Gruenberg, A. (1998). Creative stress management: "Put your own oxygen mask on first." *Young Children, 53*(1), 38–42.

Grusec, J. E., & Arnason, L. (1982). Consideration for others: Approaches to enhancing altruism. In S. G. Moore & C. R. Cooper (Eds.), *The young child: Reviews of research* (Vol. 3). Washington, DC: National Association for the Education of Young Children.

Guilford, J. P. (1981). Developmental characteristics: Factors that aid and hinder creativity. In J. C. Gowan, J. Khatena, & E. P. Torrance (Eds.), *Creativity: Its educational implications* (2nd ed.). Dubuque, IA: Kendall/Hunt.

Gundersen, B. H., Melås, P. S., & Skår, J. E. (1981). Sexual behavior of preschool children: Teachers' observations. In L. L. Constantine & F. M. Martinson (Eds.), *Children and sex: New findings, new perspectives*. Boston: Little, Brown.

Gunnar, J. R. (1996). *Quality of care and the buffering of stress physiology: Its potential in protecting the developing human brain*. Minneapolis: University of Minnesota Institute of Child Development.

Guralnick, M. J. (Ed.). (1996). *The effectiveness of early intervention*. Baltimore, MD: Brookes.

Guralnick, M. J. (1999). The nature and meaning of social integration for young children with mild developmental delays in inclusive settings. *Journal of Early Intervention, 22*(1), 70–86

Guralnick, M. J., & Groom, J. M. (1987). The peer relations of

mildly delayed and nonhandicapped preschool children in mainstream playgroups. *Child Development, 58*, 1556–1572.

Hainstock, E.G. (1997). *The essential Montessori: An introduction to the woman, the writings, the method, and the movement*. New York: Plume.

Hakuta, K. (1998). Improving education for all children: Meeting the needs of language minority children. In D. Clark (Moderator), *Education and the development of American youth*. Washington, DC: Aspen Institute.

Hakuta, K., & Garcia, E. E. (1989). Bilingualism and education. *American Psychologist, 44*(2), 374–379.

Hall, C., & Lynn, G. (1999, February 2). USA Snapshots: American mix. *USA Today*, p. 1.

Hannaford, C. (1995). *Smart moves: Why learning is not all in your head*. Arlington, VA: Great Ocean.

Hannigan, I. (1998). *Off to school: A parent's eye view of the kindergarten year*. Washington, DC: National Association for the Education of Young Children.

Harms, T., & Clifford, R. M. (1980). *Early childhood environment rating scale*. New York: Teachers College Press.

Hart, B., & Risley, T. R. (1995). *Meaningful differences in the everyday experience of young American children*. Baltimore, MD: Brookes.

Hart, L. (1996). The winning family. *Child Care Information Exchange, #126*, 83.

Harter, S. (1998). The development of self-representation. In W. Damon (Series Ed.) & N. Eisen-

berg (Vol. Ed.), *Handbook of child psychology* (5th ed.): *Vol. 3. Social, emotional, and personality development*. New York: Wiley.

Hartup, W. W. (1977). Peer relationships: Developmental implications and interaction in same- and mixed-age situations. *Young Children, 32*(3), 4–13.

Hartup, W. W. (1992). Having friends, making friends, and keeping friends: Relationships in educational contexts. *ERIC Digest: ERIC Clearinghouse on Elementary and Early Childhood Education* (EDO–PS–92–4).

Hartup, W. W., Glazer, J. A., & Charlesworth, R. (1967). Peer reinforcement and sociometric status. *Child Development, 38*, 1017–1024.

Haslett, B. B., & Sampter, W. (1997). *Children communicating: The first 5 years*. Mahwah, NJ: Erlbaum.

Haugland, S. (1999). Computers and young children: The newest software that meets the developmental needs of young children. *Early Childhood Education Journal, 26*(4), 245–254.

Haugland, S., & Wright, D. (1997). *Young children and computers: A world of discovery*. Boston: Allyn & Bacon.

Hauser-Cram, P. (1998). I think I can, I think I can: Understanding and encouraging mastery motivation in young children. *Young Children, 53*(4), 67–71.

Hawkridge, D., Chalupsky, A., & Roberts, A. (1968). *A study of selected exemplary programs for the education of disadvantaged children*. Palo Alto, CA: American Institutes for Research in the Behavioral Sciences.

Head Start Bureau. (1992). *Multicultural principles for Head Start programs.* Washington, DC: U.S. Department of Health and Human Services.

Head Start Bureau. (1998). *Head Start fact sheet.* Washington, DC: Author.

Healy, J. M. (1998). *Failure to connect: How computers affect our children's minds—for better or worse.* New York: Simon & Schuster.

Heath, S. B. (1989). Oral and literate traditions among Black Americans living in poverty. *American Psychologist, 44*(2), 367–373.

Hecht, M. L., Collier, M. J., & Ribeau, S. A. (1993). *African American communication: Ethnic identity and cultural interpretation.* Newbury Park, CA: Sage.

Hegde, M. N., & Davis, D. (1995). *Clinical methods and practicum in speech-language pathology.* San Diego: Singular.

Helburn, S. (1995). *Cost, quality, and child outcomes in child care centers.* Denver: University of Colorado.

Helfer, R. E., & Kempe, C. H. (1987). *The battered child* (4th ed.). Chicago: University of Chicago Press.

Hendrick, J. (1975). *The whole child: New trends in early education.* St. Louis, MO: C. V. Mosby.

Hendrick, J. (Ed.). (1997). *First steps toward teaching the Reggio way.* Upper Saddle River, NJ: Merrill/Prentice Hall.

Hendrick, J. (1998). *Total learning: Developmental curriculum for the young child* (5th ed.). Upper Saddle River, NJ: Merrill/Prentice Hall.

Hendrick, J., & Stange, T. (1991). Do actions speak louder than words? An effect of the functional use of language on dominant sex role behavior in boys and girls. *Early Childhood Research Quarterly, 6*(4), 656–676.

Hendrick, J. B. (1973). *The cognitive development of the economically disadvantaged Mexican American and Anglo American four-year-old: Teaching the concepts of grouping, ordering, perceiving common connections, and matching by means of semantic and figural materials.* Doctoral dissertation, University of California, Santa Barbara.

Hendricks, G., & Wills, R. (1975). *The centering book: Awareness activities for children, parents and teachers.* Upper Saddle River, NJ: Prentice Hall.

Herman, F., & Smith, J. C. (1992). *Creatability: Creative arts for preschool children with special needs.* Tucson, AZ: Communication Skill Builders.

Herzog, E., & Sudia, C. E. (1973). Children in fatherless homes. In B. E. Caldwell & H. N. Ricciuti (Eds.), *Review of child development research* (Vol. 3). Chicago: University of Chicago Press.

Hetherington, E. M. (1992). Coping with marital transitions: A family systems perspective. In E. M. Hetherington & W. G. Clingempeel (Eds.), Coping with marital transitions. *Monographs of the Society for Research in Child Development, #227, 57*(2–3).

Hetherington, E. M. (1999a). *Coping with divorce, single parenting, and remarriage: A risk and resiliency perspective.* Mahwah, NJ: Erlbaum.

Hetherington, E. M. (1999b). Should we stay together for the sake of the children? In E. M. Hetherington (Ed.), *Coping with divorce, single parenting, and remarriage: A risk and resiliency perspective.* Mahwah, NJ: Erlbaum.

Hetherington, E. M., Stanley-Hagen, M., & Anderson, E. R. (1989). Marital transitions: A child's perspective. *American Psychologist, 44*(2), 303–312.

Hewes, D. (1998). *It's the camaraderie: A history of parent cooperative preschools.* Davis: University of California, Center for Cooperatives.

Hewitt, D., & Heidemann, S. (1998). *The optimistic classroom: Creative ways to give children hope.* St. Paul, MN: Redleaf.

Hewitt, F. (1995). *So this is normal too?* St. Paul, MN: Redleaf.

Hildebrand, V., Phenice, L. A., Gray, M. M., & Hines, R. P. (2000). *Knowing and serving diverse families* (2nd ed.). Upper Saddle River, NJ: Merrill/Prentice Hall.

Hill, P. S. (1992). *Kindergarten.* Olney, MD: Association for Childhood Education International. (Original work published 1942)

Hill, S. A. (1996). Caregiving in African American families: Caring for children with sickle cell disease. In S. C. Logan (Ed.), *The Black family: Strengths, self-help, and positive change.* Boulder, CO: Westview/HarperCollins.

Hirsch, E. S. (Ed.). (1996). *The block book* (3rd ed.). Washington, DC: National Association for the Education of Young Children.

Hirsh-Pasek, K. A., Hyson, M. C., & Rescorla, L. (1990). Academic environments in preschool: Do they pressure or challenge young children? *Early Education and Development, 1*(6), 401–423.

Hobbs, T., & Westling, D. L. (1998). Inclusion, inclusion, inclusion: Promoting successful inclusion through collaborative problem-solving. *Teaching Exceptional Children, 31*(1), 12–19.

Hodges, W. (1987). Teachers-children: Developing relationships. *Dimensions, 15*(4), 12–14.

Hoffman, M. L. (1970). Moral development. In P. H. Mussen (Ed.), *Carmichael's manual of child psychology* (Vol. 2). New York: Wiley.

Hoffman, M. L. (1975). Moral internalization, parental power, and the nature of parent-child interaction. *Developmental Psychology, 11*, 228–239.

Hoffman, M. L. (1984). Empathy, its limitations and its role in a comprehensive moral theory. In W. M. Kurtines & J. L. Gewirtz (Eds.), *Morality, moral behavior, and moral development.* New York: Wiley.

Hohmann, M., & Weikart, D. (1995). *Educating young children: Active learning practices for preschool and child care.* Ypsilanti, MI: High/Scope.

Holzman, M. (1997). *The language of children* (2nd ed.). Oxford, UK: Basil Blackwell.

Hom, H. L., Jr., & Hom, S. L. (1980). Research and the child: The use of modeling, reinforcement/incentives, and punishment. In D. G. Range, J. R. Layton, & D. L. Roubinek (Eds.), *Aspects of early childhood education: Theory to research to practice.* San Diego: Academic Press.

Honig, A. S. (1982). Language environments for young children. *Young Children, 38*(1), 56–67.

Honig, A. S. (1985). Compliance, control, and discipline. *Young Children, 40*(2), 50–58.

Honig, A. S., & Lansburgh, T. (1994). The tasks of early childhood: The development of self-control—Part II. In K. M. Paciorek & J. H. Munro (Eds.), *Early childhood education 94/95.* Guilford, CT: Dushkin.

Honigman, J., & Bhavnagri, N. P. (1998). Painting with scissors: Art education beyond production. *Childhood Education, 74*(4), 205–212.

Hopkins, S. & Winerts, J. (1990). *Discover the world: Empowering children to value themselves, others, and the earth.* Philadelphia, PA: New Society.

Hosfield, D. (1998). A long day in care need not seem long. *Young Children, 53*(3), 24–28.

Housman, A. E. (1922). *Last poems, XII.*

Howes, C. (1988). Peer interaction of young children. *Monographs of the Society for Research in Child Development, 53*(1), #217.

Howes, C., & Phillipsen, C. (1992). Gender and friendship: Relationships within peer groups of young children. *Social Development, 1,* 231–242.

Hulit, L. M. (1996). *Straight talk on stuttering: Information, encouragement, and counsel for stutterers, caregivers, and speech-language clinicians.* Springfield, IL: Charles C Thomas.

Humphrey, H. H. (1977, November 1). Speech delivered at the dedication of the Hubert H.

Humphrey Building for the U.S. Department of Health, Education and Welfare, Washington, DC.

Humphrey, J. H. (1993). *Stress management for elementary schools.* Springfield, IL: Charles C Thomas.

Humphrey, J. H. (1998). *Helping children manage stress: A guide for adults.* Washington, DC: Child and Family Press.

Humphryes, J. (1998). The developmental appropriateness of high-quality Montessori programs. *Young Children, 53*(4), 4–24.

Hurwitz, S. C. (1998). War nurseries: Lessons in quality. *Young Children, 53*(5), 37–39.

Hyman, I. A. (1997). *The case against spanking: How to discipline your child without hitting.* San Francisco: Jossey-Bass.

Hyson, M. C. (1994). *The emotional development of young children: Building an emotion-centered curriculum.* New York: Teachers College Press.

Hyson, M. C., & Hirsch-Pasek, K. A. (1990). Some recent Spencer studies: Academic environments in early childhood: Challenge or pressure? *The Spencer Foundation Newsletter, 5*(1), 2–3.

Ianotti, R., Zahn-Waxler, C., Cummings, E. M., & Milano, M. (1987, April). *The development of empathy and prosocial behavior in early childhood.* Paper presented at American Educational Research Association, Washington, DC.

Ignico, A. A. (1991). Physical education for Head Start children: A field-based study. *Early Child Development and Care, 77,* 77–92.

Imhoff, G. (Ed.). (1990). *Learning two languages: From conflict to consensus in the reorganization of the schools.* New Brunswick, NJ: Transaction Publishing.

Important facts about pediatric emergency care. (1993). *Children Today, 22*(3), 3.

Infant Health and Development Program. (1990). Enhancing the outcomes of low birth-weight, premature infants: A multisite, randomized trial. *Journal of the American Medical Association, 263*(22), 3035–3042.

Inhelder, B. (1968, Fall). *Recent trends in Genevan research.* Paper presented at Temple University, Philadelphia.

Irwin, R. T., & Moore, S. G. (1971). The young child's understanding of social justice. *Developmental Psychology, 5*(3), 406–410.

Isbell, R. T., & Raines, S. C. (1991). Young children's oral language production in three types of play centers. *Journal of Research in Childhood Education, 5*(2), 140–146.

Isenberg, J. P., & Jalongo, M. R. (1997). *Creative expression and play in early childhood* (2nd ed.). Upper Saddle River, NJ: Merrill/Prentice Hall.

Isom, B. A., & Casteel, C. P. (1997/98). Hispanic literature: A fiesta for literacy instruction. *Childhood Education, 74*(2), 83–89.

Jacklin, C. N., & Baker, L. A. (1993). Early gender development. In S. Oskamp & M. Costanzo (Eds.), *Gender issues in contemporary society.* Newbury Park, CA: Sage.

Jacobs, N. L., Changler, T. M., & Hausknecht, D. R. (1996).

Unraveling the mystery of parents' work. *Early Childhood Education Journal, 24*(1), 61–64.

Jacobson, E. (1991). *You must relax.* New York: National Foundation for Progressive Relaxation.

Jacobson, J. W., & Mulick, M. A. (Eds.). (1996). *Manual of diagnosis and professional practice in mental retardation.* Washington, DC: American Psychological Association.

Jacobson, L. (1998, August 5). Hispanic children outnumber young Blacks for the first time. *Education Week,* p. 6.

Jalongo, M. R. (1988). *Young children and picture books: Literature from infancy to six.* Washington, DC: National Association for the Education of Young Children.

Jalongo, M. R. (1997). Multicultural children's literature: Resources for teachers. *Early Childhood Education Journal, 25*(1), 51–52.

Jalongo, M. R., & Collins, M. (1985). Singing with young children: Folk singing for nonmusicians. *Young Children, 40*(2), 17–22.

Jalongo, M. R., & Stamp, L. N. (1997). *The arts in children's lives: Aesthetic education in early childhood.* Boston: Allyn & Bacon.

James, A., Jenks, C., & Prout, A. (1998). *Working children: Theorizing childhood.* New York: Teachers College Press.

James, S. L. (1990). *Normal language acquisition.* Boston: Allyn & Bacon.

Jarrell, R. H. (1998). Play and its influence on the development of young children's mathematical thinking. In D. P. Fromberg & D. Bergen (Eds.), *Play from birth to*

twelve and beyond: Contexts, perspectives, and meanings.* New York: Garland.

Johnsen, E. P., & Peckover, R. B. (1988). The effects of play period duration on children's play patterns. *Journal of Research in Childhood Education, 3*(2), 123–131.

Johnson, J. E., & Roopnarine, J. L. (1983). The preschool classroom and sex differences in children's play. In M. B. Liss (Ed.), *Social and cognitive skills: Sex roles and children's play.* San Diego: Academic Press.

Johnson, L. G., Rogers, C. K., Johnson, P., & McMillan, R. P. (1993). *Overcoming barriers associated with the integration of early childhood settings.* Presented at the conference of the National Association for the Education of Young Children, Anaheim, CA.

Johnson-Powell, G., & Yamamoto, J. (Eds.). (1997). *Transcultural child development: Psychological assessment and treatment.* New York: Wiley.

Jones, E., & Nimmo, J. (1994). *Emergent curriculum.* Washington, DC: National Association for the Education of Young Children.

Jorde, P. (1982). *Avoiding burnout: Strategies for managing time, space, and people in early childhood education.* Washington, DC: Acropolis Books.

Kagan, J. (1981). *The second year: The emergence of self-awareness.* Cambridge, MA: Harvard University Press.

Kagan, S. L., & Bowman, B. T. (Eds.). (1997). *Leadership in early care and education.* Washington, DC: National Association for the Education of Young Children.

Kagan, S. L., & Cohen, N. E. (1996). *Reinventing early care and education: A vision for a quality system.* San Francisco: Jossey-Bass.

Kaiser, B., & Rasminsky, J. S. (1995). *HIV/AIDS and child care: Fact book.* Ottawa, Ontario: Canadian Child Care Federation & Health Canada.

Kaiser, B., & Rasminsky, J. S. (1999). *Meeting the challenge: Effective strategies for challenging behaviors in early childhood environments.* Ottawa, Ontario: Canadian Child Care Federation.

Kalter, N. (1990). *Growing up with divorce: Helping your child avoid immediate and later emotional problems.* New York: Free Press.

Kamii, C. (1975). One intelligence indivisible. *Young Children, 30*(4), 228–238.

Kamii, C. (1982). *Number in preschool and kindergarten: Educational implications of Piaget's theory.* Washington, DC: National Association for the Education of Young Children.

Kamii, C. (1985). *Young children reinvent arithmetic: Implications of Piaget's theory.* New York: Teachers College Press.

Kampe, E. (1990). Children in health care: When the prescription is play. In E. Klugman & S. Smilansky (Eds.), *Children's play and learning: Perspectives and policy implications.* New York: Teachers College Press.

Kanner, L. (1944). Early infantile autism. *Journal of Pediatrics, 25,* 211–217.

Kantor, R., Elgas, R. M., & Fernie, D. E. (1993). Cultural knowledge and social competence within a preschool peer culture group. *Early Childhood Research Quarterly, 8*(2), 125–147.

Kaplan, P. (1992). *A child's odyssey* (2nd ed.). New York: West.

Karnes, M. (1994). Outdoor play for children with special needs. *Scholastic Early Childhood Today, 8*(8), 55.

Karnes, M. B., & Johnson, L. J. (1989). Training for staff, parents, and volunteers working with gifted young children, especially those with disabilities and from low-income homes. *Young Children, 44*(3), 49–56.

Karnes, M. B., & Johnson, L. J. (1991). The preschool/primary gifted child. *Journal for the Education of the Gifted, 14*(3), 267–283.

Katz, L. (1991). Keynote address at the Reggio Conference, Oklahoma City, OK.

Katz, L. (1997). *Fostering children's social competence: The teacher's role.* Washington, DC: National Association for the Education of Young Children.

Katz, L., & Chard, S. C. (1991). Engaging children's minds: The project approach. Norwood, NJ: Ablex.

Katz, L., & McClellan, D. E. (1997). *Fostering children's social competence: The teacher's role.* Washington, DC: National Association for the Education of Young Children.

Katz, L. G. (1993). *Distinctions between self-esteem and narcissism: Implications for practice.* Urbana, IL: ERIC Clearinghouse on Elementary and Early Childhood Education.

Katz, L. G. (1994). All about me. In K. M. Paciorek, & J. H. Munro (Eds.), *Early childhood education, 93/94.* Guilford, CT: Dushkin.

Katzen, M., & Henderson, A. (1994). *Pretend soup and other real recipes: A cookbook for preschoolers and up.* Berkeley, CA: Tricycle Press.

Kelly, N. T., & Kelly, B. J. (1997). *Physical education for preschool and primary grades.* Springfield, IL: Charles C Thomas.

Kempe, C. E. (1962). The battered child syndrome. *Journal of the American Medical Association, 181*(17), 17–24.

Kemple, K. M., & Hartle, L. (1997). Getting along: How teachers can support children's peer relationships. *Early Childhood Education Journal, 24*(3), 139–146.

Kendrick, A. S., Kaufman, R., & Messenger, K. P. (Eds.). (1995). *Healthy young children: A manual for programs* (Rev. ed.). Washington, DC: National Association for the Education of Young Children.

Kent, J. (1983). *Silly goose.* Upper Saddle River, NJ: Prentice Hall.

Kessler, J. W., Gridth, A., & Smith, E. (1968). *Separation reactions in young mildly retarded children.* Paper presented at the annual convention of the American Orthopsychiatric Association, Boston.

Kinch, A. F., & Schweinhart, L. J. (1999). Making child care work for everyone: Lessons from the Program Recognition Project. *Young Children, 54*(1), 68–73.

King, J. R. (1998). *Uncommon caring: Learning from men who teach young children.* New York: Teachers College Press.

Kingston, J. F., Thompson, R. H., Allen, K. E., Boettcher, C., Collins, T., & Goldberger, J. (1996). Implementing play in hospitals: Values and viewpoints. In A. L. Phillips (Ed.), *Topics in early childhood education: Playing for keeps: Supporting children's play.* St. Paul, MN: Redleaf.

Kinnell, G. (Ed.). (1995). *Toilet learning in group care: A resource for child care programs and parents.* Syracuse, NY: Child Care Council of Onondaga County, Toilet Learning Task Force.

Kinnell, G. (Ed.). (1998). *Addressing the biting dilemma: A resource for child care programs serving toddlers.* Syracuse, NY: Child Care Council of Onondaga County, Task Force on Biting.

Kinsman, C. A., & Berk, L. E. (1979). Joining the block and housekeeping areas: Changes in play and social behavior. *Young Children, 35*(1), 66–75.

Kirk, E. W., & Stroud, J. E. (1997). Water, sand, and so much more. *Oklahoma Child Care, 1,* 14–20.

Kirk, S. A. (1972). *Educating exceptional children* (2nd ed.). Boston: Houghton Mifflin.

Kliman, G. (1968). *Psychological emergencies of childhood.* New York: Grune & Stratton.

Kline, P. (1988). *The everyday genius: Restoring children's natural joy of learning—and yours too.* Arlington, VA: Great Ocean.

Koblinsky, S., Atkinson, J., & Davis, S. (1980). Sex education with young children. *Young Children, 36*(1), 21–31.

Koch, P. K., & McDonough, M. (1999). Improving parent-teacher conferences through collaborative conversations. *Young Children, 54*(2), 11–15.

Kochanska, G., Casey, R. J., & Fukumoto, A. (1995). Toddlers' sensi-tivity to standard violations. *Child Development, 66,* 64–656.

Kochanska, G., & Thompson, R. A. (1997). The emergence and development of conscience in toddlerhood and early childhood. In J. E. Grusec & L. Kuczynski (Eds.), *Parenting and children's internalization of values: A Handbook of contemporary theory.* New York: Wiley.

Kohl, H. (1984). *Growing Minds: On Becoming a Teacher.* New York: Harper & Row.

Kohl, M. F. (1989). *Mudworks: Creative clay, dough, and modeling experiences.* Bellingham, WA: Bright Ring.

Kohlberg, L. (1969). Stage and sequence: The cognitive-developmental approach to socialization. In D. A. Goslin (Ed.), *Handbook of socialization theory and research.* Chicago: Rand McNally.

Kohn, A. (1993). *Punished by rewards: The trouble with gold stars, incentive plans, A's, praise, and other bribes.* Boston: Houghton Mifflin.

Kohn, A. (1996). *Beyond discipline: From compliance to community.* Alexandria, VA: Association for Supervision and Curriculum Development.

Koplow, L. (1996). *Unsmiling faces: How preschools can heal.* New York: Teachers College Press.

Koralek, D. (1992). *Caregivers of young children: Preventing and responding to child maltreatment.* Washington, DC: U.S. Department of Health and Human Services.

Koralek, D. G., Colker, L. J., & Dodge, D. T. (1993). *The what, why, and how of high-quality early childhood education: A guide for on-site supervision.* Washington, DC: National Association for the Education of Young Children.

Kosnik, B. (1993). Everyone is a V.I.P. in this class. *Young Children, 49*(1), 32–37.

Kostelnik, M. J., Whiren, A. P., & Stein, L. C. (1986). Living with he-man: Managing superhero fantasy play. *Young Children, 41*(4), 3–9.

Koster, J. B. (1999). Clay for little fingers. *Young Children, 54*(2), 18–22.

Koulouras, K., Porter, M. L., & Senter, S. A. (1986, July). Making the most of parent conferences. *Child Care Information Exchange, 50.*

Kranowitz, C. S. (1994). Kids gotta move: Adapting movement experiences for children with differing abilities. *Child Care Information Exchange, 5*(94), 37.

Kritchevsky, S., & Prescott, E. (1977). *Planning environments for young children: Physical space.* Washington, DC: National Association for the Education of Young Children.

Labov, W. (1970). The logic of non-standard English. In F. Williams (Ed.), *Language and poverty.* Chicago: Markham.

Lakeshore Learning Materials. (n.d.). *Multicultural cooking with kids.* Carson, CA: Lakeshore Equipment.

Lally, R. (1998). Brain research, infant learning, and child care curriculum. *Child Care Information Exchange, #121,* 46–48.

Lamb, S. (1993). First moral sense: An examination of the appearance of morally related behaviors in the second year of life. *Journal of Moral Education, 22,* 97–109.

Landreth, G., & Homeyer, L. (1998). Play as the language of children's feelings. In D. P. Fromberg & D. Bergen (Eds.), *Play from birth to twelve and beyond: Contexts, perspectives, and meanings.* New York: Garland.

Lansdown, R. (1996). *Children in hospital: A guide for family and careers.* New York: Oxford University Press.

Larson, N., Henthorne, M., & Plum, B. (1994). *Transition magician: Strategies for guiding young children in early childhood programs.* St. Paul, MN: Redleaf.

Lavatelli, C. S. (1970a). *Early childhood curriculum: A Piaget program.* Boston: American Science and Engineering.

Lavatelli, C. S. (1970b). *Piaget's theory applied to an early childhood curriculum.* Boston: American Science and Engineering.

Lazar, I., & Darlington, R. (1978). *Summary: Lasting effects after preschool: Final report to the Education Commission of the States.* Urbana, IL: ERIC/ECE.

Lazar, I., & Darlington, R. (1982). Lasting effects of early education: A report from the Consortium for Longitudinal Studies. *Monographs of the Society for Research in Child Development, 47*(2–2), #195.

Lazar, I., Darlington, R., Murray, H., Royce, J., & Snipper, A. (1982). Lasting effects of early education: A report from the Consortium for Longitudinal Studies. *Monographs of the Society for Research in Child Development, 47*(2–3, Serial No. 195).

Lazar, I., Hubbell, V. R., Murray, H., Rosche, M., & Royce, J. (1977). *Summary report: The persistence of preschool effects* (OHDS 78–30129). Washington, DC: U.S. Department of Health, Education and Welfare.

Leacock, E. (1982). The influence of teacher attitudes on children's classroom performance: Case studies. In K. M. Borman (Ed.), *The social life of children in a changing society.* Mahwah, NJ: Erlbaum.

Lectenberg, R. (1984). *Epilepsy and the family.* Cambridge, MA: Harvard University Press.

Lee, E., Menkart, D., & Okazawa-Rey, M. (Eds.). (1998). *Beyond heroes and holidays: A practical guide to K–12 anti-racist, multicultural education and staff development.* Washington, DC: Network of Educators on the Americas.

Lee, F. Y. (1985). Asian parents as partners. *Young Children, 50*(3), 4–9.

Lee, L. C. (1973, August). *Social encounters of infants: The beginnings of popularity.* Paper presented at the International Society for the Study of Behavioral Development, Ann Arbor, MI.

Lehrer, P. M., & Woolfolk, R. L. (Eds.). (1993). *Principles and practice of stress management* (2nd ed.). New York: Guilford.

Leight, L. (1988). *Raising sexually healthy children: A loving guide for parents, teachers, and caregivers.* New York: Avon Books.

Leonhard, B. (1963). Paper presented at the NAEYC Workshop, Santa Barbara.

Leonhard, G. J. (Ed.). (1999). *The Asian Pacific American heritage: A companion to literature and arts.* New York: Garland.

Levin, D. E. (1998). *Remote control childhood? Combating the hazards of media culture.* Washington, DC: National Association for the Education of Young Children.

Levin, D. E., & Carlsson-Paige, N. (1995). The Mighty Morphin Power Rangers: Teachers voice concern. *Young Children, 50*(6), 67–72.

Lieberman, J. H. (1968). Playfulness and divergent thinking ability: An investigation of their relationship at the kindergarten level. In M. Almy (Ed.), *Early childhood play: Selected readings related to cognition and motivation.* New York: Simon & Schuster.

Lightfoot, D. (1999). *The development of language: Acquisition, change, and evolution.* Oxford, UK: Basil Blackwell.

Lillard, A. S. (1998). Play with a theory of mind. In O. N. Saracho & B. Spodek (Eds.), *Multiple perspectives on play in early childhood education.* Albany: State University of New York Press.

Linder, T. W. (1993). *Transdisciplinary play-based intervention: Guidelines for developing a meaningful curriculum for young children.* Baltimore, MD: Brookes.

Lionni, L. (1987). *Swimmy.* New York: Knopf.

Lively, V., & Lively, E. (1991). *Sexual development of young children.* Albany, NY: Delmar.

Livingston, M. C. (1994). *Animals, vegetables, minerals: Poems about small things.* New York: HarperCollins.

Loeffler, M. H. (Ed.). (1992). *Montessori in contemporary Amer-*

ican culture. Portsmouth, NH: Heinemann.

Lonigan, C. J., & Whitehurst, G. J. (1998). Relative efficacy of parent and teacher involvement in a shared-reading intervention for preschool children from low-income backgrounds. *Early Childhood Research Quarterly, 113*(2), 263–290.

Lopez, A. (1996). Creation is ongoing: Developing a relationship with non-English-speaking parents. *Child Care Information Exchange, #107,* 56–62.

Lord, C. (1982). Psychopathology in early development. In S. G. Moore & C. R. Cooper (Eds.), *The young child: Reviews of research* (Vol. 3). Washington, DC: National Association for the Education of Young Children.

Lorenz, K. (1966). *On aggression.* New York: Harcourt, Brace & World.

Love, J. M., & Logue, M. E. (1992). *Final report of the National Transition Study: Transitions to kindergarten in American schools: Executive summary.* Washington, DC: Author.

Lowenfeld, V., & Brittain, W. L. (1987). *Creative and mental growth* (6th ed.). New York: Macmillan.

Lubeck, S. (1985). *Sandbox society: Early education in Black and White America.* Philadelphia: Falmer.

Maccoby, E. E. (1980). *Social development: Psychological growth and the parent-child relationship.* New York: Harcourt Brace Jovanovich.

Maccoby, E. E. (1999). The uniqueness of the parent-child relationship. In C. Coll, W. A. Collins, & B. Lauren (Eds.), *Relationships as developmental contexts: The Minnesota Symposia on Child Psychology* (Vol. 30). Mahwah, NJ: Erlbaum.

Maccoby, E. E., & Jacklin, C. N. (1980). Sex differences in aggression: A rejoinder and reprise. *Child Development, #512,* 964–980.

MacDonald, S. (1996). *Squish, sort, paint, & build: Over 200 easy learning center activities.* Beltsville, MD: Gryphon House.

Macfarlane, J. W. (1943). Study of personality development. In R. G. Barker, J. S. Kounin, & H. F. Wright (Eds.), *Child behavior and development.* New York: McGraw-Hill.

Macnamara, J. (1966). *Bilingualism in primary education: A study of Irish experience.* Edinburgh: Edinburgh University Press.

Maker, C. J. (Ed.). (1989). *Critical issues in gifted education: Defensible programs for cultural and ethnic minorities.* Austin, TX: PRO-ED.

Malaguzzi, L. (1992). *A message from Loris Malaguzzi: An interview by Lella Gandini, April, 1992, La Villetta School, Reggio Emilia.* Amherst, MA: Performanetics.

Malaguzzi, L. (1998). History, ideas, and basic philosophy: An interview with Lella Gandini. In C. Edwards, L. Gandini, & G. Forman (Eds.), *The hundred languages of children: The Reggio Emilia approach—Advanced reflections.* Norwood, NJ: Ablex.

Mallory, B. L., & New, R. S. (Eds.). (1993). *Diversity & developmentally appropriate practices: Challenges for early childhood educa-tion.* New York: Teachers College Press.

Maratsos, M. (1998). The acquisition of grammar. In D. Kuhn & R. S. Siegler (Eds.), *Handbook of child psychology* (5th ed.): *Vol. 2. Cognition, perception, and language.* New York: Wiley.

Marcon, R. A. (1992). Differential effects of three preschool models on inner-city 4-year-olds. *Early Childhood Research Quarterly, 7*(4), 517–530.

Marcon, R. A. (1994a). Doing the right thing for children: Linking research and policy reform in the District of Columbia Public Schools. *Young Children, 50*(1), 8–20.

Marcon, R. A. (1994b). *Early learning and early identification follow-up study: Transition from the early to later childhood grades: 1990–1993.* Washington, DC: District of Columbia Public Schools.

Margolin, E. (1968). Conservation of self-expression and aesthetic sensitivity in young children. *Young Children, 23,* 155–160.

Marion, M. (1997). Research in review: Guiding young children's understanding and management of anger. *Young Children, 52*(7), 62–67.

Marion, M. (1998). Guidance of young children (5th ed.). Upper Saddle River, NJ: Merrill/Prentice Hall.

Marshall, N. L., Robeson, W. W., & Keefe, N. (1999). Gender equity in early childhood education. *Young Children, 54*(4), 9–13.

Martin, H. P. (1976). *The abused child: A multidisciplinary approach to developmental issues and treatment.* Cambridge, MA: Ballinger.

Mash, E. J., & Barkley, R. Q. (Eds.). (1998). *Treatment of childhood disorders* (2nd ed.). New York: Guilford.

Masters, W. H., Johnson, V. E., & Kilodny, R. C. (1994). *Heterosexuality.* New York: HarperCollins.

McAfee, O. (1976). To make or buy. In M. D. Cohen & S. Hadley (Eds.), *Selecting educational equipment and materials for home and school.* Wheaton, MD: Association for Childhood Education International.

McAfee, O. D. (1985). Circle time: Getting past "Two Little Pumpkins." *Young Children, 40*(6), 24–29.

McAfee, O. D., & Leong, D. (1994). *Assessing and guiding young children's development and learning.* Boston: Allyn & Bacon.

McCadden, B. (1998). *It's hard to be good: Moral complexity, construction, and connection in a kindergarten classroom.* New York: Lang.

McCord, W., McCord, J., & Howard, A. (1961). Familial correlates of aggression in nondelinquent male children. *Journal of Abnormal Social Psychology, 62,* 79–93.

McCurdy, H. G. (Ed.). (1966). *Barbara: The unconscious autobiography of a child genius.* Chapel Hill: University of North Carolina Press.

McKay, M., & Fanning, P. (1996). *The daily relaxer.* Oakland, CA: New Harbinger.

McKey, R. H., Condelli, L., Ganson, H., Barrett, B. J., McConkey, C., & Plantz, M. C. (1985). *The impact of Head Start on children, families, and communities: Final report of the Head Start Evaluation, Synthesis, and Utilization Project.* Washington, DC: CSR Incorporated for the Head Start Bureau, ACYF, U.S. Department of Health and Human Services.

McLane, J. B., & McNamee, G. D. (1990). *Early literacy.* Cambridge, MA: Harvard University Press.

McLaughlin, B. (1987). *Theories of second language learning.* London: Arnold.

McLeod, N. S., & Wright, C. (1996). Developmentally appropriate criteria for evaluating sexual abuse prevention programs. *Early Childhood Education Journal, 24*(2), 71–74.

McLoyd, V. (1986). Scaffolds or shackles? The role of toys in preschool children's pretend play. In G. Fein & M. Rivkin (Eds.), *The young child at play: Reviews of research* (Vol. 4). Washington, DC: National Association for the Education of Young Children.

McMillan, M. (1929). *What the open-air nursery school is.* London: Labour Party.

McNamee, G. D. (1990). Learning to read and write in an inner-city setting: A longitudinal study of community change. In L. C. Moll (Ed.), *Vygotsky and education: Instructional implications and applications of sociohistorical psychology.* New York: Cambridge University Press.

McTear, M. (1985). *Children's conversations.* Oxford, UK: Basil Blackwell.

Meeker, M. N., Sexton, K., & Richardson, M. O. (1970). *SOI abilities workbook.* Los Angeles: Loyola-Marymount University.

Meisels, S. J., & Atkins-Burnett, C. (1994). *Developmental screening in early childhood: A guide.* Washington, DC: National Association for the Education of Young Children.

Menyuk, P. (1963). Syntactic structures in the language of children. *Child Development, 34,* 407–422.

Michael, R. J. (1995). *The educator's guide to students with epilepsy.* Springfield, IL: Charles C Thomas.

Micklethwait, L. (1993). *A child's book of art: Great pictures with first words.* New York: Dorling Kindersly.

Midlarsky, E., & Bryan, J. H. (1967). Training charity in children. *Journal of Personality and Social Psychology, 5,* 405–415.

Mikkelsen, E. J. (1997). Responding to allegations of sexual abuse in child care and early childhood education programs. *Young Children, 52*(3), 47–51.

Miller, K. (1989). *The outside play and learning book: Activities for young children.* Mt. Beltsville, MD: Gryphon House.

Miller, K. (1996). *The crisis manual for early childhood teachers: How to handle the really difficult problems.* Beltsville, MD: Gryphon House.

Miller, L. B., & Dyer, J. L. (1975). Four preschool programs: Their dimensions and effects. *Monographs of the Society for Research in Child Development, 40*(5–6), #162.

Miller, L. H., Smith, A. D., & Rothstein, L. (1993). *The stress solution: An action plan to manage the stress in your life.* New York: Pocket Books.

Mills, K. (1998). *Something better for my children.* New York: E. P. Dutton.

Mills, P. E., Cole, K. N., Jenkins, J. R., & Dale, P. S. (1998). Effects of differing levels of inclusion on preschoolers with disabilities. *Exceptional Children, 65*(1), 79–90.

Milner, J. S. (1998). Individual and family characteristics associated with intrafamilial child physical and sexual abuse. In P. K. Trickett & C. J. Schellenbach (Eds.), *Violence against children in the family and the community.* Washington, DC: American Psychological Association.

Mindel, C. H., Habenstein, R. W., & Wright, R. (Eds.). (1988). *Ethnic families in America: Patterns and variations.* Upper Saddle River, NJ: Merrill/Prentice Hall.

Mirandy, J. (1976). Preschool for abused children. In H. P. Martin (Ed.), *The abused child: A multidisciplinary approach to developmental issues and treatment.* Cambridge, MA: Ballinger.

Mitchell, A. (1985). *Children in the middle: Living through divorce.* London: Tavistock.

Mitchell, A., Stoney, L., & Dichter, H. (1997). *Financing child care in the United States: An illustrative catalog of current strategies.* Ewing Marion Kauffman Foundation and The Pew Charitable Trusts.

Mize, J. (1995). Coaching preschool children in social skills: A cognitive learning curriculum. In G. Carledge & J. F. Milburn (Eds.), *Teaching social skills to children and youths* (3rd ed.). Boston: Allyn & Bacon.

Mize, J., & Abell, E. (1996). Encouraging social skills in young children: Tips teachers can share with parents. *Dimensions of Early Childhood, 24*(3), 15–23.

Moffitt, M., & Omwake, E. (n.d.). *The intellectual content of play.* New York: New York State Association for the Education of Young Children.

Montagu, A. (1986). *Touching: The human significance of the skin* (3rd ed.). New York: Harper & Row.

Montessori, M. (1912). *The Montessori Method: Scientific pedagogy as applied to child education in "The Children's House" with additions and revisions by the author* (A. E. George, Trans.). New York: Frederick A. Stokes.

Montessori, M. (1967). *The discovery of the child* (M. J. Costelloe, Trans.). Notre Dame, IN: Fides.

Moomaw, S. (1997). *More than singing: Discovering music in preschool and kindergarten.* St. Paul, MN: Redleaf.

Moomaw, S., & Hieronymus, B. (1995). *More than counting: Whole math activities for preschool and kindergarten.* St. Paul, MN: Redleaf.

Moor, P. (1960). What teachers are saying—about the young blind child. *Journal of Nursery Education, 15*(2).

Moore, G. T. (1997). A place for block play. *Child Care Information Exchange #115,* 73–77.

Moore, R. C., & Wong, H. H. (1997). *Natural learning: Creating environments for rediscovering nature's way of teaching: The life history of an environmental schoolyard.* Berkeley: MIG Communications.

Moore, S. G. (1982). Prosocial behavior in the early years: Parent and peer influences. In B. Spodek (Ed.), *Handbook of research in early childhood education.* New York: Free Press.

Moore, T. E., & Harris, A. E. (1978). Language and thought in Piagetian theory. In L. S. Siegel & C. J. Brainerd (Eds.), *Alternatives to Piaget: Critical essays on the theory.* San Diego: Academic Press.

Morford, J. P., & GoldenMeadow, S. (1997). From here and now to there and then: The development of displaced reference in homesign and English. *Child Development, 68,* 420–435.

Morgan, J. (1984). Reward-induced decrements and increments in intrinsic motivation. *Review of Educational Research, 54*(1), 5–30.

Morrison, G. (1998). *Early childhood education today* (7th ed.). Upper Saddle River, NJ: Merrill/Prentice Hall.

Morrow, A. L., Benton, M., Reves, R. R., & Pickering, L. K. (1991). Knowledge and attitudes of day care center parents and care providers regarding children infected with human immunodeficiency virus. *Pediatrics, 87*(6), 876–883.

Morrow, L. M. (1997). Literacy development in the early years: Helping children read and write (3rd ed.). Boston: Allyn & Bacon.

Morse, L. W., & Shine, A. E. (1998). Sickle cell anemia. In L. A. Phelps (Ed.), *Health-related disorders in children and adolescents.* Washington, DC: American Psychological Association.

Moyer, J. (Ed.). (1995). *Selecting educational equipment and materials for school and home* (Rev. ed.). Wheaton, MD: Association for Childhood Education International.

Murphy, D. M. (1997). Parent and teacher plan for the child. *Young Children, 52*(4), 32–36.

Murray, F. B. (1972). Acquisition of conservation through social interaction. *Developmental Psychology, 6*, 1–6.

Mussen, P. H., Conger, J. J., & Kagan, J. (1969). *Child development and personality.* New York: Harper & Row.

Nakayama, T. K., & Martin, J. N. (Eds.). (1999). *Whiteness: The communication of social identity.* Thousand Oaks, CA: Sage.

National Association for the Education of Young Children (NAEYC). (1993). *Understanding the ADA: The Americans with Disabilities Act: Information for early childhood programs.* Washington, DC: Author.

National Association for the Education of Young Children (NAEYC). (1995). *National Association for the Education of Young Children position statement: Responding to linguistic and cultural diversity: Recommendations for effective early childhood education.* Washington, DC: Author.

National Association for the Education of Young Children (NAEYC). (1997). National Association for the Education of Young Children position statement on the prevention of child abuse in early childhood programs and the responsibilities of early childhood professionals to prevent child abuse. *Young Children, 52*(3), 42–46.

National Association for the Education of Young Children (NAEYC). (1998a). *Accreditation criteria & procedures of the National Association for the Education of Young Children.* Washington, DC: Author.

National Association for the Education of Young Children (NAEYC). (1998b). *Code of ethical conduct and statement of commitment: Guidelines for responsible behavior in early childhood education.* Washington, DC: Author.

National Association for the Education of Young Children (NAEYC). (1998c). NAEYC: Change agent for a changing world: NAEYC annual report. *Young Children, 53*(6), 43–54.

National Association for the Education of Young Children (NAEYC). (1998d). *Technology and young children—ages three through eight: A position statement of the National Association for the Education of Young Children.* Washington, DC: Author.

National Association for the Education of Young Children (NAEYC). (1998e). *Violence in the lives of children: A position statement of the National Association for the Education of Young Children.* Washington, DC: Author.

National Association for the Education of Young Children (NAEYC). (1998f). What would you do? Real-life ethical problems early childhood professionals face. *Young Children, 53*(4), 52–54.

National Association of Child Care Resource and Referral Agencies. (1998). *NACCRRA information.* Washington, DC: Author.

National Black Child Development Institute. (1994). Constraints and opportunities for African American leadership in early childhood education. *Young Children, 49*(4), 32–36.

National Black Child Development Institute. (1995). *Young children and African American literature.* Washington, DC: National Association for the Education of Young Children.

National briefs: Millions with bad teeth can't afford dentist. (1993, November 30). *Oklahoma Daily.*

National Center for Education Statistics. (1993). *Statistical analysis report: Profile of preschool children's child care and early education program participation: National Household Education Survey, Office of Educational Research and Improvement* (NCES 93–133). Washington, DC: Author.

National Center for Education Statistics. (1995). *Child care and early education program participation of infants, toddlers, and preschoolers: National Household Education Survey* (NCES 95–213). Washington, DC: Author.

National Center on Child Abuse and Neglect. (1992). *Child abuse and neglect: A shared community concern.* Washington, DC: U.S. Department of Health and Human Services.

National Center on Child Abuse and Neglect. (1996). *Study of national incidence and prevalence of child abuse and neglect: 1996.* Washington, DC: U.S. Department of Health and Human Services.

Nationaline: 10% of U.S. residents are foreign-born, Census says. (1998, April 9). *USA Today,* p. 3a.

National Institute of Neurological Diseases and Stroke. (1969). *Learning to talk: Speech, hearing, and language problems in the preschool child.* Washington, DC: U.S. Department of Health, Education and Welfare.

National Pediatric & Family HIV Resource Center. (1999, April 18). *Children living in a world with AIDS: Guidelines for children's participation in HIV/AIDS programs.* Available: www://pedhivaids.org.

Nedler, S., & Sebera, P. (1971). Intervention strategies for Spanish-speaking children. *Child Development, 42,* 259–267.

Needlman, R., & Needlman, G. (1997). Dispelling the myths about epilepsy. *Scholastic Early Childhood Today, 11*(4), 12–13.

Nelsen, J., Erwin, C., & Duffy, R. (1998). *Positive discipline for preschoolers: Raising children who are responsible, respectful, and resourceful* (2nd ed.). Rocklin, CA: Prima.

Neubert, D. Z. (1997). Time to grow: The history—and future of preparing youth for adults roles in society. *Teaching Exceptional Children, 29*(5), 5–15.

Neugebauer, R. (1998). Congregations that care: Child care in religious institutions. *Child Care Exchange, #124,* 22–25.

Neugebauer, R. (1999). Six national chains—six approaches to development. *Child Care Information Exchange, #125,* 35–38.

Newcomb, A. F., & Bagwell, C. L. (1996). The developmental significance of children's friendship relations. In W. M. Bukowski, A. F. Newcomb, & W. W. Hartup (Eds.), *The company they keep: Friendship in childhood and adolescence.* New York: Cambridge University Press.

Nieto, S. (1992). *Affirming diversity: The sociopolitical context of multicultural education.* White Plains, NY: Longman.

Niffenegger, J. P., & Willer, L. R. (1998). Friendship behaviors during early childhood and beyond. *Early Childhood Education Journal, 26*(2), 95–99.

Northcutt, W. H. (1970). Candidate for integration: A hearing impaired child in a regular nursery school. *Young Children, 25*(6), 367–380.

Norton, C. C., & Norton, B. E. (1997). *Reaching children through play therapy: An experiential approach.* Denver, CO: Publishing Cooperative.

Norton, D. (1999). *Through the eyes of a child: An introduction to children's literature* (3rd ed.). Upper Saddle River, NJ: Merrill/Prentice Hall.

Nourot, P. M. (1991). Perspectives from the field: Play and paradox. In B. Scales, M. Almy, A. Nicolopoulou, & S. Ervin-Tripp (Eds.), *Play and the social context of development in early care and education.* New York: Teachers College Press.

Nourot, P. M. (1997). Playing with play in four dimensions. In J. P. Isenberg, & M. R. Jalongo (Eds.), *Major trends and issues in early childhood education: Challenges, controversies, and insights.* New York: Teachers College Press.

Nourot, P. M. (1998). Sociodramatic play: Pretending together. In D. P. Fromberg & D. Bergen (Eds.), *Play from birth to twelve and beyond: Contexts, perspectives, and meaning.* New York: Garland.

Nourot, P. M., & Van Hoorn, J. L. (1991). Research in review: Symbolic play in preschool and primary settings. *Young Children, 46*(6), 40–50.

Numeroff, L. J. (1987). *If you give a mouse a cookie.* New York: HarperCollins.

O'Connor, R. D. (1972). Relative efficacy of modeling, shaping, and the combined procedures for modification of social withdrawal. *Journal of Abnormal Psychology, 79,* 327–334.

Odom, S. L., McConnell, S. R., & McEvoy, M. A. (Eds.). (1992). *Social competence of young children with disabilities: Issues and strategies for intervention.* Baltimore, MD: Brookes.

Oehlberg, B. (1996). *Making it better: Activities for children living in a stressful world.* St. Paul, MN: Redleaf.

Olds, D. L., & Kitzman, H. (1993). Review of research on home visiting for pregnant women and parents of young children. *Future of Children, 3*(3), 53–92.

Oliner, S. P., & Oliner, P. M. (1988). *The altruistic personality: Resources of Jews in Nazi Europe.* New York: Free Press.

Olson, S. L., Bayles, K., & Bates, J. E. (1986). Mother-child interaction and children's speech progress: A longitudinal study of the first two years. *Merrill-Palmer Quarterly, 32,* 1–20.

Olweus, D. (1999). Sweden. In P. K. Smith, Y. Morita, J. Junger-Tas, D. Olweus, R. Catalano, & P. Slee (Eds.), *The nature of school bullying: A cross national perspective.* London: Routledge.

Orata, P. T. (1953). The Iloilo experiment in education through the vernacular. In *The Use of Vernacular Languages in Education Monographs on Fundamental Education, VIII.* Paris: UNESCO.

Osborn, D. K. (1991). *Early childhood education in historical perspective.* Athens, GA: Education Associates.

Ostrosky, M. M., Skellenger, A. C., Odom, S. L., McConnell, S. R., & Peterson, C. (1994). Teachers' schedules and actual time spent in activities in preschool special education classes. *Journal of Early Intervention, 18*(1), 25–33.

Owens, K. (1995). *Raising your child's inner self-esteem: The authoritative guide from infancy through the teen years.* New York: Plenum Press.

Owens, R. E. (1992). *Language development: An introduction* (3rd ed.). New York: Merrill/Macmillan.

Oyer, H. J., & Hall, B. J. (1994). *Speech, language, and hearing disorders: A guide for the teacher.* Boston: College Hill.

Pacific Oaks College Faculty. (1985). *The anti-bias curriculum.* Paper presented at the National Association for the Education of Young Children Conference, New Orleans.

Parham, V. R. (1993). *The African American child's heritage cookbook.* South Pasadena, CA: Sandcastle.

Parke, R. D. (1996). *Fatherhood.* Cambridge, MA: Harvard University Press.

Parke, R. D., & Buriel, R. (1998). Socialization in the family: Ethnic and ecological perspectives. In W. Damon (Series Ed.) & N. Eisenberg (Vol. Ed.), *Handbook of child psychology* (5th ed.): Vol. 3. Social, emotional, and personality development. New York: Wiley.

Parke, R. D., & Duer, J. L. (1972). Schedule of punishment and inhibition of aggression. *Developmental Psychology, 7,* 266–269.

Parke, R. D., & Slaby, R. G. (1983). The development of aggression. In W. Damon (Series Ed.) & E. M. Hetherington (Vol. Ed.), *Handbook of child psychology* (5th ed.): *Vol. 4. Socialization, personality, and social development.* New York: Wiley.

Parrillo, V. N. (1985). *Strangers to these shores: Race and ethnic relations in the United States* (2nd ed.). New York: Wiley.

Parten, M. B. (1932). Social participation among preschool children. *Journal of Abnormal and Social Psychology, 27,* 243–269.

Parten, M. B. (1933). Social play among preschool children. *Journal of Abnormal and Social Psychology, 28,* 136–147.

Patrick, S. (1993). Facilitating communication and language development. In T. W. Linder (Ed.), *Transdisciplinary play-based intervention: Guidelines for developing a meaningful curriculum for young children.* Baltimore, MD: Brookes.

Patterson, C. (1977). Insights about persons: Psychological foundations of humanistic and affective education. In L. M. Berman & J. A. Roderick (Eds.), *Feeling, valuing, and the art of growing: Insights into the affective.* Washington, DC: ASCD.

Patterson, G. R. (1982). *Coercive family practices.* Eugene, OR: Castalia Press.

Patterson, G. R., DeBaryshe, B. D., & Ramsey, E. (1989). A developmental perspective on antisocial behavior. *American Psychologist, 44*(2), 329–335.

Payne, F. G., & Rink, J. E. (1997). Physical education in the devel-
opmentally appropriate integrated curriculum. In C. H. Hart, D. C. Burts, & R. Charlesworth (Eds.), *Integrated curriculum and developmentally appropriate practice: Birth to age eight.* Albany: State University of New York Press.

Pellegrini, A. D. (1986). Communicating in and about play: The effect of play centers on preschoolers' explicit language. In G. Fein & M. Rivkin (Eds.), *The young child at play: Reviews of research* (Vol. 4). Washington, DC: National Association for the Education of Young Children.

Pellegrini, A. D., & Boyd, B. (1993). The role of play in early childhood development and education: Issues in definition and function. In B. Spodek (Ed.), *Handbook of research on the education of young children.* New York: Macmillan.

Pepler, D. (1986). Play and creativity. In G. Fein & M. Rivkin (Eds.), *The young child at play: Reviews of research* (Vol. 4). Washington, DC: National Association for the Education of Young Children.

Perry, T., & Delpit, L. (1998). *The real Ebonics debate: Power, language, and the education of African American children.* Boston: Beacon Press.

Peterson, C., Maier, S. F., & Seligman, M. E. P. (1993). *Learned helplessness: A theory for the age of personal control.* New York: Oxford University Press.

Peterson, R., & Felton-Collins, V. (1986). *The Piaget handbook for teachers and parents: Children in the age of discovery, preschool to third grade.* New York: Teachers College Press.

Pflaum, S. W. (1986). *The development of language and literacy in young children* (3rd ed.). Upper Saddle River, NJ: Merrill/ Prentice Hall.

Phelps, L. A. (Ed.). (1998). *Health-related disorders in children and adolescents*. Washington, DC: American Psychological Association.

Phillips, C. B. (1998). Preparing teachers to use their voices for change. *Young Children, 53*(3), 55–60.

Phipps, P. A. (1998). Working with angry parents. *Child Care Information Exchange, #121*, 10–14.

Piaget, J. (1926). *The language and thought of the child*. New York: Harcourt Brace & World.

Piaget, J. (1932). *The moral judgment of the child*. London: Routledge & Kegan Paul.

Piaget, J. (1948). *The moral judgment of the child*. Glencoe, IL: Free Press.

Piaget, J. (1950). *The psychology of intelligence*. London: Routledge & Kegan Paul.

Piaget, J. (1959). *The construction of reality in the child*. New York: Basic Books.

Piaget, J. (1962). *Play, dreams, and imitation in childhood*. New York: Norton.

Piaget, J. (1963). *The origins of intelligence in children*. New York: Norton.

Piaget, J. (1965). *The child's conception of number*. NY: Norton.

Piaget, J. (1981). *Intelligence and affectivity: Their relationship during child development*. Palo Alto, CA: Annual Reviews.

Piaget, J. (1983). Piaget's theory. In P. H. Mussen (Series Ed.) & W.

Kessen (Vol. Ed.), *Handbook of child psychology* (4th ed.): *Vol. 1. History, theory, and methods*. New York: Wiley.

Piaget, J., & Inhelder, B. (1967). *The child's conception of space*. New York: Norton.

Piaget, J., & Inhelder, B. (1969). *The psychology of the child* (H. Weaver, Trans.). New York: Basic Books.

Pica, R. (1995). *Experiences in movement with music, activities, and theory*. Albany, NY: Delmar.

Pica, R. (1997). Beyond physical development: Why young children need to move. *Young Children, 52*(6), 4–11.

Pica, R. (1998). *Moving and learning across the curriculum: 315 activities and games to make learning fun*. Albany, NY: Delmar.

Piirto, J. (1999). *Talented children and adults: Their development and education* (2nd ed.). Upper Saddle River, NJ: Merrill/ Prentice Hall.

Piper, W. (1980). *The little engine that could*. New York: G. P. Putnam.

Pitcher, E. G., & Prelinger, E. (1963). *Children tell stories: An analysis of fantasy*. New York: International Universities Press.

Play, Policy, & Practice Caucus. (1999). *Play, policy, & practice CONNECTIONS*. New York: Play, Policy, & Practice Caucus of the National Association for the Education of Young Children.

Poole, C., Miller, S. A., & Church, E. B. (1998). Reassuring routines & rituals. *Scholastic Early Childhood Today, 13*(1), 25–29.

Portner, J. (1997, September 10). New report on children's dietary habits disappoints educators. *Education Week*.

Powell, D. R. (1998). Research in review: Reweaving parents into the fabric of early childhood programs. *Young Children, 53*(5), 60–67.

Powell, G. J. (1983). *The psychological development of minority group children*. New York: Brunner/Mazel.

Pratt, C. (1990). *I learn from children*. New York: Harper & Row. (Original work published 1948)

Prelutsky, C. (Ed.). (1986). *Read aloud rhymes for the very young*. New York: Knopf.

Prescott, E. (1981). Relations between physical setting and adult/child behavior in day care. In S. Kilmer (Ed.), *Advances in early education and day care: A research annual* (Vol. 2). Greenwich, CT: JAI Press.

Quisenberry, M. L., & McIntyre, D. J. (Eds.). (1999). *Educators healing racism*. Reston, VA: Association of Teacher Educators.

Rab, V. Y., Wood, K. I., & Taylor, J. M. (1995). *Child care and the ADA*. Baltimore, MD: Brookes.

Radlaver, E. (1967). *Father is big*. New York: Bowman.

Raines, S. C., & Canady, R. J. (1989). *Story stretchers: Activities to expand children's favorite books*. Beltsville, MD: Gryphon House.

Raines, S. C., & Canady, R. J. (1991). *More story stretchers: More activities to expand children's favorite books*. Beltsville, MD: Gryphon House.

Raines, S. C., & Isbell, R. (1994). *Stories: Children's literature in early education*. Albany, NY: Delmar.

Ramirez, G., & Ramirez, J. L. (1994). *Multiethnic children's literature*. Albany, NY: Delmar.

Ramsey, P. G. (1979). Beyond "Ten Little Indians" and turkeys: Alternative approaches to Thanksgiving. *Young Children, 34*(6), 28–52.

Ramsey, P. G. (1991). *Making friends in school: Promoting peer relationships in early childhood.* New York: Teachers College Press.

Raver, S. A. (1999). *Intervention strategies for infants and toddlers with special needs: A team approach* (2nd ed.). Upper Saddle River, NJ: Merrill/Prentice Hall.

Read, K. H. (1996). Initial support through guides to speech and action. In K. M. Paciorek & J. H. Munro (Eds.), *Sources: Notable selections in early childhood education.* Guilford, CT: Dushkin.

Readdick, C. A., & Park, J. J. (1998). Achieving great heights: The climbing child. *Young Children, 53*(6), 14–19.

Redleaf, R. (1993). *Busy fingers, growing minds: Finger plays, verses, and activities for whole language learning.* St. Paul, MN: Redleaf.

Reguero de Atiles, J., Stegelin, D. A., & Long, J. K. (1997). Biting behaviors among preschoolers: A review of the literature and survey of practitioners. *Early Childhood Education Journal, 25*(2), 101–105.

Reifel, S. (1982). The structure and content of early representational play: The case of building blocks. In S. Hill & B. J. Barnes (Eds.), *Young children and their families: Needs of the nineties.* Lexington, MA: Heath.

Reifel, S. (1984). Block construction: Children's developmental landmarks in representation of space. *Young Children, 40*(1), 61–67.

Reifel, S., & Greenfield, P. M. (1982). Structural development in a symbolic medium: The representational use of block constructions. In G. E. Forman (Ed.), *Action and thought: From sensorimotor schemes to symbolic operations.* San Diego: Academic Press.

Reifel, S., & Yeatman, J. (1991). Action, talk, and thought in block play. In B. Scales, M. Almy, A. Nicolopoulou, & S. Ervin-Tripp (Eds.), *Play and the social context of development in early care and education.* New York: Teachers College Press.

Reifel, S., & Yeatman, J. (1993). From category to context: Reconsidering classroom play. *Early Childhood Research Quarterly, 8*(3), 347–367.

Renck, M. A. (1997). Many people, many places, other times: An annotated bibliography of multicultural books for 3–8-year-olds. *Early Childhood Education Journal, 25*(1), 45–50.

Reppucci, R. K., Land, N. D., & Haugaard, J. J. (1998). Child sexual abuse prevention programs that target young children. In P. K. Trickett & D. J. Schellenbach (Eds.), *Violence against children in the family and community.* Washington, DC: American Psychological Association.

Resnick, R., & Hergenroeder, E. (1975). Children and the emergency room. *Children Today, 4*(5), 5–9.

Reynolds, G., & Jones, E. (1997). *Master players: Learning from children at play.* New York: Teachers College Press.

Reynolds, M. C. & Birch, J. W. (1988). *Adaptive mainstreaming: A primer for teachers and principals.* White Plains, NY: Longman.

Rheingold, H. L. (1982). Little children's participation in the work of adults: A nascent prosocial behavior. *Child Development, 53,* 114–125.

Rice, E. P., Ekdahl, M. C., & Miller, L. (1971). *Children of mentally ill parents: Problems in child care.* New York: Behavioral Publications.

Rice, M. L., & Wilcox, K. A. (Eds.), (1995). *Building a language-focused curriculum for the preschool classroom: Vol. 1. A foundation for lifelong communication.* Baltimore, MD: Brookes.

Riley, S. S. (1989). Pilgrimage to Elmwood Cemetery. *Young Children, 44*(2), 33–36.

Rinaldi, C. (1993). *Opening remarks: The Reggio Emilia approach in the United States.* Traverse City, MI: Wayne State University, Merrill-Palmer Institute.

Rinaldi, C. (1994). *The philosophy of Reggio Emilia.* Reggio Emilia, Italy: Reggio Emilia Seminar.

Robertson, J., & Robertson, J. (1989). *Separation and the very young.* London: Free Association Books.

Rodgers, D. B. (1998). Supporting autonomy in young children. *Young Children, 53*(3), 75–80.

Rodriguez, J. L., Diaz, R. M., Duran, D., & Espinosa, L. (1995). The impact of bilingual preschool education on the language development of Spanish-speaking children. *Early Childhood Research Quarterly, 10*(4), 475–490.

Roemer, J. (1989). *Two to four from 9 to 5: The adventures of a daycare provider.* New York: Harper & Row.

Rogers, C. R. (1961). *On becoming a person.* Boston: Houghton Mifflin.

Rogers, C. R., & Dymond, R. F. (1954). *Psychotherapy and personality change*. Chicago: University of Chicago Press.

Rogers, D. L., Perrin, M. S., & Waller, C. B. (1987). Enhancing the development of language and thought through conversations with young children. *Journal of Research in Childhood Education, 2*(1), 17–29.

Rohe, W., & Patterson, A. H. (1974). The effects of varied levels of resources and density on behavior in a day care center. In D. H. Carson (Ed.), *Man-environment interaction*. Milwaukee, WI: EDRA.

Rohner, R. P. (1986). *The warmth dimension*. Newbury Park, CA: Sage.

Roopnarine, J. L., & Carter, D. B. (1992). *Parent-child socialization in diverse cultures: Annual advances in applied developmental psychology* (Vol. 5). Norwood, NJ: Ablex.

Roopnarine, J. L., Johnson, J. E., & Hooper, F. H. (Eds.). (1994). *Child's play in diverse cultures*. Albany: State University of New York.

Rosenhan, D. (1972). Prosocial behavior of children. In W. W. Hartup (Ed.), *The young child: Reviews of research* (Vol. 2). Washington, DC: National Association for the Education of Young Children.

Rosenthal, R., & Jacobson, L. (1968). *Pygmalion in the classroom: Teacher expectation and pupils' intellectual development*. New York: Holt, Rinehart & Winston.

Ross, J. G., & Pate, R. R. (1987). The National Children and Youth Study: A summary of findings. *Journal of Physical Education, Recreation and Dance, 58*(9), 51–56.

Rothbaum, F., Grauer, A., & Rubin, D. J. (1997). Becoming sexual: Differences between child and adult sexuality. *Young Children, 52*(6), 22–30.

Rouse, K. A. G. (1998). Infant and toddler resilience. *Early Childhood Education Journal, 26*(1), 47–52.

Rowe, M. B. (1974). Wait-time and reward—Part 1—Wait-time. *Journal of Research on Science Teaching, 11*, 81–94.

Rubin, K. H. (1977). The play behaviors of young children. *Young Children, 32*(6), 16–24.

Rubin, K. H., & Coplon, R. J. (1998). Social and nonsocial play in childhood: An individual difference perspective. In O. N. Saracho & B. Spodek (Eds.), *Multiple perspectives on play in early childhood education*. Albany: State University of New York Press.

Rubin, Z. (1980). *Children's friendships*. Cambridge, MA: Harvard University Press.

Ruble, D. N., & Martin, C. L. (1998). Gender development. In W. Damon (Series Ed.) & N. Eisenberg (Vol. Ed.), *Handbook of child psychology* (5th ed.): Vol. 3. *Social, emotional, and personality development*. New York: Wiley.

Rudman, M. K., Gagné, K. D., & Bernstein, J. E. (1994). *Books to help children cope with separation and loss: An annotated bibliography*. New York: Bowker.

Rutherford, E., & Mussen, P. (1968). Generosity in nursery school boys. *Child Development, 39*, 755–765.

Saarni, C. (1997). Emotional competence and self-regulation in childhood. In P. Salavey & D. J. Sluyter (Eds.), *Emotional development and emotional intelligence: Educational implications*. New York: Basic Books.

Sack, J. L. (1999). Report charts rise in special education enrollment. *Education Week, 3*(17), 40.

Sacks, J. J., Smith, J. D., Kaplan, K. M., Lambert, D. A., Sattin, R. W., & Sikes, R. K. (1989). The epidemiology of injuries in Atlanta day care centers. *Journal of the American Medical Association, 262*(12), 1641–1643.

Safford, P. (1978). *Teaching young children with special needs*. St. Louis, MO: C. V. Mosby.

Saifer, S. (1990). *Practical solutions to practically every problem: The early childhood teacher's manual*. St. Paul, MN: Toys 'n Things Press.

Saltz, E. D., & Johnson, J. (1977). Training disadvantaged preschoolers on various fantasy activities: Effects on cognitive functioning and impulse control *Child Development, 48*, 367–380.

Samalin, N. (1991). *Love and anger: The parental dilemma*. New York: Viking.

Samalin, N., & Jablow, M. M. (1987). *Loving your child is not enough*. New York: Viking.

Sander, E. K. (1972). When are speech sounds learned? *Journal of Speech and Hearing Disorders, 37*(1).

Sanders, C. M. (1999). *Grief: The mourning after: Dealing with adult bereavement* (2nd ed.). New York: Wiley.

Sanders, S. W. (1992). *Designing preschool movement programs*. Champaign, IL: Human Kinetics.

Sanders, S. W., & Yongue, B. (1998). Challenging movement experiences for young children. *Dimensions of Early Childhood, 26*(1), 9–17.

Saracho, O. N. (1998). What is stylish about play? In O. N. Saracho & B. Spodek (Eds.), *Multiple perspectives on play in early childhood education*. Albany: State University of New York Press.

Saracho, O. N., & Spodek, B. (Eds.). (1998). *Multiple perspectives on play in early childhood education*. Albany: State University of New York Press.

Satter, E. (1987). *How to get your kid to eat . . . but not too much*. Palo Alto, CA: Bull.

Saunders, R., & Bingham-Newman, A. M. (1984). *Piagetian perspectives for preschools: A thinking book for teachers*. Upper Saddle River, NJ: Merrill/Prentice Hall.

Schachter, F. F., & Strage, A. A. (1982). Adults' talk and children's language development. In S. G. Moore & C. R. Cooper (Eds.), *The young child: Reviews of research* (Vol. 3). Washington, DC: National Association for the Education of Young Children.

Schellenbach, C. J. (1998). Child maltreatment: A critical review of research on treatment for physically abusive parents. In P. K. Trickett & C. J. Schellenbach (Eds.), *Violence against children in the family and the community*. Washington, DC: American Psychological Association.

Schering-Plough, & Scholastic Early Childhood Today. (n.d.) *Healthy ears, healthy learning* (Scholastic supplement). New York: Author.

Schickedanz, J. A. (1999). *Much more than the ABCs: The early stages of reading and writing*. Washington, DC: National Association for the Education of Young Children.

Schiefelbusch, R. (Ed.). (1986). *Language competence: Assessment and intervention*. San Diego: College Hill Press.

Schiller, P., & Peterson, L. (1997). *Count on math: Activities for small hands and lively minds*. Beltsville, MD: Gryphon House.

Schiono, R. H., & Quinn, L. S. (1994). Epidemiology of divorce. *Future of Children, 4*(1), 15–28.

Schirrmacher, R. (1998). *Art and creative development for young children* (3rd ed.). Albany, NY: Delmar.

Schlank, C. H., & Metzger, B. (1997). *Together and equal: Fostering cooperative play and promoting gender equity in early childhood programs*. Boston: Allyn & Bacon.

Schweikert, G. (1996). I confess, I've changed. *Child Care Information Exchange, #111*, 90–92.

Schweinhart, L. J., Barnes, H. V., & Weikart, D. P. (1993). *Significant benefits: The High/Scope Perry Preschool Study through age 27*. Ypsilanti, MI: High/Scope.

Schweinhart, L. J., & Weikart, D. P. (1993). Public policy report: Success by empowerment: The High/Scope Perry Preschool Study through age 27. *Young Children, 49*(1), 54–58.

Schweinhart, L. J., & Weikart, D. P. (1997). *Lasting differences: The High/Scope Preschool Curriculum Comparison Study through age 23*. Ypsilanti, MI: High/Scope.

Schweinhart, L. J., Weikart, D. P., & Larner, M. B. (1986). Consequences of three preschool curriculum models through age 15. *Early Childhood Research Quarterly, 1*(1), 15–46.

Scott-Little, M. C., & Holloway, S. D. (1992). Child care providers' reasoning about misbehaviors: Relation to classroom control strategies and professional training. *Early Childhood Research Quarterly, 7*(4), 595–606.

Seefeldt, C. (1987). *The visual arts in the early childhood curriculum: A review of current research*. New York: Teachers College Press.

Seitz, V., & Apfel, N. (1994). Parent-focused intervention: Diffusion effects on siblings. *Child Development, 65*, 677–683.

Selye, H. (1981). The stress concept today. In I. L. Kutash, L. B. Schlesinger, & Associates (Eds.), *Handbook on stress and anxiety*. San Francisco: Jossey-Bass.

Serbin, L. A., Connor, J. M., & Citron, C. C. (1978). Environmental control of independent and dependent behaviors in preschool boys and girls: A model for early independence training. *Sex Roles, 4*, 867–875.

Shade, B. J., Kelly, C., & Oberg, M. (1997). *Creating culturally responsive classrooms*. Washington, DC: American Psychological Association.

Shade, D. D., & Davis, B. C. (1997). The role of computer technology in early childhood education. In J. P. Isenberg & M. R. Jalongo (Eds.), *Major trends and issues in early childhood education: Challenges, controversies, and insights*. New York: Teachers College Press.

Sharmat, M. (1980). *Gregory the terrible eater*. New York: Four Winds Press.

Shatz, M., & Gelman, R. (1973). The development of communication skills: Modification in the speech of young children as a function of listening. *Monographs of the Society for Research in Child Development, 38.*

Sheldon, K. (1996). "Can I play too?" Adapting common classroom activities for young children with limited motor abilities. *Early Childhood Education Journal, 24*(2), 155–120.

Sheridan, M. K., Foley, G. M., & Radinski, S. H. (1995). *Using the supportive play model: Individualized interventions in early childhood practice.* New York: Teachers College Press.

Shipley, C. C. (1993). *Empowering children: Play-based curriculum for lifelong learning.* Scarborough, Ontario: Nelson.

Shirah, S., & Brennan, L. (1990). *Sickle cell anemia.* Paper presented at the National Association for the Education of Young Children, Washington, DC.

Shore, C. (1998). Play and language: Individual differences as evidence of development and style. In D. P. Fromberg & D. Bergen (Eds.), *Play from birth to twelve and beyond: Contexts, perspectives, and meanings.* New York: Garland.

Shore, R. (1997). *Rethinking the brain: New insights into early development.* New York: Families and Work Institute.

Shotwell, J. M., Wolf, D., & Gardner, H. (1979). Exploring early symbolization: Styles of achievement. In B. Sutton-Smith, *Play and learning.* New York: Gardner Press.

Shuchter, S. R., & Zisook, S. (1993). The course of normal grief. In M. S. Stroebe, W. Stroebe, & R. O. Hansson (Eds.), *Handbook of bereavement: Theory, research, and intervention.* New York: Cambridge University Press.

Shweder, R. A., Mahapatra, M., & Miller, J. G. (1987). Culture and moral development. In J. Kagan & S. Lamb (Eds.), *The emergence of morality in children.* Chicago: University of Chicago Press.

Siegel, D. J. (1999). *The developing mind: Toward a neurobiology of interpersonal experience.* New York: Guilford.

Siegel, I. E., & Brainerd, C. J. (Eds.). (1978). *Alternatives to Piaget: Critical essays on the theory.* San Diego: Academic Press.

Siegel, L. S. (1972). Development of the concept of seriation. *Developmental Psychology, 6,* 135–137.

Siegler, R. W. (1999). *Children's thinking* (3rd ed.). Upper Saddle River, NJ: Merrill/Prentice Hall.

Sigel, I. (1987). Does hothousing rob children of their childhood? *Early Childhood Research Quarterly, 2*(3), 211–225.

Sigel, I. E., & McBane, B. (1967). Cognitive competence and level of symbolization among five-year-old children. In J. Hellmuth (Ed.), *The disadvantaged child.* Seattle: Special Child Publications.

Sikes, R. K. (1989). The epidemiology of injuries in Atlanta day care centers. *Journal of the American Medical Association, 262*(12), 1641–1643.

Silver, A. A., & Hagin, R. A. (1990). *Disorders of learning in childhood.* New York: Wiley.

Singer, D. G., & Revenson, T. A. (1997). *A Piaget primer: How a child thinks* (Rev. ed.). Madison, CT: International Universities Press.

Singh, N. N., Osborn, J. G., & Huguenin, N. H. (1996). Applied behavioral interventions. In J. W. Jacobson & M. A. Mulick (Eds.), *Manual of diagnosis and professional practice in mental retardation.* Washington, DC: American Psychological Association.

Skinner, B. F. (1974). *About behaviorism.* New York: Knopf.

Slapin, B., & Seale, D. (1992). *Books without bias: Through Indian eyes* (3rd ed.). Philadelphia: New Society.

Smedslund, J. (1966). Les origines sociales de la centration. In F. Bresson & M. de Montmalier (Eds.), *Psychologie et épistemologie genetiques.* Paris: Dunod.

Smilansky, S. (1968). *The effects of sociodramatic play on disadvantaged children.* New York: Wiley.

Smilansky, S., & Shefatya, L. (1990). *Facilitating play: A medium for promoting cognitive, socio-emotional, and academic development in young children.* Gaithersburg, MD: Psychosocial & Educational Publications.

Smith, C. A. (1988). *I'm positive: Growing up with self-esteem.* Manhattan, KS: Kansas State University, Cooperative Extension Service.

Smith, E. (1998). What is Black English? What is Ebonics? In T. Perry & L. Delpit (Eds.), *The real Ebonics debate: Power, language, and the education of African American children.* Boston: Beacon Press.

Smith, J. R., Brooks-Gunn, J., & Klebanov, P. K. (1997). Consequences of living in poverty for young children's cognitive and verbal ability and early school achievement. In G. J. Duncan & J. Brooks-Gunn (Eds.), *Consequences of growing up poor*. New York: Russell Sage Foundation.

Smith, N. R., Fucigna, C., Kennedy, M., & Lord, L. (1993). *Teaching children to paint* (2nd ed.). New York: Teachers College Press.

Smith, P. K., & Connolly, K. J. (1980). *The ecology of preschool behavior*. Cambridge, UK: Cambridge University Press.

Smith, P. K., Morita, Y., Junger-Tas, J., Olweus, D., Catalano, R., & Slee, P. (Eds.). (1999). *The nature of school bullying: A cross national perspective*. London: Routledge.

Smith, P. K., & Sharp, S. (1994). *School bullying: Insights and perspectives*. London: Routledge.

Smitherman, G. (1977). *Talkin and testifyin: The language of Black America*. Boston: Houghton Mifflin.

Smitherman, G. (1994). *Black talk: Words and phrases from the hood to the AMEN corner*. Boston: Houghton Mifflin.

Smutny, J. G., Walker, S. Y., & Meckstroth, E. A. (1997). *Teaching young gifted children in the regular classroom: Identifying, nurturing, and challenging ages 4–9*. Minneapolis, MN: Free Spirit.

Snow, C. E. (1989). Understanding social interaction and language acquisition: Sentences are not enough. In M. H. Bornstein & J. S. Bruner (Eds.), *Interaction in human development*. Mahwah, NJ: Erlbaum.

Soderman, A. K. (1985). Dealing with difficult young children. *Young Children, 40*(5), 15–20.

Soderman, A. K., Gregory, K. M., & O'Neill, L. T. (1999). *Scaffolding emergent literacy: A child-centered approach for preschool through grade 5*. Boston: Allyn & Bacon.

Soto, L. D. (1991). Research in review: Understanding bilingual/bicultural young children. *Young Children, 46*(2), 30–36.

Spaggiari, S. (1998). The community-teacher partnership in the governance of the schools: An interview with Lella Gandini. In C. Edwards, L. Gandini, & G. Forman (Eds.), *The hundred languages of children: The Reggio Emilia approach—Advanced reflections*. Norwood, NJ: Ablex.

Speidel, G. E., & Nelson, K. E. (Eds.). (1989). *The many faces of imitation in language learning*. New York: Springer-Verlag.

Spodek, B., & Saracho, O. N. (1994). *Dealing with individual differences in the early childhood classroom*. White Plains, NY: Longman.

Spolsky, B. (1999). Second-language learning. In J. A. Fishman (Ed.), *Handbook of language & ethnic identity*. New York: Oxford University Press.

Sprafkin, C., Serbin, L. A., Denier, C., & Connor, J. M. (1983). Sex-differentiated play: Cognitive consequences and early interventions. In M. B. Liss (Ed.), *Social and cognitive skills*. San Diego: Academic Press.

Sprung, B. (1975). *Nonsexist education for young children: A practical guide*. New York: Citation Press.

Sroufe, L. A. (1983). Individual patterns of adaptation from infancy to preschool. In M. Perlmutter (Ed.), *Proceedings of the Minnesota Symposium on Child Psychology*. Mahwah, NJ: Erlbaum.

Starr, R. H. (1988). Physical abuse of children. In V. B. Van Hasselt, K. R. L. Morrison, A. S. Bellack, & M. Hersen (Eds.), *Handbook of family violence*. New York: Plenum Press.

Stebbins, L. B., St. Pierre, R. G., Proper, E. C., Anderson, R. B., & Cervan, T. R. (1947). *Education as experimentation: A planned variation model: Vol. IV–A. An evaluation of Follow Through*. Cambridge, MA: Abt Associates.

Steglin, D. A. (1997). Early childhood professionals and HIV/AIDS-impacted children and families: Strategies for professional preparation. *Journal of Early Childhood Teacher Education, 18*(3), 26–34.

Steglin, D. A., Atiles, J., & Smith, S. (1996). *Knowledge and attitudes about HIV/AIDS: A study of early childhood professionals in Georgia*. Paper presented to the Southern Early Childhood Association Annual Conference, Little Rock, AR.

Stephens, K. (1999). Toilet training: Children step up to independence. *Child Care Information Exchange, #125*, 76–80.

Stevens, J. (1995). *Tops and bottoms*. New York: Harcourt Brace.

Steward, S. (1998). *The gardener*. New York: Farrar, Strauss & Giroux.

Stile, W. W., Kitano, M., Kelley, P., & Lecrone, J. (1993). Early intervention with gifted children: A national survey. *Journal of Early Intervention, 17*(1), 30–35.

Stipek, D., Daniels, D., Galluzzo, D., & Milburn, S. (1992). Characterizing early childhood education programs for poor and middle-class children. *Early Childhood Research Quarterly, 7*(1), 21–44.

Stipek, D., Recchia, S., & McClintic, S. (1992a). Self-evaluation in young children. *Monographs of the Society for Research in Child Development, 57*(1) 1–84, #225.

Stipek, D., Recchia, S., & McClintic, S. (1992b). Study 3: The effects of winning or losing a competition with an age mate. *Monographs of the Society for Research in Child Development, 57*(1), 60–69, #226.

Stone, P. S. (1992). "You know what?" Conversational narratives of preschool children. *Early Childhood Research Quarterly, 7*(3), 367–382.

Stott, L. H. (1955). *The longitudinal study of individual development.* Detroit: Merrill-Palmer School.

Stott, L. H., & Ball, R. S. (1957). Consistency and change in ascendance-submission in the social interaction of children. *Child Development, 28,* 259–272.

Streitmatter, J. (1994). *Toward gender equity in the classroom.* Albany: State University of New York Press.

Strickland, J. (1999a). The child abuse storm scale: Part 1. *Child Care Information Exchange, #125,* 86–91.

Strickland, J. (1999b). The child abuse storm scale: Part 2. *Child Care Information Exchange, #126,* 76–81.

Strong, M. F. (1999). Serving mothers with disabilities in early childhood education programs. *Young Children, 54*(3), 10–17.

Sturm, C. (1997). Creating parent-teacher dialogue: Intercultural communication in child care. *Young Children, 52*(5), 34–38.

Sutcliffe, J. (1997). *The complete book of relaxation techniques.* Allentown, PA: People's Medical Society.

Sutton-Smith, B. (1971). A syntax for play and games. In R. E. Herron & B. Sutton-Smith (Eds.), *Child's play.* New York: Wiley.

Szinovacz, M. E. (Ed.). (1998). *Handbook on grandparenthood.* Westport, CT: Greenwood Press.

Szymanski, L. S., & Kaplan, L. C. (1997). Mental retardation. In J. M. Wiener (Ed.), *Textbook of child & adolescent psychiatry* (2nd ed.). Washington, DC: American Psychiatric Press.

Tabors, P. O. (1997). *One child, two languages: A guide for preschool educators of children learning English as a second language.* Baltimore, MD: Brookes.

Talbot, J., & Frost, J. L. (1989). Magical playscapes. *Childhood Education, 66*(1), 11–19.

Tambourlane, W. V. (Ed.). (1997). *The Yale guide to children's nutrition.* New Haven, CT: Yale University Press.

Tardiff, T. Z., & Steinberg, R. J. (1988). What do we know about creativity? In R. J. Sternberg (Ed.), *The nature of creativity: Contemporary psychological perspectives.* Cambridge, UK: Cambridge University Press.

Task Force on Children's Learning and the Arts. (1998). *Young chil-*

dren and the arts: Making creative connections. Washington, DC: Arts Education Partnership.

Tavris, C. (1982). *Anger: The misunderstood emotion.* New York: Simon & Schuster.

Taylor, K. W. (1981). *Parents and children learn together* (3rd ed.). New York: Teachers College Press.

Teele, D. W., Klein, J. O., & Rosner, B. A. (1989). Epidemiology of otitis media during the first seven years of life in children in greater Boston: A prospective cohort study. *Journal of Infectious Diseases, 160,* 83–94.

Terman, L. M., Baldwin, B. T., & Bronson, E. (1925). *Mental and physical traits of a thousand gifted children: Genetic studies of genius* (Vol. 1). Stanford, CA: Stanford University Press.

Thelen, E., Ulrich, D., & Jensen, J. (1989). The developmental origins of locomotion. In M. Woolacott & A. Shumway-Cook (Eds.), *A development of posture and gait: Across the lifespan.* Columbia: University of South Carolina Press.

Thomas, R. M. (1999). *Comparing theories of child development* (5th ed.). Monterey, CA: Brooks/Cole.

Thomason, N. D. (1999). "Our guinea pig is dead!" Young children cope with death. *Dimensions of Early Childhood, 27*(2), 26–29.

Thompson, R. (1994). The role of the father after divorce. *Future of Children: Children and Divorce, 4*(1), 210–235.

Thompson, R. (1998). Early sociopersonality development. In W. Damon (Series Ed.) & N. Eisenberg (Vol. Ed.), *Handbook of child psychology* (5th ed.):*Vol. 3. Social, emotional, and personality development.* New York: Wiley.

Thouvenelle, S. (1994). Do computers belong in early childhood? *Scholastic Early Childhood Today,* 8(5), 48–49.

Tizard, B., Mortimore, J., & Burchell, B. (1983). *Involving parents in nursery and infant schools: A source book for teachers.* Ypsilanti, MI: High/Scope.

Tobacco settlement yields new opportunities to invest in children. (1999). *CDF Reports,* 20(1), 2–13.

Tobin, J. (1997a). *Making a place for pleasure in early childhood education.* New Haven, CT: Yale University Press.

Tobin, J. (1997b). The missing discourse of pleasure and desire. In J. Tobin (Ed.), *Making a place for pleasure in early childhood education.* New Haven, CT: Yale University Press.

Tomlinson, C. M. (Ed.). (1998). *Children's books from other countries.* Lanham, MD: Scarecrow Press.

Torbert, M., & Schneider, M. A. (1993). *Follow me too: A handbook of movement activities for three- to five-year-olds.* Menlo Park, CA: Addison-Wesley.

Torrance, E. P. (1962). *Guiding creative talent.* Upper Saddle River, NJ: Merrill/Prentice Hall.

Torrance, E. P. (1977). *Discovery and nurturance of giftedness in the culturally different.* Reston, VA: Council for Exceptional Children.

Torrance, E. P. (1987). Teaching for creativity. In S. Isaksen (Ed.), *Frontiers of creativity research: Beyond the basics.* Buffalo, NY: Bearly.

Torrance, E. P. (1988). The nature of creativity as manifest in testing. In R. J. Sternberg (Ed.), *The nature of creativity: Contemporary psychological perspectives.* Cambridge, UK: Cambridge University Press.

Toussaint, P. (1999). *Great books for African American children.* New York: Penguin.

Trawick-Smith, J. (1997). *Early childhood development: A multicultural perspective.* Upper Saddle River, NJ: Merrill/Prentice Hall.

Trelease, J. (1995). *The new read-aloud handbook* (4th ed.). New York: Penguin.

Tricket, P. K., & Schellenbach, D. J. (Eds.). (1998). *Violence against children in the family and the community.* Washington, DC: American Psychological Association.

Trief, E. (Ed.). (1998). *Working with visually impaired young students: Curriculum guide for 3- to 5-year-olds.* Springfield, IL: Charles C Thomas.

Trueba, H. T. (1990). The role of culture in the acquisition of English literacy by minority school children. In G. Imhoff (Ed.), *Learning two languages: From conflict to consensus in the reorganization of schools.* New Brunswick, NJ: Transaction.

Tsai, L. Y., & Ghaziuddin, M. (1997). Autistic disorder. In J. M. Wiener (Ed.), *Textbook of child and adolescent psychiatry* (2nd ed.). Washington, DC: American Psychiatric Press.

Turnbull, R., & Cilley, M. (1999). *Explanation and implications of the 1997 amendments to IDEA.* Upper Saddle River, NJ: Merrill/Prentice Hall.

Tutwiler, S. W. (1998). Diversity among families. In M. L. Fuller & G. Olsen (Eds.), *Home-school relations: Working successfully with parents and families.* Boston: Allyn & Bacon.

Twaite, J. A., Silitsky, D., & Luchow, A. K. (1998). *Children of divorce: Adjustment, parental conflict, custody, remarriage, and recommendations for clinicians.* Northvale, NJ: Jason Aronson.

Tzeng, O. C. S., & Hanner, L. J. (1988). Abuse and neglect: Typologies, phenomena, and impacts. In O. C. S. Tzeng & J. J. Jacobsen (Eds.), *Source book for child abuse and neglect.* Springfield, IL: Charles C Thomas.

UNICEF. (1999). *Facts and figures.* New York: UNICEF House, Division of Communication.

U.S. Department of Agriculture (USDA). (1985). *Your money's worth in foods* (#183). Washington, DC: Superintendent of Documents.

U.S. Department of Labor. (1997). *Facts on working women: Women's Bureau fact sheet: Child care workers.* Washington, DC: U.S. Department of Labor, Bureau of Labor Statistics, Employment and Earnings.

Valentine, C. W. (1956). *The normal child and his abnormalities* (3rd ed.). Baltimore, MD: Penguin Books.

Van Hoorn, J. (1987). Games that babies and mothers play. In P. Monighan-Nourot, B. J. Scales, & J. Van Hoorn (with Almy, M.). *Looking at children's play: A bridge between theory and practice.* New York: Teachers College Press.

Van Riper, C., & Erickson, R. L. (1996). An introduction to

speech pathology and audiology (9th ed.). Boston: Allyn & Bacon.

Vecchi, V. (1994). *Science or magic for making rainbows*. Washington, DC: Symposium: Multiple Intelligences and Reggio Emilia Preschools.

Vogel, N. (1997). *Getting started: Materials and equipment for active learning preschools*. Ypsilanti, MI: High/Scope.

Vygotsky, L. (1962). *Thought and language*. Cambridge: MIT Press.

Vygotsky, L. (1978). *Mind in society: The development of higher psychological processes* (M. Cole, V. John-Steiner, S. Scribner, & E. Souberman, Eds.). Cambridge, MA: Harvard University Press.

Wadsworth, B. J. (1989). *Piaget's theory of cognitive and affective development* (4th ed.). White Plains, NY: Longman.

Wadsworth, B. J. (1996). *Piaget's theory of cognitive and affective development* (5th ed.). Reading, MA: Addison-Wesley.

Walk, R. D. (1981). *Perceptual development*. Monterey, CA: Brooks/Cole.

Wallach, M. A., & Kogan, N. (1965). *Modes of thinking in young children: A study of the creativity-intelligence distinction*. New York: Holt, Rinehart & Winston.

Wallach, V., & Caulfield, R. (1998). Attachment and at-risk infants: Theoretical perspectives and clinical implications. *Early Childhood Education Journal, 26*(2), 125–129.

Wallerstein, J. S., & Blakeslee, S. (1989). *Second chances: Men, women, and children a decade after divorce*. New York: Ticknor & Fields.

Wallinga, D., & Skeen, P. (1996). Siblings of hospitalized and ill children: The teacher's role in helping these forgotten family members. *Young Children, 51*(6), 78–83A.

Wang, M. C., & Gordon, E. W. (1994). *Educational resilience in inner-city America: Challenges and prospects*. Mahwah, NJ: Erlbaum.

Ward, W. C. (1968). Creativity in young children. *Child Development, 39*, 737–754.

Wardle, F. (1998). Meeting the needs of multiracial and multiethnic children in early childhood settings. *Early Childhood Research Journal, 26*(1), 7–11.

Warren, R. M. (1977). *Caring: Supporting children's growth*. Washington, DC: National Association for the Education of Young Children.

Waslick, B., & Greenhill, L. (1997). Attention-deficit/hyperactivity disorder. In J. M. Wiener (Ed.), *Textbook of child & adolescent psychiatry* (2nd ed.). Washington, DC: American Psychiatric Press.

Wassil-Grimm, C. (1994). *Where's Daddy? How divorced, single, and widowed mothers can provide what's missing when Dad's missing*. New York: Overlook Press.

Watkins, R. Z. (1993). Two-way communication: Sharing personal perspectives with parents. *Scholastic Early Childhood Today, 8*(1), 41.

Watson, M. W., & Peng, Y. (1992). The relation between toy gun play and children's aggressive behavior. *Early Education and Development, 3*(4), 370–389.

Watt, M. R., Roberts, J. E., & Zeisel, S. A. (1993). Ear infections in young children: The role of the early childhood educator. *Young Children, 49*(1), 65–72.

Weber, S., & Mitchell, D. (1995). *That's funny, you don't look like a teacher: Interrogating images and identity in popular culture*. London: Falmer.

Weikart, , D. P. (1990). *Quality preschool programs: A long-term social investment*. New York: Ford Foundation.

Weisberg, R. W. (1988). Problem solving and creativity. In R. J. Sternberg (Ed.), *The nature of creativity: Contemporary psychological perspectives*. Cambridge, UK: Cambridge University Press.

Weiss, B., & Weisz, J. R. (1986). General cognitive deficits: Mental retardation. In R. T. Brown & C. R. Reynolds (Eds.), *Psychological perspectives on childhood exceptionality*. New York: Wiley.

Weiss, K. (1997). Let's build. *Scholastic Early Childhood Today, 12*(2), 30–43.

Wellhousen, K. (1996). Do's and don'ts for eliminating hidden bias. *Childhood Education, 73*(1), 36–39.

Wenar, C. (1994). *From infancy to adolescence* (3rd ed.). New York: McGraw-Hill.

Wender, P. L. (1973). *The hyperactive child, adolescent, and adult: Attention deficit disorder through the lifespan*. Oxford, UK: Oxford University Press.

Werner, E. E. (1999). Children of the garden island. In A. Slater & D. Muir (Eds.), *The Blackwell reader in developmental psychology*. Malden, MA: Blackwell.

Werner, E. E., & Smith, R. S. (1982). *Vulnerable but invincible: A longitudinal study of resilient children and youth*. New York: McGraw-Hill.

Werner, E. E., & Smith, R. S. (1992). *Overcoming the odds: High-risk children from birth to adulthood*. Ithaca, NY: Cornell University Press.

Weston, J. (1980). The pathology of child abuse and neglect. In C. H. Kempe & R. E. Helfer (Eds.), *The battered child* (3rd ed.). Chicago: University of Chicago Press.

White, B. L. (1979). *The origins of human competence*. Lexington, MA: Lexington Books.

White, R. W. (1968). Motivation reconsidered: The concept of competence. In M. Almy (Ed.), *Early childhood play: Selected readings related to cognition and motivation*. New York: Simon & Schuster.

White, R. W. (1976). *The enterprise of living: A view of personal growth* (2nd ed.). New York: Holt, Rinehart & Winston.

Wickstrom, R. L. (1983). *Fundamental motor patterns* (3rd ed.). Philadelphia: Lea & Febiger.

Wien, C. A. (1995). *Developmentally appropriate practice in "real life": Stories of teacher practical knowledge*. New York: Teachers College Press.

Wilkerson, D. C. (1997). Easing separation anxiety: Recommendations for parents, families, and teachers. *Young Children, 24*(3), 155–160.

Williams, C. K., & Kamii, C. (1986). How do children learn by handling objects? *Young Children, 42*(1), 23–36.

Williams, V. B. (1982). *A chair for my mother*. New York: Greenwillow Books.

Willis, C. (1998). Language development: A key to lifelong learning. *Child Care Information Exchange, #121*, 63–65.

Wilmes, L., & Wilmes, D. (1997). *Easel art*. Elgin, IL: Building Blocks.

Wilmes, L., & Wilmes, D. (n.d.). *Paint without brushes*. Elgin, IL: Building Blocks.

Wilson, A. N. (1997). *The Tabitha stories*. Cambridge, MA: Candlewick Press.

Wilson, G. L. (1980). Sticks and stones and racial slurs do hurt: The word *nigger* is what's not allowed. *Interracial Books for Children Bulletin, 11*(3/4).

Wilson, M. (1989). *The good-for-your-health all-Asian cookbook*. Washington, DC: Center for Science in the Public Interest.

Wilson, M. N. (Ed.). (1995). African American family life: Its structural and ecological aspects. *New Directions for Child Development, 68*, entire issue.

Witt, J. C., Elliott, S. N., & Gresham, F. M. (1988). *Handbook of behavior therapy in education*. New York: Plenum Press.

Wittmer, D. S., & Honig, A. S. (1994). Encouraging positive social development in young children. *Young Children, 49*(5), 4–12.

Wittmer, D. S., & Honig, A. S. (1996). Encouraging positive social development in young children. In K. M. Paciorek & J. H. Munro (Eds.), *Early childhood education 96/97*. Guilford, CT: Dushkin.

Wolchik, S. A., & Sandler, I. N. (1997). *Handbook of children's coping: Linking theory and intervention*. New York: Plenum Press.

Wolf, C. P. (Ed.). (1986). *Connecting: Friendship in the lives of young children and their teachers*. Redmond, WA: Exchange.

Wolfgang, C. H. (1999). *Solving discipline problems: Methods and models for today's teachers* (4th ed.). Boston: Allyn & Bacon.

Wong Fillmore, L. (1991). When learning a second language means losing the first. *Early Childhood Research Quarterly, 6*(3), 323–346.

Wood, D. (1998). *How children think and learn: The social context of cognitive development*. Oxford, UK: Basil Blackwell.

Woodhead, M., Faulkner, D., & Littleton, K. (Eds.). (1998). *Cultural worlds of early childhood*. London: Routledge.

Woolston, J. E. (1997). Obesity in infancy and childhood. In J. M. Wiener (Ed.), *Textbook of child & adolescent psychiatry* (2nd ed.). Washington, DC: American Psychiatric Press.

Workman, S. N., & Gage, J. A. (1997). Family-school partnerships: A family strengths approach. *Young Children, 52*(4), 10–19.

Wright, J. L., & Shade, D. D. (Eds.). (1994). *Young children: Active learners in a technological age*. Washington, DC: National Association for the Education of Young Children.

Yolen, J. (1987). *Owl moon*. New York: Philomel.

York, S. (1992). *Roots and wings: Affirming culture in early childhood programs*. St. Paul, MN: Redleaf.

York, S. (1998). *Big as life: The everyday inclusive curriculum* (Vols. 1 & 2). St. Paul, MN: Redleaf.

Yoshikawa, H. (1995). Long-term effects of early childhood programs on social outcomes and delinquency. *Future of Children, 5*(3), 51–75.

Youniss, J. (1975). Another perspective on social cognition. In A. Pick (Ed.), *Minnesota Symposia on Child Psychology* (Vol. 9). Minneapolis: University of Minnesota Press.

Zahn-Waxler, C. (1991). The case for empathy: A developmental review. *Psychological Inquiry, 2,* 155–158.

Zahn-Waxler, C. Z., Radke-Yarrow, M. R., & King, R. A. (1979). Child rearing and children's prosocial initiations toward victims of distress. *Child Development, 50,* 87–88, 2, 155–158.

Zakriski, A., Jacobs, M., & Coie, J. (1997). Coping with childhood peer rejection. In S. A. Wolchik & I. N. Sandler (Eds.), *Handbook of children's coping: Linking theory and intervention.* New York: Plenum Press.

Zanolli, K. M., Saudargas, R. A., & Twardosz, S. (1997). The development of toddler's' responses to affectionate teacher behavior. *Early Childhood Research Quarterly, 21,* 99–116.

Zaslow, M. J., Oldham, E., Moore, D. A., & Magenheim, E. (1998). Welfare families' use of early childhood care and education programs, and implications for their children's development. *Early Childhood Research Quarterly, 13*(4), 535–563.

Zavitkovsky, D. (1990). Enjoy a Docia story. *Child Care Information Exchange, 74,* 62.

Zeece, P. D. (1999). And the winner is: Children's literature awards and accolades. *Early Childhood Education Journal, 26*(4), 233–239.

Zimmerman, B. J., & Bergen, J. R. (1971). Intellectual operations in teacher question-asking behavior. *Merrill-Palmer Quarterly, 17*(1), 19–26.

Zion, G. (1976). *No roses for Harry.* New York: Harper.

Acknowledgments for Chapter-Opening Quotations

1. From *Growing Minds: On Becoming a Teacher* (p. 16) by Herbert Kohl, 1984, New York: Harper & Row.
   From *Teaching in the Key of Life* (p. 56) by Mimi Brodsky Chenfield, 1993, Washington, DC: National Association for the Education of Young Children.
2. From *The Young Man Luther* by Erik Erikson, 1958, New York: Norton.
   From *Places for Children: Making Quality Happen in the Real World* (p. 6) by Jim Greenman, 1998, Redmond, WA: Child Care Information Exchange.
3. Danish proverb—traditional.
4. From *Teaching Young Children*, by Evelyn Beyer, copyright © 1968, by Western Publishing Company, Inc., reprinted by permission of The Bobbs-Merrill Company, Inc.
5. From "Beginnings Workshop: Kids Gotta Move: Adapting Movement Experiences for Children with Differing Abilities" (p. 37) by Carol S. Kranowitz, 1994, *Child Care Information Exchange, 5*(94).
6. From *Early Education and Psychological Development* (p. 5) by Barbara Biber, 1984, New Haven, CT: Yale University Press.
   From *The Child with Special Needs: Encouraging Intellectual and Emotional Growth* (p. 219) by Stanley I. Greenspan and Serena Wieder, 1998, Reading, MA: Addison-Wesley.
7. From Mother Teresa (p. 65), 1996, as quoted in *Child Care Information Exchange, #126*.
   From "The Winning Family" (p. 83) by Louise Hart, 1996, as quoted in *Child Care Information Exchange, #126*.
8. From *Last Poems, XII* by A. E. Housman, 1922.
9. From *Merrycats Brochure* by Gretchen Buchenholz, 1993, as quoted by L. G. Johnson, C. K. Rogers, P. Johnson, & R. P. Macmillan in "Overcoming Barriers Associated With the Integration of Early Childhood Settings," seminar at the National Association for the Education of Young Children, Anaheim, CA.
   From Hubert Humphrey, 1977, Dedication Speech at the opening of the Hubert Humphrey Building, Washington, DC.
10. From the preface by Urie Bronfenbrenner in *Soviet Preschool Education: Vol. 2. Teacher's Commentary* by H. Chauncey (Ed.), 1969, New York: Holt, Rinehart & Winston.

From "Having Friends, Making Friends, and Keeping Friends: Relationships as Educational Contexts" by Willard W. Hartup, 1992, *ERIC Digest*, EDO–PS–92–4.

11.   From Alma Berg Greene, personal communication, 1945.

From *There's Gotta Be a Better Way: Discipline That Works* (p. 73) by Becky Bailey, 1997, Oviedo, FL: Loving Guidance.

12.   From *Punished by Rewards: The Trouble with Gold Stars, Incentive Plans, A's, and Other Bribes* (p. 167) by Alfie Kohn, 1993, Boston: Houghton Mifflin.

From *Emotional Intelligence* by Daniel Goleman, 1995, New York: Bantam Books.

13.   Author unknown. A particularly well-sung version of this gospel hymn is available on the recording *Spirituals*, sung by Jessye Norman. A Phillips release, 416 462–2.

14.   From "The Motivation to Be Creative" by Teresa Amabile, in *Frontiers of Creativity Research: Beyond the Basics* by Scott G. K. Isaksen (Ed.), 1987, Buffalo, NY: Bearly.

From "From the Guest Editor" (p. 7) by Walter Drew, 1997, in *Play, Policy & Practice Connections*, (6)Spring.

15.   From *The Autobiography of Friedrich Froebel* (p. 25), translated by Emilie Michaelis and H. Keatley Moore, 1889, Syracuse, NY: Bardeen.

16.   From *Mind in Society: The Development of Higher Psychological Processes* (p. 28) by Lev Vygotsky. M. Cole, V. John-Steiner, S. Scribner, & E. Souberman, Eds., 1978, Cambridge, MA: Harvard University Press.

From "Learning the Mother Tongue" by Jerome S. Bruner, 1978, *Human Nature*, 1(9), 42–49.

17.   From *Literacy Development in the Early Years* (3rd ed., p. 131) by Lesley M. Morrow, 1997, Boston: Allyn & Bacon.

18.   Romanian proverb—traditional.

From *The Developing Mind: Toward a Neurobiology of Interpersonal Experience* by Daniel Siegel, 1999, New York: Guilford.

19.   From "What Do Young Children Teach Themselves?" (p. 9) by Nancy Balaban, 1984, in *Early Childhood: Reconsidering the Essentials: A Collection of Papers*. New York: Bank Street College.